Islamic Empires

JUSTIN MAROZZI

Islamic Empires

Fifteen Cities that Define a Civilization

ALLEN LANE
an imprint of
PENGUIN BOOKS

ALLEN LANE

UK | USA | Canada | Ireland | Australia
India | New Zealand | South Africa

Allen Lane is part of the Penguin Random House group of companies
whose addresses can be found at global.penguinrandomhouse.com.

First published 2019
002

Copyright © Justin Marozzi, 2019

The moral right of the author has been asserted

Set in 10.2/13.5 pt Sabon LT Std
Typeset by Jouve (UK), Milton Keynes
Printed and bound in Great Britain by Clays Ltd, Elcograf S.p.A.

A CIP catalogue record for this book is available from the British Library

ISBN: 978-0-241-19904-6

www.greenpenguin.co.uk

To J
I could not have done it without you

Contents

List of Illustrations

Photographic acknowledgements are given in parentheses.

List of Maps

Many of these maps draw data copyright to OpenStreetMap contributors, available under the Open Database Licence. The ancient city of Mecca (Chapter 1) is not mapped.

Middle East, North Africa and Central Asia today

EUROPE

ATLANTIC
OCEAN

SPAIN

Cordoba
Granada

Mediterranean Sea

Athens

Algiers   Tunis

Qairouan

Rabat
Meknes   Fez

MOROCCO

TUNISIA

Tripoli

Banghazi

Marrakech

ALGERIA   LIBYA

AFRICA

1,000 miles

1,000 km

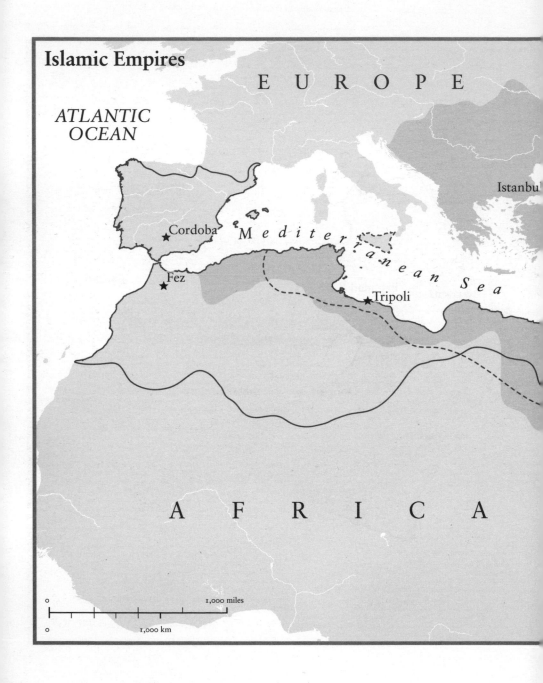

Islamic Empires

EUROPE

ATLANTIC
OCEAN

Cordoba

Fez

Mediterranean Sea

Tripoli

Istanbu

AFRICA

0   1,000 miles

0   1,000 km

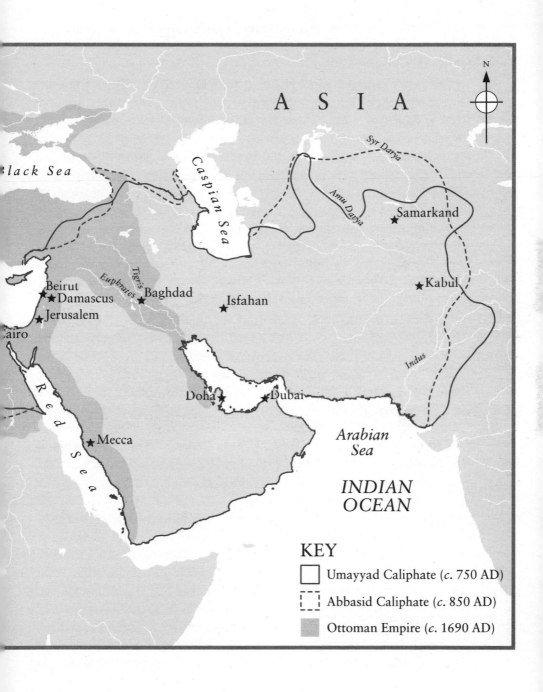

ASIA

Black Sea

Caspian Sea

Syr Darya

Amu Darya

Samarkand

Euphrates

Tigris

Beirut
Damascus   Baghdad   Isfahan

Jerusalem

Kabul

Cairo

Red Sea

Indus

Doha   Dubai

Mecca

Arabian
Sea

INDIAN
OCEAN

KEY

☐ Umayyad Caliphate (*c.* 750 AD)

☐ Abbasid Caliphate (*c.* 850 AD)

▨ Ottoman Empire (*c.* 1690 AD)

N

A Note on Spelling

Is it to be Mohammed, Muhammad or Mahomet? Should it be the Quran, Koran or Qur'an? Transliterating Arabic is fraught with danger, and can be a pedant's paradise. There are various systems for 'precise' Arabic transliteration, but they are generally very complicated and have little to recommend them aesthetically. My aim has been to make things as simple and comprehensible as possible for the general reader. I do not wish to throw diacritical marks all over the text like confetti, a dot beneath an 's' and an 'h' here, a line above an 'i' or an 'a' there, apostrophes and hyphens crowding in like unwelcome visitors. Asked to choose between *Tārīkh al-'Irāq bayna Iḥtilālayn* (Abbas al Azzawi's *History of Iraq Between Two Occupations*) and *Tarikh al Iraq bayn al Ihtilayn*, I choose the latter without hesitation.

I have transliterated the guttural Arabic letter qaf or ق as 'q', rather than 'k' – unlike in my last book, where I did the opposite, so am already guilty of inconsistency. I have chosen to ignore altogether the problematic letter 'ayn or ع – virtually unpronounceable for those who do not know Arabic, and which tends to be variously rendered 'a', 'aa' or even '3' – because what does an apostrophe, or for that matter '3', really mean to the reader who does not know Arabic or the complexities of Arabic pronunciation? Arabic experts will surely know what is meant, and others will hardly notice its absence. So the caliph Ma'mun becomes simply Mamun and 'Iraq becomes Iraq. I prefer not to hyphenate the definite article, so I have Al Mansur and Al Amin rather than Al-Mansur and Al-Amin at the first mention, Mansur and Amin thereafter.

There are, I know, a number of other departures here from the most rigorous modern scholarly practice. Responding to a plea for clarity from the much put-upon editor of *Seven Pillars of Wisdom*, T. E. Lawrence replied tartly: 'There are some "scientific systems" of transliteration, helpful to people who know enough Arabic not to need helping, but a wash-out for the world. I spell my names anyhow, to show what rot the systems are.' I would not dream of suggesting these systems are rot, but less brazenly I have followed his example. And, to answer the question with which I began, the Prophet is Mohammed and the holy book revealed to him by Allah is the Quran.

Preface

'I'm embarrassed to be an Arab these days,' a Tunisian friend said to me recently. 'Everywhere you look there's chaos, fighting, bloodshed, dictatorship, corruption, injustice, unemployment. The only thing we're leading the world in is terrorism.'

That is indeed much of the perception in the West today, as well as in the Arab world itself. But of course it is far from being the whole story – and it wasn't always like this. A thousand years ago, Islamic civilization bestrode the world. For an Arab Muslim, pride in occupying the very summit of the global pecking order, rather than shame and embarrassment at languishing in its nether regions, was the order of the day. Many of the magnificent cities of North Africa, the Middle East and Central Asia were architectural, intellectual and economic wonders in their own right. From Damascus, Baghdad and Cordoba to Cairo, Fez and Samarkand, the capitals of successive Islamic Empires were famed – and frequently feared – across the world. They represented an exhilarating combination of military might, artistic grandeur, commercial power and spiritual sanctity. They were also powerhouses of forward-looking thinking in science, medicine, mathematics, astronomy, cartography, calligraphy, history, geography, law, music, theology, jurisprudence and philosophy, each metropolis a superbly humming engine room of innovation and discovery. Outgunned, out-peopled and out-thought, Christian Europe looked south and east with envy, dread and hostility. While Baghdad could boast of a population of about 800,000 in the ninth century, London and Paris by contrast were minnows of just 20,000 in 1100. Islamic cities, then, were the embodiment of a superior civilization.

The word 'civilization' springs from the Latin *civis*, a citizen, which is in turn related to *civitas*, a city. From these etymological origins, it is only a short step to argue that a city civilizes – it removes men and women from a savage, barbarian life – and that without cities there is no such thing as civilization. It is within cities, rather than among deserts, wildernesses, steppes, mountains and jungles, however beautiful and spirit-soaring, that humankind has realized its greatest potential: excelling in the arts and sciences, exploring the human condition and leaving an indelible literary legacy.

When it comes to the geographical origins of civilization, however,

Latin offers us little guidance. Our gaze must move 3,000 miles east of Rome, to what today is Iraq, and which for much of its millennial history Ancient Greeks knew as Lower Mesopotamia, the fertile, irrigated land between the life-giving Tigris and Euphrates rivers.* It was here, from Sumerian times in the sixth millennium BC through the Babylonian, Assyrian, Achaemenid, Seleucid, Parthian, Roman and Sassanid periods, that successive empires, civilizations and great cities such as Akkad, Assur, Babylon, Ur, Uruk, Nineveh, Nippur and Nimrud first flourished. These ancient cities rose in mud-brick splendour from the Mesopotamian plain, lorded it over the world around them and wrote their names into posterity. Most had subsided into crumbling ruins by the time Islam arrived in the seventh century.

If Mesopotamia gave the world its first cities, the Islamic Empires that followed in the region bequeathed some of the most glorious and resplendent capitals ever seen. This book looks at fifteen of them, focusing on a single city in each of the fifteen centuries of Islam from the time of the Prophet Mohammed and the birth of the new faith to the present day. In its own way each has contributed decisively to the history of the Dar al Islam, or Muslim world.

Islamic Empires traces a history of this world through some of its greatest cities and during some of its most important and dramatic moments, focusing on what Herodotus, the fifth-century BC 'Father of History' called 'great and marvellous deeds'. It begins in the seventh century and ends in the twenty-first, with intermittent forays into the present day.

Our story necessarily starts in Mecca, where the history of Islam first began amid the parched Hijaz desert of Arabia, and which remains to this day the holiest place for the world's 1.5 billion Muslims, the lodestar to which they turn five times a day in prayer. It is also unique within the Muslim world for prohibiting non-Muslims, a tradition fiercely upheld ever since the new faith seized it from pagan hands, and which is scrupulously maintained to this day. Unlike every other city in this book, it is by definition an exclusive city, a sanctuary of complete purity from which outsiders are excluded. It is, to that extent, an emblem of Islam's superiority complex.

The surge of Arab horsemen out of the desert, blazing a trail of Islamic conquest during the seventh century, shook the world. From the Arabian Peninsula in the lifetime of the Prophet, the Islamic Empire rapidly spread

---

* The word 'Iraq' – from the Arabic for 'vein' or 'root' – is thought to trace its earliest origins to the Sumerian city of Uruk, dating back to around 4000 BC, via the Aramaic Erech and possibly Persian Eragh.

north and west under the rule of his first four successors as caliph – the Rashidun, or 'Rightly Guided', leaders Abu Bakr, Umar, Uthman and Ali. Its first great capital was Damascus, from where the Umayyad Dynasty (r. 661–750) expanded Islamic dominions into one of the largest empires the world had ever seen, extending from the Atlantic Coast of North Africa and the Iberian Peninsula in the west to the mountains of Central Asia and the borders of China and India in the east.

After a revolution in 750 brought a vicious and bloody end to the Umayyads, they made way for the Abbasids, who reigned from their incomparable new metropolis of Baghdad, City of Peace, from 762 to 1258. For much of these 500 years, this was the pre-eminent city on earth, a marvel of opulent palaces, sky-filling mosques and *madrassas* (religious colleges), libraries, universities and research institutes crammed with some of the world's finest, mostly Muslim, scholars, a sophisticated network of roads and canals, state-of-the-art hospitals and thriving markets. Baghdad was a quintessentially cosmopolitan capital in which art, music, wine-drinking and poetry (sometimes bawdy enough to shock modern readers) testified to the self-confident pluralism of Islam.

Over time the Islamic Empire fragmented. In 929, the emir or prince Abd al Rahman III (r. 929–61) renounced his notional allegiance to Baghdad from distant Al Andalus and declared a rival caliphate in Cordoba. With throngs of high-minded scholars beavering away in its prodigiously stocked libraries during his reign, the Andalusian city became *decus orbis*, the ornament of the world.

Jerusalem moves to the centre of my narrative in the apocalyptic First Crusade of 1099, whose infamy lives on in many Muslim minds to this day. Known as Al Quds by Arabs, the city is scarcely less holy than Mecca within Islam and bears witness at once to humankind's reverence for religion and its often fatal predilection for competition and strife. Centuries of conflict, which continue today, have given it the unwished-for moniker of most contested city on earth.

After the ignominy and humiliation of the First Crusade at the climax of the eleventh century, we move to Cairo – Al Qahira, 'The Victorious' – for more auspicious Islamic fortunes under the legendary Kurdish leader Saladin in the twelfth. The Crusaders were routed, Jerusalem was retaken, honour was restored. Sunni Islam and prestige were reinstated at the heart of the Muslim world.

Thousands of miles away at the other, western end of the Dar al Islam, one city stood out gloriously in the thirteenth century. Known as the 'Athens of Africa', Fez emerged under the Marinid Dynasty (r. 1244–1465) as a world-illuminating centre of learning to rival the Europe of Dante,

Aquinas, Froissart, Bacon and Chaucer. To this day its sprawling *medina*, or Old City, remains the largest in the world and one of the most completely bewitching sights on earth.

In the fourteenth century, no city within the Islamic world could compete with Samarkand, 'Pearl of the East', nor could any Muslim leader match the mighty Turkic warlord Timur, better known in the West as Tamerlane. A one-man empire-builder who was undefeated in battle over four decades in the saddle, he turned Samarkand into a dazzling, blue-domed metropolis of peerless monuments admired across Asia. He also turned many of the continent's finest cities, including several of those described here, into smoking wastelands surrounded by the dreadful, vulture-haunted towers made from the piled up decapitated heads of his enemies.

For much of the eight centuries since the faith first emerged, Islam was a clear and present danger to Christendom. That contest came to a climax in 1453 with the youthful Ottoman Sultan Mehmed II's extraordinary conquest of Constantinople, longed for and attempted by Muslim armies on numerous occasions since the time of the Prophet. It was a seismic event whose resonance is still felt, with pain and pride respectively, by so many Greeks and Turks today. And, although it did not happen overnight, the steady transition from Christian Constantinople to Muslim Istanbul was of enormous lasting significance.

High in the Hindu Kush mountains of Central Asia, a new Islamic Empire was born in the sixteenth century. From his diminutive capital of Kabul, Babur 'The Tiger', great-great-great-grandson of Timur, looked south for his conquests and founded the long-lived Mughal Empire that would transform the Indian Subcontinent and endure until 1857. As ambitious with the pen as he was with his sword, Babur is also widely revered as the author of the *Baburnama*, one of the greatest treasure troves of Muslim literature. With its wine-soaked, hashish-perfumed tales of wild parties and daring military missions among the mountains, this high-spirited autobiography represents a thrilling counterpoint to the view, widespread in the West, that Islam is monolithic, austere, intolerant. It is another timely and elegant reminder of the early pluralism of the Islamic world.

Isfahan is one of the few non-Arab cities included here. While most capitals in the book represent the orthodox Sunni sect of Islam, Isfahan is a glittering gem of the Shia world. It would justify its inclusion on grounds of architectural wonder alone, even without the story of Shah Abbas I, the man who created and reimagined it so brilliantly while leading the Safavid Empire (r. 1501–1722) to new heights in the seventeenth century – a formidable challenge to the Ottomans in the west and the Mughals in the east. Little wonder the poets eulogized Isfahan as 'Half the World' in and of itself.

Libyans have long known Tripoli fondly as the 'Bride of the Sea'. These days some call it the 'Widow of the Sea', following the turmoil and blood-shed since the revolution of 2011; as I write these words in early 2019, gunfire from posturing militia fighters rifles across the city. Although the eighteenth century marked neither the zenith nor nadir of the city's for-tunes, it was one of Tripoli's most remarkable chapters in the ruthless and audacious overthrow of Ottoman hegemony by the pugnacious Karamanli Dynasty. This upstart family ruled from 1711 to 1835, during which time its unruly pirate fleet became the scourge of Mediterranean shipping. With its fearsome Barbary corsairs, whose ranks included renegade European Muslim converts, Tripoli intruded upon both Ottoman and European consciousness as never before.

Where better than Beirut, the 'Paris of the Middle East', to exemplify sophisticated and leisurely nineteenth-century city life? Under the late Ottoman Empire, and with increasing European diplomatic and commer-cial engagement, here a melange of Muslims and Christians blossomed spectacularly, harnessing the indigenous genius for trade, enriching its cosmopolitan residents and setting the bar high for pleasure-seeking syb-arites. In the periodic, sometimes catastrophic, conflicts between the diverse sects and communities – at once a strength and a weakness – there is also a crueller side to Beirut's story, which is as relevant today as it was then.

Few could ever have predicted that a desperately obscure little fishing community in the Arabian Gulf, completely unknown to the outside world, would transform itself within a few decades of the twentieth cen-tury into a city-state of monumental skyscrapers famed across the planet. Yet one family's unstoppable vision, based on a reckless, bet-the-farm gamble and a visceral instinct for free trade, achieved the impossible with Dubai. It has become a beacon for Arabs fleeing repression and corruption, for fortune-seeking Western expatriates, and for impoverished manual workers of Asia and the Subcontinent in search of a better life. More than merely Arab, it is a truly global city. The Maktoums built it and the world came.

The story ends in our own time in another, no less astonishing, city-state. Like a chrysalis metamorphising into a butterfly, Doha has evolved from utterly insignificant pearl-fishing village into the world's richest twenty-first-century city. As a purely urban phenomenon, developing at breakneck speed, it has appeared almost unfathomably from the pitiless Arabian sands. As in Dubai, one family stands *primus inter pares* and is equally hungry for global recognition. The Al Thanis' international trophy-buying spree, from Harrods and the Shard skyscraper in London to the football club Paris St Germain and investments in blue-chip Western companies such as Porsche, Siemens and Credit Suisse, has put Qatar, and its mushrooming capital, definitively on the map. Like its neighbour Dubai, it is nothing less than a modern wonder of the world.

I should stress that this is a very personal selection. Though some cities, such as Mecca, Damascus, Baghdad, Cairo and Istanbul, would find their way into any history of the Islamic world, it would be perfectly possible to draw up a very different list to encompass the fifteen centuries of Islam. Jakarta, Lahore and Delhi are not included here, despite representing the three countries with the largest Muslim populations in the world. There is no Balkh, Bukhara, Khiva, Tabriz, Shiraz, Mosul, Merv, Aleppo or Ghazni, to name just a few of the cities that once sparkled across the Islamic firmament. The ancient Holy City of Qairouan in Tunisia equally fails to make my director's cut. With just one city per century, this is a competitive list. Moving into the present day, Marseille or Bradford, rather than Doha, could easily have provided a very different twenty-first century perspective. My personal experience over several decades as a journalist and historian, starting with stints in Istanbul, Cairo and Tripoli as a teenager, has been in the Middle East, North Africa and Central Asia, and it is from these three regions, which include the cradle and still the heart of the Islamic world, that I have chosen.

The Dar al Islam is diverse and diffuse, ranging ever more widely from the Far East and North America to Africa and Europe as the world's fastest-growing religion, but Arabs have long played a disproportionate role within it. Arabic will always be the original language of the Quran, the tongue in which Mohammed received the first revelation in a cave high above Mecca, and therefore the 'purest' language of Islam. The presence in the heart of the Arabian Peninsula of both Mecca and Medina, so pivotal in the history of the religion, further strengthens the focus on this region as the nucleus of the Muslim world.

A word about method. Archives, histories, biographies, travelogues, letters, maps, pictures, photographs and all the other documentary records are necessary and essential to the historian, but they do not rule out consulting the living. As the Roman tribune Sicinius asks the citizens in Shakespeare's *Coriolanus*, 'What is a city but the people?' 'True,' the citizens reply, 'the people are the city.'[1] The voices of the men and women who come from these fifteen cities offer fresh perspectives on important and enduring themes, which echo across the region today.

And if we listen carefully enough, there is an insistent dialogue between the voices of our contemporary world and its historical underpinnings. Capricious Clio, the muse of history, is more regularly discernible than one might imagine. We hear her, for example, in one man's dream of restoring a global empire that fell a century ago, when the Turkish president tells his people that Turkey is 'the only country that can lead the Muslim world'.[2] We hear her call too in contemporary conversations about Islamic history, freedom and democracy, human rights and repression, terrorism, the supposed clash between Christian West and Muslim East, foreign meddling and conspiracy theories, sectarian divisions, tolerance and intolerance, the ongoing cataclysm of *fitna*, an Arabic word encompassing division, discord and disorder, which has convulsed so much of the Muslim world in recent years – and in my Tunisian friend's embarrassment about being Arab.

Together these fifteen cities tell a very different story from that which is so prevalent today, an engrossing history of Islamic strength, scholarship and spirituality. They testify to the once boundless capacity for daring and innovation which helped make the Dar al Islam for many centuries the world's greatest civilization. Above all, perhaps, they recall a spirit of tolerance, plurality and cosmopolitanism, which were once so integral to the fortunes of the Islamic world and which many hope can once again be recaptured.

I

Mecca – Mother of All Cities
(7th Century)

Many a time have We seen you turn your face towards the sky.
We will make you turn towards a qiblah that will please you. *
Turn your face towards the Holy Mosque; wherever you be, turn
your faces towards it.

Quran 2:144

For centuries Mecca has been a mostly intangible aspiration. It haunts the imaginations of the great majority of Muslims unable to complete the arduous, often dangerous and invariably expensive *hajj* pilgrimage. Those fortunate enough to have made the journey frequently consider the *hajj* the most spiritually satisfying experience of their lives. They return describing it in hallowed tones, recalling pounding hearts, quickening pulses and flowing tears, using words like 'mind-blowing', 'mesmerizing' and 'humbling'. To a man and woman, each pilgrim is overwhelmed by an emotionally charged experience in a gathering of humanity without parallel in history.

The city of the Prophet Mohammed's birth has always drawn its potency for Muslims from both the story of his God-given revelations there in the seventh century and the totemic status of the Kaaba, the cube of black granite which is considered the House of God, at the heart of the pilgrimage. All Muslims who were physically and financially able to do so were required by the Quran to perform the *hajj* to Mecca, the only place in the world where such a visit was obligatory. The subsequent centuries of tradition and pilgrimage have only added greater brilliance to

* The *qiblah*, Arabic for 'direction', is the direction in which Muslims pray towards Mecca. It is generally indicated by a *mihrab* niche in the wall of a mosque that is oriented towards Islam's holiest city.

the city's unique lustre within the Islamic world. Mecca is the immutable and undisputed centre of Islam, the lodestar to which the world's Muslims direct their prayers; the Kaaba the single point on the planet around which pilgrims literally revolve.

Today a clock tower rears 600 metres above the Kaaba, completely dwarfing the sacred monument that inspired its erection. Were a pigeon to leave its seed-hunting colleagues at ground level for a few minutes and flutter up to these dizzying heights, it would stare down to the north at what might be taken for a vast sports stadium teeming with white-robed fans moving in procession around a rectangular object. Yet this is no sports arena. The Abraj Al Bait, or Makkah Royal Clock Tower, a sky-scraper complex of luxury hotels, apartments and shopping malls, complete with heliports, jacuzzis, saunas, steam rooms, chocolate rooms, beauty parlours, business centres, ballrooms and twenty-four-hour butler service, looms over Islam's holiest mosque, the Masjid al Haram, or Sacred Mosque, and the cube at its heart, the Kaaba. Once a year, in the world's greatest display of organized religion, a swirl of humanity circum-ambulates seven times around this thirteen-metre high stone block, directing its collective prayers to the Almighty.

Islam's holiest place has witnessed innumerable changes over the fifteen centuries since the time of the Prophet Mohammed, beginning with a series of property expropriations and 'improvements' under the caliphs Umar (r. 634–44) and Uthman (r. 644–56), yet none as rapidly introduced or so dramatically skyline-changing as those of the twenty-first. In 2002, to make way for the new clock tower complex, the Saudi authorities demolished the Ajyad Fortress, the Ottoman citadel built around 1780 to protect Mecca from invaders. Amid the international outcry that followed, the Turkish government called the destruction a 'crime against humanity . . . and cultural massacre'.[1] In a curious twist of the old adage about the mountain and Mohammed, the Saudis also levelled the Bulbul hill on which the fortress had stood.

Some footprints in Mecca, such as those of Patriarch Abraham, the legendary builder of the Kaaba, which are preserved in the heart of the holy mosque, are more revered than others. The footprint of the Makkah Royal Clock Tower stands on an estimated 95 per cent of Mecca's millennium-old buildings, including 400 sites of cultural and historical importance. The house of Abu Bakr, Mohammed's closest companion and the first caliph of the Muslim Empire (r. 632–4), was displaced by the Mak-kah Hilton. The house belonging to Khadija, the Prophet's cherished first wife, is now a block of public lavatories. Not even the Prophet's house has been spared the obliteration. It was buried beneath a new royal palace.[2]

Behemoth that it is, the Makkah Royal Clock Tower is just a small part of a vast, multibillion-dollar redevelopment programme that is utterly transforming Mecca. The wholesale destruction and construction have been met with anguish by many Muslims and non-Muslims alike. In 2014, the Ottoman section of the mosque, which contained its oldest surviving features, including beautifully carved marble columns built by a series of rulers from Sultan Suleiman to Sultan Murad IV between 1553 and 1629, was pulled down to make way for multi-storey, air-conditioned prayer halls. To the west of the Great Mosque is the Jebel Omar project, where a forest of new skyscrapers containing more luxury hotels will soar from another levelled hill. To the north is the Al Shamiya development, an extension of the mosque that will accommodate 250,000 people and add 300,000 square metres of prayer halls.

The Saudi government maintains the development is essential to accommodate the relentlessly growing number of revenue-generating pilgrims, which is expected to continue to rise sharply from around 2 million today. Saudi Arabia's Grand Mufti, Sheikh Abdul Aziz Bin Abdullah al Sheikh, says the nation should thank the government for the vital reconstruction work.[3]

Yet many Meccans mutter darkly about their holy city being transformed into another Las Vegas. Sami Angawi, the Saudi architect and founder of the Hajj Research Centre, has described the ongoing redevelopment of Islam's most sacred site as a complete contradiction of the nature of Mecca and the sacredness of the House of God. It is, he says, 'truly indescribable. They are turning the holy sanctuary into a machine, a city which has no identity, no heritage, no culture and no natural environment. They've even taken away the mountains.'[4] Critics noted that the then King Abdullah's order for a masterplan for Mecca and its surroundings came only long after the giant construction projects were well underway. To the loss of heritage from the earliest Islamic period must also be added the profound human cost of this razed-ground reconstruction. Residents of this ancient quarter were evicted with a week's notice before the most historic part of the Old City was flattened. 'Locals, who have lived here for generations, are being forced out to make way for these marble castles in the sky,' says Irfan al Alawi, director of the Islamic Heritage Research Foundation in Mecca.[5]

Among the pilgrims, reactions have been mixed. Some have seen Mecca's mega-tower as a sign that the end time is drawing near. They cite as evidence one of the *hadith*, or sayings of Mohammed, in which the Prophet told the Angel Jibril that 'When the shepherds of black camels start boasting and competing with others in the construction of higher buildings', the Day of Judgement was approaching.[6] While some admire the bold modernity and confidence of Mecca's transformation, others find the commercialism inappropriate and disorientating. 'What the Saudis have done to Mecca is completely ghastly,' says one British Muslim recalling how his pilgrimage was marred by the 'retail extravaganza' that extends right up to the Great Mosque. 'The last things I saw before turning towards the Kaaba were a Samsonite shop and Häagen-Dazs. They've turned Mecca into a shopping mall.'[7]

It is certainly true that the loss of ancient heritage strikes a common chord with those interested in cultural history, reminiscent of the Taliban's destruction of the Buddhas of Bamiyan in Afghanistan in 2001 and the self-proclaimed Islamic State's destruction of similarly 'idolatrous' heritage, including the sites of Nimrud in Iraq and Palmyra in Syria, in 2015. Yet tragic as these recent urban developments in the cradle of Islam are, there is something historically appropriate about naked commercialism thriving at the heart of Mecca, a settlement whose earliest origins – certainly in legend, probably in reality – are intimately connected with both trade and the vigorous extraction of money from pilgrims. As an ancient local saying goes, 'We sow not wheat or sorghum; the pilgrims are our crops.'[8]

It is only fair to note, too, that Mecca has never been a great source of culture. The exceptional, world-illuminating gifts of Islamic civilization in the arts and sciences, from architecture, mathematics and astronomy to geography and geometry, poetry, physics and philosophy, came not from Mecca but from cities such as Damascus, Baghdad, Cordoba, Cairo, Fez, Samarkand, Istanbul and Isfahan, among many others. Where those metropolises were cosmopolitan and open, melting-pots of Islam, Judaism and Christianity, of all faiths and none, Mecca has long been insular and closed. It remains to this day a bastion of purity, strictly forbidden to the non-Muslim visitor.

And as for the loss of history, while it is true that it can be bulldozed away in Mecca with scarcely a thought, it can also, as we shall see, just as easily be invented.

The extreme inhospitality of Mecca's location requires no such invention. Hemmed in between two steep mountains in a depression at the bottom of a narrow, poorly ventilated, riverless, treeless valley in a desolate corner of the Hijaz desert, forty-three miles inland from the port city of Jeddah, it has long been prone to head-roasting summer temperatures approaching fifty degrees Celsius – the notorious *ramdaa Makka* or burning of Mecca – and destructive flash floods brought on by violent thunderstorms bringing epidemics in their wake.[9] It is more cursed than blessed by nature. For the early Islamic poet Al Hayqatan, Mecca was a place where 'winter and summer are equally intolerable. No waters flow . . . not a blade of grass on which to rest the eye; no, nor hunting. Only merchants, the most despicable of professions.'[10] An early chronicler mentions a landscape barren but for acacias and thorny trees. Speaking to God in the Quran, Abraham described it simply as 'a valley without cultivation'.[11] It was a settlement shrouded in 'suffocating heat, deadly wind, clouds of flies', according to the tenth-century Arab geographer Muqaddasi.[12] An intermittent supply of water from the Zamzam Well offered the only respite from this parched wilderness. Dependent on caravan supplies of grain from Syria and Iraq, it was a pitiless, rocky, sterile, rain-starved world prone to regular famine. Agriculture was an impossible dream. The reader is probably entitled, therefore, to raise an eyebrow at the suggestion from Ibn Ishaq, the eighth-century historian and earliest biographer of the Prophet Mohammed, that Mecca was 'a town blessed with water and trees'.[13]

Furrowed brows aside, there is much more serious cause for concern when it comes to investigating the earliest days of Islam. The historian faces formidable difficulties here because the history of Mecca, where the human and supernatural drama first played out, is far more impenetrable than the roiling desert wastes that surround it. Navigating through shifting sands of history, faith and fable towards fixed historical references is a fraught affair since, apart from legends, the evidence on early Mecca is 'extremely scanty'.[14] Archaeology in this part of Arabia is virtually non-existent and there is precious little evidence in terms of inscriptions, coins and papyri from this pre-Islamic era of oral culture.

As a result, for the early history of the cities where Islam was born and where the Prophet Mohammed lived and died, 'we must rely almost entirely on what later – in some cases, much later – Muslims tell us'.[15] Frustratingly for the historian, Muslim sources on Mecca and Mohammed begin only in around the mid-eighth century, leaving a tantalizing 120 years or so from the death of Mohammed unaccounted for by contemporaries.

While Muslims tend to accept the traditional Islamic sources and generally do not consider this lacuna problematic, for other scholars it has become especially vexing. The dearth of first-hand material is so severe that a principal source for the birth of Islam in and around Mecca is Quranic exegesis, which is not without its own significant problems of dating and interpretation.

In recent decades a 'highly sceptical school of historical analysis regarding the origins of Islam' has arisen, casting 'grave doubt' on the traditional

Muslim accounts, which have been dismissed as 'tendentious Islamic historiography'.[16] Early Muslim biographies of the Prophet, for example, contain 'so many contradictions and so much dubious storytelling' that they are difficult to accept at face value.[17] In essence, the accusation is that these are less historical accounts than literary constructions, written long after the events they purport to describe and with a clear agenda – to promote the new faith and ground it in historical certainty.

Muslim tradition holds that Adam built God's House, the Kaaba, in Mecca shortly after the Creation according to a divine design, so that a religious sanctuary predates Mecca as a settlement. It is problematic, however, that outside Arabia nowhere within the sprawling mass of literature in Greek, Latin, Syriac, Aramaic or Coptic is there a single mention of Mecca before the Arab conquests, and yet the tradition maintains this was a thriving centre of trade and pagan religious devotion.[18] During an exhaustive survey of the western coast of Arabia in *The History of the Wars*, the first-century Roman author Procopius makes no mention of Mecca. A century later, Ptolemy's *Geography* refers to a Macoraba in the Arabian interior whose coordinates approximate to those of Mecca. We must wait until 741, more than a century after the Prophet's death, for a mention of Mecca in a foreign text, and even then the *Byzantine-Arab Chronicle* locates it far to the north in Mesopotamia.[19]

The debate over the history of seventh-century Mecca, however contentious and inconclusive, is critical because it forms the foundation of a far wider story: that of the Prophet Mohammed, the revelation of the Quran and the birth of Islam. The stakes are high because this is a contest over the very historicity of the Islamic narrative about Mohammed, Mecca and Islam. What for one person constitutes legitimate historical enquiry, for another is an unpardonable offence to the Prophet. And since the traditional penalty in Islam for apostasy – renouncing the religion in thought or deed – is capital punishment, in some cases this can be a matter of life and death.

For all the efforts of medieval Muslim scholars, however, we must conclude that certainty about the origins of Mecca, the Kaaba, and the birth of Islam itself, remains elusive. In a sense, this should not be unduly surprising or too difficult to accept. Contemporary confusion in some quarters neatly echoes the reactions of seventh-century Christians, for whom the rise of Islam was a complete and sudden mystery. In 614, midway through the ruinous Byzantine–Sasanian War of 602–28, the Persians conquered Jerusalem. It was only natural for the Byzantines to consider the Persians their principal adversary. And yet in 637, just five years after the death of Mohammed, the forlorn Patriarch Sophronius of Jerusalem was surrendering the keys of the city not to the Persian Empire, which was by then close to terminal collapse, but to the ascendant Arab caliph Umar, leader of a new, unknown and militant faith.

So much for this irreconcilable tussle between faith and doubt. Since it is impossible either to prove or disprove a religion and its foundations, and since faith by definition requires a considerable suspension of disbelief, and credence in the supernatural and divine, let us acknowledge this certain blurring at the intersection of early history and the rise of a new faith and move onto the no less contentious literary record.

To begin with Mecca and the Kaaba, the earliest source on the settlement is Al Azraqi, the ninth-century editor of *Kitab Akhbar Makka* (*Book of Reports about Mecca*), a title remarkable for being the first Arabic history of a single city. Azraqi claims that the sacred stone dates back to the very beginning of time before Creation itself. 'The Kaaba was the froth on the water forty years before God Almighty created the heavens and the earth; from it the earth was spread out.'[20] Azraqi tells his readers in a series of iterations that Adam built up the Kaaba, that Abraham and his son Ishmael rebuilt it after the Flood and that the Quraysh, the predominant pagan tribe in Mecca from the fifth century, rebuilt it again during the time of Mohammed in the dying days of what Muslim Arabs refer to as the Jahiliya, the Age of Ignorance before Islam. Later, Arab geographers referred to Mecca as 'the Navel of the Earth'. The Quran, perhaps surprisingly, contains only a few references to the Kaaba. It narrates how it was created as 'a resort and a sanctuary for mankind', a site of worship at 'the place where Abraham stood' and that it was built and dedicated by Abraham and Ishmael, who cleansed it for those who walked around it, prayed and worshipped in it.[21]

Nor is the Quran much more forthcoming on Mecca, or indeed many other locations – only nine places are mentioned by name in the entire text. Mecca is referred to by name only once,* prompting the suggestion that 'the Quran is as little interested in Mecca as the Gospels are in Nazareth'.[22] Two verses speak of 'the Mother of Cities' and are interpreted as references to Mecca.[23] Tradition has it that another reference in the Quran to Bakka is an alternative name for Mecca, but again, although the verse pulls together the related threads of a sacred sanctuary, the *Maqam*, or Station of Abraham, and the duty of pilgrimage, firm evidence remains beyond our reach.†

* 'It was He who ended hostilities between you in the Valley of Mecca after He had given you victory over them. God was watching all your actions'. Quran 48:24
† 'The first temple ever to be built for mankind was that at Bakka, a blessed site, a beacon for the nations. In it there are veritable signs and the spot where Abraham stood. Whoever enters it is safe. Pilgrimage to the House is a duty to God for all who can make the journey.' Quran 3:96–7

Together with Azraqi and Ibn Ishaq, Mohammed ibn Jarir al Tabari, the prolific, ninth-century author of the *History of the Prophets and Kings* (whose English translation runs into a whopping thirty-eight volumes, or around 10,000 pages), forms a trio of historians who date Mecca's foundation as a permanent settlement by a tribesman called Qusay ibn Kilab any time between 400 and 470. Before this the tribes had been camping on the mountain slopes above the valley. We are told that at the time of Noah's Flood, which destroyed the Kaaba, Mecca was uninhabited, and the surrounding country was populated by the Jurhum and the Amalekites. The Jurhum were the custodians of the Kaaba from around the beginning of the second century to the first half of the third. Their behaviour apparently left a great deal to be desired and their depravity was infamous. Lovers looking for a discreet spot for liaisons would on occasion sneak off into the Kaaba, including one couple who, after having sex there, were promptly 'transformed into two stones' in punishment for such sacrilege. Mecca, Tabari tells us, 'was also called Bakkah, because it used to break (*tabukk*) the necks of evildoers and tyrants when they acted wrongfully there'.[24] In time the Jurhum were displaced by the Khuzaa, who held sway at Mecca until they in turn were replaced by the Quraysh, the Prophet Mohammed's tribe.

Qusay cleared the immediate shrine area and settled his people there in what proved a decisive move from desert nomadism towards an urban community, precursor to the rise of the Islamic city. His most important construction was the Dar al Nadwa, Arabia's first council chamber, where political, social and commercial questions were discussed and settled. Other ceremonies, such as circumcisions, betrothals of marriage and declarations of war were also carried out here. The building doubled as Qusay's personal house, and a door from it opened directly onto the Kaaba. Then, as now, proximity to the Kaaba defined the status of residents and visitors alike – for every guest wafting around the air-conditioned splendour of the Fairmont in the Makkah Royal Clock Tower, there are many more poorer pilgrims sweltering in substandard, 'dangerous' and 'appalling' conditions, some even in squalor.[25] One obvious hazard of living too near the Kaaba, however, for late seventh- and early twenty-first-century residents alike, has been the tendency of the authorities, be they medieval caliphs or contemporary Al Sauds, to summarily expropriate land and property to allow ad hoc redevelopments and expansion of the shrine.

The Quraysh established the sanctuary of the Haram, an area extending in a twenty-mile radius from the Kaaba in which all violence was completely prohibited and all visitors were free from attack, a critical consideration in a place beset by tribal rivalries, constant raiding and conflict. Inveterate pagans and worshippers of idols, as the exclusively Muslim writers are always keen to remind us, each tribe had its own stone effigy god. As monopolists of the Kaaba pilgrimage, the Quraysh collected the various totems of the different tribes and installed them for their worship in the Haram. They themselves worshipped Hubal, a large reddish stone inside the Kaaba, together with the three chief goddesses of Mecca, Allat, Al Uzza and Manat.*

Muslim authors highlight a distinct vein of greed and licentiousness in pagan Mecca (for many critics, such greed remains an integral part of today's Mecca). With the aim of maximizing pilgrim revenues, the Quraysh introduced a policy prohibiting visitors from bringing their own clothes and food into the sanctuary.

It appears that from the early sixth century Arabian tribesmen were trading at a series of *suqs* or markets. They travelled in a clockwise loop, starting in Bahrain, Oman and Yemen before five consecutive markets in and around Mecca, culminating in the month of *hajj* in Mecca and its holy Kaaba. Saddle-sore and sunburnt from their journeys, once they reached Mecca the tribesmen performed the traditional rites of pilgrimage, surrounded by 360 tribal totems. First they jogged seven times between the hills of Safa and Marwa, re-enacting the frantic search for water of Abraham's discarded second wife, Hagar, with her infant son Ishmael. After running to the hollow of Muzdalifa, home of the mighty thunder god, the tribesmen then held an all-night vigil on the plain beneath Mount Arafat, sixteen miles outside Mecca. In a reference to the three times Satan tried to tempt Abraham, they hurled pebbles at three pillars in the valley of Mina, east of Mecca. The *tawaf* was the anticlockwise circumambulation of the Kaaba seven times, perhaps a re-enactment of the circular trade route. A sacrifice of the tribesmen's most precious female camels brought the pilgrimage to a hearty, blood-soaked end.

Mecca, then, was an important site to visit and a highly profitable place to control. While acknowledging the religious bias of the earliest sources, it appears that trade and religion were the main drivers in the development of pre-Islamic Mecca. Historians suggest there was a transport revolution sometime in the fifth century, during which the Arabian Bedouin invented a saddle capable of carrying much heavier camel loads. As a result, Indian, East African, Yemeni and Bahraini merchants replaced their slow-moving donkey carts with camels, obviating the need to bypass the Arabian

---

* The trio of goddesses is roundly rejected in Quran 53:23: 'They are but names which you and your fathers have invented: God has vested no authority in them.'

Peninsula for those trading in luxury goods, including incense, spices, ivory, cereals, pearls, wood, fabrics and medicines, to Byzantium and Syria. Bedouin guides and guards were employed for protection along the way.[26]

Recent studies suggest that Meccan trade was given a significant fillip by Hashim ibn Manaf, grandson of Qusay, who invented the *ilaf*, a commercial agreement which enabled the less affluent members of the community to pool their capital and invest in a caravan. Thus there was an *ilaf* with Syria to grant safe conduct for Meccan merchants trading cloths and leather. This was an innovation that helped internationalize Meccan commerce, opening up business in Busra, Gaza, Alexandria and other markets under Byzantine control, facilitating trade missions to Abyssinia, Yemen and Persia. Commerce was a fragile affair in such a remote corner of the Hijaz. With many traders periodically teetering on bankruptcy prior to the *ilaf*, Hashim's masterstroke appears to have ended the grim tradition of *itifad*, or ritual suicide, by which a merchant who had lost all his wealth would be forced to separate himself and his family from the wider clan and simply starve to death.[27]

According to the traditional view, Mecca owed its very existence to trade. 'Pilgrimage rite and trade were indivisible in this city.'[28] A word of warning is necessary here because again we are on contested territory. Some revisionists have expressed doubts as to whether Mecca was really the Quraysh's commercial headquarters; more controversially, another writer has speculated that Mohammed may not even have received his divine revelation there at all.[29] The accusation is that Muslim sources deliberately and retrospectively exaggerated the status of seventh-century Mecca to make it a more fitting home for the new faith.

These early Muslim sources are certainly determined to demonstrate that Mecca was of sufficient wealth, sanctity and importance to be the object of foreign envy and desire. They report that in 570 mighty Abraha, the Christian ruler of Himyar and former Abyssinian viceroy in Yemen, led an army to Mecca to demonstrate that the sanctuary there was neither divinely protected nor invulnerable. Since Abraha had built a splendid rival sanctuary in Sanaa, he had a vested interest in proving the point. Just as his war elephant reached the outskirts of Mecca and was ready to do its worst, it suddenly fell to its knees and, miraculously, refused to attack. Mecca survived. This was an event so momentous it was recorded in the Quran, a rarity in a holy book which, unlike the Bible, scarcely records historical figures, actions and events.* This came to be known by

---

* 'Have you not considered how God dealt with the Army of the Elephant? Did He not confound their stratagem and send against them flocks of birds which pelted them with

Muslims as the Year of the Elephant. In legend or fact, Mecca's sacred inviolability had been proven. The sources elect 570, one is tempted to suspect, because this coincided with the birth of Mohammed and therefore made it doubly auspicious.[30]

If Azraqi were alive today and whisked up to the prayer room within the giant, thirty-five-tonne golden crescent which sits atop the Makkah Royal Clock Tower, once he had recovered from the shock of his vertiginous height, the mountain-swallowing explosion of construction and the pro-liferation of cranes, he would be able slowly, if shakily, to reconstruct his 1,200-year-old account of Mecca, which begins at its heart with the Kaaba.[31] From here he radiated out, broadening his view and pausing all the while to explain the most important and sacred landmarks within the holy of holies. First the Maqam Ibrahim, or Station of Abraham, the spot on which the patriarch stood as he built the upper walls of the Kaaba with his son Ishmael, today surrounded by pilgrims jostling to see the ancient footprints hollowed out in stone beneath a crystal dome. Continuing out, twenty metres east of the Kaaba, is the famous Zamzam Well, the miraculously revealed source of water that saved the life of Hagar and her son Ishmael. Today Zamzam water, bottled eagerly by the massed crowds of pilgrims during their visit, is treasured and drunk by Muslims the world over.

It is abundantly clear from Azraqi's account that the only monuments that really mattered in Mecca were those of the Kaaba and its associated features. Most of his 500-odd pages are devoted to them. The city's living quarters were almost an afterthought. Mecca was, to a very great extent, the Kaaba and the open space known as the Masjid al Haram immediately around it.

By the late sixth century, according to the Arab historians, Mecca was gripped by a spiritual crisis. The rise of market forces was tearing apart the traditional ties of community. Some merchants were becoming fan-tastically rich while other Meccans had been left behind in a grinding drudge of poverty. Again there is a strong sense that the historians were retrospectively creating the most propitious possible environment for the arrival of Mohammed. The Mecca that comes to us from the Muslim sources was a dark, demon-haunted settlement, a pagan den of iniquity and licentiousness that was home to satans, soothsayers and sorcerers. It

---

clay-stones, so that they became like the withered stalks of plants which cattle have devoured?'
Quran 105:1–5

was no place for the faint-hearted. Only a faith-founding, world-changing prophet could alter that.

It was into this sun-scorched pagan settlement that Mohammed was born in 570. However misty the outlines, however problematic the sources, the story of the future Prophet's life, and the religion and Islamic Empires that followed, are inextricably linked to that of Mecca – for better and worse.* It might be supposed that the founder of a faith would be the city's favourite son, but for much of his life the opposite was true. Though Meccan by birth, Mohammed had a complicated and difficult relationship with the town that encompassed revelation, rivalry and redemption, persecution, violence and bloodshed.

Born into the Hashim clan of the Quraysh, he was not of a wealthy family. His great-grandfather may have been the first merchant to trade independently with Syria and Yemen, but the death of Mohammed's father Abdullah before he was born brought the inevitable difficulties for the family. Worse was to come at the age of six when his mother Amina died. We hear the young orphan lived at first with his aged grandfather, who liked to have his bed carried outside so that he could relax in the sanctified shade of the Kaaba. After his grandfather's death, Mohammed went to live with his uncle Abu Talib, chief of the Hashim clan. In time he started to work in the caravan trade through another uncle, Abbas, managing the business on the northern leg to Syria. His skills as a merchant brought him to the attention of Khadija, a wealthy and desirable widow, whom he married at her suggestion. He was twenty-five, she was around forty.

The sources pay tribute to Mohammed's judgement and powers of mediation. One story tells how the Quraysh set about rebuilding the Kaaba with alternating layers of teak and stone, following a shipwreck off the coast at Jeddah in around 605. The unexpected supplies of timber were a godsend in this inhospitable wilderness. An argument broke out between the tribesmen competing for the honour of setting the famous Black Stone in place in the easternmost corner of the Kaaba wall. When an impasse occurred, it was agreed that the next person to come into the sanctuary should determine the question. In walked Mohammed, who advised the squabbling tribesmen to place the stone on a piece of cloth, grab a corner each and lift it up together. The difficulty was resolved, the honour was shared and Mohammed installed the stone himself. He came

---

* Ibn Ishaq and Tabari were by no means alone in writing about the life of the Prophet. Among the earliest sources were additional biographies written by Mohammed ibn Umar al Waqidi (d. *c.* 820) and his ninth century contemporary, Mohammed ibn Saad, prelude to a legion of biographers that continues undimmed to this day.

to be known as Al Amin, the reliable one. Today the fragments of rock are cemented into the Kaaba within a broad silver frame. Many Muslims try to touch and kiss it as they revolve around the cube.

So far, perhaps, so unremarkable. Then, in 610, the thunderbolt struck. The forty-year-old Mohammed was in a mountain cave high above Mecca, two miles out of town. For some time he had been seeking seclusion from his townsmen and women, spending days and nights meditating in the rocky hills. Now, in the depths of a starlit desert night overlooking the town of his birth, the voice of God suddenly burst forth in all its mesmerizing majesty. 'Recite!' the voice commanded. It was the Angel Jibril. The voice ignored the perfectly reasonable response from the illiterate Mohammed that he was unable to read and the command was repeated. 'Recite!* In the name of your Lord who created man from a clot. Recite! For your Lord is most generous, who has taught by the pen, taught man that which he knew not.'[32] It was a terrifying experience. Traumatized, Mohammed felt he was being pressed so tightly he would die. He believed he had been possessed by *jinn*, or malevolent spirits, and was ready to fling himself from the mountain to end the torment. He climbed up towards the summit, resolved to do his worst, only to be interrupted by a heavenly voice saying, 'O Mohammed! Thou art the apostle of God and I am Gabriel.'[33]

It was a life-transforming moment, later commemorated as Laylat al Qadr, the Night of Decree. The man who had climbed up to the cave as a perfectly ordinary Qurayshi tribesman descended, head spinning, as God's Prophet. And the words which had been revealed to him would be the earliest verses of the Quran. Fourteen hundred years later, many of the more physically committed pilgrims routinely make a beeline for the rocky crag of Mount Hira, also known as Jabal al Nour, the Mountain of Light. Ignoring the Saudi notices announcing that an ascent to the cave is not part of the pilgrimage, they slog up flights of stairs to gaze in wonder and devotion at a little slab-roofed, graffiti-covered cave measuring four metres by one and a half. Some recite poems, some kiss the rocks, others fall to their knees in prayer.

The revelations continued to pour forth in fits and starts over the following years. Then, in around 613, the preaching in Mecca began. Mohammed started railing against idolatry and polytheism. For much of his life in Mecca from this time, he was the object of scorn and hostility. From the Qurayshi perspective, it is not difficult to determine why. Bound by ancient ties of tribe and tradition, in which the pagan rites centring on

---

* The Arabic word *ikra* can be translated as 'read' or 'recite'. Hence the Quran, literally the 'Recitation'.

the Kaaba were fundamental, Mecca became a community divided. Stung by his attacks on their traditions, infuriated by his failure to rein in the public criticism despite repeated warnings, threats and inducements, it was little wonder he was accused of being a liar, a poet, a sorcerer and a diviner, and of being possessed. Yet the verbal attacks did nothing to cool Mohammed's ardour. A group of Meccans went to his uncle and protector, Abu Talib, to deliver an ultimatum. 'By God, we cannot endure that our fathers should be reviled, our customs mocked and our gods insulted. Until you rid us of him we will fight the pair of you until one side perishes.'[34]

One can easily imagine the tensions, suspicions and animosity that gripped Mecca as Mohammed preached to anyone who would listen. His message of one God was inherently divisive and threatened the status quo, including the leadership of the community. The pagan rites of worship that had centred on the Kaaba since time immemorial were the hand that fed Mecca and its merchants. Now here was Mohammed trying to bite it off.

Invented or otherwise, there is a rationality to the story in which Mohammed's embryonic group of followers – the world's first Muslims, those who had submitted to God – largely men from the poorest, most humble sections of the community, were persecuted. Muslims of the highest social standing were told they would be branded 'blockheads' and 'fools', their reputations destroyed. Merchants were warned their businesses would be boycotted until they were reduced to 'beggary'. The harshest measures, however, were reserved for those at the bottom of Meccan society. Since, for most of the town, Mohammed's revolutionary message was anathema, they 'attacked them, imprisoning them, and beating them, allowing them no food or drink, and exposing them to the burning heat of Mecca, so as to seduce them from their religion'. In one particularly cruel punishment the slave Bilal was taken out of Mecca at the hottest time of the day and thrown on his back in an open valley beneath the broiling sun with a huge rock on his chest.[35] The persecution of the new community of Muslims grew so intense that in 615 Mohammed sent some of his followers across the waters of the Red Sea to seek refuge in Christian Abyssinia.

His position in Mecca grew increasingly fraught. In the face of constant threats against his life, his security ultimately depended on his uncle Abu Talib, by now under siege from Meccans demanding he surrender Mohammed to them. When, in 619, both he and Mohammed's wife Khadija, the first person to convert to Islam, died, the Prophet's situation became desperate. It came to a head in the summer of 622 when news reached

Mohammed that assailants were planning to assassinate him. 'O Mecca, I love thee more than the entire world, but thy sons will not let me live,' he lamented.[36] Eleven years as a prophet had brought him little but rejection, persecution and a couple of hundred followers. Drastic measures were called for. Under the cover of night he and his band of followers, including the devoted Abu Bakr, a future father-in-law of the Prophet and the first Muslim caliph, silently stole out of town and made their way to the city of Yathrib, 200 miles north. Local tribesmen here, impressed by Mohammed's earlier preaching and his obvious leadership qualities, had already assured him of a welcome when they met during the annual pilgrimage at Mecca.

The dramatic desert journey of Muslim tradition came to be known as the *hijra*, or the migration, an event of such significance it became the starting point of the new Muslim calendar. Within a couple of months the diminutive Muslim community had almost entirely relocated to Yathrib. They joined a city of two principal pagan Arab tribes, the Aws and Khazraj, and three Jewish tribes, the Qaynuqa, Qurayza and Nadir, who predated all the other communities. Overnight, Mecca became enemy territory. The once Jewish town of Yathrib, by contrast, came to be known as Medinat al Nabi, City of the Prophet, in time abbreviated simply to Medina.

From the time of the *hijra*, military struggle, raiding missions and conquest were woven into the spread of Islam. Initially this was only on the most local scale as pagan Mecca and the Muslims of Medina vied for supremacy in the Hijaz, yet in time it would expand from Arabia and emerge as an international phenomenon, one of the most remarkable feats of arms and faith in history.* In 624, Muslims faced Meccans at the Battle of Badr, where Mohammed's modest force, the first Muslim army in history, prevailed over a much larger enemy in a victory that immediately elevated the Prophet from maverick renegade to revered leader of men.

With his hand strengthened, the Prophet now moved against the Jewish Qaynuqa tribe, who represented a challenge to his position and who may have been intriguing with the merchants of Mecca behind his back. Mohammed struck swiftly. After besieging them and forcing their surrender, he expelled them from Medina in the first significant act of hostility in history between Muslims and Jews. He then divided their property among his followers, retaining a fifth share for his putative Islamic state.

---

* Among Islam's most militant adherents there are those who believe the military struggle initiated by Mohammed has not finished and should continue until the entire world has converted to the faith.

In 625, the Jewish Nadir tribe was expelled from Medina and followed the Qaynuqa into exile after being accused of plotting to assassinate the Prophet. The tribes of Arabia had been put on notice.

Victory at Badr was followed – after an indecisive encounter at Uhud in 625 – by the Battle of Al Khandaq (the Trench) in 627, where the Meccans sought to terminate the upstart Prophet's career by putting Medina under siege, apparently assisted by the exiled Jewish tribes of Nadir and Qaynuqa. Again Mohammed led his men to victory.

It was time to settle scores. Mohammed, the sources tell us, could not tolerate treachery by the Qurayza. After negotiations for safe passage out of Medina were rejected, they were reduced to unconditional surrender. Mohammed's appointed arbiter, Saad ibn Muadh, then issued a terrible order. The men were to be executed, the women and children enslaved and their property divided among the Muslims. Mohammed welcomed the sentence as the 'judgement of Allah'.[37] In Ibn Ishaq's account, the Prophet took charge of the mass execution personally:

> Then he sent for them and struck off their heads in those trenches as they were brought out to him in batches . . . There were 600 or 700 in all, though some put the figure as high as 800 or 900.[38]

While Muslim commentators over the centuries have accepted the slaughter of the Qurayza as 'lawful', 'better for Islam' and indeed incumbent upon Mohammed, it has attracted considerable opprobrium from Western historians, who have variously described the mass killings as 'savage and inhuman', 'an act of monstrous cruelty, which casts an indelible blot upon the Prophet's name' and an unjustifiable 'barbarous deed'.[39] Apart from the charge of treachery as reason for the slaughter of the Qurayza, one should not discount the compelling attraction of the booty that it liberated – in both human and physical form. Land, properties, weapons, horses and camels, together with the captive women and children – some of whom could be kept, others sold on to purchase more weapons and horses – represented a massive windfall that Mohammed was able to distribute among his growing band of Muslims. Ruthlessness towards his enemies, combined with generosity towards his supporters, raised his reputation as a leader worth following.

The Prophet's distinctly martial career, leading from the front with sword in hand, would provide *the* sacred example for Muslims for the next fourteen centuries. It would both inspire, and provide the justification for, every future generation of Islamic empire-builders, from the Umayyads of Damascus, the Abbasids of Baghdad and Timur of Samarkand to the Ottomans of Istanbul, Babur's Mughals and even today's caliphate-obsessed *jihadists*. Preaching to win new converts, as exemplified by Jesus, was one thing, but military conquest in the name of Allah and his Prophet Mohammed was a more compelling proposition.

Mohammed's work was far from done. If his adopted city of Medina had accepted him as the Prophet of God, the same could still not be said for the town of his birth, which persisted in adamant opposition. Mecca had to be brought to heel.

In 628, in what the Meccans must have regarded as an utterly brazen affront, Mohammed led around 1,400 unarmed Muslims on the pilgrimage to Mecca. They were intercepted outside the town at a place called Al Hudaybiya, where some harsh words were exchanged. After the Quraysh's intermediary had suggested that Mohammed's men would soon abandon him, Abu Bakr shot back with a memorable rejoinder lampooning the pagan rites: 'Go suck Allat's tits! Should we desert him?'[40] After some threats and scuffles, Mohammed sent his son-in-law and cousin, Uthman, the future third caliph of the Muslim Empire, to negotiate. Eventually, calm returned and more sensible discussions followed, resulting in the Treaty of Hudaybiya, which established a ten-year peace deal between Mecca and Medina and authorized Mohammed and his men to return on pilgrimage the following year. For two years the treaty held until – the Muslim writers tell us – the Bakr clan, allies of the Quraysh, attacked the Khuzaa, allies of Mohammed and the Muslims. For the Prophet this was a clear breach of the treaty. He offered the Quraysh three alternatives: end the alliance with the Bakr tribe, pay blood money or dissolve the Treaty of Hudaybiya. The Quraysh chose the last option. It was an incitement to war.

In 630, Mohammed led an army of 10,000 on Mecca. Fearing defeat and the total destruction of his people, Abu Sufyan ibn Harb, leader of the Quraysh, rode out to meet Mohammed, camped at Mar al Zahran, two stages outside Mecca, where he was strongly encouraged to 'Submit and testify that there is no God but Allah and that Mohammed is the Prophet of God before you lose your head.'[41] He duly converted to the new faith, an essential first step to the conversion of his town and tribe. After Abu Sufyan had made his submission, he returned to Mecca with news of the general amnesty pronounced by Mohammed. His wife, Hind bint Utbah, a famously ferocious woman, was unimpressed by the surrender. 'Kill this fat greasy bladder of lard!' she shouted, pulling on her husband's moustache in fury. 'What a rotten protector of the people!'[42] Hind had form. Ibn Ishaq wrote of her cutting out and chewing on the liver from the corpse of Mohammed's uncle Hamza after the Battle of Uhud and mutilating the bodies of the Prophet's other companions, making necklaces, anklets and pendants from their noses and ears.

Mohammed now marched on Mecca, his men advancing in four columns from four directions, under order only to fight those who opposed them. Resistance proved minimal. Casualties were reportedly limited to twenty-eight on the Qurayshi side and just two among the Muslims. It was an extraordinary triumphal entry, one of the most important moments in the history of the Middle East.

At a stroke Mecca became the first Muslim conquest and the sacred heart of a fledgling empire that would soon spread like wildfire, first across the Arabian Peninsula, then north into the Middle East and North Africa. Conquest, whether peacefully accepted in spiritual submission or enforced more violently at the tip of a sword by the Prophet and his followers, was the lifeblood of the religion from the outset. There lay one of the most visible differences between Christian martyrs and Islamic warriors.

Once the situation was calm, Mohammed headed to the Kaaba. He rode around it seven times on his camel, touching the Black Stone on every circuit with a stick. Then he took the keys to the Kaaba, entered it and saw the wooden figure of a dove, which he smashed and threw away. Ibn Ishaq reported that the pictures stored inside the Kaaba were all destroyed, apart from two of Jesus and Mary. Next came the 360 lead-strengthened idols, which Mohammed pointed at with his stick and smashed with a burst of supernatural power. A small number of Meccans, perhaps ten, were excluded from the amnesty and executed for a variety of offences, including those who had apostatized – a harbinger of the severity with which Islam henceforth would punish apostasy – and one or two slave-girls who had been satirizing Mohammed and ridiculing Islam. Hind, perhaps surprisingly given the ferocity of her earlier resistance, was not among them. The one-time adversary of Mohammed followed her husband and submitted to the new faith.

The conquest of Mecca was celebrated in an outpouring of poetry, an aspect of cultural continuity at a moment of profound dislocation and change. This was a predominantly oral culture in which a reverence for the sonorous beauty of Arabic verse ran deep. In the poetic imagination Mohammed's entry into Mecca represented nothing less than divine illumination:

> Had you seen Mohammed and his troops
> The day the idols were smashed when he entered,
> You would have seen God's light become manifest
> And darkness covering the face of idolatry.[43]

In reading these early accounts of Mohammed's actions during the conquest of Mecca, whether he was smashing idols, meting out justice, dividing spoils or re-establishing the boundaries of the sanctuary, there can be no doubting his complete political and military supremacy, in addition to his religious role as creator and leader of a new faith.* Uniting the competing, feuding tribes of Arabia under the banner of Islam was an inherently political and military task, which dominated the remaining years of his life, during which time he became the undisputed leader of Arabia. Islam was political, then, from its very beginnings.

The armies Mohammed put into the field grew larger as the scope of his campaigns widened. At the Battle of Hunayn in 630, his army of 12,000 defeated a much larger force made up of the Hawazin tribe and their allies south-east of Mecca. The booty was phenomenal – armour, weapons, 24,000 camels, 6,000 prisoners – and the battle merited another mention in the Quran. Muslim power started to spread across northern and eastern Arabia. Nomadic Bedouin concluded a series of agreements with Mohammed, acknowledging the suzerainty of Medina, the Muslims' political capital, and undertaking to pay the zakat religious tax in return for maintaining their cultural independence. In these earliest days of the new faith and in the context of a raiding culture, this new levy would have felt like a protection payment, 'more a tribute to a new conqueror than a religious obligation owed to God'.[44]

Reaping the spoils of war was not just a pleasant consequence of victory in battle. Having received divine sanction in the Quran, it was far more important than that.† 'In short, Muhammad had to conquer, his followers liked to conquer, and his deity told him to conquer: do we need any more?'[45] While much of the history of early Mecca and the rise of Islam has centred on the role of trade, there is no doubting the primacy of conquest as a driving principle in the spread of the new faith. The overriding financial incentive was now raiding, with booty for everyone.[46] Mohammed's military career in Arabia provided the foundation for the history-making conquests of the seventh and eighth centuries, in which Arab armies surged out of Arabia and literally put Islam on the map in a great sweep of territory seized from the shores of the Atlantic and the Iberian Peninsula in the west to the snow-shrouded mountains of Central Asia in the east.

---

* Centred on the Kaaba, the boundaries of the *haram* or sanctuary were defined as follows: a journey of one hour on the Medina road; three hours on the Yemen road; five hours on the Taif road; three hours on the road to Iraq; four hours on the Jirana road. These were later renewed by the second and third caliphs, Umar and Uthman.
† 'They consult you about the spoils of war. Say, "The spoils of war belong to God and the messenger." You shall observe God, exhort one another to be righteous, and obey God and His messenger, if you are believers.' Quran 8:1

The Prophet's death in 632, after a final pilgrimage to Mecca the same year, ended this first chapter in the history of Islam. It also ushered in a period during which both Mecca and Medina abruptly slipped off the Muslim historians' radar. Attention switched to the Islamic conquests under the first caliphs and then to Damascus, after Muawiya, brother-in-law of the Prophet and governor of Syria, seized power in 661 and established the hereditary Umayyad Dynasty (r. 661–750) with Damascus as his capital.*

The Haram soon became too small to accommodate the growing number of Muslims. The caliph Umar was the first to extend it after purchasing and tearing down the surrounding houses before constructing a wall around the holy site. 'It is you who are encroaching upon the Kaaba – this is its garden – and not the Kaaba that is encroaching upon you,' he told those who objected to the compulsory purchases.[47] Uthman continued where his predecessor left off, enlarging the sanctuary again and introducing galleries. Some Meccans refused to sell their properties. Uthman promptly demolished them. Those who protested were thrown into prison.

Under the caliphates of both Umar and Uthman, the Islamic Empire spread rapidly. Mesopotamia, Armenia and the Persian Empire had all joined the Dar al Islam by the mid-640s, by which time Arab military expeditions were also underway in North Africa and Afghanistan, with naval raids launched in the eastern Mediterranean and against the Iberian Peninsula.

The population of Mecca grew steadily across the seventh century, and the city expanded significantly to accommodate it, with new orchards planted and wells bored. The caliph Muawiya (r. 661–80) personally bought up tracts of land and also snapped up the house belonging to the Prophet's beloved first wife Khadija, turning it into a mosque, the public lavatories of today.

Sacred or not, Mecca found itself embroiled in squalid politics and under attack in 683. Attempting to overthrow the Umayyads, the Prophet's grandson Hussain ibn Ali had been slaughtered and decapitated at the Battle of Kerbala in southern Iraq in 680. This was a fateful encounter that entrenched the divide within Islam between those who thought the leader of the Islamic Empire should be chosen by consensus among Muslims (Ahl al Sunnah wal Jamaah, the People of the Traditions of the Prophet and the Consensus of the Community, or the Sunni) and those who believed he should be a descendant of the Prophet's cousin and

---

* The new dynasty took its name from Umayya ibn Abd Shams, an ancestor of the Prophet, from whom the family claimed descent.

son-in-law Ali (the Shiat Ali, Followers of Ali, or the Shia), who had also been murdered, in 661, during the turmoil over the succession.

Abdullah ibn al Zubayr, another rival to the Umayyads, took refuge in Mecca's holy of holies and the Kaaba caught fire during the ensuing siege, smashing the Black Stone to pieces. The siege was broken off only when news of the death of the caliph Yazid (r. 680–83) brought renewed uncertainty over the succession and the Syrian army hurried back to Damascus. There was one final act of drama and bloodshed to bring the seventh century to a close. Determined to wipe out Ibn al Zubayr for good, the caliph Abd al Malik (r. 685–705) sent another force to Mecca in 692.* It soon crushed the resistance and reinstated Umayyad control. Abd al Malik then issued orders for the Kaaba to be pulled down and rebuilt according to the time of Mohammed. It has remained in this form ever since.

During the lifetime of Mohammed, and in the earliest biographies of the Prophet, Mecca was comprehensively reimagined and reinvented, in a word Islamicized. The ancient, formerly pagan rituals of the settlement, such as the circumambulation of the Kaaba, the running between the hills of Marwa and Safa, the stoning of the three pillars at Mina, were removed from their original polytheistic context and retained and adapted for Islamic consumption, making acceptance of Islam a less culturally difficult pill for the Arabs to swallow.

The contested story of the Satanic Verses, in which the Prophet is said to have been tempted by the devil to utter Quranic verses acknowledging the efficacy of the trio of pagan deities Allat, Uzza and Manat, emanated from that same basic reality: the need to retain and rebrand some revered cultural traditions at a time when exceptionally radical innovations were being introduced at the point of a sword. Although Ibn Ishaq, Tabari, Al Waqidi and Ibn Saad all relate the incident of the Satanic Verses, modern Muslim scholars dismiss it. Suggesting anything to the contrary can be a dangerous business, as the writer Salman Rushdie discovered following the publication of his novel *The Satanic Verses* in 1988. A year

---

* Mecca suffered more devastating violence in 930, when the Qarmatians, a utopianist religious sect from eastern Arabia, stormed the city during the pilgrimage season, butchered up to 30,000 pilgrims, desecrated the holy mosque, threw corpses into the Zamzam Well and made off with the Black Stone, which was returned to the city only in 951, shattered into pieces. In 1314, Mecca hosted a stomach-churning instance of cannibalistic fratricide after the ruler Abu Nomay had abdicated. His son Humaida killed one of his brothers and invited the others to a dinner consisting of their brother Abul Ghaith cooked whole and served well done. Humaida later got his comeuppance. He was executed on the orders of the Egyptian Sultan Al Nasir in 1320.

later, Ayatollah Khomeini, Supreme Leader of Iran, issued a *fatwa* ordering Muslims to kill him.[48]

   Culture was never part of Mecca's centripetal attraction. Unlike some
of the great Muslim cities of the Middle East, it has never been considered
a cultural capital. For much of its life, in fact, in the words of a recent
Muslim biographer of the city, this holy enclave has been 'culturally arid
and surrounded by corruption . . . narrow, enclosed and indifferent to the
changing realities of the wider world'.[49] Other cities would emerge as cultural powerhouses of the Islamic world, leading and defining some of the
greatest civilizations on earth, while Mecca would remain introverted,
limited and austere. Its supercharged power continues to emanate from
its spiritual sanctity, allowing a remote, heat-wracked desert settlement
to transcend its unpromising geography and bring the world's 1.5 billion
Muslims together in shared reverence. For Jews, however, it has less auspicious memories as the site of the first mass slaughter by Muslims.

   From the time of Mohammed's farewell pilgrimage in 632 up to the
present day, a great swathe of humanity has beaten a path to this isolated
desert city, men and women dressed in the simple white *ihram* robes of
pilgrimage sweltering beneath a pitiless sun as they swirl around the
ancient granite cube. They have come from all parts of the world and all
walks of life. Kings and sultans, conquerors, caliphs and cleaners, travellers, writers, workers, peasants, singers, scientists and soldiers, celebrities,
students, seamstresses, bank clerks, footballers, accountants, ambassadors, politicians, farmers, butchers, bus drivers and businessmen and
women. For all its foibles and frailties that reflect the failings of its human
masters during the fifteen centuries of Islam, Mecca is the one place that
every other Muslim city – in this book and beyond – looks to and longs
for, from afar. It is the ultimate, unifying experience of Islam. And with
its pulse-quickening, prophetic and martial adventures of the seventh
century, it shook the world and set the tone for every Islamic Empire to
come.

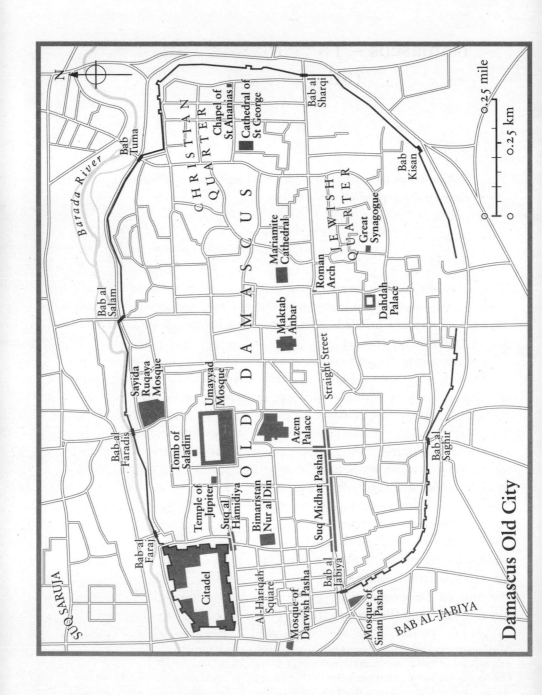

Damascus Old City

2

Damascus – The Perfumed Paradise (8th Century)

If Paradise be on earth, Damascus must be it; if it is in heaven, Damascus can parallel and match it.

Ibn Jubayr

'We may come from different communities – we have many tribes and many faiths – but we are one people and we live together peacefully, Muslims, Jews and Christians. That is our way. We are all Syrian. There are no problems between us.'

It is difficult to forget that conversation. Years ago, long before the Syrian civil war exploded on the streets of Damascus, I was walking through its Old City with a local historian. Mohammed and I wandered through the narrow-alleyed warren of Al Amin, the Jewish Quarter, where the last few members of that beleaguered community maintained a lonely vigil from once stately, now crumbling townhouses. Within the remnants of the great Roman walls we headed down the Roman street called Straight, which still bisects the Old City from east to west, where the blind Pharisee Saul, sight miraculously restored, became the Christian Paul early in the first century AD.[1] For over 1,000 years, pious pilgrims had assembled outside these walls every year before setting off on a journey of almost 900 faith-testing miles across the desert to Mecca (the last such caravan left in 1864, from which time the journey by boat to Jeddah took over). We counted the seven ancient gates,* gazed up at the Temple of Jupiter, glowing golden in the late afternoon sun, and plunged headlong into Al

---

* Running clockwise from the citadel, these are: Bab al Faradis (Gate of Paradise), Bab al Salam (Gate of Peace), Bab Tuma (Gate of Thomas, named after the Apostle), Bab al Sharqi (Eastern Gate), Bab Kisan (from where St Paul escaped Damascus by night), Bab al Saghir (Little Gate) and Bab al Jabiya (Gate of the Water Trough, still connected to Bab al Sharqi by Midhat Pasha and Sharaa al Mustaqim, the modern version of Straight Street).

Hamidiya Suq, tiny shafts of light stealing through a tin roof constellated with bullet holes from earlier conflicts. With limited time and so much to see, we bustled along to pay hurrying homage to the ghosts of this city of synagogues, churches and mosques, a shrine of Saladin here, the House of Saint Ananias, baptizer of Saul, there, as we made our way towards the greatest mosque of them all.

I still think about that long-ago visit, jasmine-scented and shot with flashes of hibiscus and bougainvillea, because the city struck me then, as it had Ibn Jubayr, the twelfth-century Andalusian poet, pilgrim and geographer, as some kind of earthly paradise.

Few visitors to Damascus today could describe it in those terms. More than 800 years after the Andalusian's panegyrics, a ruinous civil war has reduced sections of the city to what the UN has described as 'hell on earth'. Syria, once a bastion of stability and harmony between its mixed communities, has devoured itself. An entire country has been laid waste by *fitna* – that dread word for internal strife that is so feared by Arabs. Though the ancient heart of Damascus, one of the oldest continually inhabited cities in the world, has escaped the worst of the carnage, its sprawling suburbs are scenes of complete devastation. The sheer scale of damage and destruction, to roads, houses, apartment blocks, to the entire built environment, recalls the most notorious urban casualties of war from Dresden and Beirut to Kabul and Mogadishu. Drone footage from this vast wreckage site shows how years of vicious sieges and aerial bombardment carried out by the Russian-backed regime of President Assad, together with rocket fire from the myriad rebel groups, have reaped their terrible harvest: row upon row of gutted and collapsed apartment towers, walls and windows blown out so that those which still lurch up from the neighbouring rubble resemble half-finished, multi-storey car parks. Swathes of Damascus, one of the most venerable capitals in Islamic history, have been pulverized into an urban apocalypse, a world away from the cosmopolitan paradise the city once represented for Jews, Christians and Muslims.[2]

Damascus has always soared high in Arab affections. In 634 it became the first major Byzantine city to fall to Muslim warriors, a feather in the cap for the fast-spreading Islamic Empire. With a history stretching back twenty-six centuries, it is also one of the world's most celebrated cities and has long attracted florid praise. For the North African geographer Idrisi, writing in 1154, it was 'the most delightful of all God's cities in the whole world'.[3]

By the time of the Arab conquests in the seventh century, Damascus was accustomed to foreign armies arriving at its gates. Capital of the

Aramaean kingdom of Aram-Damascus in the eleventh century BC, from when its earliest rectangular street plan and network of canals date, it had been occupied by Assyrians in the eighth century BC, Babylonians in the seventh, Achaemenids in the sixth, Alexander the Great's Greeks and Seleucids in the fourth, and Nabateans and Romans in the first. In AD 612, the city fell to the Persians under the Sasanian king Khosrow II (r. 590–628), only to be restored to Byzantine hands under the ailing empire of Heraclius in 628.

Invading armies were irresistibly drawn to this emerald jewel in the desert, the lush Ghouta oasis wrapped around the city, fed by the life-giving Barada River which rises in the Anti-Lebanon and disappears into the marshes south-east of the capital. The once bucolic suburb of Eastern Ghouta has borne the brunt of some of the worst recent fighting in the Syrian War. After years of shelling, bombing, street fighting and a series of alleged chemical attacks, much of it has been turned to rubble. A local doctor called it 'the massacre of the twenty-first century'.

Just as Muslim historians provided a determinedly Islamic gloss to the history of Mecca, the lives of the Prophet Mohammed and of the four Rashidun 'Rightly Guided' caliphs who succeeded him, so Arab authors, writing long after the conquest of Damascus, went to extraordinary lengths to magnify the city's sanctity. In *Tarikh Madinat Dimashq* (*History of the City of Damascus*), the first comprehensive study of an Islamic city and its most illustrious residents, Ibn Asakir (d. 1176) had the Prophet boldly predicting the future spread of Islam, with Arab armies dispatched to Syria, Iraq and Yemen. '"Oh Messenger of God, choose one for me," one of his companions said. "Go to Syria," Mohammed replied.'[4]

Judging by the earliest accounts, the motivations of these first Muslim warriors were straightforward. Baladhuri, the ninth-century historian, whose *Kitab Futuh al Buldun* (*Book of the Conquests of Lands*) was considered the definitive account for centuries, described the caliph Abu Bakr calling on the Arabs to rise up in a 'holy war', which would win them 'booty'. Those who took up arms, he wrote, were spurred on both by 'greed' and 'the hope of divine remuneration'.[5]

Greedy or godly, 5,000 Arab warriors under Khalid ibn Walid, companion of the Prophet and the military brains behind the unification of Arabia under Mohammed, reached the eastern gate of Bab al Sharqi in 634 and prepared for battle. They were confident of victory. A string of Byzantine cities in Syria had started to fall. Blessed by Allah, the holy warriors of a new, expanding faith had momentum on their side.

Wearied by the theological dogma of Byzantine rule, perhaps mindful of the Arab general's Islamic moniker Sayf Allah al Maslul, the Drawn

Sword of God, the Christian community under Mansur ibn Sarjun, grand-father of the theologian St John of Damascus, chose not to fight the invaders. Terms of surrender were negotiated with Khalid, who pledged 'security for their lives, property and churches ... So long as they pay the poll tax, nothing but good shall befall them'.⁶ This was acceptable for the people of Damascus, who opened the gate to the Arabs in the knowledge they would now be liable for the *jizya* poll tax levied on all conquered peoples.

The fall of Damascus to Arab Muslim forces has been described as 'an event of incalculable importance', ending almost a millennium of Western, Christian supremacy.⁷ Yet it brought no disorienting revolution in its wake. While the main outdoor meeting place shifted from Roman agora to Muslim mosque, continuity was, in most aspects of life, the order of the day. The historian Hugh Kennedy has written how the Islamicization of Damascus and other Eastern cities should be understood in terms not of a few years or even decades, but of half a millennium.⁸ Staples of the Islamic city, such as *khans* (inns), *caravanserais* (large inns, typically built around a courtyard, to accommodate travelling merchants and their caravans), *qaysariyas* (covered markets) and *madrassas*, had to wait until the eleventh and twelfth centuries.

The immediate changes from Christian to Muslim rule in Syria and Iraq, then, were less dramatic than one might have expected. Historians report no administrative breakdown in fiscal or ecclesiastical affairs, no devastating physical destruction, no waves of Arab settlers turning the place upside down. Unlike the contemporary conflict in Syria, recovery from which is likely to take several generations and many billions of dollars, the seventh-century conquest has been likened to a summer thunderstorm: 'terrifying while it lasted, but soon past and the damage promptly repaired'.⁹

There was, however, one instant and profoundly symbolic change to the fabric of the city, an architectural assertion of new ownership and control. The Muslim warriors celebrated their conquest by building a small *musalla* or prayer room, in the south-eastern section of the *temenos*, or sacred precinct, of the Church of St John the Baptist, so-called because it was said to contain the saint's severed head. The church stood on the site of the Roman Temple of Jupiter, which in turn had been built on top of an Aramaean sanctuary. The city's first Muslim mosque was a make-shift structure close to Bab Tuma, where Khalid had prayed during the siege. Today it is part of the oratories of Sheikh Arslan cemetery.

There was a late attempt by Theodorus, brother of the Byzantine emperor Heraclius, to retake the city in 636, but the Arab rout of Byzantine forces at the Battle of Yarmuk, east of the Sea of Galilee, in the same year, brought Christian rule in Syria to a calamitous end. The Arabs, wrote the Greek chronicler Theophilus of Edessa (c. 695–785), killed so many Romans that their piled-up corpses formed a bridge across the river. 'Fare-well oh Syria,' said Heraclius bitterly as he retreated from the scene of his ruin. 'And what an excellent country this is for the enemy.'[10] By 637, Jerusalem and Antioch had both fallen. By 640, the same year the Arab invasion of Egypt had begun, Hellenism was not so much in retreat along the Levantine coast as completely crushed. In 641, Alexandria, ancient jewel of the Mediterranean, was taken. The Byzantine collapse at Yarmuk proved the harbinger of an extraordinary century of Muslim conquests that would bring unprecedented glory to the Islamic Empire and its resplendent capital of Damascus.

Against great odds Mohammed had managed to unite the habitually feud-ing tribes of Arabia under the single banner of a new faith that promised untold plunder. Yet division, never far from the surface, broke out cat-astrophically in 656 when Egyptian rebels assassinated the elderly caliph Uthman in his home in Medina – of Mohammed's first four successors as leaders of the Islamic world, three were assassinated. Widely resented for favouring his Umayyad family, Uthman was repeatedly stabbed and bled to death over his beloved copy of the Quran. Ali (r. 656–61), the Prophet's cousin and son-in-law, was appointed caliph in the same year, an unhappy reign that coincided with the First Fitna, or Islamic civil war. Muawiya, a Meccan aristocrat and the Umayyad governor of Syria since 639, refused to give his allegiance to Ali, demanding revenge for the murder of his kinsman Uthman, whose blood-stained robe he hung up in the mosque in Damascus to rally his supporters. In the first major conflict between Muslims, an inconclusive series of battles was fought between those who favoured Ali and those, including the Prophet's widow Aisha, who backed the Umayyads.

Neither battles nor arbitration carried the day. What ultimately proved decisive in this struggle for power was the poisoned-sword murder of Ali by a Kharijite assassin while he was praying in the mosque at Kufa in 661.* The killing of a man whom Edward Gibbon considered a rare amal-gam of poet, soldier and saint was a fateful act, inaugurating the division

---

* Kharijites, from the Arabic word for 'those who went out', were the earliest Islamic sect, separate from either Sunni or Shia Muslims. They rejected the doctrine of the caliph's infal-libility and opposed the monopolization of power by one clan. They also rejected both Sunni claims to the caliphate by the Quraysh tribe and the Shia claims advanced by Ali's descend-ants, preferring a democratic election to the highest office. Removal of any leader who had

between Sunni and Shia that has riven the Muslim world ever since.[11] On Ali's death, Muawiya, already master of the largest military force in the Islamic world, declared himself caliph. Ali's son and heir Hasan was subdued in Iraq and forced to accept Muawiya's authority.

Crowned in Jerusalem, Muawiya had no intention of maintaining the empire's capital either at Medina or at Kufa, which had been Ali's headquarters. Damascus suited for a number of reasons. It was favourably situated close to the Byzantine frontier in a central location between Iraq, Egypt, the Mediterranean ports and the desert of Hijaz. Perhaps more important, he had developed a formidable political network after serving as governor for over twenty years, allowing him to establish the makings of a central imperial administration. Moving south to the remote Arabian deserts at a time when the Islamic world was looking west for future expansion would have been a step in the wrong direction. Muawiya was a dynamic and restless leader, famed for his eloquence, elegance and finesse, virtues that were highly prized in the Arab world. He threw himself into establishing a government fit for empire. He reorganized and reinforced the army, initiated numerous agricultural and irrigation projects, established a functioning finance ministry and instituted a regular postal service between Medina and Damascus.

If it appears paradoxical that Damascus remained a majority Christian city under this vigorous founder of a world-conquering dynasty, there were substantial financial incentives, above all the *jizya* tax, to maintain the status quo. Islam was still an elite minority pursuit and pressure to convert had yet to emerge. Although officially second-class citizens, non-Muslim *dhimmis* were given legal protection and freedom of religion in return for acknowledging Muslim authority. Over time, the conversion to Islam of increasing numbers of non-Arabs, who were not accorded the same rights as Arab Muslims, together with the sharply reduced tax revenues from *dhimmis*, generated tensions and social unrest that fuelled resistance to Umayyad power as the eighth century wore on.

In this earliest period of interfaith coexistence in Damascus, Christians and Jews were well treated. 'The three communities lived together peacefully then, just as they do today,' the Damascus historian Mohammed was keen to remind me, before the civil war changed everything. The atmosphere fostered by Muawiya, well aware that most of his subjects in the Fertile Crescent and Egypt were Christian, was one of tolerance. The Christian family of St John, whose grandfather had negotiated the

sinned was obligatory for this puritanical movement, whose fanatical beliefs fuelled regular rebellions against established authority.

surrender of Damascus, was kept in charge of the treasury, the most important imperial office at a time when Muslim armies, and increasingly navies, were extending the reach of the Islamic world and being established on a more professional, rather than tribal, footing. When the famous cathedral of Edessa was severely damaged by an earthquake in the late 670s, Muawiya restored it. As a Nestorian bishop in Syria put it, his Muslim overlords did not fight against the Christian religion, 'rather they protect our faith, respect our priests and saints, and offer gifts to our monasteries'.[12]

Christians continued to dominate the Damascus court and the chronicles report high-minded debates on the relative merits of Christianity and Islam. Despite his notorious reputation as a wine-drinking womanizer, Al Akhtal (the Loquacious) basked in the splendour of his position as Muawiya's court poet, jauntily sauntering through the caliph's palace with a crucifix hanging from his neck while he composed syrupy panegyrics to the Umayyads and satires against their enemies.[13] The Christian influence in that most important inner sanctum of imperial life, the caliph's bedchamber, was particularly strong. In a flagrant breach of Medinan tradition, Muawiya's favourite wife Maysum, daughter of the chief of the powerful Jacobite Christian Kalb tribe, provided the caliph with his designated son and heir Yazid. A Christian also served as his personal physician.

Tolerance and more or less harmonious coexistence between the faiths, so rare in much of the conflict-ridden region today, were the bedrock of Damascus's success, and that of other imperial Muslim capitals to follow. The greatest Islamic cities set the tone for the empires they ruled over and reflected the boundless self-assurance of their masters. Damascus under the Umayyads, like Abbasid Baghdad, Fatimid Cairo, Marinid Fez, Ottoman Istanbul, Timur's Samarkand, Safavid Isfahan and Maktoum Dubai today, was grand, outward-looking and confident in its power. Intolerance, sectarian strife and division, the obverse of the coin and the hallmark of contemporary difficulties in the Middle East, were both the symptom and cause of the much later decline, decrepitude and loss of power and prestige.

An indication of the initial Muslim architectural inferiority complex that would soon have dramatic and long-lasting consequences for Damascus is evident in the story of a Byzantine ambassador's visit to Muawiya's capital. He was asked what he thought of the Dar al Khadra governor's palace, simply constructed from baked brick and timber. 'The upper floor will do for birds, the lower part for rats,' he sniffed.[14] History does not record what happened to this undiplomatic envoy, but Muawiya had the palace pulled down and rebuilt in stone. Acutely conscious that the central mosque of Damascus could in no way be considered a suitably imperial showcase of Islam, Muawiya negotiated with the episcopal authorities to transfer the Church of St John the Baptist to the Muslim community. But the Christians refused to budge.

Beyond Damascus, Muawiya's imperial strategy was to deputize leaders to take the fight to infidels in the east, beyond the River Oxus to Bukhara, Samarkand and Kabul in today's Central Asia and the 'Stans, while he concentrated on the Romans, to the west. In 668, only thirty-six years after the death of the Prophet, Muawiya's armies reached Chalcedon, from where they could stare across the Bosphorus at mighty Constantinople. After an unsuccessful debut siege against the triple-walled metropolis, Muawiya made another attempt in 674, launching a series of naval attacks from the Sea of Marmara that lasted up to seven years. Still Constantinople refused to buckle. It is easy to dismiss these expeditions as failures, but when one considers the city would fall to Muslim forces only eight centuries later, Muawiya's sheer audacity in the first century of Islam appears more impressive.

Breathtakingly rapid as they were, the Arab conquests were by no means the purely military, destructive affair that Christian accounts portrayed so apocalyptically. There was a strong element of cultural elision and assimilation. Alongside the inducements to surrender in the form of promises to respect life, property and freedom of worship, there were also tax exemptions to those living in remote terrain.

Equally important, however foreign and different Islam might sound to a modern non-Muslim reader, for a Middle Eastern and North African population in the seventh and eighth centuries the Islam of these horse-mounted warriors contained no shortage of reassuringly familiar features. Here was the one omnipotent God of an Abrahamic faith, together with his coterie of already revered prophets; there were the scripture, prayers, fasting, almsgiving, pilgrimage to holy sites, holy days and community buildings in which to pray. 'It was different enough from Christianity and Judaism to make it distinctive, but similar enough to make it palatable.'[15] In fact, for some contemporaries, like St John of Damascus, Islam was less a new faith than a Christian heresy.[16] And if the new *jizya* tax was unwelcome, it was probably no more so than the taxes already exacted by Constantinople.

With Muawiya's death in 680, Damascus lost her greatest patron and the Muslim Empire one of its most brilliant leaders. Politically astute and militarily precocious, he was admired for his consummate leadership and *hilm*, the use of subtlety, flattery and cunning to achieve his objectives.

The ninth-century Arab historian Yaqubi described Muawiya's philosophy of power in a memorable passage: 'I apply not my lash where my tongue suffices, nor my sword where my whip is enough. And if there be one hair binding me to my fellow men I let it not break. If they pull I loosen, and if they loosen I pull.'[17] Muawiya was also resented, however, by later Muslim tradition for turning the caliphate into a hereditary monarchy by appointing his son his heir.

As it happened, the caliphate of Muawiya's son Yazid was short-lived (680–83) and was most notable for the devastating legacy of the Battle of Kerbala in southern Iraq in 680, when several thousand Umayyad forces routed a ragtag army of 110 soldiers led by the late caliph Ali's son Hussain, grandson of the Prophet. Hussain was killed and decapitated, his family, including his baby son, were slaughtered. The massacre cemented a tradition of Shia martyrdom whose passionate force still reverberates across the Middle East fourteen centuries later as Sunni and Shia powers struggle for mastery of the Muslim world.

Damascus and the empire became noticeably more Arab under the caliph Abd al Malik (r. 685–705), who issued his own coinage of gold dinars and silver dirhams to replace the Byzantine denarius and Iraqi issues. Of more lasting significance was his institution of Arabic as the official language of administration. Gradually it replaced Aramaic as the written and spoken idiom and Greek and Pahlavi as the language of financial affairs. The professionalization of the armed forces continued. Negotiations dragged on unsuccessfully with the Christians for the transfer of the Church of St John the Baptist to the Muslims. The atmosphere, however, was changing. Michael the Syrian (d. 1199), a patriarch of the Syriac Orthodox Church, reported Abd al Malik's decree that 'crosses should be taken down and pigs slaughtered'.[18] Although it is unclear how widely this was enforced, the public display of Christianity was officially restrained and Muslim dietary taboos made universal.

Abd al Malik's greatest architectural contribution was reserved not for imperial Damascus but for holy Jerusalem, where in 692 he built the magnificent Qubba al Sakhra, Dome of the Rock, enshrining the site from which, according to Muslim tradition, the Prophet ascended to heaven accompanied by the Angel Jibril.* Lest any should doubt that Islam was the supreme faith, it loomed over its Christian rival, the Church of the

---

* 'Is it not obvious,' asked the Arab geographer Muqaddasi, 'that Abd al Malik, seeing the grandeur and magnificence of the Dome of the Holy Sepulchre, was concerned lest it dazzle the thoughts of the Muslims, and thus he erected above the Rock the Dome now seen there?'

Holy Sepulchre, in ostentatious one-upmanship and was richly decorated with Islamic inscriptions refuting the notion that God should have a son and referring to Jesus as his 'prophet and servant', rather than a divine being. Alongside the Dome of the Rock in the Noble Sanctuary, he also built the Al Aqsa Mosque, Islam's third holiest site after the Sacred Mosque in Mecca and the Prophet's Mosque in Medina. It was a bold bid to challenge Arabia's monopoly of Islamic sanctity and the steady stream of pilgrim revenues it generated.

And so Damascus entered the eighth century as the growing and self-confident imperial capital of an expanding Islamic Empire. If the Christian majority had once shared their faith, despite the theological differences, with their masters and co-religionists in Constantinople, they were now Christian subjects of a Muslim power.

The caliph Al Walid (r. 705–15) was determined to stamp his definitive Islamic mark on Damascus and there was only one way to do it. Every time the caliph left his palace, he was greeted with a sight that grated: the biblical inscription by the Roman emperor Theodosius (r. 379–95) on the southern entrance to the great church: 'Your kingship, O Christ, is a kingship for ever; your reign lasts from age to age' (Psalm 145:13), a Christian imprimatur on the converted pagan temple. Something had to give.

Unlike Muawiya and his father Abd al Malik, Walid refused to take no for an answer on the lingering question of the Church of St John the Baptist. Early on in his reign he told the inhabitants of Damascus that the city's four greatest attributes – its climate, water, fruits and baths – gave them 'a marked superiority' over the rest of the world. 'To these I wanted to add a fifth: this mosque.'[19]

For six decades Christians and Muslims in Damascus had prayed almost alongside each other, the Christians worshipping in their transcendent church next to the Muslims in their inferior mosque within the walled enclosure. All that was to change. Theophilus of Edessa left an anguished account of Walid's seizure and destruction of the church, and its replacement with a wondrous mosque of glittering mosaics. 'The wretched man did this out of envy of the Christians, because this church was surpassingly beautiful,' he wrote.[20]

Scant consolation it might have been for the Christians, but they were allowed to keep all the previously confiscated churches and monasteries in the Ghouta as well as the Church of St Mary in the Street Called Straight, which became the city's main church, as it remains to this day.

The Umayyad Mosque, which became the fourth holiest site for Muslims after those in Mecca, Medina and Jerusalem, was the defining symbol of eighth-century Damascus. With this sublime monument, which became famous throughout the world, Walid almost single-handedly made Damascus a sacred site, and all the forces at his disposal, from builders and calligraphers to poets and writers, were deployed to proclaim this triumphant message. Coexistence with Christians was all very well, but people had to understand who was in charge.

Ibn Asakir reported the caliph sending a brusque letter to the Byzantine emperor in Constantinople – whom he referred to as Al Taghiya, the Tyrant. In it he demanded 200 skilled workers 'for I wish to construct a mosque, the like of which has never been built and never will be again. If you do not comply I will invade your country with my armies. I will destroy all the churches in my territory, including those of Jerusalem, Edessa and all the Rumi monuments.'[21]

The Christian ruler, according to Ibn Asakir, meekly complied and sent the caliph the workers. Ibn Jubayr put the number of Greek craftsmen at 12,000, together with Copts, Persians, Indians and North Africans. The historian Baladhuri recorded Walid offering Christians a huge sum of money in return for their church. When they refused and the caliph threatened to tear it down, one of them warned him that whoever dared do that would go mad. The threat so enraged Walid that he immediately sent for an axe and swung the first blows against the church himself, before passing the axe around to the assembled grandees and getting the Jews to finish the job, while the devastated Christians sat groaning on the steps. The year was 706. Ibn Asakir also told the story of workers discovering the miraculously preserved head of John the Baptist in a cavity beneath the mosque. Walid ordered it to be reinterred underneath one of the columns.

A monument of such extravagance on such a scale could hardly be inexpensive. Its cost generated considerable comment from those impressed and scandalized alike. The tenth-century Persian historian and geographer Ibn al Faqih reported the final cost was several times the annual income to the treasury from the *kharaj* land tax, or in excess of 600,000–1,000,000 dinars. So many workers were employed on the construction, he wrote, that the cost of the daily supply of vegetables to feed them alone was 6,000 dinars. When the work was completed, eighteen camels were required to carry all the building receipts to Walid. No sooner had he received them, however, than the caliph, who appeared gloriously uninterested in such trifles, 'ordered them all to be burnt'.[22]

The fabulous cost of the Umayyad Mosque reverberated across the centuries. It is a mark of the serious disquiet such expenditure caused, according to the historian Tabari, that the caliph Yazid III (r. 744) felt

obliged on his accession a generation later to promise the people not to
lay 'stone upon stone, brick on brick'.[23] Muqaddasi, author of *The Best
Divisions for Knowledge of the Regions*, was the first Muslim visitor to
record a detailed account of Damascus. He asked his uncle why Walid
had squandered such huge sums on the mosque. The older man was having
none of it. He defended the caliph's project as worthy and right, the necessary architectural realization of the supremacy of Islam. Walid recognized
the outstanding grace and 'splendour' of ancient Christian churches such
as the Church of the Holy Sepulchre. 'So he sought to build for the Muslims a mosque that would be unique and a wonder to the world.'[24]

The Umayyad Mosque, probably the most sublime architectural creation since the fall of Rome, was an extraordinarily powerful symbol of
the new faith's pre-eminence. It upgraded the Muslims of Damascus from
a simple, open-air *musalla* in the south-eastern corner of a shared complex
to sole control of the most magnificent mosque anywhere within the
Islamic world. For a nomadic culture rooted in the Arabian desert it was
also a decisively urban creation and a landmark proclamation of the
virtues of settled civilization. And for the Islamic faith it was an instant
architectural paragon right across the Muslim world, a benchmark for
several centuries from Iraq to India, Andalusia to Afghanistan, Cordoba
to Cairo and Isfahan to Ghazni. As late as the thirteenth and fourteenth
centuries, the Umayyad Mosque was influencing imperial Mamluk architecture in Egypt and the Levant. For some medieval Muslim authors,
the Umayyad Mosque even counted as two wonders of the world, one
for the building, the other for its intricate mosaics and carved marble
decoration.[25]

'Think of your great cathedrals in Europe,' says Mohammed as we stand
inside a corner of the mosque's courtyard. For a moment there is an
approximation of silence, broken only by the distant sound of worshippers
click-clacking across the worn stones and a rumbustious squadron of
pigeons whose wings catch the fire of the slanting afternoon light.

'Notre-Dame, the Duomo, Cologne, St Peter's, and many more. On one
level, it's a story about religion, of course, but it's also about much more
than that. It's about power. It's about empire. Just look at this.' His right
arm sweeps across this crushing panorama. 'This is Umayyad power written in stone.'

He is completely right. As I try to gather my initial impressions, I am
merely swallowed up in its immensity. This sheer size is the first thing that
strikes the sun-dazed visitor. The outer dimensions of the sanctuary are
almost preposterous: 385 metres running east–west by 305 metres from

north to south. Within the walls, the triple-aisled prayer hall, built against the southern wall and supported on ancient marble columns with Ionic and Corinthian capitals, stretches an eye-blurring 160 metres, illuminated by hanging golden lamps along its length.

It is a glorious assault on our senses. Set against the spectacular scale of the Umayyad Mosque, the exquisite decoration on all surfaces, in lavish and fine detail, is transfixing. We step from the bleached sunlight of the sky-filled courtyard through a colonnaded portico into the cool prayer hall, beneath a façade dominated by a monumental gabled entrance that is set alight by shimmering golden mosaics beneath a central dome visible right across Damascus. 'We were nearly carried away by giddiness,' the Andalusian geographer, poet and traveller Ibn Jubayr recalled of his heart-stopping climb up and into the dome during the summer of 1184. It 'sends the senses reeling . . .' As a reminder that interfaith relations could sometimes be fraught, he also observed that 'the fires of discord burn between the two partics, Muslim and Christian', but that travellers came and went unmolested.[26] On 15 March 2011, the first discord of the Syrian revolution flared here, when around fifty protesters took to the streets outside the Umayyad Mosque after midday prayers and started calling for freedom and the overthrow of the regime.[27]

'Just look at these mosaics,' says Mohammed. 'They are the real treasures here.' Like Ibn Jubayr, we are momentarily awestruck by the interior decoration, a mesmerizing combination of minute detail and monumentality in the vast expanse of mosaics that run riot across the courtyard. They portray imagined scenes of paradise – fertile orchards and babbling streams, the grandest palaces, houses and ornate rotundas – that are the final destiny of the faithful. Forty metric tonnes of glass and stone cubes, a third of them in green, trace an iridescent band of light around the quadrangle. On the southern wall a dedicatory inscription from the Quran salutes the Almighty across four bands of gold set on a dazzling background of lapis lazuli. Then come the images of acanthus and grapes, figs, almonds, pomegranates, apples, pears and cypresses in mosaic and marble.

Above the *mihrab* a golden vine frieze, inlaid with sapphires, pearls, coral, carnelian and other gems, sprawls across the walls in glittering mosaics. It is a glorious fusion of Byzantine craft with Muslim piety and extravagance. The florid iconography sends a distinctive message. Damascus is paradise on earth, its Umayyad Mosque the pathway to everlasting paradise.

Muslim pilgrims to the Umayyad Mosque were often extravagantly impressed. Visiting in the fourteenth century, the high-spirited Moroccan traveller Ibn Battuta considered it 'the greatest mosque on earth' in terms of beauty, grace and architectural magnificence. Ibrahim ibn Abi al Layt al Katib, an eleventh-century visitor, thought it 'the paragon of the century, the marvel of the time and the curiosity of the ages'.[28]

Once the great mosque had been finished, the Muslim traditionalists could begin sanctifying it. To Walid's Islamic memorial in stone now had to be added the scholarly imprimatur in ink. Ibn Asakir's Damascus became the birthplace of Abraham, a city blessed by a visit from the Prophet and a reference in the Quran, a refuge for Mary and Jesus and home to more than 10,000 illustrious scholars, holy men, jurisprudents, historians, craftsmen and other grandees. Here was the beginning of the mystical tradition of Mount Qasiyun, at whose feet Damascus lay, with its various shrines, including the Grotto of Blood, where Cain was said to have killed Abel.[29] There, beyond the southern wall of the city, was the Bab al Saghir cemetery, final resting place for some of the most honoured Muslims in history. This was just a small part of the more than 200 pages of his door-stopping volume devoted to the Islamic conquest of Syria, a period studiously exalted to the virtual abandonment of its pre-Islamic past. It was Islamic propaganda masquerading as history – for neither the first nor the last time. 'The Saudis aren't interested in anything that happened before Islam, either,' Mohammed says later.

There is nevertheless something of the Pevsner about Ibn Asakir. An obsessive compiler of the city's monuments as well as its leading men, he listed fourteen churches in Damascus. Half a millennium after the Muslim conquest of Syria, eight were in varying degrees of ruin, one had been demolished, three had been converted into mosques – as had the synagogue – and only two were functioning.* The Church of St Mary had become the primary place of Christian worship. The great survivor of Christian Damascus, despite being burned to the ground by mobs during the 1860 Druze–Christian conflict that spread from Lebanon, it endures to this day on Straight Street as the Mariamite Cathedral of Damascus, seat of the Greek Orthodox Patriarchate. It was damaged by mortar fire in 2018.

For the Christians the loss of their beloved Church of St John was a trauma made all the more piercing by its replacement with a sublime Muslim mosque, crowning spiritual symbol of their temporal defeat. 'Then

---

* Intimate, street-level detail was a hallmark of Ibn Asakir's history. So, for instance, 'The Church of the Jacobites is the one behind the new prison. You enter via Saddlemakers' Market, which today is beside the Market of Ali, it's the street where the entrance of the Saddlemakers' Baths is, by Susi Street. Certain parts of the building are still there, it has been in ruins for a long time.' N. Elisséeff, *La Description de Damas d'Ibn Asakir*, p. 221

came Christianity and it became a church, then came Islam and it became a mosque,' wrote Masudi, the tenth-century historian known as the Herodotus of the Arabs.[30] Damascus was a palimpsest. Islam had been written over Christianity, which had been superimposed over the monuments of pagan Rome, which had replaced those of the ancient Assyrians. Only the city endured.

Eight Umayyad caliphs ruled the Islamic Empire between 715 and 750, a brief period in which the dynasty plunged from its world-illuminating zenith to its blood-spattered nadir and destruction. The fate of Damascus mirrored these political vicissitudes. Opposition to what increasingly felt like a family business grew during the first half of the century. Too much power and prosperity were centred in one family, the Umayyads' detractors started to murmur. The caliphs Walid, Sulayman (r. 715–17), Yazid II (r. 720–24) and Hisham (r. 724–43) were all sons of Abd al Malik, while Umar II (r. 717–20) and Marwan II (r. 744–50) were his nephews.[31]

While the military conquests continued unabated, opposition remained muted. Yet the catastrophic failure of a two-year siege of Constantinople during 717–18 represented an unprecedented reversal for the Umayyads. Accustomed to a string of stirring victories over the infidels, the Arabs were reduced instead to a pitiful condition, eating dead animals and scraps of pitch from their ships. A relief mission carrying grain, weapons and supplies was seized and plundered by the Byzantines, bringing an ignominious end to the expedition.

Tensions, meanwhile, were rising over the mass conversions to Islam by peasants across the empire, many of whom had left their land and enrolled in the army expressly to escape taxes. Undermined by the corresponding loss of revenues, provincial governors raised the bar for conversion, enforcing circumcision on the ranks of new Muslims and requiring them to recite the Quran to demonstrate their sincerity. In a pointed decree Umar II ordered his governors to maintain equal rights for all Muslims: 'Whosoever accepts Islam, whether Christian, Jew or Zoroastrian, of those now subject to taxes and who joins himself to the body of Muslims . . . he shall have the same rights and duties as they have . . .'[32]

For two decades under Hisham, Arab armies were kept busy, yet the continual warfare resulted in virtually no change to the empire's borders and grievously drained imperial coffers. Hisham was rarely in Damascus and, like a number of the later Umayyads, preferred to spend time in his desert palaces – at Rusafa, south of the Euphrates, in his winter palace of Khirbat al Mafjar in the Jordan Valley near Jericho, and in the vast palace-fortress of Qasr al Hayr al Sharqi, near Palmyra, a complex of 10,000 square metres, where he could enjoy the pleasures of hunting, music, wine and singing girls.

Muslim armies were marauding in the land of the Franks throughout the 720s. Then, in 733, nemesis struck. At the Battle of Tours (also known as the Battle of Poitiers), an Arab army led by Abd al Rahman al Ghafiq, governor of Al Andalus, faced Charles, duke and prince of the Franks. During fierce fighting, according to the eighth-century *Mozarabic Chronicle*, the European army remained 'immobile as a wall' and held together 'like a glacier'. Then, 'In the blink of an eye, they annihilated the Arabs with the sword.'[33] Abd al Rahman was killed, the Christian army victorious. Charles was given the honorific Martellus, the Hammer. Tours sounded the death knell for Islamic conquests in Europe. Had the Muslims prevailed, Gibbon imagined more than 1,000 years later, an Arabian fleet might have sailed unchallenged into the Thames. 'Perhaps the interpretation of the Koran would now be taught in the schools of Oxford, and her pulpits might demonstrate to a circumcised people the sanctity and truth of the revelation of Mahomet.'[34]

After Hisham's valiant efforts on the battlefield, there was an unmistakable – to many Muslims horrifying – decadence about the short-lived caliph Walid II (r. 743–4). He abjectly failed to measure up to his more impressive namesake and was instead addicted to hunting, wine, music, poetry and sex, pursuits that were memorably celebrated in the following verse:

> *I would that all wine were a dinar a glass*
> *And all cunts on a lion's brow.*
> *Then only the liberal would drink*
> *And only the brave make love.*[35]

For Muslim and Christian historians of the time, Walid was a degenerate and a libertine. Frescoes from his desert palace Qasr Amra, a UNESCO World Heritage Site in eastern Jordan, one of the earliest surviving examples of Islamic art and architecture, include images of bare-breasted women, together with scenes of wine drinking, hunting and a representation of the zodiac among the constellations. Islamic art has never been less austere, never more confidently defiant of the convention against displaying the human form. His vast and opulent desert palaces, complete with swimming pools and ornate interiors, have been called the 'Playboy Mansions' of their day.[36]

One of Walid's most sacrilegious acts was to use a copy of the Quran as a shooting target. If he upset his Muslim subjects, Walid did not endear himself to his Christian subjects in Syria either by having St Peter of

Damascus's tongue cut out as punishment for 'publicly reproving the impiety of the Arabs and the Manicheans'.[37] Peter was exiled to Yemen, where he later died.

In an astonishing sign of the times the chronicles tell the story of an encounter between Walid and Abu Harrim Utarrad, a distinguished singer and Quranic reader summoned from Medina to entertain the caliph. After a long journey across the desert, the singer found Walid in his private, marble-paved bath chamber, sitting on the edge of a stone-lined tank filled not with water but with wine. Walid ordered him to sing a song, after which he suddenly ripped his brocaded gown into two and jumped naked into the pool of wine, 'whence he drank until, God knows, the level was distinctly lowered. Then he was pulled out, laid down dead drunk and covered up.'

Flabbergasted by the caliph's behaviour, Abu Harrim beat a discreet retreat only to be summoned back the next day. The same thing happened again. Then, on the third day, Walid called for him again and warned him to keep silent about what he had seen. 'Son of a whore, I swear by God that if so much as a whisper of what happened passes your lips, and I hear of it, I'll have your head off!' With that he dismissed the singer with 1,000 dinars.[38]

While caliphs fiddled, the caliphate burned. Full-blown rebellions burst out in the 740s, starting with the Berbers in North Africa in 740 in a violent and bloody revolt that brought Christians and Kharijite Muslims together in a full-scale challenge to the empire. The year 744 was an *annus horribilis* for Umayyad authority. Three caliphs came and went, with a fourth appointed in a desperate bid to stem the chaos. First Walid was overthrown, killed and beheaded. His successor, Yazid III, had his wine-soaked head paraded around Damascus on a lance, with a man scornfully announcing to the crowds, 'this is the head of the wine-lover'.[39] Widely acknowledged as a pious man, Yazid had little time to demonstrate it. He died less than a year into his reign and was replaced by Ibrahim, who was in turn almost immediately replaced by Marwan II. Marwan was said to have disinterred Yazid and crucified his body on a wooden stake.

Of far more lasting significance for Damascus was Marwan's decision, in 744, to transfer the imperial capital to Harran in northern Jazira, an immediate blow to the prestige and fortunes of the city. The royal treasury was briskly loaded onto 3,000 camels and taken to the new seat of empire, leaving 'Damascus destitute of all the trappings of kingship'.[40] Since they had come to power, Umayyad caliphs had built palaces, castles and hunting retreats across the desert and moved the seat of government between them and other cities on occasion, but this was a more decisive shift, the first time Damascus had been sidelined so comprehensively.

If that decision was regrettable for a single city, there were far more ominous setbacks for the Islamic Empire writ large. Marwan's accession inaugurated the Third *Fitna* or civil war. In 746 a rebel in Yemen declared himself caliph and seized Mecca and Medina before he was killed in 748. A far more serious Shia revolution had been smouldering in southern Iraq from 719, when enemies of the Umayyads in the holy city of Kufa sent a messenger disguised as a perfume-seller to a village south of the Dead Sea in Jordan. His mission was to encourage a distant descendant of the Prophet Mohammed's family to champion a rebellion against the hated regime. Abu al Abbas, great-great-grandson of the Prophet's uncle Abbas, became the moral leader of the movement. Though their blood ties with the Prophet were more distant than those of the House of Ali, the Abbasids' powers of organization, and the ruthlessness of Abu al Abbas, were unequalled.

Over time, more secret missions were dispatched from Kufa to Khorasan, the easternmost corner of the Islamic Empire, a wide-skied region that today encompasses eastern Iran and swathes of Afghanistan, Uzbekistan and Turkmenistan. This was a world of steppe and snow-covered Hindu Kush mountains, of ancient cities such as Samarkand, Bukhara, Nishapur, Herat, Balkh and Merv, its capital. Captured in 650 by the Arab armies, Khorasan was home to Arab conquerors and their descendants, converted Turkish nomads, Iranian princes, prosperous Soghdian merchants and poverty-stricken peasants. The revolutionaries spoke of an Islamic revival and a new world in which Arabs and non-Arabs would be treated equally as fellow Muslims, unlike the Umayyads, who favoured Arabs over all others.

The message found a receptive audience. Divisions between the southern Arabian Kalb tribes and the northern Arabian Qays tribes were already undermining the Umayyad Dynasty from within. Marwan's preferential treatment of the Qays alienated the Kalb of Khorasan, sending increasing numbers of them into the arms of the revolutionaries. The Shia felt alienated by the corrupt Sunni clan in Damascus, who had stolen the caliphate from its rightful owners; the Kharijites detected sin everywhere and were in revolt.

Oaths of allegiance were sworn to Al Rida min al Mohammed (An Acceptable Member of the House of the Prophet), a deliberately secretive and vague form of words designed to broaden the appeal of the rebellion to the Shia. Nasr, the Umayyad governor of Khorasan, sensed impending disaster. 'I see coals glowing amongst the embers, they want but little to burst into blaze,' he wrote to Marwan. 'Fire springs from the rubbing of sticks, and warfare from the wagging of tongues.'[41] On 15 June 747, the hitherto clandestine insurgents unfurled their black banners for the first time on the outskirts of Merv. Thousands flocked to take up arms in a great coalition of Shia, Khorasanian and Abbasid forces. By 748, the Abbasids had taken Merv under their military leader Abu Muslim, victorious in a string of battles with the Umayyads, infamous for having reputedly killed 60,000 people in cold blood.[42] A year later, Al Abbas was pronounced caliph Al Saffa, 'The Shedder of Blood', in the great mosque at Kufa and issued a prescient warning to those assembled before him: 'Hold yourselves ready, for I am the pitiless blood-shedder and the destroying avenger.'[43]

In January 750 Marwan's Umayyad forces faced the Abbasid rebels on the banks of the Great Zab River, a tributary of the Tigris in northern Iraq. The imperial army, which Theophanes estimated at 300,000, massively outnumbered the men with black banners. Marwan's cavalry charged confidently, but failed to penetrate the Abbasid wall of lances. Many were impaled on the spot, many others deserted and huge numbers drowned in the foaming waters. It was a complete rout.

Damascus, commanded in the caliph's absence by Marwan's son-in-law Walid, trembled before the Abbasid advance. Then, on 25 April, the city fell, its defences breached by Abdullah ibn Ali, uncle of the self-proclaimed caliph Saffa. There was fierce fighting between Umayyads and Abbasids and possibly within Umayyad ranks. Theophilus reported indescribable scenes of bloodshed as the former imperial capital was ransacked: 'Abdullah ibn Ali's men . . . spent three hours lopping heads in the markets, streets and houses, and they seized their money . . . Al Walid was amongst those killed, and on that day a great number of Jews and Christians were killed.'[44]

The death toll inside Damascus was fearful. Masudi reported 'a great many people' killed. Captured Umayyad commanders were sent to the Shedder of Blood for execution. Many had their throats cut on the banks of the River Futros. Buried Umayyads were disinterred. Exhumed corpses were 'scourged with whips and then crucified', royal skulls were used as target practice until smashed into pieces. Remaining Umayyad family body parts were collected and burnt to ashes.[45] The city's great buildings were sacked, its defences destroyed and royal tombs profaned. Some reports claimed the Abbasids even ploughed up the cemetery in which the martyrs of the siege of Damascus in 634, including the companions of the Prophet, had been buried. But to the claim that the city's palaces were razed to the ground in 750 must be added the counter-observation from Yaqubi, who worked as an official in the Abbasid government in the later ninth century, that most houses in Damascus were former Umayyad residences or palaces and that Muawiya's palace was the governor's residence. There can be no doubt, however, that the destruction and bloodshed were devastating.

The Shedder of Blood (r. 749–54) pursued Marwan and all surviving male members of the Umayyad family with a relentlessness that suggested he intended to live up to his name. Marwan fled as far as Egypt, where he was hunted down and killed while hiding in a church, his severed head sent to Saffa. Then, in a ruse as simple as it was treacherous, eighty surviving Umayyad princes, invited to a dinner of reconciliation outside the city of Jaffa, were instead put to the sword. Saffa reportedly sat smiling on their writhing bodies as they lay dying. 'Never have I eaten a meal that did me such good or one that tasted more delicious,' he crowed.[46] Only one Umayyad prince, the nineteen-year-old Abd al Rahman, managed to escape the slaughter. Evading multiple would-be assassins who harried him for much of his marathon, five-year journey, he made his way through Palestine, Egypt and across North Africa to found the Umayyad emirate of Cordoba in the Iberian Peninsula.

Back in the heart of the Islamic world, however, the Umayyad Dynasty had been exterminated. Damascus's time in the imperial sun was over and the city slipped into the shadows for around a century after its sacking. Eclipsed hereafter by Baghdad, the new headquarters of the Muslim Empire from 762, the city was relegated to provincial obscurity, decline and irrelevance. While Damascus enjoyed something of a resurgence under the ebullient Nur al Din, scourge of the crusaders, in the twelfth century, it was only a pale imitation of its former greatness under the Umayyads. 'Never before and never after did the Syrian capital reach such a peak of power and glory.'[47]

'They didn't last long,' says Mohammed of the Umayyads, 'but my God, they built the greatest empire on earth in no time at all. And they made Islam known throughout the world. That was their finest achievement.'

It may be, as Hugh Kennedy has argued, that Umayyad rule from Syria was something of an aberration because 'the country was not populous enough, united enough or wealthy enough to sustain a vast empire'.[48] Yet from 661 to 750 the dynasty, despite the challenge of three civil wars, managed not only to hang on to but also to enlarge the Islamic Empire. For a time Damascus ruled over an empire that eclipsed that of Rome at its height.

The spread of a new religion was undoubtedly the dynasty's longest-lasting legacy. The Umayyads wrenched the seat of empire out of the stultifying, introverted Hijaz and thrust it into the more cosmopolitan world of the Levant. It is quite possible, as one recent historian of the city has suggested, that 'without the Damascus interlude Islam might never have become a world faith'.[49]

There were impressive achievements in other fields, too. Through the caliph Walid's monumental building programme, above all the Umayyad Mosque, Damascus created an architectural legacy that continued long after its relatively short-lived political ascendancy. One sublime place of worship established an entire paradigm that was revered and emulated – barely matched, let alone surpassed – from the Atlantic to Central Asia. For the French Orientalist Jean Sauvaget, the Umayyad Mosque was simply 'one of the masterpieces of architecture from any time and in any land'.[50]

To architectural innovation and the extension of Islam across three continents should be added Umayyad Damascus's role in advancing the frontiers of human knowledge. Intellectually, though Baghdad's record in the arts and sciences would be of an altogether higher order, Damascus could still claim formidable achievements. The Umayyad capital played a critical role in the rise of religious science through serious theological discourse. Disciplines that had first emerged at Medina, such as *tafsir* and *tawil* Quranic commentary and interpretation, *hadith* Prophetic trad-itions, *fiqh* canon law and *kalam* defensive apologia, all developed extensively in Damascus, and were given fresh impetus by earlier Jewish, Greek and Christian sources. To a very great degree this helped provide the underpinnings for the massive edifice of ninth-century translations of Greek scholarship into Arabic, often via Syriac, under the Abbasids. Umayyad caliphs respected learned men – public life was exclusively a male world – and, as the sprawling biographical compilations of both Ibn Asakir and Ibn al Adim (d. 1262) emphatically reveal, huge numbers of scholars made Damascus their home during this time, many under royal patronage. The caliph Hisham, for example, cultivated eminent scholars like the *hadith* specialist Ibn Shihab al Zuhri (d. 742), one of the greatest Muslim minds of his generation, and his former student, Maamar ibn Rashid (d. 770), a biographer of the Prophet and an expert in Islamic law.[51]

For the minorities, together with the non-Arab population, the Umayyad story was less glorious. Christian discourse in Syria and Iraq assumed an increasingly apologetic register, much of it in Arabic, as the eighth century wore on. So thoroughly had Christian thought been marginalized that at the Second Council of Nicaea in 787, convened to restore the use and veneration of icons, there was not a single Syrian bishop in attendance. During the debates and controversies involving Byzantine and Roman Christianity the Syrian churches played no role. The earlier atmosphere of Muslim tolerance also darkened during the late Umayyad period, when fiscal exactions on minorities grew more severe. By the end of the eighth century, the propagation of Arabic as the language of empire and scholarship had advanced to the point where Greek had virtually disappeared as a literary, scientific and theological language in Syria and Palestine.[52]

As one curtain fell on Damascus, another was raised on the city that replaced it, with a much longer blaze of imperial glory, at the heart of the Islamic Empire. The 'provincial minimalism' of Umayyad Damascus now gave way to the 'imperial grandeur' of Abbasid Baghdad.[53]

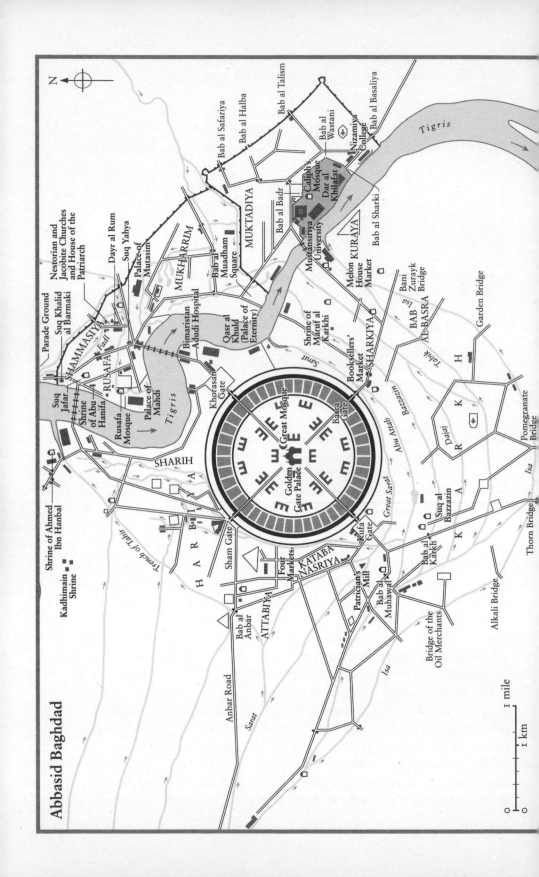

Abbasid Baghdad

N

Tigris

Bab al Talism
Bab al Basaliya
Bab al Wastani
Nizamiya College
Bab al Halba
Bab al Safariya

MUKTADIYA

Caliph's Mosque
Dar al Khilafat
Bab al Badr

Nestorian and Jacobite Churches and House of the Patriarch
Dayr al Rum
Suq Yahya
Palace of Mutasim

MUKHARRIM

Bab al Muadham Square

Mustansiriya University
Bab al Sharki
Melon Market
KURAYA
House Market

Parade Ground
Suq Khalid al Barmaki

SHAMMASIYA
Fadl
RUSAFA

Bimaristan Adudi Hospital
Qasr al Khuld (Palace of Eternity)

Shrine of Maruf al Karkhi

Booksellers' Market
SHARKIYA

Bani Zurayk Bridge
BAB AL-BASRA

Garden Bridge

Suq Jafar
Shrine of Abu Hanifa
Rusafa Mosque
Palace of Mahdi

Tigris

Khorasan Gate

Great Mosque

Golden Gate Palace

Basra Gate

Sarat

Tabik
KARKH

SHARIH

Great Sarat

Abu Attab
Bazzazin
Dajaj

Pomegranate Bridge

Shrine of Ahmed Ibn Hanbal

Kadhimain Shrine

Trench of Tahir

H A R B I

Sham Gate

Four Markets

Kufa Gate

KATABA NASRIYA

Isa

Suq al Bazzazin

Bab al Karkh

Thorn Bridge

ATTABIYA
Bab al Anbar

Patrician's Mill
Bab al Muhawal

Bridge of the Oil Merchants

Alkali Bridge

Anbar Road
Sarat

Isa

1 mile

1 km

0
0

3
Baghdad – City of Peace, City of Blood (9th Century)

Baghdad, in the heart of Islam, is the city of well-being; in it are the talents of which men speak, and elegance and courtesy. Its winds are balmy and its science penetrating. In it are to be found the best of everything and all that is beautiful. From it comes everything worthy of consideration, and every elegance is drawn towards it. All hearts belong to it, all wars are against it and every hand is raised to defend it. It is too renowned to need description, more glorious than we could possibly portray it, and is indeed beyond praise.[1]

Muqaddasi, *The Best Divisions for Knowledge of the Regions*

A staccato burst of gunfire crackles across the city, stunned into stupor by the head-spinning heat. Police sirens wail in response. Somewhere in the distance American Black Hawk helicopters spread thunder across a cobalt sky. Violence hangs in the air.

We have come to see the Mustansiriya, which proud Iraqis with an interest in history revere as the world's oldest university, founded by the penultimate Abbasid caliph Al Mustansir in 1233. My friend Dr Thair, an academic at Baghdad University, is one of these historically minded Iraqis. At great personal risk and at a time when his city has become a cauldron of killing, he has brought me here in his car. On the eastern bank of the Tigris, at the southern end of Baghdad's Old Quarter, a towering portal tapers towards the heavens. The elegant arched entrance is beautifully decorated with arabesque-sculpted terracotta, geometric motifs in masonry and a bristling forest of inscriptions. Overhead a blue-tiled dome glitters in the blinding sun beneath a stately minaret.

The Mustansiriya is one of the very few survivors of the firestorm unleashed on Baghdad by Hulagu, Genghis Khan's grandson, who attacked from the east in 1258. It is a rare jewel of Abbasid architecture that still stands in a city serially invaded, damaged and destroyed by for-eign powers. 'Just look how beautiful it is and I think you can understand how great the Abbasids were,' says Thair.

We step through the portal and find ourselves swallowed up by a paved, sun-scorched courtyard of around a hundred metres by fifty, lined with arches arranged on two storeys. Three *iwan* galleries open onto the court, a fourth side leads towards three open-air oratories. A lonely palm tree stands guard, wilting in the furnace. It is a serene space of simplicity and silencing grandeur.

Here, almost 900 years ago, students from right across the Muslim Empire toiled away on their studies of theology, the Quran, Islamic jurisprudence, medicine, mathematics and literature. In an architectural reflection of the desire to bring the rival Sunni sects together, the campus united on one site the four orthodox schools of Islamic *fikh* jurisprudence, based on the Quran, the *hadith* and the interpretations of the *ulema* clergy: Hanbali, Hanafi, Shafi and Maliki.

During those precious moments when they were able to escape the rigours of academic life and take a break from the library, heaving with tens of thousands of volumes donated by the caliph, the students could relax by soaking in the *hammam*, before tucking into dinner freshly cooked in the kitchen. Anyone requiring medical attention could be treated in the on-site hospital. A monumental, state-of-the-art, water-powered clock in the entrance hall sounded the times for prayer and study and served also as a reminder to students and teachers alike that they were living in one of the most advanced, sophisticated cities on earth.

I say something about the peacefulness of this deserted campus-cum-historical-monument. 'Not like the other Mustansiriya,' Thair laughs sarcastically. In Baghdad's second Mustansiriya University, established in the 1960s in the north-east of the city, a student gang has been murdering, torturing and raping fellow students, university professors and adminis-trators.* 'Only in Baghdad,' says Thair wearily.[2]

The bloodshed on the modern Mustansiriya campus, the gunfire rifling across the city and the American helicopters slicing through the skyline represent the darker side of Iraqi history, a story of sectarian strife and bloodshed, political turbulence and repeated foreign invasions – themes that echo through much of the Middle East.

The five centuries of the Abbasid Dynasty, however, were a vastly more optimistic time. The original Mustansiriya was opened 471 years after

---

* In 2009, Prime Minister Nuri al Maliki temporarily closed the university in an effort to purge the student gang.

Baghdad replaced Damascus as the capital of the Islamic Empire. Yet, although it opened its doors to inquisitive minds in the thirteenth century, during the last gasp of the glorious Abbasid caliphate, it still symbolized that dynasty's unflinching commitment to advancing the frontiers of human knowledge during the half-millennium it held sway. This single building represented a marriage of imperial might and intellectual endeavour with architectural grace and confidence. The university in the heart of the city was a physical incarnation of one of the most famous *hadiths* of the Prophet Mohammed: 'Seek knowledge even to China.' The Abbasid age was the Islamic Empire's answer to Greece's golden age in the fifth century BC. At no time was it more splendid than in ninth-century Baghdad.

By comparison with Mecca and Damascus, ancient settlements whose origins blur into the furthest recesses of antiquity and legend, Baghdad was an upstart arriviste. It was founded on the Tigris River in 762 by the caliph Al Mansur (The Victorious), brother of the blood-shedding Al Saffa, who died of smallpox in 754. While Saffa's greatest legacy was the Abbasid Dynasty, his brother and successor's gift to history was the even longer-lasting city which briefly bore his name: Medinat al Mansur. Its residents, however, preferred Medinat al Salam, the City of Peace, or Dar as Salam, the House of Peace, a reference to the description of paradise in the Quran.* The name Baghdad, by which the city came to be known, is probably ancient Persian in origin, derived from the elision of *bagh*, 'God', and *dadh*, meaning 'founded' or 'foundation' – thus Baghdad was the city 'founded by God', the capital of the Islamic Empire, by now an immense dominion of 5 million square miles stretching from Morocco and the Iberian Peninsula to Central Asia.[3]

Geographically speaking, Mecca and Medina reflected the earliest origins of Islam, with its priority of conquests in Arabia. Damascus, the next iteration, took the Islamic Empire out of the desert and looked west for future expansion. Then, in the closing decades of the eighth century, came the third phase. Unlike the city it supplanted, the new city of Baghdad, auspiciously located in central Mesopotamia, the wondrously fertile Land Between the Rivers, was independent from loyalties to earlier dynasties, such as the Umayyads, and studiously looked east to assimilate lands already won beyond the Oxus River. Sufficiently removed from the

---

* 'God invites you to the House of Peace. He guides whom He will to a straight path. Those that do good works shall have a good reward, and more besides. Neither blackness nor misery shall overcast their faces. They are the heirs of Paradise, wherein they shall abide forever.' Quran 10:25–6

Byzantine frontier, it was also close to Persia, which provided the bulwark of Abbasid military strength.

With abundant supplies of water from both the Euphrates and Tigris, this eastern swathe of the Fertile Crescent had witnessed a succession of flourishing civilizations from Sumerian times in the sixth millennium BC through the Babylonian, Assyrian, Achaemenid, Seleucid, Parthian, Roman and Sassanid periods. It was superbly situated at the heart of the sprawling trade and communications networks that linked East and West. In the words of Mansur, according to the geographer and historian Yaqubi, author of *The Book of Countries*, it was 'the crossroads of the universe':

> Ships on the Tigris, coming from Wasit, Basra, Obolla, Ahwaz, Fars, Oman, Yamama, Bahrain and neighbouring countries, will land and drop anchor there. It is there that merchandise will arrive by way of the Tigris from Mosul, Azerbaijan and Armenia; that too will be the destination of products transported by ship on the Euphrates from Rakkah, Syria, the borderlands of Asia Minor, Egypt and the Maghreb. This city will also be on the route of the peoples of Jebel, Isfahan and the provinces of Khorasan. By God I will build this capital and live in it all my life. It will be the residence of my descendants. It will certainly be the most prosperous city in the world.[4]

Within an incredibly short period of time it was. The speed of the Arab conquests of the seventh century has long been remarked upon as one of history's most remarkable military phenomena. The whirlwind creation of Baghdad from a miniscule, insignificant settlement to a roaring metropolis and world capital of civilization within just a few years is surely no less astonishing. There was nothing inevitable about Baghdad's success, as the four temporary capitals established in Iraq by Saffa and Mansur between 750 and 762, all of which proved unsatisfactory, clearly demonstrated.

One of the advantages of dealing with a relatively new city, unlike Mecca and Damascus, is the quantity of material available about its creation. The sources on Baghdad, while often guilty of exaggeration and hagiography in the interests of Islamic piety and keeping royal patrons happy, offer a compellingly detailed picture of a city being built from scratch. We know, for example, that Mansur, a famously hands-on leader, had workers trace the outline of his Round City on the ground in lines of cinders, a circular tribute to the geometric teachings of Euclid, whom he had studied and admired. We learn from the chronicles how he then walked through these ground-level plans and supervised the positioning of the double outer walls. Balls of cotton were soaked in naphtha, or liquid petroleum, placed along the outlines and then set alight to make a permanent mark for the builders – of whom there were a multitude, sweating in the sun alongside humble labourers, carpenters, blacksmiths, diggers, architects, engineers, surveyors and legal experts. It was a cosmopolitan, polyglot workforce, brought together from the ends of the earth by the opportunity to make a fortune on the Islamic Empire's greatest construction project by far. Perhaps the 100,000 workers estimated by Yaqubi was a wild inflation but it is nevertheless indicative of the sheer scale of the undertaking.

Mansur's Round City, when it was finished on the west bank of the Tigris four years later in 766, was an architectural marvel, the first of its kind anywhere in the world. 'It is as though it is poured into a mould and cast,' the ninth-century essayist and polymath Jahiz wrote approvingly.[5] Four gates pierced the outer walls, and straight roads from each led to the centre of the city. Both the Kufa Gate to the south-west and the Basra Gate to the south-east opened onto the Sarat Canal, a key part of the network of waterways that drained the waters of the Euphrates into the Tigris and made this site so attractive. The Sham (Syrian) Gate to the north-west led to the main road to Anbar and on across the desert to Syria. Finally, to the north-east the Khorasan Gate lay close to the Tigris, leading to the bridge-of-boats across it. Baghdad would have to wait for the arrival of the British, another foreign invasion almost 1,200 years later, for its first fixed bridge across the river. Until then, pontoon bridges were the order of the day.

The quartet of roads running towards the centre of the city from the outer gates were lined with vaulted arcades containing merchants' shops and bazaars. Smaller streets led off these four main arteries, giving access to a series of squares and houses for the as yet limited population. The heart of Baghdad, however, was preserved strictly as a royal enclosure around 2,000 metres in diameter. The outer limits of this space were home to palaces for the junior royals, staff accommodation, the caliph's kitchens, a bakery, cavalry barracks and offices for the treasury, land tax department, armoury and chancery. As a bold architectural symbol honouring the union of temporal and spiritual authority within the Islamic world, the hallowed ground at the very centre of the Round City was dominated by its two most splendid buildings: the Great Mosque and Mansur's Golden Gate Palace.

Mansur's palace, the first within a city that quickly became a byword for palatial excess, was a grand edifice of some 185 square metres, topped by a forty-metre green dome above its main audience chamber. High in the Baghdad skyline, it was surmounted by a sculpture of a lance-wielding cavalryman, who reportedly swivelled like a weathervane to indicate the direction from which the caliph's enemies would next materialize. Like so many of the Abbasid-era monuments, Mansur's great mosque, Baghdad's first, was originally built of sun-baked bricks set in clay, with a roof resting on wooden columns. Serially restored over the centuries, it somehow managed to survive the scorched-earth visitation of Hulagu in 1258 and was remarked upon by the globe-trotting Moroccan Ibn Battuta in 1327, at the start of his 75,000-mile, twenty-nine-year journey across much of the known world.

In Damascus, Walid's Umayyad Mosque had been a notoriously extravagant and expensive project. Mansur's construction of an entire city was of a completely different order. Though the precise costs are impossible to pin down, an idea can be gained from Al Khatib al Baghdadi, the eleventh-century scholar, whose *History of Baghdad* is a treasure trove on the construction of the new capital. He cited two conflicting reports. One claimed the price was 18 million silver dirhams; the other said the cost of the city, its mosque, the caliph's palace, the gates and its markets amounted to a suspiciously precise 4,000,833 dirhams.[6] However much it was we know the expenditure did not leave the famously penny-pinching Mansur out of pocket. On his death in 775, according to the gossipy historian Masudi, the founder of Baghdad left 14 million dinars and 600 million dirhams* in the treasury, the equivalent of 2,640 metric tons of silver.[7]

The population of Baghdad exploded during his caliphate. Apart from the masses engaged in the building of the city and its expanding portfolio of palaces, mosques, homes and bazaars, the ninth-century historian Tabari reported that waves of immigrants from Khorasan, Yemen, the deserts of the Hijaz, Wasit, Kufa and across the Muslim world beat a path to Baghdad, fuelling an extended property boom and transforming the nascent capital into one of the most multicultural places on earth, a melting pot of races, tribes and languages, united – with some prominent exceptions – under the banner of Islam. While the royal family prospered at the highest echelons of society, the incredible wealth spread much more widely, to the ranks of Abbasid courtiers, favourites and officials, famous singers, beautiful slave-girls, wine-quaffing poets, the most brilliant scholars and industrious merchants and traders. There was a capriciousness about life in Baghdad. A well-turned verse from a poet could result in a

---

* A single gold dinar was worth around twenty silver dirhams. A dirham weighed approximately three grams.

life-changing fortune, while an inappropriate barb could lose him his head.

Caliphal largesse was the most glittering and glamorous aspect of the resounding growth of Baghdad, yet trade was also a critical part of the mix. Within only a few years of its foundation the city could justifiably claim to be 'the crossroads of the universe' that Mansur had intended. Boats plied the lengths of the Euphrates and Tigris, two of the four ancient rivers of Paradise, caravans trudged in from Egypt and Syria, bringing their cargoes of goods to a new city, whose population, taking their cue from its leaders, was beginning to glorify in the excesses of conspicuous consumption. The city's markets were soon heaving with the products of the world: silks, gold, jewellery and precious stones, books, spices, exotic fruit, exquisite carpets and long-suffering camels, not to mention slaves and concubines. Boosted by Baghdad, the province of Iraq yielded four times as much revenue to the treasury as Egypt, the next richest province in the Abbasid Empire. Each year it paid a colossal 160 million dirhams – or about 480 tonnes of silver – to the exchequer.[8]

Both before and during the caliphate of Mansur's son and heir Mahdi (r. 775–85), eastern Baghdad or Rusafa (the Causeway, also the Compactly Built), as it is known to this day, started to emerge as a city in its own right. It was still centred on a mosque and royal palace and linked to the Round City via a pontoon bridge that reached western Baghdad, or Karkh, north-east of the Khorasan Gate, beyond an enormous parade ground. Chief officers of the military and state were granted fiefs of land, thereby extending the city both north and south along the eastern bank. Mahdi's royal patronage was supported – occasionally even eclipsed – by the Barmakids, the leading family of courtiers to the first Abbasid caliphs, who built themselves palaces so opulent they easily rivalled those of their masters.

While the 500-year Abbasid era is invariably hailed as Baghdad's most glorious period, the absolute zenith of this period can be narrowed down to the eight decades from 762 to 833, when the city, its people and its culture reigned supreme during the caliphates of Mansur, Mahdi, Hadi (r. 785–6), Harun al Rashid (r. 786–809), Amin (r. 809–13) and Mamun (r. 813–33). It was a sign of the caliphate's restlessly outward-looking ambition that Amin was the only caliph who died in Baghdad during those eight decades.

Of those half dozen names, one stands out above all others, and it is not the founder of the city, but his grandson, Harun al Rashid 'The Rightly Guided'. 'So great were the splendours and riches of his reign, such was its prosperity, that this period has been called "the honeymoon",' Masudi wrote in *The Meadows of Gold*. For Edward Gibbon he was 'the most powerful and vigorous monarch of his race'.[9]

One reason for Harun's immense fame, in East and West alike, was his starring role in the perennially popular *A Thousand and One Nights*, a masterpiece of Indian, Persian and Arab storytelling that dates back to the eighth and ninth centuries. He sashays through its stories charismatically, a nocturnal, street-prowling caliph, alternately enjoying himself in the arms of beautiful concubines, lopping off the heads of those who displease him, throwing bags of gold at those who amuse him, dashing off lines of poetry and rolling with laughter at dirty jokes. In this collection of tall stories Harun, or at least a bawdy stereotype of the caliph, carries all before him.

Behind and beyond Harun's extravagance, however exaggerated, there was real mettle and purpose. For Baghdad, Harun's caliphate was a transformative experience that built upon, often literally, the solid foundations established by his grandfather Mansur to develop the infant city into a fully fledged world metropolis. Might and magnificence combined in torrents of royal patronage and expenditure, the funds for which were regularly replenished during repeated expeditions against the Byzantines. Harun led his first *jihad* at the ripe old age of fourteen and treated Baghdad like a favourite concubine, lavishing ever more treasures on it after each new triumph against Byzantium. This was a kaleidoscope of bloodshed and conquest, pilgrimage and procreation, science and scholarship, palatial building in Baghdad and expenditure on an imperial, never-to-be-repeated scale. Such supercharged largesse should not be confused with decadence or abandon. Tabari recorded how, on his death in 809, Harun left the imperial treasury with 900 million dirhams, together with huge quantities of gold, silver and precious gems, 4,000 turbans, 1,000 pieces of the finest porcelain, 300,000 lances and shields and other treasures besides. As a mid-century caliph supposedly boasted to the Byzantine emperor in Constantinople, 'The least of my territories ruled by the least of my subjects provides a revenue larger than your whole dominion.'[10]

Cities bring together individuals from all walks of life to produce a culture that is far greater than the sum of its parts. The most brilliant men and women transform a city and are transformed by it, rubbing shoulders with colleagues in the arts and sciences, music, law, fashion, the official classes, the religious, commercial, culinary and sporting worlds. The early Abbasids were formidable incubators of urban culture, and under their enlightened leadership Baghdad became a giant ideas laboratory.

While Mansur and Mahdi dipped their toes into cultural patronage,

Harun took it to new, superlative heights. One of his finest achievements was to champion a translation movement, in which scholars in Baghdad translated some of the great works of classical Greek, Hindu and Persian scholarship into Arabic, revised and in many cases improved them, and then circulated the updated texts throughout the Islamic Empire and far beyond. Abbasid envoys returned from expeditions to Byzantium weighed down by manuscripts of seminal works by Plato, Aristotle, Euclid, Hippocrates, Galen and others. The royal library collections swelled to monumental proportions – tens of thousands of volumes – emulated by fabulously wealthy and socially ambitious private patrons, who were only too happy to fuel the translation boom. Abbasid culture was pluralist and adaptive, open to the best the outside world had to offer. The wisdom and knowledge of the ancients was transmitted from West to East, ensuring that it survived to pass back, centuries later, into Western civilization, an enormous intellectual service to which we still owe much to this day. When the first Arabic translation of Euclid was published, it was dedicated to Harun. Philip Hitti likened this period in Baghdad to the Renaissance of the sixteenth century, noting that nothing comparable happened in the Arabic-speaking world for another 1,000 years. 'It made of the Arab capital a world scientific centre comparable to that of Rome in law, Athens in philosophy, and Jerusalem in religion.'[11]

Harun personified this energizing atmosphere of intellectual curiosity and acquisition and set the tone for the city and its leading denizens. His salons included an eclectic circle of religious lawyers (Malik ibn Anas and Al Shafi), judges and historians (Al Waqidi and Ibn Qutayba), poets (Abu al Atahiya and the scandalous Abu Nuwas), musicians (Abu Ishaq al Mosuli), grammarians (Ali ibn Hamza) and humanists (Asmai and Abu Obayda) – though they had to be careful what they said. For conservative clerics with closed minds, the free-wheeling philosophical, religious and scientific discussions and debates Harun encouraged were anathema – as were the drinking bouts, lavish feasts, orgies and homosexual liaisons. Harun and his cronies enjoyed drinking bouts that raged until dawn, fortified by the ruby-red wine of Shiraz, served in golden, silver or crystal goblets, entertained by young women of the harem, who sang, strummed the lute and aroused their drunken audience with the playful scarf dance and the languorous dance of the sabres. As the poet Muslim ibn Walid wrote in verses that encapsulated the spirit of the royal court, 'What is this life but loving, and surrender to the / drunkenness of wine and pretty eyes?'[12]

Little wonder, then, that behind his back the po-faced clerics should call Harun the Commander of the Unfaithful, a play on the caliph's traditional moniker Amir al Muminin, or Commander of the Faithful. Yet this seems a little unfair in light both of Harun's distinguished record of *jihad* against the infidels and his qualification as a *hafiz*, someone who could recite the entire Quran by heart, the only caliph apart from Uthman who was said to be able to do so.

Harun's closest confidants were the astronomically rich Barmakid family, who were extravagant patrons of the arts and sciences in their own right. The loyal Yahya, son of Mansur's vizier Khalid al Barmak, was vizier and mentor to Harun, and the two together spearheaded the development of eastern Baghdad, which became the scene of palace-building on the most sumptuous scale. Yahya's son Jafar, Harun's close friend, adviser and later vizier, spent a scarcely credible 20 million dirhams building a single palace here, with a further 20 million dirhams going on its interior decoration. Diplomatically this was presented as a gift to Harun's son Mamun, who later used it as his official residence, centrepiece of the Dar al Khilafat, the glittering caliphal complex that was home to future Commanders of the Faithful. Baghdad, initially a Round City on the west bank, grew rapidly on its eastern bank under first Mahdi then Harun, the districts of Rusafa, Shammasiya and Mukharrim centred on the caliph's palace and mosque on land given as fiefs to a new, sharp-elbowed generation of courtiers.

In 803, for reasons which remain unclear to this day, Harun abruptly had Jafar beheaded and his elderly father, Yahya, thrown into prison, where he died in 805. To the horror of many Baghdadis, Jafar's body was hacked into three pieces, each of which was gibbeted for public display on the pontoon bridges and left rotting for two years. Baghdad's poets, who had benefited most from Barmakid largesse, mourned their passing in verse heavy with grief.

> *The stars of generosity are out;*
> *The hand of benevolence is closed.*
> *The seas of bounty have ebbed away*
> *Now that the Barmakids are gone.*
> *The stars of the sons of Barmak*
> *Which showed the guide the true path*
> *Have fallen.*[13]

The Islamic Empire to date had been a distinctly patriarchal place. Women were mothers, wives and concubines but not public figures. Their proper place was considered to be the private, domestic sphere, as it remains today in much of the Muslim world. In Harun's Baghdad, however, a small number of women from a very select background emerged into more public roles, either in the flesh or in the sources, which meta-phorically lifted the veil on an otherwise secret realm.

At the very pinnacle of Baghdad society with Harun was his wife and cousin Zubayda. Even without her royal marriage to the most powerful man alive, she was a formidable character. As granddaughter of Mansur, Zubayda was of royal blood, immensely wealthy and well educated in religion, poetry and literature. She won lasting fame on two counts: first for her unrivalled displays of luxury, second for her charitable and religious activities. Harun's Baghdad was a temple of conspicuous consumption and no one was more conspicuous than Zubayda. It was said that during the most important court ceremonies she was so laden with gold and precious stones that two servants were required simply to help her stand upright. At her wedding to Harun in 781 she was given 'precious stones, jewellery, diadems and tiaras, silver and gold palanquins, scents, clothes, servants and maids of honour', together with a priceless waistcoat encrusted with rows of large rubies and pearls, booty seized from the Umayyads at the fall of Damascus in 750. Huge sums of money were distributed among the awestruck guests, gold dinars in silver bowls and silver dirhams in golden bowls, bags of musk and ambergris, expensive perfumes in glass bottles and richly coloured robes of honour woven with gold. 'Nothing comparable had ever been seen in Islamic times.'[14] A stag-gering 50 million dinars was spent on the ceremony from the private treasury alone, with more coming from Harun's own purse.

Those who might have been scandalized by such imperial ostentation would have looked more approvingly on Zubayda's creation of a safe, 900-mile pilgrim route across the desert from Kufa, south of Baghdad, to the holy city of Mecca. Darb Zubayda, Zubayda's Way, as it came to be known, was a large-scale engineering project, with wells, reservoirs, cisterns, state-of-the-art dams with filtering tanks, and fifty-four major resting stations built approximately every sixteen miles, a day's march. When weary pilgrims finally arrived in Mecca, they were able to take advantage of the city's first canal, commissioned by Zubayda, to supply spring water to the shrine. Thirteen hundred years later, the mountain source is still known as Ain Zubayda, Zubayda's Well. The cost of this enormous scheme ran into millions of dinars, paid for from her own pocket. Millions of Muslim pilgrims have her to thank for it.[15]

Other women in Baghdad enjoyed fame for their beauty – and price tags that reflected the giddy spirit of the age. There was a market for everything in the capital of the Islamic world, and that included the most desirable women. Setting an example to his son Harun, Mahdi purchased a girl called Maknuna, 'who took pride in her slender hips and high chest', for 100,000 silver dirhams. Another, Basbas (Caress), cost an eye-watering 17,000 gold dinars. The caliph may have reigned supreme but did not always have things his way. Harun became obsessed by an Arabian woman called Inan. Not only was she beautiful, highly educated and flirtatious, she was also reported to be able to hold her own in poetic repartee with the legendary Abu Nuwas, a master of homoerotic verse. Twice Harun failed to buy her, the first time by refusing to pay 100,000 dinars for her, the second after being outbid by a buyer who paid 250,000 dirhams for her. Inan was not alone in winning fame as a woman. One of the most remarkable characters from the harem was surely Arib, nicknamed the 'nightingale of the court' for the sweetness of her voice and the thousands of songs and poems she composed. Originally purchased by Amin, she later joined Mamun's household, where she fearlessly cuckolded him in his own palace, spiriting in her lover for late-night trysts in an exceptionally dangerous adventure. Arib was said to have her hair massaged with rich pomades of amber and musk, later sold for a handsome price by her servants. As an old woman she was visited by two young men who asked her whether she was still interested in sex. 'Ah, my sons, the lust is present but the limbs are helpless,' she replied. She died in Samarra in her nineties, having enthralled a succession of caliphs.[16]

One of the defining features of Abbasid Baghdad – and its lifeblood as a flourishing city – was its cosmopolitanism. Arabs lived alongside Persians, Indians, Turks, Armenians and Kurds in a capital of Jews, Christians and Muslims. Tolerance was less something to boast about than a generally accepted way of life. Both Jews and Christians long predated Muslims in the region chosen by Mansur as the site of his Round City and both were firmly rooted. Had the tragic destruction of Jerusalem not occurred, it is arguable that Rome may never even have emerged as the capital of Western Christianity. As Diarmaid MacCulloch has argued, 'Still in the eighth century of the Christian era, the great new city of Baghdad would have been a more likely capital for worldwide Christianity than Rome.'[17]

Christians play a prominent role in the city's foundation stories. In Tabari's version a Christian doctor in the Sarat quarter of Baghdad told Mansur of the local tradition that a man called Miklas would one day found a city between the Tigris and the Sarat Canal. 'By God, I am that man!' Mansur exclaimed. 'I was called Miklas as a boy, and then the name fell into disuse!'[18] Nestorian monks, who were already settled in the area, supposedly advised Mansur of the district's favourable climate – comparatively cool (which Baghdadis can be forgiven for discounting as summer temperatures soar above fifty degrees Celsius today), dry and free from mosquitoes, reducing the fatal risks of fever and malaria that raged further south and along the Euphrates.

Harun might have styled himself *'Ghazi wa Hajji'*, Warrior of Islam and Pilgrim, as his special *kalansuwa*, a tall conical hat in silk, proclaimed, yet there was nothing fanatical about his religion. After his teenage debut waging *jihad* against the Byzantines in 780, he returned to Baghdad with the Christians taken as captives from the garrison at the castle of Samalu on the Armenian frontier. They were allowed to form a Christian community in Rusafa, where they worshipped in a church called Dayr al Rum, the Monastery of the Greeks. Over time it became a thriving Christian centre and remained so until the catastrophe of 1258, which reduced most of the city to ruins. The sources suggest that Nestorian and Jacobite churches jostled for space among Baghdad's many mosques.

The Nestorians had much for which to thank the Abbasids. After the rout of the Umayyads and the exit from Damascus, the Syriac Church rose to prominence over the ranks of Christian factions. The Abbasids granted the Nestorian patriarch official jurisdiction over all Christians in the caliphate, which extended from Egypt to Central Asia.[19] Caliphs also tended to value highly the well-known skills of Christian physicians. From the time of Mansur, the Bakhtishu family, a distinguished line of Syriac Christians trained originally in the Persian university of Gundeshapur, provided the Abbasid court with physicians for more than 250 years.

To understand the situation for Baghdad's oldest minority one has to wait much longer, until the later twelfth century, for the first account of Jewish life in the city. Benjamin of Tudela (in Navarre, northern Spain), an adventurous traveller who reached the city sometime around the late 1160s, discovered a prosperous Jewish population of about 40,000 living in 'security, prosperity and honour under the great Caliph'.[20] Their number included well-known sages and the wise rabbis who headed the ten Talmudic academies, many of them of illustrious lineage. Samuel, the chief rabbi, for instance, reportedly traced his family back to Moses.

Benjamin was quite clear what he thought of the caliph. He was, he wrote 'a benevolent man' who was 'kind unto Israel' and had many Jewish attendants. He was multilingual, 'well versed in the law of Israel. He reads and writes the holy language [Hebrew].' The exilarch, the head of the Babylonian Jews in exile, was a man called Daniel, invested with authority over all Jews within the Islamic Empire, from Mesopotamia, biblical Shinar (Sumer), Iran, Khorasan and Yemen, the lands of the Togarmim (Turks) and Alans (in Georgia and the Caucasus), to the wastes of Siberia and 'the gates of Samarkand, the land of Tibet and the land of India'. Jewish communities brought him 'offerings and gifts from the ends of the

earth'. He was a 'very rich' man who owned hospices, gardens and plantations in Babylon and swathes of land inherited from his father.

As a sign of Baghdad's religious tolerance under the Abbasids, there
were twenty-eight synagogues in the city at the time of Benjamin's visit.
The principal place of worship was a monument of breathtaking grandeur
with columns of many-coloured marble overlaid with silver and gold and
inscriptions from the Psalms. An indication of the importance of the city's
Jewish community can be discerned from the regular access its leader
enjoyed to the caliph. Whereas Baghdadis tended to see their caliph only
once a year in a great pageant, Daniel visited him 'every fifth day' amid
sumptuous ceremony, escorted by Christian and Jewish horsemen and
with heralds clearing his way. Having kissed the caliph's hand, he then sat
on a throne opposite the caliph, 'and all the Mohammedan princes who
attend the court of the Caliph rise up before him'. During his investment
ceremony he was escorted from the caliph's palace to his own house 'with
timbrels and fifes'.

Baghdad's Jewish community was of fundamental importance to the
Muslim authorities, not least because it provided 'much money' to the
caliph and his court, a fact of life that held true well into the twentieth
century. Reading Benjamin today, his observation that 'The Jews of the
city are learned men and very rich' proved remarkably accurate for the
following 800 years, until the tragedies of the modern age intervened.
During the second half of the twentieth century and the early years of the
twenty-first, an ancient community that dated back to the Babylonian
Captivity in the sixth century BC was hounded into extinction.

Within only two years of Harun's death in 809, Baghdad was gripped by
a ruinous internecine war between his two sons and heirs, Amin and
Mamun. The conflict, which destroyed much of the city and spelled the
end of western Baghdad as its political and social heart, was the first
instance of large-scale, explosive violence. It marked the beginning of a
pattern of fighting, bloodshed and, in many instances, maniacal cruelty
that would repeatedly recur throughout the history of the City of Peace.

During the civil war of 811–13, the city was first put under siege by
Mamun, who rained down a bombardment of stones and missiles, naphtha and fire from siege engines erected around the city. Amin retreated to
the Round City to make his last stand, but the attack was so fierce he was
forced to abandon Mansur's Palace of Eternity, though not before torching
this magnificent building so admired by Baghdadis.

For the poet Al Khuraymi, Baghdad, until recently a 'paradise on earth'
and an 'abode of happiness' with resplendent palaces, luxuriant gardens

and beautiful lute-players, had become 'as empty as the belly of a wild ass', a desolate, fire-scorched hell where war widows ran screaming through streets prowled by dogs eating headless corpses.[21] Even the Tigris, often likened to a shining mirror or a string of pearls between two breasts, had lost its beauty, reduced to a blood-soaked dumping ground for the bodies of men, women and children – as it became again during the vicious insurgency that raged for years in the aftermath of the US-led invasion of 2003. Swathes of south-western and northern Baghdad were laid waste. Hemmed in by his brother's forces, Amin tried to make a break for it in a chaotic escape by river, but was overrun by his enemies. His end came in a manner that would become painfully common during Baghdad's long, turbulent history: he was hacked down by soldiers and beheaded.

Inaugurated in fratricidal bloodshed, Mamun's twenty-year caliphate from 813 to 833 might have begun inauspiciously, but by its end he had left a glorious legacy of intellectual achievement unmatched by any Abbasid caliph. Mamun set the tone for scholarly endeavour with his extraordinarily generous patronage, luring some of the greatest scientists of the age to Baghdad with stratospheric salaries and the prospects and prestige of conducting cutting-edge research in *the* city of the world.

The latest technology of paper, which reached Baghdad from China in the later eighth century, gave free rein to a new generation of well-funded copyists and translators to turn their attentions to the sprawling fields of Roman law, Greek medicine, mathematics, philosophy and geography, Indian mysticism, Persian scholarship, cartography, astronomy and, for those of a certain literary bent, pre-Islamic poetry. Under Mamun, Baghdad's lavishly endowed Bait al Hikma, or House of Wisdom, became the nerve centre of Abbasid intellectual activity, a wonderfully Abbasid hybrid of royal archive, learned academy, library, think-tank and translation bureau, with a professional staff of scholars, copyists and bookbinders. By the middle of the ninth century, it was the largest repository of books in the world, 'the seed from which sprouted all the subsequent achievements of the golden age of Arabic science, from Uzbekistan in the East to Spain in the West'.[22]

The intellectual buzz in Baghdad reverberated across Asia. It was a time of new books, libraries, reading rooms, bookshops and a torrent of scholarship. In 828 Mamun commissioned an astronomical observatory, the first in the Islamic world, to verify the observations made by the second-century astronomer and geographer Ptolemy in his famous treatise, the *Almagest*. A lasting triumph in design and delivery, it was 'the world's first state-funded large-scale science project'.[23] He also funded a pioneering world map, in which a number of ancient-world errors, such as the size of the Mediterranean, were corrected. Ptolemy's landlocked seas became the Atlantic and Indian oceans, open bodies of water. *Surat al Ardh* (*Picture of the Earth*), a geographical study from this time, detailed the latitudes and longitudes of over 500 cities, categorizing towns, mountains, rivers, seas and islands in separate tables, each with its precise coordinates.

Mamun tasked the three Banu Musa brothers, Mohammed, Ahmed and Hassan, who were distinguished mathematicians, astronomers and engineers, to assess the accuracy of the ancients' measurement of the world's circumference. By fastening pegs and lines of cord into the ground for many miles across the level plain of Sinjar, north-west of Baghdad, and then – to verify their figures – the desert around Kufa, taking measurements of the elevation of the Pole Star, they calculated the earth's circumference at 24,000 miles, in line with the ancient-world measurement (the true figure is 24,902 miles).

Where Mamun led, others followed. Just as the Barmakids had emulated the grandest caliphal palaces during the time of Mansur, Mahdi and Harun, so some of the wealthiest Baghdadis encouraged academic discovery. Apart from being actively engaged as scientists, the three Banu Musa brothers were powerful patrons who funded missions to Byzantium to bring back new manuscripts for translation by scholars hired on extremely attractive salaries on a par with those of senior officials.

Pre-eminent among the House of Wisdom's scientific scholars, Mohammed ibn Musa al Khwarizmi (d. *c.* 850) was a master of arithmetic and astronomy, author of the ground-breaking text *Al Kitab al Mukhtasar fi Hisab al Jabr wal Mukabala* (*The Compendium on Calculation by Restoring and Balancing*), dedicated, as were so many great studies at this time, to Mamun. He is better remembered for the word 'algebra' bequeathed by his landmark work, which was also a key conduit for the passage of Arabic numerals into the medieval West. *The Book of Addition and Subtraction According to the Hindu Calculation*, another of his most substantial titles, introduced for the first time the decimal system of nine numerals and a zero, 'the tenth figure in the shape of a circle', gateway to the discovery of decimal fractions, which were later used to calculate the roots of numbers and the value of pi to sixteen decimal places.[24] Al Khwarizmi can be remembered today in a word familiar to those working at the cutting edge of the financial world: 'algorithm'. Thabit ibn Kura (*c.* 836–901) was another great mathematician and astronomer, author of at least thirty works and hyperactive translator of Archimedes, Euclid, Ptolemy, Diophantus and Nicomachus.

New advances were also made in the field of medicine, led by Nestorian

Christians and their Muslim descendants. Foremost among them was Hunayn ibn Ishaq (808–73), who gravitated to Baghdad from the ancient Christian city of Hira in southern Iraq via a scholarly sojourn in Byzantium. Nicknamed the 'sheikh of the translators', he was master of Arabic, Persian, Syriac and Greek, qualifications that saw him promoted to the position of head translator in the House of Wisdom, in addition to his responsibilities as chief physician to the caliph Mutawakil (r. 847–61). Hunayn was an early starter, translating the second-century Graeco-Roman physician Galen's great study, *On the Natural Faculties*, at the age of just seventeen. He translated many more Galen works, including *On the Anatomy of Veins and Arteries* and *On the Anatomy of Nerves*, and others by Hippocrates, and was a distinguished scientist in his own right. His *Ten Treatises on the Eye*, written around 860, includes one of the first ever anatomical drawings of the human eye and is considered 'the first systematic textbook of ophthalmology'.[25]

In Razi (c. 854–c. 935), Baghdad could boast the greatest physician of the medieval world. A pioneering physician, philosopher and prolific author of numerous medical tomes, he bestrode the medical world like a colossus. His *Kitab al Asrar* (*The Book of Secrets*), in which he classified substances into four groups (animal, vegetable, mineral and derivatives of the three), was a significant move away from alchemy and quackery and a stride towards laboratory experiment and deduction that would later lead to the scientific classification of chemical substances. His views of time as absolute and infinite, requiring neither motion nor matter to exist, was hugely innovative and has been likened to Newton's much later theories. In a haunting passage that looks tragically prescient about Baghdad's troubled future, not to mention that of much of the Muslim world today, Razi evinced contempt for his conservative religious opponents:

> If the people of religion are asked about proof for the soundness of their religion, they flare up, get angry, and spill the blood of whoever confronts them with this question. They forbid rational speculation, and strive to kill their adversaries. This is why truth became thoroughly silenced and concealed.[26]

No description of scholarship in early Abbasid Baghdad can be complete without paying tribute to Abu Yusuf Yaqub al Kindi (c. 800–c. 873), the first 'Philosopher of the Arabs', as well as a mathematician, physician, musician, astrologer and tutor to a son of the caliph Mutasim (r. 833–42), Mamun's successor. It was Kindi, more than any other ninth-century scholar in Baghdad, who was responsible for introducing Greek philosophy to the Muslim world. A broad-minded intellectual of noble Yemeni stock, he took a rational, Razi-like approach to religion that won him enemies among the conservative *hadith* scholars, who despised him for the Christian company he kept. Kindi was prolific on a grand scale, the author of 250 works that ranged in flourishing polymathic fashion from his seminal work, *On First Philosophy*, to studies of Archimedes, Ptolemy, Euclid, Hippocratic medicine, glass manufacture, music, cryptography and swords. He is even credited today with establishing what became known as the frequency analysis method, in which variations in the frequency of letters or groups of letters can be analysed to break a particular code. The first theoretician of music in the Muslim world, he added a string to the Arab lute, made pioneering advances in musical notation and even attempted to cure a quadriplegic boy through the use of music therapy.[27] He was, said Ibn al Nadim, the tenth-century author of the *Fihrist*, or *Catalogue*, a voluminous survey of the literary, scientific and intellectual elite, 'the distinguished man of his time and unique during his period because of his knowledge of the ancient sciences'.[28] He is honoured today in Baghdad's Al Kindi Teaching Hospital in Rusafa, north-east of Baghdad's most famous road, Al Rashid Street, itself a lasting tribute to Harun.

Hard science did not prosper at the expense of literary life. The Arab love of Arabic verse, which long predated the coming of Islam, continued unabated and was championed by open-handed patrons from the caliph down. Poetry, the rock-and-roll of Abbasid Baghdad, offered untold rewards to those who found favour at the highest level. Like so many scholars and scientists, musicians, physicians, mathematicians, philosophers, astronomers, geographers, historians, traders, lawyers, singing slave-girls and the most ambitious men and women from the length of the empire, the transgressive poet Abu Nuwas (c. 757–c. 814), who enjoyed some mischievous cameos in *The Arabian Nights*, made his way to Baghdad in the closing years of the eighth century to seek his fortune. His career is a powerful reminder of just how tolerant the Abbasid era – and the world of Islam – was at its height. A bold and brilliant writer who would have had his head struck off in less forbearing times, Abu Nuwas revelled in explicit celebrations of illicit sex, even going so far in one poem as to question his dangerous affection for the caliph Amin. Widely considered the greatest Bacchic poet in the Arabic language, he wrote freely and provocatively of wine-fuelled homosexual encounters:

> *Auspicious stars had risen on this night*
> *When drunkard assaulted drunkard*
> *We passed the time kowtowing to the Devil,*
> *Until the monks sounded the bells at dawn*

And a young adolescent left, dragging delightful robes
Which I had stained with my iniquitous behaviour,
Saying, 'O woe!' as tears overcame him,
'You have torn away the dignity I had preserved.'
I replied, 'A lion saw a gazelle and lunged at it;
Such is the variety of Fate's vicissitudes!'[29]

While still an adolescent he was seduced by the openly gay poet Waliba ibn Hubab. On their first tryst and after considerable quantities of wine, the story went, Waliba was admiring the younger man's naked body and kissed him on his behind. The impudent Abu Nuwas farted in his face and was immediately cursed for such vulgarity. Abu Nuwas was undaunted. 'What reward can there be for the man who kisses ass except a fart!' he retorted. One of the most popular, and certainly the most controversial, poets of his age, Abu Nuwas is remembered today in the tree-lined corniche that bears his name along the east bank of the Tigris, together with the 1972 bronze statue by the Iraqi sculptor Ismail Fattah al Turk, in which the poet nursed his trademark goblet of wine. In a sign of the far more conservative times prevailing today, the statue was vandalized in 2015 and the cup of wine removed.[30]

Abbasid poets mined a rich seam of love poetry, much of it mournful and unfulfilled, along with melancholic musings on the human condition and more riotous paeans to the joys of the grape and, in some instances, downright debauchery. Abu al Atahiya (748–825) rose from the most humble origins as a penniless pot-seller to become one of the most transcendent voices of the Abbasid era. Beaten, imprisoned, sent into exile, he was forever getting into scrapes for his high-spirited behaviour and attempts to win the heart of Utba, a beautiful slave-girl who belonged to the royal household. Once, after suffering another beating for harassing the poor woman, he declared he was giving up poetry altogether. Thrown into prison on the orders of the caliph Mahdi, he was ordered to watch a man beheaded. 'Choose either to make verses or to be sent after him,' the caliph told the poet.[31] Abu al Atahiya picked up his pen again, and somehow managed not to lose his head during the reigns of the following four caliphs. Bashar ibn Burd (d. *c*. 784), the final figure within the triumvirate of the Abbasid era's most celebrated poets, was another rags-to-riches story typifying the social and geographical mobility of the time, though his life would end ultimately in ruin. Despised by some as a libertine, he was cautioned to desist from writing love poetry but ignored the warning. Tabari recorded how Bashar offended one of Mahdi's ministers, who appears to have taken his revenge by framing the poet. He showed the caliph verses accusing Mahdi of having sex with his aunts, calling for his overthrow and demanding that Mahdi's son Musa be 'shoved back up Khaizuran's cunt', a reference to the caliph's beautiful wife.[32] Bashar was murdered before he could explain himself, a victim of deadly court intrigues.

While poets were the celebrities of the Abbasid era, with financial packages to match, writing fine prose, which was still in its infancy, could also win the caliph's attention. There was probably no one in the field more entertaining or erudite than the prolific polymath Jahiz ('The Goggle-Eyed', *c.* 776–*c.* 868), a scholar from a modest background in Basra. Like so many of the finest minds of their generation, he gravitated to Baghdad in the early ninth century, drawn to show off his talents in the greatest city in the Islamic Empire. He was 'probably the greatest master of prose in all Arab literature', a writer possessed of 'exceptional genius'.[33] An indefatigable scholar, he was the author of a stupendous 231 titles, of which the best known was *Kitab al Hayawan*, the seven-volume *Book of Animals*, which drew heavily on the works of Aristotle and, some argue, contained the kernel, a millennium before Darwin, of the theory of natural selection.[34] He was a master essayist, and the breadth of his writing caught the intellectual spirit of the times, wide-roving and utterly fearless. He discoursed on the superiority of black men over whites, pigeon-racing, Islamic theology, miserliness, the Aristotelian view of fish and whether women should be permitted to make noises of pleasure while having sex. Like today's publishers scrambling to offer the most famous writers the most monstrous advances, viziers, chief judges and the cream of Baghdad society fell over themselves to pay him substantial sums in return for dedications in his many works.[35]

Like the most notable poets of the age, the leading singers and musicians were also celebrities, some of them spectacularly rich. Ibrahim al Mosuli was a louche, wine-drinking musician who rose from impoverished traveller to become a leading luminary of Baghdad's cultural scene with his son Ishaq. Ibrahim, possibly the first-ever orchestra conductor, took spending to almost caliphal levels of extravagance. Ishaq reckoned that by the time of his death his father had spent 24 million dirhams, in addition to his monthly salary of 10,000 dirhams, much of it on feasts for friends and fans, lubricated with reckless quantities of wine. 'The beautiful concerts given at Baghdad have left memories that still last,' wrote the magisterial historian Ibn Khaldun five centuries later. The courts of Mahdi, Harun, Amin and Mamun represented 'the high point of ancient Arab musical culture'.[36]

*

In 835 Baghdad received a humiliating blow. The new caliph Mutasim abruptly upped sticks from the imperial city, moved a hundred miles north along the Tigris and built himself a new capital at Samarra. It was from this new city, and not Baghdad, that Mutasim and the next seven caliphs ruled until 892.

For many Baghdadis the city's demotion came less as an affront than a blessed relief. Mutasim had been recruiting Turkish *ghulams*, a loyal personal force of slave-soldiers, from the steppes of Central Asia. Baghdadis grew resentful of these hordes of Asiatic interlopers clattering through the streets on horseback, knocking down anyone in their path. *Ghulams* were appointed to lucrative court positions, despite being unable to speak Arabic. Clashes broke out on the streets and in the barracks, and there were a number of murders. There were additional reasons for local jealousies. The talents of the youthful *ghulams* were by no means limited to the battlefield; they made themselves attractive to the Abbasid courtiers in a variety of ways. 'The same boy could be at once slave, guard, muse and bedfellow to his master.'[37]

The dramatic move from Baghdad to Samarra was a reaction to these social tensions. The new site offered unlimited land on which to accommodate the boisterous troops. In the short term the departure from Mansur's noble city might have made sense. In time, however, the caliphs who followed Mamun saw their power steadily ebb away to the Turkish military commanders who were intended to protect them. Like the Mamluks of the Ayyubid Sultanate and the Janissaries of the Ottoman Empire, whom they anticipated, the *ghulams* steadily grew in power until it was they, rather than the caliph, who exercised real authority. The leader of the Abbasid Empire increasingly became a prisoner in his own palace.

No longer ruled by a caliph, Baghdad was reduced to the ignominy of being administered by a series of governors, a dramatic loss of political power and prestige. Worse was to follow. In 865, only half a century after the terrible siege and civil war between Amin and Mamun, the city was under attack again. After a mutiny in Samarra, the caliph Mustain (r. 862–6) fled to Baghdad. His court immediately swore an oath of allegiance to his cousin Mutazz, son of the caliph Mutawakil.

As part of his strategy to defend Baghdad, the governor Tahir destroyed bridges and flooded the canals in the Al Anbar district to prevent a Turkish attack from the north-west. This short-term decision caused long-term damage to the irrigation infrastructure that was vital to the prosperity of Baghdad and Iraq. Faced with a professional Turkish army of 12,000 outside the Shammasiya Gate, Baghdad's defenders were in such dire straits that Tahir ordered a special draft so desperate that even a party of pilgrims from Khorasan, hitherto minding their own business on the way to Mecca, were press-ganged into an irregular army of 'vagabonds', waifs and strays, armed with nail-studded clubs and tar-covered mats for shields. The Baghdad defenders chalked up an early success when they charged the Turkish camp, driving many of the attackers into the Tigris, where troops in river boats cut them down. Tabari reported skiffs piled high with severed heads, destined for gruesome display on bridges and the walls of the governor's palace. Two thousand of the attackers were killed.

In the autumn, the Turks finally smashed through the Anbar Gate fortifications on the west bank and torched everything as they advanced, causing massive damage to the Harbiya quarter. Worn down by the siege, hungry and exhausted Baghdadis took to the streets in protest against the governor, riots erupted and crowds broke down his palace gates. Mustain appeared on the roof of his palace, clad in the Prophet Mohammed's hallowed black cloak and brandishing the ceremonial spear of office, assuring the crowds he remained in control. In early 866, after an act of treachery by Tahir, Mutazz was declared caliph. Mustain was granted exile in the Hijaz but was quickly intercepted and murdered. His head was sent to his cousin Mutazz. 'Put it there,' the caliph commanded, not deigning to interrupt his game of chess.[38]

Over time the Samarra caliphs must have come to fear for their lives in their militaristic new capital. During the fifty-seven years they ruled from this purpose-built city, they met their maker in varying levels of discomfort. The methods of execution did not lack imagination and included being bled to death with a poisoned lancet (Al Muntasir, 862); decapitation (Al Mustain, 866); thirsted to death while locked up in a cell without food or water (Al Mutazz, 869); and, most agonizing of all, testicular crushing (Al Muhtadi, 870). Determined to escape such an exquisitely painful death, in 892 the caliph Mutadid (r. 892–902) returned the caliphate to Baghdad, which remained its home for the final 350 years of the Abbasid Dynasty.

Mutadid exemplified the interests of the Baghdad caliphs in the aftermath of the golden era of the ninth century. He was a prodigious palace-builder and threw himself into an ambitious reconstruction programme to repair the destruction wrought by the siege of 865. He lived in and dramatically enlarged the Dar al Khilafat complex on the east bank, creating new gardens and building the Qasr al Firdus, or Castle of Paradise, with its vast wild animal park; the Qasr al Thuraya, Palace of the Pleiades, connected by a two-mile underground passage to the Hasani Palace, allowing the women of the imperial household to come and go with complete discretion; finally, the Qasr al Taj, Palace of the Crown, later the chief official residence and gilded cage of the Abbasid caliphs.

After the inspiring heyday of Mamun's reign, power steadily slipped away from the Abbasid caliphs. The move back to Baghdad from Samarra did not arrest this decline, which saw them reduced from supremely powerful monarchs of the world to wealthy puppet-rulers kept under virtual palace arrest. Yet Baghdad remained a city to behold for some time. Visiting on a diplomatic mission from the empress Zoe of Byzantium, the ambassadors John Radinos the Patrician and Michael Toxaras arrived in Baghdad to discuss peace terms with the caliph Al Muktadir (r. 908–32) in 917. They were overawed by a calculated display of power and magnificence: 160,000 cavalry and infantry lining the route to the caliph's palaces, twenty-three of which they were invited to visit; 7,000 eunuchs; 4,000 black pages; the finest textiles, including 38,000 curtains and 22,000 carpets in a single palace; elephants mounted with fire-throwers; 100 muzzled lions, each with its own keeper; a one-and-a-half-ton tree made of solid silver and gold, complete with mechanical singing birds fashioned from the same precious metals.

So far, so splendid. Yet by the last decade of the ninth century, faced with the growing power of the Tulunids in Egypt, the Samanid Dynasty in Central Asia and the rebel authority in Persia, Baghdad's caliphal dominions were narrowing to Iraq, western Persia and parts of Arabia and its neighbours. The tenth century relentlessly chipped away at Baghdad's control of the Islamic Empire and its hard-won cultural domination. In 909, a rival Shia Fatimid caliphate was declared in Tunisia. Other eastern cities were determined to make their own mark and developed high-minded courts thronged with their own constellations of brilliant stars. It was a lengthening list of urban distinction within the Dar al Islam: Samarkand, Balkh, Khiva, Tabriz, Isfahan, Shiraz, Mosul, Aleppo, Cairo, Ghazni.

Ninth-century Baghdad glittered across the firmament like a meteor, illuminating the earth with a host of world-changing discoveries. The light started to fizzle out, said Masudi, during the caliphate of the religious hardliner Mutawakil in the second half of the century. He put an end to the freewheeling intellectual culture, so much of which depended upon the caliph's patronage. 'Mutawakil abolished free thought, philosophical disputes and the things which had preoccupied men's minds under Mutasim, Wathik and Mamun,' Masudi wrote. 'He re-established orthodoxy and submission to traditional religious values,' though such ostentatious piety did not prevent him building up a harem of 4,000 women, all of whom he was said to have slept with.[39]

When the Andalusian geographer and poet Ibn Jubayr reached Baghdad in 1184, he was cruelly disappointed by the once great metropolis of Islam. 'In comparison with its former state, before misfortune struck it and the eyes of adversity turned towards it, it is like an effaced ruin, a remain washed out, or the statue of a ghost,' he wrote.[40] Such 'misfortune' was as nothing to the annihilating visits of Hulagu in 1258, followed by Tamerlane in 1401, which collectively put paid to any further pretensions of Baghdad to world authority.

'This is where the caliphs and their families were buried in the middle and late Abbasid era,' says Manaf, a Baghdadi friend and retired diplomat. It is 2005, a vicious insurgency is raging across Iraq, Sunni and Shia death squads stalk the city and we have braved the car-choked roads of Adhamiya, a Sunni heartland in north-eastern Baghdad, for a historical excursion. Unlike the Kadhimain shrine, its great Shia counterpart almost directly across the Tigris, the Abu Hanifa Mosque is a monument of spartan simplicity behind a wall daubed with red graffiti ('Be patient, be patient, Baghdad. The army of the Invader will be swept away'). This is the shrine of Imam Abu Hanifa, founder of the Hanafi school of Islamic jurisprudence, largest of the four orthodox schools, hallowed across the Dar al Islam. 'You should see it on the Prophet's birthday,' says Manaf. 'It's the focal point for the Sunni throughout the Islamic world and the birthday celebrations are one of the major events in Adhamiya. Khaizuran, Harun al Rashid's mother, was buried nearby so it came to be known as Khaizuran's graveyard. In one of these streets is the shrine of Um Rabia, daughter-in-law of Mustasim, the last Abbasid caliph, who was slayed by the invading Mongol hordes in 1258.'

For a moment I have tantalizing visions of stumbling across the graves of the greatest Abbasid caliphs, but Manaf quickly dispels them. 'The tombs of the caliphs disappeared during the floods and devastations that afflicted the district during Baghdad's many dark periods,' he says quietly.

For the once pre-eminent capital of Mansur's Islamic Empire, all those troubles lay ahead. Yet while Baghdad's fortunes were already firmly in decline at the turn of the tenth century, at the westernmost corner of the Muslim world, in one of history's minor ironies, one Islamic city was about to stamp its mark. Destroyed completely in Damascus, the Abbasids' bitter enemies the Umayyads rose again from the ashes and declared a rival caliphate in Al Andalus in 929. Its capital was Cordoba.

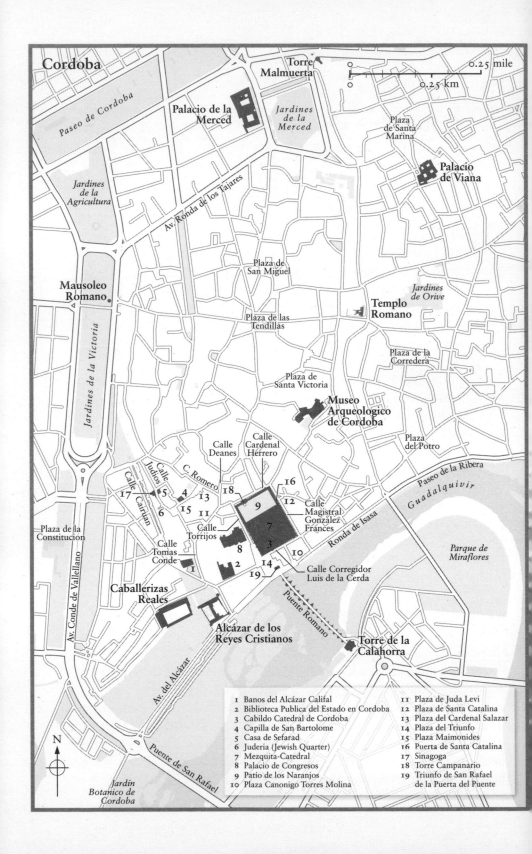

Cordoba

Torre Malmuerta

Paseo de Cordoba

Palacio de la Merced

Jardines de la Merced

0.25 mile
0.25 km

Plaza de Santa Marina

Palacio de Viana

Jardines de la Agricultura

Av. Ronda de los Tajares

Mausoleo Romano

Jardines de la Victoria

Plaza de San Miguel

Templo Romano

Jardines de Orive

Plaza de las Tendillas

Plaza de la Corredera

Plaza de Santa Victoria

Museo Arqueologico de Cordoba

Plaza del Potro

Calle Deanes

Calle Cardenal Hérrero

C. Romero

Calle Judios

16

Paseo de la Ribera

Calle Cairuan

17 5 4 13 18

9 12

Calle Magistral González Fránces

Guadalquivir

15 11

6

7

Ronda de Isasa

Plaza de la Constitucion

Calle Torrijos

8 3

Parque de Miraflores

Av. Conde de Vallellano

Calle Tomas Conde

1 2 14

10

19

Calle Corregidor Luis de la Cerda

Caballerizas Reales

Puente Romano

Alcázar de los Reyes Cristianos

Torre de la Calahorra

Av. del Alcázar

N

Puente de San Rafael

Jardín Botánico de Cordoba

1 Banos del Alcázar Califal
2 Biblioteca Publica del Estado en Cordoba
3 Cabildo Catedral de Cordoba
4 Capilla de San Bartolome
5 Casa de Sefarad
6 Juderia (Jewish Quarter)
7 Mezquita-Catedral
8 Palacio de Congresos
9 Patio de los Naranjos
10 Plaza Canonigo Torres Molina

11 Plaza de Juda Levi
12 Plaza de Santa Catalina
13 Plaza del Cardenal Salazar
14 Plaza del Triunfo
15 Plaza Maimonides
16 Puerta de Santa Catalina
17 Sinagoga
18 Torre Campanario
19 Triunfo de San Rafael de la Puerta del Puente

4

Cordoba – Ornament of the World (10th Century)

The capital city of Cordoba since the island of Andalus was conquered, has been the highest of the high, the furthest of the far, the place of the standard, the mother of towns; the abode of the good and godly, the homeland of wisdom, its beginning and its end; the heart of the land, the fount of science, the dome of Islam, the seat of the imam; the home of right reasoning, the garden of the fruits of ideas, of the earth and the banners of the age, the cavaliers of poetry and prose. Out of it have come pure compositions and exquisite compilations. And the reason for this, and for the distinction of its people before and since, as compared with others, is that the horizon encompasses none but the seekers and the searchers after all the various kinds of knowledge and refinement. Most of the people of the country are noble Arabs from the East who conquered it, lords of the troops of Syria and Iraq who settled there, so that their descendants remain in each district as a noble race. Hardly a town lacks a skilled writer, a compelling poet who, had he praised it, the least would have been great.[1]

Unknown author of *Al Dhakhira al Saniyya*
(*The Gleaming Treasure*)

'*No hay Moros en la costa!*'

Father Manuel González Muñana allows himself a smile. 'There are no Moors on the coast!' It's an old Spanish saying, he explains, the equivalent of the British expression 'the coast is clear', only in this case the enemy is made more explicit. Father Manuel, author, professor of theology and parish priest of the Immaculate Conception and St Albert the Great, has been discussing the campaign waged by local Muslims to be allowed to pray in the eighth-century Mezquita-Catedral of Cordoba. The priest is a slight, bespectacled man who cuts a modest figure in his black donkey jacket and dog collar. But there is real steel behind the gentle demeanour. Framed beneath one of the many entrance arches, with the glorious Court of Oranges – a vista of sunlit palms, cypresses, citrus trees and irrigation channels behind him with the stout minaret-turned-belltower rising beyond into the skyline – his confident presence here is a Catholic assertion of ownership and primacy. Father Manuel leaves no doubt that, were it up to him, not only would there be no Moors on the coast but there would certainly be no Muslims praying in the famous mosque-turned-cathedral. Ever. 'It is a place of Christian worship,' he says with an air of finality.

In a café across town, Abdulaziz, the local imam of Cordoba, smiles wearily while discussing the same subject over a cappuccino. '*Con la iglesia hemos topado,*' he shrugs. It's another well-known expression. 'When you get to the Church, you hit a brick wall.' The Reconquista does not brook any argument.

In the heart of Cordoba's languidly winding Jewish Quarter, or Judería, a UNESCO World Heritage Site since 1984, a tiny museum and library stand a stone's throw from a statue of Maimonides, the twelfth-century Jewish philosopher and physician. Accommodated in a house that dates back to the fourteenth century, the Casa de Sefarad is dedicated to preserving the memories of the Sephardic tradition in the Iberian Peninsula. Yet such is the state of interfaith relations and anti-Semitism in Cordoba – the museum has been daubed with hateful graffiti, so much for the *convivencia* of Al Andalus – that the director of the museum is uncomfortable even saying whether he is Jewish. 'There are some things I never discuss with strangers,' he says.[2]

Sprawling across a depression in the Guadalquivir Valley, home to the mud-brown river of the same name, Cordoba is an ancient city whose history, unlike that of Baghdad, ranges back more than two millennia to Carthaginian times.* Conquered by the Romans in the early third century BC, it became the capital of Hispania Baetica, the empire's southernmost province in the Iberian Peninsula, a port city from which Spanish wheat, wine and olive oil were shipped back to Rome. In 571 the campaigning Visigothic king Leovigild took it from the Byzantines and established a bishopric here, increasing the town's prestige and importance. Long a rich agricultural centre auspiciously located between the cattle-raising territory of the Sierra Morena mountain range to the north and the fertile farming

---

* Guadalquivir, from the Arabic *Wadi al Kabir*, the Great River.

land to the south, within just a few years of its capture by Muslim forces in 711, Cordoba – Al Qurtuba to the Muslim conquerors – had emerged as the provincial capital of Al Andalus.

Sole royal survivor of the Abbasids' slaughter of his Umayyad family in Damascus in 750, the never-say-die Abd al Rahman, grandson of the caliph Hisham, last encountered in these pages fleeing the scene of those atrocities, headed west on a perilous journey dodging Abbasid assassins. From Iraq he passed into Palestine, then Sinai and into Egypt, continuing across North Africa into present-day Morocco. After a tumultuous, five-year flight, forever fighting off spies, informants and would-be murderers, he landed on the Iberian Peninsula in 755 and quickly established a new dynasty and fledgling Muslim state, the amirate of Cordoba, in 756. It would last three centuries. During the eighth century the Christian principalities of northern Spain expanded south, so that by the tenth century Muslim Cordoba defined its infidel enemies on the peninsula as León, Castile, Navarre, Aragon and Barcelona.

After the conquests of the eighth century, when there was little time for the comforts and refinements of civilization, life grew more pleasant for the Umayyads in the ninth. Aping the sophistication of Baghdad, from where he imported the finest tapestries and carpets, Abd al Rahman II (r. 822–52) built lavishly decorated palaces and mosques and introduced a more luxurious court ceremonial with extravagant sartorial standards. After the rigours of the Middle East, the gentler Andalusian climate mellowed the descendants of the rough desert horsemen who had ridden west under the banner of Islam, so that 'soon they became sensual and pampered, fond of wine, singers and dancing-girls, and all the delights that had made Gades [Cadiz] and its women famous during the Roman Empire'.[3]

Abd al Rahman III succeeded to the amirate in 912 at the tender age of twenty-one. Though his name was quintessentially Arab, his bloodline was not; it was much more cosmopolitan. His father, Mohammed, had been born of the union between Amir Abdullah and Iñiga, a Christian princess, daughter of a king of Navarre who had been sent to Cordoba as a hostage in the 860s. Abd al Rahman's mother was the Christian slave-concubine Muzna, making her son three-quarters Hispano-Basque and one quarter Arab. His fair hair and blue eyes, physical traits he shared with a number of the Umayyads of Cordoba, hardly marked him out as the traditional Muslim leader, a presentational problem he attempted to remedy by dying his hair black to appear more Arab.[4]

It is tempting to discern in the Umayyads' mixed blood, a marriage of Muslim Arab fathers and largely Christian mothers, the genetic foundation for the remarkable cultural cosmopolitanism over which they presided in

Spain for three centuries. From the time of Abd al Aziz, son of Musa ibn Nusayr, the eighth-century conqueror who first brought Islam to the Iberian Peninsula, female Christian captives and slaves poured into the Umayyad harems. Several centuries of breeding with women of Berber, Iberian and Visigothic stock produced a royal line that had little Arab – and a good deal of fair or ginger hair and blue eyes – in it. As children, these future rulers grew up listening to Christian rituals, stories and ballads from Castile, León, Catalonia and France, living among architecture loaded with symbols as intrinsic to the heritage of their mothers as to that of their fathers.[5]

While Cordoba flourished under its succession of fair-headed Umayyad amirs, it was only in the tenth century that it entered a spectacular golden age and became, in the words of the German nun Hrotsvitha of Gandersheim (c. 930–c. 1002), *decus orbis*, the 'ornament of the world'.[6] If one man can be credited for ushering in this period of unprecedented peace, prosperity, political stability and the cultural flowering they underpinned, it was Abd al Rahman III, the stand-out figure of his age. During his long reign from 912 to 961 he proved himself neither an inspired general nor a charismatic religious leader but a shrewd and dogged politician, who steadily extended the writ of Cordoba from barely beyond its outskirts to the undisputed sovereignty of Al Andalus, master of all Muslim communities and perennial scourge of the Christians. Fundamental to this assertion and accumulation of power was his success in fashioning an organized military force from a disorganized and unruly 'war-band living off the proceeds of an annual pillaging expedition'.[7]

Faced with a peninsula swarming with perpetually feuding principalities, local lords and would-be kings, Abd al Rahman moved decisively to impose his authority, mounting a relentless series of campaigns against his rivals, be they major towns like Seville, Badajoz or Toledo or single castles halfway up a mountain. He pursued a classic policy of stick and carrot: recalcitrant powers were put under siege and blockade and, in some instances, were subjected to economic warfare by having their fruit trees and agricultural lands destroyed. Those who buckled under, however, such as Mohammed ibn Ibrahim ibn al Hajjaj, ruler of Seville, or Abd al Rahman's sworn adversary Hafs ibn Hafsun, lord of Bobastro, could expect to be rewarded with a senior vizierial or military appointment on a comfortable salary in Cordoba. Generosity was used as a weapon to buy off opposition, with magnificent robes made from the finest richly textured fabrics a favourite present bestowed on those who bent the knee and laid down their swords.

Abd al Rahman led from the front. He took personal command of *jihad* campaigns against the northern infidels in 917, 920, 924, 934 and 939. A master of strategic communications before the term existed, he was the first Umayyad ruler to employ an official historian, Ahmed ibn Mohammed al Razi (d. 955), whose work sadly does not survive in its original form, and had news of his victories announced in the mosques during Friday prayers. Panegyrics and newsletters praising his martial valour and Islamic piety were trotted off by dutiful poets and writers, who celebrated him as the courageous, just and noble warrior, the tireless reviver of religion and defender of orthodoxy, scourge of heretics with his thirsty sword, and more honorifics besides. More visually compelling evidence of his conquests came with the clusters of severed heads of his enemies dispatched back to Cordoba for public display on Bab al Sudda, one of the gates of the Alcázar royal citadel, or paraded in the markets. Those adversaries who were not executed on capture might be sent to Cordoba for a rabble-rousing public beheading on the esplanade between the royal palace and the great Guadalquivir.

In 925 we hear of a Christian archer called Abu Nasr, a follower of the rebel Omar ibn Hafsun, crucified alive while fellow archers fired a volley of arrows at him, an agonizing execution concluded with the burning of his corpse. Furtun ibn Mohammed, a traitor from the disastrous Battle of Al Khandaq in 939, had his tongue cut out before he was crucified. Writing from the safe perspective of the eleventh century, the Andalusian polymath Ibn Hazm, author of 400 titles on subjects as diverse as Islamic jurisprudence and the art of love, judged Abd al Rahman to be a cruel leader who had no qualms about shedding blood, including that of one of his own sons, whom he executed. According to one story, he once had some hapless mixed-race youths strapped to the waterwheel in one of his palaces until they died. His executioner Abu Imran Yahya was one of his busiest officials, always conveniently within reach with his sword and leather mat at his ruler's disposal.[8]

On Friday 16 January 929, Abd al Rahman made his move. It was an extraordinarily audacious decision. At a stroke he abandoned his title of amir, threw off the notional obedience to the distant authority of Abbasid Baghdad and declared himself caliph. His *laqab* or throne title was Al Nasir li Din Allah, 'He who gives victory to Allah's creed'. The fourteenth-century historians Ibn al Khatib and Ibn Idhari recorded how letters were sent to Abd al Rahman's governors announcing the news and instructing them how he should be addressed:

> We are the most worthy to fulfil our right, and the most entitled to complete our good fortune, and to put on the clothing granted by the nobility of God, because of the favour which He has shown us, and the renown which He

has given us, and the power to which He has raised us, because of what He has enabled us to acquire, and because of what He has made easy for us and for our state to achieve; He has made our name and the greatness of our power celebrated everywhere ... We have decided that the da'wa should be to us as Commander of the Faithful and that letters emanating from us or coming to us should be in the same manner ... So order the khatib in your place to pronounce [the *khutba**] using [this title] and address your communications to us accordingly, if God will.[9]

Gold coins were minted with the new caliphal legend: Al Imam al Nasir li Din Allah Abd al Rahman Amir al Muminin, Commander of the Faithful. Across the Mediterranean on the shores of North Africa, the rising power of the Fatimid Dynasty, which had declared a rival Shia caliphate in 909, was unimpressed by the Iberian upstart. 'To whom do they trace their ancestry?' one wondered in a letter of scorching contempt. 'To dogs, or to apes, or to pigs? By God these are better than the people to whom they trace their ancestry.'[10] For the first time the Muslim world now consisted of three rival caliphates, two orthodox and one Shia.

In 939, a decade into the caliphate of Cordoba, Abd al Rahman encountered defeat for the first time. Leading his army at the Battle of Al Khandaq, he only narrowly avoided being captured and killed by Christian forces under Ramiro II, King of León. His tent was stormed, his royal standard seized, together with his suit of armour and personal copy of the Quran. It was a near miraculous escape. After such a profound shock, Abd al Rahman never took to the field again at the head of an army, against infidels or otherwise.

For Cordoba and its people this proved an extraordinarily beneficial decision. Freed from a direct military role, the first caliph of Cordoba now devoted himself to providing the appropriately glorious architectural foundation for the caliphate he had established. As a poem attributed to Islam's newest caliph expressed it:

> *Kings who want posterity to talk about their elevated aims*
> *Use the tongue of their buildings.*
> *See how the Pyramids still stand,*
> *Whereas so many kings were erased by the ups and downs of time.*[11]

Nowhere was this evidenced more splendidly than in Medinat al Zahra, 'The Shining City', a city-palace complex four miles to the west of Cordoba, supposedly named after one of Abd al Rahman's favourite

---

* The *khutba* was the sermon delivered during Friday prayers.

concubines – he is said to have had a total of 6,300 women in his palace to choose from, employed for domestic service and royal lovemaking. Set in the foothills of the Sierra Morena, it measured a mile from east to west and half a mile from north to south, lording it over the plains below from three descending terraces, each one surrounded by turreted fortress walls. Building work began around 936 and continued for the rest of Abd al Rahman's reign and the best part of two decades under the caliphate of his son and heir, Hakam II (r. 961–76). Abd al Rahman's personal obsession with the project was so notorious that he was publicly chastised by a Cordoban jurist when he failed to attend prayers at the Great Mosque on several consecutive Fridays.

Everything about Medinat al Zahra was on the grandest, most fantastical scale, from its size (280 acres) and labour force (10,000–12,000 workers) to the time required to finish it (forty years) and the final cost (one third of all government revenues over the entire period of its construction). For the seventeenth-century historian Al Maqqari, who was not immune to a little exaggeration, it was one of the most splendid architectural projects ever undertaken by man. His history of Muslim Spain, *Nafh al Tib min Ghusn al Andalus al Ratib* (*The Breath of Perfume from the Green Branch of Andalusia*), contains reams of florid praise for it.[12] Ibn Hayyan, the eleventh-century Cordoban historian, claimed that during the first phase of its construction under Abd al Rahman some 6,000 blocks of stone were used daily. Pink and green marble came from Carthage, Tunis and Sfax, also from Rome, the kingdom of the Franks and, more locally, white marble quarried from Tarragona and Almeria was part of the great mass of materials hauled onto the mountain by 15,000 mules and 5,000 camels. It was said that every three days 1,100 loads of clay and plaster were used. There were at least 4,000 pillars, 140 presented by the Byzantine emperor. The sources on the construction of Medinat al Zahra are notoriously untrustworthy, but it may still be worth noting the palace servant who reported the annual cost of construction was 3,000,000 gold dinars. In an age of greater budgetary innocence that would make modern chancellors smile at the simplicity of it all, Abd al Rahman used a third of his treasury revenues for army pay, a third for household expenses and a third for the construction of this great palace fantasy and, to a much lesser extent, other new buildings.

The upper terrace, as befitted the proper place of royalty, was reserved for the caliph's palace, together with a series of handsome forts. On the middle terrace were shaded gardens, brimming with white-blossomed fig and almond trees, and a game reserve. The lower terrace consisted of living quarters for slaves, servants and a great mosque with a reception hall

overlooking the Guadalquivir. This was a walled palatine city of sumptuous residences, inns, colleges, barracks, bath-houses, workshops, kitchens,
a zoo, an aviary and pools well stocked with fish. The number of male
servants was 13,750, in addition to the 3,750 slaves and eunuchs. The
latrines were fitted with running water, an innovation that was centuries
ahead of its time in Europe. Thanks to the Byzantine sculptors and mosai-
cists, famed across the Mediterranean for their work, floral motifs
proliferated among the geometric designs, acanthus and vine leaves to the
fore. Self-consciously Medinat al Zahra was a heaven on earth.

For Ibn Hayyan, the complex's most remarkable features were two
fountains, the larger one from Byzantium in gilt bronze beautifully
sculpted with bas-reliefs of human figures, the smaller one in green marble
from either Syria or Byzantium. The latter was surrounded by twelve
grouped statues of red gold set with pearls and jewels, figures fashioned
in Cordoban workshops – lions, stags, crocodiles, and an eagle, dragon,
dove, falcon, duck, hen, cockerel, kite and vulture – each one spouting
water from its mouth.[13]

A more famous marvel was the Salon of the Caliphs, a deliberately
dazzling riot of gold and multicoloured translucent marble walls and ceiling. Some versions suggest a huge pearl, gift of the Byzantine Emperor
Leo VI, was suspended above a pool filled with mercury. Eight doors,
decorated with gold and ebony, lined each side of the hall between piers
of coloured marble and clear crystal. The drapings in this room were said
to be of gold and silver. The choice of materials was calculated to impress
forcefully the power and majesty of the caliph. When the sun shone into
the room, blinding light reflected from the walls and ceiling.

> When the Caliph wished to astonish his visitors, he would signal to one of
> the slaves to disturb the pool of quicksilver; at once the hall would be filled
> with flashes of light and those gathered would begin to tremble because, so
> long as the mercury quivered, the whole room appeared to revolve around
> a central axis following the movement of the sun.[14]

The great traveller and geographer Ibn Hawqal, who visited Cordoba
in the tenth century, described how Abd al Rahman, having provided the
essential infrastructure for his new development, then successfully encouraged people to take up residence in it:

> He invited the people to live there and ordered that the following proclama-
> tion should be issued throughout Spain: 'Whoever wished to build a house,
> choosing a spot next to the sovereign, will receive 400 dirhams.' A flood of
> people rushed to build; the buildings crowded together and the popularity

of this city was such that the houses formed a continuous line between Cordoba and Zahra.[15]

While Medinat al Zahra was the largely secular architectural stamp of the Cordoban caliphate, denoting imperial might and cultural sophistication, its spiritual counterpart was the Great Mosque, whose monumental size, allied with extraordinarily beautiful and innovative design, powerfully asserted the Umayyads' claim to Islamic legitimacy and leadership. The ghosts of Damascus were never far away from Al Andalus and the history of the Great Mosque of Cordoba bears striking parallels with the Umayyad Mosque of Syria.

Originally an eighth-century Visigothic church dedicated to St Vincent, after the Muslim conquest of 711 it was initially a shared place of worship for both Mozarab Christians and Muslims.* This period of joint worship was a prelude, as it had been in Damascus, to complete Muslim take-over. In 785, Abd al Rahman I purchased the Christian section and built a mosque over it within a year. Thereafter, every Cordoban amir and caliph altered and expanded it so that the modest and austere rectangular building of Abd al Rahman I in the eighth century swelled to the vast and astonishingly extravagant edifice of Al Mansur in the early eleventh, by which time it was one of the greatest mosques in the world. Abd al Rahman III's lasting personal contribution was the towering minaret, a striking, multi-storey edifice that dominates the skyline and is now a magnificent, quintessentially Christian belfry, with its arsenal of clanging bells, housed in arches and rectangular recesses, visible – and audible – from afar.

Today the Great Mosque, known to Spaniards as Santa Iglesia Catedral de Cordoba – or, less triumphantly, as the Mezquita-Catedral – is 'universally recognised as one of the most singular monuments of medieval architecture'.[16] Its arcaded hypostyle hall, a forest of 856 columns of multi-coloured marble, jasper, onyx and graphite surmounted with intricately decorated Roman, Gothic and Moorish capitals, beneath alternating red and white stone and brick voussoirs set in double arches, remains a richly atmospheric space, long likened to a bristling grove of palm trees in another architectural allusion to the beloved Umayyad homeland of Damascus from where the dynasty had originally hailed. Another unmistakable reference to the Umayyad line, and the great wrongs perpetrated against it, came from the late caliph Uthman's Quran, installed in the Great Mosque in 965. We know from the geographer Al Idrisi that, in an

---

* The Mozarabs were Christians living in the Iberian Peninsula under Muslim rule.

act charged with symbolism, this landmark copy, containing the blood-spattered pages rescued from the scene of his murder in 656, was taken out by servitors with great ceremony every day and recited from by an imam.[17]

One of the monument's most arresting highlights to this day, at once opulent and sublime, is the arched *mihrab* niche introduced by Hakam II and framed by bands of gold Kufic inscriptions from the Quran on a blue background set among floral mosaics. The verses remind Muslims of Allah's omniscience and their duty of complete submission to him. Hakam enlarged the mosque by a third. His most controversial creation, however, was the *maqsura* royal enclosure, a sacred space within a sacred space, drenched with sunlight beneath a breathtaking sequence of interwoven arches and a dome embellished with sparkling golden mosaics. Architecturally exquisite, it proved politically unpopular, a result both of the staggering expenses it had occasioned and the stark demonstration of distance and formal separation between ruler and ruled that it unequivocally presented, a violation of the Islamic code that all are equal before God. In the eyes of many, the Umayyads' justified pride in the Islamic community's wealth and power had tipped into overweening self-indulgence and narcissism.[18]

The signature monument of Al Andalus, the Great Mosque is also a unique embodiment of Spanish history, a palimpsest on which successive dynasties and faiths have marked their supremacy. From the Reconquista of Cordoba by Ferdinand III of Castile in 1236, the monument that had been a Muslim place of worship for almost half a millennium became a church again. Christian alterations continued over the next several centuries but the most significant, shape-shifting change occurred in 1523, when the Holy Roman Emperor Charles V authorized the construction of a Renaissance cathedral nave inside the mosque, a decision which he famously came to regret. On visiting the church to inspect the completed works, he was appalled: 'If I had known what you wanted to do, I would never have allowed it,' he thundered. 'You have taken something unique in the world and destroyed it to build something you can find in any city.'[19] In his poem 'The Mosque of Cordoba', published in 1935, the Punjabi scholar and politician Mohammed Iqbal evoked the piercing sense of nostalgia occasioned by the reconquest of Al Andalus, a loss mourned by Arab and Muslim writers ever since.

> *Shrine of the lovers of art! Visible power of the Faith!*
> *Sacred as Mecca you made, once, Andalusia's soil.*
> *If there is under the skies loveliness equal to yours,*

Only in Muslim hearts, nowhere else can it be . . .
Even today in its breeze fragrance of Yemen still floats,
Even today in its songs echoes live on of Hejaz.[20]

Even in the twenty-first century this loss can still rankle in Cordoba and is capable of stirring more than merely literary regret. In recent years Spanish Muslims have lobbied for permission to pray in the cathedral-mosque, a request that has been steadfastly rejected by both the Spanish Church and the Vatican. In 2010 violence broke out and two Muslim tourists were arrested after attacking and injuring security guards who were attempting to enforce the prohibition on Muslim prayers inside the building. More recently the Church has found itself at odds with the city's secular authorities, which have rejected its claim of sole ownership and argued in a report that the true owners of the site are 'each and every citizen of the world from whatever epoch and regardless of people, nation or culture'.[21] The case, as they say, continues.

Like the Umayyad caliphs of Cordoba who created them, both Medinat al Zahra and the Great Mosque were composite creations – a harmonious melding of Roman and Visigothic Christian influences with their Syrian and Iberian Muslim counterparts. Together they helped transform Cordoba from 'a city of marginal political, economic and cultural importance to one that could compete with the grandeur of contemporary Baghdad and Cairo'.[22]

The magnificent monuments were reflections of both the natural beauty of Andalusia and the booming economy under Abd al Rahman III. Writing to the distant king of the Khazars during his attempt to locate a semi-mythical Jewish kingdom in Asia, Hasdai ibn Shaprut, leader of the caliphate's Jewish community and a trusted vizier of the caliph, extolled the many virtues of Al Andalus:

> It is a fat land full of rivers, springs and stone-cut wells . . . It is a land of grains, wines and purest oils, rich in plants, a paradise of every sort of sweet. And with gardens and orchards where every kind of fruit tree blossoms, and those with silkworms in their leaves . . . Our land also has its own sources of silver and gold and in her mountains we mine copper and iron, tin and lead, kohl and marble and crystal . . . The king ruling over the land has amassed silver, gold and other treasures, along with an army the likes of which has never been amassed before . . . When other kings hear of the power and glory of our king they bring gifts to him . . . I receive these offerings and I, in turn, offer them recompense.[23]

When it comes to assessing the population of tenth-century Cordoba, estimates have varied unhelpfully from 90,000 to an implausible 1 million. Recent studies tend to congregate around the lower figure, at around 100,000, which would make it the largest city in Europe, on a par with Constantinople, though the usual caution about medieval sources emphatically applies. Much of our knowledge comes from Al Maqqari's seventeenth-century compilation, memorably described by a modern writer as 'nostalgia at two removes'.[24] In terms of the city's physical size, there is even greater uncertainty. The thirteenth-century Andalusian scholar Al Shakundi estimated it was ten miles long, including Medinat al Zahra, by two miles across, its centre enclosed by walls whose circumference was around seven and a half miles. Another medieval account reckoned it was twenty-four miles by six, the entire area along the banks of the Guadalquivir covered with palaces, mosques, gardens and houses. Recalling his own visit in 948, Ibn Hawqal recommended a brisk walk around the city walls. 'You can do it in an hour,' he wrote, suggesting a circumference of rather less than seven and a half miles.[25]

Whatever its precise size and population, Cordoba was in an urban category all of its own in Europe, ahead of its muddy, squalid, shivering counterparts by a country mile. Ibn Hawqal left a glowing, suitably awed description of the city in its regional context. He was in no doubt about its greatness:

> There is nothing to equal it in the whole of the Maghreb, or even in Upper Mesopotamia, Syria or Egypt, for the number of its inhabitants, its extent, the vast area taken up by markets, its cleanliness, the architecture of the mosques or the great number of baths and caravanserais. Several travellers from this city who have visited Baghdad say that it is the size of one of the quarters of that city ... Cordoba is not perhaps equal to half the size of Baghdad, but is not far off being so. It is a city with a stone wall, with handsome districts and vast squares.[26]

Modern scholars have largely echoed Ibn Hawqal in their assessments of the city's prominence. For Hugh Kennedy, Cordoba in its heyday had 'no equal in western Europe' and any realistic comparison would have to be with Baghdad or Constantinople.[27]

Enclosed by the River Guadalquivir on its southern flank, the walled city with its seven gates, the original Roman Cordoba, was primarily official territory, containing the main mosque, the magnificent Alcazar palace of the caliphs, the chancery and mint, army barracks, prison and the grand residences of the caliphate's most senior officials. North of the river prosperous suburbs fanned out in a verdant landscape of market gardens and the splendid *munya* country houses of the rich, handsomely situated on the southern slopes of the Sierra de Cordoba. Here also were well-stocked markets, industrial zones, sprawling gardens, bath-houses and cemeteries. For most Cordobans city life was a north bank affair. Across the river, via the Roman bridge that survives with its sixteen arcades to this day, the south bank was only lightly populated, a large cemetery and leper colony striking a somewhat pessimistic note alongside a clutch of riverside mansions. Most notable among these was the Munyat Nasr, home to the famous courtier and musician Ziryab in the ninth century, and in the tenth a caliphal property for accommodating distinguished visitors, such as the Byzantine envoys who arrived in 949.

There was little question Cordoba was an evocative city with its romantically named Garden of Wonders, Shops of the Sweet-Basil Sellers, a Mosque of the Rejoicing and so on. The narrow streets and quiet plazas, the small gardens with acacias and date palms unmistakably recalled the city of Damascus from which the Umayyads had so brutally been expunged, leaving only a solitary exile and his descendants to recreate the lost glory, centuries later, on another continent.

Romantic at street level, Cordoba was based on eminently pragmatic foundations. Trade and industry flourished under Abd al Rahman's enlightened rule. Within the city's perfumed streets could be heard the din of craftsmen working with metal, leather, wood, ceramics, glass, ivory, not to mention paper, silk and wool. Textiles reigned supreme within the world of Cordoban manufactures. Ibn Hawqal picked out velvet, felts, linen and silks in his survey of products. 'Their dyers work miracles,' he wrote.[28] Urban prosperity was also based on a dynamic agricultural sector and what scholars have dubbed a green revolution in the Iberian Peninsula. New irrigation technology, notably waterwheels with buckets, prepared the ground for new crops so that by the middle of the tenth century Andalusians were growing – and in many cases exporting – rice, hard wheat sorghum, sugar-cane, cotton, oranges, lemons, limes, bananas, pomegranates, watermelons, spinach, artichokes, aubergines and figs. The combination of innovative technology and novel crops brought what one historian of Moorish Spain has called 'incalculable economic and social benefits', among them greater productivity, longer growing seasons, a healthier population, resilience to capricious weather, stability of supply and prices, higher income for growers and encouragement to experiment and diversify.[29]

Andalusian Jews were highly influential figures in this commercial world. *The Book of Roads and Kingdoms* by Ibn Khurdadhbeh in the late ninth century recorded polyglot Jewish merchants who spoke Arabic, Persian and Greek travelling between the Eastern and Western worlds, exporting eunuchs, slaves, swords, fine silks, hides and fur such as beaver and weasel, returning from China by land and sea with rare luxuries such as musk, camphor and cinnamon.[30]

Agriculture and trade generated wealth, wealth produced leisure and leisure offered the space for culture to flourish, so much so that Cordoba under Abd al Rahman III and Hakam II vied with Baghdad as 'the most civilised place on earth', championing the greatest cultural efflorescence in Spain until the seventeenth century.[31] Literature led the way. We hear of 170 women in a single western suburb earning a living copying manuscripts and 60,000 books being produced annually. Hakam was Cordoba's most prodigious bibliophile, amassing a library of 400,000 volumes, including rare titles brought from the great centres of learning in the East. Royal patronage fuelled a booming book market, where splendid and exceptional titles were auctioned for fabulous sums. 'The Christians love to read the poems and romances of the Arabs,' mourned Alvarus of Cordoba, the ninth-century poet and theologian for whom the Prophet Mohammed was a precursor of the Antichrist. 'For every one who can write a letter in Latin to a friend, there are a thousand who can express themselves in Arabic with elegance.'[32]

Historical and religious writing both took off in earnest under the patronage of Hakam, having begun under his father's caliphate. Ahmed ibn Mohammed al Razi was the first to codify the rules of historical composition, setting out a new annalistic form of history writing. His son Isa wrote a history of Hakam's reign that was preserved by Ibn Hayyan. When he was not dabbling in agriculture, astronomy, zoology, botany and hawking, Arib ibn Said (d. c. 980), polymath and possible author of the *Calendar of Cordoba*, combined Eastern historical studies with original material on the Iberian Peninsula. Ibn al Qutiyya (d. 977), author of the first philological treatise on verb conjugation, also wrote a history of Al Andalus dutifully toeing the Umayyad line.

One of the most popular Islamic genres was the biographical dictionary of religious scholars, providing a window onto their writings, teachings and lives. Hakam frequently provided the royal patronage for such studies during his father's reign. Thus there were works by the Tunisian immigrant Ibn Harith al Khushani (d. 971), the Cordoban Khalid ibn Saad (d. 963) and Ahmed ibn Abd al Barr (d. c. 949), who collectively wrote about Andalusian jurists. Pious orthodox texts supported Cordoba's claim to be a leader of the Islamic world, above all in opposition to the heterodox Shia power of the Fatimids across the Mediterranean. There were also biographical dictionaries of grammarians (Al Zubaydi), doctors (Ibn Juljul), secretaries (Sakan ibn Ibrahim) and poets.

Intellects roved freely and widely, a defining sign of the Umayyad times. One of the most famous titles to emerge from tenth-century Cordoba was *Al Iqd al Farid* (*The Unique Necklace*), a sprawling masterpiece of Arabic literature by Ibn Abd Rabbih (860–940) that across twenty-five books – each one representing a gem on the necklace – drew on the Bible, the Quran, the *hadith*, history, poetry and writers like Jahiz, the ninth-century polymath and polemicist. This was one of the most sophisticated examples of *adab* literature, a kind of literary passport to polite society, containing the improving and entertaining intellectual ballast – not forgetting some humorous fripperies – that any refined individual could be expected and required to know, from government, natural history and proverbs to war, food and drink and verse. Ibn Abd Rabbih was not alone in providing this door-stopping vade mecum for aspiring officials and men of letters. Other writers, such as Abu Ali al Qali (d. 967), lured by lavish royal patronage, drifted west from Baghdad, lending further literary lustre to the booming metropolis. Poets and scholars like Said al Baghdadi and the Andalusian romantic Ibn Faraj al Jayyani were among many writers who gratefully dedicated their works to Hakam II.

Music continued to develop at the caliph's court. There was no more famous musician than Ziryab (789–857), who had brought Baghdadi refinements to a Cordoba steadily emerging under Abd al Rahman II. Trained by the great Iraqi composer and musician Ishaq al Mosuli, Ziryab, 'The Lark', headed west to seek his fortune in Andalusia. He found it immediately. His remuneration package, consisting of 200 gold dinars a month and more in bonuses, a palace in Cordoba, country villas with farmland and bushels of wheat and barley, was said to be so excessive the royal exchequer formally refused to pay it, leaving Abd al Rahman II to reimburse the musician from his privy funds. The caliph was reportedly so carried away by the beauty of the Iraqi's voice that he never listened to another singer again. Ziryab wasted little time making his mark. He introduced the *oud* (lute) and, just because he could, added a fifth set of strings, which he called the soul of the instrument. A new conservatoire was opened, setting the foundations for Andalusian music to flourish and evolve for generations to come. His influence on medieval European music was profound.

Yet Ziryab was much more than a talented musician. He became the most important arbiter of style, fashion and etiquette in Al Andalus, a one-man cultural supremo and celebrity whose pronouncements governed all aspects of life. His was the final word on elegant coiffure (gone were the women's traditional centre-partings and braids, replaced by shaped cuts and sculpted eyebrows); personal hygiene and deodorants for courtiers (Europe's first toothpaste, protoxyde of lead applied underarm); how to bleach white clothing; refined tableware (in with delicate crystal, out with clunky gold or silver goblets); seasonal changes of dress (bright colours in silks, linen and cotton in spring, white in summer, fur-trimmed cloaks in winter); table settings (fitted decorated leather covers); courtly dinners (the introduction of courses for the very first time, beginning with a starter of soup, followed by a main course of fish, fowl or meat, ending with fruits and desserts). As part of this sweeping cultural and culinary revolution, Ziryab even found time to introduce Cordobans to new recipes and delicacies like asparagus. Twelve centuries after his death, he is remembered to this day in a hearty local Cordoban speciality of roasted salted white beans, *ziriabí*, not to mention a host of streets, hotels and restaurants named after him across the Muslim world.[33]

Poetry was not always high-minded and refined. It could also be bawdy and obscene. We know of a good deal of verse by the princess Wallada, daughter of the short-lived caliph Mustakfi (r. 1023–5) and high-spirited host of Cordoba's pre-eminent literary salon. Wallada was a remarkable woman, famous both for her beauty and her daring and controversial behaviour. She was said to refuse to wear the *hijab* and decorated her robes with her own verses celebrating sexual licence, embroidered in gold.

> *By God, I am fit for greatness, and stride along with great pride.*
> *I allow my lover to reach my cheek, and I grant my kiss to him*
>   *who craves it.*[34]

As a poet she competed and excelled in an almost exclusively male world. Much of her work is love poetry directed at her lover Ibn Zaydun, ambassador, minister and the outstanding poet of his era, with whom she conducted a turbulent affair. In one poem written during a particularly difficult time in their relationship she publicly accused him of homosexual trysts, calling him a pimp, adulterer, cuckold, sodomite and thief, a line of attack she sharpened in another more graphic verse:

> *Ibn Zaydun's backside swoons for the rod in men's pants.*
> *Were it to spy a penis atop a palm tree, it would swoop*
>   *down on it like a vulture.*[35]

Anticipating reality television relationships and YouTuber 'super couples' by 1,000 years, this was a tenth-century celebrity romance played out in public that ended in tears – and reams of verse. Wallada eventually left Ibn Zaydun and took up with a vizier, who appropriated his rival's properties and had him thrown into prison. In *Qafiyya*, a nostalgia-laced hymn of praise to a garden outside Cordoba, Ibn Zaydun bade a more elevated farewell to his lover:

> *In times gone by*
> *We demanded of each other*
> *Payments of pure love*
> *And were happy as colts*
> *Running free in a pasture.*
>
> *But now I am the only one*
> *Who can boast of being loyal.*
> *You left me*
> *And I stay here,*
> *Still sad, still loving you.*[36]

Andalusian Jews were as well represented in scholarly circles as they were in trade. There was Menahem ben Saruq (d. *c.* 970), who exchanged provincial northern Spain for cosmopolitan Cordoba. He wrote *The Book of Interpretations*, the first lexicon of the Hebrew language, and became secretary of Hasdai ibn Shaprut, the most powerful and celebrated Jew in Andalusia. Born in Fez from a Baghdad family, the pugnacious scholar Dunash ben Labrat also succumbed to the centripetal pull of Cordoba, where he won fame and respect as a cantor and poet, composing and chanting liturgical hymns when not writing verses warning of the dangerous temptations of the grape:

> *We shall drink among the flower beds hedged with roses*
> *And put sorrow to flight with all manner of gaiety*
> *Partaking of sweets and drinking from goblets*
> *And then disport ourselves like giants, imbibing from basins.*[37]

Jewish literati exemplified the pluralistic nature of the cultural flowering in Cordoba at this time. There were distinguished poets and philologists (Isaac ibn Qapron, Abu Umar ibn Yakwa, Hakohen ben al Mudarram, Abu Ibrahim Isaac ibn Khalfon), respected grammarians (Isaac ibn Djikatilla, Judah ben David Hayyuj) and erudite writer-judges (Hasan ben Mar Hassan).

The combined fruits of Muslim, Jewish and, to a lesser extent, Christian intellectual endeavour reflected a self-conscious desire on the part of the Umayyads of Cordoba to rival Baghdad, the seat of Islam. To a very great degree they succeeded. 'The products of this crucible spread out towards Christian Europe and touched Scholastic Philosophy, Romanesque Art, the School of Medicine at Montpellier, the lyric poetry of the troubadours and the mystic poetry of Dante.'[38]

Any discussion of tenth-century Cordoba requires an assessment of *convivencia*, the coexistence between the faiths in Muslim Spain. In recent years it has been the focus of considerable scholarly contention, setting romantics against sceptics in a frequently polarized debate.[39] The romantics point to the brilliance of this mixed community, a society of Spaniards and Orientals, free men and slaves, professional soldiers, Jewish teachers and merchants, Christian envoys, open to and tolerant of different cultures. Culture aside, at a very basic carnal level, there was considerable coexistence, invariably heavily tilted in favour of high-born or simply affluent Muslims. We have seen how the caliph's harems teemed with beautiful Christian women. 'Poets sang of their mistresses or of the princes' favourites and from them we learn that the Spanish Moslems had a high regard for generously proportioned women,' especially fair-haired girls from Galicia and the Basque Country.[40] Unscrupulous traders even tried to pass off Andalusian women as Christians from the north.

It is probably helpful to observe that different communities within this tripartite world had very different experiences of *convivencia*. For Christians, the *dhimma* system instituted after the Muslim conquest of Al Andalus – branded 'discriminatory tolerance' by one modern Spanish writer – was a catastrophic relegation from their pole position as political rulers.[41] For Jews, however, hitherto languishing in the nether reaches of Spanish social and political life under the Visigoths, it represented a dramatic and welcome promotion to the covenanted status of the *Ahl al Kitab*, People of the Book, opening up undreamt-of opportunities for political and commercial advancement. Christians either resisted what they considered intolerable cultural oppression by heading into voluntary exile in the still Christian north or, more sensationally in the mid-ninth century, by committing suicide as martyrs to their faith – or they converted to the conquerors' creed, as the majority did. In 926, the Christian prince Pelagius was martyred at the age of thirteen, supposedly for religious offences. In her account of his life the German nun Hrotsvitha of Gandersheim follows Christian convention and attributes Pelagius's fatal downfall to the caliph Abd al Rahman's 'burning passion' for the beautiful youth. Furious at his rejection, the Muslim caliph, 'stained by pederasty' and 'enflamed with love', orders him to be hurled over the city walls from a siege engine and when that miraculously leaves Pelagius unharmed he is finally tortured, dismembered and beheaded.[42]

By contrast, Andalusian Jews took a fourth path, that of assimilation into the Islamo-Arabic culture of the Umayyads while remaining a devout religious community with their language of faith intact. A persecuted minority thereby became a protected minority, which is not to say that persecution simply ended overnight.[43]

Convivencia clearly fluctuated across the centuries. Within only a generation, triumph could easily turn to tragedy. Thus Samuel Ha-Nagid, a poet, scholar and statesman, could rise to become vizier and chief general of the neighbouring kingdom of Granada in the eleventh century, yet in 1066 his son Joseph was torn apart by a mob enraged by Jewish influence, triggering a notorious massacre of Granada's Jews. Narrowing the focus to the tenth century, a major Jewish study of the Jews of Muslim Spain concluded a survey of Abd al Rahman III's reign with an unequivocal endorsement of the climate of tolerance he fostered: 'There is no doubt that this enlightened ruler was the most tolerant of all the Umayyads who ruled in Cordoba. The chronicles of his reign include no information of any harm befalling non-Moslem communities.' This was contrasted with the Abbasids of Baghdad, who insisted Jews mark their clothes to show their faith. 'Moslem Spain was a multinational state and did not bear a clearly defined religious stamp; therefore its rule did not endanger the existence of a minority, national or religious.' The Jews' lot under Abd al Rahman III was 'a happy one'.[44]

While there was no church within the walled city from the eighth century, Christians having been ejected from intramuros, we know the Jewish quarter of Cordoba became too small for the burgeoning Jewish population in the tenth. Set in the south-west of the capital, it bordered the city walls in the west and was situated next to the royal district housing the Umayyad palace and quarters for their servants and guards, a location affording enhanced security. Today it is occupied by a bishop's palace and other Church offices, but Jewish traces are not difficult to discern in contemporary Cordoba. Named after the twelfth-century Jewish Cordoban physician and astronomer, Calle Maimonides, formerly Calle de los Judíos, was the principal street of the Jewish quarter, 160 metres long and very narrow, snaking its way through the north side of the Great Mosque courtyard to Puerta de Almodóvar, one of the city's seven early gates. North of Plaza de las Bulas, formerly the Plaza de la Judería, stands the modest fourteenth-century synagogue, perhaps sitting on the site of an earlier version dating to the Muslim period.

The story of Hasdai ibn Shaprut suggests the rich possibilities available to the most talented members of the Jewish community of Andalusia during the tenth century. For the historian Ibn Hayyan, Hasdai was the pre-eminent royal servant, famed for his manners, subtlety, patience and intelligence, often in evidence when acting as an intermediary between Christians and Muslims. In 940 Abd al Rahman III sent him to León to rescue a Muslim leader, Al Tujibi, from captivity. The same year saw him in Barcelona negotiating a commercial treaty with local counts. In 955, he was an envoy to the court of Ordono. Displaying the broadest possible range of skills, he even cured the notoriously fat king of Navarre of obesity in 958. Such a meteoric rise to greatness and the untold riches that accompanied high political office inevitably won him enemies. The twelfth-century Cordoban philosopher and polymath Ibn Rushd, better known in the West as Averroes, wrote of a fanatical Muslim cleric railing against Hasdai to the caliph himself in front of a crowd of Cordobans: 'As for the prophet for whose sake alone you are given honour, this one [the Jew] says of him that he is a liar.'[45]

One of the most revealing and fascinating episodes of interplay between Muslims, Jews and Christians came in the middle of the tenth century. In the late 940s, concerned by the rise of the Fatimids in North Africa, the Byzantine Emperor Constantine VII (r. 913–59) wanted to reinvigorate diplomatic relations with the Umayyads of Cordoba and dispatched a eunuch to Spain suggesting Abd al Rahman III send a mission to Constantinople to negotiate a treaty of friendship. In 948 the caliph's Christian envoy Hisham ibn Kulaib duly sailed east and Constantine sent a reciprocal delegation to Cordoba under Stephanos, the emperor's chamberlain and chief of protocol. Receiving the emissaries in his royal palace, Abd al Rahman was presented with a number of splendid presents, including a chrysobull, a royal epistle in Greek with gold letters on a blue parchment scroll and a heavy gold seal engraved with an image of Jesus on one side and the likeness of the emperor and his son on the other, stored inside an engraved silver box with a golden cover. Constantine's gifts also included some rare books, among them a volume by the fifth-century Spanish author Orosius and Dioscorides's *De Materia Medica*, the defining textbook on pharmacology for centuries to come. Since there was no one in the caliph's court who knew Greek, Abd al Rahman asked Constantine to send him someone to translate. A Greek monk called Nicholas arrived in around 951 and, together with Hasdai, set about working on a new translation.

A more contentious diplomatic exchange occurred around the same time. Responding to a request from the Holy Roman Emperor Otto I (r. 938–73) to rein in Spanish robber bands who had been causing havoc with trading around the Mediterranean from their base in Fraxinetum (in the Gulf of St Tropez), Abd al Rahman sent another diplomatic mission in 950, this time a Mozarab bishop bearing a letter containing distinctly undiplomatic insults against the Christian faith. The envoys were effectively detained for three years and went back to Cordoba with nothing to show for their mission. In 953, Otto I returned the compliment, dispatching an embassy with a letter containing equally unpleasant remarks about Islam, led by a single-minded German monk, Johannes of Gorze, accompanied by a deacon, two Jews and the caliph's emissaries. In a classic instance of diplomatic tit-for-tat, the monk was deliberately kept waiting, although Abd al Rahman was desperate to know the contents of the letter. On the one hand he could not tolerate any insults against Islam, on the other he was mindful of Otto's greater power. As the year 954 came to an end, Abd al Rahman still had not granted Johannes an audience. Tensions increased. The monk was allowed to worship every Sunday only under special guard and was otherwise kept isolated in his villa.

Hasdai tried to intercede with the stubborn monk. Fearing possible conflict and trouble for his fellow Christians in Al Andalus, Bishop John of Cordoba also implored Johannes to reconsider his diplomatic mission and avoid insulting Rahman with his official letter. 'Consider,' he said, 'under what conditions we exist. Through our sins we have been reduced to this, that we are subject to the sway of the pagans. The Apostle forbids us to resist legitimate power. There is only one consolation in this calamity, that they do not forbid us our law . . . In the circumstances, therefore, it seems wise to us to comply with all things which do not hinder our faith.' Johannes, who comes across as something of a zealot in the sources, was unmoved: 'You, who appear to be a bishop, are the last person who should speak thus . . . It is a thousand times better for the Christian to suffer the cruel torment of hunger than to eat the food of the gentiles at the cost of his soul.'[46] To the caliph's threat that if he executed Johannes he would also kill every Christian in Spain, the monk professed his willingness to be torn limb from limb rather than refrain from formally presenting Otto's correspondence. The caliph was at an impasse. He would be honour-bound to kill Johannes for insulting Islam if the letter was accepted, knowing full well that this course of action would precipitate war.

Eventually a diplomatic solution was reached. On the monk's advice, Abd al Rahman sent a letter to Otto asking for new diplomatic instructions. The question arose, who would lead this sensitive mission? Rabi ibn Zaid, a cultured Mozarab, agreed to go to Germany in 955, but only on condition he received proper recognition of his efforts. 'What reward are you going to give to the man who sells you his soul?' he asked meaningfully.[47] The answer was a substantial reward. Rabi ibn Zaid became Recemundus, bishop of Elvira, near Granada, a prosperous appointment he enjoyed for the next forty years. Otto, by now keen to secure a treaty of peace and friendship with Cordoba, softened his tone and the tensions were defused.

On one level the convoluted diplomatic episode was a microcosm of *convivencia* in Spain. During the sensitive manoeuvring involving Christians, Jews and Muslims there were tensions, threats, flexibility, pragmatism, fudge and, ultimately in this case, a peaceful resolution. Such animosities as existed were more apparent between Christians and Muslims, representing rival polities, than between Muslims and Jews. Hrotsvitha of Gandersheim may have admired Cordoba as the 'ornament of the world' but we should be cautious about reading too much multi-faith harmony into the remark. When it came to expressing her own views on Cordoba and the conquest of Christian Spain by the Muslims, the German nun did not pull her punches:

> In previous times this city had been fully subject to the true Christ, abounding with white-robed children baptized to the Lord. But all of a sudden a belligerent power overturned the well-established laws of the sacred faith and, spreading the error of its nefarious teachings, inflicted injury on its faithful citizens. The perfidious nation of the indomitable Saracens enticed the strong inhabitants of this city to war and forcefully took control of the destiny of this glorious kingdom.[48]

In 961, on the eve of registering half a century as the first caliph of Cordoba, Abd al Rahman III died. He left 50 million gold dinars in the treasury, an indication of the enormously prosperous state he had carved out from a hodgepodge of feuding principalities. For Andalusia his reign had been the height of good fortune, yet at a personal level there is a surprisingly mournful note about Abd al Rahman's famous comment that he had enjoyed only fourteen days of happiness in his lifetime.

Cordoba's success and glory continued under the rule of his son and heir Hakam II, a hugely cultured and cultivated man who won fame as a voracious reader and collector of books. He was a prodigious patron of scholars and attracted some of the finest minds from the arts and sciences to Cordoba. Construction continued at the palace-city of Medinat al Zahra, together with extensive and dramatic additions to the Great Mosque, architecturally transcendent but in some cases extremely controversial. Contemporaries may have baulked at the sheer ostentation, extravagance and cost of Hakam's improvements but visitors today, more than 1,000 years later, still marvel at the beauty of the carved stone, stucco and mosaic of the *mihrab*, resplendent beneath a sculpted mother-of-pearl ceiling, a triumphant creation by Byzantine craftsmen working at the peak of their powers.

Hakam II was a worthy successor to Abd al Rahman, but he was also the last Umayyad caliph of Cordoba of note. On Hakam's death in 976, Mohammed ibn Abi Amir, a ruthless and ambitious man who had worked his way up the official ladder from humble scribe to a series of influential roles, sleeping with those who would promote him, killing those who got in his way, manoeuvred to secure the succession of the twelve-year-old prince Hisham II. By 981 he had conferred on himself the regnal title Al Mansur 'The Victorious' – a nod to the illustrious founder of Baghdad – altogether hijacking the dynastic succession and ruling as the undisputed leader until 1002. Mansur's reign was the high-water mark of Muslim rule in Spain in terms of territorial security, and it was tinged with something approaching military mania and dictatorship, a veritable whirlwind of battles and bloodshed. He is credited with fifty-seven victories, the most remarkable being the violent sacking of the holy shrine-city of Santiago de Compostela in 997, which followed the sacking of Barcelona in 985. Mansur celebrated his victory over the holy city by plundering the cathedral. Christian captives were forced to dismantle its most valuable contents and then carry the doors and bells to Cordoba, for use in the Great Mosque and as lanterns respectively. The bells were returned to their original home by Fernando III of Castile only in 1236 during the Reconquista. Mansur also declared war on intellectual freedom, allowing the chauvinistic clergy to indulge their fierce disapproval of philosophical texts by burning the contents of Hakam's library, a wonder of the civilized world that disappeared in smoke.

As the tenth century ended, Cordoba's time of glorious ascendancy was also drawing to a close. Mansur's breakneck expansion of his armed forces, effected through the wholesale drafting in of Berber units from North Africa, contained within it the seeds of the caliphate's demise. Rivalries within the peninsula between Arab and Berber, already keen, were sharpened by the arrival of thousands upon thousands of armed Berbers from across the Straits of Gibraltar, more loyal to their tribal leaders than to the Andalusian state. That dread phenomenon *fitna*, denoting division, strife and rebellion against authority, now broke out with great violence. On paper the dates of Hisham II's long reign from 976 to 1013 suggest durability and resilience, but for much of that time his authority was only theoretical, while Andalusian political life was in complete disarray. Where the reign of Abd al Rahman III was marked by unprecedented peace and stability, that of his grandson Hisham II was defined by turmoil, instability and finally collapse. Indeed, within just half a century of Abd al Rahman's death the caliphate he had laboured so painstakingly to establish lay convulsed upon its deathbed, never to be revived.

In 1000 Sancho Garcia, Count of Castile, inflicted heavy losses on the

Muslim state. Then, in 1009, Sulayman, a great-grandson of Abd al Rahman III, proclaimed himself caliph Mohammed II, marched on Medinat al Zahra and devastatingly sacked it with his Berber forces. As the eleventh-century poet Al Sumaysir wrote sadly:

> I stopped at Al Zahra weeping; considering it,
> I lament its broken fragments.
>
> And I said: 'O Zahra, no, come back.'
> And she answered: 'Can someone return from the dead?'
>
> I did not cease crying, crying there,
> But, oh, how the tears were of no use, none at all.
>
> They were like the traces of tears shed by professional
> Mourners of the dead.[49]

Reflecting these same feelings of acute nostalgia and loss in prose, the historian Ibn Hayyan observed of the wholesale destruction of Medinat al Zahra that 'the carpet of the world was folded up and the beauty that had been an earthly paradise was disfigured'.[50] Time has waged its own battle against this once resplendent city and reduced it to ruins, but its natural beauty remains undimmed in destruction. Today, walking through the exquisitely evocative complex of crumbling palace and neglected gardens framed by cypresses and palm trees, it is impossible not to hear the murmuring ghosts of Cordoba's evanescent power.

From the sacking of Medinat al Zahra in 1009, Andalusia was shaken by a series of civil wars as rival warlords manoeuvred for power. The old Andalusian order, once a rock of political unity and cultural grandeur, 'exploded like a star'.[51] In 1013, having secured the formal surrender of the capital after subjecting it to the most terrible blockade, Sulayman's Berbers violated the agreement of safe passage for the city's people, stormed Cordoba and plundered it mercilessly, massacring swathes of the inhabitants, already wracked by the evil quartet of plague, siege, fire and flooding. One of the most remarkable eyewitnesses to the carnage was Ibn Hazm, later to become one of the greatest and most prolific Arab writers. He was around nineteen when Cordoba fell and later listed sixty eminent scholars cut down in the slaughter. One of them, Ibn al Faradi, author of the first history of the learned men of Andalusia, lay unburied in the street for three days.[52]

Internecine warfare, exploited by the Christian powers, especially the rising figure of Sancho the Great of Navarre, raged throughout the Iberian Peninsula as rival leaders vied for the highest office between 1008 and

1031. By the time of the caliph Hisham III (r. 1026–31), the Umayyad rulers of Cordoba had declined in popular estimation so much that they 'were objects as much of contempt as their office had once been of wonder'.[53] When he was overthrown in 1031, the caliphate was formally abolished.

The caliphate of Cordoba had enjoyed a short-lived brilliance, a meteor-like flash of illumination across the heavens. One of its greatest strengths, apart from the astute rule of Abd al Rahman III and Hakam II, was perhaps the cosmopolitanism that provided the social glue to bind it together as a more or less harmonious, unified state, where free trade and freedom of thought ruled supreme. The antithesis of such unity – *fitna* – proved its fatal undoing as the caliphate unravelled into petty *taifa* kingdoms unable to defend themselves effectively against either the Christian powers to the north or, later, the Almoravids and Almohads who surged out of North Africa into Spain. Other cities, above all Granada and Seville, quickly eclipsed the former capital of the caliphate, which remained a haunting memory of lost unity, glory and pre-eminence. Muslims have mourned the fall of Cordoba and the later, calamitous loss of Al Andalus in 1492 ever since. As for *fitna*, it would haunt Arab polities for centuries to come.

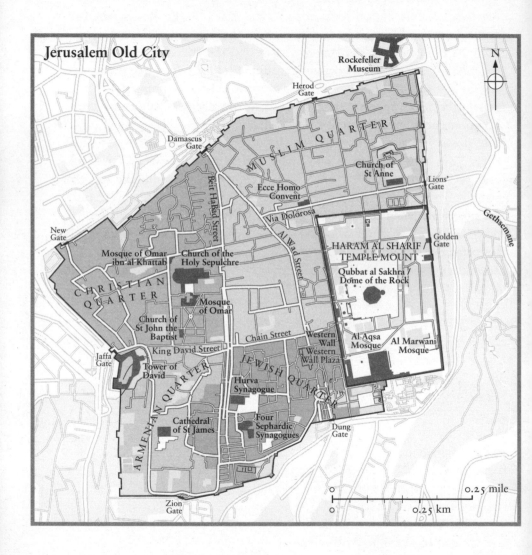

Jerusalem Old City

N

Rockefeller
Museum

Herod
Gate

Damascus
Gate

MUSLIM QUARTER

Church of
St Anne

Ecce Homo
Convent

Lions'
Gate

Via Dolorosa

New
Gate

Beit HaBad Street

Al Wad Street

HARAM AL SHARIF /
TEMPLE MOUNT

Golden
Gate

Gethsemane

Mosque of Omar
ibn al-Khattab

Church of the
Holy Sepulchre

Qubbat al Sakhra /
Dome of the Rock

CHRISTIAN
QUARTER

Mosque
of Omar

Church of
St John the
Baptist

Chain Street

Western
Wall

Al-Aqsa
Mosque

Al Marwani
Mosque

King David Street

Western
Wall Plaza

Jaffa
Gate

Tower of
David

JEWISH QUARTER

Hurva
Synagogue

ARMENIAN QUARTER

Cathedral
of St James

Four
Sephardic
Synagogues

Dung
Gate

0.25 mile

Zion
Gate

0.25 km

5

Jerusalem – The Contested City (11th Century)

Enter upon the road to the Holy Sepulchre. Wrest that land from the wicked race and subject it to yourselves.

Pope Urban II, address at Clermont, 1095

A sun-bleached morning in Jerusalem. The Old City stirs. A couple of crows are conducting aerial surveillance overhead, raucously signalling their interest in proceedings below. Street-sellers' carts clatter and clank across the cobbles through the monumental Damascus Gate. Shopkeepers open their shutters and hang out clothes and handbags, cloth and carpets in Suq Khan al Zeit, ready to do battle with the city's prowling, gimlet-eyed matriarchs. Black-brimmed fedoras share the streets with red-checked *keffiyehs*, coloured skullcaps, *hijabs*, bare heads, beards and baseball caps before scurrying off into the shadows of the Jewish, Muslim, Christian and Armenian quarters. A white-whiskered man pores over his newspaper, taking in the horrors of the world over a steaming glass of tea. The city's serpentine streets swallow up pedestrians whole before disgorging them unharmed into a fulgor of sunlight. A young man hurries out from a dark passage balancing a tray of freshly baked bread on his head. A pair of turtle doves watches on discreetly from a rooftop. Outside the desert-tinged city walls, built by the Ottoman Sultan Suleiman in the sixteenth century, traffic mounts and tempers rise amid the honking cars.

Today, like every other day in the heart of the world's religious capital, is a tableau of worship. At the foot of the vast Western Wall, Jews bob backwards and forwards in prayer beneath a cerulean sky, sidelocks waving to and fro. Others stand motionless against the wall, palms, nose and forehead pressed against it in remembered devotion. The ancient stone gives solace. On Via Dolorosa, a couple of early bird pilgrims pose for photographs in front of a Station of the Cross; then, completely overcome by the occasion, fall to their knees in prayer. A few hundred metres away in the Church of the Holy Sepulchre, a living tomb of sectarian schisms, a Coptic monk maintains a lonely candlelit vigil, hemmed in by the rival battalions and pressing claims of Franciscan friars and the Greek, Armenian and Syrian Orthodox. Theological and territorial battles continue even on the roof of this hallowed space, where an embattled community of black-robed Ethiopian monks live in penury in leaky, mud-hut hovels, squabbling with the Copts – and the state of Israel – over electricity supply and sanitation. These hoary patriarchs of Christianity's most sacred space are no strangers to scuffles. Violence between the priestly throngs breaks out with the regularity of the seasons – a tussle over a key here, a punch-up over closing a chapel door there – testament to man's genius at conjuring discord from thin air.

Squinting in the summer sunlight, I walk into a thirty-seven-acre quadrangle that has been described as one of the world's most explosive pieces of property. Jews call this sprawling esplanade the Temple Mount, the holiest site in Judaism, home to the elusive Holy of Holies and site of the first Jewish Temple. For Muslims it is the Haram al Sharif, the Noble Sanctuary, home to the Al Aqsa Mosque, the third holiest Muslim site, and the Dome of the Rock, a place of supreme religious significance for Jews, Christians and Muslims alike. Though Muslims hold the ascendancy here today, this remains the most disputed place on earth, a source of enduring conflict between the faiths over many centuries. Under the status quo arrangements for Jerusalem, which date back to Ottoman times and govern the ownership and usage of the holy sites, non-Muslims are allowed to visit but not to pray here, a prohibition that is often challenged by militant Jews in more headline-making brawls.

Yet despite these ancient enmities there is a strange, unmistakable serenity about this city. Jerusalem seems to rise like a spirit over these petty human frailties. It endures above and beyond them, an urban marvel to behold and admire. It is, as the tenth-century Arab geographer Muqaddasi put it, 'a golden basin full of scorpions'.[1] Coexistence and cosmopolitanism are seared into this city, but so too is division, and for many Jerusalemites today, whether Jewish, Muslim or Christian, the fractures within the city are deepening. Increasingly, the different communities live 'not entwined, but in isolated parallel'.[2]

A vigorously moustachioed Arab guide breaks the reverie. He has herded his flock of sunhatted Europeans in front of the Al Aqsa Mosque, where he addresses them in staccato bursts of English, explaining the importance of this holy site to Muslims. He speaks of the Prophet Mohammed's miraculous Night Journey to heaven (*Al Isra wa al Miraj*, as Arabs know it), pointing across to the shimmering splendour of the Dome of the Rock, whose glowing dome soars triumphantly above the city, architectural symbol – lest anyone doubt it – of the pre-eminence of Islam.* He speaks of Abraham and the common origin of Jews, Christians and Muslims.

A Frenchman asks him what effect the Crusades had on Jerusalem. The guide becomes more animated. Though he is too polite to refer to the tourist's distant Norman and Provençal ancestors, who played a leading role in the First Crusade, he talks of the indiscriminate slaughter of Jews and Muslims in 1099. He describes Christian knights riding their horses into the mosque before us, hacking to death innocent men, women and children in rivers of blood. 'They were killing everyone where we are standing now. Believe me, they were very proud of this,' he says, explaining how some of the soldiers and priests glorified the massacre when they wrote their later histories of the Crusades. There is an awkward silence.

'These were very terrible crimes,' he says, as though recalling a recent atrocity, rather than something that took place almost 1,000 years ago. 'The people of Jerusalem have never forgotten them.'

By the middle of the eleventh century, the Muslim world bowed to no other faith, nor any other region on earth, when it came to the sophistication of its civilization. If proof were needed of such a claim, it was hewn in stone (or sun-baked brick in the case of Iraq) right across the Middle East. Civilization was by definition an urban phenomenon, and no one did cities quite like the Muslims.

While Islamic cities encompassed growing populations in the hundreds of thousands, their Christian counterparts muddled along with tens of thousands living in rather less style and considerably less splendour. Only a handful of European cities might have intruded on Muslim consciousness at this time. There was Rome, of course, in a league of its own, and then there were Milan and Cologne, followed by the second tier of London, Paris, Rouen, Mainz, Prague, Cracow and 'a few pestilential hamlets like Venice'.[3] If medieval Europe was inching towards urban life, the Muslim world was galloping through it at full tilt. As the most obvious sign of urban success, size mattered. While Baghdad lorded it over the Islamic Empire with a population of approximately 800,000 in the ninth century, with Cairo at around 400,000 and Cordoba about 100,000,

---

* 'Is it not obvious,' asked the Arab geographer Muqaddasi, 'that Abd al Malik, seeing the grandeur and magnificence of the Dome of the Holy Sepulchre, was concerned lest it dazzle the thoughts of the Muslims, and thus he erected above the Rock the Dome now seen there?' Oleg Grabar, *Formation of Islamic Art*, pp. 64–5

within Christendom Constantinople alone came close with something like half a million. Proud European cities with illustrious histories, such as Rome, Milan and Cologne, were no larger than the mid-ranking cities of the Islamic world with populations of 30,000–40,000. In 1100, London and Paris hid their blushes with a diminutive 20,000.[4]

The Islamic city was, above all, diverse and cosmopolitan, teeming with Muslims, Jews and Christians of various persuasions. In crowded streets and thriving markets bursting with products from all corners of the world, Arabs and Kurds shared streets with Turks and Persians, Greeks and Slavs with Africans, freemen with slaves. The magnetic attraction of the cities of the Muslim world was proof positive of Islam's imperial, cultural and economic success. If Muslims gave the barbaric, sun-starved denizens of Europe's muddy, provincial backwaters a second thought, it was only with a shudder.

The Islamic world's superiority complex was founded on geographical as well as strictly religious principles. Drawing on Ptolemy in his atlas *Kitab Surat al Ard*, the master mathematician, astronomer and geographer Mohammed ibn Musa al Khwarizmi had divided the world into seven climes, each of which imparted certain characteristics to its inhabitants. According to this somewhat self-serving scheme, the third and fourth zones, which contained the Arab homelands, North Africa, Iran and parts of China, were the most harmonious and balanced. The sixth zone, however, which included the land of the Franks, Turks and Slavs, was another matter altogether. Here the people were filthy, unhygienic and treacherous, given to savagery, sexual licentiousness and warfare. The tenth-century Abbasid historian Masudi reflected the popular Muslim perceptions of Europeans at this time: 'their bodies are large, their natures gross, their manners harsh, their understanding dull, and their tongues heavy'.[5] Writing in Toledo in 1068, the Muslim judge Said ibn Ahmed did not pull his punches either. He described the contemptible European barbarians as closer to beasts than humans, pale-skinned corpulent creatures who lacked 'keenness of understanding and clarity of intelligence and are overcome by ignorance and apathy, lack of discernment and stupidity'.[6] The best that could be said about them was that they were courageous and disciplined.

Though their worldviews were poles apart, Muslims and Christians did not always disagree. Jerusalem was a city of ineffable grandeur and sanctity to eleventh-century Christians, a small, sleepy, sacred town for Muslims. Yet for Muslim, Christian and Jew alike, the city's historically charged holiness placed it in a different category altogether from its peers, irrespective of its modest size.

1. A seventeenth-century Dutch print showing a caravan of Muslim pilgrims from Istanbul arriving in Mecca. The Quran calls Islam's holiest place the 'Mother of All Cities'; early Arab geographers referred to it as the 'Navel of the Earth'.

2. A view of the sacred Kaaba in the heart of the Great Mosque of Mecca, to which the world's 1.5 billion Muslims direct their daily prayers. The Saudi authorities' extensive development of the site in recent years has been widely criticized.

3. Inside the eighth-century Umayyad Mosque, the finest monument in Damascus. The city was the capital of the rapidly expanding Islamic Empire under the Umayyad Dynasty, which ruled from 661 to 750.

4. An aerial view of Arbin, a suburb of Damascus, in 2018. Since 2011, the civil war has reduced swathes of this formerly cosmopolitan city to rubble.

5. A thirteenth-century illustration of scholars meeting in a library in Baghdad, the 'City of Peace'. Under the Abbasid Dynasty, which ruled the Islamic Empire from 750 to 1258, the Iraqi capital became the greatest city on earth and a formidable centre of scholarship.

6. A view across the River Tigris from Baghdad's Mustansiriya University, founded in 1233 by the penultimate Abbasid caliph Al Mustansir. One of the oldest universities in the world, it was a rare survivor of the devastating firestorm unleashed on the city by Genghis Khan's grandson Hulagu in 1258.

7. An evening view of Cordoba, known as the 'Ornament of the World' under the splinter Umayyad caliphate, which ruled much of the Iberian Peninsula from 929 to 1031. The eighth-century Mezquita-Catedral is one of the world's most splendid medieval monuments.

8. The sublime interior of the Mezquita-Catedral. The arcaded hypostyle hall is a forest of 856 columns of marble, jasper, onyx and graphite, topped with Roman, Gothic and Moorish capitals beneath red and white double arches.

9. The tenth-century Medinat al Zahra, 'The Shining City', a palace complex four miles west of Cordoba. Building work on the lavish project started under the great Umayyad caliph Abd al Rahman III, continued for over forty years and consumed one third of state revenues.

10. Godfrey of Bouillon, Christian hero of the First Crusade, celebrates the conquest of Jerusalem in 1099. Crusader accounts boasted of knights hacking down Muslims in the Al Aqsa Mosque and riding 'in blood up to their bridles'.

11. Jerusalem, the world's most contested city. On the right, the Dome of the Rock, built by the Umayyad caliph Abd al Malik in 692, is the oldest surviving Islamic monument.

12. The nineteenth-century Mohammed Ali Mosque (*left*) and Saladin's mighty citadel (*right*), built between 1176 and 1184, dominate Cairo's skyline.

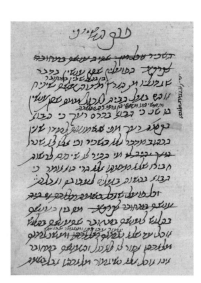

13. A draft of the *Mishneh Torah* legal code by the pre-eminent Jewish philosopher Maimonides, who came to live in Cairo around 1165.

14. Maimonides's text is just one of the more than 250,000 Geniza documents stored in Cairo's Ben Ezra Synagogue for around a thousand years. Most were taken to Cambridge by the rabbi and scholar Solomon Schechter in the late nineteenth century.

15. Bab Bou Jeloud, one of the most famous entrances to Fez's Old City. The minaret through the arch belongs to the Bou Inania Madrassa, built between 1351 and 1356 at the highpoint of the Marinid Dynasty.

16. The Chaouara tannery in the heart of Fez. For around a thousand years, workers stripped to their waist have dyed leather hides in these vats.

17. Timur, Sword of Islam and Conqueror of the World, receives a European embassy in this sixteenth-century Persian miniature. The Timurid era was a golden age for the arts but an apocalypse for much of the Islamic world.

Jerusalem, like Damascus, was a palimpsest on which the world's three greatest religions had written their stories. It was the city of Abraham, father of the three Abrahamic faiths, of King David, Jesus and Mary. Jews revered it as the site of the First Temple, also known as Solomon's Temple, which was destroyed by the Old Testament anti-hero Nebuchadnezzar, the Jew-slaying, gold-loving despot, in 587 BC. The original sanctity of the city was born of the exceptionalism of the Jews as God's chosen people. Like an edifice, this spiritual power grew with the later devotions – and constructions – of first Christians and then Muslims, who embraced and intensified this exceptionalism as their own.[7] Christians looked to Jerusalem for the two holiest sites in Christendom: the place of Jesus's crucifixion at Calvary, or Golgotha, and the empty tomb from which his resurrection to heaven took place. Both were contained within the Church of the Holy Sepulchre, described in the earliest recorded account of a Christian pilgrimage in the Holy Land as 'a church of wondrous beauty', built by Constantine, Rome's first Christian emperor, in the 320s.[8]

For Muslims, Jerusalem was the holiest city outside Arabia, the birthplace of Islam. In the earliest days of the Muslim faith it was to Jerusalem, and not Mecca, that believers had directed their prayers. Above all, the city had been sanctified as a bastion of the Islamic faith by the Prophet Mohammed's miraculous Night Journey, during which he had been taken by the Angel Jibril from the sacred mosque of Mecca to 'the farthest mosque', Al Aqsa, of Jerusalem, had a glimpse of hell before arriving in heaven, where he met all his predecessors as prophets and witnessed an enthroned God surrounded by angels. This extraordinary nocturnal voyage was commemorated in the inscriptions of the Dome of the Rock and Al Aqsa, both sited on the very epicentre of Jerusalem's sanctity – the Haram al Sharif, the Noble Sanctuary or Temple Mount. Jerusalem was the most sacred city within Palestine – Al Ard al Muqaddasa, the Holy Land – itself the most sacred district of the most hallowed land of Syria.[9]

In 637, the Muslims made it theirs. After eastern Christendom's catastrophe at Yarmuk in the same year, Byzantine rule crumbled until only Jerusalem resisted. After months under siege by Muslim forces, having seen the cities of Palestine and Syria fall one by one to the caliph's armies, with no prospect of relief and supplies perilously low, Patriarch Sophronius agreed to surrender on the condition that he submit to the caliph in person. Thus the man who only recently had warned his flock of 'the slime of the godless Saracens', the poet who had extolled his beloved Jerusalem as 'Zion, radiant Zion of the Universe', found himself handing over the keys to the city to the Muslim caliph Umar, who had made the journey to

Jerusalem and now entered the city on a white camel, surrounded by his dirty, battle-weary soldiers mounted on camels and horses.[10] It was an annihilating moment for Sophronius, who recalled Christ's words through his tears: 'Behold the abomination of desolation, spoken of by Daniel the prophet.'[11] He died soon afterwards of a broken heart.

Umar's restrained and courteous behaviour during the Muslim conquest of Jerusalem would be remembered and contrasted with later, blood-drenched depredations. He asked to see the Church of the Holy Sepulchre, only for the Muslim time of prayer to coincide with his visit. Invited by the patriarch to pray where he stood, the caliph sensitively demurred, observing that were he to do so his actions would quickly transform the church into a place of Muslim worship. He prayed nearby instead, on the site of the present Mosque of Umar, built in the late twelfth century. When Umar asked to be shown the sanctuary of David, he found the Temple Mount fouled by 'a dungheap which the Christians had put there to offend the Jews'.[12] The Christians had intended more lasting offence to Jews and Roman pagans by leaving the huge blocks of stone and rubble, remnants of Titus's destruction of Herod's Temple in AD 70, strewn across the platform. It was an instance of Christian triumphalism in Jerusalem (that would have its later Muslim echo). As Jesus had prophesied to his disciples, 'Not one stone will be left upon another; every one will be thrown down' (Mark 13:2).

Umar's visit to the Holy of Holies was more auspicious. A Jewish convert showed him the foundation stone of the Temple, the very location of Adam's prelapsarian paradise, the rock upon which Abraham had been prepared to sacrifice his son Isaac and the place where God-sent prophets and kings David and Solomon had planned their Temple.* Muslim tradition held that from this same spot the Prophet Mohammed had ascended to heaven during his Night Journey. It was just to the south of this rock, known to Arabs as *sakhra*, that Umar built his first mosque on a site occupied by the Al Aqsa Mosque today. Umar granted to both Jews and Christians the right to continue practising their religion, though there were certainly many conversions to the faith of the conquerors. We know that, initially at least, Muslims shared churches with the Christians and that Jews were invited by Umar to pray at the Temple Mount with Muslims. The differences between the faiths were far less sharply defined when Islam was in its infancy. Muslims also borrowed the names for Jerusalem

---

* All three Abrahamic faiths recognize this as the place of Abraham's would-be sacrifice. Jews and Christians maintain Isaac was the son to be sacrificed, while Muslims believe it was Ishmael.

from the Jews. Thus they referred to the city as Bait al Maqdis, the Holy House, from the Jewish name for the Temple, Bait ha-Miqdash.

Arab tradition has it that during Umar's triumphant visit to Jerusalem he gave the keys of the Holy Sepulchre to the Nuseibeh family, powerful supporters of the Prophet Mohammed in Medina and leading protagonists in the Arab conquests of the seventh century. Named after the female warrior Nuseibeh, a companion of the Prophet who fought alongside him in battle, the family claims to be the oldest in Jerusalem and the Holy Land. Appointed Custodians of the Church of the Holy Sepulchre by Umar, the Nuseibehs have maintained this role over fourteen centuries, with only the briefest hiatus during the First Crusade. To this day a member of the Nuseibeh family opens the church in a ritual at dawn and closes it in the evening. The Nuseibehs also continue to mediate in the disputes between the various Christian sects that are a regular feature of life in the Holy City and authenticate the annual Orthodox Christian ritual known as the Descent of the Holy Fire, in which fire miraculously emerges from Jesus's tomb and descends on an olive oil lamp held by the Greek Orthodox Patriarch of Jerusalem.[13]

If tolerance in Jerusalem towards the two more ancient Abrahamic faiths was set in motion under Umar, the primacy of the younger religion was quickly set in stone. Islamic Jerusalem grew in status in the early years of the new creed through concerted architectural and literary production. Partly this arose from the Umayyads' inferiority complex as a new dynasty. They were determined to proclaim their Islamic credentials both in their capital city of Damascus and beyond. The most visible manner in which Muslims expressed their faith was the transformation of the urban space they had claimed for it.

Built by the caliph Abd al Malik in 692, the outstanding Dome of the Rock, Qubbat al Sakhra, appropriated at a stroke the holy *sakhra* stone for Islam. It rose monumentally into the skyline, a simultaneously sublime and powerful assertion of Islam's supremacy. A piece of land long sacred to both Jews and Christians had been swept up and restyled in the name of Islam, a greater truth that first built upon and then displaced Judaism and Christianity alike. One monument alone dominates Jerusalem today – for many it defines the city in a single vision – and it is not the Church of the Holy Sepulchre. Arabs have traditionally referred to the Christian shrine derisively as the *Qumama* or dungheap, a play on *Kanisa al Qiyama*, the Arabic term for the church. Constantine's Rotunda, encompassing the burial site of Jesus, may have been magnificent, but it was completely eclipsed by the resplendently golden Dome of the Rock, which floats above the Old City, glittering and shimmering, drawing the eye and dazzling day and night. This was one of Islam's earliest and great-est architectural achievements, the most ancient surviving Muslim monument, and one without precedent in the brief history of Islamic architecture. For visitors approaching the city from the south, the trad-itional route taken in the Middle Ages, the Dome of the Rock, soaring ethereally towards the heavens, was the majestic first sight of Jerusalem. It was only after approaching the sacred building through the city's dark labyrinthine alleys, illuminated by occasional shafts of sunlight, and bursting into the vast, open precinct of the Noble Sanctuary, pilgrim hearts beating in excitement, that the full splendour of the Dome of the Rock was manifest. It was a harmony of sun-bright white marble, rich mosaics in blue and green, and more than 240 metres of inscriptions proclaiming the glory of God and His Messenger and reminding the faith-ful that, while Jesus was certainly a prophet and divine 'servant', he was neither Son of God nor God Himself.*

When he visited Jerusalem more than six centuries after its construc-tion, during the summer of 1326, the irrepressible Moroccan traveller Ibn Battuta was instantly smitten. 'The Dome of the Rock is a building of extraordinary beauty, solidity, elegance, and singularity of shape,' he wrote in his discursive travelogue, *A Precious Gift to Those Who Con-template the Wonders of Cities and the Marvels of Travelling*. 'Both outside and inside, the decoration is so magnificent and the workmanship so surpassing as to defy description. The greater part is covered with gold so that the eyes of one who gazes on its beauties are dazzled by its bril-liance, now glowing like a mass of light, now flashing like lightning.'[14]

Architecture was essential but insufficient for Islam's greater glory. It was just as important to represent Muslim cities in texts which exalted them to the heavens. Medieval chroniclers therefore spilled torrents of ink to dem-onstrate the special status of Syria, 'a land that God has blessed', switching the exegetical tradition into overdrive to link Jerusalem and Damascus within Al Sham as part of a new cosmological scheme fully endorsed by the Prophet.[15] Had not the Prophet Mohammed himself asserted that God had divided goodness into ten parts, nine of which were in Syria? Jerusalem's foundation narrative was reworked to present a seamless unity with the birthplace of Islam. After God's creation of Mecca, 'He joined [Mecca] to Medina and joined Medina to Jerusalem, and then he created the entire earth after 1,000 years in a single gesture.'[16] The Prophet later enjoined his followers not to set out on pilgrimage to any site other than the Sacred

---

* There was no room for uncertainty or confusion. The Islamic formula *La sharika Lahu*, God has no companion, was repeated five times in the inscriptions.

Mosque of Mecca, the Prophet's Mosque in Medina and the Al Aqsa Mosque of Jerusalem. Storehouse of memories, foundation of faiths, Jerusalem steadily rose to the forefront of the Islamic world.

Christian pilgrimage to Muslim Jerusalem, which began in earnest in the tenth century, continued apace in the eleventh. Founded in 910, the Abbey of Cluny in Burgundy, long the largest Christian building in the world, emerged as the nerve-centre of European pilgrimage to sacred sites from Spain to the Holy Land. It was thanks to the encouragement of the abbots of Cluny that the Abbot of Stavelot set off for Jerusalem in 990 and the Count of Verdun in 997.[17] Penitence was a motivating principle of pilgrimage. Thus a cast of pious, sometimes bloody, characters made the long journey to Jerusalem to atone for their sins. Looming large among them, and completely outnumbering their English and German counterparts, were French and Lorraine pilgrims, reflecting the local patronage of the counts of Anjou and dukes of Normandy. In 1001, after burning his wife alive in her wedding dress, having first pronounced her guilty of adultery with a swineherd, Fulk the Black, Count of Anjou and founder of the Angevin Dynasty that ruled England in the twelfth and thirteenth centuries, considered it prudent to make the journey to Jerusalem. King Harold of England's brother, Earl Sweyn Godinson, removed his shoes and embarked on a barefoot pilgrimage to Jerusalem after raping the virgin Abbess Edwiga. Robert Duke of Normandy, father of William the Conqueror, made the journey in 1035 but, like so many pilgrims of the time, died before he reached his destination.[18] The presence of holy relics, overwhelmingly located in the East, the birthplace of Christianity, was another compelling draw for Jerusalem, even though many were moved for safety to Constantinople over a number of centuries.

Jerusalem had a mixed and cultivated population for much of the eleventh century. Most of the doctors and secretaries were Christians, according to the tenth-century geographer Muqaddasi, while the bankers, tanners and dyers were Jews. Apart from the settled population, which included numerous Muslim scholars, both local and from all corners of the Islamic world, the flow of pilgrim traffic was constant so that 'on no day was the city free of strangers'.[19] Relations between Muslims and Jews and Christians were generally good, Muqaddasi noted, and Muslims participated in some Christian feasts. Many Muslim visitors, such as the Andalusian scholar Ibn al Arabi, who arrived in 1098, were 'desirous of seeking knowledge in the utmost extremities [of the earth]'. He was not disappointed. 'The full moon of knowledge shone for me and I was illuminated by it for more than three years.'[20]

Tolerance between the faiths was not a constant in Muslim Jerusalem. It ebbed and flowed according to the passions and prejudices of its leaders. The name of one caliph remains anathema to Jews and Christians to this day. In 1009 disaster struck the Christian community, when the formerly tolerant, now unhinged, Shia Fatimid caliph Hakim (r. 996–1021) gave the order to destroy the Church of the Holy Sepulchre. Long-standing rivals to the declining Sunni Abbasid Dynasty in Baghdad, the Fatimids had made themselves masters of Egypt and Jerusalem with the conquest of Cairo in 969. Hakim's dire decree followed his instructions for all cats and dogs in Egypt to be killed, the arbitrary arrests and executions of Christians and the forced conversion of churches to mosques. Irked by the prosperity of the Christian pilgrims, scandalized by the raucous Easter celebrations, in which the faithful marked Jesus's Resurrection with the dubiously miraculous ritual of the Holy Fire (in which light and fire emanate from the spot where Christ was thought to have been buried), Hakim gave orders for the church to be completely razed to the ground.* Stone by stone, it was levelled. Only decades later was it rebuilt.

Hakim's sectarian attacks were not confined to the Christians. Jews were also targeted and attacked, ordered to convert or leave. In a bizarrely cruel practice they were made to wear a wooden cow necklace, a crude reference to the Golden Calf. Christians were forced to wear an iron cross. Wine was banned. Synagogues as well as churches were burned to the ground. From a narrow sectarian base Hakim's savagery grew steadily wider and more psychopathic until he was attacking Muslims indiscriminately, targeting Sunni and Shia alike, banning Ramadan and executing – often dismembering – those nearest him, from loyal tutors and sycophantic poets to blameless cooks and members of the royal household.

After Hakim mysteriously disappeared on one of his nocturnal journeys in 1021, leaving only a donkey and blood-stained clothes behind, his son and heir Zahir (r. 1021–36) succeeded to the Fatimid caliphate. After Hakim's sanguinary storm, Zahir's rule was a respite for Jerusalem. There was a flurry of reconstruction and a return of tolerance. Although the city escaped human destruction for a time, it was unable to avoid natural devastation in the form of the shattering earthquake of 1033. This smashed the Byzantine walls and the Al Aqsa Mosque of the Umayyads and terrified

---

* In *The History of the Decline and Fall of the Roman Empire* Edward Gibbon was unimpressed by the miracle. 'This pious fraud, first devised in the ninth century, was devoutly cherished by the Latin crusaders, and is annually repeated by the clergy of the Greek, Armenian, and Coptic sects, who impose on the credulous spectators for their own benefit and that of their tyrants,' he sniffed.

the population. '[People] ran out from their houses into the streets because they saw the houses and the walls tremble, while the wooden beams separated from the walls and swayed back and forth' before collapsing in ruins, the scribe of the Jerusalem Yeshiva wrote in a letter.[21] Zahir demonstrated his love of the city by launching extensive restoration work, rebuilding its walls in more or less the form in which the Ottoman-era walls around the Old City stand today, and lavishing sparkling new mosaics on both the Dome of the Rock and Al Aqsa Mosque. Under Zahir and his successor Mustansir (r. 1036–94), relations with the Byzantines improved. Zahir signed a treaty with Emperor Romanus III, which paved the way for the later reconstruction of the Church of the Holy Sepulchre, together with other Christian sites in the Holy Land, by Emperor Constantine IX Monomachus between 1042 and 1048.[22]

The Persian poet, philosopher and traveller Nasir-i-Khusraw left a valuable mid-century portrait of Jerusalem. He arrived in 1047 in the early stages of a seven-year, 12,000-mile pilgrimage, having resigned from his position as a tax collector in Khorasan after hearing a celestial voice in a dream. His *Safarnama* (*Book of Travels*) contains a meticulously observed description of the 'very great city' of 20,000, surrounded by cultivated land of corn, figs and olives, especially of its most sacred Muslim sites of worship. Khusraw admired the numerous 'high, well-built and clean bazaars', each with its own artisans, the stone-paved streets and the richly endowed *bimaristan* hospital, which treated large numbers of sick people with 'potions and lotions'. It was a highly cosmopolitan place of pilgrimage for subscribers to all three Abrahamic creeds. In some years, he reported, as many as 20,000 Muslims unable to make the journey to Mecca travelled on pilgrimage to Jerusalem instead, congregating on the Haram al Sharif. 'From all the countries of the Greeks, too, and from other lands, the Christians and the Jews come up to Jerusalem in great numbers in order to make their visitation of the Church of the Holy Sepulchre and the Synagogue that is there.' Muslim worshippers thronged inside the Dome of the Rock, handsomely laid out with fine silk carpets. Carved from green, variegated marble, the balustrade around the platform of the Noble Sanctuary was like a 'meadow covered with flowers in bloom'. Above it, 'rising like the summit of a mountain', the famous dome was visible from afar. Khusraw also rhapsodized about the 'great and beautiful' Al Aqsa Mosque with its 280 marble columns, the *mihrab* niche adorned with enamel beneath a beautifully sculptured wooden roof. Nearing the completion of its reconstruction, the Church of the Holy Sepulchre was 'a most spacious building, and is capable of containing eight thousand persons. The edifice is built, with the utmost skill, of coloured marbles, with ornamentation and sculptures. Inside, the church is everywhere adorned with Byzantine brocade, worked in gold with pictures.' Jesus was portrayed on an ass, together with prophets and patriarchs such as Abraham, Ishmael, Isaac and Jacob, 'peace be upon them all!'[23]

Khusraw's visit came just a few years before the Great Schism of 1054, which cleaved the Christian world in two in a fracture which has yet to be healed almost a millennium later. After rival moves to close each other's churches in Constantinople and southern Italy, born of obscure theological and ecclesiastical differences and disputes, Pope Leo IX's papal legate briskly excommunicated the Byzantine Patriarch Michael I Celarius, who retaliated with his own excommunication. Henceforth, Latin Catholics under their popes in Rome were set against the Greek Orthodox, who recognized only the temporal and spiritual leaders of Constantinople. Already attractive to Christians, Jerusalem swiftly became the scene of intra-Christian competition for influence. Khusraw reported the local legend that the Byzantine emperor came on pilgrimage in secret 'so that no one should recognise him'. From 1059, Constantine X Doukas supported the development of a Christian quarter around the holy church.

All Christendom, Orthodox and Catholic alike, was horrified to hear the news of 1064, when, only days from Jerusalem, a huge party of 7,000 German and Dutch pilgrims led by Arnold Bishop of Bamberg was attacked by 'a most ferocious tribe of Arabs who thirsted for human blood'. The defenceless pilgrims were no match for these 'famished wolves', who slaughtered them mercilessly, according to one chronicler.[24] There were harrowing stories of pilgrims swallowing gold, only to be cut up and disembowelled by the rapacious bandits determined to get their hands on it. Five thousand were said to have been killed. Had the Fatimid governor of Palestine not arrived with a relief party, the entire caravan of pilgrims might have been massacred. It was a bloody reminder of the dangers of pilgrimage to the Holy City.

From the 1070s, instability in the Holy Land deepened. In 1071 an army led by the Seljuq commander Alp Arslan, or Heroic Lion, routed Byzantine forces at the Battle of Manzikert, in what is eastern Turkey today. The battle, which marked the beginning of Turkish ascendancy in Anatolia and the slow decline of Byzantium, was a cataclysmic defeat. Humiliatingly Emperor Romanus IV Diogenes was captured and taken prisoner.

Alp Arslan's general, the Turkish chief Atsiz ibn Abaq, pressed on south and put Jerusalem under siege. Out of respect for the city's status as 'God's sanctuary', he vowed not to fight it. Such concern for the sanctity of Jerusalem did not prevent him from starving its people into submission in

1073. By 1077 he was back beneath the walls of the Holy City after the population, buoyed by his defeat in Egypt, rebelled. This time Atsiz was less inclined to restrain his men. Three thousand Jerusalemites were slaughtered. Only those who took refuge in the Noble Sanctuary were spared in return for ransom. The Jewish poet Solomon ben Joseph Ha-Cohen described Atsiz's savagery in Cairo and Jerusalem, likening the Turkmens to beasts, harlots and adulterers:

> They . . . robbed and murdered
> And ravished and pillaged the storehouses
> They were a strange and cruel people . . .
> They laid waste the cities and they were made desolate . . .
> And burned the heaped corn and destroyed the palaces,
> And cut down the trees and trampled upon the vineyards,
> Despoiled the graves and threw out the bones.[25]

Atsiz's capture of Jerusalem conspicuously failed to usher in a more orderly era for the city. Within a couple of years Atsiz was murdered and Alp Arslan's fledgling empire was imploding, the victim of internecine rivalry and conflict. Jerusalem passed like a pawn into the hands of the Turkish warlord Ortuq ibn Aksab, who celebrated his mastery of the city by shooting an arrow into the dome of the Church of the Holy Sepulchre. Notwithstanding another attempted rebellion in 1093, Ortuq's sons held Jerusalem until 1098, when the Egyptian vizier put the city under a forty-day siege, forcing its surrender to a new governor, Iftikhar al Dawla, the loftily named Pride of the State.

The rapid coming and going of violent Turkmen warlords and Egyptian overlords might have been an inconvenience for Jerusalem and its people. It was as nothing compared to the horrors about to unfold.

In the Place de Jaude in the heart of the French city of Clermont-Ferrand there is a grand statue of the moustachioed Gallic chieftain Vercingetorix galloping on horseback over a fallen Roman legionary, sword held aloft in triumph. Set on six columns and a substantial plinth so that it rises high above street level, dominating the public space, it is a stirring monument to martial glory. The inscription takes its tone from the sculpture. *J'ai pris les armes pour la liberté de tous*, it reads. I took up arms for the freedom of all.

On 27 November 1095, more than 1,100 years after Vercingetorix had united the tribes of Gaul against Rome, another Frenchman stood in Clermont and called on his audience to take up arms for liberty. Addressing the Council of Clermont, Pope Urban II exhorted bishops and noblemen to rally to the rescue of embattled Christians in the Holy Land. He was responding to a desperate plea for help from the Eastern Orthodox Church against the marauding Seljuqs.

'Our Christian brothers, members in Christ, are scourged, oppressed, and injured in Jerusalem, in Antioch, and the other cities of the East,' he told the grim-faced council.[26] Christians were 'flogged and exiled as slaves for sale in their own land', subjected to 'unspeakable degradation and servitude'. Churches in which divine mysteries had once been celebrated were now used as stables. The Christian cities of the East were now held not by Christian holy men but by 'base and bastard Turks'. The most emotional and apocalyptic version of the pope's sermon (of which there are five) came from the chronicler Robert the Monk, writing in around 1122. Here the Muslim rulers of the Holy Land were blood-curdling savages, 'a race utterly alienated from God'.

> They ruin the altars with filth and defilement. They circumcise Christians and smear the blood from the circumcision over the altars or throw it into the baptismal fonts. They are pleased to kill others by cutting open their bellies, extracting the end of their intestines, and tying it to a stake. Then, with flogging, they drive their victims around the stake until, when their viscera have spilled out, they fall dead on the ground.

Urban roused his followers to right these abominable wrongs by taking up the cross and setting off on the road to the Holy Sepulchre to seize from this 'wicked race' the land that flowed with milk and honey, which rightfully had been given to the children of Israel. Jerusalem was 'the navel of the world', a 'paradise of delights' that God had made illustrious by His advent, beautified by His residence, consecrated by suffering, redeemed by death and glorified by burial. Held captive by godless barbarians, the city 'desires to be liberated, and does not cease to implore you to come to her aid'. Those who accepted this holy challenge would be granted 'the remission of your sins, with the assurance of the imperishable glory of the kingdom of heaven'. It was a calculatedly compelling proposition.

Christian pilgrims had been attacked and killed. The Byzantine emperor had fallen to the Muslims. Sacred Jerusalem was being passed from one barbarian savage to another. The Holy Land was awash with blood. It was time for decisive action in the service of Christ. There could be no doubt of the divine sanction for the greatest ever journey to Jerusalem, a pilgrimage that would become the First Crusade. The crowd of knights and bishops roared their approval of the pope's tumultuous address. 'Deus vult!' they thundered. God wills it!

Pope Urban might not have had a huge number of battalions at his disposal, but the timing of the bold expedition he was calling for was exceptionally fortunate. Within the past several years the Islamic world had lost its principal, long-standing leaders. Mustansir, the Fatimid caliph in Cairo, and his vizier Badr al Jamali; the Abbasid caliph Muqtadi in Baghdad; the Seljuq Sultan Malikshah and his vizier Nizam al Mulk, all had been plucked by the Angel of Death to meet their maker. Fatimid and Abbasid power had been seriously weakened. The Seljuq Empire was disintegrating.[27]

For many medieval Christians, Jerusalem was, as the pope had argued, the centre of the world. Beyond the holy relics it contained, the city itself was the most sacred relic of all. This was where God Himself had intervened to redeem mankind. It was a city, above all others, that symbolized the spiritual power of generations of prophets and holy men. It was the city of the first Christians, of Christ and his apostles. It was the place where Christ had been crucified and buried and from where He had risen again. For those who gave credence to prophetic traditions, Jerusalem was where the last emperor would be crowned before the End Times. Little wonder that the most popular rallying cry of the Crusaders was Psalm 79: 'O God, the heathens are come into thine inheritance'.

The Crusaders were men of high birth and low: nobles, knights, peasants, holy hermits, ruffians, bigots, romantics, eccentrics and adventurers united in their acceptance of Urban's call to take up the cross, the holy stamp sewn symbolically onto their clothing. Bishop Adhemar of Le Puy, the pope's spiritual leader of this great, armed pilgrimage, was the first to take the cross, followed by Raymond IV, Count of Toulouse. The leadership of this hastily assembled army was eclectic, divided, frequently feuding, occasionally kingdom-seeking, ruthless and ambitious. Predominantly Norman and Provençal, it included Robert Duke of Normandy; Robert Count of Flanders; Tancred of Lecce in southern Italy; Godfrey of Bouillon, Duke of Lower Lorraine; and the Norman knight Bohemond of Taranto.

Their way to Jerusalem was lubricated with blood. In late 1095 and early 1096, even before they had left Europe, there were pogroms against the Jews in France and Germany, still blamed, more than 1,000 years after the event, for killing Christ. In 1097 the Crusaders took their first Asian prize, seizing Nicaea in north-west Anatolia after a month-long siege and handing it over to Byzantine forces. The ancient city of Antioch followed, though not without the most gruelling, starving siege, which came close to ending the Crusade before achieving its greatest goal. Within the Crusader camp one of the soldiers, Peter Bartholomew, began having visions telling him where the Holy Lance was buried. The subsequent 'discovery' of the relic beneath a church rallied the Crusaders, who survived Antioch and lived to fight another day. Bartholomew, however, never shook off the accusation of fraud. Determined to prove his innocence, he submitted himself to ordeal by fire, walked across red-hot ploughshares and died several days later.

Conditions worsened. Supplies of food were exhausted. A plague broke out, carrying off many of the battered army. Then, in late 1098 at Maarra in north-west Syria, three days' march south of Antioch, the Crusaders stooped to new depths, still remembered with horror today. 'Our troops boiled pagan adults in cooking-pots,' the Frankish chronicler Radulph of Caen recorded. 'They impaled children on spits and devoured them grilled.'[28] These were not baseless accusations by the enemy. The cannibalism was freely confessed. 'Not only did our troops not shrink from eating dead Turks and Saracens,' the chronicler Albert of Aix reported. 'They also ate dogs!'[29]

The official explanation offered by the Crusaders, as expressed in a letter to the pope, was famine. Many Muslims saw it as fanaticism. As Osama ibn Munqidh, the twelfth-century man of letters from Syria, later wrote: 'All those who were well-informed about the Franj saw them as beasts superior in courage and fighting ardour, but in nothing else, just as animals are superior in strength and aggression.'[30] To this ghastly episode in Maarra must be added the wholesale slaughter by the Crusaders of the town's men, women and children. Those who were not killed were robbed and sold into slavery. The city walls were destroyed, houses set on fire. In a spectacular example of statistical exaggeration the twelfth-century historian Ibn al Athir claimed that 100,000 were slain at Maarra. The entire population of the town was unlikely to have been more than 10,000. Whatever the numbers, the slaughter was devastating.

Horrified by the stories of Frankish atrocities related by refugees fleeing the carnage, a slew of cities including Hama, Homs, Tripoli, Beirut, Caesarea and Acre hastily cut deals with the Crusaders, who were supported by a ragged English fleet off the coastal road. At Arsuf the army cut inland towards their sacred goal, now just fifty miles away. On 3 June 1099, with the summer temperatures rising, they took Ramla. The Norman lord Tancred rushed off to claim Bethlehem for himself. On 7 June, in buoyant mood and with some of the Crusaders barefoot, already 'rejoicing and exulting' at their achievement, the exhausted army reached Jerusalem.[31] According to Raymond of Aguilers, a chaplain of Raymond of Toulouse, it numbered 12,000, of which around 1,200 were knights, with many more armed peasants and non-combatants.

For the inhabitants of the Holy City, the sight of yet another army camped beyond the city walls was a particularly chilling one. It was only nine months since the city had surrendered to the Fatimids after a destructive forty-day siege. Yet their position was far from hopeless. The city had robust defences and a substantial garrison. The army that faced them across the parapets was dangerously exposed, shattered after a series of forced marches, perilously short of supplies and riven with the usual divisions between its lordly leaders. Summer temperatures were escalating. Wells had been blocked and supplies of water were limited. Most seriously of all, news quickly reached both defenders and Crusaders that a large Egyptian army under Al Afdal was already on its way to destroy the infidel invaders. The Crusaders did not have time on their side. After another divine vision, this time by a hermit on the Mount of Olives, who urged an immediate attack on the city, the Crusaders launched a lightning ladder assault without recourse to the siege engines required to storm the walls. The defenders beat back the advance and the Crusaders retreated ignominiously with heavy losses.

The defeat prompted a more considered approach – and a fresh round of bickering as the leaders discussed who would attack which stretch of the city walls. After protracted arguments, Raymond of Toulouse took his forces to press on the southern section at the Zion Gate beneath Mount Zion. Tancred and the two Roberts, of Normandy and Flanders, took up positions to the north, facing the New Gate and Damascus Gate respectively, while Godfrey set about building his siege tower out of range of the defenders. The twin-flank approach divided the garrison's defensive preparations at a stroke, forcing them to protect their walls with sacks of straw and chaff, enormous wooden beams, ropes, even tapestries and mattresses stuffed with silk – anything to help withstand the relentless pounding from the mangonels. There was another stroke of good fortune for the Crusaders when Genoese ships touched in at Jaffa on 17 June. The vessels were taken apart and their timbers quickly transported to Jerusalem, where they were transformed into the mobile siege engines without which the city could not be taken.

By 6 July the temperature was becoming unbearable for the fair-skinned Europeans. Another divine vision intervened. A priest claimed that the late bishop Adhemar Le Puy, a man 'of revered character and immortal memory', who had died the previous year at Antioch, had appeared to him and was calling on the Christian host to process around the city walls in the spirit of Joshua at Jericho.[32] A three-day fast was agreed. Then, marching barefoot behind ranks of bearded, relic-bearing priests, the light-headed army set about its surreal circumnavigation of the Holy City, galvanized by a barrage of trumpets and a sea of Crusader banners, mocked every step of the way by the defenders, for whom this bizarre sight must nevertheless have been disconcerting. A sermon preached beneath the city walls at this time, as related by Abbot Baldric of Bourgueil, brilliantly conveys the feverish, fanatical atmosphere of Christian duty and destiny that now gripped the camp:

> Rouse yourselves, members of Christ's household! Rouse yourselves, knights and footsoldiers, and seize firmly that city, our commonwealth! Give heed to Christ, who today is banished from that city and is crucified . . . and forcefully take Christ away from these impious crucifiers . . . If an outsider were to strike any of your kin down would you not avenge your blood-relative? How much more ought you to avenge your God, your father, your brother, whom you see reproached, banished from his estates, crucified; whom you hear calling, desolate, and begging for aid?[33]

By nightfall on 13 July the Frankish army had completed its spiritual and military preparations for the assault. Two enormous siege towers loomed menacingly out of the night, their sides covered in newly flayed animal skins soaked in vinegar to resist the defenders' Greek fire. Tancred, Robert of Flanders and Robert of Normandy moved their positions further to the north-east, close to what Godfrey of Bouillon had identified as the most vulnerable section of the city walls, a little to the east of Herod's Gate, opposite today's Rockefeller Museum, a vision of white limestone.[34] Godfrey had reserved this spot for his own attack, in which he awarded himself the leading role on his siege tower, climbing to its summit, from where, wielding his heavy crossbow, he loosed off volleys of sharpened steel bolts into the ranks of the defenders. A sky-filling barrage of missiles flew between the mangonels on both sides.

On the morning of 14 July, signallers stationed on the Mount of Olives with sun-catching reflectors cleverly coordinated the simultaneous attacks on the city's northern and southern defences. Ibn al Athir records how Raymond's tower on the southern flank was attacked and burned by the garrison, killing everyone inside. But while the Fatimids had concentrated their defensive efforts in the south, by noon Godfrey's tower, fighting off concerted attacks of missiles and Greek fire, was in place alongside the north-eastern walls. From here his men could storm the ramparts and force an entry into the city, followed soon afterwards by Tancred's Normans. On the other side of the city, frustrated by their slow progress, Raymond's men finally broke through and, with a zeal born of their impatience, rushed on furiously towards the Tower of David, to where, with their outer defences breached, much of the garrison had retreated under the command of governor Iftikhar. Jutting out from the western walls, the ancient octagonal citadel, complete with monumental found-ations welded in lead, was virtually indestructible, but Iftikhar understood the city was falling around him. Pressed to surrender by Raymond in return for the lives of his men, he agreed and was allowed to depart later for Ascalon.

For Jerusalemites there was no such escape. Panic-stricken, the ordinary men, women and children of the city sought refuge on the Temple Mount, a natural place of sanctuary. Instead of finding relief there, though, they met only with slaughter, in scenes so sadistic, blood-crazed and merciless they can hardly be explained by messianic fervour. Nor can these atroci-ties be blamed upon enemy propaganda. They are described in all their graphic horror within the Crusaders' chronicles, in which Pope Urban's *milites Christi*, his soldiers of Christ, glorify the violence and revel in the blood-spilling. One such was Raymond of Aguilers, who described the massacres with a pride that borders on the jaunty:

> Wonderful sights were to be seen. Our men cut off the heads of their enemies, others shot them with arrows so that they fell from the towers, others tortured them longer by casting them into the flames. Piles of heads, hands and feet were to be seen on the streets. It was necessary to pick one's way over the bodies of men and horses.[35]

There was no question of surrender, no prospect of mercy. Years of privations and suffering on the 2,700-mile road to Jerusalem were forgot-ten in an orgy of killing and plunder. The most infamous Crusader accounts do not seek to minimize the indiscriminate slaughter of innocents, the dashing to death of babies against walls, the hurling of victims over the ramparts. The tone is instead one of bombastic exaggeration and glorifi-cation, as though each documented killing lent further lustre to their Christian honour. So we hear that the knights who were pursuing Fatimid soldiers towards the Dome of the Rock entered the Al Aqsa Mosque, con-tinued hacking down everyone in front of them and 'rode in blood up to their bridles'. For Raymond of Aguilers again, it was 'a just and splendid judgement of God that this place should be filled with the blood of un-believers'.* Perhaps, some historians wonder, the Crusaders saw themselves as agents of the wrath of God.[36]

Eleventh-century Muslims had likened the Franks to beasts. Fulcher of

---

* William of Tyre, the archbishop and great chronicler of the Crusades, sounded a dissenting note in the twelfth century, observing that the carnage was so grotesque that even the blood-soaked victors themselves were struck with 'horror and disgust'. See Benjamin Kedar, 'The Jerusalem Massacre of July 1099 in the Western Historiography of the Crusades', *Crusades* 3, pp. 15–76.

Chartres, a priest who participated in the First Crusade as chaplain to Baldwin of Boulogne and later wrote a chronicle of the expedition, compared the Jews and Muslims of Jerusalem to 'rotten fruit':

> With drawn swords our people ran through the city;
> Nor did they spare anyone, not even those pleading for mercy.
> The crowd was struck to the ground, just as rotten fruit
> Falls from shaken branches, and acorns from a wind-blown oak.[37]

Ten thousand are thought to have been killed on the Noble Sanctuary, 'a large number being imams, ulema, righteous men and ascetics, Muslims who had left their native lands and come to live a holy life in this quiet spot'.[38] While later Muslim accounts speak of up to 100,000 slaughtered – Ibn al Athir reported 70,000 were killed in the Al Aqsa Mosque alone – modern historians reckon on one-tenth of that. 'Many people were killed,' Ibn al Qalanisi, one of the few contemporary Muslim chroniclers, reported simply. 'The Jews had gathered in their synagogue and the Franj burned them alive. They also destroyed the monuments of saints and the tomb of Abraham, peace be upon him!'[39]

Tancred ordered the remaining 300 Muslims on the roof of the Al Aqsa Mosque to be spared, then turned from slaughter to plunder. The next morning, ignoring Tancred's command, Raymond's forces mounted the roof and embarked on another wild spree of murder and maiming, torture and beheading.

'Today if God pleases we will all become rich' had been one of the most popular rallying cries from the earliest days of the Crusade. Now it was a free for all. The ancient Temple Mount surrendered its prodigious treasures sacred shrine by sacred shrine. Ibn al Athir wrote of the Franks systematically stripping the Dome of the Rock of more than forty silver candelabra, each weighing 3,600 dirhams, a huge silver lamp weighing forty-four Syrian pounds, 150 smaller silver candelabra, more than twenty gold ones and untold quantities of other booty. The Crusaders took to the looting with the same frenzied spirit they had exhibited during the killing spree, combing every inch of the city, according to another eyewitness, 'seizing gold and silver, horses and mules, and houses full of all sorts of goods', all the time 'rejoicing and weeping from excess of gladness'.[40]

Blood ran in the streets, already choked with piles of corpses. Parties of Jews and Muslims, who until this point had escaped the massacres, were ordered to remove the bodies and burn them on pyres before being cut down themselves in cold blood and consigned to the flames.

On 17 July, after all this killing in the name of Christ, the exhausted knights, wiping away tears of joy, required spiritual succour. 'With the fall of the city it was rewarding to see the worship of the pilgrims at the Holy Sepulchre, the clapping of hands, the rejoicing and singing of a new song to the Lord. Their souls offered to the victorious and triumphant God prayers of praise which they could not explain in words.'[41]

The Franks were brutal even to their co-religionists. Asserting Latin control over the city's holiest Christian site, Arnulf, the newly elected Norman Patriarch of Jerusalem, expelled the Eastern Orthodox priests – the Greeks, Georgians, Armenians, Copts and Syrians – from the Holy Sepulchre. When those priests refused to reveal the hiding place of the True Cross, they were subjected to torture.

In addition to all the physical plunder, there was profit to be had from selling prisoners into slavery. The most valuable were ransomed, those who failed to find the money to pay for their release joined their colleagues on the burning pyres of corpses. In the throbbing summer heat, bodies started to decompose immediately and the city became a stinking charnel house. 'Oh, what a stench there was at that time around the walls, within and without, from the dead bodies of the Saracens rotting there until then,' Fulcher of Chartres wrote a full five months after the sacking of Jerusalem.[42]

Jerusalem had been gutted in a matter of days, its people killed without mercy, its sacred Jewish and Muslim shrines destroyed, its treasures sacked and stolen in an ugly storm of Christian fury. The land that had flowed with milk and honey ran with blood and rotting human flesh. It now needed a new Christian leader.

Since there was no shortage of candidates, fresh disputes broke out between the posturing leaders of the Crusade. Offered the throne, Raymond refused, delicately asserting his unworthiness of becoming a king in the city of Christ. Chaste and unmarried, Godfrey, the tousle-haired hero of the siege, was the God-fearing choice. Refusing to be crowned king on the grounds that he would never wear a crown of gold in the city where Christ had worn a crown of thorns, Godfrey was anointed instead Advocate of the Holy Sepulchre. His first duty was to lead out the remnants of the Crusader forces to fight the Egyptian relief army, which he bested at Ashkelon, crushing any immediate threat. Raymond skulked off to establish a new Crusader kingdom in Tripoli, the last of the initial quartet of Crusader states that included Antioch, Edessa and now Jerusalem.

Collectively they became known as Outremer – Overseas – a tapestry of Christian territories born in a sea of Jewish, Christian and Muslim blood. Jerusalem's fall to Christian forces, together with the virtuous destruction of the detestable enemies of God, was nothing less than a miracle. As the roused rabble of knights and clerics had shouted at Clermont less than five years earlier, *Deus vult*.

The Islamic world was horrified. In a poem written in the aftermath of Jerusalem's fall, Abu Muzaffar al Abiwardi, an Iraqi poet of the late eleventh and early twelfth centuries, dwelled on the shame, ignominy and dishonour to the faithful, asking how Muslims could dare sleep peacefully after such an outrage. The Prophet Mohammed was calling out from his grave, exhorting the believers to holy war:

> *This is war, and the man who shuns the whirlpool*
> > *to save his life shall grind his teeth in penitence.*
> *This is war, and the infidel's sword is naked in his hand,*
> > *ready to be sheathed again in men's neck and skulls.*
> *This is war, and he who lies in the tomb at Medina seems*
> > *to raise his voice and cry: 'O sons of Hashim!*
> *I see my people slow to raise the lance against the enemy:*
> > *I see the Faith resting on feeble pillars.*
> *For fear of death the Muslims are evading the fire of battle,*
> > *refusing to believe that death shall surely strike them.'*[43]

Distraught by the loss, appalled by the slaughter, Abu Saad al Harawi, grand *qadi*, or judge, of Damascus, rushed to Baghdad with a wretched gaggle of refugees from Jerusalem. After a punishing, three-week journey across the desert in the torrid heat of summer, he burst into the royal chamber. Gone was his sumptuous silk turban, removed to reveal a sunburnt head shaved in mourning. His anguish turned immediately to anger at the sight of the youthful Abbasid caliph Al Mustazhir reclining languorously in his *diwan*, surrounded by his court favourites. Al Harawi forgot himself.

'How dare you slumber in the shade of complacent safety, leading lives as frivolous as garden flowers, while your brothers in Syria have no dwelling place save the saddles of camels and the bellies of vultures,' he thundered. 'Blood has been spilled! Beautiful young girls have been shamed, and must now hide their sweet faces in their hands! Shall the valorous Arabs resign themselves to insult, and the valiant Persians accept dishonour?'[44]

The cowering refugees from the Holy City told harrowing tales which reduced their audience to tears. Begging for help, they spoke about the killing and enslavement of men, women and children and the plunder of Muslim property 'in that revered, august place'.[45] Mustazhir, still in his early twenties, was ill equipped to mount a robust response to the Crusaders' assault on the heart of the Islamic world. A gentle soul, his passion was for architecture and love poetry rather than holy war and martial glory. He burst into tears at the *qadi*'s devastating news, a reaction that received short shrift from his distinguished visitor. 'Never have the Muslims been so humiliated, never have their lands been so savagely devastated,' he chided the caliph.

Like many a modern politician seeking to calm an eruption of righteous public anger, Mustazhir ordered an inquiry, to be conducted by seven grandees. 'It is perhaps superfluous to add that nothing was ever heard from that committee of wise men.'[46] The man whose position had once embodied the power, glory and restless energy of Arab civilization was an impotent, indolent puppet.

This was not the first time the Islamic world had felt the force of Christian steel. The Dar al Islam had already suffered from Christian offensives and invasions, not least during the Byzantine wars of the ninth century, but the First Crusade and the fall of Jerusalem were of a different magnitude. That they were overtly religious in their motivation made the Muslim loss more painful to bear.

For Muslims the most straightforward explanation of the Christian triumph was not difficult to discern. Ali ibn Tahir al Sulami, the twelfth-century Syrian preacher and author of the *Book of Jihad*, was the first Muslim author to discuss the Crusades. The leaders of the Muslim world, he wrote, had been guilty of abandoning their responsibilities for waging *jihad*. God had divided them as punishment, leaving them vulnerable to the Frankish invasion. 'The rulers were all at odds with one another . . . and so the Franks conquered the lands.'[47] It was another ruinous demonstration of the consequences of *fitna*, disunity among the believers. Sulami called for Muslims to retake Jerusalem but was met with a resounding silence.

Perhaps the most baleful and most enduring consequence of the First Crusade, and those that followed until the late thirteenth century, was the sealing of enmity between the Christian and Muslim worlds. The Crusades brought Christendom into wholehearted conflict with the Dar al Islam. For many the Crescent and the Cross to this day elicit bitter memories of a conflict that can be traced back a millennium to the Crusades. Turks never forgot the cannibalism at Maarra, Jews and Muslim Arabs still recall the depredations in Jerusalem.

'There came to be an association between Christianity and Western invasion, a confusion that still lingers today,' says Dr Hazem Nuseibeh, a Jerusalemite and former foreign minister of Jordan. 'We don't call it the Crusades, we call it Harb al Faranja, the Wars of the Franks. We never recognize it as war between Christianity and Islam. Never – because we revere Christianity as much as Islam. But there still is that confusion.'[48]

A thousand years after the Crusades, Jerusalem remains as sacred as ever to Jews, Christians and Muslims. For many Israelis it is the 'undivided, eternal capital of the Jewish people'. Millions of Christians still flock to the city on Holy Land pilgrimages. Uneasily shared between the three faiths, it remains the most disputed city in the world, a spiritual battleground, a place of competition and cosmopolitanism, piety and bloody conflict. 'It means all my life, it means all my dreams and aspirations,' says Nuseibeh. 'It's been the city of my family for fourteen centuries and is the dearest thing to me. I feel a great pain about Jerusalem. It is the most beautiful city, even though it is being systematically decapitated and devoured. It's extremely sad. But nothing lasts for ever.'

Born out of hope, desperation and necessity, this is a very Muslim sentiment in today's Jerusalem. 'Look, nobody here lasted,' says Chris Alami, a Palestinian hotelier in the Old City. 'Not the Romans, not the Turks, not the Christians, not the Muslims, not the Jews, not the British. No matter how powerful they were, no matter how great they were, no one has lasted in Jerusalem. In the end, Jerusalem has always belonged to Jerusalemites only.'[49]

Frankish control of the Holy City, Crusader capital of Outremer, didn't last for ever, either. Jerusalem remained in Christian hands for less than a century after its tumultuous fall in 1099. The Crusader states lasted a little longer, but with the fall of Tripoli in 1289 and Acre in 1291, the messianic movement imploded.

All that was yet to come. One of the most immediate legacies of the First Crusade was to elevate Jerusalem to the highest possible importance for Muslims. That the believers had failed in their duties, and been grievously chastised by God, was clear enough. It became equally evident, as the years passed, that Jerusalem had to be retaken.

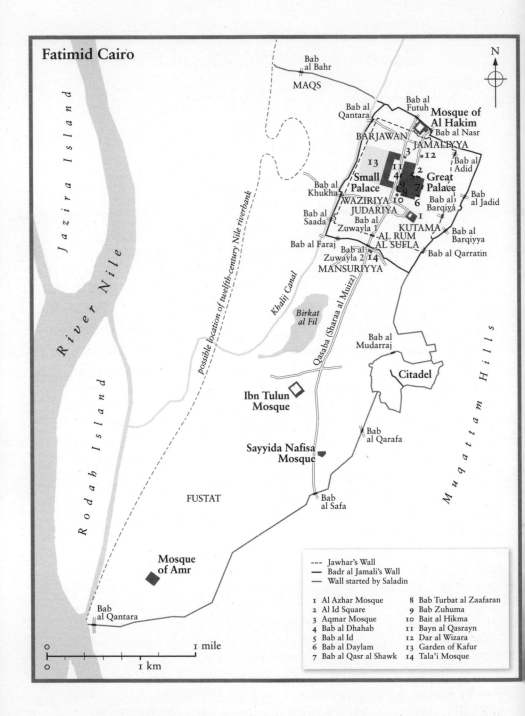

Fatimid Cairo

N

Bab
al Bahr
MAQS

Bab al
Qantara

Bab al
Futuh

**Mosque of
Al Hakim**

Bab al Nasr

BARJAWAN

JAMALIYYA

3   12

Bab al
Adid

13   11   2
**Small   4   5
Palace**   9   7

**Great
Palace**

Bab al
Khukha

WAZIRIYA   8   6

JUDARIYA   10

Bab al
Barqiya

Bab al
Jadid

Bab al
Saada

Bab al
Zuwayla 1   1

KUTAMA

AL RUM

Bab al
Barqiyya

Bab al Faraj

Bab al
Zuwayla 2   14

AL SUFLA

Bab al Qarratin

MANSURIYYA

*Birkat
al Fil*

Bab al
Mudarraj

Citadel

M u q a t t a m   H i l l s

**Ibn Tulun
Mosque**

Bab
al Qarafa

**Sayyida Nafisa
Mosque**

FUSTAT

Bab
al Safa

**Mosque
of Amr**

Bab
al Qantara

o   1 mile
o   1 km

- - -   Jawhar's Wall
──   Badr al Jamali's Wall
──   Wall started by Saladin

1 Al Azhar Mosque   8   Bab Turbat al Zaafaran
2 Al Id Square   9   Bab Zuhuma
3 Aqmar Mosque   10 Bait al Hikma
4 Bab al Dhahab   11 Bayn al Qasrayn
5 Bab al Id   12 Dar al Wizara
6 Bab al Daylam   13 Garden of Kafur
7 Bab al Qasr al Shawk   14 Tala'i Mosque

J a z i r a   I s l a n d

R i v e r   N i l e

R o d a b   I s l a n d

possible location of twelfth-century Nile riverbank

Khalij Canal

Qasaba (Sharaa al Muizz)

6

Cairo – The City Victorious
(12th Century)

In times gone by, when storms and tempests threatened us, we
wandered from place to place. But by the mercy of the Almighty
we have now been able to find a resting place in this city.

Maimonides, *The Guide for the Perplexed*

For the most commanding view over Cairo in all its sprawling, steaming, stinking, minaret-studded magnificence, there is only one place to go. Set on a spur of the 200-metre Muqattam hill, the great Qalaa or Citadel of Saladin has lorded it loftily over the city for eight centuries. Brainchild of an Iraqi Kurd, built by captive European Christians, home to generations of caliphs and concubines, sultans and slaves, warlords, pashas, ruffians and chancers, it has become one of the defining symbols of the Egyptian capital. Crowned by the nineteenth-century Mosque of Mohammed Ali Pasha with its many domes and twin twenty-five-metre minarets lancing towards the heavens, it is instantly recognizable from afar.

Many times over the years I have stood on these ramparts and stared across a city which transfixes the eye and fires the imagination like no other. I have wrestled with the demons and furies of classical Arabic and conversational Egyptian here, interviewed dissidents, Islamists and a world-famous dentist-novelist. There have been encounters with an Herodotean Egyptologist, the grim-faced sheikh of Al Azhar, the mild-mannered head of the Anglican Church, an infamous single-mother feminist who told tales of free-spirited girls fellating in veils, hot-headed revolutionaries and cold-blooded regime apparatchiks gloating over the 9/11 terrorist attack ('We warned you in the West about the Islamists, but you wouldn't listen to us'), languorous belly-dancers and a hip-swinging, secretly gay film star. I have haggled pathetically over trinkets in the tourist trap of Khan al Khalili, clambered over the pyramids in moonlight, smoked *shisha* in

Heliopolis, been pursued down narrow alleys by incandescent taxi-drivers, dodged Egyptian secret police on mopeds and waged futile war with Egyptian officialdom at the monumental Mugamma in Midan Tahrir, Cairo's answer to Kafka's Castle, in the throbbing heart of the city, as the mercury rose above forty degrees Celsius. During a feverish forty-eight hours I lay pinned to my bed, wrapped in clammy sheets, moving in and out of delirium while all around, from every minaret in the broiling city, came the pounding symphony of the call to prayer – *Allahu akbar! Allahu akbar!* – searing itself into my consciousness.

There have been many happy hours nosing about in the cramped book-shops of Talat Harb and the literary landmark that is Madbouly, before retiring, sated, for tea in the famous Café Riche, where Cairo's intellectuals have long gathered to while away the hours, despairing of the state of affairs to the sound of classical crooners such as Farid al Atrash and Mohammed Abd al Wahab. Historical explorations come no grander than a wander along Sharaa al Muizz, named after the swashbuckling Fatimid caliph, Glorifier of the Faith of Allah, a stretch of a little over half a mile linking Bab al Futuh in the north to Bab al Zuwayla, a grand procession of mosques, *madrassas*, minarets and dusty domes that together represent the highest concentration of medieval architectural treasures in the Islamic world. And where better to get lost than in Qarafa al Arafa, the City of the Dead, an Islamic necropolis that rambles along for five miles beneath the Muqattam cliffs and is home to the dead and the living alike, from the shrines of Imam Hussain and the mausoleum of the incomparable diva Umm Kulthum, queen of Arab music, to the humblest and most pitiful family hovel?*

As an impoverished teenager I used to hone my backgammon skills in dirt-cheap coffeehouses, slamming down the counters deep into the early hours, delaying until as late as possible the return to the notoriously filthy furnace that was Oxford Pension, where nights were spent fighting off scuttling battalions of fleas, lice and cockroaches. As a marginally more pecunious adult I have swished through the air-conditioned splendour of the Khedive Ismail's nineteenth-century palace on the river, also known as the Marriott. There have been forays up and down the Nile in battered feluccas and prostitute-filled riverboats, watching the setting sun sucking down plumes of golden light into the sands that roll out beyond the city. At night the immortal, imperturbable river is a slick of pitch-black oil,

---

* 'Rarely in history has one artist entranced so vast an audience for such a span of years. Umm Kulthum was Edith Piaf and Maria Callas, Frank Sinatra and Luciano Pavarotti rolled into one. To 150 million Arabs she was the Star of the East, the Nightingale of the Nile, the Lady of Arabic Song. To Cairenes she was simply *al Sitt*, The Lady.' Max Rodenbeck, *Cairo: The City Victorious*, pp. 328–9

stained with the smudged glares of reflected lights as it oozes its way north towards the delta. Then there have been days immersed in the sepulchral cool of the Egyptian Museum, not so much walking through the centuries as moving through entire millennia.

'When a man is tired of London, he is tired of life,' said Samuel Johnson. Yet by comparison with the Egyptian capital, London seems almost insipid. Cairo *is* life. It is vital and visceral, overwhelming, suffocating, intoxicating, squalid, august, monumentally inspiring and profoundly depressing. It sucks the life out of you in snarling traffic jams reverberating to the score of a thousand drivers sitting on a thousand horns. Its overflowing markets throng with shouty shoppers, overly vocal vendors and products from all over the globe. It luxuriates in shabbiness, monumental grandeur, colonial splendour, ugliness, kitsch and tat. It stinks and sweats, has a life of its own, is all-consuming, and you drown in it, carried this way and that by a tide of humanity that seems never to disappear, whatever the hour. With a population of 21 million, rising and plunging by several million with the daily influx and exodus of rush-hour commuters and country-dwellers bringing their offerings to market, it is a pulsating, dizzying megalopolis bursting at the seams. Many centuries before Dr Johnson was dispensing his *bons mots*, when London was merely a Viking-ridden backwater, Cairo was the cynosure of the world. In *A Thousand and One Nights* Cairo co-stars alongside Baghdad as the setting for many scrapes and adventures. In 'The Jewish Doctor's Story' on the 28th Night, for example, we hear travellers lauding it as the most beautiful city on earth:

> *He who hath not seen Cairo hath not seen the world.*
> *Her soil is gold,*
> *Her Nile is a marvel.*
> *Her women are as the bright-eyed houris of Paradise;*
> *Her houses are palaces; and her air is soft, more odorous*
>   *than aloes-wood, rejoicing the heart.*
> *And how can Cairo be otherwise when she is the Mother*
>   *of the World?*[1]

And during all these visits, sooner or later I find myself back at the Citadel, a fixed point amid the maelstrom of a city that never stops shifting and growing. This vast fortress-city provides the most arresting overview of Cairo, the Nile Valley and Egyptian history through several thousand years. There is nowhere better to find your bearings in space and time. Beyond the glimmering Nile, ten miles to the west and barely perceptible through the smog and skyscrapers, is the neat beige triangle of the Great Pyramid of Cheops at Giza, built around 2467 BC and visited by Herodotus in the fifth century BC, when it was already as ancient to him as he is to us today. Farther south, enclosed by date palms, are the ruins of impenetrably ancient Memphis, while beyond them the western suburbs blur into the distant Sahara, a desert that swallowed up the invading army of Cambyses 2,500 years ago and which runs all the way to the Atlantic 3,000 miles away.

Countless pharaohs over countless centuries followed the processional way from Heliopolis, City of the Sun, in the north, to Memphis in the south, which remains the main traffic route across the city to this day. Closer to hand beneath the citadel begins the maze of medieval Cairo, guarded by the mighty bulk of the Mosque and Madrassa of Sultan Hasan with its quartet of staggered minarets and, a little to the left, the ninth-century Ibn Tulun Mosque, its squat, corkscrew minaret perching over an immense, sun-fired courtyard. East of the corniche is a site that is curiously barren for one of the world's largest and most densely populated cities. This rubble-scattered plain, scarred by partial excavations of villas and aqueducts, strewn with debris from long-abandoned pottery kilns, is all that remains of Misr al Fustat, the City of the Tents, founded by the victorious Arab general Amr ibn al As after routing the Byzantines here in 641. Here, on the ruins of the Roman and later Byzantine garrison town of Babylon, is where the story of Islamic Cairo began.

Within a century of the Arab conquest of Egypt, Fustat had become a great city. The tenth-century Persian geography book *Hudud al Alam* (*Boundaries of the World*) described it as the richest in the world. The Iraqi traveller and geographer Ibn Hawqal, who visited twice in the tenth century, admired its great markets and commercial centres, the flowering gardens and verdant parks. High praise also came from our old friend Muqaddasi, the Arab geographer from the same period, who compared its teeming population to locusts. What Baghdad had once been, he wrote, Fustat now was. 'I know of no city in all of Islam that is more impressive . . . Al Fustat has eclipsed Baghdad. It is the glory of Islam and the commercial centre of the universe. More magnificent than Baghdad, it is . . . the hub of the Orient.' Muqaddasi recorded a lovely moment of urban one-upmanship, a trait that survives in the ebullient Cairene show-off of today:

> One day as I was walking along the banks [of Fustat] and marvelling at the multitude of ships at anchor or just setting sail, a man said to me: 'Know, sir, that the ships moored in this port added to those that have sailed from here to other cities and settlements are so numerous that if they travelled

to your native town they could take on board all its population, all its machinery, all its stones, all its beams, so that, as one might say, they could carry off your entire city.'[2]

Fustat spawned a succession of separate royal and military suburbs in the same neighbourhood, from Al Askar (The Cantonment) in 751 to Ibn Tulun's settlement of Al Qatai (The Wards) in the 860s. Over the centuries each would be eclipsed and encompassed in turn by the royal city of Al Qahira, founded two miles to the north of Fustat in 969 by the Fatimid caliph Muizz li Din Allah's general Jawhar to mark the victorious campaign in Egypt. He chose a site slightly to the north of the Ibn Tulun Mosque, the Muqattam hills rising to the east, immediately to the west of the banks of the Khalij canal, a former pharaonic project rebuilt by Trajan to connect the Nile to the Red Sea and the holy cities of Arabia. This would be the new royal city, home to both the *rijal al sayf*, the men of the sword or military, and the *rijal al qalam*, the men of the pen or administrators.[3] Sweeping in from what is today Tunisia at the head of an army of 100,000, Jawhar caused a sensation when he arrived in Egypt. For a start, he carried with him 1,200 chests filled with money. Then there were countless camels loaded with huge millstones made of gold. A proclamation was issued promising freedom of religion for all Egyptians, be they Sunni Muslims, Christians or Jews. It set the tone for two centuries of Fatimid tolerance.

Al Qahira was the Victorious – from which Europeans derived Cahere, Caire and Cairo. Different legends surround the city's foundation. According to one version, the name came from the planet Mars, Al Qahir, which was in the ascendant when the first ground was broken – the court astrologers had judged this the most auspicious time. Another states that Muizz li Din Allah had ordered Jawhar to build a city, Al Qahira, which would rule the world. Of lasting significance for the Egyptian capital and the wider Muslim world to the present day was the foundation in 972 of Al Azhar, the Resplendent, a propaganda centre charged with promoting the minority sect of Shia Islam, and the first mosque and theological college built in Fatimid Cairo.

Muizz, the fourth Fatimid caliph, had succeeded his father Al Mansur in 953, and in his early twenties already ruled over most of what is today Morocco, Algeria and Tunisia. Having now displaced the once mighty Abbasids as masters of Egypt without much of a fight, and resolved to shift his imperial headquarters here, Muizz was determined to make the grandest possible entry.* In 972 or 973, at the head of a lavish,

---

* The first three Fatimid capitals were all in today's Tunisia, initially in Raqqada (909–21), southwest of Qairouan, then in Mahdia (921–48), before moving again to Al Mansuriya (948–72).

elephant-led procession that included three coffins containing the remains of his predecessors, he dismounted from his horse, led the prayers marking the end of Ramadan at the Eid al Fitr festival and delivered the Friday sermon, before resuming the procession to his palace, where he took his seat on a golden throne and assumed formal control of the city. Officially the Fatimids claimed descent from the Prophet Mohammed through his daughter Fatima – hence the name – and the caliph Ali. Shia Fatimid power, therefore, represented a decisive and highly controversial break from the orthodox Sunni rule of the Abbasids. Unofficially their legitimacy came down to power and money. When challenged by a Cairene on his contentious claim to the title of caliph, Muizz simply drew his sword. 'Here is my lineage,' he said. Then he thrust his hand into his purse, threw gold coins onto the ground and declared, 'And here is my proof.'[4]

Muizz's enthronement as caliph was a moment that reverberated long and loudly across the Middle East. For the first time in a millennium Egypt was once again a sovereign state. From this time until the Ottoman conquest five and a half centuries later, it would be at the forefront of the Dar al Islam with the expanding, merging city of Fustat-Cairo as its capital. Over time the Fatimid Empire would range across North Africa, encompass the Holy Cities of Mecca, Medina and Jerusalem and would spread east as far as the Tigris River in Iraq, west to the coast of Sicily, south into Yemen and north up to the Taurus Mountains in southern Turkey.

Muizz (r. 953–75) established a clear Fatimid strategy of administrative reform, religious tolerance and economic revival through trade, a direction continued by his son Aziz (r. 975–96), whose name was acknowledged in the Friday *khutba* across a great swathe of the Muslim world from the Red Sea to the Atlantic.* So sure was Aziz of his coming triumph over the Abbasid caliph in Baghdad that he spent 2 million dinars on a gilded palace ready to house his Iraqi captive. It was not to be. The maniacal persecutions of Jews and Christians, as well as Muslims, by the caliph Hakim (r. 996–1021) have been touched upon already. His caliphate proved the exception to the Fatimid rule of tolerance and pluralism. Arbitrary executions – of slaves, courtiers, concubines, Jews, Christians,

---

* Muizz will also be remembered as the man who commissioned the world's first fountain pen, in 953, as recorded in the tenth-century Fatimid manuscript *Kitab al Majalis wa 'l Musayarat* (*The Book of Sessions and Excursions*): 'We wish to construct a pen which can be used for writing without having recourse to an ink-holder and whose ink will be contained inside it. A person can fill it with ink and write whatever he likes. The writer can put it in his sleeve or anywhere he wishes and it will not stain nor will any drop of ink leak out of it. The ink will flow only when there is an intention to write.'

Muslims, anyone who incurred the caliph's displeasure, in fact – became commonplace. In 1017, egged on by some of his more enthusiastic supporters, Hakim proclaimed himself an incarnation of the deity, a move that would have lasting consequences to this day with the birth of a new cult.* Henceforth, the Fatimid caliph was at once imperial ruler and Ismaili imam, the temporal and spiritual leader of the faithful.†

A bright spot for Cairo amid the darkness of his caliphate was the foundation in 1005 of the Dar al Hikma, the House of Wisdom, an Egyptian counterpart to the institution of the same name in Baghdad. It quickly became an important centre for the study of astronomy, medicine and religion. Al Musabbihi, the court chronicler and friend of the caliph Hakim, described lectures given by Quranic readers, jurists, astronomers, grammarians, mathematicians, logicians, philologists and physicians, many of whom were appointed by the caliph on princely salaries. The Dar al Hikma was open to 'people of all walks of life'. Serious scholars and amateur bookworms alike were entitled to read and copy the books, making use of free ink, writing reeds, paper and inkstands. With something like 100,000 'manuscripts in all the domains of science and culture', it was, said the historian Ibn Abi Tayyi, a 'wonder of the world'.[5] The greatest achievement of the institute was a new *zij*, a set of astronomical tables compiled by Ahmed ibn Yunus al Hakimi, a substantial improvement on those produced under the intellectually inquisitive caliph Mamun in Baghdad in the ninth century. The most renowned scholar was Ibn Haytham, the father of optics and a pioneering theoretical physicist, known to medieval Europeans as Alhazen. Then there was the ophthalmologist Ammar ibn Ali, an innovator in the treatment of cataracts. A little over a century after this flourishing intellectual scene, the caliph Al Amir (r. 1101–30) established the Dar al Ilm, or Hall of Knowledge, close to the Western Palace.

Just as he had provided a priceless account of Jerusalem from his visit in 1047, the Persian poet, philosopher and traveller Nasir-i-Khusraw left a swooning portrait of Fustat and Cairo a year later. He described in detail the Suq al Qanadil, the Market of the Lamps, and the products it contained. It was without equal, he wrote, full of the most rare and precious

* The eleventh-century preacher Al Darazi embraced the new creed of caliph-as-incarnation-of-God. It took root in Lebanon and Syria, where its followers are now known as the Druze.
† The Ismailis represent a minority branch of Shia Islam, which differs from the largest school, the Twelvers. While Twelvers believe in twelve divinely ordained imams, the last of whom is Mohammed al Mahdi, destined to reappear on earth one day from occultation, Ismailis instead recognize the succession of the imamate through the seventh imam, Ismail ibn Jaafar, from whom they take their name.

goods from all over the world. There were tortoiseshell caskets, combs and knife handles, rock crystal worked into beautiful creations by skilful artisans, huge elephant tusks from Zanzibar, Abyssinian ox hide to be made into sumptuous slippers, copper vases from Damascus that shone so brightly one would swear they were gold. Khusraw listed the products he found in the market one day in December: roses, lilies, oranges, lemons, grapes, apples, dates, sugar-cane, gourds, garlic, onions, carrots and many other fruits, flowers and vegetables. He was particularly taken by the exquisitely delicate faience, 'so fine and so diaphanous that one can look through the walls of a vase and see one's hand on the outside'.[6]

Less than a century after its foundation, according to Khusraw, 'Cairo is a great city to which few cities can be compared'.[7] There were eight imposing mosques in Cairo and the same number in Fustat. He estimated the sultan owned 20,000 shops in Cairo and the same number of houses in Fustat. As for the caliphal palace, it boasted a retinue of 30,000, including 12,000 servants and 1,000 foot and horse guards. One of the most remarkable sights recorded by Khusraw was the seven- to fourteen-storey communal houses of Fustat, forerunners of the city's residential skyscrapers 1,000 years later. He writes about one resident who laid out a garden on his seventh-floor terrace and installed a water-wheel powered by an ox, which brought water up from ground level to irrigate his orange, banana and other fruit trees. Khusraw's account is no Marco Polo fantasy. It is supported by Ibn Hawqal and Muqaddasi, who both speak of houses up to seven storeys high. Fatimid Cairo was an urban marvel, and in time became the greatest city in the Islamic world. It was a triumph of architectural innovation and neck-craning verticality in which high-rise living became completely normal almost 1,000 years before skyscrapers first sprouted in Manhattan.

Two opulent palaces stood at the heart of the walled imperial capital. The Great Eastern Palace was a complex of buildings enlarged by successive rulers. It rambled magnificently over nine hectares and boasted imperial proportions – nine gates, 4,000 rooms and a western façade 345 metres long. There were gardens stocked with rare birds and exotic animals. Fourteen camel loads of snow were delivered daily from Mount Sinai to the royal kitchens where fifty staff prepared the caliph's favourite delicacies. Opposite the Eastern Palace was the smaller Western Palace, designed to accommodate Bayn al Qasrayn, literally Between the Palaces, a huge esplanade measuring 255 metres by 105 metres, the centrepiece of lavish Fatimid ceremonial and large enough to hold 10,000 cavalry. The north–south route through the city was the Qasaba – today's Sharaa al Muizz – which fed into Bayn al Qasrayn as it ran south from Bab al Futuh to Bab al Zuwayla. Al Azhar the Resplendent lay south-east of the Dar al Hikma and a little south of the Eastern Palace.

What lay behind this rapid rise to greatness and prosperity? In a word, trade. During the two centuries of Fatimid rule from 969 to 1171, Fustat and Cairo together became the great entrepôt of the West and a major player in the commerce between the Mediterranean and India. In his study of Cairo, Max Rodenbeck notes how, through this continent-spanning commercial nexus, Arabic trading terms steadily infiltrated into the English language:

> There was *fustian*, the tough blend of *cotton* – from the Arabic *qutn* – and linen made at Fustat. There was the *dimity* of Damietta, the *damask* of Damascus, the *gauze* of Gaza, the *muslin* of Mosul and the watered silk of Baghdad's Atabi quarter known as *tabby* cloth. There was soft *mohair* and delicate *chiffon*; and the *camisole*, the *ream*, the *sash*, the *sequin*, the *mattress* and the *sofa*. A shipment leaving Fustat might comprise *jars* of *camphor* or *syrup* or *sherbet*; sugar, *candy* and spices like *cinnabar*, *caraway*, *carob*, *cumin* and *sesame* seeds, enough to fill a *magazine* or *arsenal*, and certainly to require payment of a hefty *tariff*. An *admiral* of the highest *calibre* might command the vessel. Having consulted his *almanac* and imbibed a *carafe* brimming with an *elixir* of *attar* of *jasmine* when the sun reached its *zenith*, he would have himself *massaged* with a gentle *drubbing* before the *mizzen* mast, to the accompaniment of a *lute*.[8]*

All the world – its goods and its people – came to Cairo. Perhaps the most fascinating source for this period is the collection of Geniza documents of the Jewish community in Fustat, named after the storeroom (*geniza*) of the Ben Ezra Synagogue, where for around 1,000 years Jews routinely retained all papers bearing the name of God. There are more than a quarter of a million such documents, 193,000 of which were taken to Cambridge by the scholar Solomon Schechter after he had inspected them in Egypt in 1896–7. Most of them cover the period between the beginning of the eleventh century and the later years of the thirteenth and offer an extraordinarily rich insight into the medieval world of Mediterranean Jews. Apart from the

---

* Mohair from the Arabic *mukhayyar*, chosen; chiffon from *shafaf*, transparent; camisole from *qamis*; ream, *ruzma*; sash, *shash*; sequin, *sikka*; mattress, *matraha*; sofa, *suffa*; jar, *jarra*; camphor, *kafur*; syrup, *sharab*; sherbet, *sharbat*; sugar, *sukkar*; candy, *qandi*; cinnabar, *zunjufr*; caraway, *karawiya*; carob, *kharrub*; cumin, *kammun*; sesame, *simsim*; magazine, *makhzan*; arsenal from *dar al sinaa*, House of Industry; tariff, *taarifa*; admiral from *amir al bahr*, Lord of the Sea; almanac, *al manakh*; carafe, *gharrafa*; elixir, *al iksr*; attar, *itr*; jasmine, *yasmin*; zenith, *samat*; massage, *masaha*; drub, *daraba*; mizzen, *mizan*; lute, *al oud*.

predictable religious works, such as Bibles, prayer books and compendia of Jewish law, there are marriage contracts and divorce deeds, tracts on Sufi and Shia philosophy, Arabic fables, medical books and vast numbers of everyday documents.[9] Colourful vignettes and anecdotes abound, such as the twelfth-century letter from a teacher to a father, informing the man that, although his swotty son has been making great strides in his lessons, regrettably the boy's fellow students have smashed up his wooden writing-board.[10] The Geniza documents reveal, too, that Jews, Christians and Muslims lived together in Fustat, not in separate enclaves or ghettos.

Commercial contracts, letters, shopping lists, shipping details and information about customs and taxes in the Geniza documents reveal the sheer dynamism and commercial cosmopolitanism of the age. Fustat was connected to Africa and Europe, to Al Andalus, east across Asia to Samarkand and Ceylon. The papers show how the markets heaved with silk turbans from Spain, slave girls from Abyssinia and Europe, Egyptian flax, cheese from Jerusalem and Baalbek, Yemeni mattresses, ostrich feathers and hides from Abyssinia, Armenian rugs and carpets, fine Chinese porcelain and delicate silk, soaps, saffron, glue and resin from Sfax in Tunisia, steel swords from Damascus, Tabaristan brocade and upholstery, Arabian Sea pearls, Baltic amber, Indian teak furniture, copper from Mosul. In an inventory of the Fatimid caliphs' treasures, the fourteenth-century Egyptian historian Maqrizi listed priceless jewels, crystal vases, cups of amber, steel mirrors, gold plates, ivory inkstands, phials of musk, bejewelled swords and daggers and richly embroidered fabrics. According to the senior official Ibn al Say-rafi, the vizier Ibn Killis, a converted Jew from Iraq, left linen and cloth worth an extraordinary 500,000 dinars at his death in 991.[11]

Egyptian complaints about government inefficiency are the stuff of legend. 'Oh my God,' says my old friend Essam, an engineer. 'Everything that is bad about Egypt is in *that* building.' He is talking about the infamous Mugamma, nerve centre of 'a system of bureaucratic torture' that has bedevilled the lives of Egyptians for decades.[12] Yet it wasn't always like this.

In Fatimid Cairo, imperial grandeur, underpinned by a highly efficient administrative and tax system, was the order of the day. The caliph Aziz (r. 975–96) is said to have raised 220,000 dinars, the equivalent of a ton of refined gold, in three days. Importantly, trade did not depend on harmonious political and diplomatic relationships across the region, as elusive then as they are today. Since Fatimid Egypt was a heterodox Shia state in an almost exclusively orthodox Sunni world these relationships inevitably waxed and waned. Yet even when Sunni Tunisia and Fatimid Egypt were at war, merchants were still able to come and go as they pleased.

Medieval Muslims might have scorned the barbarian ways of European infidels, but they were not averse to doing business with them. From 996, the maritime republic of Amalfi maintained permanent representation in Fustat, while those inveterate traders, the Genoese and Venetians, were granted formal rights to do business in Egypt. In 1143 a trade agreement was signed with Roger II of Sicily. Around the same time Pisan merchants were given the use of a *funduq* or caravanserai. The Fatimid gold dinars minted in Cairo became standard international currency and held their value across the Middle East, Europe and Africa for two centuries.

While trade was the lifeblood of Fatimid Cairo, tolerance was its beating heart. They were two sides of the same coin. A sarcastic epigram from the time of Aziz exhorted the faithful to 'Become a Christian, for Christianity is the true religion, so much is patently clear today. Have faith in three persons and forsake all others as useless: the vizir Yakub is the Father, Aziz is the Son, and Fadl is the Holy Ghost.'[13] During the high summer of Fatimid rule under Mustansir (r. 1035–94), the longest ruling Muslim leader of Egypt, Jews and Christians were consistently promoted to the highest office, so much so that Muslim resentment occasionally burst out in literary form. The poet Rida ibn Thawb came up with the following satirical verses:

> These days the Jews have reached their dream
> They're rich; they reign supreme . . .
> O Egyptians, here's my advice to you
> Turn Jewish, since the heavens have turned Jew![14]

Badr al Jamali, an Armenian Christian, served as vizier from 1073 to 1094, during which time he assiduously promoted fellow Christians to senior positions. The Armenian community came to be highly respected by generations of caliphs. The caliph Hafiz (r. 1130–49) liked to receive twice-weekly history lectures from the Armenian patriarch, and a number of his successors enjoyed retreats in the quiet gardens of Coptic monasteries, where they were well looked after by hospitable monks. Generous royal donations for the upkeep of convents and churches flowed in return.

As minority Ismaili Shia in a majority Sunni region, the Fatimids were acutely sensitive to the perils of religious persecution. In 1136 the caliph Hafiz issued a decree whose language captures the Fatimid spirit of tolerance and respect for other faiths. It also strikes the modern reader as extraordinarily progressive for the time:

> We believe that we should spread wide the mantle of justice and benevolence and embrace the different religious communities with mercy and

compassion. Measures to improve conditions should include Muslims and non-Muslims alike, who should be provided with everything they might hope for in the way of peace and security.[15]

Tolerance and openness were not incidental to the roaring political and economic success of Fatimid Cairo. They were its very foundation, allowing the free flow of goods and ideas across the empire and beyond.

The Geniza documents provided literary testament to the prevailing cosmopolitanism of Fatimid Cairo. The city's architecture offered more monumental proof. A new style emerged from the late tenth century, born of the new dynasty's imperial pretensions. The promotion from tribute-paying governorate under the Abbasid caliphate of Baghdad to full-blown rival caliphate with its own royal capital needed to be reflected in appropriately grand fashion. The Fatimids chose to do so by melding a broad range of what they saw as the finest forms and styles from Iran and Iraq to Byzantium and Syria, fusing them into a markedly original departure from the more austere examples that had come before. The Iranian influence was felt in the domes and cupolas, the Syrian in the use of stone for gates and minarets. Byzantine decorative styles, already appropriated by the Umayyads of Damascus and Cordoba, were visible in the shell patterns adorning niches. Uniquely the façades of mosques in Fatimid Cairo were aligned to the streets, seen for the first time in the heavily decorated Aqmar Mosque. The style of minarets changed dramatically to what has been nicknamed the *mabkhara* or 'incense-burner' style, after the ribbed helmet sitting above a round or octagonal section supported by a rectangular shaft – the term was coined by the Orientalist Sir Richard Burton after hearing stories of the caliph Hakim burning incense in his minarets to perfume the mosques. Elaborate geometrical and floral designs and arabesques traced their way across public monuments in stone, stucco and wood, richer and more intricate than the Islamic world had ever known.

In what was likely an architectural bid to reach out to the Sunni majority as well as the Shia minority, the Fatimids built *mashhad* shrines to saints venerated by both schools, such as those to Sayyida Nafisa, Sayyida Ruqaya, Sayyida Zaynab and Imam al Hussain, whose severed head was brought from Ashkelon to Cairo in 1153 and rests in the Al Hussain Mosque next to Khan al Khalili to this day. Though the highpoints of Fatimid architecture – the royal palaces – have long since disappeared, traces of the imperial style nevertheless remain in a number of mosques, such as those of Hakim, Aqmar and Salih Talaai, as well as the trio of massive Fatimid gates, built between 1087 and 1092, that survive: the great rectangular towers of Bab al Nasr, Gate of Victory, round-towered Bab al Futuh, Gate of Conquest, complete with shafts for defenders to throw stones, grenades or burning oil on the heads of attackers, and the incomparable, fortress-like Bab al Zuwayla with its twin minaret towers and ramparts on which severed heads were displayed as late as the nineteenth century and which still offers one of the best views over Old Cairo.[16] Cairo's defensive architecture was decisively upgraded under the viziership of the Armenian Badr al Jamali, whose immense city walls and fortified gates provided a second layer of protection and whose style reflected the tastes and conventions of the Armenian and Syrian architects and builders employed. His introduction of stone, so elusive in Baghdad, proved an enduring architectural innovation for the Egyptian capital.

The later eleventh century saw renewed turbulence at the heart of the Fatimid Empire. Precipitated by drought and the inevitable ensuing famine, *Al shidda al uzma*, the Greatest Calamity, also known as the Mustansir Crisis of 1065–72, brought much of Egypt to its knees. Egypt, wrote the Ancient Greek historian Herodotus, was 'the gift of the Nile'. The river was a generous but capricious force, bringing great bounty one year, misery and death another. From the time of the pharaohs, the authorities had kept close watch on the river levels. A sophisticated Nilometer, still standing on the southern tip of Roda Island, was built after the Muslim conquest. The optimum summer flood level was sixteen cubits (each cubit was approximately fifty centimetres), which equated to decent agricultural production, government tax revenues and food prices. Less than sixteen cubits threatened drought and famine, often accompanied by plague, disorder and crime. More than this could mean devastating floods. According to the historian Masudi, Egyptians referred to the levels marking thirteen and fourteen cubits as Munkar and Nakir, the angels of the grave. Famine duly set in from 1065 and the prices of basic foodstuffs soared. Public standards of behaviour plummeted in parallel, to the point where the famished poor, having eaten horses, donkeys, cats and dogs, fell to new depths. 'So many dogs and cats were consumed that dogs became scarce,' Maqrizi wrote. 'Conditions worsened to the degree that people ate each other.' There are stories of men 'fishing' for human flesh on the streets from their terraces, using meat hooks attached to ropes to snare unwary passersby.

The hapless Mustansir was ruined, brought so low he was reduced to selling off his treasures one by one until his throne consisted of a ragged mat on the floor and he was left dependent on charity from a scholar's family, a loss of prestige so severe that the royal women of the household abandoned him, leaving a diminished entourage of three slaves. The imperial stables that had once housed 10,000 sleek horses now provided shelter to three distressed, mangy beasts. Political instability was rife. Twenty-two viziers came and went between 1062 and 1066. Large numbers of Jews emigrated and donations to religious foundations dried up. Houses in Fustat were abandoned. Unpaid soldiers and officials plundered the caliph's palaces, treasuries and libraries. 'Countless indescribably beautiful books' were stolen from the Dar al Hikma. Slaves and maids ripped off the covers of the less valuable volumes to make sandals, tearing out or burning the pages in between. Turkish soldiers looted 18,000 scientific volumes, together with 2,400 priceless manuscripts of the Quran, illuminated with gold and silver. In one day alone twenty-five camels loaded with books plodded from the caliph's palace to the home of the vizier Abu al Faraj, from where they were later stolen in turn. A general bought emeralds worth 300,000 dinars for the knockdown sum of 500 dinars.[17]

If the narrow picture in Cairo was grim, the broader regional scene was hardly more encouraging. The Fatimid Empire was fragmenting. The Barbary possessions slipped free from the mid-eleventh century. Then, in 1076, the Fatimid state lost the greater prize of Syria to the Seljuqs, occasioning a massive loss of government revenues – some 1.5 to 2.6 million dinars. The loss of this eastern bulwark left Egypt immediately exposed from the east, a threat made material with the Crusaders' invasion of the Holy Land and the sacking of Jerusalem in 1099.

Exceptional in so many ways, the Fatimids were not immune from the forces of history. In a process that would be understood by the great Arab historian of the fourteenth century, Ibn Khaldun, master theorist on the rise and fall of empires, the Egyptian Dynasty rose dramatically to prominence and power under forceful and energetic founders before – like the Umayyads of Damascus and the Abbasids of Baghdad before them – declining inexorably into indolence and irrelevance. Of the eight caliphs who succeeded Hakim from 1021, most ascended to the throne as children, leaving them vulnerable to the ambitions of predatory viziers, who were themselves battling for influence with competing parties of Egyptian, Berber, Turkish and Sudanese army generals. From 1135 Sunni resistance to the heretical Fatimids was so confident that new *madrassas* to promote orthodox Islam began to appear. The external threat started to take on a more menacing aspect from the middle of the twelfth century. In 1149 Christian forces sacked the port cities of Alexandria and Damietta. Five years later, the Turkish ruler Nur al Din, Light of the Faith, seized power in Damascus, putting Cairo squarely in his sights. Then, in 1167, the year that the Holy Roman Emperor Frederick Barbarossa defeated the forces of Pope Alexander III at the Battle of Monte Porzio, a clear danger appeared at the gates of Cairo itself.

On a fine spring morning that year, two Christian knights, Sir Hugh of Caesarea, a Knight Hospitaller, and Sir Geoffrey Fulcher, a Templar, envoys from King Amalric of Jerusalem, rode into Cairo on official business. Their mission was to conclude a deal that would bring pride and honour to the Franks and abject humiliation to Fatimid Egypt. Taking advantage of Egypt's vulnerable eastern flank, a Christian army had ridden across from Palestine and now pressed its cause.

The infidels' arrival followed treachery and disarray at the highest reaches of the Fatimid court. In 1163 the vizier Shawar was deposed, a move to which he responded by approaching the powerful ruler of Syria, Nur al Din, and offering him a third of the Egyptian tax haul in return for reinstating him as leader. No sooner had he been restored to office by an army led by the Kurdish commander Shirkuh than Shawar, duplicitous to the core, immediately reneged on his commitment to Nur al Din, entreating King Amalric for help against the Syrian. The ruse worked in the short term, but in 1167 Shirkuh was back again from Syria after the caliph Adid (r. 1160–71) requested foreign assistance against the Crusaders, who were moving against Cairo. This time Shirkuh brought along his nephew, a young man called Saladin – or Salah al Din al Ayyubi, Rectitude of Faith. Shawar once again called on the Franks. The diplomatic mission was dispatched to Cairo.

Some people have the knack of being in the right place at the right time. William, Archbishop of Tyre, was one such man. It is to this medieval prelate and diplomat that we owe the *Historia Rerum in Partibus Transmarinis Gestarum* (*History of Deeds Done Beyond the Sea*), which contains an extraordinary eyewitness account of the embassy to the Egyptian caliph. Reading it today, there is no mistaking the utter shock and awe of the European knights at the extravagance of the Fatimid court. Escorted by a detachment of infantry, they marched through Bab al Futuh and along the great processional way of Bayn al Qasrayn. Whichever way they looked came the overwhelming sight of imperial architecture, secular and spiritual by turns. Here first of all, just south of the gate, was the Mosque of Al Hakim, a spectacularly conceived monument on an epic scale – 120 metres by 113 metres – announced by two minarets presiding over a courtyard the size of a parade ground. Just before they reached the city's main esplanade, Between the Palaces, they passed the Aqmar Mosque on their left, a splendid edifice with a highly decorated façade of patterned niches, carved wood and stone medallions, a celebration of the return to splendour for Cairo and its divinely chosen leader, the tenth Fatimid caliph Amir (1101–30) bringing light and joy to his people.[18]

Adid's vizier marshalled the knights down long halls and past doors guarded by Sudanese soldiers with unsheathed swords, through another courtyard open to the elements, surrounded by arcades of marble pillars with fine mosaic floors and panelled ceilings carved and inlaid with gold. There were marble fountains, species of richly plumed exotic birds completely unknown to the European visitors, who may have felt increasingly unrefined with every step they took towards one of the greatest leaders of the Muslim world. Passing through another even more ornately decorated hall merely added to their confusion with the sight of parrots, giraffes and beasts so strange they could surely have been invented only by an artist.

> At last, after many turns and windings, they reached the throne room, where the multitude of the pages and their sumptuous dress proclaimed the splendor of their lord. Thrice did the vezir, ungirding his sword, prostrate himself to the ground, as though in humble supplication to his god; then, with a sudden rapid sweep, the heavy curtains broidered with gold and pearls were drawn aside, and on a golden throne, robed in more than regal state, the caliph sat revealed.[19]

Adid was around eighteen, little more than a pawn in the hands of his unscrupulous vizier Shawar, who related to him the great friendship and understanding that existed between the Fatimid state and King Amalric. It was shorthand for an alliance based on a large payoff from Muslim Egypt to Christian Jerusalem – in this case 400,000 dinars, in addition to an annual tribute of 100,000 dinars. Another way of looking at it would be to consider it protection money. Either way, the bluff knight Sir Hugh insisted on marking the treaty with a handshake with the imam-caliph, a diplomatic faux pas that scandalized the court. With a forced smile, the youthful Adid removed his glove and the deal was sealed.

The Franks were not going to withdraw without some sort of assurance that the tribute would be paid. Humiliatingly for the Fatimid state, a Treasury of Debt was established, complete with its own high commissioner and armed cavalry units to encourage prompt payment of the tribute. For a bastion of the Islamic faith like Cairo it was a galling reversal of fortune. For the Franks, however, it was a moment for exultation. 'The day Christian forces entered this large Muslim city was a glorious day. The entire length of the ramparts, all the towers and gates . . . the caliph's residence itself were ceded to the Christian knights,' who were all granted free access to the caliph whenever they liked. An ignominious insult to the faithful, the treaty that made a vassal state out of Fatimid Egypt proved extremely short-lived. This was a time when leaders held little store by fixed alliances. Scarcely had the ink dried on the agreement than, in 1168, Amalric launched his fourth invasion of Egypt. Closing in on Cairo, he first seized Bilbeis, forty miles north-east of the city, massacred the local population to a man, woman and child, and took Shawar's son prisoner. 'Your son Tari wonders whether I thought Bilbeis a piece of cheese that I might eat,' he wrote mockingly to the vizier. 'Yes, in truth, Bilbeis is my cheese and Cairo is my butter.'[20]

In the latest round of opportunist, on-again-off-again alliances, Adid now appealed to Nur al Din for urgent military help against the infidels. Yet this was not enough to resist the invasion. Desperate measures were required for the defence of the city. Orders were given to evacuate, then torch, Fustat, probably to prevent another massacre as well as to stop the Crusaders using it as a staging ground from which to launch the final assault on Cairo. The combination of 20,000 barrels of naphtha and 10,000 lighted torches produced an inferno that lasted fifty-four days and turned Fustat into a sandy ruin.* This, and the news that Shirkuh was fast approaching with a relief force, persuaded Amalric to retreat yet again. Reflecting the new balance of power, the Kurdish general appointed himself vizier for a couple of months, then bestowed the title on his nephew Saladin. To this role the Fatimid puppet caliph Adid added the honorific Al Malik al Nasir, the Supporter-king.

Adid died in 1171, leaving Saladin in charge in Cairo on behalf of Nur al Din. The funeral completed, there followed unexpected excitement in the caliph's palace. Ibn al Athir, whom we last met recounting the sacking of Jerusalem, described Saladin's discovery of fabulous royal treasures and enormous precious stones in the vaults. 'One mountain-size ruby was seventeen dirhams or miskals [2,400 carats]. There can be no doubt about it; I saw it with my eyes and weighed it myself. The pearls also had no peer. Among the emeralds was one four fingers long.'[21] Rather than use these treasures to enrich himself, Saladin sent a share to his overlord Nur al Din, distributed a good deal among his soldiers *pour encourager les autres* and sold off the rest to increase the reserves in the treasury. In an exceptional example of statesmanship that might serve as a reproof to

---

* There is considerable uncertainty about the causes of the fire and the extent of the destruction. The archaeological evidence is elusive, the Geniza documents are completely silent and the survival of Amr Mosque and Qasr al Sham, the five-hectare stronghold that encompasses Coptic Cairo today, is mysterious, to say the least. There are some suggestions that the fire may have been more limited than claimed by the medieval sources, part of anti-Christian riots, as tensions within the city escalated with the Crusaders arriving at Cairo's eastern gates.

some of the region's more kleptocratic leaders today, he took nothing for himself. Much of the caliph's library of 120,000 volumes he gave to his chancellor, the *qadi* Al Fadil. Generous with one hand, Saladin was steely with the other, evicting 18,000 officials, courtiers, assorted hangers-on and family members from the palace and segregating the 250 or so Fatimid males strictly from all women to ensure that over time the Fatimid Dyn- asty would be altogether extinguished. Nur al Din died in 1174, creating the opportunity for Saladin to seize outright power, capture Damascus later that year and receive his proclamation as Sultan of Egypt and Syria from Mustadi, the Abbasid caliph in Baghdad, in 1175. There was a decided irony in the fact that the young man originally sent to Cairo to prop up the ailing Fatimid Dynasty was the man who finally destroyed it. Then he went one step further by founding his own dynasty in its place, named after Saladin's father; the Ayyubids reigned over Egypt and Syria until 1250.

If Saladin brought down one edifice that had endured through two centuries, he raised another that would last more than 800 years and survives gloriously today. He had witnessed first-hand the vulnerability of Cairo's defences. The formidable citadel, combined with new city walls, was to end that weakness. The imperial capital of Cairo and the trading emporium of Fustat would together be enclosed within a single outer perimeter.

Work started immediately on the citadel, built between 1176 and 1184. It became the greatest fortress in the Middle East and the seat of govern- ment in Egypt until the late nineteenth century. From these ramparts generations of Ayyubids, Mamluks, Ottomans and the khedival rulers held sway. And with the exception of the hiccoughs that were the Fifth Crusade (1217–21), the Seventh Crusade (1248–54) and the Alexandria Crusade (1365), Egypt would be free of Frankish invaders until Napoleon's arrival in 1798.

Meticulous in his preparations, just as the caliph Mansur had been in choosing the location for Baghdad along the Tigris, Saladin picked the site of his great fortress carefully. Pieces of meat were hung up in various locations across the city. Those put up in the breezy Muqattam hills stayed fresh longest. Set on elevated land above Cairo that put it beyond the range of siege weapons of the time, it occupied a completely dominant position. The foundation inscription on Bab al Mudarraj, the western gate, hails 'this magnificent citadel close to the God-protected city of Al Qahira, on the strong hill of Armah, which combines utility and beauty and gives sanctuary to whoever seeks shelter in the shadow of his kingdom'.[22]

Ibn Jubayr, the itinerant geographer from Andalusia, sailed into Cairo in the early summer of 1183. He was in time to see the final stages of construction of this 'strong and impregnable fortress' being completed at breakneck speed. A devout Muslim, he had been overjoyed to see Saladin's latest batch of Christian captives, bound behind camels, being marched from Alexandria to the Egyptian capital, where they were put to work on one of the medieval world's greatest forced-labour projects – Al Maqrizi reckoned there were 50,000 prisoners slaving away on the citadel. After the embarrassing bending of the knees to the Crusaders in 1167, a disgrace to the Muslim world, Islamic Cairo was once again demonstrating the power and glory of the true faith. The citadel was 'a wonder amongst wonders'.[23]

Baha al Din Qaraqush was the man entrusted with its construction. Building materials came from far and wide, in addition to the locally available limestone of the Muqattam. Many pyramids in Giza were demolished, the stones transported on a giant, specially constructed causeway. More came from fifteen miles south of Cairo.

Apart from the commanding view the citadel gives, its scale is what most impresses. The nearest thing England has to it is the Tower of London or Westminster Hall, finished by William II in 1099 as the Crusaders ransacked Jerusalem and the largest hall of its kind in Europe. Yet these are mere minnows when compared with Saladin's citadel, which is a city in its own right. The sunburnt walls of the north-eastern military section alone – a bulging thirteen-hectare polygon of around 560 metres by 320 metres containing two museums and the Mosque of Suleiman Pasha – are more than a mile long, three metres thick and on average ten metres high. Separated from it by a curtain-wall and towers, the heavily fortified southwestern section, which contained the royal residence, is almost exactly the same size. Today it is home to the nineteenth-century Mohammed Ali Mosque, two further mosques, the Spiral Well and the Al Gawhara palace-museum, a nineteenth-century complex which consisted of military barracks, schools, a gunpowder factory, an arsenal and a mint. The Crusader castle of Krak des Chevaliers in Syria is often held up as the benchmark for medieval castles in the Middle East. T. E. Lawrence considered it 'perhaps the best preserved and most wholly admirable castle in the world'. It is unarguably a great feat of engineering and construction, and aesthetically its setting on the summit of a 650-metre hill in the Homs Gap is sublime, but it too is a showy upstart when held up against Saladin's citadel. More tragically, it has been severely damaged during recent fighting in the Syrian civil war.

Almost equally impressive, but largely invisible by definition, is the Spiral Well, a remarkable engineering project to supply water to the growing city on a hill. Workers dug two shafts, almost entirely through rock, which together measured ninety metres. Waterwheels, driven by oxen which spent their whole lives underground, brought the water up in two stages, first to a cistern halfway up the upper shaft, thence to the surface. The first shaft was wide enough to accommodate a sloping ramp to take the uncomplaining beasts of burden to their subterranean duties – hence the spiral.

Work on the citadel outlasted Saladin, as did that on the hugely ambitious wall, which was to run from the Nile to the Nile via the citadel at its heart. Much of it was indeed finished, as we know from the twelfth-century wandering scholar, physician and early Egyptologist Abd al Latif, who wrote of a stone wall enclosing Fustat, Cairo and the citadel.

The citadel unquestionably represents Saladin's greatest architectural legacy to Cairo. Equally enduring for Egypt and the wider Middle East on a more spiritual level was his swift and decisive return to Islamic orthodoxy after the 200-year Ismaili Shia experiment of the Fatimids. Work began on his first *madrassa* as early as 1170 in the heart of Fustat, appropriately next to the Mosque of Amr ibn al As, the first mosque in Egypt. Saladin had personally founded another four by the time construction of the citadel and city walls began, with nine more established during the rest of his reign. They represented all four of the orthodox schools of Islam and were at the vanguard of what has been termed a 'Sunni revival' stretching from Baghdad to Damascus and Cairo, turning out new generations of more or less homogeneous Islamic scholars and leaders to define, unify and strengthen the faith. Politically speaking, it has been argued, 'the madrassa saved Islam', spearheading a concerted Sunni revival and striking a blow for greater Islamic unity.[24] Originally established to propagate the Fatimids' brand of Ismaili Shia Islam, Al Azhar was stripped of its powers and influence as a congregational mosque and school by Saladin and his immediate successors. It was radically realigned by the Mamluks (r. 1250–1517) to provide and promote the theological underpinnings of orthodox Sunni Islam. Today its influence in the Sunni Muslim world is considerable, with Muslims from far beyond the borders of Egypt consulting its teachings on all aspects of Islamic law and the *fatwas* it pronounces.

In 1182, Saladin left Egypt, 'the mistress who tried in vain to separate me from my faithful spouse', Syria.[25] Called away to wage the long *jihad* against the Crusaders, above all Reynald de Châtillon and Baldwin IV, the 'Leper King' of Jerusalem, he was never to return. By 1187 he was ready to move against the Holy City, weak and divided under its new monarch, Guy de Lusignan. He took to the field against a thirsty and exhausted Frankish army at the Battle of Hattin. 'They were closely beset as in a noose, while still marching on as though being driven to death that they could see before them, convinced of their doom and destruction and themselves aware that the following day they would be visiting their graves,' wrote the twelfth-century Kurdish historian Baha al Din, one of Saladin's advisers.[26]

Their fears were well founded. Saladin's forces routed the Christians, capturing or killing the great majority. The few thousand who survived were marched back to Cairo as prisoners and pressed into forced labour on the city walls alongside their fellow Christians. Saladin treated King Guy graciously, presenting him with iced sherbet and sparing him – 'It is not the custom of kings to kill kings.' The despised Reynald, however, was executed on the spot after repeated attacks on caravans of Muslim pilgrims and merchants and his wilful failure to respect the sanctity of Mecca and Medina, which he attacked in 1182, attempting to seize the Prophet Mohammed's body and exhibit it for a fee. Hospitallers and Templars were felled where they stood. After Hattin, the Crusader kingdoms never recovered.

Saladin himself waited until 2 October 1187, the anniversary of the Prophet Mohammed's Night Journey, before making his triumphal entry into Jerusalem. Ibn al Athir recorded how 'Saladin ordered the purification of the Aqsa Mosque and the Dome of the Rock of all the filth and impurities' of the eighty-eight-year Christian occupation. There were tears of joy as the Friday sermon was preached in front of the victorious commander. Imad al Din, the Persian historian and favourite of Saladin, described how his beaming master looked as though he was surrounded by 'the halo of the moon'.[27] After the horrors of 1099, the Holy City was once again in Muslim hands.

Richard the Lionheart's Crusaders never recaptured Jerusalem. It remained under Muslim control until 1229, decades after Saladin's death in 1193. One should also recall that, on taking Jerusalem, Saladin was petitioned to destroy the Church of the Holy Sepulchre. He refused. Though the dynasty he founded proved short-lived, his personal career was extraordinarily successful. He managed to eliminate the Fatimids, unite Syria and Egypt and retake Jerusalem, winning a place in Arab and Muslim history. Perhaps the final irony beyond the grave is the fact that, though he was a Kurd, more than 800 years after his death, his coat of arms, the Eagle of Saladin, remains the coat of arms for staunchly Arab Egypt, Iraq, Palestine and Yemen.

The last years of the twelfth century saw Fustat's fortunes fading.

Ravaged by the fire of 1168, undermined by the growing political and commercial power of Cairo, increasingly it played second fiddle to the newer royal settlement. Just as Fustat had swallowed up Memphis, so Cairo expanded over Fustat. Egyptians started referring to Cairo as Misr (Egypt)– as they do today – relegating Fustat to Misr al Qadima, Old Cairo.

With a scholarly disregard for such trifles, the pre-eminent Jewish philosopher Maimonides, author of *Dalalat al Hairin* (*The Guide for the Perplexed*), came to settle in Fustat in around 1165. Born in Cordoba, the polymath first spent several years in Fez before moving to Egypt, where he became the leader of its Jewish community, chief of the Jewish judiciary and doctor of Saladin's eldest son, Al Afdal. Notwithstanding his exceptional career, intellectual life in Cairo was withering under the more restrictive, less tolerant atmosphere of the Ayyubids. The lasting victory for orthodox Sunni Islam, ousted for two centuries by the Fatimids, was imposed at the cost of the freewheeling intellectual spirit that had animated Cairo for so long. It was a case of more religion, less philosophy, and the scholarly compass narrowed accordingly. 'Debate about the correct Islamic manner of washing, or eating, or over questions like whether a woman need perform ritual ablutions after a visitation by jinns, replaced philosophical conjecture and scientific invention.'[28]

The twelfth century ended in another Nile-driven apocalypse for Cairo. In 1200 the flood level was less than thirteen cubits, its second lowest since the Arab conquest more than half a millennium earlier. It spelled disaster for the city and its people. The Iraqi scholar Abd al Latif saw the rich leave Cairo in their droves, abandoning the poor to fend for themselves in a more macabre version of dog eat dog. They were reduced, he wrote, to eating 'carrion, corpses, dogs and the excrement and filth of animals'. That was already disgusting but worse followed when 'they began to eat little children'. At first it was a surreptitious novelty. Later the practice became normal and people 'developed quite a taste for these detestable foods'. A large number of cannibals moved across to the island of Roda, from where they launched human-hunting raids, stockpiling corpses in impromptu larders. Whichever street you walked along, it was impossible not to see or touch dead bodies or those in their death throes. The death toll in the city was 'incalculable'. The total number of registered dead was 100,000, he reported, with the true figure far higher.[29] The famine eviscerated Fustat and swung the pendulum still further in Cairo's favour.

In his *Histories*, Herodotus told his audience that the waxing and waning of cities was part of the wider pattern of history, noting that 'human prosperity never abides long in the same place'.[30] And so it was that while the Egyptian capital was undergoing its ghastly torments at the dawn of the thirteenth century, 2,000 miles to the west another Arab city, the 'Mecca of the West', was about to enjoy its greatest golden age.

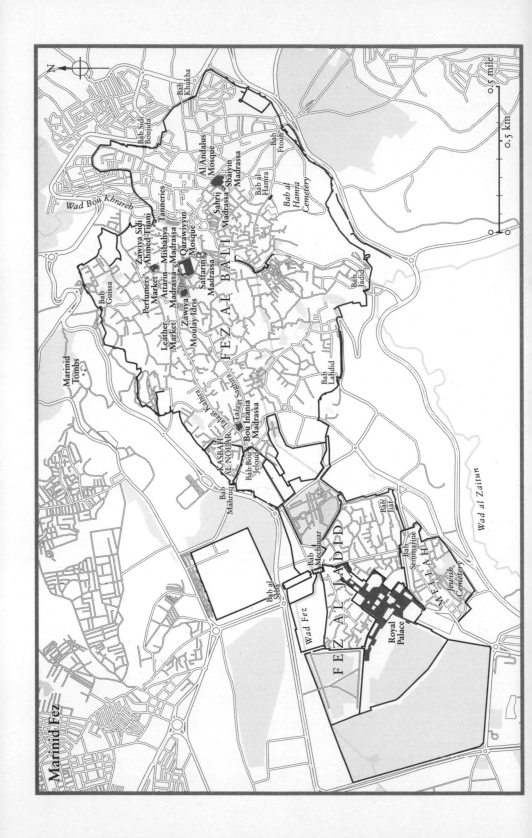

Marinid Fez

7

Fez – The Athens of Africa
(13th Century)

A World it is to see, how large, how populous, how well-fortified and walled this citie is.

Al Hassan ibn Mohammed al Wazzan al Fassi
(also known as Leo Africanus), *Description of Africa*, 1550

You get lost in Fez. It can be maddening, intimidating, sometimes even marriage-straining, but it is also essential. It takes time to realize this, but the elegant paradox about Fez is that to find this elusive city you must first lose yourself in it. In other words, the discovery, which can only ever be partial, must come from loss. While multicoloured and many-scented life explodes on the streets, much of it outwardly unchanged over the centuries, high walls and closed doors still hide some of Fez's finest, most intimate treasures. Step into one of the city's grander homes, with an orange tree and fountain resplendent in the centre of a tiled courtyard sheathed in marble, and the contrast between blandness without and brilliance within still entrances. 'A noncommittal expanse of earthen wall in the street hides a little Alhambra of one's own, a miniature paradise shielded from the gaze of the world,' wrote the American author Paul Bowles, who lived half a lifetime in Morocco.[1]

Within these dozen or so miles of encircling sandstone walls 250,000 Fassis still live in a bewildering medieval warren of 10,000 streets and alleys, making it the largest car-free urban space on earth. The confusion came not through accident but design. More than half of the Old City's streets were deliberately built as culs-de-sac, which were conducive to the residents' security while providing all the amenities they required in their self-contained quarter. I got comprehensively and repeatedly lost on my first visit to Fez and, thirty years later, on my last. When my phone's navigation app announced that it was 'unable to find a route' during one foray into this intense and tumultuous labyrinth, the news came as a thrill rather than a disappointment. Medieval Fez had outsmarted the Californian prophets of technology.

'For me the medina of Fez is like a veiled, conservative, sly woman,' chuckles Hassan al Janah, a veteran guide. 'You need time, for the woman to trust you. Maybe she'll take off her veil, maybe her *jalaba*.' He looks at my wife, laughs again less confidently and decides to end the analogy there.

Eventually, we find our way down to Sahat al Saffarin, or Coppersmiths' Square, where metal workers pound away in a symphony of sound and fury. This ancient quarter of Fez thrills to the random rhythms of their orchestra, as it has done for more than 1,000 years of banging, beating, bashing, smashing, crashing, tapping, knocking and hammering. Here in the very heart of Fez, pots, pans and platters, trays, trinkets, tajines and teapots, beakers and buckets, cups, colanders and cauldrons big enough for a small child to swim in, incense burners, samovars and couscous steamers, boxes for tea, sugar, jewellery and any number of unknown treasures take shape under this staccato barrage. Fez is a mirror, says an old proverb; a moment of silence here is as extraordinary as the din and racket would be anywhere else.[2]

Could quiet study and contemplation be possible amid this thunderous, concentration-breaking cacophony? Were medieval students even able to hear themselves think as they tried to navigate through the most brain-tormenting courses – the tortuous rigours of *fiqh* Islamic jurisprudence, *faraid* law of inheritance, *tasawwuf* mysticism, *mantiq* logic, *balaghah* rhetoric, poetry, prose and panegyrics, science, astronomy and arithmetic? The questions occur because just across from the squatting smiths, only a few metres away beneath a sloping fringe of green tiles and a limp Moroccan flag, right next to the green-awninged Crémerie de la Place, which is doing a brisk business in mint teas and soft drinks, a carved wooden screen door beneath a tall arch marks the entrance to one of the world's oldest and most remarkable libraries.

Khizanat al Qarawiyyin, the Qarawiyyin Library, is the nucleus of Fez's defining architectural and cultural landmark. In 859, a century before Cairo's Al Azhar was established, Fatima al Fihri, the pious, intellectually curious daughter of a wealthy merchant originally from Qairouan in present-day Tunisia, used her life-changing inheritance to found the Qarawiyyin Mosque and Madrassa – the first woman known to have done so in the Islamic world (extraordinarily the library still retains her ninth-century diploma, a wooden board bearing writing barely legible beneath the accumulated murk of a millennium). Her sister Mariam founded the Andalusian Mosque on the opposite, eastern bank and the city grew in two settlements around these two mosques: Adwat al Qarawiyyin on the western bank of the river and Adwat al Andalus on the eastern. From its earliest incarnations as a modest little mosque with four transverse aisles, the Qarawiyyin grew to include a university and library over the following centuries, during which it was repeatedly restored and enlarged. Under the Almoravid Dynasty's massive remodelling of 1135, which raised the number of aisles to twenty-one, it swelled to accommodate 22,000 worshippers, its surface area more than quadrupling to almost 6,000 square metres. The forest of arched colonnades mushroomed in parallel, giving rise to a local saying, 'The man who should count the columns of Qarawiyyin would go mad.' Today, almost 1,200 years after its foundation, it is internationally recognized as 'the oldest existing and continually operating educational institution in the world'.[3]

The leading lights among the Qarawiyyin alumni represent a roll-call of some of the greatest minds in the medieval Islamic world. In the twelfth century the Jewish scholar Maimonides, the pre-eminent Jewish philosopher of the Middle Ages and sometime physician in Saladin's household, studied here, together with 'the greatest master', Ibn al Arabi, the Andalusian mystic, poet and philosopher. Ibn al Khatib, the Granadan polymath, poet, historian, physician, politician and exile, came to the Qarawiyyin in the fourteenth century, alongside his prodigy and fellow Andalusian poet and politician, Ibn Zamraq, and Ibn Marzuq, the Moroccan author of the self-aggrandizing hagiography *The Correct and Fine Traditions About the Glorious Deeds of Our Master Abul Hasan* (r. 1331–51). Towering above his fourteenth-century counterparts was the magisterial Ibn Khaldun, pioneering historian, historiographer and author of the genre-breaking *Muqaddimah* universal history, father of sociology, political addict and most distinguished Qarawiyyin alumnus bar none. In the sixteenth century Ibn al Wazzan, the Andalusian diplomat, traveller and author better known in the West as Leo Africanus, who led one of the most picaresque lives and later left a long, trenchant and wonderfully detailed account of Fez, was a student here. He was staggered by the sheer size of the Qarawiyyin, 'being of so incredible a bigness' that 900 oil lamps were required to light it every night. Its circumference measured one and a half miles, with thirty-one major gates in its encircling wall. And if you listen to some of Fez's more enthusiastic guides, the Qarawiyyin's alumni in the tenth century even included Gerbert of Aurillac, the future Pope Sylvester II, although hard evidence of his attendance appears vanishingly elusive.[4]

Founded by one woman in the ninth century, the Qarawiyyin was restored by another in the twenty-first. In 2012 the Moroccan-Canadian

architect Aziza Chaouni, who grew up in Fez, was educated at Harvard
and Columbia and had long been drawn to the 'magical aura' of the
Qarawiyyin, was selected to restore the library. By then it was suffering
from myriad structural problems: abysmal drainage, inadequate insul-
ation, broken tiles, damaged wooden beams and suicidal electrics. 'It was
like healing wounds,' she says. There was also a strong family connection
that resonated. In the nineteenth century Chaouni's great-grandfather
used to travel into Fez from the countryside on the back of a mule, just
for the honour of studying at Qarawiyyin. A great-uncle was a copper-
smith who contributed to the clashing symphony of Sahat al Saffarin in
a workshop a stone's throw away.

Over the next four years the library was transformed through the sensitive introduction of new technologies. 'I didn't want the building to
become an embalmed cadaver,' Chaouni says. 'There has to be a fine balance between keeping the original spaces, addressing the needs of current
users, including students, researchers and visitors, and integrating new
sustainable technologies – solar panels, water collection for garden irrigation, and so on.'[5] A new sewerage system with subterranean canals has
resolved – for now – the problem of moisture. Digital locks guard access
to the rare books room, while air-conditioning controls the humidity levels
that caused such damage in the past.

Among its 4,000 books and ancient manuscripts are a number of literary treasures: a manuscript on the Maliki school of Islamic jurisprudence
by Ibn Rushd, better known in the West as Averroes; some of the oldest
accounts of the life of the Prophet Mohammed, including Imam al Bukhari's *Hadith*; an original, personally annotated fourteenth-century
manuscript of Ibn Khaldun's *Muqaddimah*; and a priceless ninth-century
copy of the Quran, elegantly transcribed in dancing Kufic script on camel
skin, still retaining its binding after more than 1,100 years. Some of the
library's holdings flowed from the Marinid Dynasty's ascendancy of the
thirteenth and fourteenth centuries, when battlefield victories in the Iberian Peninsula won literary, as well as territorial, prizes. The library's
security was always at a premium, according to Al Jaznai, author of *Kitab
Zahrat al As fi bina Madinat Fez* (*Account of the Myrtle Flower in the
Foundation of the City of Fez*), a chronicle published around 1365. The
books were kept behind three iron doors, with three separate keys held
by three different men.[6]

Today, if you manage to talk your way into the private library, dash up
a flight of green-tiled steps for a glimpse into the restored reading room –
an oasis of calm for a couple of disconsolate students wading through
books, notwithstanding the coppersmiths' *Sturm und Drang* – the

timeworn caretaker, his pockets full of jangling keys, still has to find his way through a series of locks on the wrought iron door at the end of a corridor that once connected the library to the mosque. To adapt a saying of the fifth-century BC Greek philosopher Heraclitus, nothing changes in Fez, everything stays the same.

Yet perhaps that is not quite true, because today the once diminutive Qarawiyyin completely lords it over Fez al Bali, the Old City *medina*, in whose centre it stands. At street level this is most evident in the high, buff-walled perimeter, punctuated by a series of grand arched entrances, beyond which non-Muslims cannot go. The streets here narrow suddenly, as though overcome by the sacred space at which they have arrived. All roads in Fez, one way or another, lead to the Qarawiyyin. Its architectural dominance is even more emphatic in an aerial view of the city, which reveals a vast green quadrangle topped with a grey, green-lined courtyard. The Qarawiyyin marks the south-eastern point of what Fassis refer to proudly as the 'golden triangle' of the city. Immediately to the west, so close the two structures virtually merge into each other, is the Zawiya Moulay Idris, the extravagantly decorated shrine dedicated to Idris II, co-founder of Fez and son of Idris I, first founder of the city and of the Idrisid Dynasty (r. 788–974) of Morocco and great-great-great-grandson of the Prophet Mohammed. Then, a few streets north of the Qarawiyyin, is the last of the trio of green-roofed centrepieces, the Zawiya Sidi Ahmed Tijani, home to the tomb of the eighteenth-century Sufi sheikh and founder of the eponymous Tijani order, whose shrine regularly draws in crowds of joyful Muslim pilgrims from right across Africa and beyond.

'It's one of the oldest and greatest cities in the world,' says Ahmed Sentissi, bespectacled doyen of Fez restaurateurs and hoteliers. He is sitting grandly in his Mnebhi Palace on the famous Talaat Saghira street, once the head-quarters of Marshal Lyautey, the first French Resident-General of Morocco from 1912 to 1925.

Sentissi is right, though it is difficult to pinpoint exactly how old the city is. Long before its golden age, under the Berber Marinid Dynasty (r. 1244–1465) during the thirteenth and fourteenth centuries, the foundation of Fez is buried deep in myth and legend. Early Muslim authors predict-ably give the story a strong Islamic underpinning, establishing Fez as a holy city from the outset.

One of the earliest Marinid accounts to survive, written around 1326 and attributed to the shadowy author Abu al Hassan Ali ibn Abi Zar, is *The Entertaining Companion Book in the Garden of Pages from the Chronicle of the Kings of Morocco and the History of the City of Fez.*

The *Rawd al Qirtas*, as it is known, describes a fantastical, completely impromptu meeting between Idris II, who is preparing to stake out his new city, and a Christian monk 'over 150 years of age'. The monk tells Idris that there used to be a city called Zef on the site, and that one day a man named Idris, descended from the Prophet, would 'renew it, revive it from oblivion, make stand its ruins; and that its importance would be great, its destiny momentous'.[7] In a scene remarkably similar to the foundation legend of Baghdad, Idris declares he is that man.*

Both Al Jaznai and Ibn Abi Zar record how the city acquired its name. 'The name of that [earlier] town was Zef,' says Idris. 'I shall reverse this name' and call the city Fez.[8] Another, more plausible, legend claims that Fez derives from the word for an axe, which was supposedly unearthed during the construction of the walls. The legends attribute the foundation of Fez to either Idris I in 789 or his son Idris II in 807. Most probably Idris senior founded a city on the right bank and Idris junior another on the left.[9] By the later twelfth century the two separate walled settlements merged into one city.

Like many great cities, its location was auspicious. It lay at 400 metres of altitude on the edge of the Sais plain, near the confluence of the Fez and Sebou rivers at the intersection of two major trade and communication routes: the first running north–south from the Mediterranean coast across the Sahara, Middle Atlas and High Atlas mountain ranges and into West Africa and the 'Land of the Blacks', passable all year round; the second running west–east from the shores of the Atlantic across to Algeria and, for many pilgrims and merchants, onwards to Arabia and Mecca – owing to its rich Islamic pedigree, one of Fez's nicknames is the 'Mecca of the West'. To its advantageous location on established routes should be added the proliferation of water supplies, so abundant that unlike in Jerusalem, where invaders, from Seleucid times in the fourth century BC to the British and Israelis in the twentieth, were able to hijack its water supply in Bethlehem, even if an enemy diverted the course of the Fez River, the city could survive, such were the stores of subterranean water, with 360 springs and numerous wells all around.

Blessed with ever-running water, Fez was lavishly provided with the finest construction materials. It was close both to quarries, which offered

---

* In his *History* the ninth-century scholar Tabari tells the story of a Christian doctor meeting the Abbasid caliph Al Mansur at the moment he is about to found Baghdad in 762. The Christian tells him of a local tradition: a man called Miklas will found a city between the Tigris and Sarat Canal called Al Zawra, or the Crooked. 'By God, I am that man!' Mansur exclaims. 'I was called Miklas as a boy, and then the name fell into disuse!' Nestorian monks also feature in a number of the foundation legends of Baghdad.

up immense quantities of stone, sand and lime, and the forests of the Middle Atlas, which supplied plenty of oak and cedar. It was also surrounded by fertile arable land, which produced sufficient food – cereals, olives, vines and fruit – to supply a growing city, together with grazing for livestock – sheep, goats and cows.[10] Although in the head-scrambling heat of summer, when the mercury rises well into the forties, it might stretch the visitor's imagination to regard Fez as a place of mild weather, Ibn Khaldun, while developing his theory on the influence of climate on human character, contrasted the hot-spirited 'Negroes' and Egyptians ('dominated by joyfulness, levity and disregard for the future') with people from more temperate climes, who were thriftier, moodier and more preoccupied with planning ahead. Fez, he wrote, was 'surrounded by cold hills', its inhabitants 'sad and gloomy and ... too much concerned for the future'. Although a man in Fez might have years' worth of wheat stored at home, he still goes to the market early 'because he is afraid to consume any of his hoarded food'.[11] Ibn Khaldun was not the last writer to remark on the Fassis' tendency towards thriftiness, seriousness and even melancholy.

Although located on the edge of the Sais plain, the ancient Idrisid city of Fez, as opposed to the wide-avenued Ville Nouvelle built by the French in the first half of the twentieth century, actually sprawls down into and across a scooped-out hollow. 'Even at first glimpse, Fez startles by its strangeness,' wrote Rom Landau, the Polish-British sculptor, who spent more than twenty years writing over a dozen books about Morocco from 1948 until his death in 1974. 'It clings to the sides of a hill-ringed valley, as though to the inside of a bowl, and all of it is visible from the opposite hill. There is nothing expansive or truly romantic about these densely-packed blocks of houses, jostling and crowding one another like the tightly interlocked pieces of a child's building set.' There was no dazzling white-ness as one might find in, say, Tripoli, but instead 'the impersonally morose grey-white of unwashed bed-sheets'.[12]

From a confirmed romantic who was completely bewitched both by Morocco in general and Fez in particular, it is a curious verdict. Though the houses do indeed tumble pell-mell down into the bowl, hiding their rich, treasure-filled interiors behind high, mostly windowless walls and closed doors, the view across the city from the Marinid Tombs, site of a former palace designed to give the most panoramic outlook over the *medina*, is unquestionably one of the world's great sights. The broader outlook from here takes in the rambling Sais plain, retreating hills of olive groves and, farther afield, the sometimes snowy summits of the Middle Atlas. Close in on the city itself and at dusk the eye is drawn irresistibly towards the sacred, green-tiled monuments which loom magnificently from the gloaming, as lights all around begin to twinkle beneath the stars and the Qarawiyyin's *Maghrib* evening call to prayer ignites an aural conflagration across the city. According to centuries of tradition, other mosques in Fez must wait until the Qarawiyyin calls the faithful before sounding their own *adhan*.

Literary visitors over the centuries have mostly been mesmerized by this special urban setting. 'The view of Fez from afar, with its emerald roofs emerging from the shimmering mist, can induce a state of poetic exuberance in even the most jaded traveller,' says one. The Swiss scholar Titus Burckhardt, who worked with the Moroccan government on the preservation of the ancient *medina* and helped it become a UNESCO World Heritage Site in 1981, fell in love with the city.* 'A geode of amethyst, brimful of thousands of tightly packed crystals and surrounded by a silver-green rim: this was Fez, the Old City of Fez, in the twilight,' he wrote in a loving study. Though she found Fez 'profoundly melancholy' during her visit in the aftermath of the First World War, the American writer Edith Wharton was nonetheless captivated by its setting. 'It is as though some powerful enchanter, after decreeing that the city should be hurled into the depths, had been moved by its beauty, and with a wave of his hand held it suspended above destruction.'[13]

The history of Fez is a story of Moroccan dynasties, rising up and crashing down like dunes in the ever-shifting Saharan sand. The Almoravids, a bristling new dynasty of Berber camel-drivers, surged out of the Sahara in the late eleventh century. Around 1070 their leader, Yusuf ibn Tashfin, founded the city of Marrakech, one of the four imperial cities of Morocco with Fez, Meknes and Rabat. Though the exact date at which Fez fell to him is unclear – 1069 or 1075 is most likely – it marked a critical moment in the history of the city because it was Yusuf who combined the rival dual settlements across the river and unified them for the first time into the single city of Fez. Although his numbers, like those of most medieval chroniclers, are deeply suspect – he claims an implausible 30,000 were killed during the subjugation of Fez – Leo Africanus gives a strong sense of Yusuf imposing himself on the city, reducing the two towns into 'firm unity and concord'

---

* In 1981 UNESCO declared the Medina of Fez a World Heritage Site. It is considered one of the most extensive and best conserved historic towns of the Arab Muslim world: 'It not only represents an outstanding architectural, archaeological and urban heritage, but also transmits a life style, skills and a culture that persist . . .'

after a bloody conquest.* This effectively brought to an end a fractious, competitive relationship that had hindered urban development, and opened a new era for the rise of Fez as a great Islamic metropolis. Yusuf was a stickler for his religion. 'Whenever he found a district without a place of worship, he scolded the inhabitants and forced them to build one,' Ibn Abi Zar recorded. Yusuf displayed his commitment to the faith, and to the demands of *jihad*, on a grander, more aggressive scale, too, sending a fleet of seventy ships to Palestine during the First Crusade.[14]

Under the three-quarters of a century of Almoravid rule (*c.* 1075–1145), Fez luxuriated in newfound prosperity. The modest Qarawiyyin was pulled down, with the exception of its minaret, and transformed into a vast mosque of more imperial dimensions, beautifully ornamented by Andalusian architects, masons and craftsmen, who commuted between the two Mediterranean shores. A new *mihrab* niche consciously echoed the Cordoban style of horseshoe arch within a rectangular *ijmiz* frame rich with floral and geometric patterns and Kufic calligraphy. Another Cordoban import, which arrived in 1144, was the *minbar* pulpit, again extravagantly adorned with scrolling flowers and eye-catching geometrical designs. Most triumphant of all was the monumental bronze chandelier donated by the Almohad ruler Al Nasir in 1203, a symbolically Islamic reincarnation of a giant Christian bell won from the infidels in Gibraltar. Extensive Almoravid waterworks introduced running water into the city, which Fez enjoyed from an extremely early time by comparison with other cities around the world.[15]

Glorious though they undoubtedly were, with an empire stretching from West Africa to Al Andalus, the Almoravids were a relatively short-lived affair. In 1145 they gave way in Fez to the Almohads (those who proclaim the unity of God), religiously fired Berbers from the High Atlas bent on Islamic reform. Although the Almohads' capital was in Marrakech, Fez retained its importance as a military centre for their operations in Al Andalus, as well as a growing commercial city whose population continued to rise with the arrival of well educated Andalusians, scholars, administrators and merchants.

Al Idrisi left a rare picture of Fez from the second half of the twelfth century that paid tribute to its 'noble' architectural grandeur, its urban sophistication, the famous fertility of its surroundings ('everything is green and fresh') and the industriousness, pride and independence of its people.[16]

---

* 'Muslim writers with a very few exceptions are utterly heedless of statistical accuracy,' say the editors of *Medieval Trade in the Mediterranean World*, recommending stated figures are reduced by 50–75 per cent.

It was a mixed city of Berbers and Arabs, Muslims and Jews, Andalusians, black slaves and Christian soldiers, merchants and scholars, artisans and holy men. From 1166 to 1168 it was also home to the peripatetic Jewish philosopher Maimonides, whose family fled Cordoba after the Almohads overran Al Andalus. Faced with the choice of conversion to Islam, death or exile, Maimonides headed south and, two decades later, was composing his commentary on the *Mishna*, the Jewish 'Oral Torah' collection of laws, in his house in Fez. A worn plaque marks his home in the narrow alley of Derb Margana, just off Talaat Kabira, one of the two main streets running through the *medina* towards the Qarawiyyin.

The dawn of the thirteenth century saw the stirring of a new power. The Marinids, or Banu Marin as they were known in Arabic, were a confederation of Zenata Berber tribes, nomadic shepherds who gave their name to the much prized merino wool which, by the early fourteenth century, was being profitably exported to Europe via Genoese merchants. They first entered the Arab chronicles at the close of the twelfth century, fighting alongside the Almohads in a decisive defeat of King Alfonso VIII's Castilian forces at the Battle of Alarcos in Al Andalus in 1195. Originally based in the territory between Figuig in eastern Morocco and Sijilmasa on the northern fringes of the Sahara, they moved northwards under pressure from incoming Arabs. In the *Rawd al Qirtas* chronicle they emerge as austere and warlike nomads:

> They knew neither money nor coins and were not subject to any prince. Proud and disdainful by nature, they brooked neither attack nor alliance. They knew nothing of agriculture or commerce and occupied themselves exclusively with hunting, horse-breeding and raiding. Their possessions consisted of horses, camels and black slaves. They nourished themselves on meat, fruits, milk and honey.[17]

In 1213, sensing *fin de régime* weakness on the part of the Almohads, who had been humiliatingly defeated by the Christians at Las Navas de Tolosa the year before, Amir Abu Said I addressed an assembly of his fellow Marinid Berber chiefs. His message was both revolutionary and, in its use of religious justification for rebellion, deeply traditional. The anonymous fourteenth-century author of the chronicle *Al Dhakhira al Saniya fi Tarikh al Dawla al Mariniyya* (*The Magnificent Treasure of the History of the Marinid State*) recorded his epoch-making call to arms:

> The Almohads are guilty because they neglected their duty towards the Islamic community. They neglected to provide an efficient government. They forgot their obligation towards their subjects ... This negligence is

an affront to the religious law and an insult which needs to be punished. Their annihilation, therefore constitutes a mission, and the Marinids should take up this mission to further the wellbeing and salvation of the Muslims.[18]

The Marinids, Abu Said urged his chiefs, would conquer the Maghreb under the banner – yet again – of Islamic reform. Some of this Islamic zeal was likely for popular consumption and retrospectively attributed to the Marinids as part of the official historiography. Thus we find Ibn Abi Zar, who was probably being paid for his literary compositions by the Marinid sultan Abu Said Uthman II (r. 1310–31), describing the Marinids as the 'first and most noble' descendants of the Zenata tribe, who had always distinguished themselves by 'the grandeur of their character and virtues. With the softest of manners, brave warriors and profoundly religious, they never broke their word.' This unsubtle emphasis on the Islamic virtues, which contrasted with the Almohad priorities of 'wine, luxury and debauchery', was aimed at the urban centres, especially Fez, where a powerful and entrenched religious community, initially at least, regarded these uncouth nomads with profound suspicion and misgivings.[19]

Whatever doubts there might have been about motivation, fewer uncertainties surrounded their military success. In 1220 Abu Said declared independence from the Almohad yoke. Over the next several decades the Marinids spread like 'a swarm of locusts', increasingly encroaching on Almohad territory until they posed a direct threat to the main cities. 'Energetic and courageous in battle', they proved irresistible to their enemies. Meknes fell in 1244, followed by Fez in 1248, Sijilmasa in 1255 and Marrakech in 1269.[20]

A period of consolidation was necessary before the Marinids could direct their attention fully on their new capital and the economic and administrative foundations of the state. For much of the thirteenth century Marinid rulers were more preoccupied with fighting the infidels on the Iberian Peninsula than in building their own kingdom. In 1248, Christian Castile captured Muslim Seville, following the earlier conquests of Valencia and Cordoba, and the kingdom of Granada and Malaga, the sole remaining bulwark of Islam in Al Andalus, was at serious risk.

Marinid mettle was tested – and proven – in a revolt in 1250, brutally suppressed by the ruler Abu Yahya Abu Bakr (r. 1246–58), who executed six of its ringleaders, including the *qadi* chief judge and his son. 'That punishment brought about the capitulation of the people of Fez to the Marinid dynasty,' Ibn Khaldun wrote. 'Up to this very day they invoke its memory with terror, and never will they dare raise their voices, or resist the orders of the government, or conspire against it.'[21] According to the

Dhakhira chronicle, two people would not even dare to speak to each other in private for fear of being considered rebels.

Fez was to reach its most glittering apogee under the Marinids, but this in no way meant that they were welcome arrivals in this stately citadel of Islam. Fassis saw themselves, not without reason, as sophisticated, civilized and refined – as they do today – unlike their new masters, whom they considered brutish nomads. Founded by a descendant of the Prophet Mohammed, Fez had enjoyed the grandest and most noble beginnings, was a city of Islamic distinction and scholarly renown. Friction between the nomadic warriors and the gilded urban elite would last well beyond the city's Marinid conquest.

This helps explain the otherwise curious decision in 1276 by the Marinid sultan Abu Yusuf Yaqub (r. 1258–86) to commission an entirely new city, initially proclaimed as Medinat al Baida, the White City, but later known as Fez al Jadid (New Fez), 700 metres away from the Idrisid Fez al Bali (Old Fez), as his military and administrative capital. According to Ibn Abi Zar, the decision to build a new capital came the day after a massacre of Jews in the city.

> Fourteen Jews had been killed by the time news reached the *Amir al Muslimin* [leader of the Muslims], who came riding with his soldiers to drive the mob away from the Jewish quarters and stop the pillage. Without his intervention none of the Jews would have survived; later he publicly warned the inhabitants of the *medina*, the old quarter, that no one should bother the *dhimma* Jews, under the threat of a severe punishment.[22]

The famous Mellah of Fez, the Jewish quarter whose name comes from the Arabic word for salt and was later used to describe Jewish quarters across Morocco, was not established, however, until much later.* Leo Africanus reported that the Jews of Fez were transferred to the new quarter during the reign of Abu Said Uthman III (r. 1398–1420), following repeated attacks on Jewish property. Residence in the Mellah was both a blessing and a curse. For some it offered security, the protection of proximity to the royal palace. Others, such as Rabbi Abner Hassarfaty, author of a sixteenth-century Jewish chronicle of the city, considered it 'a bitter and wicked exile'. Many Jews even preferred conversion to Islam to the loss of their homes and places of work in the Old City.[23]

New Fez lay behind a 'high and impregnable wall' studded with numerous towers and merlons. It was divided into three sections. The first was home to the royal palace, nobles' houses and gardens, a Great Mosque

---

* A salty stream, Wadi Mellah, ran through this neighbourhood, or close to it.

and royal mint. The second section contained the large royal stable, court-iers' palaces and a market place along a main east–west axis one-and-a-half miles long. Two more royal stables were built at the western gate for the 300 horses of the royal guard. The final district housed the king's guard and attendants, together with barracks for two distinct corps of the Mari-nid army: the Christian mercenaries from Castile or Catalonia, recruited with Moroccan gold, and Syrian archers from Homs, whose district later became the Jewish Mellah. On the northern side of the city stood the massive Lion's Gate, flanked by two crenellated towers, providing Marinid monarchs with a royal entrance to their new city.

If Leo is to be believed, it was a case of beauty within and squalor without. Beyond the city walls came an immediate contrast to all this pomp and majesty. The suburbs of Fez were home to 'great swarms of sluttish and filthy harlots', Leo reported contemptuously. They also con-tained rambling gardens and orchards from which 500 cartloads of peaches were delivered daily and where black African slaves were also traded.

On one level Abu Yusuf's creation reversed the eleventh-century move by Yusuf ibn Tashfin to forge one city from two. But in practice, Old Fez remained the commercial and intellectual capital, while alongside it New Fez emerged as the military, political and administrative heart of the growing Marinid state, home to everyone responsible for its efficient func-tioning, from the sultan in his palace to the lowliest soldier in his barracks. It was a premeditated expansion of Fez whose success can be gauged by both the flourishing Marinid era that followed and the city's endurance until today as magnificent urban design writ large.

By the time Leo was writing, the city's Jews had moved to Fez al Jadid. They lived on one long street 'and their number is marvellously increased ever since they were driven out of Spain'. As far as interfaith relations were concerned, however, the picture was not encouraging. 'These Jews are held in great contempt by all men and not allowed to wear shoes,' he reported.[24]

A word or two is in order before taking Leo's stark comments at face value. Captured off the coast of Tunis by Spanish corsairs, who quickly recognized a man of unusual talents and education, rather than being pressed into service in the galleys he was instead presented as a prize to Pope Leo X in 1520. Impressed by this enterprising and extraordinarily well travelled North African man of letters, the pontiff became his patron. Baptized in the Basilica of Saint Peter in Rome, Ibn al Wazzan became Johannes Leo de Medicis (though he preferred Yuhanna al Asad al Ghar-nati, John the Lion of Granada) and spent the next eight years writing about his travels. First published in Venice in 1550, his *Description of Africa* was a seminal work, the most authoritative text on North Africa until the nineteenth-century age of exploration. When it came to Jews and Muslims, however, he wrote with the zeal of the convert, describing Islam as 'Mahometan impiety' and 'pestilence'.[25]

Like all practised courtiers, Ibn Abi Zar knew which side his bread was buttered on. He penned a hundred hagiographical pages devoted to the reign of Abu Yusuf and, more interestingly, also left a fascinating survey of thirteenth-century Fez. Notwithstanding the caution over his figures, it leaves no doubt about the exceptional development of the city in the late Almohad period under Al Mansur (r. 1184–99) and his son Al Nasir (1199–1213). In a list of rent- and tax-paying establishments, he included 89,236 houses, 9,082 shops, 3,490 looms, 1,170 ovens, 785 mosques, 472 mills, 467 inns, 188 potteries, 135 bread ovens, 116 dye houses, 93 public baths, 86 tanneries, 47 soap-making shops, 12 copper foundries, 11 crystal manufacturing stores, 2 *qaysariya* bazaars, 2 minting houses, and possibly 400 paper-manufacturing workshops.[26] Thanks to the city's growth by this time, there were no gardens or orchards within the walls.

Such prosperity had not arisen in a vacuum. The Marinids' mid-century rise to power coincided with, and enabled, the return of European gold minting, which had been in abeyance for around half a millennium from the eighth century. While production in western Christendom had stalled during the economic decline of the Middle Ages, when silver coinage predominated across the continent, the Dar al Islam was awash with gold. As early as the eleventh century the territory of today's Morocco – especially Fez, Marrakech, Sijilmasa, Nul and Aghmat – was renowned for gold production. Of the two gold routes from sub-Saharan Africa recorded by Ibn Khaldun, one brought 12,000 caravans a year to Egypt, the other headed north from Timbuktu to Fez and the Mediterranean coast. The security of these trade routes, enabled by Marinid military might and the strength of the dynasty's administrative institutions, lit the touchpaper of economic growth as huge shipments of gold bullion and gold dust passed through Fez on its way to Europe. Traders, merchants and commercial agents flocked to the metropolis. 'There is no city, no country, that does not have representatives in Fez,' wrote Al Jaznai. 'They engage in trade, live there, and are active there. Traders, along with craftsmen, have come there from every region, and every kind of commercial dealing is gathered there.'[27]

The fall of both Cordoba and Seville, and the downgrading of Marrakech under the Marinids, made Fez *the* place for North African and

Andalusian high society to see and be seen in, from 'Banu Ziyan princes from Tlemcen, Nasrids from Granada, Hafsid princes . . . ambassadors, travellers, mystics, students or straightforward parasites'. The Marinids were so rich they could afford to fund a standing army of 5,000 Christian mercenaries from Castile, Aragon and France. The fine fourteenth-century Marinid gold dinars minted during the reign of Sultan Abu Inan (r. 1348–58) were considered unrivalled in the Islamic world. When he ransomed Tripoli for 50,000 gold dinars, he dismissed the sum as 'a trifle'. Such regal complacency can be excused when one hears that in the tenth century, according to Ibn Hawqal, Sijilmasa alone made 400,000 gold dinars a year from the trade. Little wonder, then, that the Islamic gold currency of North Africa provided the model for European coinage.[28]

Nowhere did the Marinids make their mark more magnificently across Morocco than with their construction of *madrassas*, which went into overdrive in the thirteenth and fourteenth centuries. The *madrassa* was Marinid soft power incarnate.

Step out of the swirling, fast-flowing current of traffic on Talaat Kabira – merchants, grocers, spice-sellers, students, scholars, artists, perfumers, butchers, bakers, babouche-makers, booksellers, hoteliers, cooks, carpenters, carpet-weavers, cobblers, children, housewives, electricians, plumbers, jewellers, tailors, touts, toddlers, tourists, shoppers, scroungers, stationers, dressmakers, drunkards, staggering donkeys submerged beneath high loads on sharp-edged iron panniers that could easily split your head open if you're not looking where you're going – and draw your breath in one of Fez's most peaceful, heartachingly beautiful quadrangles.

Named after Sultan Abu Inan, who had it built between 1351 and 1356 at the pinnacle of Marinid grandeur, the Bou Inania Madrassa is one of Fez's most important architectural jewels. It was commissioned, so legend has it, as the result of a scandalous love affair between the sultan and one of his favourite concubines, whom he married. Designed and ornamented with reckless extravagance and an imperial disregard for budget, it represents a highpoint of Marinid architecture. At its inauguration Abu Inan asked his scholars if prayers in this new college were valid. Indeed they were, the men replied. The sultan nodded. 'In the same way that this dump has become a prayer hall, a prostitute can become a great lady.' Later, when informed of the final, colossal cost of the monument, he brushed the sum away as a mere bagatelle. 'A thing that enthrals is never too dear,' he said.[29]

The accumulation of detail in Bou Inania borders on the overwhelming. Whichever way you gaze within the courtyard, the eye is dazzled by pattern in one of the world's greatest displays of mixed-media Islamic art. A robust minaret, crowned with iridescent green tiles on a background of Yorkstone beige, keeps watch serenely over the architectural opulence below. Seen today through the blue gate of Bab Bou Jeloud, one of the Old City's most popular entrances, it has been an icon of the Fez skyline for eight centuries.

Inside the *madrassa*, *zellij* tiles and mosaic work running vertically, horizontally and in gravity-defying niches and revetments alternately compete with and complement acres of carved plaster, dancing arabesques, fretted *mashribiyya* panels, corbels and architraves of sun-bleached cedar, gilded ceilings that dissolve into a thousand geometric patterns and a pair of vast bronze entrance doors with giant bosses. The layers of counterpoint – cool tiled floors, glazed dados, complications of filigree stucco, splintering, weather-worn cedar – mix in apparently endless combinations of tone and texture, shade and colour. 'It is like stepping inside a casket of jewels,' writes the Islamic art historian Robert Hillenbrand.[30]

Directly opposite the *madrassa* stood another of Fez's most famous monuments, the Dar al Margana clockhouse, an ingenious fourteenth-century weight-powered clepsydra or water clock, a wonder of its day. There were other water-powered Marinid marvels, too, such as the enormous noria waterwheels installed to irrigate the royal palace and the nobles' rambling gardens. During the reign of Sultan Abul Hassan we hear of numerous structures with fresh running water, from fountains and ablution rooms to full-blown swimming pools.

In the same way that visitors to the Bou Inania are often overcome by its beauty (with the possible exception of the young Chinese women who spend hours posing for selfies in studied poses), so the effervescent, Moroccan traveller Ibn Battuta, who arrived in Fez in October 1349, was overawed both by the imperial majesty of Fez and by his royal audience with Sultan Abu Inan, 'may God establish his grandeur and crush his enemies'.

Ibn Battuta was not easily impressed. He had been on the road for twenty-four years and was coming towards the end of his 75,000-mile odyssey that would see him known for ever after as 'the traveller of Islam'. In 1325, just as craftsmen were putting the finishing touches to the luminous Attarin (Perfumers) Madrassa in Fez, he had fastened his sandals, picked up his bags and set off from Tangier on his *hajj* to Mecca. Now, having performed his pilgrimage and begun the return journey west through Jerusalem, Cairo and Alexandria, he succumbed to a forgivable pang of homesickness and reached the Marinid capital of Sultan Abu Inan at the summit of the city's splendour:

I presented myself to him, and was honoured by a sight of him. The awe that surrounded him made me forget that of the King of Iraq; his elegance, that of the Emperor of India; his politeness, that of the King of Yemen; his bravery, that of the King of the Turks; his mildness, that of the Emperor of Constantinople; his religious carriage, that of the Emperor of Turkistan; his knowledge, that of the King of Sumatra; for he so overwhelmed me with his favours, that I found myself quite unequal to express my gratitude.[31]

Fascinated by the traveller's tales, the stories of foreign potentates and the reports of Islam in the East, Sultan Abu Inan commissioned an account of his compatriot's wanderings. *The Precious Gift of Lookers into the Marvels of Cities and Wonders of Travel* is one of the world's greatest travel narratives, at once scholarly, anecdotal, gossipy, humorous, humane and consistently entertaining.

Marinid *madrassas* – known locally as *medersas* – dated to Abu Yusuf's inauguration of the Saffarin Madrassa in 1271, the opening salvo in a century-long flourish of religiously inspired architecture. It set the standard for many of its successors, blending small size with lavish-to-the-point-of-decadence ornamentation, mixed media and multiple functions – religious college, mosque, charitable institution, student lodging, community centre and setting for official ceremonies.

Built between 1323 and 1325 during the reign of Sultan Abu Said Uthman II (r. 1310–31), the Attarin (Perfumers) Madrassa at the entrance to the Spice and Perfume Market right next to the Qarawiyyin Mosque is another of the most magnificent Marinid monuments of Fez. Set around a central courtyard with a fountain, it is a riot of epigraphic friezes, mosaic panels, *muqarnas* stalactite niches, sculpted plaster, lambrequin arches, cursive inscriptions and floral curlicues. Rare stained-glass windows beneath the dome send a delicate, many-coloured sparkle over the worshippers below.

The Marinid *madrassas* of Fez were far more than the show-off creations of monarchs with more gold than sense. These baroque Islamic institutions provided the Marinid Dynasty with the spiritual and intellectual firepower it required. They also represented the architectural frontline in a campaign to promote the dynasty's Islamic legitimacy – and control over a sometimes truculent religious establishment used to having its own way. Having been challenged once in the 1250 revolt, from which time imams were required to keep the authorities informed about all assemblies held in mosques, the Marinids would brook no further opposition from troublesome clerics. Those preachers who enjoyed large audiences were bought off by the state. Doctrinal orthodoxy according to the Maliki

school of Sunni jurisprudence was strictly enforced and state control of
the religious authorities reached new, micro-managing heights. To give
just one example, between 1283 and 1300, the clergy sought the sultans'
approval seven times just for permission to make specific renovations to
the Qarawiyyin Mosque.[32]

The centrality of Fez to the Marinid project can be gauged by the pro-
liferation of new *madrassas* here. Seven were built between 1271 and 1357.
Others opened their dazzling doors the length and breadth of the king-
dom. According to Ibn Marzuq, Sultan Abul Hassan (r. 1331–48), who
was briefly able to unite Morocco with Tlemcen (in Algeria) and Ifriqiya
(Tunisia, western Libya and eastern Algeria), alone built *madrassas* in Fez,
Meknes, Salé, Tangier, Anfa, Azemour, Safi, Aghmat, Marrakech and Al
Ubbad.

The wave of new *madrassas* allowed the Marinids to create a new class
of loyal, well-educated, Berber-speaking jurists and clergy devoted to the
sultan, to whom they owed their living. The *madrassas* also bolstered the
city's reputation as a seat of Islamic learning. As the Andalusian geographer Abu Said al Gharnati wrote, 'the residents of Fez are well educated,
learned and intelligent; the town is a true arsenal where one finds more
physicians, jurists, scholars, and nobles, sharifs, than in any other city'.[33]

Marinid magnificence was also stage-managed in the most opulent
royal cortèges, in which the pick of the sultan's stables, caparisoned with
gold and precious gems, paced majestically through Fez, riders resplendent
on jewel-studded saddles beneath the white standards of the dynasty, to
the martial accompaniment of drums and pipes. Wildly extravagant celebrations of Mawlid al Nabi al Sharif, the Prophet's birthday, provided the
Marinids with the opportunity to demonstrate royal piety and generosity
both to the Ahl al Bait, the descendants of the Prophet, and to the poor,
who feasted greedily on abundant leftovers from the banquets.[34]

While the *madrassas* constituted the architectural proof of the dynasty's piety, the community of *sharifs*, descendants of the Prophet, who were
invited from the length and breadth of the Islamic world to come and settle
in Fez, a city founded by the great-great-great-grandson of the Prophet,
were their human counterpart. Handsomely provided with pensions and
assorted privileges, they grew into a powerful and increasingly independent caste free from civil jurisdiction – with fateful consequences for the
dynasty.

Like Ibn Battuta before him, Leo Africanus was transfixed by Fez. His
voluminous African travelogue included seventy pages given over to 'A
most exact description of the City of Fez', in which he paid particular

attention to the almost 700 'stately and sumptuously built' mosques and religious colleges, above all the 'most beautiful and admirable' Qarawiyyin and the Bou Inania Madrassa.[35] Leo was also enthralled by the city's vast series of markets, where 20,000 weavers and 20,000 millers, 150 grocers and apothecaries, 150 tailors, 100 potters and 100 saddlers, 50 needlemakers and 50 fruit-sellers plied their trade. 'Nowhere, either in all of Africa, or in Asia, or in Italy, have I seen a market where so many kinds of goods are to be found. It is impossible to set a value on it all.'[36]

By the time Leo's book was published in 1550, the Marinids had long departed, though the glories of the Islamic city they had laboured so assiduously to enhance were still the envy of the Muslim world. The assassination of Ibn Battuta's munificent patron Sultan Abu Inan, strangled by his vizier in 1358, ushered in a steady decline for the dynasty, whose fate was anticipated by Ibn Khaldun, the Marinid era's most formidable intellect, in his *Muqaddimah*, a brilliant and far-reaching dissection of the rise and fall of empires. Indolent sultans, overreaching viziers, ambitious pretenders and a series of palace coups and murders brought anarchy and disorder to Fez and the wider Marinid state. In 1465, a popular revolt led by Fez's gilded community of *sharifs* broke out. Sultan Abd al Haq II and his Jewish vizier had their throats slit. By 1472, a new dynasty had arisen in the form of the Wattasids, fellow and related Zenata Berbers. Fez's zenith had passed. The Marinids had breathed their last.

Fashions come and go, but Fez discreetly and triumphantly manages to stay the same. Shaded by an ancient plane tree, the unhurried spice- and perfume-sellers of Suq al Henna, one of the city's oldest and most beautiful market squares, still discuss the finer arts of perfuming with their customers while blending heady concoctions of oud, jasmine, musk, gardenia, geranium, bergamot, rose oil, cedar wood and cinnamon, aniseed, pepper, camomile, frankincense and patchouli. The softly spoken perfumer Rachid Ouedrhiri mixes up a head-turning 'Royal Amber' fragrance before pointing out a crumbling building a few metres away. The Maristan Sidi Frej was one of the world's first psychiatric hospitals, built by Abu Yusuf in 1286, long before Valencia's Hospital de los Inocentes of 1410. Fez honours its traditions and memories and moves at its own pace.

Unlike its fellow imperial city of Marrakech around 300 miles to the south, prettified and gentrified beyond recognition in recent decades, there is a gritty, sometimes brutal, authenticity to Fez. You see it in the crumbling townhouses, in the crippled beggars whose deformities challenge you not to look away in shame and embarrassment, in the butchers' prize exhibits of fly-infested severed camels' heads nailed to their shopfronts. It is there for all to see and smell in the notorious stench of the Chaouara tannery where, like generations of their predecessors on this same site for almost 1,000 years before them, tanners navigate across a honeycomb grid of stone wells filled with the olfactory delights of cow urine, pigeon faeces, quicklime, salt and water to strip and soften hides before plunging them into dyes of fuchsia pink, magenta, burgundy, blues, yellows and any other tones Fassi leather goods merchants think will sell well this season. The tanners, whose guild dates back to the very dawn of Fez, still stand waist-deep in these giant inkwells, kneading the hides in natural vegetable dyes – indigo for blue, henna for orange, mint for green, saffron for yellow, cedar wood for brown and poppy flower for red. Time stands still.

Visiting in 1931, the Swiss modernist Le Corbusier deplored what he saw as the disorder and confusion of the ancient city. 'The medina is too compressed,' he complained. It was 'the destiny of the West to act, to compose, to create modern life'. Fez shrugged and life went on. Half a century later, Paul Bowles cast his eye over the 'unimaginable squalor' of the *medina*, saw Fassi families leaving the Old City to make new lives in Casablanca, and forecast 'doom'. Fez carried on regardless.[37]

When Titus Burckhardt returned to his beloved city in the 1950s after an absence of twenty-five years, he fretted about how it might have changed, how perhaps it might have lost its veneration for the sacred under the encroaching tide of modern European culture, all 'money, haste and dissipation'.

He needn't have worried. The minarets still sent their call to prayer across this green-roofed city, spice-sellers thronged the narrow streets of Suq al Attarin, advocates and notaries clustered around the ancient Qarawiyyin, mule-drivers and porters hurried through the twisting streets crying their time-honoured warning, '*Balak! Balak!* Watch out! Watch out!', wool weavers weaved, spinners span and the coppersmiths of Saffarin Square still crashed away on their pots and pans. There it was before him in all its visceral glory, just as it is today, 'unalterable, indestructible Fez'.[38]

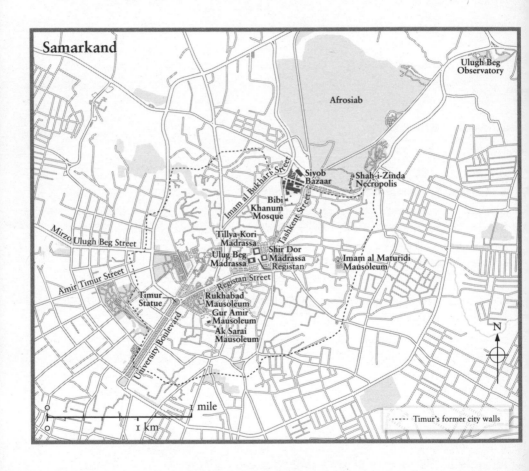

Samarkand

Ulugh Beg
Observatory

Afrosiab

Imam al Bukhari Street

Siyob
Bazaar

Shah-i-Zinda
Necropolis

Bibi
Khanum
Mosque

Tashkent Street

Mirzo Ulugh Beg Street

Tillya-Kori
Madrassa

Ulug Beg
Madrassa

Shir Dor
Madrassa
Registan

Imam al Maturidi
Mausoleum

Amir Timur Street

Registan Street

Timur
Statue

Rukhabad
Mausoleum
Gur Amir
Mausoleum
Ak Sarai
Mausoleum

University Boulevard

N

1 mile

1 km

- - - - - Timur's former city walls

8

Samarkand – Garden of the Soul
(14th Century)

*Samarkand, the most beautiful face the Earth has ever turned
towards the sun.*

Amin Maalouf, *Samarkand*

A ferocious and magnificent new power arose in Central Asia in the second
half of the fourteenth century. He was not of royal blood and inherited
neither a kingdom nor an empire from his father. He was instead one of
history's greatest self-made men, an illiterate military commander who
carved out one of the world's largest empires with an army of soldiers
loyal only for as long as their leader remained victorious. His illustrious
career on the battlefield, undefeated during thirty-five years in the saddle,
placed him firmly in the top tier of world conquerors, alongside Alexander
the Great and Genghis Khan. He enjoyed many extravagant titles that bore
witness to this pre-eminence: Lord of the Fortunate Conjunction (a reference to the auspicious position of the stars at his birth in 1336); Conqueror
of the World; Emperor of the Age; Unconquered Lord of the Seven Climes.
Christopher Marlowe called him 'the scourge and wrath of God / The only
fear and terror of the world' and named his most bloodthirsty play after
him. His name was Timur, or Tamerlane. To the Muslim leaders of his day,
who contemplated him with fear and loathing on a grand scale, he was an
illiterate barbarian. In his own mind he was the supreme leader of the
Muslim world – self-styled Sword Arm of Islam and Warrior of the Faith –
and his imperial capital, the peerless Pearl of the East, was Samarkand.[1]

Founded around the eighth-century BC, the city lay on the Zarafshan
River in the heart of what Arabs called Mawarannahr, the Land Beyond
the River, a region extending across the cotton basket of the former Soviet
Union, today's Central Asian republics of Uzbekistan, Kazakhstan, Turkmenistan, Tajikistan and Kyrgyzstan, running into north-west Xinjiang

in China. The territory was also known as Transoxiana, whose centre was a 300-mile-wide corridor of land sandwiched between the two greatest rivers of Central Asia, the Amu Darya and Sir Darya. Better known by their classical names, Oxus and Jaxartes, these were two of the four medieval rivers of paradise, slivers of fertility rushing through a barren landscape.

On the banks of these hallowed waterways and their tributaries rose the noble cities of antiquity, whose names echoed with the memories of Alexander and the Mongol warlord Genghis Khan: Samarkand, Bukhara, Termez, Balkh, Urganch and Khiva. The Persian king Cyrus the Great captured Samarkand around 550 BC, a conquest followed by Alexander, who took Marakanda, as the Greeks knew it, in 329 BC. Beyond the rivers were the deadly sands and rasping winds of the desert. West of the Amu Darya stretched the spirit-shattering wilderness of the Qara Qum (Black Sands) desert. East of the Sir Darya, the equally inhospitable Hunger Steppe unfurled, a vast flatness melting into the horizon. Even between the two rivers, the pockets of civilization and lush farming land were under siege from the burning Qizil Qum (Red Sands) desert of the north. In the summer, the heat was stupefying and the skins of those toiling in the fields blistered and turned to leather. In winter, snows gusted down on a lifeless land and the nomads and settled population alike retreated behind lined felt tents and mudbrick walls, wrapping themselves in furs and woollen blankets against winds strong enough to blow a man out of his saddle. Only in spring, when the rivers tumbled down from the mountain heights, when blossom burst forth in the orchards and the markets heaved with apples, mulberries, pears, peaches, plums and pomegranates, melons, apricots, quinces and figs, when mutton and horsemeat hissed and crackled over open fires and huge bumpers of wine were downed in tribal banquets, did the country at last rejoice in plenty.

Central Asia had existed as a crossroads between East and West ever since the Silk Road – 3,700 miles from China to the Mediterranean ports of Antioch and Alexandria via Samarkand – came into being around the beginning of the first century BC. In a snapshot of Samarkand in its heyday under Timur, the city's markets offered up the products of the world: furs and falcons, wool, gold, silver and precious stones; leather and linens from Russia and Tartary; porcelain, musk, balas rubies, diamonds and pearls, the finest silks and spices from China; nutmeg, cloves, mace, cinnamon, ginger and manna from India; cloth, glass and metalware from Syria and Asia Minor. These were in addition to the local factories making silks, crêpes and fur linings – and the most delicious, locally grown fruit and vegetables.

Timur, a Turkic Mongol or Tatar, grew up a century after Genghis Khan's scorched-earth invasion of Central Asia in the 1220s, by which time his tribe and many others had converted to Islam. It was a turbulent region of shifting alliances and divisions between the settled nobility in the towns and villages, largely in Mawarannahr, which had embraced Islam, and the nomadic, military aristocracy to the east, which rejected it and clung on to pagan beliefs. In this land of desert, steppe and mountain he learned the martial and equestrian skills required of any would-be leader.

Then in 1360, at the age of twenty-four, he vaulted out of obscurity and into the official histories with an audacious and opportunist move. Taking advantage of the chaos into which Mawarannahr had fallen after its ruler's assassination in 1358, a rival khan invaded from the east. Timur's clan leader decided to flee. Spotting an opportunity, Timur assured him he would lead the resistance, only to then offer his services to the invading khan as his vassal ruler. At a stroke Timur had boldly seized the leadership of his Barlas tribe. There followed years as a highwayman, bandit and mercenary honing his talents for leadership. At some point during this period he suffered the serious injury which left him crippled in both right limbs, an affliction which gave rise to the nickname Timur the Lame, from which Tamerlane. The lasting handicap at a time when, as the proverb went, 'Only a hand that can grasp a sword may hold a sceptre', made his subsequent career on the battlefield more extraordinary still. By 1370 he had eliminated all rivals and was undisputed master of all Chaghatay, the dominion named after Genghis Khan's second son, of which Mawarannahr formed the western half. The ever more ambitious conquests began from this time.

The quickest way to understand Timur and the scale of his achievement is to consider a map of his campaigns from 1370 to 1405. Lines stretch hyperactively across Asia through natural obstacles, across deserts, over mountains, past powerful enemies, as far west as the gates of Europe on the Turkish coast, east until deepest Siberia, from the outskirts of Moscow in the north, across the roof of the world to Delhi in the south. A map of his empire shows a giant ink stain spreading across 1.7 million square miles of Central Asia, the Caucasus, Asia Minor, the Levant and swathes of the Indian Subcontinent.

The Islamic world was already divided and fragmented at this time. Genghis Khan's grandson Hulagu had put Baghdad to the sword in 1258, annihilating the last vestiges of the Abbasid Empire, which had held sway over much of the Middle East for half a millennium. The Ottomans had yet to emerge in earnest in the fourteenth century, and North Africa was divided into minor kingdoms, leaving the Mamluks masters of Egypt and the Levant. Timur would become the most powerful Muslim monarch in the world, toppling these rival Islamic empires and shifting the focus of the Dar al Islam much farther east, away from largely Arab (and partially Berber) North Africa and the Middle East, towards the ethnically more diverse Asian steppe.

The paradox of his martial career was that beneath his rampant banner of Islam lay the millions of overwhelmingly Muslim casualties of his conquests. Though he consistently argued he was bringing glory to the Dar al Islam, others saw only wholesale destruction and the smoking ruins of those Islamic cities which had dared oppose him. As Tacitus had observed, 'To ravage, to slaughter, to usurp under false titles, they call empire; and where they make a desert they call it peace.'[2] The difference with Timur was that he then built on that desert on an imperial scale, leaving a potent architectural and cultural legacy paid for in torrents of blood and centred on Samarkand.

The whirlwind career began in the 1370s with success close to hand in Khorezm and Moghulistan. From the 1380s his compass widened, starting in Khorasan, Afghanistan and Persia. The bloody Three-Year Campaign of 1386–8 saw Timur and his Tatar armies of mounted archers victorious in Persia and the Caucasus, ransacking the dominions that Genghis's grandson Hulagu had formed into the Ilkhanid Empire. Timur deployed terror calculatingly to project and increase his power, to strike fear into the hearts of his adversaries and minimize the risks of rebellion. Two thousand prisoners were piled on top of one another and cemented alive into towers of clay and bricks in Isfizar in 1383. In the Persian holy city of Isfahan, 70,000 were slaughtered in cold blood. In 1400 he launched the Seven-Year Campaign, bringing fresh atrocities to swathes of the Levant, Middle East and Turkey.

His armies raged across Asia like a firestorm, unleashing desolation on a fearful scale. One by one, the great cities of the East fell, in an alphabet of destruction and slaughter. Antioch, Acre and Aleppo, Balkh, Baalbek, Beirut and Baghdad, Damascus and Delhi, Hama, Homs and Herat, Isfahan and Isfizar, Kabul, Urganch and Zaranj, all were sacked and torched. He took Bukhara, sacred Dome of Islam, Sultaniya and Shiraz, Termez and Tabriz. His men killed, raped, plundered and burned their way through an entire continent. Single-handedly Timur brought most of the Islamic world to its knees in slaughter and submission. Islamic civilization was under threat like never before, facing nemesis not at the hands of the hated Frankish infidels but of a savage Muslim warlord.

From the darkness of this Asian apocalypse one city rose to its most sparkling zenith.

First performed in Her Majesty's Theatre in 1923, eight years after its author, James Elroy Flecker, had died of tuberculosis, *Hassan* brought the heady adventure of the East to London's West End. It also popularized the idea of a 'golden road to Samarkand'.* The city had long shimmered in Western imagination as the most romantic of cities, distant and exotic – to many minds, it still does. Its very name conjured up images of caravans bearing spices and fabulous treasures, struggling against the fiercest desert sandstorms, of superb palaces and manicured gardens stretching enticingly before the eye. It was the essence of opulence and majesty, a blue-domed oasis of grace and serenity in a world of Oriental barbarism.

But even in the first decades of the twentieth century these fondly cherished impressions were illusory. The Great Game, an age of elegance and chutzpah in which the Russian and British empires fought for influence in the high mountain passes and royal courts of Central Asia during the nineteenth century, was long over. The nascent Soviet Empire was spreading south to encompass the former realms of Timur.

In 1917, two years after James Elroy Flecker's death in Switzerland, six years before Samarkand came to the London stage, the Russians seized the city and the red flag fluttered over the great Registan (literally 'sandy place') Square. In 1924, the Uzbek Soviet Socialist Republic was born and, a year later, Samarkand was declared its capital, ushering in a new age of progress and modernity. The regime embraced the identikit paraphernalia of the Soviet experiment. Factories, schools, hospitals and high-rise housing sprang up. Broad, tree-lined avenues replaced the clutter of labyrinthine streets. Timur, a potentially dangerous and destabilizing symbol of Uzbek nationalism, was banished from public discourse and made a pariah – barbarian tyrant and destroyer. The site of Timur's Blue Palace became Lenin Square, repository of the new culture in the form of a House of Soviets, an opera house and ballet theatre. The sprawling, disorganized romance of Samarkand was tamed. As for the great monuments of the city, these were to be restored in orderly Soviet fashion after centuries of abandonment.

When I first visited Samarkand twenty years ago, when Timur's

---

* A verse from the play, 'We are the pilgrims, master; we shall go / Always a little further . . .' is inscribed on the clock tower at the headquarters of Britain's Special Air Service in Hereford.

homeland of Uzbekistan was ruled by a dissident-boiling Communist dictator, there was nothing golden any more about the road to Samarkand. Here and there cottonfields popped up and then disappeared into the horizon, little changed since the days of Timur, but they told a sad rather than romantic tale. Cotton remained the key cash crop of Uzbekistan, where old Communist habits died hard. One clear autumn morning I approached the city from Tashkent, passing through the drab poverty of the suburbs. A convoy of more than a hundred antiquated buses filled with young men and women drove past in the opposite direction. I asked Farkhad, my Uzbek travelling companion, who they were and where they were going.

'Oh, they're just students going to pick cotton,' he said.

It was a surprise to hear that such punishing work could attract so many volunteers.

Farkhad looked at me askance. 'Of course they're not volunteers. They have to pick cotton or they'll be kicked out of university by the government. No cotton-picking, no degree.'

He had left university prematurely in the days of the Soviet Union because he could not cope with the compulsory, physically gruelling work. 'These days it's still the same. Nothing's changed, only now it's better hidden. The cotton fields are mostly far away from the main roads, so foreigners can't see what's happening.'

Timur, it was said, loved Samarkand 'as an old man loves a young mistress'. Perhaps it would be more accurate to say he wooed her with the ardour of a young man trying to win the love of a beautiful older woman. The romance began in 1366, when Timur took the city by the sword. It was his first significant victory, the first notable conquest, and brought into his orbit a city whose name, like Rome and Babylon, echoed through the millennia. He always cherished this moment as the foundation of his bid to rule the world. From that time the capital occupied an unchallenged position in his aesthetic universe. 'Samarkand indeed was the first of all the cities that he had conquered, and the one that he had since ennobled above all others, by his buildings making it the treasure house of his conquests,' wrote Ruy González de Clavijo, the Spanish ambassador from Henry III's court of Castile, who visited Samarkand in 1404.[3]

The Samarkand Timur conquered had fallen on hard times and was living on its reputation. Visiting in 1333, the Moroccan traveller Ibn Battuta considered it 'one of the largest and most perfectly beautiful cities in the world', yet of its large palaces and impressive monuments, 'The greater part are ruined and a portion of the city is also devastated – it has no wall or gates and there are no gardens outside the city itself'.[4] Timur's first action was to dress his new lover, encircling her with a five-mile girdle of fortified walls, surrounded by a deep ditch, to protect her from invaders. Broad, stone-paved avenues were built – a tradition that survives in the wide boulevards of the city today – running from the six gates in the defences to the domed bazaar in the centre of the city. This was all out of character, insofar as it flouted the Mongol traditions established by the nomadic Genghis, for whom a settled life and its associated infrastructure – towns, markets, agriculture – were complete anathema.

For the rest of his life, Timur hurried across the world, storming, sacking, torching, razing, plundering, all for the greater glory of his adored metropolis. He rampaged through the continent as though nothing else mattered, always returning to adorn her with his latest trophies and embellishments. Over four decades the city soaked up Timur's offerings like an insatiable lover. There were blue-tiled, marble-clad palaces, azure-domed mosques, mausoleums and *madrassas*, rambling gardens and parks with exquisite pavilions, there was gold, silver and precious stones without count, exotic beasts, fabulous cloths, silks, tapestries, slaves and spices, yet it was never enough. Each time he returned with more, she sent him back out into battle. Her glorification required ever increasing spoils from countless victories. Only constant campaigning could deliver them.

The human capital Timur seized was just as important, perhaps more so, than the physical plunder. Captured abroad, scientists and scholars, writers, philosophers and historians congregated in the new academies and libraries he built, adding intellectual sparkle to the city. Timur, said the fifteenth-century Syrian chronicler Ahmed ibn Arabshah, a bitter critic of the man who had sacked Damascus, 'gathered from all sides and collected at Samarkand the fruits of everything; and that place accordingly had in every wonderful craft and rare art someone who excelled in wonderful skill and was famous beyond his rivals in his craft'.* Clavijo made a similar observation after a long overland journey across Timur's empire from Constantinople. The emperor always fostered trade to make his capital 'the noblest of cities', the Spaniard wrote, and during each conquest Timur 'carried off the best men of the population to people Samarkand, bringing thither together the master-craftsmen of all nations'.

---

* The chapter headings of Arabshah's *Tamerlane or Timur the Great Amir* make no attempt to disguise the animosity: 'This Bastard Begins to Lay Waste Azerbaijan and the Kingdoms of Irak'; 'How that Proud Tyrant was Broken & Borne to the House of Destruction, where he had his Constant Seat in the Lowest Pit of Hell'. Arabshah calls Timur 'Satan', 'demon', 'viper', 'villain', 'despot', 'deceiver' and 'wicked fool'. Any praise from this writer is therefore not to be taken lightly.

Asia surrendered her finest musicians, artists and craftsmen to the regal vanity of Samarkand. From Persia, cultural capital of the continent, came poets and painters, miniaturists, calligraphers, musicians and architects. Syria sent her silk-weavers, glass-makers and armourers. India provided masons, builders and gem-cutters, while Asia Minor supplied silversmiths, gunsmiths and rope-makers. Plunder aside, peaceful trade was the bedrock of the empire's prosperity. It was Timur's boast that a child could carry a purse of gold unmolested from the western borders of his empire to its farthest reaches in the east, a claim Clavijo endorsed with his observation that 'the whole country is now at peace under the rule and government of Timur'.[5]

Priests and holy men preached to their flocks in the mosques, which multiplied like mushrooms throughout the city, blue domes glimmering among the clouds, interiors bright with gold and turquoise. Parks sprang up one by one, oases of tranquillity sprawling through the suburbs that were contemptuously named after the great cities of the East that Timur had conquered – Baghdad, Damascus, Cairo, Shiraz and Sultaniya – to demonstrate that by comparison with this imperial metropolis, Garden of the Soul, they were no more than provincial backwaters.

Timur's Samarkand was one of the most cosmopolitan cities in the world, though this owed as much to the forced movement of people and prisoners as it did to the magnetic attraction of the place. Among the Muslim population there were Turks, Arabs and Moors, the Christians represented by Greek Orthodox, Armenians, Catholics, Jacobites and Nestorians, joined in lifelong servitude by the Hindus and Zoroastrians. Jewish weavers and dyers were an important community, together with their co-religionists in Bukhara, Timur's religious capital. With a population estimated at 150,000, Samarkand was a melting-pot of languages, religions and colours, an exercise in imperial splendour and an act of devotion by one man, constant in his love.

Western historians have generally not been kind to Timur. John Joseph Saunders, the chronicler of the Mongol conquests, criticized 'the agglomeration of sheer power built on the corpses of millions', concluding that until the advent of Hitler Timur was history's 'supreme example of soulless and unproductive militarism'. Recognizing the continental scale of the destruction Timur unleashed, there is much to be said for this verdict. For much of Asia he was a one-man apocalypse. Where the judgement falls short, however, is in one critical area – highly visible more than 600 years later – which was at the heart of Islamic civilization. Blood-drenched destroyer though Timur undoubtedly was, his militarism was anything but unproductive. He was a dynamic builder of empire and monuments, whose architectural record saw much of Asia, above all its cities, remodelled in a style that took its name from the emperor. Under his enforced patronage, literary culture, music and the visual arts flourished. However unwillingly, the Dar al Islam became more united than it had been for centuries. The Sword Arm of Islam first ran roughshod over the Islamic world, then comprehensively redefined it.

Timurid architecture was characterized above all by a monumentality informed by a rationalism evident in the strong sense of proportion. Not only did Timur introduce a new aesthetic across the continent, he did so using new engineering technologies and the most opulent materials available. Unlike the often sprawling and ill-defined architecture of his predecessors, the Timurid vision imposed form and clear lines onto his monumental canvas. In practice this meant geometric shapes such as cubes, rectangular solids, stalactites, cylinders and octagons. Transverse arches and innovative vaulting allowed windows to be built into walls, illuminating interiors of dazzling gold with natural light.[6]

To the colossal scale of Timur's buildings, be they secular or spiritual, was married the richest decoration. Before Timur few buildings, apart from smaller scale funerary monuments, were so lavishly embellished. From the later fourteenth century it became the norm. Palaces, mosques and *madrassas* were wrapped in fine glazed bricks and tiles, replete with dancing frescoes and arabesques, to provide an iridescent counterpoint to the sun-bleached colours of the steppe. Bold inscriptions in Kufic script ran around marble plaques at the base of decagonal minarets, rising into sparkling lozenges of blue flowers and amber petals outlined in white faience of thousands of tiny glazed tiles. In these arid lands the blue was a refreshing reference to water and a homage to the heavens. Dados became the repositories of semi-precious stones shaped into geometric patterns, enlivened with hexagonal tiles of jet-black onyx and tracery of gold and lapis lazuli.

In the heart of Timur's city was the symbol of its strength, the heavily fortified Gok Sarai or Blue Palace, simultaneously a citadel, treasury, prison and armaments factory where captive artisans and armourers were put to work. The great walls reverberated with the din and clattering of burly men hammering plate armour and helmets, making bows and arrows. Others blew glass for the emperor's palaces, alongside cobblers cutting leather for army boots and sandals. The rope-makers were set to work on piles of flax and hemp – new crops which Timur had introduced to the agricultural lands outside the city expressly to supply the ropes for the mangonels and other siege engines with which he overwhelmed defiant cities and castles. Here also were the archives, the coin-filled treasury, rooms full of Asia's plundered treasures and formal reception halls where the emperor occasionally held court.

One of the greatest buildings from this time was Timur's Ak Sarai, or White Palace, built not in Samarkand but in his birthplace of Kesh (now Shakhrisabz), sixty miles to the south. With twin entrance towers rising to a height of almost seventy metres, flanking a grand portal arch of forty metres, this was his greatest palace. Masons and thousands of other crafts-men had been toiling on its construction for twenty years by the time Clavijo arrived. It was designed to overawe the visitor, to convey in stone the absolute power of this world-conquering monarch. The monumental scale was conscious and deliberate. As Timur said, 'Let he who doubt our power look upon our buildings.'[7]

It is impossible not to admire all these creations more than six centuries later, whether they are in a state of evocative ruin or Disneyfied over-restoration of the Soviet period. Head-craning – with the occasional gasp at the beauty and phenomenal scale – is a rite of passage on any visit to Timurid monuments in Samarkand and right across Asia.

Timur spanned the transition from Central Asian nomadism to a settled lifestyle. The unique culture of the Timurid court grew out of this fusion of nomadic heritage and military prowess with the more refined visual arts of the sedentary life. He preferred his luxuriously appointed royal camps to sleeping within brick walls, and tended to hold his most important meetings – audiences with foreign ambassadors, family marriages and celebrations of yet another victory on the battlefield – inside these rich mobile camps.

Always the movement continued. A raging blur of mounted archers, piercing arrows and slashing swords leaving smoking ruins, piled corpses and towers of skulls in its wake, with trains of horses and camels bearing off the most fantastic treasures of the world looted from its richest cities.

Yet for all his restless roaming, Samarkand was the centre around which Timur revolved. During thirty-five years of campaigning, the city invariably marked first the launch and – with ominous regularity for his enemies – the triumphal homecoming of his expeditions. He returned in 1381 following the sacking of Herat, and again in 1384 after taking Sistan, Zaranj and Kandahar in southern Afghanistan. He was back in 1392, having routed his ruthless adversary Tokhtamish, Khan of the Golden Horde. Samarkand watched on in wonder all the while as her illustrious emperor trampled the universe. In 1396, after the latest catalogue of vic-tories in Persia, Mesopotamia and the Kipchak steppes, Timur returned again to Samarkand. Only once in his entire career did he stop for a sig-nificant time in the city. That time was now.

*

The people of Samarkand roared their welcome as the Lord of the Fortunate Conjunction rode into his beloved capital after an absence of four
years. With its great parks and vineyards, its gardens and orchards in full
bloom, Samarkand arranged the most sumptuous decorations to greet the
emperor at the head of his army. It was a reception designed to reflect the
magnificence of Timur's triumphal procession, when it seemed that half
the world trooped into town carrying before it the booty of all Asia.

'On all sides were to be seen garlands of flowers with crowns, amphi-
theatres, and musicians performing the newest pieces of music to the
honour of his majesty,' wrote Sharaf al din Ali Yazdi, the Persian court
historian of the early fifteenth century, in *Zafarnama* (*Book of Victory*).
'The walls of the houses were hung with carpets, the roofs covered with
stuffs, and the shops set off with curious pieces. There was a vast multitude
of people, and the streets were covered with velvet, satin, silk and carpets,
which the horses trampled underfoot.'[8]

In this gorgeous tableau walked slaves with bowed heads, scarcely
knowing where to look as they moved through this opulent city. Behind
them rode the mounted archers, endless columns streaming in in their
most luxurious livery, drunk with the tumultuous celebrations whose din
seemed to touch the heavens. The rapturous reception was crowned with
Timur's proclamation of a three-year tax exemption for his subjects. Feasts
were ordered, booty distributed to the leading princes and commanders,
prisoners and criminals were paraded in chains and hanged before the
crowds. It was, said the court panegyrist Yazdi, a 'golden age'.

The Five-Year Campaign had been completed in four. Persia had been
brought back into line, recalcitrant Georgia had been reconquered, the
seat of the Abbasid Empire had folded and the Golden Horde had been
exterminated. Mawarannahr now faced no external threats. With the
immense treasures plundered from the campaign being carried into Samarkand on the backs of exhausted horses and camels, the empire had never
been stronger. Within the Muslim world, at the dawn of the fifteenth
century only the Ottoman Empire was beginning to emerge as a mean-
ingful future challenge, and that would quake before him soon enough.
As for Christian Europe, ravaged by Black Death, impoverished by political strife, endless wars and ignominious Crusades, it wasn't even worth
the journey.

Timur's most sacred construction in Samarkand during this time was
the necropolis of Shah-i-Zinda, the Living King. Though the site, which
lay beyond the city walls in the north-east of the capital over the ancient
settlement of Afrosiab, predated Timur by several centuries, under his
lavish patronage it developed into an important centre for Muslim

pilgrims, an integral part of his attempt to make Samarkand the Mecca of Central Asia. Arabia itself never fell under Timurid control; only, one is tempted to conclude, because it did not offer sufficient treasure for his armies to plunder.

Mausoleums had existed here from at least the twelfth century, but with one prominent exception Genghis's hordes had erased them from the face of the earth. The solitary survivor of the Mongol invasion and the centrepiece of the complex was the tomb of Kussam ibn Abbas, cousin of the Prophet Mohammed, who is supposed to have arrived in the province of Sogdiana, which encompassed Samarkand and Bukhara, in 676. Brimming with missionary fervour, Kussam was on a mission to convert the Zoroastrian fire-worshippers to Islam. The local population did not take kindly to this foreign preacher, however, and Kussam was quickly apprehended and beheaded. Notwithstanding his decapitation, legend has it, he managed to pick up his head and jump down a well, where he has remained ever since, ready to resume his work when the time comes. Arabs venerated him as a martyr and the cult of the Living King was born. Over the centuries, the tomb continued to attract the faithful, as it does today. 'The inhabitants of Samarkand come out to visit it every Sunday and Thursday night,' Ibn Battuta reported. 'The Tatars also come to visit it, pay vows to it and bring cows, sheep, *dirhams* and dinars; all this is used for the benefit of the hospital and the blessed tomb.'[9]

Timur sought to increase the popularity and prestige of the Shah-i-Zinda by converting it into a royal burial ground. Two of Timur's sisters were laid to rest here, together with other relatives and amirs, or princes, who had loyally served him. It was a feast of fine craftsmanship, masonry, calligraphy and art, a street of the dead awash with all hues of blue majolica tiles. Blue domes glowed like beacons in the white light, while all around them plainer domes of terracotta baked slowly in the sun.

For most of the twentieth century, in a cruel twist of history orchestrated by the Soviets, Shah-i-Zinda languished as an anti-Islamic museum. Freed from the shackles of communism, these days it is enjoying its latest renaissance as one of Samarkand's most impressive attractions. Farkhad and I visited the necropolis one afternoon in a latter-day pilgrimage. Our driver, a retired army officer, vigorously objected to the then government's use of Timur as part of its official regime propaganda. While the Soviets, fearing his power as a nationalist symbol, had alternately suppressed and vilified his name for seven decades, independent Uzbekistan was championing him with a vengeance. Streets and squares were named after him, newlyweds celebrated their marriages in front of statues of him, his portrait appeared on the highest-denomination banknotes, on newspaper mastheads and street hoardings. Timurabilia was everywhere, but our driver was having none of it.

'You know, in the army now they teach soldiers about Timur, how he was such a great warrior, how he won his many battles and how the new army of Uzbekistan fights in his spirit. "Strength in justice" they call it. All this talk of Timur is rubbish. It's all very well mentioning him all the time, but what does any of it mean? The comparisons aren't even accurate. Timur treated his soldiers very well. The pensions we get aren't enough to live on. This government can't even feed its own people.'

With this disheartening note ringing in our ears, we filed through the elaborate portal and domed entrance halls, built by the astronomer-king Ulugh Beg, Timur's grandson, and stepped into the complex. At once we were confronted by the familiar blue cupolas which top the Qazi Zadeh Rumi mausoleum, the largest on the site and thought by some to hold the body of Timur's wet-nurse. Down a narrow street shaded on both sides by tall monuments stand two of the finest tombs. The first, the mausoleum of Shadi Mulk-agha, built in 1372, housed a niece of Timur – 'This is a garden in which lies buried a Treasury of good fortune, And this is a tomb in which a precious pearl has been lost' reads the inscription – and the emperor's eldest sister Turkhan-agha. This was only the second dome of plain brickwork I had seen – the Rukhabad mausoleum in the centre of Samarkand was the first – its restrained simplicity forming a counterpoint both to the azure sky above and the intricate panels of carved and glazed terracotta and majolica on the portal below. It is justly considered one of the most brilliant examples of early Timurid ceramic revetments, with its entire façade and interior, including the dome, sheathed in tiles.

Inside the shaded tomb, the exuberance of the decoration shows no sign of restraint. Large rectangular panels containing medallions against a background of hexagrams stretch across the walls, framed by borders of knotted Kufic script to give the impression of a particularly fine carpet. The interior angles are filled with tumbling *muqarnas* or stalactite ornament. Above them, in the crown of the dome, a magnificent star shines forth, its eight points running down into lines which divide the heavens into eight panels, each with a teardrop medallion containing a sun and six planets in red, green and bright yellow.

Directly opposite is the tomb of Shirin Bika-agha, another of the emperor's sisters, erected a decade later, traced with mosaic faience in spiralling floral patterns of blues, yellows, white and green, vying for attention with scrolling vegetal decorations and the ornate ochre calligraphy running across the mosaics. Inside, beneath a double dome, a sixteen-sided drum tapers into an octagonal zone illuminated by shafts of sunlight stealing in through plaster-grille windows of coloured glass to reveal golden murals and a dado of green hexagons and flying cranes, the birds of heaven.

Towards the end of the street lies the Tuman-agha Mosque and mausoleum complex, named after one of Timur's favourite young wives, a twelve-year-old whom he married when he was in his early forties. The Paradise Garden was also designed in her honour. Tuman-agha had the complex erected in 1405, the year of her husband's death. At the foot of a portal twinkling with colourful faience is a carved door and above it the sombre inscription: 'The tomb is a door which everyone must enter.' On the portals of the mosque is the slightly more encouraging reminder: 'The prophet of God, peace be upon him, said, "Hurry with prayer before burial, And hurry with repentance before death." ' Within the mausoleum, Timur's bride sleeps beneath a dome of eternal night, a blue sky with scattered stars of gold watching over a country landscape of trees and flowers.

At the end of the street, past the tomb of Kutlug-agha, yet another of the emperor's wives, is the object of this pilgrimage, the deliciously cool Kussam ibn Abbas Mosque, supreme in the skyline with a trio of grand cupolas. The centre of the edifice, the *ziaratkhona* pilgrimage room, rebuilt in 1334, is ablaze with bright tiles. An elegant dado of light blue hexagons encircles the chamber, trimmed by mosaic faience in blue, green and white.

The holy heart of Shah-i-Zinda appears in a small chamber visible through a wooden lattice frame. There lies the grand four-storey tomb of Kussam ibn Abbas, its several tiers loaded with ornamented majolica and crammed with Quranic inscriptions: 'Those who were killed on the way of Allah are not to be considered dead,' reads one. 'Indeed they are very much alive.'

On 8 September 1404, after a journey of fifteen months and almost 6,000 miles from Cadiz, the dust-covered Spanish ambassador Ruy González de Clavijo rode wearily into Samarkand with his modest entourage. Arriving with the European ignorance of the East that was typical of his age, he was staggered to discover the city was larger than Seville.* It was a

---

* We have the whims of Black Sea weather systems in November 1403 to thank for Clavijo's brilliantly observed portrait of Timur and Samarkand in its finest hour. Clavijo originally intended to meet Timur in the eastern Caucasus, where the emperor and his army were wintering after campaigning in Georgia. The itinerary did not go according to plan. Shipwrecked on the edge of the Bosphorus, the Spaniards were forced to wait for four months in Constantinople until more favourable conditions arrived. The following spring they

revelation. 'The richness and abundance of this great capital and its district is such as is indeed a wonder to behold,' he exclaimed. Christendom, he had always believed, was unrivalled in the world. The rout of the Crusaders by the Ottoman sultan Bayazid at Nicopolis in 1396 had certainly challenged his confident outlook, but in his heart he was certain that the sword of Christianity would prevail over these Eastern heathens. Now, as he gazed up at the unearthly portals of Samarkand, its gorgeous turquoise domes, its heavenly parks and palaces, perhaps he suppressed a host of troublesome thoughts. Travelling overland, he had already seen enough of this empire to know that Christendom could boast no equal to the man who ruled it. Europe suddenly seemed a small place, a long, long way away.

Samarkand was approached through 'extensive suburbs', densely populated and neatly laid out with orchards, vineyards, streets and markets in open squares.

> Among these orchards outside Samarkand are found the most noble and beautiful houses, and here Timur has his many palaces and pleasure grounds. Round and about the great men of the government also here have their estates and country houses, each standing within its orchard: and so numerous are these gardens and vineyards surrounding Samarkand that a traveller who approaches the city sees only a great mountainous height of trees and the houses embowered among them remain invisible.[10]

By the time Clavijo arrived, Timur had won new distinction – and immeasurable treasures – from landmark victories during what Arabshah dubbed his 'pilgrimage of destruction' across the Middle East and Indian Subcontinent. In 1398, having traversed the snow-bound Hindu Kush mountains, he self-consciously outdid both Alexander the Great and Genghis Khan by storming Delhi, plundering gold and silver without end, jewellery, pearls and precious stones, coins and rich clothing and so many slaves that the poorest soldier in his army seized at least twenty. The extraordinary wealth amassed by generations of Indian sultans vanished in a matter of days. Ancient Aleppo was put to the sword in 1400 until 'it stank with corpses', according to the fifteenth-century historian Ibn Taghribirdi. Damascus, after a remarkable meeting between Timur and the great historian Ibn Khaldun, followed in 1401, its people tortured and slaughtered, its finest monuments, mosques, palaces and caravanserais

---

continued their journey, by which time Timur had left for Samarkand. Clavijo was obliged to play catch-up and arrived only the following autumn. He remained in Samarkand for three months. It was one of history's most auspicious shipwrecks.

burnt to the ground. The great Umayyad Mosque, one of the Islamic wonders of the world, was devastated by the inferno, desecrated by an army of Muslims under the command of a man who sought recognition as the Ghazi or Warrior of the Faith.* In the same year Baghdad paid for rebellion with its complete annihilation, a triumph Timur celebrated with his dreadful battlefield signature, 120 towers built from the 90,000 heads of his victims. The Tigris ran red with blood and blue with ink from the books ransacked from its libraries. Then, in 1402, Timur trounced the Ottoman Sultan Bayazid I at the Battle of Ankara, the only time in Ottoman history that the sultan suffered the ignominy of being captured in person. His victory allowed Constantinople, under mounting pressure from the Turks, to survive another half-century. Almost as an afterthought, he also sacked Smyrna, the last Christian outpost in Asia Minor, putting the finishing touches to this victory by bombarding the fleeing knights with the severed heads of their colleagues.† He stood, then, at the summit of the Islamic world.

'From the Irtish and Volga to the Persian Gulf and from the Ganges to Damascus and the Archipelago, Asia was in the hands of Timour,' wrote Edward Gibbon. 'His armies were invincible, his ambition was boundless, and his zeal might aspire to conquer and convert the Christian kingdoms of the West, which already trembled at his name.' While Timur stood at the gates of Europe, its feeble, divided and penurious kings – Henry IV of England, Charles VI of France, Henry III of Castile – did indeed tremble at the ease with which this unknown warlord had dispatched their most feared enemy. They rushed off sycophantic letters of congratulation and professions of goodwill to 'the most victorious and serene Prince Themur' in the hope of forestalling invasion. They needn't have worried. Timur had a far greater prize in mind.

---

*   Having seen them camped outside the walls of Damascus shortly before the city's sacking, Ibn Khaldun left a compelling picture of Timur's Tatar hordes: 'The people are of a number which cannot be counted. If you estimate it at one million it would not be too much, nor can you say it is less. If they pitched their tents together in the land, they would fill all empty spaces, and if their armies came even into a wide territory the plain would be too narrow for them. And in raiding, robbing and slaughtering settled populations and inflicting upon them all kinds of cruelty they are an astounding example.' Walter J. Fischel, *Ibn Khaldun in Egypt*, pp. 99–100
†   Yazdi provides an entertaining summary of the pre-battle correspondence between the two mighty monarchs, including Timur's warning to Bayazid: 'Since the ship of your unfathomable ambition has been shipwrecked in the abyss of self-love, it would be wise for you to lower the sails of your rashness and cast the anchor of repentance in the port of sincerity, which is also the port of safety; lest, by the tempest of our vengeance you should perish in the sea of punishment which you deserve ...' *The History of Timur-Bec*, vol. 2, pp. 148–50

Clavijo's audience with the emperor was held in the evocatively named Baghi Dilkusha, the Garden of Heart's Delight, one of Timur's most fabulous parks, designed and laid out during the emperor's two-year residence in his capital to mark his marriage in 1397 to princess Tukal-khanum, daughter of the Moghul khan Khizr Khoja. The garden lay a little to the east of Samarkand among the famous meadows of Kani-gil. From the Turquoise Gate in the city walls a straight avenue of pines led directly to the summer palace. In his memoirs, Timur's great-great-great-grandson Babur, founder of the Mughal Empire, noted its many paintings celebrating his ancestor's Indian campaign. With three storeys, a glittering dome and a forest of colonnades, it was a building of imperial dimensions.

Clavijo was led first through a great orchard, entering via a towering gate beautifully decorated with the finest blue and gold tiles. Six elephants, trophies from Delhi, guarded the entrance with imperial doorkeepers armed with maces next to them, each beast bearing a miniature castle on its back and performing tricks at the behest of its keeper. Clavijo and his companions were then escorted from one courtier to the next until they reached the emperor's grandson Khalil Sultan, who took their letter from King Henry and directed them to the Conqueror of the World. The audience could now begin. The scrupulously attentive ambassador left us a portrait of the magnificent Oriental despot, seated on a dais beneath the portal of a beautiful palace. Red apples bobbed about in a fountain which threw a column of water high into the air.

> His Highness had taken his place on what appeared to be small mattresses stuffed thick and covered with embroidered silk cloth, and he was leaning on his elbow against some round cushions that were heaped up behind him. He was dressed in a cloak of plain silk without any embroidery, and he wore on his head a tall white hat on the crown of which was displayed a balas ruby, the same being further ornamented with pearls and precious stones.

The audience passed off successfully, although Timur left the Spaniard in no doubt that he regarded himself as sovereign of the world, referring to the Spanish monarch as 'my son your King'. Henry III, Timur acknowledged, was 'the greatest of all the kings of the Franks who reign in that farther quarter of the earth where his people are a great and famous nation', but that was only in small-time Europe, land of the Franks. Timur's power and riches were on an altogether more impressive scale, hence the condescension to a petty princeling of the infidel West.

Clavijo's description of Samarkand in the early years of the fifteenth century, the highpoint of Timur's empire, is unparalleled. The envoy could

hardly believe his eyes. There were at least fifteen formally laid-out parks
with names like Garden of Paradise, the Model of the World and Sublime
Garden, all with palaces, immaculate lawns, meadows, babbling streams,
lakes, orchards, bowers and flowers. There was the Garden of the Square,
home to the two-storey Palace of Forty Pillars, then the Baghi Chinar, or
Plane Tree Garden, where Clavijo saw an extravagantly beautiful palace
in the process of construction. And Baghi Naw, the New Garden, lined
with four towers surrounded by a high wall a mile long on each side. In
the centre of the garden was an orchard and in the orchard was a palace.
Inside were marble sculptures and floors with exquisite mosaics of ebony
and ivory. According to Babur, a verse from the Quran was inscribed over
the doorway in letters so large they could be read two miles away.

Through this network of palaces and gardens Timur glided like a gilded
lion, spending several days in one before moving serenely to another. A
week after his arrival, Clavijo was invited to an imperial banquet in
another garden planted with fruit trees and paved with paths and walk-
ways. All around him were silk tents with coloured tapestries to provide
shade. In the centre of the garden was a richly furnished palace where the
Spaniard glimpsed the emperor's sleeping chamber, an elegant tiled alcove
with a silver and gilt screen in front of which a small mattress of silk
worked with gold thread lay on a dais. The walls were covered with rose-
coloured silk hangings ornamented with silver spangles containing
emeralds, pearls and other precious stones. Silk tassels rustled in the
breeze. In front of the entrance to these chambers were two tables of gold
and on them seven golden flasks, two of which were set with large pearls,
emeralds and turquoises with balas rubies at their lips. Next to them stood
six cups of gold, similarly set with pearls and rubies. Clavijo took it all
in, entranced.

The Northern Garden, one of Timur's most extravagant creations, was
another of the grandiose projects conceived between 1396 and 1398. It
was typical insofar as it made use of the empire's finest materials and its
most famous craftsmen. The marble for the palace was imported from
Tabriz, the artists and painters likewise came from Persia. The images in
these paintings, like those of the Registan public square which survive to
this day, were a direct challenge to Islam's discouragement of figurative
art, symbolic perhaps of Timur's unrivalled ascendancy, boundless self-
confidence and also of his ambivalent attitude towards the faith, not least
in the pictures of Timur and his men drinking bumpers of wine.

It was not just the outstanding beauty of these parks and palaces that
so moved Clavijo. It was also their sheer size. During his two years in and
around Samarkand, Timur laid out another park, the Takhta Qaracha

Gardens, an enclosure so vast, said Arabshah, that when one of the build-ers working on it lost his horse, the animal roamed about grazing quite happily for six months before he found it again. There were so many fruit trees planted throughout the city that one hundred pounds of fruit 'would not sell for a grain of mustard'.

This was a land of plenty, watered by the Zarafshan River, with fertile soil producing bumper crops of wheat and cotton. Vineyards were plen-tiful. The grazing was excellent for cattle and sheep. 'The livestock is magnificent, beasts and poultry all of a fine breed,' the envoy remarked approvingly. There were sheep with tails so fat they weighed twenty pounds. Even when Timur and his army were camping in the outlying meadows of Kani-gil and demand for meat was high, a pair of sheep still cost no more than a ducat. Wherever he looked, Clavijo saw food. Although he was teetotal – much to Timur's displeasure – the Spaniard was something of a gourmand, and noted with wonder the range of pro-duce. Bread was available in all parts, while rice was sold cheaply in great quantities. Everywhere there were open squares with butchers selling meat ready-cooked, roasted or in stews – fowl, pheasants and partridges were particularly popular. Fruit and vegetables, including the delicious Samar-kand melons, were grown in such abundance that many were cured and kept for a year.

During his three months in the city, Clavijo was especially impressed by the well-stocked markets. Standing on the great Khorasan road, run-ning east from Baghdad to the border with China, Samarkand had become a major trade centre during Timur's reign, the more so once the northern trade route had been diverted south after his destruction of the Golden Horde. While the Zarafshan watered the city, trade fed it and made it rich. Caravans regularly poured into town bringing plunder from the latest campaign, and tribute was always arriving from the growing ranks of vassal rulers. But commerce, and the taxes it generated for the imperial exchequer, was the backbone of prosperity throughout the empire, and was always attended to by Timur with the greatest care. Timur was that rarest of political and military leaders, an amalgam of scorched-earth conqueror and strategic empire-builder. The Islamic world had never seen anything like it, and never would again.

From the top of the minaret on the Ulugh Beg Madrassa in the Registan – which George Curzon, the future viceroy of India and British foreign secretary, considered 'the noblest public square in the world' – Samarkand is a sea of blue domes and portals almost as far as the eye can see. Only in the very farthest reaches of the horizon, where the desert lurks on the shores of this ocean, as if ready to reclaim the city in an instant, is the effusion of light dimmed slightly. And there, in the midst of this blaze of sunshine, several hundred yards north-east of the Registan, stands Timur's pride and joy, the Bibi Khanum Mosque, or Mosque of the Mother Queen.

The Cathedral Mosque was one of his greatest projects, a towering edifice among the most colossal monuments ever built in the Islamic world, a tribute to his numerous victories. Its construction began in 1399. Perhaps in these late years the emperor was growing increasingly aware of his own mortality and decided on a building to honour the Almighty, rather than a secular project as was generally his wont.

In Timur's earlier buildings, the domes tended to follow the Persian style – pointed without flowing outwards from their base. With their majestic pomegranate domes the Bibi Khanum Mosque and the Gur Amir mausoleum were harbingers of a new style, embraced by the Timurids after the emperor's death, and passed on to the Mughals of India, who used it to most notable effect in the Taj Mahal. The style was later exported to Russia, where it is seen in its full glory in the Kremlin.

This was a project on which Timur unleashed his fearsome instincts for control. Instructed to send him daily progress reports, two amirs, Khoja Mahmud Daoud and Mohammed Jalad, presided over a huge, highly skilled army of workers: master craftsmen from Basra and Baghdad, stonemasons from Azerbaijan, Fars and India, crystal workers from Damascus and artisans from Samarkand. Ninety-five elephants, never seen before in Samarkand, caused a sensation hauling 200 blocks of marble from Azerbaijan, Persia and India.

In 1404, as the mosque neared completion, the workers were surprised by the emperor's arrival, fresh from his triumphant Five-Year Campaign. Unimpressed by the modest size of the portal, the incandescent Timur ordered it to be torn down immediately and new foundations dug. The two amirs in charge were sentenced to death, Timur reserving the most gruesome punishment for Mohammed Jalad, who was dragged on his face by horses until torn to pieces.

The Conqueror of the World then took personal charge of the construction. Although in poor health and unable either to stand for long or to mount his horse, he had himself carried to the site every day in a litter, throwing coins and pieces of meat down to the workmen in the foundations 'as though one should cast bones to dogs in a pit'.

With Timur on site, the building continued night and day. The result was breathtaking. Its scale was unique, contained within an area spanning over 150 metres by 107 metres. The portal reached over thirty metres, outdone only by the forty-six-metre minarets, which looked down on a great courtyard bordered by a gallery of 400 cupolas supported by 400 marble columns. 'The dome would have been unique but for the sky being its copy; the arch would have been singular but for the Milky Way matching it,' the court historian simpered.

But however magnificent was Timur's Cathedral Mosque, it had been built too quickly. The emperor's execution of the two amirs had doubtless caused a frenzy among the workers. Perhaps they cut corners in their efforts to finish the building and save their heads. Perhaps the foundations were too shallow. The exact reasons are unknown, but no sooner had the mosque been completed than it started falling down. It was not long before worshippers, their devout reflections shattered by tumbling masonry, decided to take their prayers elsewhere. By the nineteenth century it was doubling as a cotton market and stables for tsarist officers, Bukharan amirs having plundered it of anything valuable. In 1897 an earthquake hit Samarkand, and the mosque was dealt a lethal blow.

From the top of the towers I stared over a burnished Samarkand in the warm streaming wind, past the mosque's immense dome, the azure sheen pockmarked with terracotta where missing tiles should have been. In his description of the Cathedral Mosque Yazdi seized upon its otherworldly dimensions. 'How marvellously high is the building whose upper rooms are Paradise,' he wrote. 'To estimate its loftiness must confound the greatest minds.' For once the court sycophant was hardly exaggerating.

There is no better place in which to bid farewell to Timur than the Gur Amir mausoleum where he is buried. In 1405, at the age of sixty-nine, he died in the saddle en route to war with the Ming emperor of China, the only adversary left whom he considered worthy of war. He had nothing more to achieve.

With its forty-metre blue-ribbed dome, flanked by two slender minarets, it is the finest building in Samarkand and the most inspired piece of Timurid architecture the world ever saw. Built by the emperor to honour his cherished grandson Mohammed Sultan, it became the final resting place of the Conqueror of the World, interred here by his grandson Khalil Sultan, embalmed with camphor, musk and rose-water, in a coffin of ebony beneath 'star-candles of gold and silver in the sky of the ceilings'.

Built on an octagonal plan by Mohammed ibn Mahmoud Isfahani, a celebrated architect from Persia, the mausoleum is a triumph of scale, style and simplicity, a noble building which celebrates the life of a prince, the sway of a dynasty and the omnipotence of God. Beneath the textured surface of the dome, shining with tiles of navy blue, turquoise, yellow and green, runs the inscription, in huge Kufic script over three metres high, 'God is Immortal'. Moved by the enormity of the cupola, a poet declared: 'Should the sky disappear, the dome will replace it.'

The heart of the mausoleum was a cavernous square chamber directly beneath the dome. Beyond the upper vaults, at neck-craning height, amber light streamed in from marble lattice windows, illuminating the golden furnace of the inner dome above and the tumbling stalactites of gold and blue, resplendent amid geometric panels of iridescent stars. Six tombs belonging to the leading lights of the Timurid Dynasty lay in the centre of the chamber: the valiant prince Mohammed Sultan; Ulugh Beg, the polymath astronomer king; his father, Shahrukh, wise patron of the arts; Miranshah, the emperor's most troublesome son. Raised on a marble plinth in the centre lay Timur's tomb, a slab of the darkest, most intricately engraved jade, once the largest piece of the stone in the world, brought to Samarkand by Ulugh Beg in 1425 to adorn his grandfather's cenotaph. It lay next to another sepulchre, belonging to Shaykh Sayid Baraka. The emperor's instructions to be buried at the feet of his spiritual and religious mentor had been honoured to the letter.

In death Timur managed to intertwine the two conflicting strands of his identity. The long inscription detailing – and mythologizing – his genealogy, pronounced him the descendant of both Genghis Khan and the Caliph Ali, uniting the traditions of the Mongols with the heritage of Islam in an audacious, mendacious piece of state propaganda. In death, just as in life, he was supremely pragmatic. Here, though he hailed from a conventionally Sunni tradition, he was represented as a Shia Muslim, buried alongside his Sufi guide and soulmate. Petty theological divisions were beneath the interest of the man who ruled the world.

An elderly caretaker in a ragged suit and tatty skullcap arrived, pointing at his watch, and started turning off the lights. Then he paused. For a couple of dollars, he could show me Timur's 'real grave'. My heartbeat quickened. The ground-level tombstones were merely decorative. Carefully, we made our way down a hidden flight of stairs, opened a heavy door and stepped into a glacial, pitch-black crypt. The flick of a light switch revealed a plain vault of brick and stone.

Timur's burial place was a simple slab of carved stone engraved with Quranic inscriptions. After the pomp and colour of the mausoleum above, the drab, dark chamber was a sombre sight. This was the grave of the man who had blazed across Asia like a comet across the heavens. For a few years his descendants watched over the glowing embers falling through the sky until the Timurid Empire crashed to earth in the middle of the fifteenth century, extinguished altogether. The greatest gifts it bequeathed – the mosques and *madrassas*, the dazzling minarets, the exquisite parks and palaces – lay scattered across Asia like funerary monuments to a lost civilization. Only in the Mughal Empire, founded across the roof of the world by Timur's most illustrious descendant Babur, did echoes of its splendour survive.

In the West, Timur has been all but forgotten. Those who know his name perhaps remember the fire and brimstone of Marlowe's play about a blood-crazed tyrant. But to all but a few, the greatest Islamic empire-builder in history remains little more than that: a name. The city he built so brilliantly and decorated so lovingly, once the envy of the world, lies in a neglected southern outpost of the old Soviet Empire. Only here does his memory burn brightly. Above the door was a short inscription:

> This is the resting place of the illustrious and merciful monarch, the most great Sultan, the most mighty warrior, Lord Timur, Conqueror of the World.

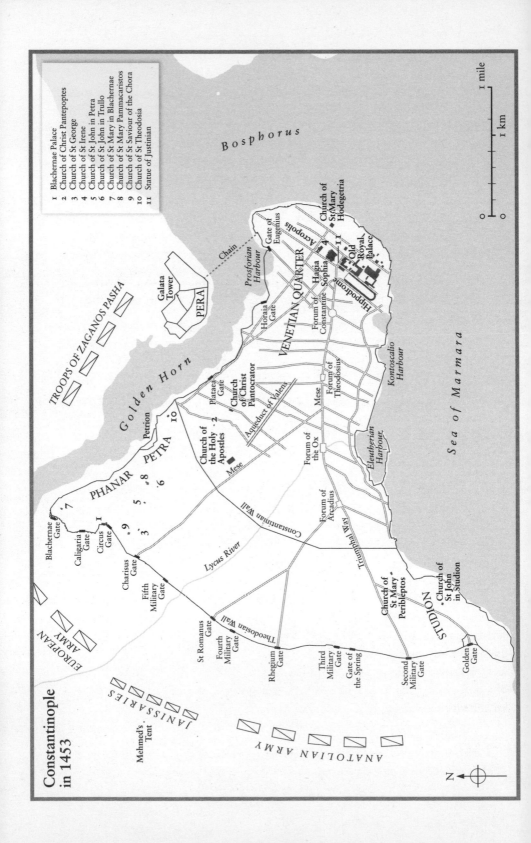

Constantinople
in 1453

Legend (key)
1 Blachernae Palace
2 Church of Christ Pantepoptes
3 Church of St George
4 Church of St Irene
5 Church of St John in Petra
6 Church of St John in Trullo
7 Church of St Mary in Blachernae
8 Church of St Mary Pammacaristos
9 Church of St Saviour of the Chora
10 Church of St Theodosia
11 Statue of Justinian

Bosphorus

Golden Horn

PERA

Galata
Tower

Chain

TROOPS OF ZAGANOS PASHA

Gate of Eugenius
Prosforian Harbour
Acropolis
Church of St Mary Hodegetria
Old Royal Palace

Horaia Gate
VENETIAN QUARTER
Hippodrome
Hagia Sophia
Forum of Constantine

Plataea Gate
Church of Christ Pantocrator
Aqueduct of Valens
Mese
Forum of Theodosius
Kontoscalio Harbour

Petrion
PHANAR
PETRA
Church of the Holy Apostles
Mese
Forum of the Ox
Eleutherian Harbour

Blachernae Gate
Caligaria Gate
Circus Gate
Charisius Gate
Fifth Military Gate
Lycus River
Constantinian Wall
Forum of Arcadius
Triumphal Way
Sea of Marmara

EUROPEAN ARMY

St Romanus Gate
Fourth Military Gate
Theodosian Wall
Rhegium Gate
Third Military Gate
Gate of the Spring
Second Military Gate
Church of St Mary Peribleptos
STUDION
Church of St John in Studion
Golden Gate

Mehmed's Tent
JANISSARIES
ANATOLIAN ARMY

N

1 mile
1 km
0

9

Constantinople – City of the World's Desire (15th Century)

Istanbul was Constantinople
Now it's Istanbul not Constantinople . . .

Lyrics by Jimmy Kennedy and music by Nat Simon, 1953

In 1400, four years after Ottoman Sultan Bayazid routed the pick of European chivalry at the Battle of Nicopolis, two years before Timur in turn annihilated Bayazid's army at the Battle of Ankara, a weary Eastern monarch arrived in London. With his imperial capital of Constantinople under siege from the Ottomans, Manuel II Palaiologos, the only Byzantine emperor ever to visit England, had come to seek support from his Western cousins in Christendom. He and his courtiers had already traipsed across Europe to Venice, Padua, Rome, Milan and Paris before crossing the Channel to try their luck. Moved by the plight of his venerable guest, Henry IV entertained Manuel lavishly over Christmas in Eltham Palace, where jousts, banquets and a masquerade were laid on in his honour. English scholars familiar with the classical Greek works of history and philosophy thrilled to meet the highly educated soldier-statesman and man of letters. Yet for all the royal honour, courtesy and generosity of his reception in this damp, grey-skied kingdom, there was no offer of military assistance. Adam of Usk, the Welsh lawyer and chronicler who worked in Henry's court, wrote of his sadness that this great Christian leader had been driven by 'the power of the infidels' to cross an entire continent in the desperate, unfulfilled hope of finding help. Constantinople, cynosure of the world, was in the greatest danger:

> Oh God! What has become of you, ancient glory of Rome? Today your imperial greatness lies in ruins for all to see . . . Who would ever believe that you, accustomed as you were to sitting on your throne of majesty, and

ruling the entire world, would now be reduced to such straits that you cannot afford any help whatsoever to the Christian faith?[1]

The sense of loss underpinning the Welshman's narrative revealed the profound grip Constantinople had exercised on the Christian imagination for many centuries. Unlike once pagan Rome, the city founded by Constantine in 324 on the ancient site of Byzantium, had been Christian from its very beginning. By the close of the fourth century it had become the Christian capital of a Christian empire. Spread out across seven hills like Rome, it was ostentatiously imperial in design. Statues of Alexander the Great, Caesar, Augustus, Diocletian and Constantine presided over broad colonnaded avenues running towards the monumental Chalkoun Tetrapylon, a four-sided triumphal arch reveted with bronze that stood at the intersection of the Mese (Middle Way), the city's principal street, and an avenue connecting the Golden Horn with the Sea of Marmara – approximately the crossroads where tomb-lined Divanyolu and Uzunçarşi Streets meet today.[2]

The ancient Roman circus, though now bereft of the four great bronze horses that had been carted off to adorn St Mark's Basilica in Venice during the Crusader apocalypse of 1204, had evolved into another victory monument, consciously harking back to the greatest glories of classical antiquity. Constantine had taken away the great Serpent Column or Plataean Tripod, the bronze column erected at Delphi to commemorate the momentous Greek victory over the Persians at the Battle of Plataea in 479 BC, to decorate the new seat of his empire.

This was a city of imperial palaces, a stock market, law court, hippodrome and library. Traders roved the markets and ship-filled harbours, while scholars pored over ancient texts and pious, hoary-bearded monks and earnest nuns bustled about beneath the broad domes of churches and monasteries, worshipping to the endless tolling of church bells and ancient chants among glittering icons, sacred relics and priceless Christian treasures.

Constantinople's architectural centrepiece both reflected and defined this Christian heritage in the monumental form of Hagia Sophia (Holy Wisdom), the church completed by Justinian in 537 that so awed the sixth-century Byzantine historian Procopius – and all who saw it. 'For it soars to a height to match the sky, and as if surging up from amongst the other buildings it stands on high and looks down upon the remainder of the city, adorning it, because it is a part of it, but glorying in its own beauty . . .' It 'exults in an indescribable beauty', he continued, pronouncing the great edifice 'altogether incredible'. Had it not been for the rich, sense-stirring liturgy that visitors from the Kievan Rus federation witnessed in Hagia Sophia on a reconnaissance mission to Constantinople in the tenth century, Russia might never have turned Orthodox. 'We knew not whether we were in Heaven or earth,' they reported, overwhelmed by such ritual. 'For on earth there is no such splendour and beauty, and we are at a loss how to describe it. We only know that there God dwells among men.'[3]

Fulcher of Chartres, the priest whom we last encountered likening the slaughtered Jews and Muslims of Jerusalem to rotten fruit in 1099, spoke for many in Christendom – profound sectarian divisions between Catholic and Orthodox notwithstanding – when he praised Constantinople to the heavens:

> Oh, what an excellent and beautiful city! How many monasteries, and how many palaces there are in it, of wonderful work, skilfully fashioned! How many marvellous works are to be seen in the streets and districts of the town! It is a great nuisance to recite what an opulence of all kinds of goods are found there; of gold, of silver, of many kinds of mantles, and holy relics. In every season merchants in frequent sailings bring to that place everything that man might need.[4]

Incredible to Procopius, breathtaking to the Russians, staggeringly beautiful to the cleric Fulcher, Constantinople was scarcely less exceptional in terms of its setting. It occupied a vast, slightly compressed triangle of land, two sides of which were bordered by sea, the third land flank delineated by massive defensive walls arcing gently from north to south. To the north lay the deep waters of the Golden Horn, a perfect port. Further east, the narrow Bosphorus channel led north to the Black Sea, while to the south the Sea of Marmara provided access, via the chokepoint of the Dardanelles, to the Aegean and Mediterranean. Marvellous to behold, Constantinople was protected by the swirling waters, fierce currents and devastating storms of the Sea of Marmara, which posed nigh insuperable obstacles to any naval offensive. A 300-metre iron chain of giant links suspended on wooden floats, pulled across the Golden Horn between the eastern tip of the city and the Genoese city-state of Galata in time of need, militated against attacks from that quarter.

Yet the most impressive man-made defences by far were the colossal city walls raised during the reign of the boy emperor Theodosius II (r. 408–50). Running for four miles on the landward side of the triangle, these formed an extraordinarily elaborate fortification. First came a twenty-metre-wide moat with crenellated wall on the inner side, then a *parateichion* outer terrace or killing field, where attackers who had managed to cross the water could be picked off easily from the walls. This terrace led to an outer wall, nine metres high and topped with towers and a battlemented walkway. Beyond a *peribolos* terrace loomed the mighty inner wall, up to six metres thick and twelve metres high, strengthened with ninety-six towers and fighting ramparts. Together, this complex system of moat and walls with towers, battlements and gates represented the ancient world's most formidable – and for attackers utterly spirit-sapping – defences ever constructed.[5] They were completed by a wall defending the Marmara coastline, reinforced with 188 towers, and another protecting attack from the Golden Horn, which had a further 110 towers. To all intents and purposes the city was impregnable.

So vital were its walls to the life of the city that Constantinople even had its own Count of the Walls, a senior official whose responsibility was the upkeep of the defences with the obligatory assistance of every citizen. Over the centuries the limestone, brick-banded walls had, with the sole exception of the Crusaders' invasion of 1204, withstood everything their enemies had thrown at them. They had seen off a long line of would-be conquerors, from Attila the Hun in 447, to the Avars in 626, the Umayyad caliph Muawiya from 674 to 678, the Umayyad prince Maslama in 717–18, the Russians in 860, the Nicaean Empire in 1260 and the Ottomans in 1422. In all, by the middle of the fourteenth century Constantinople had been put under siege twenty-three times and only once had it bowed to enemy forces. Such was the aura of protection around the walls that powerful legends had grown up around them. During moments of crisis holy relics were paraded along the ramparts to seek divine intercession and victory over the empire's enemies. As a modern historian has noted, while the Hagia Sophia offered spiritual succour to the citizens of Constantinople, the walls represented more concrete reassurance. 'If the church was their vision of heaven, the wall was their shield against the battering of hostile forces, under the personal protection of the Virgin herself.'[6]

Grandest and richest city in Europe from the middle of the fifth century to the beginning of the thirteenth, successor to Rome as imperial capital, source of pride to Christians of the Byzantine Empire, Constantinople had long attracted covetous Muslim eyes. Ever since the Prophet's standard bearer Ayyub had been martyred at the gates of Constantinople around 674, since Muawiya's repeated naval operations had ended in ignominy and his death as a broken man in 680, the faithful had begun to attribute special Islamic sanctity to the city, spurred on by a series of *hadiths* or sayings of the Prophet, some with greater legitimacy than others, that prophesied its eventual fall to the Muslims. One of them reassured believers that, 'In the jihad against Constantinople, one third of Muslims will allow themselves to be defeated, which Allah cannot forgive; one third will be killed in battle, making them wondrous martyrs; and one third will be victorious.' Another, still quoted in twenty-first-century Istanbul, confidently asserted: 'Verily they will conquer Constantinople. Truly their commander will be an excellent one. Truly their army will be an excellent one.'[7]

The fourteenth century was not kind to Constantinople. In its opening decades a new Muslim power began to emerge from the ancient Roman province of Bithynia in north-western Anatolia. Its rising strength under its founder Osman (d. c. 1324), a shadowy Turkman tribal leader who was able first to rally and then to command a large number of independent Turkman tribes, came almost entirely at the expense of the declining Byzantine Empire.[8] In 1326, the Byzantine city of Bursa, one hundred miles south of Constantinople, fell and became the first capital of the fledgling Ottoman – from Osman – state. Today the city is home to Osman's ornate, tent-like tomb. Rebuilt after a shattering earthquake in 1868 by Ottoman Sultan Abdulaziz in high baroque style, it is shrouded in silver-embroidered velvet and surrounded by a screen inlaid with mother of pearl, fitting tribute to the founder of a dynasty that would become one of the world's greatest empires. Other landmark cities fell before the new Muslim power. Smyrna became Izmir, ancient Nicaea – famous for giving Christians the Nicene Creed – Iznik.

The globetrotting Moroccan traveller Ibn Battuta, who visited and admired Osman's tomb in Bursa, arrived in Constantinople in 1332. He was impressed by its great size, though he considered the imperial capital more a collection of thirteen individual villages, separated by fields, than a single city. There is an unmistakable whiff of decline – broken bridges, filthy markets – in his description of the city, counterbalanced by a recognition of the powerful Christian identity, heritage and practice, not least in the Hagia Sophia, as big as a city in its own right, which he was told contained 'thousands' of monks and priests, in addition to another church that was home to 'more than a thousand virgins'. Ibn Battuta, an inveterate social climber, managed to secure an audience with the emperor Andronikos III Palaiologos, who gave him a robe of honour and assigned him a horse on which, to the accompaniment of 'trumpets, fifes and drums', he was paraded around the city to admire its 'marvellous and rare sights'.[9] The Moroccan was made to sing for his supper. He was quizzed by the curious emperor on a number of Islamic cities, including Jerusalem and its Dome of the Rock and Church of the Holy Sepulchre, Damascus, Cairo and Baghdad.

From the 1340s, the Byzantine Empire was beset with civil wars, doctrinal controversy and invasions by both Ottomans and Serbs. In 1347 it earned the dubious distinction of becoming the first European city to be overrun with rats carrying the Black Death plague. During the coronation of John VI Cantacuzenos in the same year, it was noticed that his crown jewels were made of glass, rather than diamonds and precious stones, which now sat in the treasury of St Mark's in Venice. The once dazzling banqueting plates had been reduced to clay and pewter.[10] Then, in 1362, the Ottomans took the city of Adrianople (Edirne in Turkish), 150 miles north-west of Constantinople, and the writing was not so much on the walls – tried and tested as they had been – but on the map. Increasingly, the metropolis was starting to resemble a beleaguered Christian island in an expanding Muslim sea. Decisive Ottoman victories at the Battles of Maritsa in 1371, from which time the Byzantine emperor became a vassal of the sultan, and Kosovo in 1389 completely overwhelmed the Serbs, putting paid to any hopes of support from Constantinople's Christian neighbours against a Muslim power in the ascendant. A trio of Hungarian-led Crusades in the later fourteenth and early fifteenth centuries shared a similar fate: ignominious defeat at the hands of a better organized, more united adversary, revelling in the opportunities provided by Europe's first fully professional army since the Roman Empire.

By the beginning of the fifteenth century, the Ottoman state ran from the Danube in the west to the Euphrates in the east. After the death of its founder in 1405, the Timurid Empire under Ulugh Beg was a diminishing force confined to Central Asia. As Byzantium had shrunk in on itself, so the nascent Ottoman Empire had grown in tandem. Osman's famous dream, in which he had seen a tree springing from his body with branches covering the whole world, its leaves transformed into swords turned against Constantinople, looked rather less improbable than it had been during his lifetime. This dream would become a resonant foundation myth of the Ottoman Empire.

A brief portrait of the city in the opening years of the fifteenth century comes from Ruy González de Clavijo, the Spanish ambassador from Castile, who had marvelled at Timur's frenzy of imperial construction in Samarkand. Arriving in Constantinople in 1403, Clavijo caught the ambivalent tone of glory and decline. 'Everywhere throughout the city there are many great palaces, churches and monasteries, but most of them are now in ruin. It is however plain that in former times when Constantinople was in its pristine state it was one of the noblest cities in the world.' There were many houses, too, but mostly 'falling to decay'. Like so many visitors before and since, he swooned at the sight of the 'mighty dome' of Hagia Sophia, whose nave he judged 'the most spacious and the loftiest and the most beautifully and richly wrought that I think anywhere in the world can be seen'. The church was so immense and so full of 'wonderful' sights that it defied 'complete examination'. Given what followed half a century after his visit, Clavijo's last words on Constantinople, recalling Ottoman Sultan Bayazid's abject failure to take the city after a decade-long siege from 1394 to 1402, positively leap out at the modern reader: 'Indeed for so great a nation as are the Turks, it is strange how unskilful they are in their siege operations, and on this occasion they entirely failed.'[11]

They failed again in 1422. This time the new Ottoman Sultan Murad II launched a full-scale siege, determined to bring Constantinople to heel after Manuel II and his son John VIII Palaiologos (r. 1425–48), deprived of European military support, had resorted to the classic Byzantine ruse of interfering with the Ottoman succession upon the death of Sultan Mehmed I in 1421 by backing the claims of first one rival prince and then another. Murad constructed a huge rampart of earth running from the Sea of Marmara to the Golden Horn, from which volleys of fire and stone were unleashed into the city. During a furious contest for the walls, the Ottomans suddenly panicked, retreated and fled. Although the walls had once again rebuffed the invaders, the Greeks attributed the victory to their prize supernatural guardian, the *Theotokos* or Mother of God. As was her wont during moments of crisis for Constantinople, the Blessed Virgin Mary herself had reportedly appeared on the walls during one of the fiercest Ottoman attacks, inspiring the defenders to heroic resistance and victory. In his account of the 1422 siege the eyewitness and Byzantine historian John Kananos wrote of the defenders breaking into prayers and hymns to the Most Holy Virgin, paying tribute to 'a rich, celebrated, memorable, extraordinary and remarkable miracle worthy of admiration'.[12]

Victory did not come without a heavy cost, however. In a striking recognition of the shifting balance of power, the elderly Emperor Manuel came to terms with Murad in 1424, negotiating a settlement under which Constantinople was reduced again to tributary status and an annual payment of 300,000 silver coins, according to the Byzantine historian Doukas.[13] There were wider costs to the empire. Although Constantinople had escaped again, 370 miles to the west Thessalonica, which had been defended by the Venetians during a simultaneous Ottoman siege, was not so fortunate. In 1430, Murad appeared at the head of a vast army, offering the empire's second city the chance to surrender. Its refusal to submit peacefully guaranteed it a dire fate in the event of its conquest. This quickly followed, triggering bloodshed and the three days of wholesale plunder allowed under Islamic law. Several thousand were carted off into slavery, churches and other buildings were ransacked. Murad wasted little

time rehabilitating the now Muslim Thessalonica. The venerable church
of the Virgin Acheiropoietos was swiftly converted into a mosque. The
second city of Byzantium had been swallowed up by the Ottomans with
barely a fight.

Western powers could hardly fail to take notice. Bertrandon de Brocquière, the Burgundian spy who worked for Philip Duke of Burgundy,
arrived in Constantinople in the early 1430s. In *Le Voyage d'Outre-Mer*,
the story of his travels, it is not difficult to discern a grudging admiration
for the qualities of the Turks, their hardiness, military acumen, efficient
organization and proven ability to put large armies into the field.

> They are diligent, willingly rise early, and live on little . . . Their horses are
> good, cost little in food, gallop well and for a long time . . . Their obedience
> to superiors is boundless. None dare disobey, even when their lives are at
> hazard . . . Their armies, I know, commonly consist of two hundred thou-
> sand men.

Notwithstanding their martial prowess, the Frenchman, who was mounting the case for another Crusade on behalf of his master, thought it 'no
difficult matter' to defeat the Turks, who were not 'so terribly formidable'
as many thought.[14]

The Cordoban traveller and historian Pero Tafur, who reached Constantinople in 1437, offered a similarly arrogant verdict typical of
Europeans at this time: 'I am of opinion that if the Turks were to meet the
armies of the West they could not overcome them, not because they are
lacking in strength, but because they want many of the essentials of war.'
Tafur also paid tribute to the city's mighty defences, quoting an earlier
Turk who had led mining operations during an earlier siege and who had
reportedly told the sultan that Constantinople could not be taken by mining because 'the walls are of steel and will never fail'.

The Spaniard was a gimlet-eyed observer of Byzantine decline. Like the
city itself, the emperor's palace, despite boasting a marble loggia crammed
with 'many books and ancient writings and histories', had fallen into a
state sadly revealing 'the evils which the people have suffered and still
endure'. Appearances were being kept up wherever possible, but the real
state of affairs was abundantly clear. 'The emperor's state is as splendid
as ever, for nothing is omitted from the ancient ceremonies, but, properly
regarded, he is like a bishop without a See.'[15]

In fact, the sea Constantinople faced was the still rising tide of Ottoman
power, which was lapping almost at the gates of the city. It was time for
John VIII to play the quintessential Byzantine hand with a nod to the
advice his father, Manuel, had offered his children from his deathbed:

Whenever the Turks begin to be troublesome, send embassies to the West at once, offer to accept union, and protract negotiations to great length; the Turks so greatly fear such union that they will become reasonable; and still the union will not be accomplished because of the enmity of the Latin nations![16]

Forced to such measures by the threat of the encroaching Ottomans, John responded positively to Pope Eugenius I V's proposal to convene a council to bring about the long-sought union of the Catholic and Orthodox Churches.

On paper, the 1439 Council of Florence was a triumph because it achieved precisely that. By steering a deft path around the central doctrinal controversy of the use of *filioque* in the Orthodox creed, it brought together two hotly adversarial Churches. In practice, though, the agreement was seen by many in Constantinople as the abject and completely unworthy surrender of ecclesiastical independence. It succeeded only in enshrining division at the heart of the city when unity against the far greater existential menace of the Ottomans was most needed. Broadly speaking, the agreement was favoured by the emperor, his entourage and senior officials and bitterly resented by most of the clergy and the common people. Such was the strength of feeling against union that clerical signatures to the agreement were hastily withdrawn in Constantinople. There was to be no joyful celebration in the Hagia Sophia, which skulked instead in silence.

The 1440s brought a series of reversals that deepened the gloom. In 1442 the emperor John's brother Demetrios, supported by the Ottomans in a counterpoint to traditional Byzantine machinations, marched on Constantinople, albeit without success. While the city fell prey to internecine passions and officials manoeuvred for grandly titled but meaningless positions within what one historian has called the 'Lilliputian' court, the centre was falling apart. 'The empire had a High Admiral but no fleet, a Commander-in-Chief but few soldiers.'[17]

Despot of the Morea (as the Peloponnese was known at this time) from 1443, another of John's brothers, Constantine, determined to stop the rot. He first reinforced his defences by constructing the *Hexamilion*, a six-mile wall across the isthmus at Corinth, then flexed his military muscles by overrunning the Ottoman territories of Athens and Thebes. This could not be allowed to pass unchallenged. Heavy recrimination followed in 1446 when Sultan Murad led a bristling army against the Morea, storming the defensive wall and plundering the province so completely that 60,000 Greeks were enslaved. Prospects of Crusader relief from the growing

Ottoman danger were dashed in 1444, when a combined Christian army under Vladislav III of Hungary was routed by Murad at the Battle of Varna. Constantinople's isolation was increasingly entrenched.

A year after John's death in 1448, the Despot of the Morea became Constantine XI Palaiologos. 'Constantine Palaiologos, in Christ true Emperor and Autocrat of the Romans', to give him his official title, now presided over an empire consisting of Constantinople and a handful of suburbs, some territories in the Peloponnese and a smattering of islands. His state was a virtually bankrupt vassal of the Ottomans, hamstrung by a perennially feuding family, his capital wracked by religious division. The city that had boasted a population of around 1 million in the twelfth century had declined to around 100,000. This was already an inauspicious beginning. More disquieting for the superstitious medieval mind was the anomaly of Constantine's investiture. Highly unusually he was crowned not in the Hagia Sophia but in the provincial city of Mistra. Popular feelings against union with the Catholic Church remained so inflamed that the new emperor feared a full-blown coronation by Patriarch Gregory III, the leading clerical unionist, would only add fuel to the fires of religious discord.[18] As a sign of the troubled times, not only did he have to hitch a ride to Constantinople on a Catalan ship due to lack of funds to provide him with appropriate transport, but there was to be no subsequent coronation in the imperial capital. In a small but significant way he was damaged from the outset.

In 1451, two years after Constantine's disappointingly damp-squib accession to the throne, Murad died. He was succeeded by Sultan Mehmed II (r. 1451–81), a shrewd, energetic, calculating and ruthless nineteen-year-old, whose childhood years had been spent plotting the conquest of Constantinople. For far too long the Christian city had been, as the popular saying went, 'a bone in the throat of Allah'. It was time to remove it.

The story of the siege of Constantinople has been told many times. When related by Western historians, it has tended – for reasons of cultural sympathy one is tempted to assume – to accord centre stage to Constantine and the defenders of Constantinople. Mehmed and his Ottoman forces too often have been shunted off to one side almost as an embarrassing or uncomfortable afterthought, as if the tumultuous events that unfolded owed everything to Byzantine disarray and disunity and nothing to the sultan's exceptional ingenuity and military command. For Steven Runciman, for example, the pre-eminent historian of the Byzantine Empire of his generation, the Greek people, praised in the opening pages for their 'unquenchable vitality and courage', represented 'the tragic hero' of the story. At its worst, Western historiography has been crude, crass and parochial. Betraying the prejudices of his time, Edward Gibbon accused the Ottoman Muslims of being inherently 'profane and rapacious'. Deploring Mehmed's 'savage and licentious nature' and his resort to 'the basest arts of dissimulation and deceit', he went on to plunge the dagger deeper still: 'I will not transcribe, nor do I firmly believe, the stories of his fourteen pages whose bellies were ripped open in search of a stolen melon, or of the beauteous slave whose head he severed from her body to convince the Janizaries that their master was not the votary of love.' The 'native cowardice' of the Greeks and 'the repugnant state and spirit of Christendom' explained the final outcome.[19] Never mind Ottoman agency in any of this. And yet, for all the undoubted stirring heroism of Greek resistance and defence, too little credit has been given to the youthful sultan for achieving what none before had managed.

In Constantine and Mehmed Byzantine–Ottoman relations suddenly had two new protagonists at the helm. Clues about the sultan's character and how he might approach this turbulent relationship can be gleaned from a fascinating portrait of Mehmed by a young Venetian merchant called Giacomo de' Languschi sometime from late 1453. He described a monarch with a fanatical interest in history, geography and military affairs, a leader who was extraordinarily determined to win his own place in posterity. He was 'obstinate in pursuing his plans, bold in all undertakings, as eager for fame as Alexander of Macedonia'. An accomplished linguist, he instructed officials to read to him daily from historical works on military campaigns, the seat of the papacy, the various kingdoms of Europe and stories about Aeneas, Anchises and Antenor. 'He has them read Laertius, Herodotus, Livy, Quintus Curtius, the chronicles of the popes, the emperors, the kings of France, and the Lombards. He speaks three languages, Turkish, Greek and Slavic . . . he burns with desire to dominate.' It is clear from the Venetian's account that Mehmed already saw himself as a world-changing, history-making ruler. Under his reign the rules of the game would change profoundly. He 'declares that he will advance from East to West as in former times the Westerners have advanced into the Orient. There must, he says, be only one empire, one faith, and one sovereignty in the world. To achieve this unity, no place was more fitting than Constantinople.'[20] With much of the Middle East still recovering from the Timurid holocaust, the quintessentially Christian city stood out as the most illustrious prize for this Muslim warrior and statesman.

An official Turkish source provides a similar picture of a young man of restless imperial ambition. Although he had inherited a great kingdom and army, 'he did not believe that these were enough for him nor was he content with what he had: instead he immediately overran the whole world in his calculations and resolved to rule it in emulation of the Alexanders and Pompeys and Caesars and kings and generals of their sort'.[21]

Those then were Mehmed's ambitions. While he was set on nothing less than world conquest, Constantine's horizons had narrowed to mere survival. Envoys criss-crossed Europe seeking help from Christian allies, above all the papacy. Disgusted with the popular opposition to union between the Churches, Patriarch Gregory slunk off to Rome, deepening the sense of foreboding that hung over the city.

In late 1451, Constantine presented the sultan with his first direct challenge, threatening to release Prince Orhan, the sole rival claimant to Mehmed's throne, from Constantinople unless the Ottomans doubled the allowance provided for his upkeep. The elderly vizier Halil Pasha, all too familiar with such Byzantine ruses, fired off an impatient riposte stressing the new sultan was an altogether different proposition from his more lenient and accommodating father. Carry on with such intrigues, he warned, and 'All that you will achieve is to lose what little you still have.'[22] Constantine's gambit merely strengthened the hand of those within the Ottoman court who were urging the sultan to war.

In the spring of 1452 Mehmed broke ground on the construction of the ominously named Bogaz Kesen, the Throat Slitter, a prodigious fortress six miles upstream from Constantinople. Also known as Rumeli Hissari, the European Castle, it was completed in less than five months by a workforce of 6,000. From vantage points at the top of Hagia Sophia the appalled Greeks watched the looming structure take shape, unwelcome evidence that Mehmed was working methodically to a clear plan. In the face of Byzantine diplomatic protests that this was in breach of their treaty, Mehmed was defiant and brusque: 'The next man to come here on a mission like this will be flayed alive.' Tolls were imposed on all vessels sailing between the Black Sea and the Mediterranean, a direct challenge to Venetian and Genoese maritime trade. Mehmed had seized complete control of all sea traffic on the Bosphorus, ensuring that no relief could easily come from either Greek settlements on the Black Sea or from the Mediterranean to the south. It was a lesson he had learned from his father Murad's unsuccessful siege of 1422, which had failed to incorporate a naval component. A punitive land expedition into the Peloponnese later that autumn, meanwhile, ensured no assistance would be forthcoming from that quarter either.

While Mehmed's dogged preparations continued and wider Christendom dithered, divisions within Constantinople intensified after a highly controversial service held in Hagia Sophia to celebrate the union on

12 December 1452. The Greeks were more sensitive to the alien imposition of unleavened bread than they were to the mounting military threat from without. In an expression of self-righteous fury, one of the leading opponents of Church union, George Scholarios, took his vows under the monastic name of Gennadios and retreated to the great Pantokrator monastery – today the Zeyrek Mosque – where he posted an inflammatory denunciation, warning his fellow citizens that, 'In losing your faith, you will lose your city.'[23]

By comparison with the more numerous and detailed European accounts of the siege of Constantinople, Turkish sources are relatively scarce. The dominant Western narrative is derived from the Greek historians Sphrantzes, a senior diplomat and eyewitness to the siege, Doukas and Chalcondyles, who all inevitably tell their story from a Western, anti-Turkish perspective. Given the prominence of these accounts and their use by successive generations of historians, it is especially important to pay proper notice to the Turkish version of events. A critical source is Krito-voulos, a Greek former governor of the island of Imbros in the northern Aegean, later a confidant of the Ottoman sultan, whose *History of Mehmed the Conqueror* provided a lucid counterpoint to the pro-Byzantine chronicles.

As far as the *casus belli* was concerned, the picture could hardly have been clearer. Over eight pages Kritovoulos presented Mehmed addressing a war council sometime in early 1453, recalling the rise to power of the Ottoman Dynasty and how Constantinople had consistently opposed it from the outset. Summarizing the events of recent decades, he emphasized how the city had encouraged Sigismund of Hungary, leader of the Crusade at Nicopolis in 1396 that Bayazid had routed. How it had then urged on the Turkic warlord Timur, scourge of the Ottomans at Ankara in 1402, who had humiliatingly captured the sultan in person. How only recently it had been intriguing again with John Hunyadi, the Hungarian leader and sworn enemy of the Turks, a man who was dedicated to their removal from Europe. The present situation, the would-be world conqueror rea-soned with some justification, was 'no longer tolerable'. More to the point, the balance of power had shifted decisively in the Ottomans' favour. While they were rich and powerful with a large, well-equipped army, Constan-tinople was at its weakest ebb. Struggling on with a depleted population with scant resources, it had little hope of real support from the Italians, was riven with religious division, 'sedition and disturbance' and was there-fore ripe for the taking. There was only one course of action to take. 'The city has not ceased, nor will it ever cease, withstanding and resisting our forces. Nor will it give up warring against us and stirring up trouble, as long as we allow it to remain in their possession. We must entirely destroy it, or else be enslaved under their hand.'[24] It was a direct call to war. Summoned to vote on the sultan's proposal, Mehmed's council gave him the answer he wanted: unanimous approval.

Thus far everything had been decisive. Yet Mehmed was not a man to rush into anything unprepared. That Constantinople was weak everyone knew. But it had resisted so many efforts to conquer it in the past, Muslim and otherwise, that a powerful sense of invulnerability had grown around it. The chronicles describe the sultan at pains to persuade his court that, rather than being impregnable, Constantinople was instead destined to fall to the faithful, as the *hadiths* themselves maintained, in one of the most glorious acts of *jihad* ever witnessed. The sources reveal a leader meticulously studying the accounts of previous efforts to take Constantinople to understand how and why they had failed, immersed in treatises about siege warfare, questioning his Italian advisers about the latest military technology available in the West, doing everything within his power to tip the balance in his favour.

A compelling opportunity came when a Hungarian engineer called Orban made his way to Edirne for an audience with Mehmed in the summer of 1452. The mercenary had already tried to seek his fortune in Constantinople as the founder of large cannons, the key new weapon within the emerging technology of artillery. Yet the penurious Constantine, although keen to retain his services, had been unable either to pay him what he needed or provide him with the raw materials required. Orban acted accordingly and made his way to the Ottomans, where he was welcomed with open arms by the sultan, who pressed him closely on what he was able to produce. Could he, for instance, manufacture a cannon capable of shattering the walls of Constantinople? The reply was unequivocal: 'I can shatter to dust not only these walls with the stones from my gun but the very walls of Babylon itself.'[25] The first cannon he produced for Mehmed was installed on the walls of the Throat Slitter castle, where it was used to devastating effect on 26 November 1452. Trying to run the gauntlet of the sultan's blockade, the Venetian captain Antonio Rizzo ignored warning shots and pressed on, only to see a barrage of artillery fire destroy his ship. Well aware of the sensation a horrible execution would produce among his enemies, Mehmed beheaded the survivors of the crew and had Rizzo impaled. The Venetian died an agonizing death with a stake through his anus.

Delighted with the results from the Hungarian's first cannon, the sultan immediately ordered the construction of another, this time double the size. With a barrel length of around nine metres and an ability to fire cannonballs weighing more than half a tonne, it was the world's first supergun. Doukas called it 'a terrible, unprecedented monster', Kritovoulos considered it so 'frightful', its power so 'unbelievable and inconceivable', that no one would believe it unless they saw it with their own eyes.[26] Mehmed ordered it to be test-fired near his palace in Edirne in January 1453. The fuse was lit, there was an almighty explosion that shook the earth and sent up a vast cloud of smoke, and the cannonball flew over a mile before smashing six feet into the earth. The thunderclap could be heard ten miles away. It was a resounding triumph, amplified by Mehmed's machinations to ensure that news of this monstrous artillery piece swiftly reached Constantinople. Psychological warfare was to be an essential feature of his campaign. A force of 200 men was ordered to level the 140-mile road from Edirne to Constantinople. Sixty oxen then hauled the cannon slowly but steadily towards the city it was intended to destroy, two and a half miles a day.

On 23 March Mehmed set off from Edirne at the head of a formidable army of infantry and cavalry. 'When it marched, the air seemed like a forest because of its lances and when it stopped, the earth could not be seen for tents,' wrote Tursun Beg, an official who was with Mehmed during the fight for Constantinople and later wrote the *History of the Conqueror*, an important panegyric which contains a rare Ottoman account of the siege.[27]

Estimates of the size of the Ottoman army Mehmed fielded against Constantinople vary wildly. An authoritative recent study settles on the combined figure of 200,000, first advanced by the slightly shadowy Florentine merchant and eyewitness called Tetaldi, who reckoned 60,000 of that number were soldiers – over half of them cavalry – with the rest comprising the giant army of camp followers from cooks to blacksmiths, tailors to thieves. Whatever the precise size of Mehmed's force, we know first that it arrived outside the city walls on 5 April and second that it comprehensively outnumbered the pitiful defensive force Constantine was able to muster. According to Sphrantzes, who had been tasked by the emperor to conduct a census, there were fewer than 5,000 Greeks, around 3,000 Genoese and Venetians from the colony of Galata across the Golden Horn, and a couple of hundred foreigners. In all the defence of the once mighty capital of the Eastern Roman Empire, including the twelve miles of walls that required appropriate manning, now rested on the shoulders of a haphazard force of fewer than 8,000. The figure was so demoralizing that Constantine and Sphrantzes resolved to keep it secret.

The sultan took his place in a gorgeous red and gold tent pitched on Meltepe hill opposite the *Mesoteichion*, the stretch of Middle Wall

between the St Romanus and Charisus Gates where the ground fell into
the Lycus Valley. This was one of two vulnerabilities identified in a forensic
Ottoman study of the walls, the second being an unmoated section to the
north towards the Golden Horn. To further terrorize the defenders
Mehmed stormed two nearby castles at Therapia, on a hill above the
Bosphorus, and at Studius, killing or capturing their garrisons. All survivors were then impaled within sight of the city walls to show what torments
awaited those who dared resist the sultan.

'A duel begins,' wrote Stefan Zweig, 'between the 1,000-year-old walls of
the emperors of eastern Rome and the new Sultan's cannon.'[28] With the
army in place, Mehmed's artillery, around seventy cannons, including
Orban's behemoth, set to work battering the city walls in an unremitting
barrage that targeted the *Mesoteichion* from 12 to 18 April. It was the
first sustained artillery bombardment in history and struck fear into the
hearts of Constantinople's defenders.

The sultan was leaving nothing to chance. This was to be a comprehensive assault by land and sea. A huge fleet had been assembled,
headquartered on the European shore of the Bosphorus at the Double
Columns quay – where the Dolmabahçe Palace now stands in the Beşiktaş
district, east of Taksim Square. Numbering around 140 vessels, consisting of war galleys, transport barges and brigantines, it manoeuvred into
position under the command of Admiral Baltaoglu and around 18 April
launched its first attack, attempting unsuccessfully to force the defensive
iron boom across the Golden Horn. Two days later a Genoese relief
convoy sailed towards Constantinople. Furious about the earlier failure
to smash through the boom, Mehmed ordered his admiral to acquit
himself more manfully. He was to seize the Genoese or not to return
alive.

The Ottomans closed on the European vessels and for several hours
there was frenzied, hand-to-hand fighting watched with grim fascination
from the city walls by the Greeks and from the opposite shore by the
Ottomans as each side raked the other with fire. The balance shifted now
in favour of the Genoese, now the Ottomans, until a favourable wind
suddenly gave the Genoese flotilla the chance to force their way through
to the city, bringing desperately needed supplies in a rousing display of
superior European seamanship. It was a stunning and very public victory,
an enormous fillip to the besieged and a correspondingly savage blow to
the besiegers. Tursun Beg reported 'despair and disorder' in the army's
ranks, while the Sufi Sheikh Akshemseddin, Mehmed's spiritual adviser,
warned of growing dissent, recommending severe punishments to

concentrate minds. Constantine chose this moment to offer Mehmed peace terms and an honourable way out. Ignoring the approach and stung by this second ignominious reversal at sea, Mehmed tore strips off Baltaoglu for his supposed cowardice and incompetence and gave the order for him to be impaled. It was only through the concerted pleas of the admiral's commanders and senior courtiers, who reminded the sultan how bravely the admiral had fought, even to the point of losing an eye in the thick of battle, that Mehmed relented. The penalty was commuted to one hundred publicly administered lashes, immediate loss of rank and total confiscation of property. The naval veteran Hamza Bey was appointed in his place. This was not an army for the faint-hearted. Success was extravagantly rewarded, failure ruthlessly punished.

Within several days of the land bombardment Mehmed had brought down a section of the outer wall and several towers on the inner wall, forcing the defenders, under the inspired leadership of the Genoese commander Giovanni Giustiniani Longo, to frantic nocturnal activity repairing the breaches, rebuilding the defences with ramparts of earth, stone and timber and desperately clearing the fosse that the Ottomans with equal determination had been filling in during the day. It was an exhausting pattern of activity, especially gruelling for the far smaller number of defenders. Encouraged by the damage his cannons had inflicted on the walls, Mehmed launched his first assault two hours after sunset on 18 April to the terrifying martial sounds of pounding drums, clashing cymbals and pipes. The sultan's elite corps of Janissaries surged forward beneath the light of flares, cannons roared away and bells within the city tolled urgently in alarm as close combat raged for four hours. In the tightly enclosed space the Ottomans were at a disadvantage and eventually withdrew. It was another reversal for Mehmed, who responded with characteristic chutzpah, ordering the artillery to step up its bombardment, straining the besieged to breaking point.

At dawn on 22 April, having wrestled for several days with the deepening conundrum of how to conquer this seemingly impregnable city, visiting his troops stationed north of Galata and assessing the strength of the fleet moored at the Double Columns, Mehmed, well aware that a prolonged siege might result in a mutiny of his army, exhibited a stroke of genius as a military strategist and leader. If the sultan could only seize control of the Golden Horn, he would be able to launch withering attacks on the city from another flank, forcing Constantine to dilute still further his scarce resources, removing more men from their defence of the embattled land walls to protect the northern ramparts. Having failed to force his fleet through the defensive boom and seize control of the Golden Horn that way, he resolved on an imaginative, wholly unpredictable alternative. Under cover of a distracting artillery barrage directed against the boom and Constantine's ships that were defending it, the Ottoman fleet was lifted out of the water onto cradles, manhandled vessel by vessel onto rollers on a hastily prepared wooden track greased with animal fat, and hauled up the steep slope for one and a half miles by men and oxen to the top of a ridge behind Galata, seventy metres above the water. To the horrified Christian sailors watching with dread and disbelief, it was an astonishing sight. Seventy or so ships rose from the sea one by one, their progress made yet more surreal and unwelcome by crews following Mehmed's impromptu orders to take their place at the oars and row through the air, cheering wildly while others hoisted sail, flew colourful pennants and sounded their trumpets. From the top of the ridge it was a careful descent down into the waters behind the defensive boom at the Valley of the Springs.

In a brilliantly executed manoeuvre characterized by dash and diligent preparation, the Ottomans had effectively seized control of the Golden Horn without a fight. The Venetians, who had taken charge of naval operations, had been undone. To compound the dire situation at sea, on 28 April what was intended to be a surprise attack to capture and torch the Ottoman fleet backfired spectacularly after Genoese posturing with the Venetians ensured the secret mission was first delayed and then discovered before its execution. In another furious encounter Venetian losses were heavy and became grimmer still when those survivors who had managed to swim ashore were captured and impaled in public before the city walls. Constantine responded to the savagery with his own display of cold-blooded killing, ordering the 260 Ottoman prisoners he held to be slaughtered on the ramparts, one by one, their corpses hung from the walls in full view of Mehmed's army.

All the while Mehmed maintained the bombardment against the section of wall close to the St Romanus Gate and the northern stretch next to the Blachernae Palace, a relentless barrage that drained the energies and morale of the defenders, who knew that without the still elusive relief from the West they were surely doomed. Envoys were still beating paths across the continent seeking supplies from the Peloponnese and military assistance from the pope, from Italian princes and the courts of Europe. Yet Christendom remained studiously half-hearted and noncommittal in its response. Catholic–Orthodox divisions, dating back to the Great Schism of 1054, were proving more compelling than Christian unity against a towering Muslim threat.

In late April and then again on 6 May, Mehmed ordered massive attacks on the walls that were beaten back in more scenes of chaotic hand-to-hand fighting. On 12 May, a breach was forced in the northern section of the wall and Ottoman cavalry surged into the city. Rallying his troops with Giustiniani, Constantine plunged into the battle and the advance was held off.

Lesser men might have given up after these repeated reversals. Yet Mehmed's commitment to the cause was never less than total. With the Horn in his possession, he continued to display a combination of ingenuity and tenacity that was terrifying for the besieged to behold. Saxon miners were sent into action in mid-May, tunnelling quietly towards the northern wall to conduct subterranean warfare that tied the defenders down in laborious countermining operations under the leadership of a canny Scot and professional soldier called John Grant. A series of tunnels was discovered within the city walls. One by one they were collapsed just before the enemy was able to use them to devastating effect. Refusing to let up the pressure for a moment, Mehmed had a siege tower secretly built and under cover of night wheeled across to the wall opposite the Charisus Gate. At dawn on 19 May the beleaguered soldiers on the ramparts were met with a staggering sight: a huge structure loomed menacingly from the gloaming only ten metres in front of them. 'They were all struck down with fear like dead men,' reported Nicolo Barbaro, a Venetian ship's doctor who kept a diary of the siege.[29]

Safely protected within the tower, Ottoman soldiers were methodically excavating earth, tipping the spoil into the moat, which their fellow soldiers could then cross before breaching or storming the walls. A covered channel ran from the tower and ditch to the Ottoman camp, allowing many men to move freely and safely between the lines. Faced with Mehmed's latest act of ingenuity, Constantine prepared emergency counter-measures. That night he ordered barrels of gunpowder to be rolled down the ramparts towards the tower. Almighty explosions lit up the inky sky, Ottoman soldiers were hurled into the air and then showered with burning pitch. The city had survived another trial, but something had to give.

With diminishing supplies of men and materiel, it was surely only a matter of time before the city bowed to the inevitable. Yet as both Mehmed and Constantine knew, it was not just the emperor of the Eastern Roman Empire whose time was running out. Mehmed needed to move quickly before the growing rumblings in his army became mutinous roars. The longer the Ottoman army was kept in the field without taking the city, the greater the doubts of success and the likelier the prospects of a mutiny against a sultan seen by many of the old guard as young and impetuous.

Everyone knew that Muslim forces had failed to capture Constantinople twelve times over nine centuries. Loyalty to the as yet untested and unsuccessful sultan was finite. From the Ottoman perspective a decisive assault was now essential. As far as Constantine was concerned, if only help could come from the West, the capital could still be saved.

And then, on 23 May, a ship managed to break through the Ottoman blockade, bringing the news that all had been dreading. There was no large fleet or horizon-filling army coming to rescue the Byzantine capital. In response to Constantine's despairing pleas, Europe had looked the other way. In its hour of greatest need Constantinople was on its own.

Kritovoulos reported a troubling series of 'divine portents' that shook the city's population around this time. There were 'unusual and strange earthquakes and boilings of the earth, and from heaven thunders and forked lightnings and frightful thunderbolts and brightness seen in the sky, and fierce gales and floods of rain and torrents'. Stars moved irregularly or, 'pouring out smoke', did not move at all. The terrified citizens believed God was ordaining 'a new order of things and a complete change'. Pictures, pillars and statues of holy men sweated in the churches while 'soothsayers prophesied many misfortunes', recalling old oracles 'pointing to no good', not the least of which was the ancient prophecy that Constantinople would be founded and lost by an emperor called Constantine. 'These all brought great terror and agony to people, totally confounded them, and gave no hope for the future.'[30]

Faced with destruction, on 25 May the God-fearing Greeks fell on their last resort. They prayed to their great protector the Virgin Mary for salvation, processing their most precious icon of the Hodegetria, said to have been painted by the apostle St Luke, through the streets. And then disaster struck. The icon slipped and fell to the ground in an apocalyptic storm that brought thunder, lightning, driving rain, a volley of hail and torrents of floodwater so severe that the procession had to be abandoned. On 26 May, as Mehmed's bombardment continued, the barrage of doom-filled portents intensified with a thick, unearthly fog, followed by a blast of light emanating from the dome of Hagia Sophia and then disappearing into the heavens. These, surely, were the end times. God had abandoned the city. Mehmed's holy men were not slow to divine the true meaning of these ghostly happenings. 'This is a great sign,' they told him. 'The city is doomed.'[31]

On the evening of 27 May, Mehmed rallied his army commanders and fixed the date for the final assault for 29 May. He reminded them of the glory and honour of taking Constantinople, a city that had been hostile to Muslims from the earliest days of the faith. Appealing to less exalted

motives, he laid out visions of the plunder that would be theirs, the retinues
of slaves and the treasures of 'gold and silver and precious stones and costly
pearls' to which they would be entitled during the official three days of pillage. In a nod to his soldiers' more basic needs, he described the multitude
of 'very beautiful women, young and good-looking, and virgins lovely for
marriage . . . till now unseen by masculine eyes'. For those with other incli-
nations there would be noble, beautiful boys. Countering fears of the city's
impregnability, he emphasized how the army had already filled in the moat
and brought down the mighty land wall in three key places, the perfect
preparation for a cavalry attack. The Christian army, which had probably
declined to around 4,000 of the original 8,000, was now so depleted that
the guard force on each tower was just two or three men. Constantinople
was 'surrounded, as if in a net, by land and sea' and could not escape.

To capitalize on the defenders' exhaustion and reduced numbers, the
Ottomans would launch rolling attacks of fresh men so that the battle
would be 'continuous and uninterrupted' until the enemy, shattered by
lack of food and sleep, simply folded. To loud cheers Mehmed announced
he would be in the vanguard of the attack. Detailed orders were then given
to his commanders. Hamza Bey was to surround the city with his fleet,
forcing the defenders to man the sea walls, and storm the defences if his
ships could run aground. Once a specially constructed pontoon bridge,
built from Genoese wine barrels in Galata, had been extended across the
Golden Horn, Zaganos Pasha would lead his men across and attack the
northern walls. Karaja Pasha and his Christian troops from the Balkans
were to attack near the royal palace. The sultan would take pride of place
among his elite Janissaries opposite the vulnerable *Mesoteichion*, reinforced by Halil Pasha and Saraja Pasha, while Ishak Pasha and Mahmud
Pasha would hammer away at the walls farther south. After weeks of
devastating siege and bombardment, destiny – and Constantinople – was
theirs for the taking.[32]

At 1.30 a.m. on 29 May, sky-filling Ottoman horns, supported by beating drums and clashing cymbals, sounded the attack. With bellowing,
blood-curdling war cries, Mehmed's most expendable troops, largely
Christian irregulars and conscripts, surged out of the darkness under a
furious artillery barrage and advanced against the walls and improvised
stockade. For the besieged it was a stomach-churning sight. Under the
indefatigable Giustiniani the defenders shot Greek fire and hurled burning
oil against the ill-disciplined mob, whose attempts to withdraw were
blocked off by a double line of military police and Janissaries under strict
orders to hack down anyone trying to retreat. Shortly after 3.30 in the
morning, the expendables having served their purpose, Mehmed threw in

his Anatolian heavy infantry. Under savage fire from cannons, crossbows and archers they pressed forward 'like lions unchained against the walls', Barbaro the Venetian recalled, taking heavy losses as they scrambled up the stockade, eventually forcing a way through into the terrace between the inner and outer walls. It was a triumphant moment. Yet the defensive architecture swiftly worked against the Anatolians, who suddenly found themselves hemmed in within an enclosed space against a larger force who cut them down where they stood. It was 5.30, the sky was perceptibly lightening, and still the defence held. Though Constantine's Greeks and Italians were stretched to breaking point, they had withstood everything – including the unsuccessful naval offensives on the shores of the Golden Horn and Marmara – that Mehmed had hurled against them.

The sultan's hand was running out. He was now within hours either of history-making victory or ignominious, possibly fatal, defeat. His last option was his elite reserve, a 5,000-strong force of heavy infantry, bowmen and lancers, his imperial bodyguard and the Janissaries, 'men who were extremely well armed, daring and brave, and far in advance of the rest in experience and valor'.[33] They were the last cards he had to play. If they failed to make the breakthrough, the game was over. To rally his troops, Mehmed led his archers and musketeers to the edge of the ditch, where they unleashed a fearsome volley of arrows, rocks and shot. Then there was another resounding barrage of noise – a thunderous war cry as the infantry advanced to the accompaniment of drums, pipes and cymbals. On the other side of the barricade, Constantine, Giustiniani, the great nobles and the elite soldiers stood their ground as the fighting became more desperate. It was an inferno of shouting, charging soldiers, hacking swords, stabbing blades and lances, thudding death blows, swooshing arrows, the crash of cannon into stone walls and earthen ramparts, choking smoke, scalding oil, burning fires, the harrowing cries of the wounded and dying. The tide ebbed and flowed between the two forces as now one side, then the other, seized the advantage. And then the balance seemed to tip and the Ottoman attack started to falter and lose its intensity.

Accounts of the siege at this point tend to emphasize two events, which together helped turn the course of the battle. The first was a party of Ottomans storming through the Circus Gate, a postern within the fortifications around the Blachernae Palace that the defenders had left open after one of their regular sorties to harass the attackers. It was through this tiny entrance that a contingent of fifty Janissaries now rushed, raising the Ottoman standards from the ramparts before they were cut down. The second incident, which completely rattled the Genoese, was the sudden and serious wounding of their commander, Giustiniani, who by this time had become, alongside the emperor, the talisman of Constantinople's defence. The injury was sufficiently severe for him to insist on withdrawing from the battle at once and being carried to his ship down in the harbour for urgent treatment. His exit through a gate that had been locked by Constantine to ensure the defenders would fight it out to the last was a self-fulfilling catastrophe, triggering a mass of panicking Genoese to follow him. Other Greeks, fearing the battle was lost, tried to rush through the tiny gate.

Sensing the defence wavering, Mehmed urged his men on. 'Friends, we have the City!' he roared. 'We have it! They are already fleeing from us!'[34] The Janissaries rushed forward again, allowing one of the soldiers to thrust himself onto the ramparts and beat off all resistance long enough to raise the Ottoman standard. A giant of a man called Hassan of Ulabat, he was soon cut to pieces, but in inspiring a new wave of soldiers to follow his rousing example and overrun the defences he had done his job. The Ottoman tide overwhelmed all before it. Somewhere in the blood-soaked chaos Constantine made his heroic last stand alongside his most faithful comrades before they were slaughtered to a man. Ottoman flags flew triumphantly from the ramparts. The city had fallen.

The Ottoman tide now swelled into a torrent, soldiers flooding through the St Romanus and Charisus Gates down the three miles of streets that led from the western gates into the heart of the city that had resisted them so long. After weeks of privations, after endless taunts from the ramparts, they were 'like wild and ferocious beasts' and immediately 'turned to plunder, robbing everything in their way, and falling on it like a fire or a whirlwind, burning and annihilating everything, or like a torrent sweeping away and destroying all things'. Men, women and children – even babies – were cut down in cold blood, but many more were immediately enslaved. Houses were looted, tombs were destroyed, libraries were consigned to the flames, young women and boys were seized and hauled off to desperate fates, children were separated from parents, wives from husbands, 'and ten thousand other terrible deeds were done'.[35]

The soldiers tore past the Forum of Theodosius and the Forum of the Ox, charging greedily down the Mese towards the centre, meeting sailors who had fought their way in from the Golden Horn in the Augustean Forum, proudly decked with a millennium's worth of imperial spoils and victory monuments, from the famous *Milion* zero-mile marker, from which all distances within the Byzantine Empire were measured, to the stately statue of the emperor Justinian. Then there was the famous but faded Hippodrome, home to the Serpent Column of Delphi and the far more ancient Egyptian column of Pharaoh Thutmose III.

Yet all eyes were turned towards the awe-inspiring domes of Hagia Sophia, storehouse of Constantinople's Christian soul and the city's greatest millennial survivor. The soldiers had heard wild stories of hidden treasures. Smashing their way in with axes, they turned the sacred space into a scene of frenzied looting and occasional bloodshed, hacking away at icons and the main altar, grabbing precious relics and every item of gold and silver they could lay their hands on. After 1,123 years of Christian worship, the great cathedral had celebrated its last service in the name of Christ. The terrified congregation, who had been praying fervently for a miracle during matins, were slaughtered or enslaved on the spot. Hagia Sophia was completely ransacked and hollowed out, together with Saint John in Petra, the Church of the Chora and Saint Theodosia.

Mehmed bided his time. He wanted proof that the emperor was dead. It came later that day in the blood-smeared form of Constantine's severed head. He mounted it on a column in the Augustean Forum to show the Greeks their emperor was dethroned and dead, before having it stuffed with straw and sent on a tour of the courts of the Muslim world that he now wished all to know he gloriously bestrode.

For Turks to this day, the iconic image of 1453 is the triumphant entry on horseback of Sultan Mehmed – from this moment with the sobriquet 'Fatih, the Conqueror' – through the corpse-strewn Charisus Gate (henceforth the Edirne Gate). Raising aloft his crescent-topped standard with its green banner of Islam, towering above his turbaned officers who crowd around him on foot, he strikes a pose of indomitable power. Smoke rises from the battlefield behind him, partly obscured by a forest of lances, turbans and red and green banners. The vigour of Mehmed and his warriors is an obvious counterpoint to the pile of lifeless bodies, symbol of Islam's victory over the infidels. For Halil İnalcik, Turkey's greatest historian of the Ottoman Empire, this was 'conquest as an act of faith'.[36]

Mehmed made his way to the great cathedral of Hagia Sophia where, after bowing in submission to Allah and declaring an immediate end to the ransacking, he summoned an imam to issue the *adhan* call to prayer, mounted the altar in another sign of Islamic ascendancy and performed his prayers. The Ottoman historian Tursun Beg wrote of how Mehmed later climbed up onto the cathedral roof, from where he surveyed his new imperial possession, a glorious, beautiful, legend-filled, hard-won, decaying, bloody, plundered city. In a moment which has echoes of the tearful Abbasid caliph Harun al Rashid reflecting on the transitoriness of life after reading a poem by Abu al Atahiya in his palace in Baghdad six centuries earlier, Mehmed is supposed to have quoted lines from the Persian poet Saadi:

The spider weaves his web in the palace of the Caesars
And the owl sings her watchsong on the towers of Afrosiab.*

Kritovoulos argued the sacking of Constantinople was worse than the fall of any other city in history – more devastating than the sacking of Troy, Babylon, Carthage, Rome and Jerusalem – because it had been emptied of 'wealth, glory, rule, splendour, honour, brilliance of population, valour, education, wisdom, religious orders, dominion – in short, all'. The once mighty and splendid city had been reduced to 'want and disgrace and dishonour and abject and shameful slavery'. After a titanic struggle between two monarchs and a calamitous siege lasting fifty-three days, Mehmed had finally brought it crashing down into 'the abyss of misfortune and misery'.[37] After so many centuries of fruitless effort, after all the *hadiths* foretelling it, a Muslim army had finally conquered Christian Constantinople. Destiny had been achieved. For the ensuing five centuries the Islamic Empire of the Ottomans would rule the world from the western Mediterranean to Central Asia.

'I find it pitiful and pathetic,' Professor Çiğdem Kafescioğlu sniffs. We are sitting in an attic office in Boğaziçi University, high on a hill overlooking the sludge-grey Bosphorus, in the shadow of Mehmed's menacing Rumeli Hissari fortress. 'We don't have a city museum but we have a "conquest" museum. It just shows how central the notion of conquest is being made. As though this is the moment when the nation realizes itself.' The professor checks her disappointment in mid-flow. 'To say the least it's unfortunate.'[38]

We are talking about the Panorama 1453 Historical Museum, opened in 2009 by Prime Minister Recep Tayyip Erdoğan. I have found my way there after traipsing along the Theodosian walls from the Yedikule Hisari, Fortress of the Seven Towers, which marks their southern conclusion at

---

* *Will you be warned by the example of him who has left*
His palaces empty on the morning of his death?
By him whom death has cut down and who lies
Abandoned by kinsfolk and friends?
By him whose thrones stand vacant,
By him whose daises are empty?
Where now are the kings and where
Are the men who passed this way before you?
O you who have chosen the world and its delights,
You have always listened to sycophants,
Take what you can of the pleasures of the world
For death comes as the end.

Abu al Atahiya (748–825), Baghdad

the Sea of Marmara, along alternately dangerously crumbling and zeal-
ously over-restored sections. Walking along these walls is one of the finest
ways to understand and fully appreciate the sheer scale of Mehmed's
achievement. The museum is located around halfway on the wall's south–
north line, appropriately close to the Edirne Gate through which the sultan
made his victorious entry, commemorated today by prowling cats and a
large plaque. Along with several hundred other visitors, I have spent a
couple of hours wandering wide-eyed through this triumphalist monument to Turkish nationalism, pepped up with a stiff dose of Islam,
surrounded by crowds of veiled Arab women, proud Turkish men visiting
from the provinces, the occasional couple in beanies and puffa jackets and
a sprawl of intermittently interested schoolchildren.

 Here in all its Technicolor, 360-degree glory is Mehmed's conquest of
Constantinople. Cannons boom away at the city's pulverized walls to the
accompaniment of the pounding drums, shrill pipes and crashing cymbals
of the Janissaries' band. The Ottoman cavalry, a sea of red and white
turbans with scimitars to the fore, charges towards the breached defences,
roaring each other on in a delirium of conquest. Terrified horses neigh
frantically amid the tumult of explosions and flames bursting out from
incoming missiles. Shattered cannon lie among scattered shields, arrows
and discarded helmets. Far off on the Sea of Marmara to the south, the
Ottoman fleet keeps its brooding vigil. Closer to hand a vast banner
emblazoned with the double-headed eagle of Byzantium is falling from
one of the towers, just stormed by Hassan of Ulabat, who raises a billow-
ing red banner from the ramparts moments before he is cut down. A
thicket of red, white, green and gold banners beneath a spreading plane
tree provides a focal point. It is from this spot, mounted on a white horse
and regally clad in a red and gold cloak, left arm aloft in imperial command, that Mehmed directs the final assault alongside a monumental
cannon, black smoke rising from its dreadful muzzle. The scene is one of
mayhem and bloodshed, death and destruction, but it is also one of glorious conquest. The Ottomans are winning.

 The voice in my earpiece provides a steady commentary in the same
vein as the dizzying, wraparound picture emblazoned across the thirty-
eight-metre diameter hemisphere: 'The dominance of the Ottomans would
get stronger . . . Istanbul had to be conquered.' The guide hails Mehmed's
final beseeching prayer as a dutiful Muslim on the eve of conquest, his
promise to Allah 'to fight for *jihad*' against the 'deniers'.

 For Turks reared on a diet of liberal Kemalist secularism, who for the
best part of a century have learnt that the history of the modern nation
began on 29 October 1923 with the election of Kemal Atatürk as

president, this is strong, disruptive and unpalatable stuff.* 'The disruption unsettles Turkish national identity not only because the scales of national time are thrown off by about half a millennium, but also because the celebrated moment is part of the Ottoman era, which has been evoked as the "other" against which modern Turkish national identity was constituted,' writes the political scientist Alev Çinar.[39]

Six centuries after the conquest, Mehmed is caught up in a very different contest over national identity, a livewire issue in twenty-first-century Turkey. 'I'm a real Turk, you bastards: one quarter Albanian, one quarter Kurd, half Greek Orthodox.' Faruk Birtek, a pugnacious, chain-smoking historian, guffaws, recalling what he said in a recent television interview. 'Ninety-five per cent of Turks are mixed but Turks don't want to hear that.' Faruk takes a dim view of the recent political reinvention of Mehmed the Conqueror. 'They're fighting the republic and they have to create alternative heroes to Atatürk,' he says of the country's leadership. 'These guys don't recognize Mehmed was the founder of an ecumenical empire. The top viziers for 150 years were from the Balkan and Byzantine aristocracy. People didn't make much of a fuss about religion then.'

Across town in Beşiktaş, a stone's throw from the football stadium, Agah Karliaga of the Civilization Studies Center, offers a different, post-Kemalist critique: 'There are six really important historical figures for us: Alp Arslan, Osman, Fatih Mehmed, Suleiman the Magnificent, Sultan Abdulhamid and Atatürk. If you ask me to choose just one, Fatih is the greatest without question. He alone brought one era – the medieval period – to an end and ushered in another. He is *the* national figure. He's our number one hero, a great example for the younger generation. Even today you can find children called Fatih in his honour. Nowadays we're looking for leaders like that.'

The truth, as the historian Edhem Eldem sees it, is that Mehmed has been reimagined from the very beginning according to the whims of those who champion him. 'It's nostalgia for a certain past, the idealization of a lost paradise.'[40] For some he is the supreme Islamic warrior, conqueror of Christian Constantinople, the man who finally and spectacularly fulfilled the Prophet Mohammed's prophecy that the city would fall to Muslim forces. For others he is the enlightened, secular emperor, a cosmopolitan and controversial figure who clipped the wings of the Islamic clergy, enjoyed a collection of nudes, disgusted his son Bayazid for his lack of

---

* As part of his secularizing reforms Atatürk turned the Hagia Sophia from a mosque into a museum in 1935. Efforts to turn it back into a mosque resurface periodically in Turkish politics.

Islamic zeal, looked to Alexander the Great as his role model and was even rumoured to be considering a conversion to Christianity.

The Panorama 1453 Historical Museum tells visitors that, for Europeans, Mehmed's conquest was 'one of the biggest disasters in the history of humanity', on a par with the destruction of Jerusalem and the crucifixion of Jesus. While that verdict may be attributed to contemporary Turkish triumphalism and historical European exaggeration, for the Greeks of the time it was certainly apocalyptic. The fall of Constantinople spelled the savage end of a once world-illuminating empire and its emperor, the death of almost all the soldiers who had defended it so valiantly and the enslavement of a further 50,000.

Yet the city did not die. The demise of an empire did not mean the end of a metropolis that had survival and adaptation seared into its genes. As Gibbon presciently remarked in the eighteenth century, 'the genius of the place will ever triumph over the accidents of time and fortune'.[41] Mehmed saw himself as the inheritor of Rome's imperial crown, and his new capital of Islambol ('Islam abounds' – the name never caught on and Turks continued to call it both Kostantiniyye and Istanbul, from the Byzantine Greek *is tin polin*, literally 'to the city') was to be his cosmopolitan seat of empire, forcibly resettled with Greeks, Armenians, Latin Christians and Jews, under a Muslim majority. It was the pivot upon which the transformation of the Ottoman state into the Ottoman Empire turned.

Greeks were resettled around the Golden Horn in the Phanar or Fener neighbourhood, which became the new seat of the patriarchate and remained a Greek quarter into modern times. Mehmed liberated the diehard anti-unionist monk Gennadios from slavery and appointed him patriarch of the Orthodox flock, initially from the Church of the Holy Apostles, which was second in size and importance only to the Hagia Sophia, then from the Pammacaristos, one of many churches to survive intact. Although he was above all an empire-building warrior, Mehmed was also a man of culture and tolerance who commissioned works on the Christian faith, received humanists and Greek scholars at his court and invited the Venetian artist Gentile Bellini to come to Istanbul to paint palace frescoes and his famous portrait – dated 25 November 1480 and now hanging in London's National Gallery.[42] 'He was a kind of hybrid,' says Özalp Birol, head of the Suna and İnan Kiraç Foundation's Pera Museum and the Istanbul Research Institute, combining the powers of a Caesar with those of a sultan and caliph. 'He was an intellectual and a poet, a patron of the arts who never let the religious scholars interfere in state affairs, or have an equal say in politics, especially after the conquest of the city. For me that was his best move. He created a kind of secular environment.'[43]

Dramatic on one level, the reinvention of the city was far more subtle than the move from Christianity to Islam might suggest. 'The view entrenched in Turkish nationalist history is that the Turks came and created the Turkish Muslim city of Istanbul and there was an end to the Byzantine Empire,' says Kafescioğlu. 'This notion of Istanbul as a suddenly Turkish Islamic city is a very reductionist, nationalist view. I want to tell the alternative story, that it was much more layered and more complex than that. It's not so much about erasure but patterns of continuity, patterns of change and references to the past.'

For most of the six centuries that followed the 1453 conquest, Istanbul remained, like Jan Morris's Alexandria, 'a gallimaufry of miscellaneous cosmopolitans'. Greeks continued as a considerable population well into the twentieth century. In 1927, the Greek Orthodox community of Istanbul stood at 100,000. In the aftermath of the Istanbul Pogrom of 1955, Greeks fled in their droves, so that by 1965 their numbers had halved to 47,000. Today, according to the Greek foreign ministry, there are only 3,500 ethnic Greek residents in Turkey.[44] The new Atatürk republic hastened the end of the polyglot, multicultural Istanbul of the imperial age.

In time, the all-pervasive sense of tragedy for the Greeks, which for many lingers even today, would find its anguished echo in the *hüzün*, or melancholy, felt by the Turks in the wake of the Ottoman Empire's collapse. For the Turkish Nobel Prize-winning writer Orhan Pamuk, the bitter-sweet *hüzün* still stalks the city in the memories of the old wooden *yalis* mansions on the Bosphorus, in the dilapidated ferries lurching from Kadiköy to Karaköy, in the crumbling *tekkes* or dervish monasteries, the teahouses packed with unemployed men, the apartment buildings discoloured by dirt, rust and soot, in ships' horns booming through the fog, in the once glorious now broken marble drinking fountains. 'Even the greatest Ottoman architecture has a humble simplicity that suggests an end-of-empire melancholy, a pained submission to the diminishing European gaze and to an ancient poverty that must be endured like an incurable disease,' he writes; 'it is resignation that nourishes Istanbul's inward-looking soul'.[45]

All that, though, lay far ahead. One change above all others was immediately visible after 1453. It was only natural, in the days, months and years that followed the tumultuous conquest, for Istanbul to be steadily Islamicized. Six churches were quickly converted into mosques, another into an Islamic college. The pealing of church bells gave way to the call of *muezzins* from multiplying minarets. Mausoleums were constructed for the Companions of the Prophet at Eyüp on the Golden Horn where, almost 600 years later, Muslim pilgrims still come in their crowds to venerate these ancient heroes of the faith.* A citadel, palace and huge bazaar – all essential components of the model Islamic city – were constructed in quick order. New, obviously Muslim, neighbourhoods were founded around a mosque complex, complete with religious schools, a charitable foundation, *hammam*, caravanserai and public kitchen, a number of whose names – such as Fatih, Aksaray, Karaman Pazari – survive to this day.[46]

Most spectacular of all was the Fatih Mosque, the Conqueror's Mosque, constructed on the site of the dilapidated Church of the Holy Apostles and completed in 1470. In the most powerful symbol of the shift from Christian to Muslim power, the church, which could trace its origins to the fourth century and its dedication by Constantine to around 330, was demolished to make way for it. In its original form the complex contained eight *madrassas*, a library, hospice, market, *hammam* and kitchen for the poor.

Rising magnificently from the Golden Horn side of Fevzi Pasha Street against an indigo dawn sky, its twin minarets and cascading domes are an integral part of the city's skyline today. Seagulls wheel around them, maintaining a noisy aerial surveillance over the complex, while cats search for snacks among the turban-topped tombstones of illustrious Ottomans, and pigeons, crows and jackdaws march briskly across the plaza to find their own crumbs from the faithful. Tacizade Cafer Çelebi, the sixteenth-century state official and poet, was moved to raptures by this crowning monument:

> Its dome rose to the highest point of the heavens
> It touched the eye of the moon and the sun
> Growing in stature that eminent one of the times
> Its crown reached the roof of the heavens.[47]

Mehmed chose the hill on which it was built so that his Greek architect Atik Sinan could build a mosque whose dome would soar over the old Hagia Sophia. He intended the new edifice to vie with, if not outstrip, every church in the city 'in height, beauty and size'.

Legend has it that when it failed to do so, notwithstanding Çelebi's

---

* The shrine, and wider district, is named after Abu Ayub al Ansari (d. 674), one of Prophet Mohammed's closest brothers in arms, whose tomb is one of Istanbul's most sacred places of pilgrimage.

dutiful praise, the sultan amputated his hand. Understandably upset by this agonizing stroke of summary justice, Sinan appealed to a judge, who bravely ruled in his favour, permitting the architect to amputate the sultan's hand. So impressed was Sinan by this display of Islamic justice, the story goes, that he pardoned the sultan and converted to Islam. In what sounds like a distinctly apocryphal postscript to this story, Mehmed is supposed to have drawn his sword, telling the judge that, had he ruled unfairly in the sultan's favour, he would have killed him there and then. Undaunted, the judge drew his own sword and replied that had Mehmed refused to submit to Allah's justice, he would have struck the sultan dead.[48]

The Islamic art historian Gülru Necipoğlu has shown how quickly Mehmed stamped his mark on a city that was at once ancient Christian metropolis and new Islamic capital. He was determined to restore the tattered city to its former greatness within an Islamic mould. First came Yedikule Fortress, cleverly built onto the city walls around the Golden Gate, infamous as a state prison from the sixteenth century. Scorning both the restoration of Constantine's ruined Great Palace and the rehabilitation of the Blachernae Palace, traditional seat of Byzantine power from the eleventh century, the young sultan chose his own distinctive path. A first Ottoman palace, complete with council hall, harem, sumptuous pavilions, a royal hunting reserve stocked with wild animals and vast gardens with elegant fountains, a monumental Theodosian column, peacocks, ostriches and other exotic birds within walls measuring at least a mile, was built where a monastery had stood on the site of the fourth-century Forum of Theodosius.

Then, in 1459, work began on a much grander project. Mehmed wanted to build 'a palace that should outshine all and be more marvellous than the preceding palaces in looks, size, cost and gracefulness'. Set on 600,000 square metres of the ancient acropolis on a series of levelled terraces at the easternmost point of the city's European shore, the New Palace evolved over two decades into an elaborate procession of three principal court-yards, each with its own monumental gates. As one advanced through the palace, the courts steadily shaded from the public to the private realm, from the mint, hospital, administrative offices, palace kitchens, stables and council hall of justice to the treasury, offices for senior officials, mosque, sultan's audience hall, harem and royal quarters. A smaller fourth courtyard contained a walled hanging garden surrounded by outer gardens and vineyards tumbling down to the shore, with pavilions for the sultan's private enjoyment. The architecture expressed in tangible form the separation of the glorious sultan from his ordinary subjects. Today Topkapi Palace, as it is now known, is one of Istanbul's most visited attractions alongside Hagia Sophia, a one-site exercise in imperial Ottoman magnificence. As a seventeenth-century European saying had it: 'If you seek wealth, go to India. If you seek learning and knowledge, go to Europe. But if you seek palatial splendour, come to the Ottoman Empire.'[49]

A string of further conquests at the expense of European Christians unravelled before the man who saw himself as a new Alexander and who, after 1453, styled himself 'Sovereign of the Two Lands and of the Two Seas' – a reference to Rumelia, Anatolia, the Black Sea and the Mediterranean.[50] Serbia and the Peloponnese fell in the late 1450s, followed by Wallachia, Bosnia and the Genoese and Greek colonies on the Black Sea in the 1460s. Albania and Genoese Crimea were overrun in the 1470s. In 1480 Otranto fell and Rome quivered at the irresistible advance of 'The Thunderbolt of War', 'The Lord of Power and Victory on Land and Sea'.

Only in 1481, with Mehmed's death close to his beloved capital, could Europe breathe a tentative – but only brief – sigh of relief. By that time, the Conqueror had established an Ottoman Empire that less than a century after his death, under the vigorous leadership of Sultan Suleiman the Magnificent (r. 1520–66), would extend across three continents, from Belgrade to Baghdad, North Africa to Yemen, and cause sleepless nights in Christendom with an army at the gates of Vienna.

For many Turks – sceptical academics notwithstanding – Sultan Mehmed II is the celebrated, holy warrior *ghazi*, 'Emperor of the Romans and of the Terrestrial Globe', true founder of the Ottoman Empire, with the city he so famously conquered at the age of twenty-one its dazzling Islamic capital and one of the world's greatest, frenetic cities to this day.

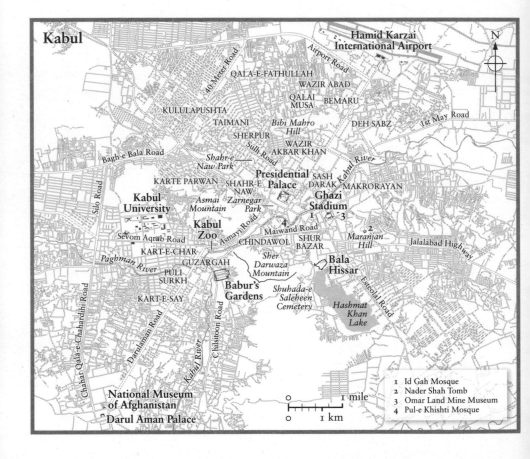

Kabul

Hamid Karzai
International Airport

N

40 Meter Road

Airport Road

QALA-E-FATHULLAH

WAZIR ABAD

QALAI
MUSA

BEMARU

KULULAPUSHTA

TAIMANI

Bibi Mahro
Hill

DEH SABZ

1st May Road

SHERPUR

Sulh Road

WAZIR
AKBAR KHAN

Bagh-e Bala Road

Shahr-e
Naw Park

Kabul River

Silo Road

KARTE PARWAN

SHAHR-E
NAW

Presidential
Palace

SASH
DARAK

MAKRORAYAN

Kabul
University

Asmai
Mountain

Zarnegar
Park

Ghazi
Stadium

Sevom Aqrab Road

Kabul
Zoo

Asmayi Road

Maiwand Road

4

CHINDAWOL

SHUR
BAZAR

1

3

2

Maranjan
Hill

Jalalabad Highway

KART-E-CHAR

GUZARGAH

Sher
Darwaza
Mountain

Bala
Hissar

Paghman River

PULI
SURKH

KART-E-SAY

Babur's
Gardens

Shuhada-e
Saleheen
Cemetery

Esteqlal Road

Chahar Qala-e-Chahardihi Road

Darulaman Road

Chilsitoon Road

Kabul River

Hashmat
Khan
Lake

National Museum
of Afghanistan

Darul Aman Palace

0   1 mile
0   1 km

1 Id Gah Mosque
2 Nader Shah Tomb
3 Omar Land Mine Museum
4 Pul-e Khishti Mosque

10

Kabul – A Garden in the Mountains (16th Century)

*Drink wine in the castle of Kabul and send the cup round without
   pause
For Kabul is mountain, river, city, lowland in one.*

Mullah Mohammed 'The Riddler', quoted by Babur, *Baburnama*

It was winter 1996. The Taliban had taken the Afghan capital a couple of months earlier and were busy telling the city's shivering inhabitants what to do and how to live their lives.

The street signs were everywhere. DRUG ABUSE IS UNLAWFUL IN ISLAM, INTOXICANTS DESTROY WISDOM AND CONSCIENCE, DRUG ABUSE EXERTS HARMFUL IMPACTS ON EDUCATION, DRUG ABUSE IS SUBMISSION TO A GRADUAL DEATH.

Kabul was a comprehensively ruined city, its historical monuments shot up, bombed into smithereens, plundered, smashed, swept away by decades of conflict. The past had been forcibly erased by the present. It was a city of derelict palaces, destroyed factories, devastated parks and gardens, hollowed houses, broken mud walls and torn-up roads. Just as the physical infrastructure of Kabul had been demolished, so too the lives of its inhabitants had been shattered. War had whittled down the city's depleted population into a sorrowful cast of victims: *burqa*-covered widows, impoverished teachers, desperate beggars, landmine cripples and amputees, malnourished children, poverty-stricken mothers and fathers, the flotsam and jetsam washed up by the retreating tides of conflict.

I was visiting Afghanistan to research a history of Timur, and Kabul, in its near total destruction and with its immiserated hordes, felt like the reincarnation of a city he had visited in annihilating fury six centuries earlier. Dust-white-faced children emerged from bombed-out ruins like ghosts in a holocaust. Young boys chased down cars roaring along tracks in clouds of dirt, drivers opening their windows to throw confetti of tiny denomination banknotes at these volunteer pothole repairers. The worldly possessions of stricken families bumped along wrecked roads in homemade carts. Young Talibs whipped women out of decrepit restaurants and into mosques. Nothing could have been more forlorn. It was an urban apocalypse.

Yet despite this devastation on an unholy scale, Kabul somehow managed to hang on to its otherworldly beauty, born of one of the most remarkable settings of any city in the world. Tucked into a narrow valley at an altitude of 1,800 metres, it was lifted from its urban squalor – or at least it appeared to be – by the amphitheatre of Hindu Kush peaks, known to medieval Arab geographers as the Stony Girdles of the Earth, that rose protectively around the city beneath a pristine covering of snow.

Forty miles north of Kabul in his headquarters in the Panjshir Valley – at the precise spot where Alexander the Great had encamped in 329 BC during his conquest of the Persian Empire – I met Ahmed Shah Massoud, the charismatic *mujahideen* leader already famous for having led the successful resistance to the decade-long Soviet occupation of Afghanistan that ended in 1989. Handsome to a dangerous degree, the Lion of the Panjshir, as he was known for his heroic exploits defying the Russians there, wore his Afghan *pokol* hat at a rakish, gravity-defying angle. Surrounded by devoted commanders and all manner of military hardware, Massoud was the quintessential man of war, embroiled in this latest existential conflict against the Islamist iconoclasts. Tanks rumbled through muddy streets past armoured personnel carriers, rocket launchers and freezing soldiers armed with the ubiquitous Kalashnikovs. Amid this noisy military orchestra, four-wheel-drive Toyotas with tinted windows ferried its conductor Massoud to and fro at breakneck speed.

Massoud talked predictably enough about the war and how he was winning it, but he also spoke about his love of literature and his library of 3,000 volumes that he had just relocated to the Panjshir when the Taliban had taken Kabul. Among his particular favourites were the poets Sanayi Ghaznawi and Abdul Qadir Bedil, and those two Persian masters of mysticism, Rumi and Hafiz. Massoud might have been the world's most celebrated *mujahid*, or holy warrior, but he was also a bookish man of quiet dignity and moderation. Two years later, in his 'Message to the People of the United States of America', he wrote of his mission to defeat the Islamists. 'We consider this as part of our duty to defend humanity against the scourge of intolerance, violence and fanaticism.'[1]

With his tolerant outlook, passion for poetry and admiration for Hafiz (a lover of wine and scourge of religious hypocrites), Massoud reminded me of another great warrior-writer who had fought his way to prominence and glory in this mountainous corner of the world. The memory of Babur (1483–1530), the sixteenth-century founder of the Mughal Empire, is still treasured in the city that he adored and made his capital. While I had searched in vain for Timurid monuments – 'I'm afraid you won't find much in Kabul,' Professor Abdul Baqi said sadly in his office in the university's damaged cubist campus, 'They're all long gone' – there was a more promising possibility in the form of Babur's Gardens.

Descended from Timur on his father's side, and from Genghis Khan on his mother's, the blue-blooded Babur inherited the Turkic conqueror's love of stately parks and gardens. His passion for the natural world and all things horticultural earned him the nickname of 'Gardener King'.* He built ten gardens in and around Kabul alone, of which Bagh-e Babur, Babur's Gardens, was his favourite. Laid out in the middle of the sixteenth century, it occupied a large rectangular sweep of ground tumbling down the western slopes of Mount Sher-i-Darwaza to the foaming Kabul River. One of the grandest projects the city had ever seen, in their prime the eleven-hectare gardens offered blooming evidence of Babur's magnificent cultural legacy, a tantalizing indication of what the city would have looked like in its heyday.

Writing in 1977, two years before the Soviet invasion, Nancy Hatch Dupree, an expert on the cultural heritage of Afghanistan, wrote admiringly of Babur's Gardens with their 'charming summer pavilion' built by Amir Abdur Rahman (r. 1880–1901) and 'shaded by magnificent plane trees so beloved by the Mughals', overlooking 'terraced gardens dotted with fountains'.[2]

Two decades of fighting had changed the place beyond all recognition. Dupree's description was of another world. Babur's Gardens were no more than a giant slope of wasteland overlooking a visibly shattered city. Mortars had ripped into the park and craters had replaced flowerbeds. The neat lawns that once stretched down the mountain towards the city had disappeared altogether. Fountains and waterworks had been smashed and removed, landmines laid in their place. The once magnificent plane trees were charred trunks, hacked down and burned as precious firewood. The cypress trees had vanished.

My guide in the gardens was Shukur, an Afghan in his early thirties. He had fled to Pakistan after both his parents were killed in a rocket attack

---

* In *The Garden of the Eight Paradises* the historian Stephen Dale has described Babur, in modern terms, as 'a memoirist, poet, warrior, politician, administrator, nominal Muslim, hypocrite, drunkard, drug user, chronicler, gardener, aesthete, betrayer, avenger, social critic, correspondent, loving father, bisexual, literary critic, nominal Sufi, egotist, bigot, self-flagellant and philanthropist'.

on Kabul sixteen years earlier. As a boy he used to visit the gardens regularly with his family, but had not returned to the capital since his parents' death. Seeing the extent of the damage to Babur's cherished gardens, victim of the civil wars between rival *mujahideen* groups in the 1990s, was a terrible shock. As we surveyed the desolation he grew tearful. 'There used to be so many plane trees here,' he said, pointing to another charred tree trunk. 'There were flowerbeds filled with colourful flowers, lots of green bushes everywhere. Many families came here for picnics in the afternoons and weekends. It was a very beautiful place. It's all gone now. Fighting has killed everything.'

We continued up the barren slope to Babur's tomb, next to a badly damaged marble mosque, built in 1646 by the Mughal emperor Shah Jahan (r. 1628–58) to celebrate his capture of the ancient city of Balkh. Next to it was an empty swimming pool with cracked tiles and a broken diving board. The tomb itself consisted of a simple slab of marble on a raised platform grazed by random bullets. Above it was an elegiac inscription:

> Only this mosque of beauty, this temple of nobility, constructed for the
> prayer of saints and the epiphany of cherubs, was fit to stand in so venerable
> a sanctuary as this highway of archangels, this theatre of heaven, this light-
> garden of the God-forgiven angel king whose rest is the garden of heaven,
> Zahiruddin Mohammed Babur the Conqueror.

An instinctive aesthete, Babur had chosen his burial place with care. It gave by far the finest views over his city. War had disfigured this picture, and many of the buildings which rose into the skyline were skeletal wrecks beyond repair. On the plain far beneath these ruined gardens loomed the jagged outline of Habibiya high school, a building which had been hit by rockets so many times it looked like a concrete colander. In the distance beyond that was the war-torn outline of Darulaman Palace, built for King Amanullah Khan in 1923. But still Kabul retained its natural beauty. Beneath a shameless blue sky a veil of haze drifted upwards from the ring of mountains girdling the city. Fighting had raged here in recent times, but the flourishing pockets of green suggested that some parks and gardens had weathered the onslaught. Just as it had done since Kabul was founded at least 2,500 years ago, the Kabul River meandered dreamily through the city.

Babur had asked that nothing should cover his grave, so that rain could fall and sun could shine on him. For a long time after his Afghan wife Bibi Mubarika (Blessed Lady) Yusufzai brought his body back from Agra to Kabul, his instructions were honoured. But in the reign of King Nadir

Shah (r. 1929–33), a marble stone was installed over the grave, together with a pavilion to protect it from the elements. In a perverse twist of fate the recent fighting had helped fulfil Babur's last wish. Gunfire had removed much of the roof, which now contained more rectangles of sky than tiles. It seemed a tragically inauspicious monument to a man of genius, but at least it had survived.

'The people who did this had no respect for our history,' Shukur said softly. 'They were not good men. Looting and destroying, that was what interested them. That was all they knew.'

Listening to these wistful recollections, the stories of urban destruction and plunder six centuries after Timur's rampages across Central Asia, I recalled Ibn Battuta's description of Kabul. He had passed through in 1332 in the course of his epic travels across the world. Then, as now, destruction was the order of the day. Kabul, he wrote, was 'once a large city; but it is now, for the most part, in ruins'.[*3]

When Babur stood at the gates of Kabul in October 1504, he had already come a very long way. Born in 1483 in the city of Andijan in the Ferghana Valley east of Samarkand in what is today Uzbekistan, the great-great-great-grandson of Timur lost his father in a bizarre accident in 1494. Umar Sheikh Mirza, ruler of the Ferghana Valley and a keen pigeon fancier, fell to his death when the dovecote in his castle, built on the edge of a ravine, crashed into the river in a landslide. Babur put it more poetically: 'Umar Shaikh Mirza flew, with his pigeons and their house, and became a falcon.'[4] On 9 June 1494, at the tender age of eleven, Zahiruddin Mohammed – Defender of the Faith, but nicknamed Babur, the Tiger – became the ruler of one of the world's more fractious kingdoms. The heart of Central Asia from the Aral Sea to the Hindu Kush was at this time a melting-pot of tribes and territories ruled by the forever feuding descendants of Genghis Khan and Timur. The unity imposed first by the Mongol Empire, then by the Timurid, had long gone, splintering the territory into petty kingdoms. Babur, who from an early age was gripped by an 'ambition for rule and desire of conquest' and felt it in his blood, wanted more than this meagre slice of Asia.[5]

Before he could look farther afield for his conquests, he had to fight off two uncles outside Ferghana and ambitious nobles within it to secure his throne, which he was able to do only with the support of a wily grandmother. At the age of fifteen, and after a siege lasting seven months, he

---

* Ibn Battuta took a dim view of the Afghans. 'These are a powerful and violent people,' he wrote, 'and the greater part of them highway robbers.'

next seized Samarkand, which the would-be empire-builder saw as his ancestral Timurid home. Bloodline was well and good, but Babur knew only too well that advancement in this brutal world of ever-shifting loyalties was inconceivable without excelling in the martial arts. Winning the famous cities of antiquity was not the same thing as holding onto them. A rebellion broke out back in Ferghana and, while he was marching back to put it down, a rival seized Samarkand, leaving the fledgling conqueror Babur bereft of both. Efforts to retake them came to naught, forcing the frustrated young king without a kingdom to seek his fortune elsewhere. Ferishta, the sixteenth-century Persian historian, described this decade of destitute wandering across Central Asia, during which 'Babur was like a king on a chess-board, moved from place to place, and buffeted about like pebbles on a seashore'.[6]

And then, in 1504, with his fortunes at their nadir, an opportunity suddenly presented itself four hundred miles to the south. The ruler of Kabul, another relative of Babur, had died, and his infant son had been unable to prevent an unpopular usurper seizing control. Although it was winter and some of his men urged delaying until conditions were more favourable, Babur made his move and determined to lay siege to Kabul. The ruler, Muqim, resorted to delaying tactics and subterfuge, convincing Babur that a show of strength was required to force the pretender's hand. Approaching the city with his army, he ordered his men to put on their armour and their horses' chain mail in sight of the walls 'to strike terror on those within'. An advance party galloped up to the walls. It had the desired effect. Defenders at the Curriers' Gate, the large eastern gate north of the ancient citadel, turned tail and fled into the city without making a stand. 'A crowd of Kabulis who had come out to see the sight raised a great dust when they ran away from the high slope of the glacis of the citadel.' Hidden pits had been dug along the approaches to the city and some of Babur's cavalry were thrown from their horses. There was minor skirmishing in the streets before Muqim offered to surrender the town to Babur. Terms were agreed and Muqim was allowed to make a dignified departure the following day with his family, retainers and possessions. At dawn, Babur's *mirzas* and *begs*, his senior officers, reported 'much mobbing and tumult of the common people'. The city was completely unstable. 'Unless you come yourself, there will be no holding these people in,' Babur was told. Another show of strength was needed to calm the population. The man who would be king understood exactly what was required. 'In the end I got to horse, had two or three persons shot, two or three cut in pieces, and so stamped the rising down.' Muqim was escorted to a camping ground nine miles north of Kabul. So it was that in October 1504, 'without a fight, without an effort, by Almighty God's bounty and mercy', Babur made himself master of Kabul.[7]

We know what Babur thought of Kabul because he wrote about it at length in one of the most sparkling and swashbuckling histories of his time. The *Baburnama* (*Memoirs of Babur*), a literary masterpiece of enormous historical importance, begins with his inheritance of his father's kingdom in 1494 and ends abruptly in 1529, a year before his death. Through those decades it tells, in enchanting prose and with a piercingly distinctive voice, the story of Babur's tumultuous life and his interests, the career-changing triumphs and humiliating reverses. As an Islamic historian recently argued, he wrote so directly, openly and extensively about himself that 'he represents for Islamic civilisation what his Italian contemporary Benvenuto Cellini represents for European civilisation: the most completely revealed individual of the 16th century'. Among the many admirers of the *Baburnama* was the writer E. M. Forster, who likened it to a 'mountain stream', with 'sentences that jostle against one another like live people in a crowd'. What was most striking for Mountstuart Elphinstone, the nineteenth-century Scottish statesman and former governor of Bombay, who toiled for seven years on an English translation of the *Baburnama*, was that instead of the stately, ponderous and artificial style that one might expect from an official memoir, 'we find him natural, lively, affectionate, simple, retaining on the throne all the best feelings and affections of common life'.[8] There was nothing pompous about Babur on the page.

His memoirs demonstrate his thrill in the natural world, in wildlife, flowers and orchard-filled, river-crossed mountain vistas. He writes with authority and sharp judgement on some of the most famous poets of their time and their work. His reverence for the written word was deep-seated and, although his reputation as a poet has always been modest, his prose was exceptional. Which writer today would disagree with Babur's advice to his eldest son Humayun (r. 1530–40; 1555–6) in a letter of 27 November 1528? 'In future write without elaboration. Use plain, clear words. It will be less trouble for you and the reader.'[9] There are hair-raising accounts of expeditions across snow-bound mountain passes, descriptions of bloody battles, considered judgements on some of the leading thinkers and singers, sheikhs and *sadrs* (religious scholars), of their day, light-hearted tales of wine-drenched parties and gentle warnings about the dangers of mixing alcohol and hashish.

'A hashish party never goes well with a wine party,' he writes in one such portrait of an evening that went awry:

> the drinkers began to make wild talk and chatter from all sides, mostly in allusion to hashish and hashish eaters. Baba Jan, even, when drunk, said

many wild things. The drinkers soon made Tardi Khan mad-drunk, by giving him one full bowl after another. Try as we did to keep things straight, nothing went well; there was much disgusting uproar; the party became intolerable and was broken up.[10]

The lightning, almost bloodless conquest of Kabul, as related in his memoirs, was the spur for twenty-eight pages of what amounts to an extended eulogy to the city.[11] The city was not large, broadly encircled by mountains and more narrowly confined within walls connected to another mountain whose lower slopes were covered with gardens watered by the Bala Jui Upper Canal, which still irrigates Babur's Gardens today. Describing the topography in scrupulous detail, he concluded – in a line whose truth has echoed through the following centuries – 'The country of Kabul is a fastness hard for a foreign foe to make his way into.'

The ancient citadel, the Bala Hissar, close to which Babur's men had launched their attack on Kabul, stood defiantly on a detached spur of rock on Uqabain, the Hill of the Two Eagles, with the walled town at its northern end, overlooking three meadows and a large lake. The north wind brought refreshing cool, even in the fiercest heat of summer. While talking about the citadel Babur cannot resist quoting a couplet from the poet Mullah Mohammed 'The Riddler', which also reveals one of his own great loves, and sometime source of inner conflict:

> Drink wine in the castle of Kabul and send the cup
>   round without pause
> For Kabul is mountain, river, city, lowland in one.

Unlike the Taliban half a millennium later, Babur was generally more relaxed about intoxicants.

Geography and topography completed, it was onto his next keen interest: trade. Kabul, he wrote, was one of two markets on the land route from India to Khorasan, with caravans arriving from Kashgar, Ferghana, Turkistan, Samarkand, Bukhara, Balkh, Hisar and Badakhshan. 'Kabul is an excellent trading centre; if merchants went to Khita [northern China] or Rum [Turkey], they might make no higher profit.' Every year between 7,000 and 10,000 horses came to Kabul, while from India came caravans of 10,000–20,000 merchants bringing slaves, white cloth, sugar-candy, refined and common sugars and aromatic roots. It was such a prosperous business that many traders were not even content with a profit of 300–400 per cent. Despite his obvious interest in trade, judging by the brevity with which fiscal and financial affairs are mentioned here, they did not move Babur to poetic heights. The section headed 'Revenue of Kabul' consists of a solitary sentence revealing that taxes from tolls, cultivated lands and rural populations generated the modest sum of '8 laks of shahrukhis', calculated by the British editor to be the equivalent of £33,333 in 1922 – or £1.74 million today.

Babur's priorities with regards to Kabul were elsewhere. He marvelled at its favourable weather and the flourishing natural produce it brought. Within a day's travel from Kabul one could reach a point where snow never fell, and within two hours a place where it never thawed. South-west of the city were 'great snow-mountains where snow falls on snow', from where supplies were fetched to cool the drinking water when Kabul's ice-houses had run out. Like so much about Kabul he found the climate perfect. 'If the world has another so pleasant, it is not known. Even in the heats, one cannot sleep at night without a fur coat.'

Fruit, as a result of these variable conditions, was incredibly abundant. Green-fingered Babur had sour cherry cuttings brought to Kabul, which grew nicely. He counted thirty-two varieties of wild tulips on the mountainsides and admired the fecundity of the fields and orchards, which produced 'grape, pomegranate, apricot, apple, quince, pear, peach, plum, almond and walnut' in abundance. Oranges, lemons, rhubarb, melons and sugar-cane also grew plentifully, and apiaries produced large quantities of honey. Throughout the city and among the valleys of the outlying villages, birds filled the air with their song. There were nightingales, herons, mallards, blackbirds, thrushes, doves, magpies, egrets, waterhens and, most stately of all, cranes, the birds of heaven, 'great birds, in large flocks, and countless numbers'. In the rushing waters of the Kabul River and its tributaries, fishermen took to the banks and hauled in generous catches.

There was no shortage of firewood, described in Babur's quintessential style, an attractive blend of the meticulous and jaunty. Of the mastic, holm oak, almond and saxaul, the mastic was his favourite:

> It burns with flame and a nice smell, makes plenty of hot ashes and does well even if sappy. Holm oak is also first-rate fire-wood, blazing less than mastic but, like it, making a hot fire with plenty of hot ashes and a pleasant smell. It has the peculiarity in burning that when its leafy branches are set alight, they fire up with amazing sound, blazing and crackling from bottom to top. It is good fun to burn it.

The rhapsodies continued over the six meadows around Kabul, detailed according to those which were home to horse-troubling mosquitoes – no minor consideration for Babur's growing army, founded on a well-equipped cavalry – and those which were free of such nuisances. The type of grass that grew here provided excellent grazing. As the *Cambridge*

History of India observed, 'These portions of his memoirs read like the notes of a peace-loving naturalist rather than those of a restless warrior.'[12]

Babur was as fascinated by the human population of Kabul of which he had made himself master as of its wildlife. He was especially struck by the cosmopolitan, polyglot inhabitants of the territory. There were many tribes, including Turks, Mughals, Arabs, Persians and Sarts, who spoke up to twelve languages, from Arabic, Persian, Turki, Mughuli, Hindi and Afghani to Pashai, Paraji, Gibri, Birki and Lamghani. 'If there be another country with so many differing tribes and such a diversity of tongues, it is not known.' Just like his world-conquering ancestor Timur before him, Babur took care to promote the liberalizing forces of commerce, which brought in numerous foreign traders and an accompanying spirit of tolerance, which he proved determined to uphold. An orthodox Sunni, he nevertheless forged marriage ties to Sufi Naqshbandi orders in Kabul at the same time as supporting the Shia Qizilbash troops in his army, a military exemplar of diversity, encompassing Arabs, Tajiks, Uzbeks, Pashtuns and other peoples of Central Asia.

When it came to the pleasures of the grape, Babur demonstrated both gay abandon and bouts of tortured doubt and shame. His relationship with alcohol was complicated and evolved during his life. He offers up a rivetingly candid internal discussion over the should-I-shouldn't-I temptations of drinking for the first time in 1506 during his visit to the city of Herat, a model of urban glamour and sophistication, in an episode described as 'a classic instance of the country cousin come to town'.[13]

> Although at that time I had not committed the sin of drinking to tipsiness, had not experienced drunkenness and did not know the delight and pleasure of being drunk as it should be known, not only was I inclined to have a drink of wine, but my heart was actually urging me to cross that valley.

Reading this extraordinary account, you can feel the temptation – and tension – increasing with every sentence. He thinks back to his childhood, during which his father had offered him wine, which he had refused. By the time he was gripped by 'the desires of young manhood and the promptings of the carnal soul', there was no one to offer him a drink. And now he had arrived at the 'fabulous', pleasure-filled city of Herat, former seat of the Timurid Empire under Timur's son Shahrukh (r. 1405–47), legendary patron of the arts and sciences: 'If I didn't drink now, when would I?'[14] Inevitably, perhaps, he succumbs to the temptation and a discreet drinking evening is arranged. One of the party is 'high as a kite', there is singing and dancing and 'the conviviality really waxed warm'. But then the drunkenness became excessive and the evening descended into 'taste-less impertinences' – as they so often do.

Babur had reached Herat on 27 October. His first impression was inaus-picious. He was understandably unimpressed by the undignified reception from his young cousins and princes, who rode out to meet him, arriving late and hung over after yet another drinking bout. Babur's visit to his cousins' court at Herat at a time when the city was a cultural lodestar shining brilliantly from a Timurid Dynasty on the brink of implosion was an eye-opener. On one level he admired it intensely, declaring it had 'no equal in the world'. Gatherings were convivial, entertainments sophisti-cated, conversations witty. The art, poetry, singing and dancing raised cultural life to its dazzling zenith. The great fifteenth-century Herati poet Ali Sher Navai (1441–1501) reigned supreme as the poet laureate of his era and a great philanthropist and patron of artists. But for Babur, at least, there was a darker side to this gorgeous refinement. The decadence of the court, liberal to the point of libertine, brought out an inner censoriousness. He found it distasteful that the great king of 'an Islamic city like Herat' presided over a family, people and nation where 'vice and debauchery were rife and rampant'. He castigated the religious entourage, which he con-sidered effete, witty, depraved and debauched. There were 'pseudo-Sufis' guilty of 'tasteless and impious' work that amounted to 'near blasphemy' and 'a pack of lies'. As for the 'deviation' and 'pederasty', the less said about that the better.

It is clear from Babur's shrewdly observed account of his stay in Herat that, much as he admired the cultural sophistication of the city and its royal court, the passion for poetry and traditions of philosophical debate, the architectural refinement and sublime artistry from miniaturists to calligraphers, jade carvers and bookbinders, there was something omin-ously and unmistakably lacking from the leadership in this dangerous world. 'Although these mirzas were outstanding in the social graces, they were strangers to the actuality of military command and the rough and tumble of battle.' They were prancing and posturing as enemies rumbled on the horizon.

His words proved prescient. In 1507, within a year of Babur's visit, the city fell to the warrior Mohammed Shaybani Khan's Uzbek army, putting the final light out on a Timurid Dynasty that, from the time of Shahrukh, had illuminated Central Asia for a century. Herat gave up its priceless treasures – 'so many lustrous pearls, emeralds, Badakhshan rubies and other gems and gold vessels were obtained that not a decimal of a tenth could be contained in the imagination of any emperor'.[15] As the only Timurid left standing in any position of power, however limited in practice, Babur used the fall of Herat to promote himself from *mirza* to *padshah*, prince to emperor.

From being the political and cultural capital of the once resplendent Timurid Empire, Herat had declined to the status of weak and tempting target for empire-builders on the make. One such was Shah Ismail I, founder of the Safavid Dynasty, who, over a decade of bloody conquests from 1501, had reunited Iran for the first time since Arab armies had stormed through in the mid-seventh century, thereby ending 850 years of rule by Arab caliphs, Turkish sultans and Mongol khans. Ismail's Iran was once again under Iranian rule, with the Shia faith established as the official state religion. At the Battle of Merv in 1510, he defeated Mohammed Shaybani Khan and took Herat. The body of his adversary was dismembered, his skull set in gold and turned into the ultimate warrior trophy, a gem-studded drinking vessel that he later sent to Babur as a gesture of goodwill and a reminder of the new balance of power in the region.

If Herat's effete Timurid princes had failed to demonstrate toughness and resolution on the battlefield, the same could not be said of Babur, who left his cousins on 23 December 1506 and, forced to overcome appalling conditions brought on by 'an amazing snowstorm', demonstrated characteristic leadership and resilience on the return journey to Kabul. With each step through the snow the men sank as far as their waist or chest. The terrified horses, sinking down to their stirrups or even girth straps, were soon exhausted. Babur's ears were frostbitten. Many got frostbite in their hands and feet. 'During those few days, much hardship and misery were endured, more than I had ever endured in my whole life,' he remembered.

Babur was to suffer further vicissitudes, including another agonizingly brief and final tenure of Samarkand from 1511 to 1512, amid the swirling currents of dynastic conquests and rebellions in a Central Asia whose default setting was unsettled, unruly and opportunistic. With the Uzbeks and Safavids having carved up the ancestral Timurid lands to the north and west respectively, the man who would be emperor necessarily needed to look elsewhere for his empire.

'Strangers and ancient foes,' he wrote, 'are in possession of all the countries once held by Temur Beg's descendants . . . one remains, I myself, in Kabul, the foe mightily strong, I very weak, with no means of making terms, no strength to oppose.' Faced with 'such power and potency', it was imperative to put distance between themselves and their enemies.[16] Some of Babur's men favoured Badakhshan to the north-east. Babur had grander ideas. His eyes turned south towards Hindustan or India.

Like his greatest ancestor, Babur was conscious of his place in history.

The *Baburnama*, encompassing his life story from childhood to just before his death, is a one-volume testament to the importance he attached to posterity. Timur had measured himself against his predecessors, eclipsing both Alexander the Great and Genghis Khan by crossing the Indus and taking Delhi. Babur, a regular reader of Sharaf al din Ali Yazdi, Timur's court historian, was determined to seek his fortune away from his kingdom's snowy mountains on the burning plains of the Punjab and beyond.

From 1519 he launched a series of expeditions that combined reconnaissance with pillage, satisfying his men's constant desire for booty, while probing his enemies' defences and assessing their strength. His army was modernized and reformed while he did this, with the introduction of artillery to supplement the fire from his musketeers. In November 1525 he left Kabul for the last time, making an unhurried approach to India enlivened by a series of wine-soaked banquets among the mountains.

Unlike Timur before him, who had used the Kurram River Valley, Babur's chosen passage into India was through the Khyber Pass. It is a wildly romantic, legend-filled route, entwined with the invasions of world-conquering empire-builders such as Darius I, Alexander the Great and Genghis Khan. Twisting and turning through battalions of fortress-mountains dashed chiaroscuro across the skyline, the dramatic route was made famous to the British after the country's ill-fated entanglements in Afghanistan in the nineteenth century and then again in the twenty-first, remembered today in the colourful regimental plaques hewn into the rock. For thousands of years these rippled mountains with dimpled slopes shading from ochre to slate-grey to white, poised above crashing, white-foamed, grey-blue waters, have played the spectacular backdrop to history-makers on the move.

On 21 April 1526, having passed through the Khyber with an army that had numbered 12,000 when he left his kingdom and was unlikely to have grown much beyond 20,000 with the arrival of new contingents, he faced off against the much larger Afghan force of Ibrahim Lodi, Sultan of Delhi, at Panipat, fifty miles north of the Indian city. Babur estimated his enemy's army at 100,000 with 1,000 war elephants. With a brilliant series of manoeuvres and feints – and a dash of good fortune – Babur hemmed his adversary into a narrow front and organized an ingenious series of defences that simultaneously allowed his cavalry to charge between spaces within a line of 700 bullock carts protecting his matchlockmen on the one hand and his cannons on the other. It was a masterful adaptation of traditional steppe and mountain warfare with the innovations of Ottoman artillery, the first time such heavy artillery had been used in India. The barrage of guns and cannons sent Lodi's war elephants into a blind panic. They turned tail and trampled their own men in their disarray.

By midday the battle was over, Lodi was dead and the Afghan casualties, in Babur's estimation, were around 16,000. Through the grace of Allah, 'This mighty army, in the space of half a day, laid in the dust.'[17] It had taken Babur less than a day to topple an empire. No time was wasted to press home his victory. His son and heir Humayun was dispatched 'to ride fast and light' to occupy Sultan Lodi's capital of Agra, while another contingent was ordered to move on Delhi. On 10 May, having finished a round of visits to palaces, shrines and gardens in Delhi, Babur made his ceremonial entrance into Agra, riding into his late adversary's imperial citadel in triumph. The Gardener King had become the first Mughal emperor, ushering in a new Asian dynasty that would be far more successful and last far longer than anything Timur had established. His men were rewarded with lavish distributions from the Agra treasury.

With this momentous conquest Babur became the fourth Turkic-speaking ruler within a century to found a major state in the Middle East, Central Asia and the Indian Subcontinent. He was thereby following in the martial footsteps of Ottoman Sultan Mehmed II, conqueror of Constantinople; Safavid Shah Ismail I, the firebrand Shia ruler of Iran; and the Uzbek ruler Mohammed Shaybani Khan, a descendant of Genghis Khan. Successful leaders in their own right, they nevertheless demonstrated, in their rival realms and kingdoms, how much the Islamic Empire had splintered since the time of its greatest unity under the Rashidun, Umayyads and the early centuries of the Abbasids. Only the Ottomans would come close to achieving such unity again, but even with their continent-spanning empire, great swathes of the Islamic world, especially Iran and the Subcontinent would always elude them. Collectively the four men also revealed the strength and depth of the eastern, non-Arab Islamic world. Each of the quartet ethnically or culturally was either a Turk or Turkicized Mongol, and respected Genghisid and Timurid political legitimacy more than blood ties with the Arab world. Each, moreover, valued Persian, not Arabic, as the language and literary culture of eastern Islam.[18]

Perhaps it was only to be expected that Babur should celebrate his triumph by laying out the Garden of the Eight Paradises in Agra. This was one of a number of evocatively named gardens – Garden of Rest, Lotus Garden, Gold-Scattering Garden – that he designed and constructed in India, tribute to his love of the natural world and an echo of his ancestor Timur's imperial horticultural projects in Samarkand. Babur particularly treasured the fruits that grew so successfully in the Garden of the Eight Paradises, especially because they reminded him of his homeland of

Mawarannahr, the Land Beyond the River, and his capital, Kabul. As he wrote later, 'to have grapes and melons grown in this way in Hindustan filled my measure of content'.[19]

For Babur's men, accustomed to the spine-chilling mountains, verdant valleys, orchards and crashing rivers of Afghanistan, the furnace of the Indian plain was intolerable. Many left after a year with their emperor's permission, job done and booty won, prompting a regretful verse from Babur:

> *Ah you who have gone from this country of Hind,*
> *Aware for yourselves of its woe and its pain,*
> *With longing desire for Kabul's fine air,*
> *You went hot-foot forth out of Hind.*[20]

To judge by his descriptions of his new kingdom, a long passage infamous to Indians to this day, Babur was not immediately captivated. 'Hindustan is a country of few charms,' he wrote.

> Its people have no good looks; of social intercourse, paying and receiving visits there is none; of genius and capacity none; of manners none; in handi-craft and work there is no form or symmetry, method or quality; there are no good horses, no good dogs, no grapes, musk-melons or first-rate fruits, no ice or cold water, no good bread or cooked food in the bazaars, no hot-baths, no colleges, no candles, torches or candlesticks.[21]

Amid this pessimistic gloom there was at least a ray of light. 'Pleasant things of Hindustan are that it is a large country and has masses of gold and silver.' There were, besides, 'numberless artisans and workmen', many of whom were soon put to work by Babur in a rush of construction. He noted how Timur had used 200 stone-cutters on one of his mosques, while he went one better and employed 680 stone-cutters in Agra alone, or 1,491 if you added his building projects in Sikri, Bayana, Dholpur, Gwaliar and Kol. Babur knew that the majority of his soldiers and officers, appalled by the heat, the hostility of the Indians, the lack of provisions and the pestilential winds which were killing off droves of his men, wanted to leave India and return home to Afghanistan. Recognizing this 'unsteadi-ness' of his men, he held a council and reminded them of the sacrifices they had made together. They had endured several years of hardship, long travels and 'deadly slaughter' to win new lands. 'And now what force compels us, what necessity has arisen that we should, without cause, abandon countries taken at such risk of life?' he asked. 'Was it for us to remain in Kabul, the sport of harsh poverty?'[22]

That last line is worth dwelling on. We may recall Babur's modest section – a single sentence – on his revenues from Kabul. One of the reasons he had looked south to carve out a kingdom was that the city was too small to house and finance an expanding army and serve as an imperial capital. In a later entry in his memoirs, recorded in 1528, he includes a table headed 'Revenues of Hindustan from what has so far come under the victorious standards', detailing the various sources from Agra to Sialkot, Delhi to Dipalpur, Lahore to Lucknow. Tentatively estimated at approximately £4.2 million by Babur's English translator William Erskine in a study published in 1854, that equates to £429 million today – or almost 250 times his revenues in Kabul. The calculations may be somewhat shaky, but whatever the precise figures there can be no doubt that the conquest of India had raised Babur's treasury to a more appropriately imperial level.

Though imperial destiny had impelled him south from Kabul, Babur never lost his deep affection for the city. On 10 February 1529, he wrote a letter to his governor and old friend Khwaja Kalan confessing how 'boundless and infinite is my desire' to return to Kabul, where the melons and grapes were so exquisite he had wept on eating a melon recently in India. Apart from Baburian digressions on poetry, gardening ('The best of young trees must be planted there, lawns arranged, and borders set with sweet herbs and with flowers of beautiful colour and scent') and his longing for a drinking bout ('sometimes the craving for wine brought me to the verge of tears'), the letter contained detailed instructions for the repair and provisioning of the fort, the allocation of revenues to construct a congregational mosque, the repair of the caravanserai and hot baths and the completion of a building within the citadel in 'a gracious and harmonious design'. The detail was exhaustive, the tone conversational to the point of breezy. Once he had settled affairs in India, he told his comrade, he would be back 'at once' to his beloved Kabul.[23]

It was not to be. In 1530, the year after his heartfelt letter to Khwaja Kalan, he died at the age of forty-seven, ruler of an empire that stretched from the Indus in the west to Bihar in the east, from the soaring Himalayas in the north as far south as Gwalior in Madhya Pradesh.

In the time-honoured traditions of Genghis Khan and Timur of dividing up a ruler's territories among his sons, a certain precursor of interfamilial conflict, Humayun was given Mughal territories in present-day India, while his half-brother Kamran Mirza was given Kabul and Lahore. From being the seat of an emerging power, Kabul drifted out to the periphery of an expanding empire that was headquartered, successively over the following four centuries, at Agra, Fatehpur Sikhri, Lahore, Agra again, Shahjahanabad and lastly Delhi.

Babur's lasting fame was twofold. Emulating his ancestral hero Timur, he had brilliantly overcome the throneless travails of his youth to found the Mughal Empire which, at its pinnacle in the late 1600s, controlled the destinies of up to 150 million people, around a quarter of the world's population, scattered over 1.5 million square miles of the Indian Sub-continent, and would endure until the British displaced it in 1858.[24] As with Timur, glory on the battlefield was the foundation of cultural splendours beyond it. Timur's challenge, 'Let he who doubt our power look upon our buildings' could equally have been uttered by the Mughals. Their archi-tectural record alone – including such gems as Humayun's Tomb, Agra Fort, Lahore Fort, Fatehpur Sikhri and Shah Jahan's heartbreaking Taj Mahal – has entranced hundreds of millions and filled the world's libraries with admiring volumes. Under Babur's successors, 'Mughal' became a byword for power and prosperity, religious tolerance, administrative excel-lence, opulence and ostentation: marble-decked palaces with perfumed fountains and fragrant gardens, lavish banquets and state receptions, the 'heaven-depleting grandeur' of the Peacock Throne commissioned by Shah Jahan, Emperor and Shadow of God, an extravagance of gold, pearls and innumerable precious jewels, complete with twelve pillars of emerald and two golden peacocks, each carrying a flashing ruby in its beak. Eight feet deep by seven wide and fourteen high, it was fashioned from almost 1.2 metric tonnes of solid gold and is said to have cost twice the price of the Taj Mahal.[25]

One of the earliest indications of the riches that had suddenly become available to Babur in his new kingdom came when Humayun presented the world's most famous diamond – the Koh-i-noor, or Mountain of Light – to his father on the latter's arrival in his just-conquered capital. Although over the course of its turbulent history it has captivated kings and queens, rulers and brigands, in India, Iran, Afghanistan, Pakistan and Britain – the 105-carat gem was the centrepiece in the crown of Queen Elizabeth the Queen Mother, placed on top of her coffin during the lying-in-state in 2002 – it failed to excite Babur. 'Humayun offered it to me when I arrived at Agra. I just gave it him back.'[26]

To his achievements as empire-builder in the tradition of Genghis Khan and Timur before him, albeit without the blood-spilling atrocities both men perpetrated on an epic scale across the continent, must be added the formidable literary record. Memoirist and poet, Babur was also formally trained in poetics and musical theory and was an authority on rhyme and metre. He was not only a patron of high literary culture but an energetic, genre-bending writer in his own right. His breadth of intellectual interest was as wide as the Asian steppe from which his ancestors had emerged and he produced works on Sufism, law and prosody, together with poems in

Persian and Chagatay Turkish. His writings in the latter language are considered second only to those of the poet Ali Sher Navai, whom Babur
reckoned 'had no equal'. The *Baburnama*, enthusiastically hailed as 'among
the most enthralling and romantic works in the literature of all time', has
proved even more long-lived than the empire founded by its author.[27]

When assessing Humayun, there were unmistakable echoes of the
father in the career of the son. Humayun spent the period from 1530 to
1540 beset by rebellions, fraternal dissension and continued opposition
from Afghans and Rajputs. The kingdom he inherited in 1530 had been
lost by 1540, defeated by an Afghan soldier of fortune called Sher Shah
of Sur, so that, like his father, Humayun became a destitute wanderer. In
1543 he was reduced to retreating first to Kabul, thence to Kandahar and
Herat, his entire royal entourage pathetically reduced to forty men subsist-
ing on scraps of meat boiled up in his soldiers' helmets. After enduring
this ignominy he can surely be forgiven for launching into an anguished
discussion with his hosts on the 'world's faithlessness and the instability
of external circumstances'.[28]

Although his imperial career was at its nadir, the Safavid chancellery
was determined that Herat should honour Humayun's arrival with a
sumptuous reception, for who knew what alliances might be contracted
in the future with the Mughal emperor, 'sphere rider, sun cupola, pearl of
consciousness and sovereignty's ocean, goodly tree ornamenting the garden of government and worldly sway'?[29] Such precautions and politesse
were well founded on the part of Shah Tahmasp. It was ultimately only
with Safavid assistance – conditional on Humayun's controversial conversion to Shia Islam – that the Mughal was able to regain his empire in India
in 1555, having taken Kabul three times from his serially disloyal brother
Kamran Mirza, whom he reluctantly had blinded and sent into exile.
Humayun's restoration, supported by a large court of Iranian nobles,
marked a significant cultural shift in the life of the Mughal Empire, the
traditional Turko-Mongol influence from Central Asia steadily eclipsed
by a much greater emphasis on Iranian schools of art and architecture,
language and literature.

Babur loved literature with a passion. Had he been less of a bibliophile,
had he not sown the seeds of reading with such gusto in his son and
heir, perhaps Humayun might have escaped one of history's more perverse
literary deaths. On 24 January 1556, Humayun heard the call to prayer
as he was descending the stairs of his library carrying a pile of books.
Instinctively bowing his knees, he took a tumble, smashed his head and
died. His tomb in Delhi, a sumptuous edifice of red sandstone, centred
around a dome sheathed in cream marble among representations of the

Quran's four rivers of paradise running through neatly clipped lawns, is the first garden-tomb in the Indian Subcontinent and the first great masterpiece of Mughal architecture.

One evening in the bone-freezing depths of winter in 1556 – the same year that Thomas Cranmer, Archbishop of Canterbury, was declared a heretic and burned at the stake in Oxford – a severed head arrived at Kabul's ancient fortress the Bala Hissar. This was good news. The traditional, blood-smeared war trophy originally belonged to Hemu, a saltpetre trader and greengrocer turned military ruler and Hindu thorn in the Mughal Empire's side. At the Second Battle of Panipat, the army of Humayun's thirteen-year-old son and heir, Akbar (r. 1556–1605), had triumphed over his Indian adversary. When Hemu was wounded and captured, the teen-aged emperor was given the opportunity of beheading his illustrious prisoner but demurred, leaving his commander-in-chief and guardian Bairam Khan to finish off proceedings with a stroke of his sword. While Hemu's head made its way 600 miles to Kabul, his body was gibbeted on a gate in Delhi.

We know about the excitement caused by the arrival of Hemu's head at Kabul from the *Tadkhira Humayun wa Akbar* (*Memoir of Humayun and Akbar*). Its author, Bayazid Bayat, was a military officer who recorded the outbreak of fighting which erupted in and around Kabul on the death of Humayun and the accession of his young son. With predictable opportunism, a senior Mughal, Mirza Suleiman of Badakhshan, sent a force estimated at 10,000 south to put the Bala Hissar and its garrison, together with the royal wives and children, under siege. Mirza Suleiman met his son's army at what is today the sprawling cemetery of Shuhada-e Saleheen on the southern outskirts of the city. Bayat was given the keys of the fortress-palace during the six months the siege lasted.

His eyewitness account provides a rare glimpse of Kabul in the mid-sixteenth century amid the clashes and skirmishes between the besiegers and defenders. When, anxious to strike a deal and bring the siege to an end, Mirza Suleiman sent an envoy to the palace to parley, 'he was entertained with the best fruits, drinks and cooked dishes, for 40 days, as a propaganda show, as if to say, "Look, we lack nothing here in the fort! Help is on its way from India and will arrive today or tomorrow – just wait till our two forces combine! How will you get over the Hindu Kush passes back to Badakhshan?" '[30] Terms were eventually agreed allowing Mirza Suleiman to save face by having one Friday sermon read in his name before lifting the siege and returning to Badakhshan with his dignity more or less intact.

When Hemu's head arrived, Bayat was instructed to display it over the Iron Gate of the Bala Hissar, overlooking the Old City, where it would have the greatest, morale-boosting effect on the population. An orchestra was ordered to play fanfares celebrating the great victory. According to Akbar's memoirs, the *Akbarnama*, 'the drums of joy beat high' and there was great 'thanksgiving and rejoicing' at the downfall and death of this enemy, 'a whip of warning to the arrogant and self-willed'.[31]

Raised in Kabul by his uncles while his father was in exile, Akbar spent his youth learning how to hunt and fight, classic martial skills which were called upon repeatedly during a forty-nine-year reign spent enlarging and consolidating his empire far beyond the city of his childhood across most of the Indian Subcontinent. Although Kabul was of secondary importance to his shifting capitals in India, it remained significant as a centre of trade – particularly for horses – and as the gateway to Central Asia, where the Mughals dreamed one day of reclaiming their lost ancestral lands.[32]

For Mughal historians the third emperor was always Akbar the Great, an epithet awarded after an unbeaten military career based on superbly trained standing and irregular armies, a prodigious arsenal of cannons and war elephants, and a network of strong forts.[33] Mughal tentacles spread steadily across the continent in a series of conquests. Gujarat fell to Akbar in 1573, Bihar in 1574, flood-riven Bengal in 1576. In 1580 Akbar's half-brother Mirza Hakim led a rebellion against the emperor. 'On every side there was a fire of sedition, and the dust of strife rose high.' At the head of an army of 50,000 cavalry, 500 war elephants, infantry and camel corps, Akbar moved against his disloyal brother, who had 'left the highway of obedience on account of the intrigues of wicked wretches', among them prominent clerics who considered the emperor's religious policies unacceptably liberal, and the uprising was snuffed out.[34] Hakim fled and Akbar, indulging a desire for imperial nostalgia, temporarily moved into his grandfather Babur's citadel. He annexed and took direct control of Kabul in 1585, from which time it was held by the Mughal emperors of India until Nadir Shah captured it in 1738. Kashmir fell in 1586, Sindh in 1590, parts of Orissa in 1592–3 and much of the Deccan from 1596 to 1601. Akbar's consolidation of the maritime and commercial province of Gujarat with the agricultural powerhouse of the Punjab and Ganges basins laid the economic foundations of a flourishing and productive trading empire.[35]

The cultural flowering of the Mughal Empire under Akbar's enlightened and tolerant rule was hardly less remarkable. Although illiterate himself, Akbar took pleasure in having courtiers read to him daily from his royal library of 24,000 manuscripts in Hindustani, Persian, Kashmiri,

Sanskrit, Arabic, Greek and Latin. His courts at Agra and Fatehpur Sikhri glittered not only with gold, gems and precious stones but from the intellectual sparkle of their leading lights. Abul Fazl ibn Mubarak, author of the *Akbarnama*, was one of Akbar's *Navaratnas*, or Nine Jewels of the emperor's court, a stellar group which included his brother Faizi, the poet laureate, the classical musician and singer Tansen and Raja Todar Mal, the warrior-writer turned finance minister.

In around 1575 Akbar built the Ibadat Khana, or House of Worship, a forum for discussion of Islamic law. Then, in 1579, he made his move against the conservative *ulama* clergy, first by reading the *khutba* sermon in his own name as caliph, then by extracting a declaration from some senior clerics that he outranked the formally qualified *mojtaheds* in interpreting Islamic law. With Akbar's personal blessing, the Ibadat Khana broadened into what today would be called an interfaith think-tank, with debates and discussions opened to an ever widening circle of thinkers, from Shiite scholars and Sufi dervishes to Hindus, Jains, Parsis and Christians. His favourite slogan, 'Peace to all', defined his outlook as an emperor who governed over millions of Muslims and non-Muslims alike, a tolerance that was both instinctively personal and deliberately political, aimed at promoting imperial strength and unity and undermining those pursuing more narrow, divisive interests and agendas, be they Muslim, Hindu or otherwise.[36] For conservative clerics his abolition of the *jizya* poll tax on unbelievers was anathema, a lapse of judgement exceeded only by his attempt to devise his own Sufi-influenced form of divine monotheism, Din-i Ilahi (literally Religion of God), a syncretic blend primarily of Islam and Hinduism, with added elements of Christianity, Zoroastrianism and Jainism thrown in. It never caught on.

One of the most eloquent testimonies to Akbar's qualities comes from an unlikely source. Father Pierre du Jarric, the early seventeenth-century French Catholic missionary and historian of the Jesuit missions, left a positively glowing account of the emperor.

To the entirely conventional Catholic view that, as a Muslim, Akbar would be 'unable to escape everlasting torment', du Jarric added a much longer eulogy commending his many virtues as a ruler and singling out for particular notice the emperor's tolerance of, and justice towards, all faiths. 'He was a prince beloved of all, firm with the great, kind to those of low estate, and just to all men, high and low, neighbour or stranger, Christian, Saracen or Gentile; so that every man believed that the King was on his side.'[37] In the course of his long reign he had strengthened and expanded his empire more remarkably than his counterpart Elizabeth I of England. She, though, had laid the foundation for imperial acquisitions and, in granting a royal charter to the East India Company in 1600, had planted the seeds for the Mughals' much later demise.

Akbar died in October 1605, a multiculturalist before his time.

In 2018, I returned to Kabul for the first time in a decade. It was a city transformed. Four decades of continuous fighting had taken their toll. A 'war on terror' brutalism had turned Kabul into an urban dystopia. Sprawling across the northern district of Wazir Akbar Khan, a new 'Green Zone' had sprung up, a heavily defended enclave in which embassies lived in compounds within secure compounds, protected by security guards, security fencing, security cameras, sniffer dogs, sandbags, checkpoints, barriers, barbed wire and blast walls so high it was impossible to see the snow-sprinkled mountains that encircled the capital. Yet hope somehow survived. 'Kabul the Peace City' read the most popular graffiti stencilled on the blast walls. A suicide bomber killed six Afghans on my second day in town. A week later, another killed fifty-five at a gathering of religious scholars.

I made my way to Babur's Gardens, not knowing what to expect. The eleven-hectare site has evolved repeatedly over more than 500 years, from the late Timurid period into the Mughal era and the various constructions of Babur, Jahangir (r. 1605–27) and Shah Jahan, through the intrusive late nineteenth-century additions of Amir Abdul Rahman (r. 1880–1901) and the Europeanizing alterations of King Nadir Shah (r. 1929–33). Now it was a different place again. Drab brown wasteland had been transformed into green wonderland. A central east–west axis of pools and stone paving rose directly – Babur would have recognized and approved of the strict geometry – through fifteen landscaped terraces of lawns, marble-lined water channels, chutes and basins, trees and flowers. It was magnificent, a swathe of green serenity in a turbulent city.

In the intervening years the Aga Khan Trust for Culture had restored the gardens as part of a programme to rehabilitate some of Afghanistan's most important, war-damaged heritage. With scholars from Afghanistan, India, Germany and South Africa, the cosmopolitan aspect of the restoration team carried with it echoes of the multiethnic Mughal Empire. New marble was brought in from Babur's Ferghana Valley in Uzbekistan and then carved by expert masons in India. Mines and other unexploded ordnance were carefully removed.

Engineer Abdul Latif Kohistani, the chief horticulturalist, emerged as a local hero, contacting plant-growing associations right across Afghanistan as far afield as Herat, riding his motorbike far and wide over the hills and mountains to collect the more than 5,000 species of vegetation that now adorn the garden. Here were the plants and trees that once gave so much pleasure to the Gardener King: roses, pistachios, walnuts, an avenue of plane trees interspersed with peaches and pomegranates, apricots, apples and cherries, and, of course, the Arghavan or Judas trees so beloved by Babur – 'If, the world over, there is a place to match this when the Arghavans are in full bloom, their yellow mingling with red, I do not know it.'

'My favourites are the plane trees, the Judas trees, sweet and sour cherry and the pomegranates,' Abdul Latif says proudly. A little under a third of the planting was fruit trees, he says, with more than 40 per cent given to ornamental trees and shrubs, in line with the original balance stipulated by Babur when the gardens were laid out. Seeing the completely restored garden is 'very exhilarating'.

These days fighting in Kabul is the least of Engineer Latif's worries. He has to contend with plant-wilting temperatures of up to forty degrees in summer and minus twenty in winter as well as the city's wretched, leaf-browning air pollution. 'Each tree is like a child to me and I hate to see them suffer,' he says.

I ask an Afghan friend in Kabul how Babur is remembered today. 'People can't think about Babur at times like these,' he replies. 'Everyone is just struggling to survive.'[38]

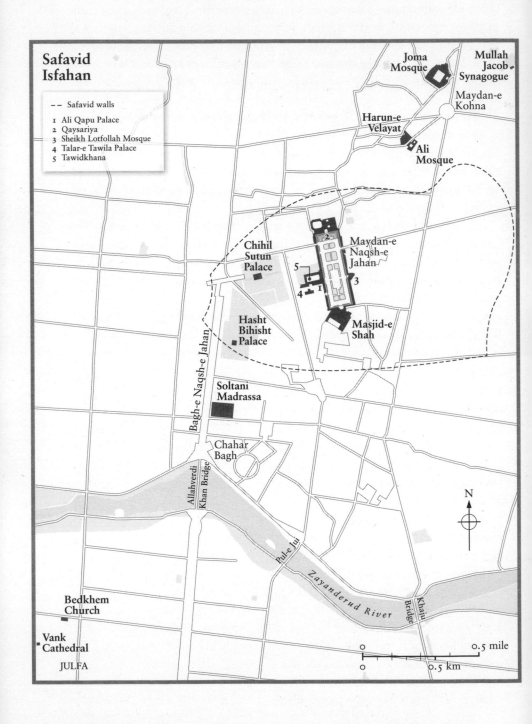

Safavid
Isfahan

-- Safavid walls

1 Ali Qapu Palace
2 Qaysariya
3 Sheikh Lotfollah Mosque
4 Talar-e Tawila Palace
5 Tawidkhana

Joma Mosque

Mullah Jacob Synagogue

Harun-e Velayat

Maydan-e Kohna

Ali Mosque

Chihil Sutun Palace

Maydan-e Naqsh-e Jahan

Hasht Bihisht Palace

Masjid-e Shah

Soltani Madrassa

Chahar Bagh

Bagh-e Naqsh-e Jahan

Allahverdi Khan Bridge

Pul-e Jui

Zayanderud River

Khaju Bridge

Bedkhem Church

Vank Cathedral

JULFA

N

0.5 mile
0.5 km

11
Isfahan – Half the World
(17th Century)

Esfahan nesf-e jahan, *Isfahan is half the world.*

Iranian proverb

Let us look at an aerial view of Isfahan for a moment. The first thing that grabs our attention is the Zayanderud, the sludge-grey River of Life that flows ponderously from west to east and bisects the city into two unequal halves. Our eyes are next drawn to a very long, slim shape that stands out prominently in the heart of the city in the larger, northern section. Zoom in a little more closely and that observation becomes an understatement. Poised north of the river, an elongated rectangle slants flamboyantly from north-west to south-east, an annihilating space that completely lords it over the residential and commercial property all around. Enlarge the view again and more details start to emerge. Smaller rectangles of dark green cluster around a pale inner core within a perimeter studded with round, shadow-making blobs. A slim avenue runs down the middle, crossing half a dozen smaller lines to form a neat grid. Tightly wrapped around this enclave is a corrugated border, the same buff colour of the desert plain from which the ancient city has sprung. When set against the broad roads, winding streets and tree-filled parks around it, this carved-out space in the centre of a vast, throbbing city seems wholly out of scale, too large to comprehend.

Its name, appropriately for such an immense edifice, is Maydan-e Naqsh-e Jahan, Image of the World Square. It is the work of one man, who lived four centuries ago and reimagined Isfahan so brilliantly and so thoroughly that he might have created a new city. It is often said about a person that he left his mark on a place. In a small, usually modest way that is sometimes true: a monument here, a new road there, this or that attraction. Very rarely, however, are there examples of more enduringly comprehensive creation. The caliph Mansur's Baghdad, perhaps Baron Haussmann's Paris and Pierre Charles L'Enfant's Washington.

Yet few men or women in history have left such a lasting, wonder-making imprint on a city as Shah Abbas, the Iranian monarch who reigned for over forty glorious years from 1588 to 1629, taking Safavid power to its absolute zenith. The territories of 'the expansive realm of Iran' ranged from parts of Turkey in the west to Pakistan and Afghanistan in the east, from the Caucasus to Kuwait. It was politically stable, martially self-confident and architecturally pre-eminent, and its awesome artistic achievements were envied across the world.[1]

Peerless in the seventeenth century, Isfahan had been a great city long before that. Dating back to pre-Islamic times, in the tenth century it was the stately seat of Iran's Buyid Dynasty (r. 932–1055), which in 945 had seized Baghdad from its indolent Abbasid caliph to usher in a century of heterodox Shia rule in one of Islam's holiest cities. After this period of Iranian history, often known as the 'Iranian intermezzo' between the rule of the Abbasid caliphate and the Seljuq Empire, from 1040–1194 Isfahan served as the capital of the Great Seljuqs, a thrusting Central Asian confederacy of tribes whose empire at its apogee in the closing years of the eleventh century stretched from the Hindu Kush mountains in the east to the Aegean coast in the west. At this time, according to the footloose Persian poet and writer Nasir-i-Khusraw, who gave us those rich portraits of Jerusalem and Cairo, Isfahan was one of the world's most splendid cities under the rule of Malikshah (r. 1072–92). 'The city has a high, strong wall with gates, embrasures and battlements all around,' he wrote. 'Inside the city are courses for running water, fine tall buildings, and a beautiful Friday mosque.' In *Mahasen Isfahan* (*The Beauties of Isfahan*), the eleventh-century writer Al Mafarruki extolled the many virtues of the city and its people, lavishing particular praise on its rambling gardens and handsome monuments.[2]

Alas, with the notable exception of Isfahan's Friday Mosque, one of the oldest in the country, none of those 'fine tall buildings' that predated Iran's Safavid Dynasty (r. 1501–1722) survive today. The dearth of this earlier architectural heritage is easily explained. A devastating barrage of invaders overwhelmed Isfahan in the thirteenth, fourteenth and fifteenth centuries. First came the firestorm of the Mongols, who launched repeated attacks against the city between 1228 and 1241 and put the inhabitants to the sword in a series of bloody massacres. A century later the city had recovered sufficiently for Ibn Battuta to judge it 'one of the largest and fairest of cities', despite the ruins.[3]

Then, in 1387, resolved to plunder the wealth of a city that glittered invitingly before him on the desert plain like an emerald and sapphire brooch with its cool waters and verdant orchards, Timur moved against the city. A prompt surrender usually staved off wholesale destruction but in this case, after his garrison of 3,000 soldiers had been killed in an overnight uprising, Timur issued one of his most vengeful commands. The Syrian chronicler Ahmed ibn Arabshah, eyewitness to Timur's sacking of Damascus in 1401, wrote how the conqueror 'ordered bloodshed and sacrilege, slaughter and plunder, devastation, burning of crops, women's breasts to be cut off, infants to be destroyed, bodies dismembered, honour to be insulted, dependants to be betrayed and abandoned, the carpet of pity to be folded up and the blanket of revenge to be unfolded'.[4] What this meant in practice was the slaughter of every man, woman and child. A market in severed heads sprang up instantly as soldiers scrambled to bring the allotted number to their commanders on pain of death. The price rapidly collapsed from twenty dinars a head to half a dinar once they had overcome their initial scruples at cutting down fellow Muslims in cold blood. On Timur's orders, and following his personal example, 7,000 children under the age of seven were then taken out onto the plain and trampled to death by his cavalry. In all, 70,000 Isfahanis were killed in the bloodbath. The fifteenth-century Timurid court historian Hafiz-i-Abru walked halfway around the city shortly after the slaughter and witnessed Timur's customary battlefield signature with his own eyes. He counted twenty-eight towers, each one built from 1,500 heads.

In the wake of these horrors, the fifteenth century was only marginally kinder. The city's rising against its Qara Qoyunlu (Black Sheep) overlords, an unruly confederation of pastoral Turkmen tribes, was met with savage retribution in the later years of Jahanshah's reign (r. 1438–68). This time 50,000 Isfahanis were killed.

Having endured three successive centuries of external onslaught, perhaps Isfahan was overdue more auspicious times. The opening years of the sixteenth century saw Iran renascent. A new power burst forth in the fiery form of Ismail, grandson of the Aq Qoyunlu (White Sheep) ruler Uzun Hassan and a descendant of the celebrated Sufi ascetic Sheikh Safi, founder of the eponymous Safavid holy order in Ardabil, north-western Iran. Ismail rose to power at the head of the Qizilbash (literally Red Head), a militant Shia movement from the Turkmen tribes of Anatolia, Azerbaijan and Kurdistan, named after their red-topped turbans. After a rousing procession of victories on the battlefield, the holy warrior proclaimed himself Shah Ismail in 1501 as a precocious fourteen-year-old. Under his brilliant, often brutal leadership, Iran, after nine centuries of being ruled by foreigners, was at last back under Iranian control and, for the first time since those spellbinding Arab conquests of the seventh century, was a distinct entity once again within its traditional borders. Ismail's capital was Tabriz, a thriving entrepôt in the silk trade that underpinned Iranian prosperity.[5]

For Isfahan, however, the benefits of this native leadership were not immediately apparent. Ismail, who was nothing if not sectarian in his outlook, marked his capture of the city with the massacre of 5,000 of its Sunni population. When he seized Baghdad in 1508, he celebrated by executing the leading Sunnis, levelling the venerated shrines of Abu Hanifa, founder of one of the four Sunni schools of Islamic jurisprudence, and that of the distinguished preacher Sheikh Abdul Qadir al Gilani, and ordering the city's Sunni mosques to be converted to Shia mosques.

Founder of the Safavid Dynasty that would raise Iran to imperial greatness over the next two centuries, Ismail was as much spiritual trailblazer as secular warlord. His proclamation of Twelver Shiism as the official state religion had extraordinarily important consequences, which still reverberate explosively across the Middle East and wider world half a millennium later.[*] Ismail's reign also established a pattern of Safavid military rivalry with both the Ottomans to his west and the Uzbeks to his east. Victorious over the Uzbeks in 1510, Ismail was defeated by the Ottomans at the Battle of Chaldiran in 1514, a reversal that took the wind out of his puffed-up sails and put paid to all intimations of messianic invincibility. The victorious Ottoman Sultan Selim entered Tabriz in triumph, a humiliation – together with further Ottoman campaigns against the city in 1535 and 1585 – which would long be remembered by Safavid shahs, to Isfahan's advantage. By 1517, Selim had conquered the Mamluks of Egypt in a decisive war that transformed a growing territory into a full-blown Sunni Empire encompassing the Middle East and, critically for the legitimacy of the Ottoman sultan's claim to supreme authority over Islamic lands, the Holy Cities of Mecca and Medina.

From Tabriz in the early years of the sixteenth century, the Safavid capital shifted to Qazvin in the wake of a peace treaty with the Ottomans agreed by Shah Tahmasp (r. 1524–76) in 1555. Given the regularity of Ottoman incursions into Iranian territory prior to that agreement, the decision to move the seat of Safavid power almost 300 miles south-east made sound strategic sense.

On 1 October 1588, less than a month after Elizabeth I had seen off the Spanish Armada, the seventeen-year-old Abbas I was proclaimed shah,

---

[*]   Twelver Shiism is the largest branch of the Shia faith and takes its name from its followers' belief in the Twelve Imams, divinely ordained leaders, of whom the last, Mohammed al Mahdi, the hidden imam who lives in occultation, will one day reappear as the promised Mahdi and rid the world of evil.

having managed to survive a youth ominously punctuated with the murder or blinding of at least nine of his uncles and other relatives. They were the unfortunate victims of the short-lived Shah Ismail II (r. 1576–7), who had ferociously sought to eliminate all rival royal princes and their patrons. Abbas's childhood experiences understandably left a lasting impression. Suspicion – and detection – of possible intriguers against his throne became a growing, almost maniacal obsession during his long reign and accounted for the murder of a number of his relatives.

To forestall filial intrigue his sons were unusually confined to the harem, rather than given the traditional provincial governorates as a way of learning kingship. In the short term of Abbas's reign this proved brilliantly effective, creating the politically stable polity that allowed the new shah to extend and amplify Safavid influence. In the longer timeline of the Safavid Dynasty, however, it became a practice that 'effectively put a stop to the training of competent successors' and was 'undoubtedly one of the major causes of Safavid decline'.[6] One son was assassinated, two others were blinded.

So much for the family. The other source of rivalry lay among the bristling red-and-white turbans of the Qizilbash. Although they had raised Abbas to power in a palace coup, they could just as easily dispose of him, as they had killed both his mother and his elder brother. Abbas moved quickly to crush the Qizilbash, cutting back their sway in the administration and smashing their military monopoly by raising an alternative source of civil and military power in the *ghulams*, converted Circassians, Georgians and Armenians who were slaves of the royal household owing personal allegiance to the shah. Approaching half a million prisoners, including as many as 300,000 Armenians and 160,000 Georgians, were deported from the Caucasus to Iran in the wake of the Safavid–Ottoman wars of 1604–5 and Abbas's two campaigns against Georgia between 1613 and 1617.[7] They took up positions as soldiers and generals in both the cavalry and infantry units, as civil administrators, governors, farmers and artisans. In one of his most innovative acts, Abbas created a standing army of 40,000 from these new arrivals. A shrewd modernizer, he introduced artillery on a grand scale for the first time in Iranian history, bringing in the most technologically advanced cannons in addition to a new corps of musketeers.

Brutal scourge of familial pretenders to his throne, ruthless military commander on the battlefield, Abbas was sweetness, light and munificence when it came to the city of Isfahan. From his accession to the throne he wasted little time setting to work on the city, which hitherto had been a royal retreat for hunting, feasting and leisure and which he now planned to make his capital. Poised on the desert plain east of the Zagros

Mountains at 1,600 metres above sea level, watered by the lazy Zay-anderud, Isfahan lay another 300 miles south-east from Qazvin, safer still from Ottoman attack, closer to his eastern rivals, the Uzbeks, whom he defeated in 1598, and nearer, too, to the strategic port of Hormuz, which he was resolved to retake from the Portuguese.

Work began in 1590 with a bold, typically decisive act. Isfahan was declared crown land – always a handy royal prerogative in advance of major building works – and a senior official, Mirza Mohammed Nishapuri, was appointed in charge of fiscal administration. Sheikh Baha al Din, often known simply as Sheikh Bahai, a polymathic poet, philosopher, mathem-atician, astronomer and Islamic scholar, was designated chief architect.

Abbas's Isfahan was no accident in the making. It was no happy co-incidence that raised it in quick order from an unremarkable old city of 50,000 to one of the greatest metropolises on earth with a population of 600,000 in the later seventeenth century, putting it on a par with Istanbul, Paris and London. It was no chance of fortune that accounted for what one recent historian of Iran has called 'perhaps the most splendid and impressive gallery of Islamic architecture in the world'.[8] This was a cal-culatedly imperial project based on an urban masterplan conceived of the shah's unbending will to elevate the Safavid Dynasty to global greatness and project this power through his capital with unparalleled magnificence. Istanbul, imperial seat of the Safavids' great adversaries, might well have been 'the city of the world's desire'. No matter. Isfahan would eclipse it entirely, becoming, during its seventeenth-century heyday under Abbas and his successors, *nesf-e jahan*, half the world.

Where better to begin than with a *tabula rasa*? At first Abbas directed his energies to remodelling the Old City, a traditionally Islamic warren of narrow, winding streets within defensive earthen walls, but when he ran into resistance from local property owners, rather than riding roughshod over them and alienating his own people, which would have constituted a needlessly inauspicious beginning to his reign, he decided to move imme-diately south-west of the walls and start from scratch. He thereby gave himself an infinitely broader canvas on which to mark out his monumen-tal, uniquely personal design – a city whose composition would deliberately and dazzlingly reflect the Safavids' synthesis of Islamic, political, social and economic priorities.[9]

The centrepiece of Abbas's Isfahan, and his first creation, the most enduring and the most resplendent to this day, was the great Maydan-e Naqsh-e Jahan, a square measuring 560 metres by 160, dimensions to which the word 'imperial' does little justice. Its surface was levelled and then enclosed within a perimeter of arcaded shops, initially on one storey, later on two – the second floor providing accommodation, as well as premises from which prostitutes could ply their nocturnal trade. The square was set within a triple border consisting of a water channel of black marble, a paved promenade and shade-giving *chinar* plane trees. Its surface was the fine beige sand hauled from the Zayanderud. The square was eminently functional as a public space given over to market traders and occasional polo players by day, and both delightful and depraved entertainment by night – from dancing, juggling and poetry recitals to sky-filling fireworks displays and the discreet temptations of courtesans – yet there was nothing utilitarian about its design. This was an architecture that flaunted extreme ostentation and sophistication, a marriage of pomp and practicality.

Prostitutes aside, one of the most eagerly awaited attractions in the Maydan was the Parthian shooting competition, an ancient tradition in which riders galloped at full tilt past a tall column erected in the middle of the square. Once they had passed it, they would then swivel in their saddles and fire off an arrow over the horse's tail, trying to hit a golden cup set on top of the column. The winner was presented with a golden quiver of arrows. This was a noble martial pursuit, often championed by the shah. The French traveller Jean-Baptiste Tavernier, whom we shall meet shortly, said he personally had seen Shah Safi (r. 1629–42) shoot down three cups in five attempts. Some of the Maydan was also given over to animal fights staged for the shah's entertainment featuring lions, bears, bulls, rams and cocks.

Rising monumentally above the commercial premises on the western flank of the square was the gateway of the Ali Qapu palace, a portal through which one left the public space of the square and entered the strictly royal quarter of Bagh-e Naqsh-e Jahan, the rambling garden retreat that dated back to Timurid times. Abbas loved this park, in which he hosted special ceremonies throughout the year. We find him celebrating the Nowruz, New Year, festivities there in 1609, as faithfully recorded by his seventeenth-century biographer, Eskandar Munshi Beg.

In his precious study *Tarikh-e Alamara-ye Abbasi* (*History of Shah Abbas the Great*), he described how Abbas took his place among his viziers and courtiers, distinguished citizens, merchants and members of guilds. Each group had been allocated certain places and pavilions along the stream that ran through the park into a lake in a scene he likened to 'the gardens of paradise'. 'The whole night long the stars of the firmament looked down with envy at the brilliantly lit scene,' he wrote, Abbas wandering freely to talk to whomever he pleased: 'sweet-voiced singers and dexterous musicians banished everyone's cares, and rosy-cheeked girls passed the wine and kept the revellers in a happy mood'.[10] This was Abbas's style of rule: personal, accessible, arbitrary and absolute.

Disparagingly dismissed by the English travel writer Robert Byron in 1937 as 'that brick boot-box' on account of its blocky design, the Ali Qapu was the Lofty Gate, Isfahan's answer to Istanbul's Sublime Porte.[11] It was also a place of sanctity. Walking over the threshold was strictly prohibited and even the shah was required to dismount before entering the royal precinct. In another symbol of growing Safavid might, a line of cannons captured from two rival powers – the Portuguese at Hormuz and the Ottomans at Baghdad – guarded the entrance to it.

While the western flank of the Maydan represented royal political power, its northern side reflected purely economic concerns, the commitment in stone to promote trade and prosperity. Here was the entrance to the Qaysariya Bazaar, the snaking connection between old Isfahan – with its crowd-thronged market hub of Maydan-e Kohna, Old Square – and the new. Unlike the open market space of the Maydan-e Naqsh-e Jahan, where traders sold everyday goods and essentials, the broad streets of the Qaysariya Bazaar catered to the more upmarket consumer, who could browse in Isfahan's luxury goods world among jewellers selling gold, silver, pearls, emeralds, rubies and other precious stones. Here, too, were the mostly Indian moneychangers, the brocade sellers and the Isfahan mint, which minted coins in gold, silver and brass. As the seventeenth-century scholar Mullah Salih Qazvini put it, 'The epitome of the world is Iran, the epitome of Iran is Isfahan, and the epitome of Isfahan is the Qaysariya, and there I am.'[12]

Today this famous market is a one-and-a-quarter-mile stretch of shops heaving with spices, fruit, nuts, miniatures, handicrafts, many-coloured inlaid boxes for jewellery, pens and trinkets, leather goods, carpets piled from floor to ceiling, clothing, fabrics, mannequins wrapped in black *abayas*, shining pots, pans and metalware, smoke-filled teahouses crammed with men sitting by coiled hookah pipes and restaurants busy with harassed waiters rushing to bring steaming *beryani* minced lamb and kebabs to shopped-till-they-dropped visitors.

So far so secular. There were now two flanks on the Maydan awaiting their own centrepiece. In 1602 Abbas started work on the eastern side, building the Sheikh Lotfollah Mosque, named after the shah's father-in-law, a saintly and widely venerated Shia preacher. Amid the reams of descriptions of seventeenth-century Isfahan left by European travellers, which we shall discuss shortly, little mention was made of this mosque and its extraordinary interior for the very good reason that they were not known either to Christian visitors or ordinary Isfahanis. It was a strictly private mosque for the royal household. Externally, it steers towards understatement, its squat dome eschewing the more traditional flashing turquoise for a more muted cappuccino enlivened with dancing arabesques in white, turquoise and midnight blue. The mixture of glazed and unglazed tiles offers a subtle interplay between sunlight, sparkle and a quieter glow.

'If the outside is lyrical, the inside is Augustan,' wrote Byron, who was not given to excessive praise. He had never experienced such splendour before, he confessed, comparing its richness to Versailles, the porcelain rooms at Schönbrunn, the Doge's Palace or St Peter's, while acknowledging that each one fell short.[13] While Isfahan is Abbas's very personal creation writ large, the Sheikh Lotfollah Mosque is one of his most sublime creations.

Whatever one's faith, whatever one's background, exploring the mosque is a transcendental experience. The inside of the soaring dome is mesmerizing, an apotheosis of the tileworkers' art, whose intricacy is so hypnotic it draws the eye unwaveringly into the centre of shimmering golden arabesques that melt into myriad constellations. The gloriously tumbling *muqarnas* stalactites in iridescent turquoise and the exquisite ornamentation of the *haft-rangi*, seven-coloured tilework by Ali Reza Abbasi, the miniaturist and calligrapher supreme, set the monument ablaze in white script on midnight blue. Directly opposite the royal gateway of the Ali Qapu across the Maydan – Abbas had a tunnel built to provide discreet access – the Sheikh Lotfollah Mosque was the Safavids' heavenly architectural symbol of Islamic legitimacy. It was the monument, above all others, that persuaded Byron to rank Isfahan alongside Athens and Rome, architecturally speaking, as 'the common refreshment of humanity'.[14]

That left a single stretch of arcaded shops free for the fourth and last monumental intervention. Set on the southern side of the Maydan, directly opposite the entrance to the Qaysariya Bazaar, the Masjid-e Shah, the Royal Mosque, was the Safavids' first congregational mosque in any major city. Where the Sheikh Lotfollah Mosque was intimate and royal, this was immense and quintessentially public, conceived by Abbas to be 'without equal in Iran and possibly in the entire civilized world'. In the words of its foundation inscription, 'A second Kaaba has been built', as concise an expression as exists of the Safavids' vaulting ambition to lead the Islamic world.[15]

Built towards the end of Abbas's reign, when time was at a premium and the shah feared he might not see its completion, the Masjid-e Shah was more rushed than his earlier creations. Like Timur in Samarkand, who drove on his architects and workers with a head-scrambling combination of carrot (cash rewards) and stick (off with his head), Abbas brooked no opposition. Shortcuts were taken and foundations were too shallow, causing difficult problems for future generations. Yet these were insignificant details when set against the final result, the greatest monument built during a long reign that occupied the commanding heights of Iranian art and architecture.

Visitors enter beneath a grand portal thirty metres high, golden *muqarnas* stalactites within a green-ribbed *iwan* recess flanked by more white-on-blue calligraphy and two balcony-topped minarets. A half-turn to the right thrusts the awestruck visitor into the improbably immense courtyard, aligned with Mecca, from where the loftiest dome in Isfahan at fifty-two metres height rises ethereally towards the heavens. The scale is as arresting as the beauty of the ornamentation. Something like 18 million bricks and half a million tiles were used in its construction. Though open to the public, it remained officially closed to Christians, who, if recognized, were 'driven out with cudgels like a dog', according to the French traveller Jean de Thévenot, who visited Isfahan in 1664.[16]

There was no question about the focal point of Abbas's Isfahan. It followed that the approach to his city had to be equally imposing. In 1596, he launched the construction of the Chahar Bagh, the Four Gardens, named after the vineyards that were originally planted here. This was to be the grandest possible avenue, a stately one-and-a-half-mile procession from his vast Hazar Jarib, Thousand Jarib Park – a rambling estate of terraces, trees, orchards, pavilions and babbling streams at the foot of Mount Takht-e Rustam, Throne of Rustam – over the Allahverdi Khan Bridge and on to the Imperial Gate next to the royal palace. This was no mere highway. Around fifty metres wide, on the northern palace side of the river it consisted of a series of terraces and onyx-bordered basins either side of a central marble water channel. During the long summer months cut roses bobbed prettily in the pools of water beneath a first row of plane trees, followed by an open section for horseback visitors, a paved promenade, flower-filled parterres and a final line of plane trees, each one said to have been planted in front of Abbas, who buried a gold and silver coin beneath them one by one.

This was at once a royal road designed to impress foreign envoys and a more intimate space for ordinary Isfahanis to gather and gossip and catch a glimpse of the city's grandees strutting ostentatiously in their finest linens or sitting cross-legged for an elegant evening picnic among the flowers and fountains, over endless cups of coffee with smoke curling lazily upwards into the trees. Traders set up shops and stalls along the avenue, adding to the bustle of the place. A two-storey pavilion at the northern end of the avenue allowed Abbas's royal wives and concubines to indulge their fill of people-watching, discreetly removed from prying eyes. Arch-ways off the avenue, bordered by a latticed mud-brick wall, led into Abbas's evocatively named royal gardens with handsome pavilions and coffeehouses, open to the public: the Garden of the Nightingale, Mulberry Garden, Garden of the Dervishes, Octagon Garden and Garden of the Throne. Designed and laid out by the ubiquitous Sheikh Bahai, the Chahar Bagh was a blend of the public and the private, part diplomatic ostenta-tion, part pastoral retreat, and an exuberant celebration of the natural world in complete harmony with man's architectural design. The German Adam Olearius, a member of the Duke of Holstein's commercial embassy to Isfahan in 1637, was enchanted. He thought it 'one of the most beautiful and charming spots in the world'. It was, as one art historian has dubbed it, the 'Champs Elysées of Isfahan'.[17]

In Abbas's Isfahan, the sumptuous became the everyday, a yardstick for the glory of Safavid civilization and architecture. The Chahar Bagh crossed the Zayanderud not over a simple bridge but across one of the most beautiful ever built. Constructed between 1602 and 1607, the Allah-verdi Khan Bridge, or Si-o-se pol, the Bridge of Thirty-three Spans, was named after Abbas's most trusted general, a Georgian *ghulam* who had risen to the summit of the Safavid state. Running for around 300 metres, by day and night it remains one of the great sights of Isfahan more than four centuries after its construction. All who saw it were captivated. 'So long as the wheeling stars of the sky above circle this world, the like of this bridge will never come before their gaze,' wrote Mirza Beg Junabadi, contemporary of Abbas and author of *Rauzat al Safawiya* (*The Garden of the Safavids*), a history of the dynasty from 1501 to the end of Abbas's rule. For once this was not just another sycophantic flourish from a court panegyrist who knew who paid his bills. Lord Curzon had a similar re-action after seeing the bridge in 1889. He thought it 'the stateliest bridge in the world'.[18]

When Ruy González de Clavijo, the Spanish ambassador from Henry III of Castile, visited Timur's Samarkand in 1404, he did so as the represen-tative of a state that, by comparison with the empire carved out by the Sword Arm of Islam and Conqueror of the World, was a piffling power. By the seventeenth century, however, the balance of power between East and West was more nuanced. The Battle of Lepanto in 1571, then the largest naval battle in history, had convincingly demonstrated the Otto-mans could be beaten at sea. European powers started to consolidate forces against the Ottomans in the later seventeenth century and, under Pope Innocent XI's direction, formed the Holy League in 1684. Fifteen years later, the Treaty of Karlowitz of 1699 brought a decisive end to the Ottoman Empire's control of much of Central Europe, establishing the Habsburgs as the dominant power in its stead. At the same time, contact between Christendom and the Islamic world increased dramatically with new opportunities to travel allowing both sides to get a much better look at each other. They may not always have liked what they saw, and old prejudices died hard, but when it came to visiting Safavid Iran positive experiences overwhelmingly, perhaps surprisingly, proliferated.

Virtually nonexistent in Iran before 1600, European travellers swelled from the feeblest trickle into a veritable torrent during the reigns of Abbas and his Safavid successors, offering the shah far more compelling commercial, technological, military and diplomatic opportunities than Clavijo had been able to muster. These travellers came from a broad range of European society. Silk-tongued diplomats rubbed shoulders with profit-seeking mercenaries, wealthy merchants and more spiritually motivated missionaries, such as the Barefoot Carmelites and faith-fired Augustinians. Here were knowledge-seeking scholars, thrill-seeking adventurers and artists searching for new perspectives and experiences. Europe represented new technology, from artillery experts to the latest binoculars, diamond-cutters, watchmakers, jewellers and goldsmiths. This was a wonderfully eclectic group of Westerners, many of whom left a treasure trove of travelogues, memoirs and diaries.

A list of distinguished European visitors to Iran from 1601 to 1722, as a recent study noted, makes fascinating reading. There was the Spanish diplomat Don García de Silva y Figueroa, the first Western traveller to identify correctly the ruins of the ancient Iranian capital of Persepolis; the Italian composer and traveller Pietro Della Valle; the German scholar Adam Olearius; Cornelis Speelman, governor-general of the Dutch East Indies in the 1680s. The French were also well represented. Among their ranks were Jean-Baptiste Tavernier, traveller and diamond-dealer *par excellence*, the man who discovered the 112-carat Tavernier Blue diamond and sold it to Louis XIV in 1669 for the cash equivalent of 147 kilograms of gold; the natural scientist and linguist Jean de Thévenot; Jean Chardin, another jeweller and traveller, author of a magisterial ten-volume study of Iran and the Middle East, one of the most comprehensive and valuable Western sources for this period; the youthful priest François Sanson; the German naturalist and explorer Engelbert Kaempfer; Father Raphaël du Mans, the celebrated Capuchin priest and Safavid court interpreter, who lived in Isfahan for half a century from 1647 to 1696 and won the admiration of Iranians and Europeans alike; the Russian statesman and diplomat Artemy Volynsky; the Dutch artist and traveller Cornelis de Bruijn; Dr

John Fryer, the East India Company surgeon; and the buccaneering Sherley brothers, Sir Anthony and Sir Robert, mercenaries, sometime diplomats and inveterate chancers.[19]

European diplomats also presented Abbas with the chance to divide and rule while he pursued his own objectives, an opportunity he embraced enthusiastically when it came to forming alliances against the Ottomans and exploiting rivalries between the Portuguese, Dutch and English over the East Indies trade. In 1622, he successfully pressed the English into removing the Portuguese from Hormuz using the naval fleet that he lacked, a service for which the English were repaid with the grant of half of the toll receipts from Bandar Abbas.

Whatever country they represented, European traders had to beware the rules of the shah's highly autocratic game. Woe to those who failed to do so. In 1628 Sir Dodmore Cotton, England's first accredited ambassador to the court of Shah Abbas, observed a caravan arriving at the city of Qazvin with forty camel loads of tobacco, blithely unaware of the shah's latest ban on a product he had come to loathe especially. Furious at this breach of his edict, Abbas ordered a savage punishment. The caravan drivers all had their ears and noses cut, while the tobacco was piled into a pit and set alight.[20] We hear another European story about the shah's disapproval of tobacco from the French traveller Jean Chardin, who described how, after Abbas had very publicly given up smoking, he ordered horse manure to be used as a substitute by his courtiers. When he asked his bewildered officials what they made of the new substance, they told him it was exquisite, the best they had ever smoked, all too aware that angering the shah with a careless word could easily result in a swift execution. Abbas was unimpressed. 'Cursed be the drug that cannot be distinguished from horse-dung!' he roared in disgust.[21]

Abbas took a dim view of some of the coffeehouses that sprang up across Isfahan and became the height of fashion for polite society. This was where of an evening 'men assembled to talk and prattle of State affairs', according to Jean-Baptiste Tavernier, who shared the shah's disapproval of these 'tobacco whiffers and coffee quaffers'.[22] Many of the customers came from the cream of Isfahani society, including fabulously wealthy merchants, powerful ministers, senior officials and sometimes Abbas himself. A smattering of intelligentsia in the form of languid, loose-tongued writers, poets and intellectuals gave the coffeehouses a bohemian charm as they discussed the issues of the day while hurling down backgammon counters or absorbing themselves in quieter games of chess amid thick wreaths of smoke. Others came to enjoy the notorious pleasures of heavily made-up, suggestively dressed Georgian and Circassian boys, who staged erotic dances and whispered filthy stories to whet the older men's carnal appetites before disappearing together on commercial trysts. In a somewhat forlorn attempt to elevate the tone Abbas sent in the mullahs to provide religious instruction, together with legal and historical education, but perhaps unsurprisingly this failed to have the desired effect. Chardin called these coffeehouses 'sodomy shops', and they were eventually closed down by Shah Abbas II (r. 1642–66), great-grandson of Abbas I, in 1656.[23]

The European accounts of seventeenth-century Iran are priceless for a number of reasons. They describe the city of Isfahan, together with its principal monuments and places, often in tremendous detail in the wake of Abbas's ground-breaking urban masterplan. While often reflecting the Eurocentric prejudices of their time to the Islamic world – bigotry which was more often than not heartily reciprocated – the most open-minded writers strikingly convey their appreciation and admiration of Abbas's achievements. The tone of their accounts, by and large, is a world away from the contemptuous screeds of the Crusader era. The evident glories of Isfahan and its people in particular, Safavid Iran and its civilization more widely, had the effect of suspending the traditional piercing European criticism of the Islamic world.

Nowhere is this more true than in the built environment. Almost without fail, Western visitors sang the praises of the Safavid capital to the heavens. The Frenchman Jean de Thévenot stayed in Isfahan with Father du Mans for five months in 1664. He, like so many visitors, was bowled over by its sheer magnificence. 'Of all the regular piazzas, it is the greatest and finest place in the world,' he wrote of Abbas's landmark Maydan-e Naqsh-e Jahan. Dr John Fryer, the East India Company surgeon who visited Iran in 1677, compared London's markets unfavourably with their counterparts in Isfahan. They were, he wrote, freely admitting his surprise at this unexpected discovery, mere 'Snaps of Buildings' when held up against the 'Lofty-Ceiled and Stately-Erected Buzzars' of Abbas's city. The exception to this almost universal admiration was the Frenchman Jean-Baptiste Tavernier, surely the prissiest and most mean-spirited of these seventeenth-century travellers. He objected to the narrow streets of old Isfahan with their deposits of manure and animal carcasses causing 'a most filthy stench'. Men urinated in the street, washing their members with running water or rubbing them against the wall if no water was to hand, 'which they take for a great piece of gentility and modesty'.[24]

Abbas was exceptional, too, in rising above the wearily familiar contests and conflicts between the faiths. When it came to toleration and mutual respect between the Abrahamic religions, he provided an unmistakable and powerful royal lead. Father Paul Simon, the first Carmelite leader who arrived in Isfahan in late 1607, wrote of how in former times the Iranians had been extremely superstitious and abhorred Christians as 'a foul race', to the point where, if a Christian even touched a man's clothes, the latter, horrified by the contamination, would immediately take them off and have them washed. Then, under Abbas, such prejudices had quickly faded away. 'Nowadays, because the Shah shows great regard for Christians, passes his time with them and sets them at his table, they have abandoned all this and act towards them as they do towards their own people: only in some distant districts and among the common folk is it still kept up.' Father Paul reckoned Abbas 'very vivacious and alert', sturdily built and so strong and fit that 'with his scimitar [he] can cut a man in two'.[25] Abbas's enlightened stance towards Christians was not entirely altruistic. Developing strong relations with the courts of Europe, through envoys and the Christian missions alike, was all part of the grand plan to form alliances against the constant menace of Istanbul.

After centuries of differences and difficulties, regular enmity and conflict, more harmonious diplomatic relations between East and West were all to the good. On the Iranian side they rested on a Safavid *Weltanschauung* of complete religious and cultural supremacy. 'They have small regard either to Foreigners or their Countries, in respect of their Native Soil or Abilities, conceiting themselves superlative in everything,' John Fryer reckoned. In this 'affectation', he added in a quintessentially English dig, they were not unlike the French.[26]

Iranian cultural prejudices were by no means restricted to infidels. The official Safavid worldview held that Arabs were stupid, coarse, hypocritical, violent and oversexed 'lizard eaters'. The Turks were rustic, stubborn and dim-witted, Afghans despicable, primitive, ignorant thieves. Uzbeks were inherently devilish, dirty and 'devoid of religion'. Worst of all were the Russians, the 'most base and the most infamous of all Christians'.[27] Multiculturalism had its limits.

An interest in the outside world, and diplomatic relations with it, did not translate into significant notice of the West, or of Europeans in Iran, in the literary record. Official Iranian historiography paid scant attention to it, bar the passing comment about *Farangiyan*, or Westerners. The Sherley brothers, for example, were household names in Elizabethan England as travelling adventurers, diplomats and mercenaries – Sir Anthony Sherley was appointed an envoy of Abbas, while his brother, Sir Robert, played a key role in modernizing the Safavid army. In a turbulent life crammed with adventure, Sir Anthony was imprisoned by Queen

Elizabeth I and King James I, knighted by King Henry IV of France, made a prince and envoy by Shah Abbas I, sent to Morocco by the Holy Roman Emperor Rudolph II and appointed admiral of a fleet by King Philip III of Spain. High-spirited tales of his self-enriching hobnobbing with the Safavid shah, known to Englishmen as the 'Sophy', even found their way into Shakespeare's *Twelfth Night*.* Despite all their work in Iran at the very summit of Isfahani society, however, there was not a single reference to the Sherley brothers in any Iranian chronicle. Eskandar Munshi Beg briefly acknowledged the English role in helping Abbas eject the Portuguese from Hormuz, but in general there was a resounding silence about Westerners, symptomatic, perhaps, of the Islamic world's innate sense of superiority.[28]

European visitors were wont to remark positively on what they found a surprisingly open intellectual climate in which foreigners were actively encouraged to debate with their Iranian colleagues, even with the shah. The Italian Niccolao Manucci, an official in the Mughal court and author of the *Storia do Mogor*, a history of the dynasty, contrasted the freewheeling freedom of expression in Safavid Iran with the draconian atmosphere of Turkey, Arabia, Uzbekistan, and the lands of the Mughals and Pathans, where questioning the law of the Prophet Mohammed could easily cost you your head. In Iran, however, 'you may use arguments, make inquiry, and give answer in matters of religion without the least danger'.[29] Self-confident senior Shia clerics took pleasure in challenging foreigners to debate religion with them, an opportunity that was regularly taken up by the resident European population, which grew in size during the century.

With his restless energy and his quick-fire creation of a magnificent new capital city, Abbas echoed the history-making urban record of the Abbasid caliph Mansur. A truly great city, as both men understood, relied on more than indigenous talents and was open to the world. In remarkable parallels with eighth-century Baghdad, Abbas's Isfahan was vibrantly, extraordinarily cosmopolitan.

Whatever the parallels between the two cities, Isfahan and Baghdad remained profoundly different in perhaps the most important matter of religion. From the Safavid shah's perspective the sectarian split between Sunni and Shia that had torn the Islamic world apart for a millennium, and continues to do so today, proved more difficult to overcome than the traditionally fraught, often fatal interactions with Christians and Jews.

---

* Act II, Scene 5: Fabian: 'I will not give my part of this sport for a pension of thousands to be paid from the Sophy.'

   Act III, Scene 4: Sir Toby Belch: 'Why, man, he's a very devil; I have not seen such a firago . . . They say he has been fencer to the Sophy.'

In this enduring schism, the Dar al Islam had unwittingly followed the example of the Christian world, divided first from 1054 between Eastern Orthodox and Western Catholic, and then with an additional schism between Protestants and Catholics from the advent of Martin Luther in 1514. The doctrinal divergence between Sunni and Shia has proved an insuperable obstacle to Islamic unity.

In 1623, Abbas captured Baghdad and was unable to resist the temptation of meting out wholesale destruction to the Sunni community, together with its properties and most treasured places of worship. Thousands of Sunni, including the *mufti* of Baghdad, were killed. Thousands more were taken back to Isfahan and sold into slavery. The incomparable Sunni shrines of Abu Hanifa and Sheikh Abdul Qadir al Gilani were sacked and almost completely destroyed in a vicious sectarian echo of the outrages committed in Baghdad by Ismail, the first Safavid shah, in 1508.

Baghdad aside, the story of Abbas's long reign was one of cosmopolitanism, freely expressed in the expanding architectural composition of his capital. The new suburb of Abbasabad sprung up west of the Chahar Bagh avenue to accommodate refugees from Tabriz who had lost their homes during the war between Safavids and the Ottomans in 1610. From a settlement of 500 houses, it quadrupled in size within half a century, its broad, tree-shaded streets and pretty water channels making it a fashionable district.

South of the Zayanderud was Julfa, a more stately suburb for the Christian Armenian community that Abbas had deported to his capital. It boasted its own cathedral, built in 1606, and a series of grand palaces that strikingly marked the prosperity of their merchant owners. By the time of the demise of the Safavid Dynasty in 1722, Julfa contained around thirty churches and a convent. Other churches were built in the north of the city and across Isfahan. Armenian merchants had their own caravanserai close to the Ali Qapu palace, but they also enjoyed equal footing with their Muslim counterparts with shops in the old bazaar. Abbas allowed a noticeable degree of autonomy for Julfa's Armenian community, which had its own *kalantar*, or mayor, who was responsible for taxation, working beneath a Muslim *darugha*, or governor, with overall administrative command.

This was a mixed city of Iranians, Georgians, Armenians, Turkmens, Indians, Chinese and a distinctive European community. Muslims traded alongside Christians and the smaller, prosperous Jewish community, which was well represented in the commercial, artisan and fledgling banking sectors and had its own Yahudiyya, or Jewish quarter, and three synagogues. The treatment and fortune of Isfahan's Jews worsened over the century, however, with periodic persecutions. The same was true of other minorities in the later decades.

Languishing at the bottom of Isfahani society was the most ancient community of all. The fire-worshipping Zoroastrians, scornfully referred to as *gebr*, pagans or infidels, lived south of the river, east of the fine suburb of Julfa in the eponymous canton of Gebrabad. Brought in as labourers to help build the Islamic city of Abbas's dreams, the Zoroastrians were far removed from the splendour they toiled so hard to create. Jean Chardin, who lived in Isfahan during the 1670s, found a beleaguered community that had withered away to just 200 families.

Forced into proximity with so many different races and multiple faiths by the outward-looking disposition of their ruler, the Isfahanis were, according to the Spanish diplomat Don García de Silva y Figueroa, 'very open in their dealings with foreigners, because of having to deal every day with people of several other nations'. Chardin was completely charmed: 'The Persians are the most kind people in the world; they have the most moving and engaging ways, the most complaisant temper, the smoothest and most flattering tongues, avoiding in their conversation stories or expressions which may occasion melancholy thoughts.'[30]

On 19 January 1629, as Charles I moved to dissolve the English parliament and embark upon his fateful eleven-year Personal Rule, Abbas died. The world, according to the dutiful Eskandar Munshi Beg, was immediately plunged into mourning: 'A radiant sun, in the shadow of whose justice men had lived in tranquillity, had set.' In his fulsome obituary of Abbas, the royal biographer included a letter from Pope Urban VIII, acknowledging Abbas as 'a king who is the model and source of guidance for people throughout the world', and who, when compared to the most powerful princes of Europe, was 'their superior in grandeur, majesty and dominion'.[31]

Abbas had been the guiding light of Isfahan, kindling a flame that would burn long after his death. Although history has not remembered them with the same regard and, in some quarters at least, reverence, his immediate successors managed to keep the cultural blaze alight for most of the century. Due to the mutilation and murder of his heirs, Abbas was succeeded not by a son but a grandson, Safi, who celebrated his accession to the throne at the age of eighteen with a killing spree – royal rivals, senior courtiers and the military top brass – that came straight from his grandfather's playbook. His talents on the battlefield, however, were less formidable than those of Abbas, and the Ottomans were able to make incursions into Safavid territory in both Armenia and Iraq. They retook Baghdad after Sultan Murad put the city first under siege, then to the sword, in 1638. Safi's reign was noteworthy, too, for concluding the interminable series of Ottoman–Safavid wars over the southern Caucasus and Iraq. The war of 1623–38 finally ended with the Treaty of Zuhab in 1639, a border-shifting victory for Istanbul over Isfahan. Eastern Armenia, together with eastern Georgia, Dagestan and Azerbaijan henceforth fell under Iranian control, while western Georgia, western Armenia and Iraq were recognized as Ottoman possessions.

Away from politics and the battlefield, history has remembered Safi as one of his dynasty's most dissolute drinkers and drug abusers. Ambiguity is often proclaimed over the Safavids' relationship with wine, but there was nothing ambiguous about Safi's addiction to the grape, nor about his use of opium. European envoys witnessed important matters of state being decided when the shah was in his cups. Royal inebriation could have fatal consequences. In 1633, Safi's drinking session with Imam Quli Khan, son of Abbas's general Allahverdi Khan and governor of Shiraz, ended with the shah's abrupt order for the man's execution, together with two of his sons. Perhaps it was divine retribution for such wanton cruelty when drunk that accounted for Safi's untimely death in 1642 at the age of thirty-one, 'over-much drinking and other ryots [having] hastened his end'.[32]

The popularity of drinking and smoking ebbed and flowed between the Safavid shahs. Following a notorious decade of drinking at his father's court, Shah Abbas II proclaimed a ban on wine after his accession to the throne at the age of nine in 1642. Such good intentions were fine as a child. By 1649, when he was seventeen and ruling in his own right, the commitment to a teetotal reign was thrown aside and royal quaffing resumed in earnest. Tobacco also rose and fell in royal favour. In 1650, as the young Abbas embarked upon his drinking career, the stern cleric Ali Naqi Kamarahi, a former Sheikh al Islam of Isfahan who had long railed against the devilish weed in fire-and-brimstone treatises directed at the faithful, died. One can almost hear the sound of louche courtiers picking up their pipes again. Had Abbas taken greater notice of the venerable older man, he might have lived longer himself. His death in 1666 at the age of thirty-four – only slightly older than his father – was equally brought on by alcoholism, a case of familial history repeating itself.

Europeans frequently experienced these royal bacchanals first-hand – it was unwise to decline a royal invitation. Huybert de Lairesse, the representative of the Vereenigde Oost-Indische Compagnie (VOC), the Dutch East India Company, was invited to drink with Abbas II in Mazandaran in 1666, a drinking bout from which it took the shah two weeks to recover. The popularity of drinking at the royal court can be gauged from the level of wine production for the royal court in the same year: 50,000 *man*, equivalent to 145,000 litres.[33] Some shahs took pleasure in forcing reluctant colleagues to drink with them, irrespective of whether they usually abstained. Shah Sulayman (r. 1666–94) was notoriously fond of humiliating his teetotal grand vizier Sheikh Ali Khan in this fashion. On one occasion the unfortunate official was temporarily dismissed for refusing to indulge the shah. Sulayman liked nothing more than seeing paralytic drinking companions hauled out of the royal presence like corpses.

Isfahan, meanwhile, continued to bloom. The same aerial view in which Maydan-e Naqsh-e Jahan flaunts its royal dimensions so brazenly is remarkable also for another sprawling quadrangle of dark green just to the west, criss-crossed with spidery avenues. This is the Chihil Sutun (Forty Columns) Palace, built by Abbas II in 1647 as the grandest venue for royal receptions and entertainments, its name derived from the elegant wooden columns supporting the pavilion reflected in the limpid waters that stretched before it. At the time it was the largest palace within the *Daulatkhana* palace complex, set within a formal walled garden of seven hectares. While the architecture is Safavid grace and the projection of political power exemplified, the interior is notable for the finest preserved Iranian murals in existence. Large-scale, richly coloured paintings tell the Safavids' story in a series of eye-catching setpieces: Shah Ismail I doing battle with the Uzbeks; Shah Tahmasp receiving the Mughal emperor Humayun; Shah Abbas I receiving the Uzbek ruler Vali Mohammed Khan. There are stylized depictions of Europeans at the Safavid court, alongside feasting and hunting scenes. In a bold and joyful defiance of the Islamic prohibition of alcohol, the royal wine cup is a recurrent, ubiquitous motif. Taken together, the Chihil Sutun is a dynastic boast writ large.[34]

Immediately to the south-west is the third and final expanse of green in the heart of Isfahan. Built by Shah Sulayman around twenty years after the Chihil Sutun, the Hasht Bihisht (Eight Heavens) Palace is an almost solitary reminder of the sumptuous Safavid pavilions which once adorned Isfahan's skyline in the heyday of the dynasty. It took its name from the eight rooms surrounding a central domed chamber on two floors.

The later years of the seventeenth century were less fortunate for Isfahan than the opening decades under Abbas I. The records teem with mournful tales of famine, which hit the city in 1662, 1668–9 and then again, catastrophically, in 1678–9, when more than 70,000 people were reported to have died.

Like the Abbasid caliphs of Baghdad before them, the Safavid shahs of Iran over time retreated from all-powerful monarchs to palace-bound shadows of their former selves. Abbas II was the last of the dynasty's shahs to earn his spurs on the battlefield. In the dying decades of the century the royal universe steadily drew in upon itself to focus on beautiful parks and gardens, palaces and pavilions, rather than looking outward to the field of battle and imperial expansion.

The public and political role of women in the Islamic world tended to be minimal over the centuries, with the domestic sphere generally considered their proper place, as it remains in a number of Muslim countries today. Yet women could play extraordinarily influential roles at the highest levels of the Safavid state. This was most evident when shahs acceded to the throne at a very young age – as was the case with Abbas II – a delicate, frequently fatal period requiring deft navigation through the treacherous currents of court politics. 'The power of mothers of Persian kings looms large when they [shahs] are at a young age,' Chardin observed. 'Abbas II's mother had much influence, which was absolute. They [queen mothers] were in close contact with the prime minister and they would help each other mutually . . . Saru Taqi was the agent and confidant of the queen mother; he would gather immense fortunes for her. She governed Persia at her will through her minister.'[35]

The shahs' loss of political power could be offset by vigorous architectural flourishes, as was the case under Shah Soltan Hosayn (r. 1694–1722), the last Safavid king, who threw himself into building a complex of *madrassa*, bazaar and caravanserai. Soltan Hosayn was another ruler who declared war on alcohol and opium, while enjoying mammoth drinking sessions among the crystal, diamond-studded carafes of ruby-red Shiraz wine which had so bewitched his royal predecessors. 'His proclivities toward extreme religiosity and his abandonment of the reins of authority to the powerful clerical class went hand in hand with his complete retreat into the bosom of the harem, speaking both figuratively and literally.'[36] With this display of Safavid laissez-faire it was no surprise that the authority and influence of the Shia clergy reached its apex at a time when the *ghulam* eunuchs were also all-powerful.

Religious discrimination and persecution rose accordingly under Soltan Hosayn. Orders were given for the forced conversion of Zoroastrians, while their temple was destroyed and replaced with a mosque. A poll tax was imposed on Jews and Christians. If any one measure could indicate the otherworldly, fiddling-while-Rome-burned atmosphere of the time it was surely the decree prohibiting those who were not Shia from leaving their houses when it rained for fear they would pollute those who were.[37]

Remembered with a spirit of regret as the last of his line, from a narrowly architectural point of view Soltan Hosayn is more auspiciously celebrated as the guiding light behind the Soltani Madrassa, a feast of Safavid baroque that paid tribute to royal patronage, Islamic piety and scholarship. Clad in bright tiles that raised the eye from the vast courtyard and its water-fed flowerbeds towards a sunlit dome flanked by two flashing minarets, the religious college revelled in its stately position, its pair of tall silver doors of breathtaking expense opening onto the royal Chahar Bagh avenue. It was the last great monument built in Isfahan until the twentieth century.

In the dying embers of the seventeenth century and the opening decades of the eighteenth, the sense of decadence and decline under the reign of Shah Soltan Hosayn – it is difficult to call it rule – is compelling and unmistakable. The shah's complete disinterest in politics earned him the nickname *Yakshi dir*, 'It is good', the inevitable response to any proposal from his senior officials. The records tell of one instance in which the mullahs removed 60,000 bottles of wine from the royal cellars and smashed them in public.[38] Anathema to the clerics, such royal indolence and alcoholism was a heaven-sent opportunity for the Safavids' enemies.

A series of attacks on Iran's frontiers tested the waters. In 1699 Baluch tribes overran Kerman, then in 1717 the short-lived Afghan Hotaki Dynasty attacked Khorasan, prompting a desperate attempt from another important royal woman to stop the rot. Soltan Hosayn's great-aunt Maryam Begom, daughter of Safi I, who had been instrumental in securing his accession to the throne, warned him that if he did not get a grip of the worsening situation he would lose his kingdom and she would lose her liberty. She galvanized financial and diplomatic support for a military expedition, including assistance from the East India Company and the Dutch VOC, but it was too little to stem the tide. In 1721 the Lezgins of the southern Caucasus moved against Dagestan and Shirvan. A year later, far worse was to follow.

After incursions in 1720 and again in 1721, a small, poorly equipped Afghan army under the warlord Mir Mahmud Ghilzai reached Golnabad, twelve miles from Isfahan, early in 1722. The attacks were born of ruthless Safavid attempts to convert Sunni Afghans to the Shia faith, a dangerous policy that led initially to rebellion then to revenge and all-out invasion. Soltan Hosayn's response was twofold. He delayed battle until the astrologers ruled the time was auspicious, then issued orders for his troops to eat a magic soup that would render them invisible to the Afghans. It seems superfluous to note the Safavid army was routed.[39]

From March Isfahan was under siege, and conditions inside the city steadily worsened. Nicholas Schorer, chief merchant of the Dutch VOC, kept a *Dagregister*, a diary of the siege, between March and August. There were reports of desperate people reduced to eating shoe leather and tree bark – even instances of cannibalism. Mahmud's demand for a punitive ransom, meanwhile, led to plotting, intrigues and betrayal, together with frantic, fruitless efforts to raise the money.

Christian Constantinople had fallen to Sultan Mehmed in a blaze of glorious conquest and heroic defence. It was arguably asking too much of Soltan Hosayn to similarly rise to the occasion at this fateful hour. The fall of Isfahan, when it came, was appropriately bathetic. Shorn of money, the last Safavid shah picked his way through the stinking streets of his capital, strewn with corpses and a near-mutinous population wracked with hunger, and formally surrendered to Mahmud on 21 October 1722. The end of the most brilliant period in Iranian history had arrived with a whimper.

The postscript to Soltan Hosayn's ruinous reign was correspondingly inglorious. For the Safavid family it was a catastrophe. In a ravening fury brought on by mental disorder, Mahmud personally butchered almost every surviving Safavid prince. For Iran it was no less of a calamity. Rival powers, above all the Russians and Ottomans, fell on Iran, dividing much of the Safavid carcass between them in the Treaty of Constantinople, signed in 1724 while Soltan Hosyan remained in gilded confinement. To the ignominy of losing swathes of its territory amid the turmoil unleashed by the fall of Isfahan was added the further insult of another Ottoman invasion, led by the commander Ahmed Pasha in 1726. He dispatched an offensive letter to the new Afghan leader Ashraf Ghilzai, who had proclaimed himself shah, calling him an illegitimate usurper and threatening to reinstate Soltan Hosayn on the throne. There was a brutally simple way to prevent that. In the dazzling Hall of Mirrors in his palace the toppled Safavid shah was made to kneel and was beheaded. His head was sent to the Ottoman general with a few lines from Ashraf to the effect that this was just a holding message. A fuller reply would follow at the point of his sword.[40]

The Safavids had established Iran's greatest empire since Sunni Islam arrived in the seventh century. Though their final demise was inglorious, the legacy they bequeathed proved more resilient. An effective state bureaucracy was introduced, artistic patronage and architectural self-confidence returned with a vengeance, and through the enlightened trade policies they pursued Iran became once again an economic force to be reckoned with. Most enduring of all, the Safavids successfully made Iran the spiritual bastion of Shia Islam, which – as the country's allies and enemies alike would acknowledge – it remains defiantly, often militantly, to this day.

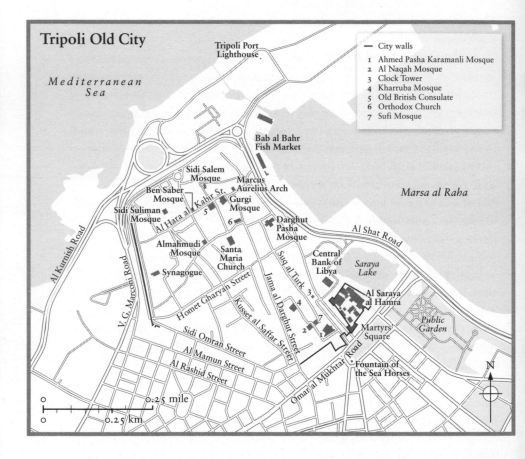

Tripoli Old City

Mediterranean Sea

Tripoli Port
Lighthouse

— City walls
1 Ahmed Pasha Karamanli Mosque
2 Al Naqah Mosque
3 Clock Tower
4 Kharruba Mosque
5 Old British Consulate
6 Orthodox Church
7 Sufi Mosque

Bab al Bahr
Fish Market

Marsa al Raha

Sidi Salem
Mosque
Ben Saber
Mosque
Marcus
Aurelius Arch
Sidi Suliman
Mosque
Gurgi
Mosque
Al Hara al Kabir St.
Darghut
Pasha
Mosque
Al Shat Road
Almahmudi
Mosque
Santa
Maria
Church
Central
Bank of
Libya
*Saraya
Lake*
Synagogue
Al Saraya
al Hamra
Homet Gharyan Street
Kusset al Saffar Street
Jama al Darghut Street
Sug al Turk Street
*Public
Garden*
Sidi Omran Street
Martyrs'
Square
Al Mamun Street
Al Rashid Street
Omar al Mukhtar Road
Fountain of
the Sea Horses
V. G. Marconi Road
Al Kurnish Road

0.25 mile
0.25 km

N

12

Tripoli – Pirates' Lair (18th Century)

I do not fear war, it is my trade.

Yusuf Karamanli, Pasha of Tripoli (1795–1832)

'Yes, I suppose you could call it *fitna*,' says Adel, a Libyan banker friend.

We're sitting on his first-floor terrace overlooking the Mediterranean on a warm, early summer's evening on the cusp of Ramadan. In the near distance young couples on romantic trysts stroll along the beach holding hands, men in swimming trunks are playing beach tennis, children rush giddily around and the odd solitary walker hurries along the shore or trudges through thick sand deep in his thoughts.

Adel and I are discussing the situation in Libya, where I have been working for the past three years. In the turbulent, often bloody aftermath of the 2011 revolution there are now three governments, two parliaments, two central banks, two investment authorities, two national oil corporations and militias beyond counting. Libya is a divided country beset by conflict.

Like many Arabic words, *fitna* has a variety of meanings. It appears in various forms in the Quran, where it can mean, among other things, trial, temptation, persecution, dissension and discord.* In its modern usage it often refers to conflict and strife, rebellion, disorder and division. Our conversation is happening in Tunis, rather than Tripoli, precisely because of such troubles. Kidnapping has become such a scourge that travelling to Tripoli is prohibitively dangerous for Adel, who hasn't been able to return to the city for several years. Security has collapsed, disorder is the order of the day.

---

* 'They would have wormed their way through your ranks, seeking to sow discord among you . . . They had sought before this to sow dissension, and hatched plots against you.' Quran 9:47–8

It wasn't always like this. Tripoli was the first Arab city I visited, accompanying my father on a business trip as a teenager. It was the beginning of a thirty-year love affair with a city Libyans proudly called *Arus al Bahr*, Bride of the Sea. There was no question, in the late 1980s, of *fitna*. However feared and despised he was in many quarters, the authority of Colonel Muammar Gaddafi was absolute and virtually unchallenged, the population he ruled over cowed into acquiescence and submission. Those brave enough to defy the regime were swiftly incarcerated. Many were eliminated. Even those dissidents who fled Libya into exile and opposition overseas were not safe. Gaddafi's 'Stray Dogs' policy targeted them for assassination abroad.

'Don't talk to taxi drivers or anyone else about politics,' my father warned, looking around the lobby of our seafront hotel, the Bab al Bahr, where men in suits lurked for hours, quietly taking an interest in the comings and goings. 'Anyone here could be an *antenna*.' This was how Libyans referred to an informer.

In those days there was no escaping Gaddafi. His defiant portrait greeted you whichever way you looked. He was ubiquitous on television and on the radio, in newspapers, on street hoardings and on stamps, in businesses, factories, shops, restaurants, hotels and homes. Gaddafi as fist-pumping revolutionary; Gaddafi as sanctions-busting hero of the masses; Gaddafi as the cunning Falcon of Africa; Gaddafi as Brother Leader; Gaddafi as Universal Theorist, Supreme Guide of the Great Socialist People's Libyan Arab Jamahiriya, or GSPLAJ, as it was often written. I once admired a remarkable propaganda portrait of Gaddafi as the Great Man-River Builder in which torrents of water gush from a vast pipe, transforming a desert panorama of camels, date palms and rolling sand dunes into fertile agricultural land, complete with grazing sheep, combine harvesters and sensational quantities of shiny fruit and vegetables, all under the benevolent eye of a dictator festooned with gold braid. The hotel manager was immediately notified and the portrait was presented to me in a grand gesture of brotherly goodwill from the GSPLAJ. Thirty years later it still hangs in my study as I write this sentence.

Tripoli was a beautiful, melancholy place, dazzling in its sun-bleached brightness, yet strangely mournful for a city so evocatively sited on the Mediterranean. My father's old friend Mohammed, a small, careworn chain-smoker, used to take us on long expeditions across the city in his ramshackle car. Often we'd park in Green Square, named after Gaddafi's revolution of 1 September 1969, fringed with tall palm trees and guarded by the ancient fortress. Though the focal point of the city hadn't altered in decades, its name had changed repeatedly, a bellwether for Libya's twentieth-century history. During the occupation of the Italians, who invaded Libya in a colonial land-grab in 1911 and later under Mussolini, who rebranded the country as Italy's *Quarta Sponda*, or Fourth Shore, in 1939, it was Piazza Italia. During the monarchy of King Idris, who ruled Libya from 1951 to 1969, it became Maydan al Istiqlal, Independence Square. Today, it is Maydan al Shuhada, Martyrs' Square, in honour of the victims of the 2011 revolution.

Sometimes, before heading into the Old City, we would patrol the ramparts of the great hulk of Al Saraya al Hamra (Red Castle) that stared out across the Mediterranean, impassive witness to almost 3,000 years of wars, conquests and intrigues led by Phoenicians, Carthaginians, Greeks, Romans, Vandals, marauding corsairs, Byzantines, Arabs, Normans, Spaniards, Ottomans, Italians and the British. Here were the glistening waters of Tripoli harbour, established by those incorrigible, coast-hugging sailors the Phoenicians, first to settle the site of Tripoli, which they called Uiat, later Oea, around the seventh century BC.

Wind streamed in from the sea as we wandered down through the austere Bab Hawara, gateway to the teeming medieval market of Suq al Mushir. From the octagonal minaret of the Ahmed Pasha Karamanli Mosque, built in 1737–8 by the bold founder of a new dynasty, came the *muezzin*'s haunting call to prayer. Ignoring these insistent demands of the Almighty, prodigiously built matrons, some in the traditional white, sheet-like *farrashiyya* worn for centuries by their forebears, others in gaudy *hijabs*, did battle with stoic shopkeepers, haggling ferociously over dresses and jewellery in the nearby Suq al Harir (Silk Market) and Suq al Dahab (Gold Market).

Carried along by a tide of men, women and children, we drifted into the quiet, whitewashed streets of the *medina*, padding past a procession of mosques – Al Naqah Mosque, the city's oldest; Shaib al Ayn Mosque; Kharruba Mosque – and once handsome townhouses in tumbledown disrepair with crumbling walls and balconies, taking up our places in a dilapidated café, its courtyard open to the sky, alongside men playing cards and drinking teeth-rotting sweet tea, languidly propped up over bubbling, tobacco-filled *shisha* pipes. At the eastern end of Al Hara al Kabir Street, a stone's throw from the nineteenth-century Gurgi Mosque, was Tripoli's sole Roman survivor, the quadrifrons triumphal Arch of Marcus Aurelius, dedicated to the emperor and his adoptive brother Lucius Verus in 164 to mark their victory over the Parthians. Sublime on one level, it was stinkingly unattractive on another: Tripoli's young male population used it as a urinal. In more recent years, British politicians and diplomats have taken to using it as the photogenic backdrop for social media posts showing them hard at work in Tripoli.

For bibliophiles in Tripoli all roads led – and still lead – to Dar al Fergiani, the venerable bookstore then on 1 September Street, now on the renamed 24 December Street (the date of independence in 1951). Here I first came across *A Narrative of Travels in Northern Africa in the Years 1818–20*, an account of a British expedition that inspired a much later journey across the desert and offered myriad insights into Libyan culture. Visitors are often struck by the elaborately long greetings Libyans routinely exchange on meeting each other. The etiquette was little different two centuries earlier, as the English explorer George Francis Lyon discovered in 1819:

> Very intimate acquaintances mutually lift their joined right hands in such a manner that each kisses the back of the other's hand, repeating with the greatest rapidity, 'How are you? Well, how are you. Thank God, how are you? God bless you, how are you?' which compliments in a well-bred man never last less than ten minutes; and whatever may be the conversation afterwards, it is a mark of great good breeding occasionally to interrupt it, bowing solemnly and asking 'How are you?' though an answer to the question is by no means considered necessary, as he who asks it is perhaps looking another way, and thinking of something else.[1]

Sometimes we drove off to nearby Sabratha or Leptis Magna, the two cities which, together with ancient Oea, as Romans knew Tripoli, formed the *provincia Tripolitania*, province of the three cities, created by the Emperor Diocletian in around 303. Sabratha was intimate, elegant and compact. With its towering, three-storey *scaenae frons* allowing stolen views onto the Mediterranean, the theatre was one of the world's most evocative ancient sites. Drunk with plans to recreate the Roman Empire, Mussolini was so taken by the theatre he reinaugurated it in 1937 with a performance of Sophocles' *Oedipus Rex*. 'Between the Rome of the past and the Rome of the future,' he wrote in Sabratha's visitors' book, before visiting Leptis, whose nymphaeum fountain he christened 'Mussolini's Belvedere'.[2] One almost forgives his presumption. From 2015, Sabratha became infamous for two unwelcome reasons. It was, for a period, one of North Africa's largest migrant-smuggling centres, as well as a safe haven for the multinational terrorist fighters of Daesh, who were seeking, unsuccessfully, to rebuild their so-called 'Islamic State', a caliphate for the twenty-first century. It was not to be. They were forced out by local militias in 2016.[3]

Where Sabratha offered bijou charm, Leptis was crushingly imperial and vast, an august monument to the vanities of Septimius Severus, Rome's first African emperor (r. 193–211). A combination of deep pockets, the local boy's desire to honour the place of his birth and the finest materials, architects and craftsmen available across the empire elevated Leptis to the summit of urban grandeur. Among its setpieces was the two-storey, marble-paved basilica, overwhelming in scale, gorgeous in design and ruthlessly decadent, with soaring colonnades of Corinthian columns embellished with shafts of red Egyptian granite.

Leptis's treasures proved irresistible to English and French monarchies alike. In 1692, Mohammed Shaib al Ayn, the ruler of Tripoli, granted the French the right to whisk away columns from Leptis to France, where they were pressed into service at Versailles. Leptis marble can also be found in Rouen Cathedral and the Abbey of St-Germain-des-Prés in Paris. Not to be outdone, the British took their share in the nineteenth century as explorers began to penetrate the African interior from Tripoli on desert-bound journeys of geographical and commercial discovery – the camels they used were descendants of the animals whose breeding Septimius had encouraged almost two millennia earlier to promote Saharan trade. Thirty-seven granite and marble columns were plundered on behalf of George IV in 1817, together with ten capitals, twenty-five pedestals and assorted slabs. Sir Jeffrey Wyatville, the king's architect, arranged them, a decade later, into the pastiche splendour of a 'ruined Roman temple' at Virginia Water, which stands there to this day.[4]

Extraordinarily, given the site's magnificence, visitors frequently have Leptis to themselves. Wandering along the shore and clambering undisturbed over these neglected buildings, past piles of fallen columns and discarded pedestals lying strewn under a wide African sky is one of life's great treats. Deep in drifts of sand and choked by spreading trees and plants, Septimius's city sleeps beneath the softly stirring wind. The hot, deadening silence of the place can be overpowering. For the art historian Bernard Berenson, who visited in 1935, the ruins of Leptis Magna were 'evocative and romantic to a degree that it would be hard to exaggerate'.[5]

There was no sign of *fitna* in Tripoli in September 2011. The mood, instead, was one of revolutionary euphoria. Far from being divided, Libyans were united in their joy at having toppled Gaddafi. Long-standing fear of the regime prevented Tripolines from coming out onto the streets for a few days after the liberation of the city in late August, but the celebrations in Martyrs' Square swiftly grew from tentative hundreds to ebullient and jubilant tens of thousands until they filled the square in a tumultuous sea of red, black and green tricolours, the old Libyan flag during the monarchy, belting out the newly restored national anthem against the booming backdrop of celebratory fire from anti-aircraft guns and AK47s. '*Arfa rasuk fawq! Enta Leebee hour!*' they sang. 'Hold your head high! You are a free Libyan!' People sang and danced in the streets, pressed foreigners to their chests and cried, sprayed walls with miles of Gaddafi-mocking graffiti. Doctors and engineers held hands with businessmen, digital activists and soldiers, pious imams with impassioned human rights protesters. The revolution had ignited in the east, before burning down the foundations of the regime in the west, under banners proclaiming 'Tripoli is our capital'. There was no division. Not yet. Libyans were one people.

Women, as much as men, came to the fore. Yusra al Massoudi, a civil engineer, was determined to speak to a foreign journalist. 'This is the real picture of Libya,' she told me one evening in the square, beaming from ear to ear. 'This is fantastic. I feel great. We can't believe any of this. All of my life I never felt this was my country. Libya was like Gaddafi's farm. Now, only now, for the first time in my life, I feel proud to be Libyan. This is my country.'

It was a new Libya. In those exuberant days of 2011 anything seemed possible. After languishing under the dead hand of dictatorship for forty-two years, Libyans had at last broken free from their shackles. The prophet of world revolution had been brought down by a revolution on his own soil. Now Tripoli would become the capital of a country in which Libyans freely determined their own future. It would be a peaceful Muslim country, an Islamic democracy, a Dubai on the Mediterranean or anything else Libyans could collectively conjure from the ashes of the Gaddafi regime. As Aristotle observed in a saying that was already old almost 2,500 years ago: 'Always something fresh in Libya'.[6]

In 643, 1,368 years before the revolution that brought a bloody, sodomizing end to Colonel Gaddafi's life, eleven years after the Prophet Mohammed's death, Tripoli received something fresh. It came in the form of an Arab army under Amr ibn al As, conqueror of Egypt, and its name was Islam. From that time Tripoli – *Trabulus* in Arabic – was an Arab Muslim city until 1510, with a short-lived Christian interlude of 1146 to 1158, when the Normans, fresh from conquering Sicily and Malta, established a garrison there.

In his *Description of Africa* the tenth-century traveller and geographer Ibn Hawqal recorded Tripoli as 'a most wealthy and powerful city, with vast markets ... Merchandise is plentiful there, as, for example, local wool and vivid blue and fine black stuffs of great value. These goods are loaded onto ships that call continuously from Europe and the Arab lands with cargoes of merchandise.'[7] What Ibn Hawqal did not say was that much of this wealth came both from the Muslim fleets that regularly raided Sicily and southern Italy, and from the trade in Christian flesh, especially women. These two activities – piracy by the notorious Barbary corsairs, and the desert slave trade – would be pillars of Tripoli's economy for more than 1,000 years.

A more anecdotal continuity through many centuries is the description of travellers dazed by the intensity of the light in Tripoli. 'When we approached, we were blinded by the brilliant whiteness of the city from which the burning rays of the sun were reflected,' wrote the learned Tunisian traveller Abu Mohammed Abdullah al Tijani in 1307. 'I was convinced that rightly is Tripoli called the "White City"', a reference to the city's nickname of Al Bayda, today a city in eastern Libya. 'The extreme whiteness of square flat buildings covered with lime, which in this climate encounters the sun's fiercest rays, is very striking,' Miss Tully, the Tripoli diarist and sister of the British consul, noted in 1785, during a decade observing the customs and culture of the city. The Spanish explorer and spy Domingo Badia y Leblich arrived in Tripoli in 1804, travelling under the pseudonym Ali Bey al Abbassi, and had a similar reaction. Tripoli was far more handsome than any town in Morocco, he wrote. 'Its houses are regular, well-built and are almost all of a dazzling white.' More recently the Libyan writer Hisham Matar has described the light in the eastern city of Benghazi as so all-consuming it constitutes a material in its own right, architecturally more important even than stone: 'You can almost feel its weight, the way it falls and holds its subject.'[8]

In his *Rihlah* travelogue Al Tijani admired Tripoli's clean, wide streets, modelled on the pre-existing Roman plan, that criss-crossed the city easily from one end to another, intersecting like 'a chessboard'. He marvelled at the 'astonishing precision and astounding solidity' of the 'ancient and wonderful' Arch of Marcus Aurelius and was startled by the ghoulish cemetery, which was so crammed with corpses that 'you could not see a hand's breadth of soil without a skull or a bone lying upon it'.[9]

Disaster struck for Tripoli's faithful on 25 July 1510, when Count Pedro Navarro of Spain took the city after overcoming local resistance. It was Christian Europe's latest offensive against the Dar al Islam on the western front, following Ferdinand of Aragon and Isabella of Castile's history-changing defeat of Granada's last Arab king in 1492. The Arabs had been expelled from Spain altogether in 1502, and Al Andalus went from being a cherished home and way of life to a remote, searing memory. Navarro shared the admiration of earlier visitors to Tripoli. He wrote how 'among all the cities I have seen in the world, I do not find any that is comparable to it, both for its fortifications and for its cleanliness. It seems rather an imperial city.' By now the city lay behind a deep moat and a double wall with towers and ramparts one mile in circuit, overlooking a large port capable of accommodating 400 ships. From 1530 until 1551 Tripoli was occupied by the Knights of the Order of the Hospital of St John of Jerusalem, who were sworn to defend this 'Christian oasis in a barbaric desert'.[10]

Their time on these shores was limited. By the middle of the sixteenth century, Ottoman power in North Africa was resurgent. Once Roman Mare Nostrum, the Mediterranean was becoming Mare Ottomanicum. In 1551, the Turks attacked Tripoli in a land and sea offensive that left nothing to chance. Sinan Pasha's bristling fleet consisted of 112 imperial galleys, two enormous galeasses, fifty brigantines and transport ships carrying 12,000 soldiers and siege engineers. It was a hybrid Ottoman navy and pirate force, strengthened with the corsair renegades of Darghut Pasha, later known as the 'Terror of Tripoli', and Murad Agha.* Within eight days of the first artillery fire the diminutive and barely reinforced force of the Knights of St John, a contingent of no more than 1,000 men, surrendered. The Spanish attack, and subsequent plundering, had caused considerable damage to Tripoli, forcing the Ottomans to rebuild their newly acquired city's fortifications, repair the Al Naqah Mosque and construct a palace for Darghut Pasha, who succeeded Murad Agha as Beylerbey, or chief governor, of Tripoli in around 1554.

After the ignominy of falling under infidel rule, the Turkish conquest of Tripoli restored the city to the hands of the faithful, albeit these were foreign overlords. It also ushered in a period lasting 360 years in which, despite a number of attempts to retake the city by the Knights of Malta and Philip II of Spain, Muslim power in this corner of the Mediterranean remained firmly in the ascendant. The Ottoman victory at Tripoli, which followed the capture of Algiers in 1516, was the precursor to further advances across North Africa as they went on to take Qairouan, the ancient centre of Islamic learning, in 1557, Jerba in 1558 and Tunis in 1569 and again in 1574.

Together with its neighbours of Algiers to the west and Tunis to the east, the regency of Tripoli fell under a series of *deys*, rulers who were appointed by Ottoman sultans in Istanbul. Though they varied in the level of loyalty to their overlord, tribute payments to the Sublime Porte were maintained. Financing these payments required a brisk and steady trade.

The most immediately obvious consequence was a surge in piracy.

---

* Renegades were European Christians who had converted to Islam, or 'turned Turk', as the English put it, and joined the Barbary corsair fleets raiding shipping from their bases on the North African coast from the sixteenth century.

Barbary corsairs sailed amok in the western Mediterranean, mostly in swift, shallow draft vessels, along the Atlantic coast of West Africa and even into the North Atlantic and South America in larger vessels from the sixteenth century. From their bases in Tripoli, Tunis, Algiers, Salé and Rabat, the pirates launched deadly, predatory raids on commercial shipping and coastal towns, seizing vessels and capturing Christian slaves for onward sale into the Ottoman slave trade.

Far from being a negligible sideshow of the African slave trade, a romantic tale of adventure on the high seas, the white slave trade was a hugely significant, immensely destructive phenomenon. As many as 1 million victims from Britain, Ireland, France, Spain, Italy, Holland, the Americas and Iceland were seized by Barbary corsairs between 1500 and 1800. The situation was already so desperate by 1580 that the most popular farewell to sailors leaving Italy was, 'May God preserve you from the galleys of Tripoli.' The great majority of the corsairs were Muslims, none more famous than Hizir Reis (c. 1478–1546) and Oruç Reis (1474–1518), better known as the Barbarossa brothers, whose spectacular careers in piracy led them from the island of Midilli (Lesbos) to the heights of political power in Algiers. In the case of Hizir it went further still: promotion to the rank of Grand Admiral of the Ottoman navy, Beylerbey of North Africa, the honorific Hayreddin (Best of Islam), and the government of a few Greek islands, including Rhodes, Euboea and Chios for good measure. The corsairs included in their ranks some of the most notorious European renegades, such as the Englishman John Ward, who boasted, 'If I met my own father at sea I would rob him and sell him when I was done.' Sir Henry Wotton, the English ambassador to Venice in the early seventeenth century, considered him 'beyond a doubt the greatest scoundrel that ever sailed from England'.[11]

Europeans began to dread Ottoman naval supremacy in the Mediterranean. Then, in 1571, the allied forces of Spain, Genoa, Venice and the Papal States routed an Ottoman fleet against the odds at the Battle of Lepanto. The Ottomans lost a shattering 230 warships. In all, more than 40,000 were killed and 10,000 wounded, the second largest body count in a single-day European battle after the carnage of Cannae in 216 BC, when 58,000 lost their lives in Hannibal's rout of the Romans.[12] The lasting importance of the encounter was perhaps more psychological than anything else. In the same way that the Battle of Marathon in 490 BC had, according to Herodotus, liberated Greeks from their fatalism towards Persian military supremacy ('for until that day came, no Greek could hear even the word Persian without terror'), Lepanto, in the words of Cervantes, the author of *Don Quixote*, who lost his left arm in the battle, 'broke the pride of the Osmans and undeceived the world which had regarded the Turkish fleet as invincible'.[13] Nevertheless, the Turks wasted little time in restoring their savaged fleet. By the summer of 1572, they had managed to build 150 fully equipped ships in only five months. A year later, Venice humiliatingly surrendered Cyprus to the Sublime Porte.

In response to the constant threat to its commercial shipping and the recurring need to negotiate ransoms and treaties, Europe launched a diplomatic offensive in North Africa. In Tripoli, Holland, Britain, France and Venice led the way by establishing consulates, whose *raison d'être* was to safeguard their seaborne trade and ensure the treaties were duly honoured. The first English consul in Tripoli was Samuel Tooker, who arrived with a fleet of war in 1658. Agreements to protect merchant vessels from the corsairs were struck in return for hefty payments. It was a protection racket plain and simple. Faced with still fearsome Ottoman naval power, which was underwritten by the marauding corsairs, the Europeans had little option but to play the game or face the direst consequences. A new commercial-diplomatic quarter sprang up alongside the city's harbour, containing the consulates and their *fanadiq* warehouses, together with new markets and additional storage facilities strung along the ancient Roman *cardo maximus* running north–south and now renamed Bazaar Street.

The later seventeenth century brought renewed unrest to the shores of Tripoli. In 1675 the English Admiral Sir John Narborough, tasked with suppressing the Barbary corsairs, sailed to Tripoli and demanded the release of three English ships seized by the corsairs operating there. When this was refused, he blockaded the port, bombarded the city's defences, sent gunboats into the harbour at midnight to set the fleet alight and freed all the English slaves. As the naval chaplain Henry Teonge recorded in his diary entry for 30 January 1676 from Malta: 'Here we are told of the joyful news of Sir John's burning of four Tripoli men-of-war in their own harbour; and how we took their guardboat first and killed all that were in her, and so went in and fired the ships, and came out again without any man being hurt.'[14] A decade later the French did almost exactly the same, bombarding the city, burning the enemy fleet and setting free the city's multinational group of slaves.

One of the earliest English consuls in Tripoli was Thomas Baker, who served from 1677 to 1685 and whose diaries offer a riveting portrait of the city on the cusp of the eighteenth century. On 9 June 1679 he recorded how the 'Silly, but wicked Animal' the Dey of Tripoli 'most Barbarously dismembered of their Leggs and Armes' eight young *kuloghli*. These were an ethnically mixed group employed as cavalry and officials, the products of marriages between Turkish Janissaries and local Arab and Berber women. This unfavourable view of local government was by no means uniquely European. The eighteenth-century chronicler Ibn Ghalbun, a scholar from the Libyan city of Misrata and one of the few Arab sources for this time, concurred. 'He was of evil character, vicious, following his whims in a tyrannical way,' he wrote of the *dey*. Baker's time in office coincided with a particularly chaotic period in the history of Tripoli. Between 1672 and 1711 a total of twenty-four *deys* came and went in quick succession. It was said by one Franciscan in 1686 that a *dey* rarely lasted more than a year in office. As soon as his rule became unpopular 'any drunk can rouse the city and have the rulers' heads off'.[15]

In the midst of this turmoil, in 1711 one man made his move. It was a moment of unprecedented disorder. In the space of three weeks three *deys* had been elected, murdered and replaced by competing factions. Ahmed Karamanli, whose family probably hailed from Karaman in Anatolia, was a leading figure in the *kuloghli*. Displaying a level of cunning and subtlety that would serve him well in the years ahead, he began by outsmarting one claimant to the throne in Tripoli, who was trying to have him killed, then outfoxed and assassinated another, this time Khalil Pasha, the governor Istanbul was attempting to reinstall. Karamanli's position was steadily strengthening but not yet secure. There was a final obstacle to remove. Having thanked the Janissaries for their support in beating off Turkish troops sent by Istanbul, Karamanli then announced he would hold a grand celebratory banquet in their honour in his house in the *menshia*, an oasis of summer retreats and villages a mile outside the city walls, containing date palms, fig, pomegranate, olive and jasmine trees. The *menshia* was traditionally home to the *kuloghlis*, who were not permitted to enter Tripoli without special permission, and even then only unarmed.

After the hors d'oeuvre of his initial manoeuvres there followed a breathtaking *pièce de résistance*. One by one the senior officers rode up to the house and dismounted amid the fanfare of musicians beating drums and playing pipes. After entering through the double doors they stepped into a narrow passage from which a series of small rooms issued. Here in these dark recesses Karamanli's black slaves waited, grabbing hold of each soldier as he came in, hauling him into the room and strangling him within seconds. It is a tribute both to their strength and Karamanli's Machiavellian planning that 300 Janissaries reportedly went to their suffocating deaths within an hour. To forestall the inevitable retribution from the Porte for this treacherous massacre, Karamanli plundered the houses and properties of the slaughtered officers and dispatched the treasures to Sultan Ahmed III. A florid letter accompanied these goods, requesting the sultan's gracious approval of this naked power grab, which at this early stage was only partially forthcoming.[16] Karamanli has been likened to thirteenth-century English barons and the Medicis of Italy for his combination of military and diplomatic prowess allied to administrative flair and a perspicacious judgement of his fellow Libyans, not to mention a certain aptitude for murder when the situation appeared to require it.

The prevailing anarchy in Tripoli was quickly stamped out by a purge of the remaining Janissaries, the establishment of a small standing army and the elevation of loyal officers, relatives and European renegades to senior positions. Murderers were swiftly dispatched, robbers summarily dismembered, marauding tribesmen pegged back. A new tax was imposed on the Jewish community, trade started to pick up after the recent turbulence and advantageous peace and commerce treaties were concluded with the Dutch and Genoese in 1712. Against a series of uprisings from within and efforts to replace him from without Ahmed Karamanli proved remarkably resilient during his first decade in power, so much so that after one final effort to install its man as governor in 1721, a year later Istanbul pragmatically bowed to reality and dispatched two ships carrying the official *firman* declaring him the Ottoman's supreme ruler and Pasha of Tripoli. A new dynasty had begun.

Ruthlessly effective at maintaining domestic peace and security, shrewd and wily in his relations with his nominal overlord in Istanbul, Ahmed Karamanli was no less deft in managing relations with the encroaching European powers. His first challenge was the French, who sent a squadron of six men of war, two galleys and three bomb ketches to Tripoli in 1728. Their mission was to renew a peace treaty and seek an indemnity for protected ships previously taken by the Tripoli corsairs. Karamanli was unmoved by the French threat to bombard his city. Ibn Ghalbun recorded his response, having first taken soundings from his *diwan* council: 'As to payment, no one consents to make it, and no one will give it. As for your bombs, we do not fear them; you can throw them if you wish.'[17] He then withstood a punishing barrage of heavy bombs, waiting it out until the French fleet, unable to land to take in water and fresh supplies, at the mercy of winds that might wreck them on a lee shore, and eventually exhausted of bombs to rain upon the city, offered to make peace. Displaying admirable chutzpah Karamanli flatly refused. The French fleet sailed off without having achieved its mission, the damage to the city was quickly repaired through the extensive use of slave labour and the Tripoli corsairs resumed their work, capturing twenty-one more French vessels in quick order. A year later, under renewed threat from another French force, Karamanli agreed a peace treaty, demanding as his price French military assistance to successfully put down an internal rebellion in the southern province of Fezzan. The mutinous governor and his son were captured in the capital of Murzuk and, rather than condemning them to summary execution, as would be expected, the pasha instead had them clapped into irons and put on sale in the slave market. He then purchased them for the degrading sum of two copper coins and sent them on their way. It was a masterclass in dealing with truculent rivals. They never rebelled again.

The ingenious pasha left a more lasting mark on Tripoli with the magnificent mosque that bears his name to this day. Built in 1738, the Karamanli Mosque dominates the entrance to the Old City with its green and white balconied minaret rising above the many-domed roof and elegant, columned arcade. Lured by generous fees, Italian masons worked alongside Egyptian fresco artists to create a monument treasured by Libyans three centuries later. Its interior is admired especially for the beauty of its carved frescoes, ceramic tiles and decorations in marble, much of which fell victim to an assault by gunmen, who removed tiles and vandalized the mosque in 2014 – the year *fitna* returned to Tripoli, as some Libyans will tell you. The insecurity took its toll on other parts of Tripoli's architectural heritage. At about the same time, Islamist militias were accused of removing, and probably destroying, the famous bronze statue of a naked woman stroking a gazelle, another cherished Tripoli landmark that dated to the Italian era of the 1920s.

Karamanli also constructed an aqueduct to bring water to the castle and built new markets and warehouses to service the needs of a city steadily growing in prosperity through trade and piracy. Corsair raiding yielded fresh supplies of Christian slaves and ships to be sold on for greater profit. Treaties with Britain, France, Holland, Sweden and Denmark brought large payments into the pasha's treasury, and ambassadors were sent from Tripoli to strengthen diplomatic relations with Europe's major maritime powers. When Qasim Chelebi, the pasha's nephew, was appointed Karamanli's first ambassador to London in 1728, he caused a sensation at the Court of George II, swishing around Westminster and the West End in extravagant silks festooned in gold and silver brocade, surrounded by an entourage that included 'a court jester, a dwarf mute, his tailor, a barber and wardrobe servants, cooks and coffee makers and several negro slaves, all dressed richly in the different costume of their service'. Ambassadorial quirks aside, London understood the necessity of keeping Tripoli's ebullient pasha onside. As the long-serving English consul Benjamin Lodington observed in a letter requesting yet more gifts for Ahmed Karamanli, 'tho' they cannot do us any good, they may do us a great deal of harm in interrupting our Turkey and Levant trade'.[18]

While piracy continued to bolster the pasha's revenues, the age-old

African slave trade was economically indispensable. Once Karamanli had imposed security across the province of Tripolitania, allowing the routes from Tripoli to the interior to reopen, it could continue apace. Three of the four major African caravan routes during the eighteenth and nineteenth centuries passed through Libya, of which two – Tripoli–Fezzan–Kawar–Bornu and Tripoli–Ghadames–Ghat–Air–Kano – started and terminated in the pasha's capital.[19] Though a consequence of the lawlessness and anarchy of the post-revolution years in Libya, the recent incidence of migrant-smuggling from Libyan shores also harks back to this much earlier trade in human flesh. In 2017, the American network CNN caused an international storm with its story alleging slave auctions were taking place inside Libya, a charge denied by the government.[20]

If they survived the frequently fatal journey of around 1,500 miles across the desert, haggard, sun-frazzled caravans straggled into the city with their miserable retinue of African slaves, gold in dust and small bars or rings, ivory, ostrich feathers and hides, civet, cottons, leather, ornamental sandals, *gerbas* (water skins made of goats' hides), honey, pepper, elephants' teeth and *gooroo* nuts, a prized luxury. South along the same routes went merchants with horses, beads, coral, needles ('four of which purchase a fine fowl'), silks, copper pots and kettles, looking-glasses, swords ('very long, straight and double edged; bought greedily by the Tuarick'), occasional pistols and guns, gunpowder, carpets from Tripoli, Venetian glass, muslins, silk and cotton kaftans, shawls and woollen cloaks.[21]

One of Ahmed Karamanli's last actions in office was a brutal echo of his first. In the fierce summer of 1742 a caravan of pilgrims was returning to Algiers from the *hajj* to Mecca. Among its group was Haj Mohammed, the pretender to the throne of Algiers. Informed by his spies of the young man's plans to seize power and having consulted his neighbour the Dey of Algiers, the pasha invited the traveller to rest over in Tripoli as an honoured guest. The guileless Haj Mohammed left his armed guards outside the city and entered the castle with a small entourage, the cue for Ahmed Karamanli's men to fall upon the group and strangle them. Outside the city gates the pasha's Janissaries surrounded Haj Mohammed's Algerian soldiers and slaughtered them to a man. The pasha's prize for this pitiless massacre was the caravan, which he lost no time in plundering. It yielded him 500,000 *sequins*, 200 Arabian horses and 250 camels, a handsome return on the work of a few moments. Old habits died hard.

By 1745, Ahmed Karamanli was an old man, going blind and in declining health. Having written his name illustriously in the history of Tripoli as the founder of a dynasty that bore his name and operated more or less independently from the Ottomans, he summoned a *diwan*, handed power to his younger son and heir, Mohammed, and died shortly afterwards, possibly by suicide, at the age of around sixty.

During the short reign of Mohammed Karamanli (1745–54), treaties were reaffirmed with England and France and piracy resumed in earnest against Neapolitan, German, Dutch and Genoese shipping, swelling the pasha's treasury and infuriating the courts and commercial houses of Europe. Tripoli harbour teemed again with European slaves clanking wretchedly in their chains.

After Mohammed's death in 1754, power was transferred dynastically to his son Ali Pasha, whose long reign from 1754 to 1793 witnessed a gradual decline from the golden age established by his grandfather. Government under Ali consisted of the pasha as supreme head of state, beneath whom came the *bey*, who was commander of the troops, the *agha* as chief of the Janissaries, the *kahya* as prime minister, the pirate-in-chief *rais*, the state treasurer *khaznadar*, a sheikh to administer Tripoli, a mayor and a team of clerks. Important decisions of state were taken in the *diwan* council of notables.[22]

History's verdict on Ali has been almost universally negative. 'In his reign the reins of authority became more and more loose and thefts and murders made life in Tripoli miserable; the troops were no longer paid regularly,' says the *Encyclopedia of Islam*. 'He was a vicious character, unworthy of his high rank, and it was to his bad qualities that he owed the loss of his throne and life,' wrote the traveller Ali Bey al Abbassi. In the later years of Ali Pasha's reign the French consul offered an especially scathing judgement: 'He rules, but is not obeyed. Shut up in his harem . . . he builds nothing, repairs nothing, lets all collapse.' Ali was popularly seen to be under the undue influence of the Jewish community through a woman known as 'Queen Esther', who was said to control him by ministering expertly to his sexual passions, according to the French vice-consul Vallière in the 1780s.[23]

From the riches and general prosperity of the first half of the eighteenth century, Tripoli was plunged into several ruinous famines in the second. Famine struck first in 1767–8, then again in 1778 to 1780, accompanied by a slide in the value of the currency and economic collapse. It returned with the plague in 1784–5, by which time the situation inside the city was being closely recorded by the indefatigable diarist Miss Tully, the British consul's sister. 'The place is, at present, in so dreadful a state of famine, that it is become horrid to walk or ride out, on account of the starved objects that continually die in the streets,' she wrote from the consulate on 2 August

1784. Since mid-century, this had moved to the grand and graceful marble-paved courtyard house on Sharaa al Kuwash, Baker Street, today on Al Hara al Kabir Street, next to the Gurgi Mosque. Originally built for the ageing Ahmed Karamanli in 1744, within a few years it had become the seat of British diplomacy. During Gaddafi's time the building was marked by a plaque that clearly expressed the regime's verdict on the European role in Africa: 'The so-called European geographical and explorative scientific expeditions to Africa, which were in essence and as a matter of fact intended to be colonial ones to occupy and colonize vital strategic parts of Africa, embarked from this same building.'

During the plague many of the city's Jews fled to Leghorn, making purchases more difficult and expensive because 'trade here is chiefly carried on by the Jews', Miss Tully reported. Hundreds were dying daily. By 20 July 1785, the Englishwoman noted that 40 per cent of the Muslim population, half of the Jews (of a total of around 3,000) and a staggering 90 per cent of the Christian community, had died. For a small city whose population she estimated at 14,000, this was devastating, yet worse was to follow.

Though quarantine was the most effective remedy against the plague, she reported, such a response was 'inconsistent with the ideas of the Moors', who preferred to seek the intercession of a *marabout* holy man or an *imam*. While Christians did their best to fumigate their houses with a curious mixture of bran, camphor, myrrh, aloes and gunpowder, one of the pasha's senior officials told Miss Tully that 'sovereignty is the greatest shield'. Rather than advise Ali Pasha to take the recommended precautions in hygiene and isolation, it was 'necessary to give the Moors an example not to try to resist the hand of fate'. Fatalism prevailed in the highest quarters, and in the narrow, crowded passages and airless rooms of the castle, the plague ran amok. Many in the royal household, including princes, princesses and almost all the senior officials, died in great agonies.

To have survived in Tripoli at this time was to have stared into the abyss and lived to tell the tale. Covered in red spots and excruciating swellings, those who had succumbed to the plague frequently lay where they collapsed, vomiting in the streets, panting and dying in torment alongside growing heaps of the decomposing dead. Distraught relatives clustered around them, ululating in distress. Others stumbled through the streets in a 'raving mad' stupor. With hundreds succumbing daily the city stank terribly. Faced with a tax for every burial outside the city walls, the Jews in the Jewish Quarter were said to be burying their dead in shallow graves in their own courtyards. Corpses were putrefying quickly in the summer heat, spreading the invisible infection further across the city. For once

Miss Tully was lost for words. 'The general horror that prevails cannot be described,' she wrote. Yet, whatever she thought about Muslim fatalism, she was ready to admit that the calamity equally brought out the most generous, selfless displays of humanity from the local population. 'The Moors perform acts of kindness at present which, if attended by such dreadful circumstances, would be very rarely met with in most parts of Christendom.' Amid the unspeakable horrors she had witnessed, the redoubtable Miss Tully, who had been housebound with the consul behind closed doors for thirteen months, managed to survive and tell her story. The consul's house was the last to remain in quarantine.[24]

Like any other sources, European accounts must be treated with caution for they carry the cultural assumptions and prejudices of their time. When it comes to opening a window onto the very private world of women in Tripoli during the later eighteenth century, Miss Tully nevertheless offers a rare and valuable perspective. Women from the grandest families travelled in some style, she wrote, in 'a sort of palanquin, entirely enclosed with linen, and placed on the back of a camel'. Royal women walked in the city only 'with the greatest circumspection' to visit a mosque or make an offering. Often they would set out from the castle at around midnight with a large guard, protected by an outer cordon of black women slaves and Muslim servants and an inner ring of personal attendants. The guards called ahead, warning people of their coming so the streets would be empty. Together they would have made an arresting sight. Attendants carried numerous lights and 'a vast quantity of burning perfume' in silver filigree vases and large silver ewers of rose water and orange-flower water to dampen the burning perfume so that the royal women wafted along in a dense cloud 'of the finest aromatic odours'. Woe to any man who deliberately or otherwise stole a glance at the royal procession since 'their law decrees no less a punishment than death for any person who may be in the streets and remain there while their ladies are passing by, or for any man who may look at them from a window'. Outside this rarefied world, middle-class women generally walked on foot but very rarely without a female slave or attendant. 'They are then so completely wrapped up, that it is impossible to discover more of them than their height, not easily even their size,' cocooned within a *baracan* measuring one and a half metres by five, with only the tiniest slit to see through. Jewish women were dressed very similarly with the exception of a clear space left for one eye, 'which a Muslim woman dares not do if she have a proper regard for public opinion, as her reputation would certainly suffer by it'.[25]

The desert slave trade, meanwhile, continued to provide the economic foundations of the regency of Tripoli. Described by James Richardson, the nineteenth-century English missionary, explorer and campaigner against the trade, as 'the most gigantic system of wickedness the world ever saw', it carried hundreds of thousands of captive Africans through Tripoli. In the 1700s consular reports suggest the numbers of slaves passing annually through Tripoli was 500–600, rising to 2,000 in the 1750s, before reducing to around 1,500 towards the end of the century. In the late eighteenth century Tripoli had two covered bazaars, one very large and offering 'every sort of merchandize', the other a much smaller slave market. 'The very idea of a human being, bought and examined as a bale of goods, is repugnant to a feeling heart; yet is this one of their principal modes of traffic,' Miss Tully reported.[26]

In 1778 Consul Tully received an instruction to provide 'an account of the Trade in Slaves carried on in the Dominions of the Bey of Tripoli', including the numbers brought in and sold annually, a break-down of their origin, details of where in Africa and Asia they came from 'and stating whether the male slaves are usually castrated'.

Public opinion against the trade was hardening in England. In 1787, the Committee for Effecting the Abolition of the Slave Trade was founded in London by a group of Quakers. Prime Minister William Pitt the Younger spoke in favour of abolition and Edmund Burke and Charles James Fox, a future foreign secretary, joined the chorus. But it was William Wilberforce, the young Member of Parliament known as 'the nightingale of the House of Commons' for the sweetness of his voice, who emerged as the political champion of abolition. Speaking in the House of Commons in 1789, he launched a coruscating attack on the 'warped and blinded' slave trade apologists. 'By their conduct they had placed the inhabitants of Africa in a worse state than that of the most barbarous and savage nation,' he thundered.[27] After vociferous opposition, Parliament eventually voted to make the slave trade illegal in 1807. In 1848, the Ottoman Sultan Abdulmejid I prohibited the Turkish governor of Tripoli and his officials from trading in slaves, which was then outlawed throughout the empire in 1856.

In practice, however, the trade continued, albeit in reduced volume. In 1878, exactly one hundred years after the letter to Tully, Frank Drummond-Hay, the then British consul, was telling the Foreign Office that 'the vigilance required in watching the Slave Trade, in thwarting the devices resorted to by the local authorities in order to evade the execution of the orders for its suppression, in obtaining information on the arrival of slaves by the caravans from the Interior, of intended shipments and other numerous matters' justified a substantial pay rise.[28] Everyone had an interest.

Within the castle, so often a hotbed of plotting, Ali's sons were starting to manoeuvre for power. In 1790 Yusuf, the youngest and most ambitious, lured his brother, the *bey* Hassan, into a carefully prepared trap within the castle and killed him in their mother's arms, shooting the hapless man at close range before his black slaves finished him off in a flurry of knife stabbings. Yusuf staged a loud, triumphalist celebration in the *menshia*, then, a year later, launched an attack on Tripoli, sending panic through the city as son turned against father. *Fitna* had reappeared and the people would suffer.

The British consulate was suddenly transformed into a refuge for 'Greeks, Maltese, Moors and Jews', together with the French and Venetian consuls, who brought all their property with them.[29] Sailing into this chaos at the head of a Turkish fleet in the summer of 1793 and armed with a *firman* from the Porte reasserting Ottoman rule, the opportunist Georgian renegade Ali Burghul, a pirate chief recently ejected by the Dey of Algiers, deposed the ailing Ali Karamanli and seized power. As one historian of the Karamanlis put it: 'To be expelled by an Algerian Dey for cruelty and rapacity puts Ali Burghul very high on the list of bad rascals.'[30]

Terrified Jews were driven from the streets as the new pasha made his way in state to the castle to the thundering salutes of the Turkish ships and the marine batteries. Jewish merchants were seized and tortured to extract their fortunes, the infamous 'Queen Esther' was slung into a dungeon, clapped into chains and ransomed to her family for 100,000 *pataques* (£33,000) and the most prominent Karamanli supporters were rounded up and strangled. On the ancient ramparts of the castle, from the rooftops of official buildings and the European consulates, the Karamanli flag was hastily pulled down and replaced with the fluttering crimson flag with star and crescent.

Ottoman rule proved a brutal but exceedingly brief interregnum. The Turkish threat served to galvanize and, for a while at least, unite the feuding Karamanlis. Supported by the Bey of Tunis, the brothers Ahmed and Yusuf Karamanli led an army of 30,000 to retake the city in 1795. Realizing the odds were against him, Ali Burghul ordered his men to evacuate the city after a final round of plunder and the summary execution of all prisoners in the castle dungeon. The shuffling and stammering Ali abdicated in his son Ahmed's favour in 1795 but the ever bold Yusuf shut the city gates against his brother and installed himself as pasha.

He began his long reign (1795–1832) with a ferocious crackdown on security, making liberal use of the death penalty for even minor offences. Just as his great-grandfather had brought an end to disorder and anarchy, so Yusuf's draconian measures provided the necessary fillip to commercial activity. To encourage Jewish traders, lifeblood of the economy, back from

exile in Italy, he relaxed punitive measures against the community, including the requirement for Jews to wear black clothes from head to toe.
Tripoli harbour was soon a bristling forest of tall masts again as commercial shipping returned to take advantage of the renewed desert caravan
trade. Spanish shipwrights from Cartagena worked overtime to build a
new fleet of fast corsair vessels under the command of Murad Rais, a
Scottish renegade who had escaped from an English ship as Peter Lyle and
converted to Islam, throwing in his lot with the new pasha. In 1800 the
Tripoli fleet consisted of eleven ships. By 1805 that number had more
than doubled to twenty-four, in addition to the many smaller skiffs.[31] To
those who were keeping a beady eye on the Barbary Coast and its easternmost new ruler, there could be little doubt about Yusuf Karamanli's
intentions.

The dawn of the nineteenth century found the international powers
taking renewed interest in Tripoli. Yusuf was required to navigate the
turbulent waters of European power politics, starting in 1798, when
Napoleon called on the pasha to facilitate possible troop movements
between Paris and Cairo to support his conquest of Egypt. Countervailing
pressure to resist the French came in the ominous form of Lord Nelson's
fleet on the one hand, and an official messenger from Istanbul ordering
Yusuf to support the blockade of Toulon and Malta and provide troops
for an assault on Egypt on the other. The pasha maintained tacit support
of the French while pragmatically hedging his bets.

From 1795 to 1805, Tripoli's increased maritime power resulted in lucrative (for Yusuf) treaties with Spain, France and Venice. Those who failed
to reach agreement with the pasha, such as Denmark, Holland and Sweden, who may have baulked at the price and principle of this protection
racket, soon discovered that the alternative cost of running the gauntlet
and risking captured shipping and the enslavement of their crews was
hardly more palatable.

America found itself in a special position. British protection was no
longer forthcoming for American vessels, following independence in 1776,
leaving Washington first to rely on the French and then, when that policy
was found wanting, to take measures into its own hands. Talks held in
1786 between the United States, represented by John Adams and Thomas
Jefferson, and Sidi Haji Abdul Rahman Adja, Tripoli's ambassador in
London, were remarkable on one level – they were 'the first direct US
diplomatic exchange with the Muslim world' – but yielded nothing.[32] In
fact, the conversation between the two Americans and Tripoli's ambassador owed more 'to AD 100 than 1786', thought Jefferson's biographer
James Parton. Asked why Tripoli would make war on nations that had

done it no harm, the ambassador is said to have uttered a response that must have given Jefferson and Adams an uncomfortable pause for thought:

> It was written in their Quran, that all nations which had not acknowledged the Prophet were sinners, whom it was the right and duty of the faithful to plunder and enslave; and that every Mussulman who was slain in this warfare was sure to go to paradise.[33]

Whatever the Quran had to say on the subject, a treaty was eventually concluded between the US and Tripoli in 1796 and an American consulate was opened the following year. Peace on paper was one thing, but in the years immediately after the treaty the pasha started to feel his protection had been purchased too cheaply by comparison with what his more powerful neighbour in Algiers had managed to extract. He began to request more money, but was consistently rebuffed.

Yusuf was not afraid to pick a fight. On 11 May 1801, the pasha's troops surrounded the American consulate, forced a way in and cut down the flagpole. It was a characteristically bold declaration of war, brought on by Washington's refusal to pay a sudden demand for $25,000 and agree to a revised treaty yielding an annual tribute of $250,000, the equivalent of about $450,000 and $4.5 million respectively today. Both sides fatally misunderstood the other. While America was treating Tripoli as a dependency of Algiers, Yusuf was insisting he negotiated as a sovereign power.

Confident in America's growing sea-power – the Naval Act of 1794, establishing a permanent navy, was a direct response to the challenges of Barbary Coast depredations on its shipping and resulted in the construction of six frigates at a staggering cost of $688,888.82 – the newly elected President Jefferson decided on a harder line with Tripoli, the weakest of the Barbary powers, and dispatched a squadron of three frigates to the Mediterranean.[34] In the first military encounter, on 1 August 1801, American sailors from the schooner *Enterprise* captured the *Tripoli*, one of the pasha's cruisers, and threw her guns and equipment overboard to Yusuf's intense fury. To punish him for this humiliating loss, the pasha had his defeated captain ignominiously paraded through Tripoli on a donkey, long an object of ridicule in the Arab world, with a reeking garland of sheep's entrails around his neck.

In 1802 Jefferson gave the orders for a new, larger squadron of six ships to blockade Tripoli, burn enemy shipping and take prizes. In 1803 the 1,240-ton, thirty-six-gun frigate *Philadelphia* ran aground outside Tripoli harbour, forcing the commander to strike his colours. More than 300 officers and crew were imprisoned, the frigate seized and plundered. While the officers were well treated, the crew, according to Seaman William Ray, were spat on by the Janissaries, armed with sabres, muskets and pistols, as they were shoved into 'the dreadful presence of his exalted majesty, the puissant Bashaw of Tripoli', sitting on a dais on a throne inlaid with fine mosaics and covered with a rich, gold-fringed velvet cushion 'bespangled with brilliants'. Neapolitan slaves stole their clothes before the Americans were clapped in heavy irons and put on meagre rations for two weeks. They were then forced into the slave-labour construction of Tripoli's city walls, hauling stone and sacks of sand. In a later account Seaman Elijah Shaw wrote how he and his comrades, bareheaded, barefoot and badly burned by the sun, were regularly whipped with heavy knotted rawhide whips while toiling at their back-breaking work in chain gangs. 'The Turkish drivers seemed to take great pleasure in severe treatment and when they thought we did not draw hard enough they applied their whips with an unsparing hand.'[35]

Determined that the *Philadelphia* should not remain in enemy hands and become the pasha's most powerful pirate ship, Lieutenant Stephen Decatur led a disguised boarding party of sailors and marines into Tripoli harbour on *Intrepid*, a captured ketch, on the night of 16 February 1804. After boarding the frigate and killing twenty of the corsair crew silently with cutlasses, the Americans realized the ship was in no condition to be sailed away and set it on fire with explosives with the loss of no men. It was considerably more than a shot across the bow. Nelson was in no doubt about the audacity and significance of the raid. It was, he declared, 'the most bold and daring act of the age'.[36] The US then went one step further, launching a military expedition to topple Yusuf and install his brother Ahmed on the throne, the first American attempt to remove a head of state. It resulted in the capture of the eastern Libyan city of Derna, America's first land battle on foreign soil, after a stirring, 600-mile march from Alexandria led by William Eaton, former consul in Tunis, followed by a peace treaty swiftly agreed by Yusuf in 1805. Two centuries later the First Barbary War of 1801–5 is still remembered in the opening lines of the US Marines' Hymn:

> From the Halls of Montezuma
> To the Shores of Tripoli;
> We fight our country's battles
> In the air, on land, and sea . . .

Initially resisted by the pasha, who had boasted, 'I do not fear war, it is my trade', the Americans had emerged victorious in a landmark war that thrust them decisively onto the world stage as a military power. As Pope Pius VII is said to have remarked, 'The United States, though in their infancy, have done more to humble the anti-Christian barbarians on the African coast than all the European states had done for a long period of time.'[37]

Having survived American efforts to oust him by land, Yusuf manoeuvred cunningly through the heaving seas of the Napoleonic Wars, a state of chaos and uncertainty that admirably suited this pirate state. In the years that followed, however, under increasing pressure from resurgent European powers, his revenues and authority declined in tandem to the point where the British consul Hanmer Warrington, who served in Tripoli from 1814 to 1846, was considered, in the words of his French counterpart, 'more master of the country than the Pasha himself, so much so that a gesture on his part is enough to make the Pasha tremble'.[38] Dramatic evidence of this came in 1816, when Warrington controversially insisted on the hanging of a corsair captain who had seized a Hanoverian ship sailing under British protection. Underlining his own authority, the consul successfully demanded that his Christian sailors, and not the pasha's Muslim officials, carry out the public execution from the ship's yardarm.

Further humiliations were to follow. In 1819 a Franco-English fleet forced the pasha to liberate Christian slaves and prisoners held in Tripoli and accept peace treaties that equated to the virtual suppression of piracy and protection payments. In 1827, following orders from the Ottoman sultan for naval support during the Greek War of Independence, Yusuf dispatched the feeble remnants of his corsair fleet – more akin to a few poorly armed fishing boats in the derisive verdict of the Turkish admiral – only to see it swiftly destroyed at the Battle of Navarino. What had begun as a gentle ebbing of royal power soon became a full-blown retreat.

In a brazen turning of the tables Britain and France started demanding punitive compensation payments from Yusuf for insults – real or imagined, it made little difference – towards its consuls. France demanded 800,000 francs for this reason in 1830, Britain 200,000 piastres for another diplomatic offence around the same time.[39]

The Europeans were on the rise. In 1830, the French occupied Algiers, a hammer blow to the Barbary corsairs. By the mid-1830s the combination of British and French naval power had purged the Mediterranean of corsairs for perhaps the first time since the Roman era, a devastating shock to Tripoli's vulnerable economy.[40] Shorn of tribute payments, unable to increase revenues from the under-attack slave trade, heavily indebted to foreign creditors, Yusuf's extravagantly maintained regency of Tripoli started to resemble a bankruptcy waiting to happen. In 1832 a revolt and attempted coup brought on by his desperate efforts to raise taxes to pay debts totalling $500,000 to Britain and France led to his public, tearful abdication in favour of his son Ali, whom he advised 'not to govern by caprice: the fall and sin of my government are owing to this'.[41]

It was the final manoeuvre by a ruthless ruler who had always prized pragmatism and survival over all other considerations. Yet the independent regency of Tripoli was no longer viable. On 26 May 1835, responding to the new pasha's request for military assistance during a civil war, and conscious of growing European power in North Africa, a Turkish fleet of twenty-two ships sailed into Tripoli. The next day a force of 5,000 disembarked with artillery pieces, occupied the mosques and strategic positions across the city and issued orders prohibiting the carrying of weapons and the use of Tripoli's local currency. On 28 May Ali Pasha Karamanli was invited to board the flagship of the sultan's representative, Mustafa Najib Pasha, where he was immediately detained. Najib landed and went directly to the castle, where he announced the sultan had resumed direct control and nominated him as pasha. Mehmed Bey committed suicide, his brother Ahmed fled to Malta and all the remaining Karamanlis were taken to Istanbul, with the sole exception of the old pasha Yusuf. Frail to the point of senility and cruelly impoverished after his son Ali had plundered his personal property and estates, he was allowed to live out his remaining days in the city from which he had once lorded it so triumphantly.

Launched with a rebellion, the Karamanli Dynasty had been snuffed out 134 years later in a coup. The demotion was immediate. The grand Regency of Tripoli was reduced within a few hours to a humble Ottoman *vilayet*, or province.

The Gadaffi regime likewise had been born out of rebellion against a remote monarchy. It, too, had brought some prosperity to Libya and become a thorn in the side of Europe and America, like the Karamanlis, with whom it also shared a murderous ruthlessness. Yet, unlike the audacious Karamanlis, the Gaddafi regime was merely a one-generation affair, little lamented by most Libyans at its bloody demise in 2011. It is a mark of the depths to which the country has fallen in recent years that many Libyans already mutter that life was better under Gaddafi, just as many Iraqis complain that life was better under Saddam Hussein. Arabs need a strong leader, they say, they're not ready for freedom and democracy. Not true, argue those who refuse to accept Arabs can do no better than dictatorship. The chaos, carnage and broken politics are precisely the legacy of those very regimes, not the fault of those fighting for freedom and something better.

Either way, the imagined democratic utopia of a post-Gaddafi Libya has descended into dystopia. Rival militias run amok in Tripoli. Murder, kidnapping, ransom and extortion flourish. In the country with Africa's largest oil reserves, ordinary Libyans struggle to fill up their cars with petrol, while men and women sleep overnight on the streets waiting to withdraw money from the banks. A new generation has been impoverished and immiserated. '*Nakba wa naksa*,' says my friend Jalal, an official in the beleaguered government in Tripoli. A disaster and a setback. *Fitna* has carried all before it.

In the early twenty-first century, then, Tripoli's fortunes have sunk to their pitiful nadir. Two hundred years earlier, by contrast, in the other, easternmost end of the Mediterranean, a far happier story within the Ottoman Empire was about to unfold. One city was poised to attain its greatest glory.

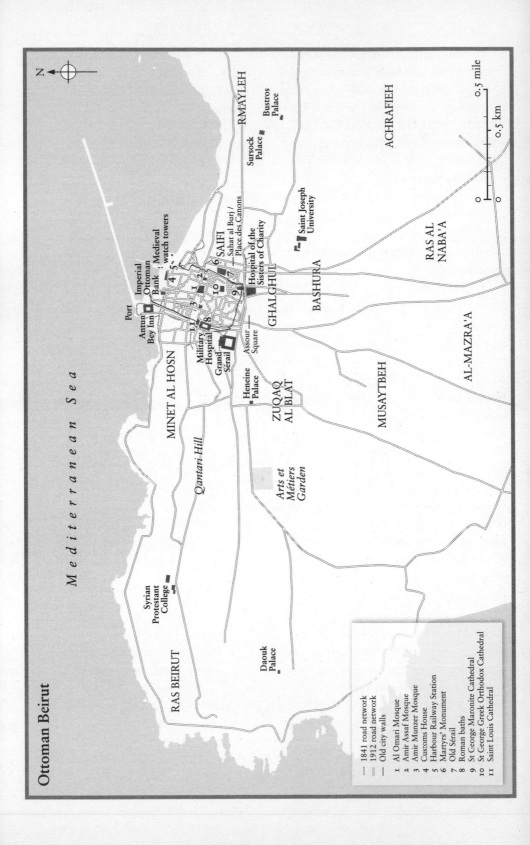

Ottoman Beirut

N

Mediterranean Sea

RMAYLEH

Bustros
Palace

ACHRAFIEH

Sursock
Palace

Saint Joseph
University

RAS AL
NABA'A

SAIFI

Sahat al Burj /
Place des Canons

Medieval
watch towers

Imperial
Ottoman
Bank

Port

Hospital of the
Sisters of Charity

GHALGHUL

BASHURA

Antun
Bey Inn

Military
Hospital

Grand
Sérail

Assour
Square

AL-MAZRA'A

MINET AL HOSN

Heneine
Palace

ZUQAQ
AL BLAT

MUSAYTBEH

Qantari-Hill

Arts et
Métiers
Garden

Syrian
Protestant
College

RAS BEIRUT

Daouk
Palace

0.5 mile

0.5 km

---- 1841 road network
—— 1912 road network
···· Old city walls
1 Al Omari Mosque
2 Amir Assaf Mosque
3 Amir Munzer Mosque
4 Customs House
5 Harbour Railway Station
6 Martyrs' Monument
7 Old Sérail
8 Roman baths
9 St George Maronite Cathedral
10 St George Greek Orthodox Cathedral
11 Saint Louis Cathedral

13

Beirut – Playground of the Levant (19th Century)

... elle est mille fois morte, mille fois revécue.

Nadia Tuéni, 'Beyrouth', 1986

Beirut dazzled. Not just on an exceptional spring day, when the voluptuous setting on the shores of the Mediterranean beneath snow-dusted Mount Lebanon and a cobalt sky offered up the city at its most sybaritic, but for most of the nineteenth century, when the once languid little port roused itself from its slumbers and thrust itself with élan onto the world stage, becoming a booming merchant republic, the pulsating heart of the Arab cultural awakening, a playground for pleasure-seekers and an idealized 'Paris of the Middle East'.

There was little to suggest, at the turn of the nineteenth century, that Beirut was destined for such heady times. Much is made of the blessings conferred by nature and geography, on the city's location almost exactly halfway up – or down – the eastern coast of the Mediterranean between Antioch in the north and Gaza in the south, midpoint of the great coastal plain that shades into Syria after traversing the mighty Mount Lebanon, rising more than 3,000 metres above sea level at the range's greatest height. Yet with a few variations the same could be said of any number of ports along the coast, places such as Sidon, Tyre, Tripoli and Acre, some of which enjoyed more illustrious histories, none of which were to experience the riches, fame and glories, or indeed the tragedies, that would define Beirut in the nineteenth century and beyond.

Beirut's remarkable rise was not inevitable. Yet on the broadest level it is certainly true that a visceral trading instinct has animated this coastline's outward-looking inhabitants from the earliest times. Emerging from the prehistorical murk of the late fourth millennium BC, the irrepressible maritime, merchant and manufacturing force that was the Phoenicians 'took to making long trading voyages' from the eastern Mediterranean, Herodotus tells us, sailing the seas in their mighty ships loaded with Assyrian and Egyptian goods.[1]

Phoenician prowess and superiority on the water were admired and feared across the Mediterranean. When the Persian Great King Xerxes decided to hold a sailing competition for his multinational fleet as part of the preparations for his invasion of Greece in 480 BC, it was the Phoenicians of Sidon who won.*

The astonishing growth of Beirut in one of the most eye-catching stories of any city, anywhere, at this time, cannot be explained by geography alone. Rather it was born of a pulse-quickening combination of indigenous talent and chutzpah, cosmopolitan vigour, Great Power meddling and rivalry – primarily Ottoman, French, British and Egyptian – and a measure of that most elusive of ingredients, good fortune, that together raised Beirut within a few decades from a dingy, unremarkable medieval hovel to the summit of urban grace, glamour and sophistication.

Nature had certainly smiled on Beirut. As visitors closed in on the port from the sea, their eyes were drawn first to the bold triangular cape on which the Old City lay between two hills, Achrafieh and Musaytbeh, craggy outliers of the overhanging mountain looming above. Their gaze then rose steadily from the cypresses, carobs, sycamores, prickly pears, figs and pomegranates of the diminutive settlement to the banana trees, gnarled olives, oranges, lemons and mulberry groves beyond it and up towards the sturdy pines that delineated the lower slopes of Mount Lebanon. It was almost indecently picturesque. When they made it a colony in 14 BC, Pompey having conquered it in 64 BC, the Romans named ancient Beirut Colonia Julia Augusta Felix Berytus, in honour of Augustus's daughter and in recognition of this 'happy shore'.

Although religion was no guarantor of happiness in this life or the next, as Beirut's much later history would bloodily attest, the city's proximity to the Holy Land ensured it an early role in the spread of Christianity, and at least one source claimed Jesus himself preached here. The early Christian traditions surrounding Berytus also report that St Peter stayed here and that this was the scene of the apostle Jude's martyrdom and the death of Saint Barbara. Legend makes Beirut the place where Saint George slew the dragon, a tradition remembered in the name of Saint George Bay on the city's northern coast, home today to the forlorn, war-damaged hulk of the Saint George

---

* The Father of History also claimed the Phoenicians were the first civilization to devise an alphabet and were responsible, too, for giving us the name Europe, transmitted via Greek mythology in the story of the Cretan tit-for-tat kidnap of Europa, princess of Tyre, that opens *The Histories.*

Hotel, a 1930s icon that finds itself in a titanic struggle for survival against Solidere, the city's biggest and most controversial developer.*

Ahead of Constantinople and Alexandria, Berytus was to become the leading centre for legal scholarship in the later Roman Empire, its law college responsible for the great codification of Roman law embarked upon by Theodosius II (builder of Constantinople's long-lived walls) and later Justinian. Though it was an important trading colony that earned its bread by producing silk and wine, its legal prowess brought it the epithet Berytus Nutrix Legum, Beirut Mother of Laws.† Anticipating its nineteenth-century return to greatness, the city became a celebrated seat of learning for the study of philosophy, languages and literature. In *Dionysiaca*, at forty-eight books the longest surviving poem of antiquity, the fifth-century Greek epic poet Nonnos of Panopolis describes Byzantine Beirut, or Beroë, as 'the keel of human life, harbour of the Loves, firm-based on the sea, with fine islands and fine verdure . . . root of life, nurse of cities, the boast of princes, the first city seen, twin sister of Time, coeval with the universe . . .'[2]

From these Elysian heights, alas, there was a long way to fall. After this golden age that lasted from the third century to the sixth, the city was brought crashing down to earth – tragically and literally – in the ravaging earthquake of 551, whose tidal wave killed as many as 30,000 and smashed the Mother of Laws into ruins. In the wake of this early cultural and intellectual pre-eminence, brought to a brutal end by that apocalypse, followed by a devastating fire in 560, the city slunk off into the shadows and became a quiet backwater of the Levant with only the shattered statues and tumbled columns of the law college and the well-trodden *cardo maximus* (main north–south road) to remind its inhabitants of its former greatness. It is a glaring sign of its insignificance that by the time the rampaging Arabs swept through in the seventh century they barely acknowledged it among their many conquests. In *Kitab Futuh al Buldun* (*Book of the Conquests of Lands*), Baladhuri, the ninth-century historian last encountered at the fall of neighbouring Damascus, mentions it almost

---

* The hotel's website explains: 'The Saint George Hotel is located on Saint George Bay, named after the legendary hero who slew the dragon terrorizing its shores. Today the bay and its inhabitants are under renewed attack from a hybrid corporate monster: Solidere; which – neither private nor public – is devouring public and people's property to line the pockets of its backers. The giant development firm has driven all legal owners and lease-holders of property from the shores of Saint George Bay, leaving only the Saint George Hotel fighting a "David and Goliath" battle to stop Solidere's long term plans to land-fill the bay and build more high-rises.'

† To this day Berytus Nutrix Legum forms part of the emblem for the Beirut Bar Association, founded in 1919.

as a footnote in the long list of towns that had succumbed to the irresistible warriors of Islam in the aftermath of that far more glorious conquest
in 635.

From Muslim rule, Beirut – or Baruth, as European knights knew it –
passed into Christian hands and the Kingdom of Jerusalem in 1110, when
it was seized and sacked by King Baldwin I. Apart from a brief, nine-year
interlude that followed Saladin's capture of the city in 1187, the city
remained in Crusader hands until 1291, when the Mamluks of Egypt took
it after another damaging siege. The Crusader Church of Saint John the
Baptist became, with the addition of a brace of minarets, the Al Omari
Grand Mosque, today a stone's throw north downtown across the con-
fessional divide from the Saint George Greek Orthodox Cathedral, the
oldest seat of Christian worship in the city, dedicated in 1767. At this time
the port was shaped like a half moon, two defensive towers rising from
the outermost points, a chain drawn across the water between them whenever required to protect ships and the town from attack.

In their persecution of Shia Muslims in the Kisrawan district north of
Beirut during the fourteenth century, the Mamluks planted the seeds of
later religious strife, attracting Maronites (an ancient local Christian sect
in communion with Rome) into Mount Lebanon over the following centuries at the expense of the Druze, an esoteric and eclectic offshoot of
Ismaili Shiism, who had settled there long before.

While some of the foundations for religious conflict were indigenous,
rooted in the steep slopes of the Mount Lebanon range, others came from
further afield. By 1450 the Maronite patriarch had a resident Roman
Catholic adviser, the beginning of a long trend of European interference
and protection. The most decisive intervention, however, with profound
and long-lasting consequences, was the announcement in 1639 by the
French king Louis XIII that the Maronites of Mount Lebanon were henceforth under his 'protection and special safeguard'.[3] It was a marker for
the Ottomans, whose imperial protection was being explicitly challenged,
and an encouraging signal to those Maronites who longed for liberation
from their Muslim masters. The later Druze–Christian contest would
haunt much subsequent Lebanese and Beiruti history. It lay at the heart
of the 1860 crisis and formed part of the wider 1975–90 civil war that
reduced the city to ashes.

The sixteenth century brought a new power to the eastern Mediterranean. Within six decades of Sultan Mehmed's conquest of Constantinople,
the Mamluks went the way of all flesh. The Ottoman Sultan Selim
the Grim's annihilating defeat of the Mamluks, first in Syria at the Battle
of Marj Dabiq in 1516, then outside Cairo in 1517, was seismic, an

earthquake that upended the reigning order of the Middle East. It transferred a swathe of Muslim lands stretching from Syria and Palestine to
Egypt and the Arabian Peninsula from an ailing Islamic power to an
altogether more vigorous Muslim successor. Not that the Sublime Porte's
sway was always unopposed. During the Russo-Turkish War of 1768–74,
a Russian fleet bombarded and occupied Beirut in 1772 and again in
1773–4, when the population was estimated to be no more than 6,000. It
was the briefest of interregnums, during which Beirutis were required to
dismount and bow before a large portrait of Catherine the Great attached
to the main gate.[4] More importantly, it was a harbinger of European challenges to the weakening empire. Yet, for all these local and international
difficulties, Ottoman control of Beirut, and most of the Middle East,
including the Holy Places, would last until the biggest cataclysm yet: the
First World War.

Through the profound trials and tribulations of these preceding centuries
the alluring beauty of Beirut had been a constant, as much a defining feature of the city as the Kaaba of Mecca, the Umayyad Mosque of Damascus
or the walls of Constantinople. Reading the accounts of more adventurous
European travellers, who began to arrive in a trickle in the early decades
of the nineteenth century as travel became more accessible, before swelling
into a constant stream from the 1840s, the sense of bewitchment at the
town's preternatural loveliness is palpable. The French writer, photog-
rapher and traveller Maxime Du Camp accompanied Flaubert to Beirut
in 1850 and was immediately besotted, less with the city than its immediate surroundings. He wrote in florid prose about the 'forest of parasol
pines', of roads fringed with bursts of nopal, myrtle and pomegranate and
the purity of the lines of 'wooded summits of the Lebanon' etched across
the sky. To this romantically inclined Frenchman, Beirut was 'a retreat
made for the contemplative, for the disillusioned, for those who have been
wounded by existence; it seems to me that one can live happily there doing
nothing but looking at the mountains and the sea'.[5]

   Travel-writers are prone to such purple rhapsodies, of course, but Du
Camp was hardly alone. 'We approached the city through a region of
luxuriance and beauty such as seldom greets the eye in the environs of an
Oriental town,' the American traveller Stephen Olin wrote in 1840. 'It is
covered with gardens and mulberry trees now literally burdened with their
rank and deeply verdant foliage.' Much more recently the late Lebanese
historian Samir Kassir, author of a loving study of the city of his birth,
has written of 'a peninsula that seems to have fallen to earth from the
heavens'. It is 'as if, when talents were distributed among Arab cities, the

fairies decided that Beirut was to be the capital of relaxation and easy living'.[6]

All are agreed, then, on Beirut's blessed setting. Yet before we get too carried away it is worth noting that the city itself did not impress Du Camp, who thought it 'pitiful and lacking in grandeur'. If that was a pithy verdict from the mid-nineteenth century, a visitor fifty years earlier would have been far more disappointed still. Beauty without, for much of the nineteenth century, was yet to be accompanied by beauty within.

Beirut at the dawn of the century was a shabby little fortified medieval town with seven main gates. It measured a paltry 570 metres from north to south by 370 from east to west, beyond which began the verdant landscape that always drew the eulogies. The heart of Beirut was built around its lifeblood – the port and mole – protected by the twin towers of Burj al Silsilah (Chain Tower) and Burj al Fanar (Beacon Tower). Architecturally speaking, apart from the port, interest focused on a trio of monuments. First, there was the Crusaders' fortress, Burj al Hashesh, on the north-eastern corner of the ramparts. A second New Fortress, Burj al Jadid, occupied higher ground on the most prominent hill that was later used to site the Grand Sérail in 1853 and remains the seat of the Lebanese prime minister today. Lastly, there was the Burj al Khashef watchtower on the south-eastern corner of the walls in a spot that would later become Sahat al Burj, Tower Square, the very heart of Beirut. It was not until the accelerating growth from the 1860s that the population of the town started to spill beyond the medieval walls in earnest.

Within this irregular quadrilateral it was less a story of light and cheer than darkness and gloom, filth and stench. Narrow, winding avenues between high-walled, three- or four-storey, windowless houses formed a labyrinth that confused many a visitor. Donkeys piled high with goods clattered through the dense alleys and low archways of the suqs, hurried along by their impatient owners. Porters pulled carts piled high with their parcels, the occasional camel loped disdainfully through the fortified gates. The sanitation was primitive, the smells immemorial.

Arriving in the early 1830s, by which time the population of Beirut was around 8,000, little changed from its size at the time of the Russian bombardment and occupation sixty years earlier, the French historian and writer Jean Joseph François Poujoulat claimed he had never seen anything 'so bizarre, irregular and extraordinary' as the architecture of the medieval Arab town; 'archways, secret outlets, dark alleys; narrow and winding streets inspire at first a kind of fright in the traveller who wishes to walk through the town; each house stands as a sort of great inaccessible dungeon'. In 1832 the French Romantic poet and politician Alphonse de

Lamartine, awed by the fertility of the landscape, the 'incomparable climate and . . . the magnificence of its situation', found Beirut completely 'captivating'. Flights of fancy about the female 'prisoners in the harems' and the 'harsh and doleful groans of the camels' kneeling to receive their cargoes at the port struck what would become a familiar, Orientalist tone. Lamartine's fellow countryman and writer Édouard Blondel, who lived in Beirut from 1838 to 1839, was less romantically inspired. He observed the half dozen mosques, several churches, the couple of hotels for foreign visitors and thought them 'shabby and devoid of interest'.[7]

To call this state of affairs picturesque torpor might be excessive, but Beirut had to wait for the sudden and unexpected arrival of the Egyptians before it could change gear. In the late eighteenth century the Russians had tested Ottoman power on these shores. In 1831 it was the turn of the Egyptians, who did so much more boldly and with more lasting effects. Having subdued the House of Saud and laid waste to much of Greece in earlier campaigns, Ibrahim Pasha, the hyperactive eldest son of Mohammed Ali Pasha, the 'Father of Modern Egypt' (r. 1805–48), blazed a trail of conquest along the eastern Mediterranean littoral. Gaza, Haifa and Jaffa were the first to fall to the invader, followed by a string of fabled ancient cities including Tyre, Sidon, Acre, Tripoli, Homs, Lataqiya and the old Umayyad capital of Damascus. Beirut succumbed in 1832 without a fight. Although Ibrahim briefly threatened a move against Istanbul, he later retreated to consolidate his power in the newly conquered territory of Syria.

Fortuitously for Beirut, the Egyptian conquests coincided with the invention of the steamship and a shipping revolution, led initially by Britain, then joined by France and other European powers, that would transform it from a sleepy entrepôt serving the Syrian interior of Damascus and Aleppo to its east into a westward-looking port city thriving on Mediterranean trade, exporting silk and raw materials and importing the products of the world, from cotton shirts made in Lancashire to Brazilian coffee. Ships with deeper drafts and immense cargoes required deeper ports, putting Beirut ahead of neighbours and rivals such as Sidon, Tyre and Tripoli. The soon-to-be-city was in the right place precisely at the right time.

At once brutal and unexpectedly beneficial, Ibrahim Pasha's demolition of Beirut's soft sandstone ramparts opened the way for the town to extend beyond the densely populated confines of its walls. To gauge the game-changing nature of this 'Egyptian' decade from 1831 to 1840, it is enough to study the record of customs receipts and ships entering the port. In 1824, according to Sir John Bowring's House of Commons report on

British trade with Syria, fifteen ships entered the harbour of Beirut, rising
to twenty-two in 1830 and twenty-eight in 1833. By 1840 around 150
British ships alone had called in. Customs receipts quadrupled between
1830 and 1840. As president of Beirut's advisory council under Ibrahim
Pasha, Mahmud Nami Bey proved an industrious and energetic leader for
the city. In 1835 a new jetty was built to accommodate the increased traffic, and in that year a total of 310 ships entered the port. By 1838 the figure
had more than doubled to 680. The British consul could report at this
time that Beirut had been 'transformed from a third-rate Arab town into
a flourishing commercial city – the residence of Europeans of various
nations'.[8] Within a few years these residents included American, Russian,
Austrian, Prussian, Tuscan, Sardinian, Spanish, Dutch and Greek consuls,
who had flocked in to take advantage of the multiplying commercial
opportunities in the wake of the British and French.

As the decade drew to a close there were sixty-nine companies established in Beirut, half of them foreign. Infrastructure and sanitation were
improved, paved streets were introduced, a lazaretto was established to
provide quarantine facilities and port and customs procedures were regu-
larized under the Egyptians' modernizing reforms. 'Truly it has become
the port of this Orient,' a Jesuit missionary reported in 1836. 'It is expanding and the Christians of the country are growing in number at a most
remarkable rate.' From 50,000 tons a year in the 1830s, total shipping
entering Beirut mushroomed twelvefold to 600,000 tons in 1886.[9]

Foreign interest in Beirut was a double-edged sword that cut deep into
society. On the one hand, it drove commercial expansion, the pace of
which grew ever more frenetic as the century wore on, and helped make
many local fortunes. On the other, it began to alter the demographic balance and later fuelled full-blown sectarian conflict. A forewarning of the
turmoil to come arrived in 1838, when the occupying Egyptians used
Maronite forces to put down a Druze rebellion in Mount Lebanon, which
was traditionally governed by emirs from the Sunni Muslim Shihab family,
at once poisoning relationships between the two communities with ominous results.* The Druze, Christians and Shia alike began to petition the
Porte to liberate them from Egyptian tyranny, opening the door to foreign
intervention.

The Ottoman Empire was under growing pressure. Internally, nationalist
movements were on the rise. Christian Serbs and Greeks led the way, fighting

---

* Emir Bashir Shihab II, who ruled Mount Lebanon from 1789 to 1840, was a Maronite,
the first of his dynasty to govern the mountain emirate as a Christian after the family's
conversion.

18. A view of the Sher Dor (Lion Bearing) Madrassa, one of a trio of Islamic religious colleges on Samarkand's Registan.

19. The Gur Amir Mausoleum, Timur's burial place in the heart of his imperial capital of Samarkand, 'Garden of the Soul'.

20. The Venetian artist Gentile Bellini's 1480 portrait of Ottoman Sultan Mehmed II, conqueror of Constantinople in 1453.

21. The Hagia Sophia, Church of Holy Wisdom, completed by Emperor Justinian in 537. Spiritual centrepiece of Christian Constantinople, later the grandest mosque in Muslim Istanbul, today it is a museum and World Heritage Site.

22. An aerial view of Istanbul, 'City of the World's Desire'. The Suleimaniye Mosque, inaugurated in 1557, remains one of the defining landmarks of the former Ottoman capital.

23. Babur, great-great-great-grandson of Timur, founder of the Mughal Empire, oversees the laying out of a garden in this sixteenth-century miniature.

24. An Afghan caretaker keeps watch at Babur's sixteenth-century tomb, which overlooks Bagh-e Babur, Babur's Gardens, in Kabul. Severely damaged during fighting in the late 1990s, the site has been restored by the Aga Khan Trust for Culture.

25. American helicopters fly over the mountain-ringed Afghan capital Kabul in 2011. Since the Soviet invasion of 1979, Afghanistan has been almost continuously at war.

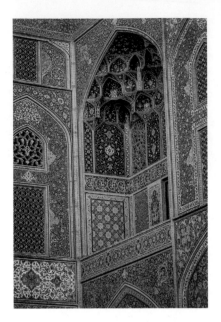

26. An eighteenth-century Mughal portrait of Shah Abbas I, who reigned from 1588 to 1629. The greatest leader of Iran's Safavid Dynasty, he made his imperial capital of Isfahan one of the most magnificent cities on earth.

27. Detail from Sheikh Lotfollah Mosque, the private royal place of worship on Isfahan's Maydan-e Naqsh-e Jahan, Image of the World Square, fêted as a crowning masterpiece of Iranian art.

28. A nineteenth-century French chromolithograph of Masjid-e Shah, the Royal Mosque, crown jewel of Isfahan's colossal main square. 'A second Kaaba has been built,' reads the foundation inscription, an expression of the Safavids' ambition to rule the Islamic world.

29. American Commodore Edward Preble's fleet attacks Tripoli, Libya, during the First Barbary War of 1801–5, America's first war as an independent nation.

30. A young boy flashes the revolutionaries' 'V' for Victory during the Libyan revolution of 2011, which brought Muammar Gaddafi's 42-year rule to an end.

31. A view in Tripoli's crumbling Old City. The minaret belongs to the Mosque of Darghut Pasha, named after the sixteenth-century Ottoman leader known as the 'Terror of Tripoli' and 'uncrowned king of the Mediterranean'.

32. An 1860 engraving showing the fast-growing city of Beirut at the foot of Mount Lebanon. The late Lebanese historian Samir Kassir wrote of 'a peninsula that seems to have fallen to earth from the heavens'.

33. A fighter from a Christian militia takes aim in Beirut, 1976. The civil war from 1975 to 1990 reduced much of the multifaith city to ruins.

34. Boats in Dubai Creek, 1975. Sheikh Mohammed bin Rashid al Maktoum, Ruler of Dubai, has called the waterway 'the very heart and soul of Dubai – its *raison d'être*'.

35. Dubai's Sheikh Zayed Road at sunset. 'Build it and they will come,' was the ruling Al Maktoum family's approach to developing this extraordinary city-state.

36. Designed by the Chinese-American architect I. M. Pei, the Museum of Islamic Art is one of the Qatari capital's most ebullient landmarks.

37. West Bay, Doha by night. Behind Tornado Tower on the left is Burj Doha, Doha Tower, unofficially known as 'the Condom'.

successfully for autonomy and independence in the Serbian Revolution (1804–17) and the Greek War of Independence (1821–9). Externally, European powers were on the march and threatening escalating intervention in Ottoman affairs under the guise of protecting Christian minorities. In 1827, a combined British, French and Russian fleet routed an Ottoman fleet under Mohammed Ali (half-heartedly supported by Yusuf Karamanli in Tripoli) at the Battle of Navarino, which marked the arrival of European hegemony in the Mediterranean. The days of mighty Muslim Empires lording it over enfeebled Western infidels seemed an increasingly distant memory.

In 1839, in a bid to modernize the empire, keep up with the advancing Western powers, win over disaffected Ottoman subjects within Europe and forestall further interventions, the Sublime Porte issued the Gülhane imperial edict proclaiming equal rights to all subjects of the Ottoman Empire, irrespective of religion or ethnicity. A series of free trade agreements struck between the Ottoman Empire and European powers from 1838 to 1840 added more grist to the commercial mill. The liberalizing Tanzimat reforms, which started under Sultan Mahmud II in 1839 and continued until 1876, represented a fundamental reordering of the state and its institutions through a series of imperial edicts and decrees. Ottoman subjects were granted rights guaranteeing their security and property. The army was reorganized and professionalized. A new criminal code was introduced, based on the French model, with European-style courts and equality before the law, irrespective of religion. Tax collection was standardized, again according to the French system, and the traditional *jizya* (capitulation) tax on non-Muslims was ended. New paper currency was launched. Factories replaced guilds, ministries of health and education were established, together with universities, teaching schools, a central bank, stock exchange, post office and Academy of Sciences. Slavery was abolished in 1847 and homosexuality was decriminalized in 1858, more than a century before Britain. Much of what the reformers adopted was considered best European practice. But the bitter irony of these promises of equality, from Beirut's perspective, was that in the eyes of some – the Druze in particular – the suddenly emboldened Maronites were fast proving more equal than others.[10]

When Europeans began to acquire interests in Beirut, they simultaneously discovered reasons to intervene to protect them. In 1840 Richard Wood, the powerful British agent of Lord Ponsonby, British ambassador in Istanbul, stirred up both the Maronite and Druze communities to revolt against their Egyptian overlords. On 11 September 1840 a combined Anglo–Ottoman–Austrian fleet appeared at Saint George Bay and began a heavy bombardment, prior to landing troops, artillery and rifles for the

Maronites. The Egyptians surrendered in October and Mohammed Ali, after a whirlwind, reforming decade, had lost Syria. Among his local legacies, he had turned 'a well fortified tax farm into an open port-city servicing Mediterranean trade'.[11] Less auspiciously, albeit with fine intentions, through the establishment of a town council divided equally between Muslims and Christians he had also helped introduce a form of sectarian politics that has bedevilled Beirut, and wider Lebanon, ever since. In the same year of the Egyptians' departure, the city's rising importance was recognized when it became the capital of an enlarged *vilayet*, or Ottoman province, of Sidon at the expense of Acre. This conferred an immediate advantage over the other Levantine ports of Tyre, Sidon and Tripoli that Beirut, already home to growing numbers of European consulates, was not slow to exploit.

Notwithstanding the outbreak of violence, beneath the pines and mulberry groves of Mount Lebanon, Beirut was on the move. The 'Paris of the East' moniker was current from the late 1830s. The British traveller Frederick Neale, who lived in the Levant for eight years between 1842 and 1850, offered a revealing insight into the state of the city. He reported how on each of his many visits he noticed that 'vast improvements' had been made. Beirut was 'steadily and rapidly increasing in wealth, population and dimensions . . . Stupendous new mansions, the property of opulent merchants, were daily being built,' together with grand country houses and summer retreats for the burgeoning class of wealthy merchants. Hotels, billiard rooms and steam-powered silk-reeling factories, equipped with European machinery, were 'springing up in every direction', providing employment for hundreds of boys and girls. Beirut deftly blended 'utility' with 'magnificence'. Social life was enlivened with evening quadrille parties. Grandees hosted balls, where the cream of Beirut's mixed Arab and European society eyed one another benevolently across the cultural divide. Europeans threw themselves into polkas and waltzes in front of the pipe-smoking, punch-drinking Turkish pasha and his entourage, who were only slightly scandalized by the 'indecorous' dancing of the Christian women. The younger European blades pulled in all-nighters, tearing themselves away from the dance floor only to dash straight into their offices 'where a great deal of soda water is consumed and very little business done'. Within this high-spirited account of mid-century Beirut, the line about the 'oft-arising disputes between the Druzes and the Maronites' casts a long shadow. It chimes with the remark from Richard Wood that the various sects were 'particularly remarkable for the great hatred they bear to each other' – in 1860 this animosity would spread catastrophically from the Mountain to Beirut.[12]

One of the most striking developments in nineteenth-century Beirut was the foreign-led, Ottoman-enabled education drive, which would have fundamental ramifications for Beirut reverberating into the twenty-first century. Spearheaded initially by Protestant missionaries from the 1820s, schools sprang up across the city to educate a generation of Beirutis whose opportunities hitherto had been extremely rudimentary at best. Nor was this a uniquely Western project since the Ottoman administration consistently placed a premium on a good Muslim education, in part competing against, in part supplementing, the charitable-cum-imperialist endeavours of the Europeans and Americans. Among the leading Muslim schools were the Maqasid Benevolent Society, established in 1878 and soon to be the primary medical and educational centre for Sunni Muslims, and the Dar al Funun primary school, founded two years later.

By the eve of the First World War, when the population had mushroomed to around 130,000, the French, whose cultural influence became steadily more pervasive across the nineteenth century, could congratulate themselves on having established schools and institutes in Beirut representing virtually every French Catholic order under the sun. Here were the Jesuits and the Lazarists, the Franciscans and Capucins, Frères des Écoles Chrétiennes, Marist Brothers and Sisters galore: the Soeurs de Besançon, the Soeurs de Saint-Joseph, the Soeurs de Saint-Joseph-de-l'Apparition, the Soeurs de la Charité de Nazareth and the Soeurs de Notre-Dame de Sion. Sister Gélas of the Soeurs de la Charité de Nazareth, who arrived in Beirut in 1847, became a local heroine for her selfless work fighting a trio of epidemics (smallpox, typhus and cholera) a year later. The Protestants could not quite match this Gallic blitz, establishing the American School for Girls and the British Syrian School for the Blind, while Greek Catholics could attend the Patriarchal College, leaving the National College for the Orthodox. The influence was such that some neighbourhoods even drew their names from these foreign institutions: Batraqiya on Musaytbeh Hill from the Patriarchal College, Yasuiyyeh from the Jesuit district around Université Saint-Joseph, Nasra on Achrafieh Hill from the Dames de Nazareth.[13]

Less creeping than charging, foreign influence was hardly unique to Beirut. British and French fingerprints – and gunboats – spread right across North Africa and the Middle East as the century progressed. Napoleon's conquest of Egypt in 1798 led the way with the first large-scale Western invasion of the Islamic world since the Crusades. It was an opening salvo in what would become an accelerating colonial assault, forerunner of the Anglo-French carve-up of the Middle East in 1916 and an anticipation of twenty-first-century wars in Iraq and Libya. The most powerful force in the Muslim world by far remained the Ottoman Empire, but it looked less and less mighty as the nineteenth century progressed. With increasing speed it was the Europeans, led by Britain and France, who were making the running. In 1820 the British imposed a treaty on the Trucial States of the Gulf, the prelude to establishing a strategically important protectorate there in 1892. France revisited the Barbary Coast with its capture of Algiers in 1830, ahead of the French protectorate in Tunisia that began in 1881. Not to be outdone, the British took Aden through the East India Company in 1839, established a protectorate over Egypt in 1882 and Sudan in 1899.

In the long nineteenth century, no city better exemplified the rapid rise to riches and glory on the one hand, and the deepening vulnerability to Western influence and intervention on the other, than Beirut.

Kaleidoscopes are beautiful, magical things. With their revolving, ever-changing patterns of colours they mesmerize young children. They are also fragile and delicate. Their harmonious balance can be damaged. When shaken too violently they can easily be broken.

In 1860 the cosmopolitan balance of Mount Lebanon, which had been under growing strain for several decades, suddenly shattered. The signs of a breakdown had been coming. The Egyptian occupation, which had been supported by the Maronites and resisted by the Druze, had torn apart the traditional ruling structures and injected poison into the bloodstream of communal relations. The subsequent Ottoman reorganization of the administration of Mount Lebanon into a dual governorate – two *qaim-aqamat* administrative regions, with Maronite control in the north and Druze control in the south – merely reinforced the growing sectarian divide, not least since both communities spanned this arbitrary border.

Then, in 1856, the Ottomans revisited the thorny question of privileges for non-Muslim communities in the Reform Decree. 'Every distinction or designation pending to make any class whatever of the subjects of my empire inferior to another class, on account of their religion, language, or race, shall be forever effaced from administrative protocol,' the Porte proclaimed. A bounty for the Christians of Mount Lebanon, the privileges conferred were conversely an outrage for many of the faithful across the empire. In the words of a Muslim judge in Damascus, they represented disgraceful 'violations of the eternal Islamic law'.[14]

How the bloody summer of 1860 unfolded remains contested territory to this day with each side claiming the other started hostilities. What is clear is that what began with looting, a handful of murders of Maronites and Druzes and a series of skirmishes in the spring of 1860 quickly escalated into full-blown civil war in the Mountain, so that by the end of May pitched battles between the different communities were in full swing. On the 27th of that month, 3,000 Christians fought a much smaller Druze force of around 600 near the village of Ain Dara and were roundly beaten, the prelude to the wholesale destruction of more than 200 Christian villages and the mass extermination of their inhabitants. Blood ran in the streets as the Druze seized control of the southern Mountain and the Bekaa Valley. The final number of casualties on Mount Lebanon hovered around 11,000, in Damascus 12,000. At least double those figures were wounded, with tens of thousands displaced. It was 'the greatest upheaval in the history of Ottoman Syria'.[15]

European pressure on the Porte, forerunner of the 'something must be done' school of foreign policy that would urge Western interventions in the Middle East during the following two centuries, led first to the dispatch of foreign minister Fuad Pasha to the region at the head of a force of 4,000. The governor of Damascus was summarily executed. Heads rolled. It was decisive action but insufficient to forestall a French intervention with an expeditionary corps of 6,000 under the command of General Charles de Beaufort d'Hautpoul landing in the Levant in mid-August.

Refugees from the bloody clashes descended from Mount Lebanon to Beirut in their droves. Within a fortnight in August the number doubled from 10,000 to 20,000. Beirut was overwhelmed by the influx. Its houses, schools, religious institutions, cemeteries, squares and gardens, even ships lolling in the harbour, teemed with traumatized refugees, who continued to pour in throughout 1860. Notwithstanding the heart-warming charity and hospitality displayed by Muslims and Christians alike, conditions in the city were desperate, the sanitation dire. While the dispossessed streamed in, many of the city's richest citizens, aghast at the horrors on the streets and fearful of an impending health crisis, took one look and voted with their feet, sailing serenely away on steamers to Alexandria, Athens and Smyrna.[16]

One of the most significant consequences of the 1860 massacres in Mount Lebanon was the end of the *qaimaqamat* dual governorate. A year after the bloodbath, Beirut hosted a conference of the Great Powers, where the Ottomans struck a deal with Britain, France, Russia, Prussia and Austria under which the Mountain fell under a single autonomous district or *mutasarrifiya*, governed by a Christian subject of the Ottoman Empire and entrenching Maronite control.

For Beirut itself, the immediate aftermath of the cataclysm in the mountains was no less dramatic, resulting in the complete redrawing of its demographic map. In 1838, the estimated percentage of Muslims and

Christians in the city stood at 45 per cent apiece. In 1846 the communities were still equal at 47 per cent. By the end of 1861, however, following the mass exodus of Maronites fleeing the carnage in the Mountain, Muslims represented 38 per cent of the population, compared to 58 per cent for the Christians. This balance continued to tip in favour of the Christians as the century progressed so that Muslims, at 29 per cent in 1882, were only half the Christian total of 58 per cent. By 1895 the figures stood at 30 and 63 per cent respectively. Beirut in quick order had become a Christian-majority city. The mass movement also rebalanced the proportions of the three major Christian sects. In 1846 the Greek Orthodox represented 23 per cent of the city, to the Maronites' 9 per cent and the Greek Catholics' 7 per cent. By the end of 1861, the Maronites (21 per cent) were running the Greek Orthodox, on 29 per cent, a much closer second.[17]

Numbers told only part of the story. The other important result of the influx of Christian refugees was that it altered the distribution of wealth across the city, putting Christians decidedly ahead of their Muslim counterparts. The civil war also put the seal on a transformation in the relationship between city and Mountain. Where once Mount Lebanon had been a place of refuge for the people of Beirut at times of crisis, henceforth people would flee the Mountain – and the Syrian interior – to Beirut, a place of safety.

Sectarian tensions had also begun to emerge from the first round of the Tanzimat reforms, before exploding violently in 1860. Before that, as the historian Leila Tarazi Fawaz has written, 'stories of persecution of Christians by other Christians are far more common than stories of persecution of Christian converts by Muslims . . . sectarian hostility in the city was as much within as among the major communities'. Yet attitudes could harden between the communities in the second half of the century, during which many Christian – and no shortage of Muslim – fortunes were made. In this period there are repeated references in the sources to outbreaks of violence between Muslim and Christian communities, ranging from the petty and banal to the more bloody and significant. In 1871, a group of Christians was attacked by Muslims with wooden clubs. A decade later, in 1881, a minor quarrel between Muslim and Christian boys playing games quickly escalated into stabbings and deaths involving adults from the rival communities. In 1888, some Christian boys found their missing goat decapitated and shot at Bedouin women, almost triggering a full-blown riot. Wooden clubs soon gave way to more powerful weapons. In 1896, 1897 and 1899 firearms were used repeatedly in a series of sectarian incidents. By the beginning of the twentieth century, 'Christian-Muslim clashes were so common that rarely did a week go by without an assas-sination, or a year without a riot.'[18]

Intercommunal suspicion was entrenched by this time, according to the Anglo-Lebanese author and activist Edward Atiyah, born in 1903, whose writings also foretell much later troubles. 'Christians versus Moslems: this was my first notion of collective human relationships,' his chapter on 'Beyrouth' begins in *An Arab Tells His Story*. 'To my mind at the age of five or six the world consisted of Moslems and Christians in antagonism to one another . . .' Atiyah, like so many others before and since, could not help admiring the city's 'superb natural beauty' in the shadow of Mount Sannin, but by 1925 he found Beirut 'incapable of breeding any-thing but fear and suspicion and hateful strife'. It was, he shuddered, a 'sordid human sore'.[19]

This was the stark verdict of a man writing from the vantage point of 1946, who had lost his great-grandfather in the 1860 civil war and had lived through the turbulent French Mandate for Syria and the Lebanon from 1923 to 1946 (most Muslims had rejected the new state of Greater Lebanon on its creation in 1920 and looked towards Damascus for their destiny). But it belied the daily cooperation and collaboration between Beirut's Christians and Muslims, evidenced most regularly in the com-mercial sector, where profit invariably came before passion for most of the nineteenth century. The instances of violence, however frequent and unwelcome, were a distinct background hum, more prevalent among poorer Beirutis, rather than the dominant mood music of the city. Extrem-ists on both sides of the sectarian divide may have fanned the flames, but the great majority of the population refused to ignite a conflagration. Muslims and Christians continued to find common ground, not just in commercial endeavours but on city committees, where equal represent-ation was maintained, in literary societies and even in political underground movements.

In the absence of a strong and effective police force, rival Christian and Muslim gangs maintained – and threatened – security in Beirut in the closing years of the century. The gangs ran the criminal underground: gambling, smuggling, protection rackets and murder. One of the most infamous *abadis*, or gang leaders, was Osta Bawli, a member of the Greek Orthodox community. 'He was a redoubtable champion, loved and admired by the Christians, dreaded by the Moslems,' Atiyah wrote. 'Every Christian in difficulties with the Moslems or with the Turkish Government was his protégé; every Christian murdered was sure to be avenged by him or his lieutenants', wearing kaftans with belts flamboyantly stuffed with daggers and revolvers.[20] Osta Bawli, like his fellow gang leaders, operated within a fatal, endless cycle of murder and revenge between Muslims and Christians.

In 1896, Osta Bawli's luck ran out, as it always does in the end. He was stabbed in the back while promenading along the corniche, a favourite pastime in *fin-de-siècle* Beirut. His funeral brought much of Beirut to a standstill and had the rare effect of uniting the traditionally antagonistic Orthodox, Maronites, Catholics and Protestants, who were at one in their grief at his demise. Mourners lined the streets belting out songs disparaging Muslims and Ottomans. Women sang to their folk hero and martyr. Then, moments before the coffin was closed, one of his admirers, immaculately turned out with a rose buttonhole and scented handkerchief, walked up to the casket, bent over the body to kiss it and muttered something unheard by the mourners. It was likely a promise to avenge the gangster chief's murder. Three days later the same man walked into a tobacconist's and shot dead three Muslims completely unconnected to Osta Bawli's assassination. 'Honour' had been served.

Walk east along the tree-lined Sursock Street in the heart of Achrafieh and a bijou palace, languidly overlooking the harbour from its private hill, springs splendidly from this expensive residential district, the Mayfair of Beirut. Walk through the wrought-iron gate, sweep up the double flight of marble steps into the house, past a pair of seventeenth-century Flemish tapestries, and the view down the thirty-five-metre Great Hall, a sumptuous visual procession through four sets of triple Lebanese arches, supported by fluted marble pillars among antique Oriental carpets, is sublime. A throng of palms and cypresses frame an otherwise uninterrupted glimpse of the Mediterranean, source of so much of this family's fantastic wealth.

Sursock Palace was built in 1860, while blood still ran in the Mountain, by Musa Sursock, doyen of the city's nouveau riche Christian merchant nobility. Today it is the largest private palace surviving from the nineteenth century as a family home, and it stands opposite the Nicolas Ibrahim Sursock Museum, a white wedding-cake hybrid of Venetian and Ottoman influences and an even grander palace originally built as a private residence in 1912. Bequeathed to Beirut by Nicholas Sursock on his death in 1952, it was later used by President Camille Chamoun (r. 1952–8) to host visiting dignitaries, before becoming a museum in 1961 and home to buzzing, *le-tout*-Beirut salons in the swinging 1960s. 'We were all full of ourselves,' the Lebanese novelist Hanan al Shaykh recalls wistfully. 'Everyone used to go, the crowds were amazing . . . only the crème de la crème of society. People went because it was prestigious, not because they were interested in the art.'[21]

Today, almost three centuries after their fortune was first made, the Greek Orthodox Sursock family, who swaggeringly bestrode Beirut at the height of its mercantile success, remain one of the city's greatest families. Together the members of this inventive, acquisitive and deeply ambitious clan achieved 'the most spectacular social climb in the nineteenth century'.[22] From Ottoman tax farmers in Turkey, they rose, like many other Christian businessmen at this time, by acquiring consular protection and the game-changing privileges it conferred, tax exemption not least among them. In 1832, for example, Dimitri Sursock was dragoman, or interpreter, to the newly appointed American consular representative. Other members of the family had Greek, French or Russian consular protection.

The Sursocks were grain-shippers and agents, bankers, stock exchange speculators and property tycoons who owned whole villages in present-day Lebanon, Syria, Egypt, Turkey, Israel and the Palestinian Territories. They were also cotton manufacturers and frenetic traders in silk, which from 1853 represented the leading export from Beirut. They invested readily and prodigiously in great infrastructure projects such as the Suez Canal, the Beirut–Damascus road and the port. Their business empire stretched from Beirut, Istanbul and Alexandria to Cairo, Paris and Manchester. When Russian Grand Duke Nicholas visited Beirut in 1872, he was whisked off immediately to meet Nicholas Sursock, whose annual income at that time was said to be £60,000, the equivalent of £6.2 million today. The Sursocks glided effortlessly among, and married into, the European aristocracy, while retaining close links to the upper echelons of the Ottoman Empire and foreign powers such as the Khedive Ismail, who ruled Egypt from 1863 to 1879, kept afloat partly through vast Sursock loans and investments. Their rambling palaces and villas were 'equal in elegance to any Italian palazzo'. In short, the Sursocks rose to the surface of the city's society to take their place among 'the cream of Beirut's merchant nobility'.[23]

The Sursocks were not alone. As Lewis Farley, an accountant from 1857 to 1858 at Beirut's newly opened Ottoman Bank and author of *Two Years in Syria*, reported: 'A few years ago, our principal merchants were foreigners, now they are natives; they now do all the exporting and importing business, and to them foreign ships come consigned.'[24] Though there was no shortage of foreign firms operating in Beirut, such as the British shipping and insurance group Henry Heald, who arrived in Beirut in 1837 and remain in business there today, the driving force was home-grown.

The Bustros family were fellow Greek Orthodox merchants, who enjoyed a similarly meteoric rise through M. Bustros and Nephews, a commercial and investment house with business in land, trade and finance, together with olive and mulberry plantations. Like the Sursocks they were agents, grain-traders and speculators, well connected with Ottoman officials and European consuls-general alike. Spitting distance from Sursock Palace, Bustros Palace is today the home of the Lebanese foreign ministry. Among the other Greek Orthodox merchant families were the Aramans, Boutroses, Bassouls, Fayads, Fianis, Fernainis, Jbeilis, Gedays, Trads and Tuénis (this chapter began with a line from the late Nadia Tuéni's poem 'Beyrouth'), all jostling for a place among the tantalizing, never-quite-agreed 'Seven Families of Beirut', which also has its Muslim equivalent.

The Greek Orthodox may have occupied the summit of Beirut's merchant class, but there was space for others to amass large fortunes. Among the leading Greek Catholics were the Medawar family from Mount Lebanon, who rose to prominence with a portfolio of landholdings, trading enterprises and financial interests, all assisted with consular protection from the French, together with the Pharaon and Zananiri families.

Like the city from which they sprang or in which they had settled, the Christian merchants were a smorgasbord of sects. There were the Maronite Malhamas and Khazens, feudal dynasts from the Mountain, and the Roman Catholic Abelas, businessmen and property owners *par excellence*, descendants of a Maltese doctor who had accompanied Napoleon to Acre.

Mercantile prosperity on a fantastic scale was by no means an exclusively Christian affair. In general, while Christian businessmen looked west for their fortunes, their Muslim counterparts, who had fewer European connections and less consular protection, looked east into the Syrian hinterland. Thus in the late 1840s, of the twenty-nine merchant houses in Beirut trading with England, only three were Muslim, a proportion that altered little for the rest of the century. By the first decade of the twentieth century, Muslim-owned silk exports represented less than 1 per cent of the total.

There were both established families, such as the feudal dynasties of the Shihabs, Barbirs and Bayhums, the Itanis and Aghars, and newer arrivals like the Anutis and Ayyases, Sarduqs and Salams, Ghandurs, Iraysis, Daouks, Yasins, Husamis, Tabbaras, Biqdashes and Bayduns, most of whom traded within a Muslim sphere encompassing Damascus, Baghdad, Egypt and the Ottoman Empire more widely. The Bayhums were merchant grandees with close connections to the Shihabi emirs, traditional rulers of Mount Lebanon, and owned enormous urban and rural estates, trading in agricultural products, notably spices, silks and cotton. As a rule, the richest Muslims were those who had thrown themselves whole-heartedly into Western trade, importing cheap European manufactures to sell on to the Syrian market.

Muslim or Christian, Sunni or Shia, Orthodox or Catholic, trade was the lifeblood of nineteenth-century Beirut. As the French consul remarked as early as 1827, Beirut was 'a republic of merchants who have their [own] strength and their [own] laws'.[25] Lebanon's highly entrepreneurial, risk-embracing merchants and traders are famous – sometimes infamous – throughout the Mediterranean and Middle East to this day.

Business success lifted Beirut's merchants to the commanding heights of society. If no one does conspicuous consumption quite like Beirutis today – in 2012 Beirut displaced Los Angeles as the plastic surgery capital of the world – the flashiness and flamboyance of the super-rich was, in the nineteenth century, literally set in stone. The Greek Orthodox triumvirate of Sursocks, Bustroses and Tuénis showed the way by building palaces in Achrafieh; the Sunni Muslim Daouks followed in Ras Beirut and the Greek Catholic Pharaons opted for Zuquq al Blat. Opulence was the defining theme, ostentation the guiding principle.

The taste for all things European meant houses with private gardens and windows facing outwards, a striking departure from the Muslim tradition of blank walls looking inwards onto a closed courtyard. The baroque met the neo-Gothic with a nod to the Moorish in an eclectic style that embraced interior marble columns, painted ceilings and furniture and furnishings that consciously aped the grandest houses of European aristocracy. Tables and chairs replaced cushions on the floor and separate bedrooms and dining rooms started to appear in earnest in the last quarter of the century. Mirrors, knives and forks became de rigueur and kaftans increasingly gave way to tailcoats. Even names were Europeanized: Sursuq became Sursock, Firaawn Pharaon, Frayj de Freige, Tuwayni Tuéni and so on. Christian names followed suit: Jirjis was now Georges, Butrus Pierre and Yusuf Joseph.[26]

By definition this gilded world of the very rich was not for everyone. The wrought-iron palace gates firmly excluded the poor, unkempt masses. In *Al Arwa al Mutamarrida* (*Spirits Rebellious*), his 1908 collection of short stories, the Lebanese-American poet and exile Kahlil Gibran cast a pitiless eye on what he considered a corrupt *al khassa* merchant elite. 'Look towards those fine dwellings and noble mansions, that is where the rich and the powerful of human kind are living . . . Between the walls hung with woven silk lives treachery with hypocrisy . . . and beneath ceilings of beaten gold stay lies and falseness.' For every fortune made, there was a corresponding tale of poverty and oppression. Sometimes this came violently to the surface in strikes and worker unrest, as at the port in 1903 in a dispute over the employment of porters, described venomously by the British consul-general as 'the scum and riffraff . . . of the Levant'.[27]

The pinnacle of Beirut's society may have looked west in their rush to make fortunes and affirm their status. The European influence in these quarters was certainly ubiquitous. Yet there were those, such as Michel Chiha (1891–1954), the indomitable Christian banker, politician, journalist and later father of the Lebanese constitution, who peered much further into history to identify the most ancient origins of the city's commercial vigour, which he considered indigenous to the core. He saw this booming merchant republic as the Phoenician city-state reborn. Like the port of Tyre, as described by the biblical prophet Ezekiel, Chiha's Beirut was

> The city that stands at the edge of the sea,
> And does business with people living on every seacoast . . .
> When your merchandise went overseas,
> You filled the needs of every nation;
> Kings were made rich by the wealth of your goods.[28]

At the burning height of summer, on 5 July 2013, Syrian protesters in Darayya, a suburb of Damascus, took to the streets to demonstrate against the Assad regime. They named this weekly protest 'The Friday of Awaken and Arise, O brigades'. It was a self-conscious tribute to the long poem composed in 1878 by Ibrahim al Yaziji, 'Awake, O Arabs, and arise!', which the Lebanese historian Fawwaz Traboulsi has called 'the rallying call for the early generations of Arab nationalists', a cry to rise up against the Ottoman Empire. Within two years of its first recital – it was too dangerous to publish such revolutionary verse openly – the poem appeared on the walls of Beirut and Damascus, causing a scandal which led both to the sacking of Midhat Pasha, governor of Syria, and the exile of its writer.[29]

For Beirut this was the time of the *nahda*, a profound cultural awakening or renaissance that challenged the traditional hold of religion, asserted a vigorous brand of secularism and, in the process, thrust Beirut to the forefront of Arab cultural life and made it the intellectual capital of the Arab world. Seeded in Cairo by the Egyptian scholar Rifaa Tahtawi, who founded a publishing house in 1821, infused with the ideals of the European Renaissance, the *nahda* 'was at once an era and an attitude'.[30] Money might have made the world go round, trade might have been an unalloyed good, but from their earliest days, long before they built some of the world's finest cities, the Arabs had revered their desert-forged culture and, in particular, the glories of the spoken and written word. Now, with new technology at their fingertips, intellectuals, writers and journalists in Beirut wasted no time in launching themselves into the tempestuous world of ideas.

Born in Beirut in 1847, Ibrahim al Yaziji, like his father Nasif al Yaziji (1800–1871), a fellow grammarian and translator, who helped liberate the Arabic language from its formal, classical constraints, was one of the brightest stars in the firmament of the *nahda*. He was a restless polymath, a translator of the Bible, who also published a dictionary of synonyms and works on medicine, music, art and astronomy. Apart from his controversial poem he is best remembered for creating the first Gregorian calendar in Arabic and inventing a simplified, typewriter-friendly font that reduced the number of Arabic characters from 300 to sixty, thereby enabling the rapid reproduction of texts.[31]

This was made possible by a publishing revolution every bit as remarkable as the explosion in Beirut's commercial life. Initially at least, there was a strong Christian impetus – the first publishing press, run by Greek Orthodox priests, came in 1751. The second came in 1843, courtesy of American missionaries from Malta. Newspapers suddenly appeared, and then multiplied with dizzying speed. The first, published in 1858, was *Hadiqat al Akhbar* (*Garden of News*), followed soon afterwards by *Al Haqiqa* (*The Truth*), *Nafir Suriya* (*The Clarion of Syria*), *Lisan al Hal* (*The Mouthpiece*), the Jesuits' *Al Bashir* (*The Herald*), *Thamarat al Funun* (*Fruits of the Arts*), the first Islamic newspaper and *Al Jinan*, *Al Janna* and *Al Junayna*, variations of the Arabic word for paradise. Within a few years Beirut could boast more newspapers, magazines and periodicals than any other city in the Arab world. As Baedeker reported, there were thirteen printing offices and twelve Arabic newspapers in 1894.[32] The old Arab saying 'Cairo writes, Beirut prints and Baghdad reads' obscured the greater truth that nineteenth-century Beirutis did all three with aplomb.

Here was Butrus al Bustani, nicknamed *Al Muaalim* ('The Master'), a Protestant convert, publisher, journalist, encyclopaedist, editor, educator, founder of the region's first secular institution, Al Madrasat al Wataniya (National School), and one of the earliest advocates of Syrian Arab nationalism. His watchword was emblazoned on his newspaper *Nafir Suriya*: 'Religion belongs to God, the country to everyone'. Then there were novelists like his son Salim al Bustani (1848–84) and Jurji Zaydan (1861–1914), perhaps none so contentious as Ahmed Faris al Shidyaq (1805–87), author of the heretical, genre-busting *Leg over Leg*, often considered the first novel in Arabic, a travelogue-cum-novel revelling in the richness of the Arabic language and a full-frontal assault on religious prudery with long lists of medieval Arabic euphemisms for the vagina ('the gripper', 'the sprayer', 'the large floppy one'), the penis ('the falcon's stand', 'the little man'), the anus ('the whistler', 'the catapult', 'the toothless one') and sex ('to stick the kohl-stick in her kohl pot'). In the spirit of the time, intellectual exploration transcended religious divides. There was the Druze emir Mohammed Arslan, who co-founded Al Jamiya al Ilmiya al Suriya (the Syrian Scientific Society) in 1857 and, in the wake of the 1860 tragedy on the Mountain, forsook politics entirely for literature. Among the most distinguished Muslim minds were the judge, author and sheikh Yusuf al Asir (1815–89), co-founder with Abdul Qadir Qabbani (1847–1935) of *Thamarat al Funun* and mastermind of a highly respected Arabic translation of the Bible.[33]

The *nahda* was given added impetus by the Syrian Protestant College, founded in 1866 on a vast swathe of land sprawling across virtually the entire northern promontory of Ras Beirut east of the Old City, where it remains to this day as the august campus of the American University of Beirut. This is no ordinary university. Those students lucky enough to win a place in AUB discover that even education in Beirut has its own glamour and extravagance. The sixty-one-acre campus contains athletic fields, a bird sanctuary, archaeological, geological and natural history museums, a publisher, an important collection of indigenous and non-native trees and plants and – because this is Beirut – a private beach across from the corniche. Its setting is borderline heavenly – Bliss Street, named after the Protestant missionary and founder of the college Daniel Bliss, runs immediately south of the campus and has a certain ring to it – and its intellectual record is no less starry. From its first graduates of 1870, its alumni have risen to the top of Lebanese social, political and commercial life. They also played a critical role in the modernization of the city, the first batch of medical students graduating in 1871. By 1889 it had educated fifteen pharmacists. Young doctors graduating from SPC and its Catholic counterpart, the Université Saint-Joseph, founded as the College of Jesuits in 1875, quickly took their professional places in a growing cohort of hospitals. The first was the Ottoman military hospital, established in 1846, followed by the German Johanniter Hospital in 1867 and the Greek Orthodox Saint George Hospital in 1878. By the time the French geographer Vital Cuinet reached Beirut in the early 1890s, he counted six hospitals, fifty medical practices and thirty pharmacies in the city – not to mention three casinos, two circuses, twenty-five hotels, thirty clockmakers, thirty bazaars, twenty-three police stations and, in recognition of Beirut's enduring love of shooting the breeze over a coffee and its passion for luxury and ostentation, fifty-five cafés and forty-five jewellers. By 1900 he might have added forty brothels to that list.[34]

Coffee drinkers, shoppers, *flâneurs* and pleasure-seekers of all shades were drawn irresistibly to Sahat al Burj, the serially renamed square to the east of the Old City walls that was the heart of Beirut's public life, a place for leisure, commerce and calculated forays into the sensual and downright seedy. It was a hubbub of hotels and cafés, music kiosks, businesses, shops, gambling joints, carriage companies, bars and brothels. Paradise for people-watchers, it was a more daunting prospect for the young Jurji Zaydan, who, while working as a bellhop for his father in the 1870s, was forced to run the gauntlet of derelicts and deviants, drunks, gamblers and prostitutes who roamed the rundown streets around the square. The Red Light district that from the late nineteenth century sprang up around the square on Mutanabbi Street, named after the tenth-century Iraqi poet, was later made famous – and notorious – by the extraordinary career of Marica Espiredone, who arrived penniless in Beirut in 1912 as an abused Greek orphan, became a prostitute and then the most beautiful, celebrated and rich *patrona*, or madam, in the city, owner of the legendary Marica establishment that employed a hundred girls who catered to the desires of the rich and famous during the 1940s and 50s. With its neon signs brazenly advertising each establishment's prize attractions – like Leila al Chacra the Blonde, French Antoinette or English Lucy – the Red Light district, known ironically as Suq al Awadem, Market of the Virtuous, lasted until its destruction in the early years of the 1975–90 civil war.[35]

While the Burj grew into 'a place of imperial and bourgeois ostentation', likened to some of the great public squares in Europe, the second main square in Beirut, scruffier, more popular and less structured by far, was Sahat al Sur, immediately south-west of the Old City. It was home to a new Ottoman telegraph office, the public *hammam* bath-house, the intersection of the main tramway lines, a cluster of cafés, swings, merry-go-rounds and, at dawn, crowds of hopeful labourers desperate for a day's work on a building site. It was converted to a public park in 1869, resplendent with an eight-metre-high white marble fountain in 1900, and today is Riad al Solh Square, named after the first and two-time prime minister of independent Lebanon (1943–5 and 1946–51). The two very different squares were connected, as the century came to a close, by the handsome, tree-lined, pavement-fringed boulevard of Rue Emir Bashir. As part of the Ottoman modernization of the city, the two main streets were widened dramatically from five and a quarter to fifteen metres in 1894.[36]

Perhaps the Ottomans were as disgusted by the confident march of European influence within the empire as Jurji Zaydan was by Beirut's dissolute and dispossessed. Their response was to fight back in the built environment with an architecture that emphasized imperial might and modernity. Under the guiding hand of the Ottomans, urban development and improvement – transport, infrastructure, street lighting, sanitation, entertainment – accelerated at breathtaking speed during the latter half of the century. A succession of monumental creations soared into the sky-line, starting in 1853 with the Qishla, later the Grand Sérail, the austere imperial barracks on Qantari Hill overlooking the city from the same place chosen by Ibrahim Pasha for his troops during the Egyptian occu-pation of Beirut from 1832. A faithful reflection of the Ottoman *Nizam-i Djedid*, or New Order, it was, and still remains, a vast edifice, with wings over eighty metres long, containing 430 rooms and 588 arches and arcades. Today, restored to full splendour and enlarged after the ravages it suffered during the civil war, it is home to the prime minister of Lebanon.

In 1856, the Imperial Ottoman Bank opened, adding commercial power and prestige to the military symbolism of the Qishla, initially from the imposing premises of the Antun Bey Inn, whose façade gave onto the water and had its own private dock. In 1863 the Saint Louis Cathedral, a Roman–Byzantine hybrid designed by the French architect Edmond Duthoit, staked the Capucin claim to a skyline already occupied by the Greek Orthodox and the Greek Catholics. The same year witnessed the completion of the road to Damascus by the concessionaire Compagnie Impériale Ottomane de la Route Beyrouth à Damas, headed by the French entrepreneur and long-time resident of Beirut, Comte Edmond de Perthuis. It slashed an expensive, difficult and dangerous journey of four days along a rough caravan path used by mules and donkeys – not to mention brigands – to a mere fourteen hours in a stagecoach.

To Ottoman imperial direction was added local architectural innov-ation. The trio of Yusuf Aftimos, Mardiros Altounian and Bechara Affendi became the founding fathers of Lebanese architecture. Commis-sioned by Ibrahim Fakhri Bey, the municipal president, and designed by Bechara Affendi, the elegant Petit Sérail on the northern side of the Burj, inaugurated as the seat of local government in 1884, was a playful burst of 'eclectic "Occidentalism"', its solid geometric structure lightened by a scrolling entrance gable, ornate vaults and miniature octagonal turrets protruding from diminutive battlements. It formed an elegant backdrop for promenaders in the Hamidiye public garden in the centre of the square, named in honour of Sultan Abdul Hamid II, whose reign from 1876 to 1909 brought new schools, hospitals, police stations, drinking fountains and an Ottoman post office. A city landmark that housed a succession of Lebanese presidents from the 1920s, the Petit Sérail fell victim to develop-ers in 1950 – an increasingly insistent theme in free-for-all Beirut – when it was demolished to make way for the Cinema Rivoli, itself demolished in the post-civil-war reconstruction of the 1990s.[37]

The Ottoman-led modernization of Beirut, which introduced town planning for the first time, went far beyond the symbolic and aesthetic.

The port, engine room of the city's prosperity, was comprehensively modernized and enlarged from 1889 to 1894 with a new quay, jetty and warehouses. The Compagnie Impériale Ottomane du Port, des Quais et des Entrepôts de Beyrouth managed the work under the energetic stewardship once again of Comte de Perthuis and his partner Salim Melhame, encouraged by Beirut's large merchant tribe. The razing of what remained of the city walls and the old Crusader fort was the price to pay for commercial expansion.

The pace of development in late nineteenth-century Beirut was so fast and furious that many Beirutis lost their sense of time. The situation was not helped by the complete absence of clocks telling the time for Muslims. As the governor-general wrote in a pleading letter 'To His Exalted Court Chamberlain' in 1897, a number of foreign institutions had clocktowers with bells, each with a Western clock, yet 'Because there is no public clock which shows the mandatory Muslim (prayer) times Muslims, even officials and (other) civil servants have regrettably had to adapt to the time of foreign clocks.'[38] If the Syrian Protestant College could have its own clocktower, never mind the Maronites, the Jesuits and the French hospital, what about the faithful? The answer, designed by Yusuf Aftimos, was the Ottoman Clocktower, the Big Ben of Beirut, a twenty-five-metre triumph of verticality that towered over every other building, with two faces of Arabic numerals and two of Latin. Just as its architectural style blended Ottoman with the Gothic and neo-Orientalist, its composition was a mix of Jounieh limestone, Beiruti sandstone, Damascene basalt and Dair al Qamar red stone. Like the Grand Sérail it stood next to, the clocktower was visible for miles from sea and shore alike.

Beirut was buzzing. In 1888, following petitions and protests, it became the capital of the newly created *vilayet* of Beirut, an indication of its irrepressible economic growth and importance. A year later, it had a lighthouse, whose history over the subsequent century revealed the classic tension in Beirut between the competing needs of public architecture and private development and, in this case, ended in the monument's complete eclipse by a phalanx of high-rise apartment buildings in the mid-1990s. New additions to the cityscape of Beirut multiplied with breakneck speed as the nineteenth century closed. In 1893 a new racecourse opened. In 1895 the train station arrived.

On the morning of 5 November 1898, the German royal yacht *Hohenzollern* anchored in the port of Beirut. Crowds of cheering, flag-waving schoolchildren lined the shore. At the landing place, beneath flagpoles and leaf garlands, a sumptuous pavilion had been erected, beside which Beirut's leaders had assembled in full state uniform to greet the imperial couple, the bewhiskered Kaiser Wilhelm II and his wife Augusta Victoria, the last German emperor and empress, the last king and queen of Prussia. After a train journey to Damascus, past Maronite villagers perched on rocky ledges waving palms and flowers, and a visit to the ruins at Baalbek, the couple returned to Beirut, through which the Kaiser paraded on horseback with his wife in a carriage beside him, surrounded by Turkish generals and uproarious crowds in a triumphant reception. The official account of the visit notes that 'the cheers, the joy and the grateful farewells exceeded the limits of imagination'. Beirut, the Kaiser was moved to pronounce, was 'the jewel in the crown of the *padisha*' (the name for the Ottoman sultan).[39]

For a city that owed its meteoric rise to trade, whose people would, in the decades ahead, be renowned around the world for their devil-may-care consumption, love of the good life and flamboyance even in the face of tragedy, there was something perfectly fitting about the arrival, in 1900, of the elegant department store Orosdi Back, 'the Harrods of the East'. What better way to open the twentieth century – on 1 September 1900, to mark Sultan Abdul Hamid's silver jubilee no less – than with this resplendent, triple-domed temple to consumerism, principal exhibit in an ambitious gentrification project on a landfill site where the quay met the port's warehouses and customs offices on Rue de la Douane? Behind the two sea-facing façades of tall windows, pilasters, pediments, corbels, shell niches, statues, more balustraded windows, Ottoman stars and turrets, impeccably uniformed doormen would swing open gleaming, brass-handled glass doors and welcome customers into the store, where a dash of French perfume would set shoppers' pulses racing. Little wonder that Beirut's new emporium, which wowed customers with an in-store lift and telephone and offered the latest treasures from Bally shoes and cashmere jumpers to fine bone china, sterling silver cutlery and silk eiderdowns, routinely outperformed its counterparts in Tunis, Alexandria, Cairo and Aleppo.

My father was born in Beirut in 1938 to an Italian father and Prussian mother. Fleeing the war that was coming in Europe, they had first sought refuge there, before moving on to Cairo, Jerusalem and Damascus. Though he had never known it well as a child, Beirut still occupied a special place in the memory of my father. He returned there frequently for business over the years and later seemed to suffer at an exile's remove the pain of the 1975–90 civil war that killed an estimated 120,000 and reduced the city of his birth, one of the world's most beautiful but delicate, to rubble. Like Beirut itself, he was a cosmopolitan. His grandmother, I discovered while researching this chapter, was a Lebanese Maronite from the mountain town of Jezzine, twenty-five miles south of Beirut.

Years ago, on my first visit to the city, I wandered across Sahat al Shuhada, Martyrs' Square, as the Burj had been named from 1931 in honour of the fifteen nationalists executed there by Jamal Pasha Al Jazzar ('The Butcher'), the Ottoman governor of Syria, on 6 May 1916. Soullessness seemed to have descended on downtown Beirut. Streets were spotless. Buildings glittered and gleamed. Shops sparkled. Order – perhaps too much – had been restored by Solidere, the development behemoth founded and part-owned by the late president and billionaire Rafik Hariri. At one level this risen-from-the-ashes Beirut was an inspiring triumph of urban renewal, consigning the destruction of the war to history in the world's largest reconstruction of a city. As nineteenth-century French geographer Élisée Reclus wrote of Beirut, 'This city is one of those that must live and relive, come what may. The conquerors pass on and the city is reborn behind them.'[40] Yet in their annihilating *tabula rasa* reinvention of Beirut after the devastation wrought by the civil war warriors, the corporate developers had sucked the life out of the place. Bustling *suqs* had become air-conditioned malls. The old, French-inspired idiom of sandstone façades, red-tiled roofs and arcaded streets had reappeared in saccharine pastiche.

During the civil war, Martyrs' Square had been the demarcation line that slashed the city in two. This, wrote the poet Nadia Tuéni, was a 'city heated white hot by the word'.[41] Passions had calmed since that bitter conflict, but feelings still ran high over Solidere's redevelopment of 455 acres (1.8 million square metres) of downtown Beirut, the entire footprint of the city up to 1830. They still do.

Solidere is a new sectarianism. Among its defenders it counts the veteran Lebanese sociologist Samir Khalaf, doyen of the American University of Beirut and historian of his beloved city. Critical of his countrymen's 'very casual, often abusive' attitude to their built environment, Khalaf accuses the Lebanese of having 'a built-in cultural aversion for any maintenance or special regard for upgrading the quality of their living space'. Solidere's work, he maintains, is 'a byword for high-quality restoration and reconstruction'. Its many detractors, however, consider it a corrupt, empty and intensely commercial reordering of the cityscape, describing it variously as 'prosthetic history', 'fake', 'a dead city', 'Disneyland', 'a fairytale', 'a surrender to international capital', 'a form of vigilantism', a never-never land somewhere 'between amnesia and nostalgia'. For the Lebanese architect and city planner Assem Salaam, 'more irreparable damage has been done to the centre of Beirut by those who claim to be interested in salvaging and rebuilding it than had been done during the course of the preceding fifteen years of shelling and house-to-house combat'. Fady al Khoury, the owner of the Saint George Hotel, who has been embroiled in a two-decade legal fight against Solidere, calls it 'the robbery of the century. They have illegally seized the city from the people who own it, and put back an empty maquette of Beirut without any of the people. What they have done to the city is apocalyptic.'[42]

The genius of Beirut from the nineteenth century was to draw upon the widest architectural vocabulary, from Ottoman arcades, Venetian arches and Genoese corbels to Islamic friezes and French Mandate portals, fashioning from this eclectic mix a harmonious, uniquely Levantine urban text. This was made possible only by Beirut's corresponding talent, its ability to bring together a mixed population of different faiths, sects and people into a greater, more or less peacefully coexisting, whole. Cosmo-politanism today is official policy in Lebanon under a constitution which recognizes eighteen distinct groups.*

The darker side of Beirut's story, the reverse face of that shining cosmo-politan mirror, is a murky tangle of sectarianism and competing national identities, a tussle over what it means to be Lebanese in the shadow of larger, more powerful Syria. These inherent divisions did not disappear on the conclusion of the civil war in 1990. The stories of three of the people mentioned in this chapter bear tragic witness to their enduring role in the history of Beirut.

On Valentine's Day 2005, former prime minister Rafik Hariri was killed by a massive car bomb as his motorcade was driving past the Saint George Hotel. The assassination ignited what the Lebanese called *Inti-fadat al Istiqlal* (Independence Uprising), better known in the West as the Cedar Revolution. A month later, Nadia Tuéni's son Gebran, a leading journalist and politician, addressed a jubilant crowd of around 1 million, a quarter of the country's population, who in the latest instalment of that uprising had crammed into the deeply symbolic Martyrs' Square waving the red and white flags of Lebanon. 'In the name of God, we, Muslims and Christians, pledge that we shall remain united to the end of time to better defend our Lebanon,' he cried.[43] On 12 December he was assassin-ated in another car bombing.

At 10.30 on the morning of 2 June 2005, Samir Kassir got into his Alfa Romeo, started the engine and was instantly killed by a huge bomb planted

---

* The eighteen groups consist of four Muslim sects (Sunni, Shia, Alawi and Druze); thirteen Christian sects (Assyrian, Syriac Catholic, Syriac Orthodox, Chaldean, Maronite, Roman Catholic, Greek Catholic, Greek Orthodox, Armenian Orthodox, Armenian Catholic, evan-gelical, Coptic and smaller Christian sects); and Jews.

under his car. He had yet to finalize the corrections to his fine history of Beirut, the city which had made him and which, through its interlinked antagonisms, had also destroyed him. No arrests were made in the aftermath of this flurry of political murders, which were almost universally attributed to Syria. Beirut is sun-kissed, sybaritic and welcoming, but it is also dangerous, blood-stained and cruel.

Beirut soared resplendent from the second half of the nineteenth century and continued its reckless money-making and revelries deep into the twentieth. The Saint George Hotel rocked to parties attended by everyone from the Aga Khan and Brigitte Bardot to David Rockefeller and the British spy Kim Philby in the 1950s and 60s, while the rival Phoenicia Hotel, a two-minute drive down Fakhreddine, played host to celebrities such as Marlon Brando, Umm Kulthum, Fairuz and Catherine Deneuve. The agonies of the civil war of 1975–90 pulled the curtain down on all that fun.

The twentieth century brought shattering, end-of-Islamic-Empire changes to the wider Arab world. In 1916, the Sykes–Picot Agreement brazenly drew a line across the Ottoman Middle East 'from the "e" in Acre to the last "k" in Kirkuk', north of which was given over to French influence and control, south of which to the British. Empires were now Christian, not Islamic.

Further degradations and disappointments were to follow. After the devastation of the Second World War, which tore apart swathes of North Africa and the Middle East, much of the region fell in thrall to the siren promises of Arab nationalism, Arab socialism, pan-Arabism and Nasserism. All proved tragically inadequate to the demands of the times and the needs of the people. Repressive dictatorships were the order of the day.

Yet for one city in the Arab world above all others, the twentieth century brought fame and riches so unexpected and untold that they made those of Beirut look almost modest by comparison. It was an achievement all the more remarkable for the fact that before the turn of the century the city had barely even existed.

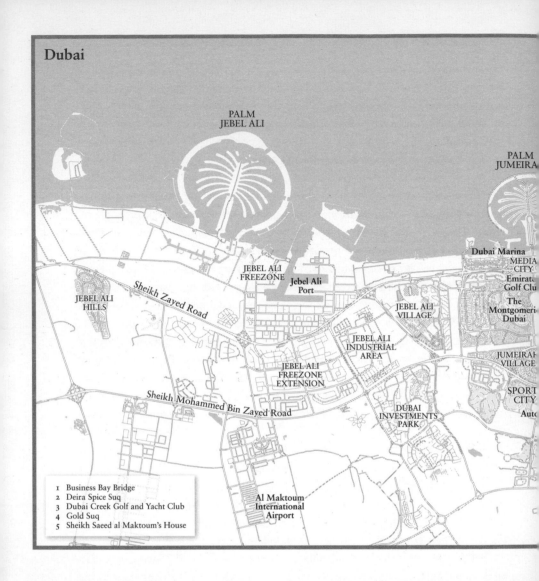

Dubai

PALM
JEBEL ALI

PALM
JUMEIRA

Dubai Marina

MEDIA
CITY

Emirat
Golf Clu

The
Montgomeri
Dubai

JEBEL ALI
FREEZONE

Jebel Ali
Port

JEBEL ALI
HILLS

Sheikh Zayed Road

JEBEL ALI
VILLAGE

JUMEIRA
VILLAGE

JEBEL ALI
INDUSTRIAL
AREA

SPORT
CITY

Auto

JEBEL ALI
FREEZONE
EXTENSION

Sheikh Mohammed Bin Zayed Road

DUBAI
INVESTMENTS
PARK

1 Business Bay Bridge
2 Deira Spice Suq
3 Dubai Creek Golf and Yacht Club
4 Gold Suq
5 Sheikh Saeed al Maktoum's House

Al Maktoum
International
Airport

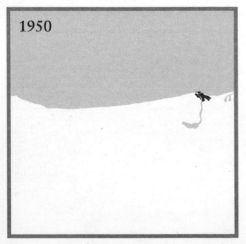

1950

1972

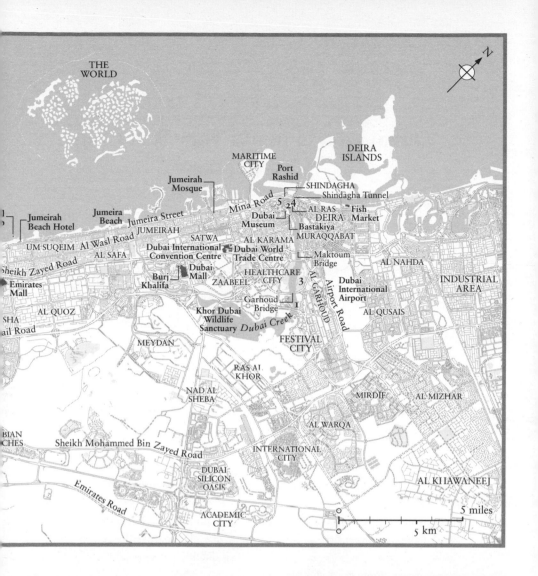

THE WORLD

DEIRA ISLANDS

MARITIME CITY

Jumeirah Mosque

Port Rashid

SHINDAGHA
Shindagha Tunnel

Mina Road

5 2 4

AL RAS   Fish Market

DEIRA

Jumeira Beach

Jumeira Street

Dubai Museum

Bastakiya

Jumeira Beach Hotel

JUMEIRAH

MURAQQABAT

UM SUQEIM   Al Wasl Road

SATWA

AL KARAMA

AL NAHDA

AL SAFA

Dubai International Convention Centre

Dubai World Trade Centre

Maktoum Bridge

heikh Zayed Road

INDUSTRIAL AREA

Emirates Mall

Burj Khalifa

Dubai Mall

ZAABEEL

HEALTHCARE CITY

3

Dubai International Airport

SHA

ail Road

AL QUOZ

Garhoud Bridge

1

AL GARHOUD

Airport Road

AL QUSAIS

Khor Dubai Wildlife Sanctuary

Dubai Creek

FESTIVAL CITY

MEYDAN

RAS AL KHOR

BIAN CHES

NAD AL SHEBA

MIRDIF

AL MIZHAR

Sheikh Mohammed Bin Zayed Road

AL WARQA

INTERNATIONAL CITY

Emirates Road

DUBAI SILICON OASIS

AL KHAWANEEJ

5 miles

5 km

ACADEMIC CITY

1994

2019

14

Dubai – Build It and They Will Come
(20th Century)

What's good for the merchants is good for Dubai.

Sheikh Rashid bin Said al Maktoum

It started with a pearl. Sometime more than 7,000 years ago – the dates are as murky as the limpid waters of the Arabian Gulf are clear – a luck-chancing diver dropped to the seabed, scooped up a cluster of oyster shells and, lungs bursting, rushed back to the surface coughing and spluttering for air. Somewhere in his catch, once the shells had been prised open, was the world's first lustrous pearl.

While our nameless Stone Age diver could have no inkling how life-changing his discovery would prove for the inhabitants of the Gulf Coast and far beyond for the next seventy-three centuries – the much later fortunes that would be made, the shattering drudge he had inspired for future generations of pearl divers, the numbers of rich, beautiful women around the world whose necks would be garlanded with these iridescent ocean stones – the pearl trade had begun.*

Over time pearls in this region likely became an integral part of one of the world's earliest recorded long-distance maritime trading networks as the Neolithic inhabitants of eastern Arabia did business with the south-ernmost villages of Mesopotamia.[1] There is a tantalizing reference to what sounds very much like pearl diving, or at least its techniques, in *The Epic of Gilgamesh*, often considered the world's first great literary work with its origins in the third millennium BC. Here the eponymous mythical hero from Mesopotamia descends to the watery depths on the trail of the elusive Flower of Immortality:

---

* The earliest pearl known to have been used in jewellery, pierced through its centre, was discovered in northern Kuwait and has been dated to around 5,300 BC.

Heavy stones he tied to his feet,
And they pulled him down to the Ocean below.[2]

Difficult though it is to imagine in the desert furnace of our time, swathes of Stone Age Arabia were then home to wet grasslands where nomadic herders and fishing communities moved their sheep, cattle and goats from one grazing spot to the next. Over the millennia the climate, and the landscape it sculpted beneath the fiery Arabian sun, became more punishing. Fishing and pearl fishing became the main sources of income for these isolated coastal populations. The years and the centuries rolled by, yet the way of life remained broadly the same. It was a tough, spirit-shattering existence, scratched out in an inhospitable patch of land caught in a vice between the rasping *simoom* (poison wind) of the desert and the skin-cracking ocean. Men and women gave birth to new generations, from which those who survived into adulthood continued their toil, gave thanks to their God, died and were buried in shallow graves beneath the sands. This was the rhythm of life.

For most of these past seven millennia there was little to differentiate one coastal settlement from the next. Yet it was surely only fitting, given this region's history, that the ancient quest for pearls lay behind the first reference to Dubai, which came in 1590 at the hands – and pen – of Gasparo Balbi, the Venetian state jeweller, merchant and traveller. *Viaggio dell'Indie Orientali*, the long-winded account of his journey across the Middle East and India in the 1580s, may have been as dry as the desert, but it included 'Dibai' in a list of places where the best, biggest and most beautiful pearls could be found.[3]

Balbi also helpfully set out the mechanics and techniques of pearl fishing. He described how temporary settlements of tents and straw huts sprang up along the coast opposite those sites at sea which were considered most auspicious for finding oysters. Protected by a handful of armed ships, the pearl-fishing fleet anchored in sixteen to eighteen fathoms (twenty-nine to thirty-three metres) of water and dropped several stone-weighted ropes to the sea floor. Divers with horn pincers to keep their noses closed and ears greased with oil to resist the water pressure then followed the ropes down, filled their bags or baskets with oysters and, when they were ready to come up, gave a sharp tug on the rope to be pulled back to the surface. 'If they do not do it quickly,' Balbi explained, 'they will die, which has often happened.' Diving continued until the evening, when the exhausted crews returned to the coast with their hauls. The oysters were opened later, when 'dead and almost rotten' to make the job easier, and the pearls were then classified into four grades using copper sieves. The Portuguese favoured the most round pearls, while the more irregular and less perfectly spherical stones were destined for Bengal and Kanara in eastern and south-western India respectively, with the 'meanest and smallest' pearls going to Gujarat once merchants had arrived to buy them 'at a known price'.[4] With a few variations, not least the demise of the requirement to pay the Portuguese king for the right to fish for pearls here, this was the essence of the Gulf Coast pearl trade.

From Portuguese military and commercial influence and control in the Gulf in the sixteenth and seventeenth centuries – Hormuz was occupied in 1515 and the Portuguese were displaced by an Anglo-Persian force only in 1622, encouraged by the Safavid ruler Shah Abbas – the colonial baton was passed on to the British, who increased their regional power during the eighteenth century before consolidating it decisively in the nineteenth.

After Balbi's one-word mention in 1590, we hear little or nothing from Dubai until 1822, when Lieutenant Cogan and a couple of his fellow offi-cers of the Bombay Marine, the East India Company's naval force, compiled a 'Trigonometrical Plan of the Back-water of Debai'. Cogan and his col-leagues, faithful servants of the British Empire, whose nautical chart eloquently demonstrated their countrymen's enduring mania for measure-ment, especially when it came to matters of trade, made a meticulous series of soundings off the coast and inland. They were more interested in the 'back-water', that is Khor Dubai or Dubai Creek, than the settlement itself, which was a genuine backwater in the more common meaning of the word. Looking at this painstakingly sketched chart almost 200 years later, what strikes you first is its artless beauty. West of the bold rows of numbers marking the sea depths and inland from a protective peninsula and sand-bank that loop south like a witch's nose, 'Debai' – also delineated in the Arabic دبي – is a tiny, entirely unremarkable cluster of twenty-five buildings clinging to the western bank of the Creek behind a 'C'-shaped mud wall. It is so small, in fact, that just four topographical features suffice to describe it: the 'Sheik's house', a watchtower at the north-eastern tip of the settle-ment and two gates, to the north-west and south-west. Two plantations of slim-trunked date palms and 'wells of fresh water' lie within easy striking distance of the village in the desert to the west. The population of this obscure little fishing community, dependent on the sheikhdom of Abu Dhabi around ninety miles south-west along the coast, hovered around 1,000 souls. That, in summary, was early nineteenth-century Dubai.[5]

Cogan's map was no idle sketch. It was graphic testament to Britain's growing assertion in the Gulf and its determination to stamp out what it saw as an unacceptable threat to its shipping from this dangerous 'Pirate

Coast', above all from the Qawasim ruling family of Sharjah.* In 1819 Britain decided on punitive action in high imperial fashion, dispatching the largest naval force ever sent to the Gulf. In a nineteenth-century antici- pation of American shock-and-awe, it then laid waste to the Qawasim fleet and reduced forts and ports for sixty miles all along the coast – from Al Rams in Ras al Khaimah to Sharjah – to smouldering ruins. Within a few days the coastal sheikhs were suing for peace. Starting in 1820, Britain concluded a series of treaties with the principal sheikhs of the coast to protect its vessels from attack. In 1835, in return for the cessation of all hostilities at sea, including fights between the various tribes, Britain agreed to assume responsibility for the defence of what became known as the Trucial States (those which had agreed a truce) in a treaty that included the sheikhs of Abu Dhabi, Dubai and Ajman and the Qawasim rulers of Sharjah, Ras al Khaimah and – across the water on the Iranian side – Lingah. Similar arrangements were reached with Oman (1829), Bahrain (1861), Kuwait (1899) and Qatar (1916).

Perspectives today inevitably tend to differ markedly between those, especially British writers, who have emphasized the active solicitation by Gulf sheikhs of British protection and those, especially Arab historians, who regard these treaties, and the resulting Pax Britannica they brought, as imposed from above.[6] Benefiting from peace on the high seas, which was a boon to pearling and wider trade, the ruling sheikhs reaffirmed the treaties annually until the Perpetual Maritime Truce of 1853. One might argue that, facing overwhelming British military power in case they demurred, they had little alternative. The treaties were overseen by the British Political Resident, based in Bushir until 1936, thereafter in Bah- rain, a senior post so important that Lord Curzon called its holder 'the uncrowned king of the Gulf'.[7] In 1892 the Trucial States of Abu Dhabi, Dubai, Sharjah, Ajman, Ras al Khaimah and Umm al Quwain agreed to cede complete control of their foreign relations to the British crown in return for guarantees of protection.

British power was a two-sided coin. It brought stability to the Gulf, allowing the development of seven increasingly robust monarchies that would join together in the later twentieth century to form the United Arab Emirates (UAE), a peaceful and progressive country by comparison with its Middle Eastern neighbours, whom it has long since galloped past. Yet it also 'ossified the region', doing little to encourage liberalizing reforms

* This British version of history has long been forcefully refuted by Sharjah, whose current ruler, Sultan bin Mohammed al Qasimi, has written energetically on the subject. His books include *The Myth of Arab Piracy in the Gulf* and *Under the Flag of Occupation*.

in health, education and politics. 'Overweening British agents treated Arab leaders like children,' argues a recent American history of Dubai that accuses Britain of bullying and 'bombardment diplomacy'.[8] Whichever view one takes of Britain's formal relationship with the Gulf sheikhdoms, it was long-lived and survived intact until independence arrived abruptly in 1971.

The greatest period in the history of Dubai was to come in the twentieth century in what was arguably one of the most spectacular urban transformations ever witnessed anywhere on earth. It was made possible, however, only by a critical development much earlier. In 1833, a decade after Lieutenant Cogan and his fellow Bombay Marine officers had bobbed around on the surface of Dubai Creek taking their soundings, and in the immediate aftermath of the bloody suppression of two attempted rebellions against Sheikh Khalifa bin Shakhbut Al Nahyan of Abu Dhabi, around 800 tribesmen and women led by warriors from the Al Bu Falasah subsection of the Bani Yas tribe seceded from the sheikhdom, rode across the desert and settled in Dubai, hitherto dependent on Abu Dhabi, on the Shindagha Peninsula at the mouth of the Creek.* The leaders of this exodus were Ubaid bin Said, who died shortly afterwards in 1836, and his nephew Maktoum bin Buti, who became sole ruler from that time until his death in 1852, by which time Sheikh Khalifa had formally accepted the bitter reality of Dubai's secession. The Al Maktoum Dynasty of rulers, which has led Dubai ever since, was born.

Poised between larger, more powerful and frequently antagonistic neighbours – particularly the Al Nahyan Dynasty of Abu Dhabi and the Qawasim, or Al Qasimi family, whose territory included Ras al Khaimah and Sharjah – the Maktoums opted for neutrality and regional balance, a policy that encouraged stability and quickly attracted traders to its shores. We know from Sheikh Maktoum bin Muti that shortly after he took power there were more than forty shops and one hundred traders in the *suq* of Dubai. By the 1880s, foreign visitors noted, although Abu Dhabi

---

* Shindagha became something of a Maktoum family enclave from the late nineteenth century. Overlooking the entrance to the Creek, the source of Dubai's growing prosperity, it had an obvious strategic attraction for the ruling family, who could keep a beady eye on all the dhows coming and going. Restored from ruins in 1986 and converted into a museum, Sheikh Said's vast, 2,000-square-metre house, oriented towards Mecca, with four wings and four *barjeel* wind towers, gives an enduring sense of Dubai's growing prosperity in the first half of the twentieth century. In the words of the government, it provides 'testimony to the will of a nation overcoming with ingenuity the harsh environment to achieve what very few have achieved'.

remained politically and militarily pre-eminent, Dubai was already 'the principal commercial port on the Gulf coast'.[9]

Under Maktoum's grandson Sheikh Maktoum bin Hasher al Maktoum (r. 1894–1906), Dubai started motoring ahead, fuelled by what would henceforth become the family's quintessential – and independent – economic policy: light-touch, tax-free and trade-friendly. No questions asked. He began bullishly in 1894 by granting tax exemption to foreign traders and proceeded to tear down other trade barriers, stripping away customs fees and the requirement for ships to have licences. The results were immediate. The pearl-fishing sector and trade more broadly flourished, quickly attracting new waves of Gulf merchants so that, by the turn of the twentieth century, Dubai had swelled to a town of 10,000, living in three main quarters: Shindagha to the north of the Creek; Dubai to the west as the focal point, with a large and growing Indian population centred around Al Fahidi Fort and several places at which boats could be unloaded; and Deira on the east, the largest section of town, home to a mixed, polyglot community of Arabs, Iranians and Baluchis with 1,600 houses and 350 shops.* All in, Dubai was a modest but expanding settlement of simple, palm-frond *arish* or *barasti* houses stretching around 3,000 metres by 1,000.

The 1900s saw Dubai emerging confidently as 'a growing multinational, sea-oriented pearling and trading community' in the words of one of the foremost historians of the UAE.[10] In 1902, as Iran moved to increase taxes at the port of Lingah, home to a considerable population of Sunni Arab traders, Sheikh Maktoum sent a powerful signal to the region's merchants by doing precisely the opposite, abolishing customs duties on all imports. It had the desired effect. Lingah's traders voted with their feet, boarded their ships, sailed across the Gulf and made their homes in Dubai – initially temporarily, soon enough permanently when they realized there was no prospect of Tehran improving the business environment. Indian goods flooded into Dubai, which rapidly became the Gulf's centre for re-exporting. The boundary between legal trade and illegal smuggling was blurred from the start. 'When I was young the dhows took smuggled goods to India,' says Arif Sayed al Kazim of Dubai Financial Services Authority (one suspects they still do).[11] Everyone knew what was

---

* Built in 1787, Al Fahidi Fort is the oldest surviving building in Dubai and once served as the original residence of Maktoum bin Buti, founder of the ruling dynasty. In the shadow of the city-state's high-rise towers and a stone's throw from the Creek-side Ruler's Court, today its buff-coloured fortifications, trio of towers and motley collection of cannons are a diminutive, evocative and increasingly elusive reminder of the city's past.

going on, but the Maktoums were not going to be difficult. They had a
city to build.

We get another glimpse into both Dubai's commercial thrust and the
British Empire's statistical zeal in the two-volume, 5,000-page form of
John Gordon Lorimer's *Gazetteer of the Persian Gulf, Oman and Central
Arabia*, published in 1908 and 1915. This soberly records, among many
other details, that Dubai had the largest number of men employed in
pearling on the Gulf Coast (6,936) and was second only to Abu Dhabi in
the size of its pearling fleet (335 boats to Abu Dhabi's 410) and in the tax
revenues levied by its ruler (41,388 rupees to Abu Dhabi's 43,964 rupees).
With a population of 45,000, the largest of the Trucial States by far was
Sharjah (which then included the future independent emirates of Fujairah
and Ras al Khaimah), ahead of Abu Dhabi (11,000) and Dubai (10,000).[12]

In Lorimer's summary description of 'Dibai', two other comments
stand out. First, he refers to the 'shallow and difficult entrance' of the
Creek, a fundamental constraint which would bring about one of the
greatest, make-or-break gambles in Dubai's history half a century later.
Second, he acknowledges the 'considerable' and 'rapidly expanding' trade
of the town, which he attributed to the 'enlightened' policy of the recently
deceased Sheikh Maktoum. More than a century later, the Maktoum
family continues to define Dubai as *the* trade-friendly place in which the
world can do business. So much so that the current ruler, Sheikh Mohammed bin Rashid al Maktoum (r. 2006–), even coined the phrase 'Dubai
Inc.' to describe the city-state's business empire, which the American
business magazine *Forbes* hailed as 'one of the most extraordinary success
stories in global investment and development'.[13]

But we are getting ahead of ourselves. Long before Dubai embarked
upon its global buying spree, it depended for what limited prosperity it
had on the pearl trade. Ancient in origin, this reached its zenith in the
early twentieth century, peaking around 1912 before coming to a swift
and, for many, catastrophic end in the early 1950s.

Although this highly specialized trade already belongs to a bygone era,
it nevertheless dominated life in Dubai within living memory. In a recent
oral history, the pearl diver Bilal Khamis recalled his career in terms that
serve as a grim reminder that, though romantic in the imagination, the
pearl trade was often a living hell on the sea. In boats carrying up to sixty
people, divers would spend three to four months away from their families
at sea in the height of summer, testing human endurance to the very limit.

Rations were meagre, conditions spartan. Fish, rice and dates. A few
drops of coffee in the morning and so little water that 'we felt thirsty for
the whole day'. Diving lasted from morning to evening, divers treading

water on the surface for a few precious minutes to recover between dives before breathing in deeply for a minute and then embarking on another – and another, and another – heart-pumping, lung-bursting descent in waters up to fifteen metres deep. More than 300 years since Balbi's description of pearl diving, little had changed. Divers wore a *fatam* or nose plug to keep water out, a *diyyin* palm-rope basket around the neck to load the oysters and stone or zinc weights around the ankles. Some wore leather finger-guards and a cotton body suit to protect against jellyfish. It was gruelling work.

Exhaustion was no excuse not to continue. 'We knew we had to go down again. Some of the *nokhadas* [representatives of the financiers of the expedition] would beat the people if they didn't go down because the captains had spent a lot of money going diving and they had to bring pearls back. The divers couldn't do anything – they had debts with the captains. They never said no. They had to dive.'

After months at sea with no freshwater for washing, the divers' skin grew rough, cracked and painful. At night, completely shattered, they flopped onto crude mats of date palm leaves thrown across uncomfortable piles of living shells. Fear haunted their waking hours. 'When we were under the water we could see jellyfish or a shark coming near, but we wanted to eat. We were diving for money, for food – to live. It was life.' Jumaa al Batishi, another pearl diver, gave a similarly baleful verdict on the trade. 'Diving was a piece of hell,' he said of his underwater tribulations more than half a century ago. 'It was hard work and very, very tough and difficult. It wasn't a trip.'

Pearling had a language all of its own. In colloquial Gulf Arabic the pearl is *lulu*, *dana*, *hussah*, *gumashah* and *hasbah*. There were names to describe pearls of all shapes, sizes and colours: the pear-shaped *sujani*, the *khaizi* with an elongated upper half and semi-spherical bottom, the pink *sindaali*, the yellow *sofri* and the most prized black pearl of all, the *sinjabassi*. Most mysterious of the lot was the *majhoolah*, an ugly large pearl, which very occasionally contained within it a smaller perfect stone.

Once the sore-limbed divers had been hauled out of the tepid waters and unloaded their piles of oysters onto the deck, the shells were later prised open and the pearls removed under the vigilant eyes of men stationed there expressly to discourage light fingers. They were then graded into seven classes from the most precious *jiwan*, to *yakka*, *golwa*, *badlah*, *khashar*, *nawaem* and *bouka*.* The best and most prized *jiwan* pearls

---

* *Jiwan*, from G-one or Grade One. This is also said to be a corruption of the Persian or Farsi word *jawan*, meaning young or premature.

were rose-tinted white, perfectly round, with an impeccable surface showing off a radiant lustre. With these valuable, infinitely concealable items
on board, it is hardly surprising that stealing, despite the precautions,
was not uncommon and the *nokhadas* kept the treasured pearls in a
wooden box with them at all times. 'He would sleep on that box,' Bilal
remembered.[14]

Flush with the profits of the booming pearl trade, Dubai grew richer
and bigger in the 1920s. In 1925 the insular and ineffective government
in Tehran imposed more swingeing import and export restrictions,
prompting those traders from Lingah who earlier had settled in Dubai
temporarily to take advantage of the offer of permanent residence from
Sheikh Said al Maktoum (r. 1912–58) and bring in their families. Another
wave of merchants came from across the water, many from Bastak in the
southern Iranian province of Fars. They were given land on which to build
their homes immediately east of Al Fahidi Fort, conveniently close to the
Creek, where their boats could be loaded and unloaded, giving rise to the
new district of Bastakiya, which is home to the few historical buildings
that have escaped the bulldozers in Dubai. Today, though the restoration
can feel overdone, it retains vestiges of an old-world charm, with its narrow, winding streets, low buildings and traditional architecture.

Apart from bringing a worldly commercialism to Dubai, with their
extensive trading networks across Africa and Asia, the Iranian immigrants
also brought a new architecture with them, which represented a dramatic
and effective upgrade from the rudimentary *arish* houses. Soaring as much
as fifteen metres from ground level, *barjeel* wind towers started to thrust
themselves boldly into the new district's skyline, precursors of the modern
skyscrapers which would alter Dubai beyond recognition within just a
few decades. Built on foundations of Iranian red clay and manure from
stone, gypsum, limestone, teak, sandalwood, chandel wood, palm fronds
and trunks, they had four concave faces, often decorated with elaborate
pillars, arches, plasterwork and coral, which funnelled cooling wind from
any direction down into the living quarters below in what has been called
the world's earliest form of air conditioning.

Dubai and the pearl trade engine that powered it had been cruising
along steadily for decades. Then, in 1929, the wheels came off in a terrible
crash. Starting in America, the Great Depression spread like a virus to
Europe and rapidly infected the rest of the world. Demand for Dubai's
single, shimmering export collapsed at a stroke. Based on credit, which
was no longer forthcoming, the pearl trade could not function. When the
pearlers rowed back into Dubai on the traditionally joyful last day of the
season in 1930, a time to celebrate their safe return and the financial

rewards that awaited them, they were horrified not to find the foreign pearl merchants who would always greet the boats on shore. 'It was a disaster of unimaginable proportions,' according to the Dubai business-man Abdulmajid Seddiqi, who helped grow the family business from a single store in Suq Bur Dubai in the 1950s into the largest distributor of Swiss watches in the Middle East. 'In days, towns that had existed for generations were thrown into a crisis from which there was no answer.'[15] Pearls had to be sold at a fraction of their usual price to merchants from India. From an industry valued at £3 million a year in the 1920s, pearling contracted to just £250,000 in the 1940s.[16]

Nor was this a simple question of demand for Gulf pearls returning once the global economy had recovered. The Great Depression was one thing, but a far worse development signified lasting ruin for the Gulf. Led by a bowler-hatted entrepreneur called Kokichi Mikimoto, the Japanese perfected the technique for creating cultured pearls, which were being produced by farmers in their millions by the 1930s. Mass produced, high quality and around 25 per cent cheaper than their natural ocean counter-parts, cultured pearls were highly desirable and spelled the abrupt, calamitous end of the 7,000-year-old Gulf pearl trade. Between 1929 and 1931, the price of pearls plummeted 75 per cent. Introduced in 1947, the Indian government's new tax on imported Gulf pearls was the final death blow. The last significant pearling fleet limped out of Dubai Creek in 1949.[17] For Dubai and its coastal neighbours, for whom pearling was an ancient way of life and virtually the only work in town, it was nothing less than a catastrophe.

The profound economic shock, and the destitution, malnutrition and misery that it unleashed on Dubai, knocked the stuffing out of Sheikh Said, a traditional, easygoing sheikh, who was ill-equipped to govern a large community in crisis from his rambling house on the Creek. When stocks of fish, rice and dates ran out, the beleaguered population was reduced to eating leaves, locusts and the spiny lizard, or *dhub*.[18] His pos-ition was severely weakened.

Efforts to diversify the economy began in earnest in 1937 with an air agreement between Britain and Dubai paying the sheikh for landing rights for Imperial Airways flying boats in one of the first indications of the ren-tier state model that would dominate in the years ahead. In the same year Sheikh Said signed a major oil exploration deal with Petroleum Conces-sions Limited, a wholly owned subsidiary of Britain's Iraq Petroleum Company. In exchange for 60,000 rupees on signature, with more money to follow in the event of oil being discovered, Sheikh Said gave Britain exclusive rights for twenty-five years. For decades, however, the promise of oil remained no more than that, a cruel mirage that regularly raised hopes, only to dash them every time.

Economic ruin, a vicious, unprecedented and unwelcome phenomenon for Dubai, brought political instability in its wake. At times, as in the unsuccessful 1929 plot by Sheikh Said's cousin Mani bin Rashid to topple him, this was acute. In 1934 there was another showdown and assassination attempt, which was only resolved with a British show of strength – a traditional display of gunboat diplomacy that was given added weight by a squadron of RAF fighter planes buzzing the town.

The challenges to Said's rule came from an increasingly powerful reform movement whose principles continue to be felt almost a century later, notwithstanding the autocratic Maktoum family's retention of absolute power. Matters came to a head in 1938, when the most powerful families among Dubai's emboldened merchant community established a consultative *majlis*, or assembly, of fifteen members, led by Sheikh Hasher bin Rashid al Maktoum under the chairmanship of Sheikh Said. It was intended to clip the ruler's wings and force him to share 85 per cent of state revenues, monies which would henceforth be used for public expenditure. A new education department was created to reopen Dubai's schools that had been closed following the economic collapse. The *majlis* introduced welfare plans and had ambitious ideas to enlarge the port. Said attended a few meetings half-heartedly and then refused to have anything more to do with the assembly. The challenge became a standoff.

Tensions reached boiling point on 29 March 1939. A fortnight after Nazi troops had occupied Czechoslovakia, and as Chamberlain wrestled with Hitler's threats to Poland, Dubai's new *majlis*, flexing its muscles, declared that Sheikh Said would have a fixed personal income of just 10,000 rupees. Revenues from the oil and air deals which he had struck with Britain would now revert to the state treasury rather than his private funds. From Said's perspective this was a public humiliation and an unacceptable affront. Fearing military action in response, the reformers seized control of and blocked access to the Deira side of the Creek. Dubai teetered on the edge of all-out conflict.

There followed a bold and brilliant counterattack by the embattled Said. His son Rashid was preparing at this time for his wedding to Sheikha Latifa bint Hamdan Al Nahyan, a union designed to cement the Maktoums' alliance with Abu Dhabi's ruling family. Ahead of the marriage, Said encouraged hundreds of his loyal Bedouin allies to make their way peaceably to Deira, where the celebrations were to be held, in an apparent gesture of goodwill towards the merchants. It was a crafty ruse. Once in Deira, the Bedouin took up positions behind sandbags on rooftops and later that evening fired on the sheikh's opponents, killing Sheikh Hasher bin Rashid al Maktoum and his son. The merchant families lost heart and quickly surrendered before much more blood was spilled. Said had triumphed. The troublesome and ever-ambitious Sheikh Mani was spirited away, but continued to conspire to remove Said. Later that year, after hearing rumours of yet another plot against him, the sheikh had five men arrested. Determined to crush any further opposition for good, he had their eyes put out with hot irons. 'There is general disgust at this act of savagery,' the British Political Agent reported – notwithstanding Britain's historical willingness to resort to violence in the Gulf when it saw fit to enforce its will.[19]

All these trials had taken their toll on Said, who, from the 1940s, still haunted by fears of assassination, started to hand over some of the reins of power to his ambitious eldest son and heir Rashid. Though the Second World War did not directly touch the Trucial Coast, its baleful effects were felt far and wide. Today it is remembered as *waqt al ji*, the time of hunger, a period of bankruptcies, famines, British ration cards and smuggling to survive. There were acute shortages of rice, tea and sugar. Fish sometimes had to be eaten raw because there was no firewood. Those still wealthy enough to own slaves were reduced to selling them for money to buy food. Stricken with hunger, people boiled empty date sacks to wring the last nutritious drops out of them. Some grew rich smuggling rations to Iran, forerunners of the gold smugglers who would make fortunes in the 1950s and 60s.

The later 1940s saw Dubai beginning to emerge from its bleakest hour into the modern age. The first clinic came in 1943, followed in 1946 by the arrival of the first bank. The British Bank of the Middle East opened its doors on the Creek in Deira in a place known as Times Square in Al Ras. It was noticeable both for its prominent wind tower and the most visible lavatory in Dubai, which protruded out over the water and was more than once mistaken for a postbox. Although primitive, it was still a luxury for the time. Most privies were deep open holes in the ground, many with a brick either side to squat on. With Dubai's precariously shifting soil, relieving oneself could be a dangerous business. The city's folk memory still includes dreadful stories of cesspits collapsing and burying people alive.[20]

In *Arabian Sands*, the celebrated story of his wanderings across the Empty Quarter by camel, the British writer and explorer Wilfred Thesiger left a brief but valuable portrait of Dubai in 1949. It was then home to a bustling, multicultural population of about 25,000, centred on the boat-filled Creek and the markets around it. 'There were *booms* from Kuwait, *sambuks* from Sur, *jaulbauts* and even a large stately *baghila*.' Naked children splashed around in the shallows while rowing boats ferried passengers across the water in this Venice of the East. Leisure, courtesy and conversation were highly valued and 'life moved in time with the past'. Behind the teeming waterfront, merchants sat cross-legged in the gloom of the covered markets, surrounded by piles of merchandise. Flies buzzed around carcasses suspended from butchers' hooks as donkey carts clattered through narrow lanes past haughtily loping camels and the odd herd of tufty goats. 'The *suqs* were crowded with many races – pallid Arab townsmen, armed Bedu, quick-eyed and imperious, Negro slaves, Baluchis, Persians and Indians. Among them I noticed a group of Kashgai tribesmen in their distinctive felt caps, and some Somalis off a *sambuk* from Aden.'[21] Thesiger's visit, before electricity had arrived, came on the brink of the oil age that would utterly transform the Trucial Coast. While he romanticized the time-honoured way of life in the Arabian Peninsula, with its material poverty, tribal nobility and traditions, most Arabs willingly embraced the riches promised by the subterranean 'black gold'. Dubai may have had less than some of its neighbours, above all oil-rich Abu Dhabi, but that proved conversely advantageous. It was enough to get started and had the unexpected benefit of proving too little to rely on. Wealth, in other words, had to be earned elsewhere and required ingenuity. If they wanted to hang onto power, it was the Maktoum family's duty to demonstrate it.

Gold-smuggling from Dubai took off in earnest in the 1950s. Imported from Britain and the US at a market price of $35 an ounce, gold was sailed discreetly across to India, where under Nehru's government gold imports were illegal, and sold there for more than double. 'Lots of people had lots of money in their pockets,' the dhow builder Saif Mohammed al Qaizi recalled of this time. He was often busy twenty-four hours a day building new boats and repairing old ones for the energetic smugglers, who played a dangerous cat-and-mouse game with the Indian coastguard and police. Once they had reached the Indian coast, the smugglers would transfer their precious cargo into belts around their waists and signal a prearranged code to waiting fishing boats, which would then sail out to meet them if the coast was clear. Al Qaizi made good money with his boat business and did his own bit of smuggling on the side. 'I built a new house and I married two ladies. It was a golden time. We thought it would last for ever.'[22]

On 10 September 1958 these happy times were interrupted by sorrowful news. Shortly after 7.30 in the morning, Dubai's *muezzins* burst into mournful song, spreading a pall of gloom across the town. The Quranic verses tumbling out from the minarets brought the news that everyone had been dreading. Sheikh Said, who had weathered all the storms life had thrown at him – the collapse of pearling, economic depression, repeated coup attempts and efforts to assassinate him – and who had guided Dubai into the stability of a newly prosperous modern age, had died. 'Inna Lillahi wa inna Ilayhi rajaun,' townsmen and women dutifully mumbled through their tears in the traditional Muslim response to a death, 'From God we come and to God we return.' In the sweltering heat of summer Dubai came to a standstill. Most had known no other ruler. Later that day up to 15,000 men and women, almost half the city's population, came out to witness or join the funeral procession snaking through the streets. Women wailed as the bier swayed past, prayers were offered to Allah and tears mingled with the dust to mark the end of an era.

It was the greatest gamble in the history of Dubai: £200,000 raised locally through bonds, special levies and local banks and a staggering £400,000 loan from Kuwait, in total the equivalent of several years of Dubai's GNP then and almost £13 million today. Sheikh Rashid had bet big and could not afford to fail. 'Everything depends on it,' he told his *majlis*. 'Dredging the Creek was the first great gamble in the 1950s,' says Ammar Shams, a retired Emirati banker. 'It would have broken Dubai if it hadn't come good. Rashid borrowed to the hilt. He bet the farm on it.'[23] Dubai's revenues at this time were extremely modest. Even a 4 per cent tax on imported goods would raise only 60,000 rupees per annum, not remotely enough to fund such a major infrastructure project.

The Creek was the city-state's lung, its connection to the world, 'the very heart and soul of Dubai – its raison d'être'.[24] The city depended and thrived on trade but if boats could no longer get in and out, that was the end of it. The Creek, we may remember, suffered from a 'shallow and difficult entrance', as Lorimer had reported back in 1908. In the years since he had written those words, it had become much shallower and more difficult still, silted up to the point where each winter the mouth of the Creek shrank by more than 600 metres. At low tide, it was less than one metre deep, so cargo-laden Dubai-bound ships had no choice but to anchor a mile offshore and laboriously unload their goods onto barges, which even then could enter the Creek only at high tide. Captains in a hurry simply gave Dubai a miss. It wasn't worth the trouble.

Rashid had made up his mind. Against all the odds the vast sum of money was raised. Dredgers, diggers and lifters lumbered into the Creek in late 1959. By the end of 1960, the British firm Sir William Halcrow and Partners and Austria's Overseas AST had virtually finished the job. Aerial photos from the time show the white-tinged, silt-filled, sandbank-narrowed

Creek transformed into clear dark water. Five-hundred-ton vessels could now navigate the waters. As if to show the perils of inactivity, a severe *shamal* summer wind blew down from Iran in 1960, rolling untold tons of sand into Sharjah's larger port and blocking it completely. It remained closed for a decade, totally hammering the economy and forcing another wave of merchants to up sticks and relocate to Dubai. Many of them built homes and businesses on the new land reclaimed from the Creek on the Deira side during the dredging and sold on profitably by the relentlessly entrepreneurial Rashid. Time and again Dubai had pinched business from Lingah on the Iranian side of the water. Now it was attracting merchants from its immediate neighbours.

The Creek was merely the start. To the question why did Dubai not have its own airport, the British Political Agent told Sheikh Rashid he didn't need one, drawing his attention to next-door Sharjah, which had been operating an airport since 1932. Rashid was not looking for caution and restraint. 'The Ruler is determined, against advice [from the British], to press on with the construction of a jet airport,' an agent's report read in 1962.[25] Displaying the Maktoum family's healthy scepticism about British officialdom, Rashid went behind the agent's back, secured approval from his superior the Political Resident by assuring him no British funding would be sought, and went ahead.* 'Dubai must lead, not be led,' he told his hand-picked *majlis*, later dubbed the 'Arabian Camelot', the Gulf's counterpart to JFK's presidency.[26] The airport opened on 30 September 1960, complete with the region's first duty-free shop, another telling symbol of Dubai's laissez-faire approach. In the triangle of business, politics and religion, business always came at the top. The first asphalt runway opened in 1965, and, by the mid-1980s, more than forty airlines were using Dubai airport. Trouble came in 1984, when Abu Dhabi-backed Gulf Air, the main operator in Dubai, attempted to pressurize Rashid into offering the sorts of incentives, such as preferential landing rights, that were available elsewhere in the region. When the airline abruptly slashed its scheduled weekly flights from eighty-four to thirty-nine to force the issue, Rashid was in a quandary. Rather than buckling, however, he responded with typical Maktoum chutzpah and against the advice of his advisers (again), borrowing $10 million to lease Boeing 737s from Pakistan International Airlines and launching his own airline, Emirates, in 1985. By 1999 Dubai airport had overtaken Jeddah as the region's busiest. Today

---

* The trait lives on in Sheikh Rashid's son and later successor. 'Bureaucrats are self-declared enemies of change,' Sheikh Mohammed bin Rashid al Maktoum writes in *My Vision*. 'There is nothing like bureaucracy to kill creativity and simple, efficient problem-solving. I do not like bureaucracy and bureaucrats.'

Emirates is the largest carrier in the Middle East and one of the biggest in the world.[27]

Traditional empires, Islamic or otherwise, were out of fashion. In 1922, around 600 years after Osman had founded it in north-western Anatolia, the once mighty Ottoman Empire was dissolved in the wake of the Young Turk Revolution and the sultanate abolished. In 1923, a republic of Turkey was declared under President Mustafa Kemal Atatürk and, a year later, the once ascendant caliphate was brusquely eliminated, though not without a struggle by Abdülmecid II, the last caliph, who had tried and failed to secure an increase in his allowance. 'Your office, the Caliphate, is nothing more than a historic relic,' came Atatürk's scathing reply. 'It has no justification for existence. It is a piece of impertinence that you should dare write to any of my secretaries!'[28]

The curtain was coming down, too, on the British Empire. As the twentieth century advanced, the global sway of Britain, virtually bankrupted by two world wars, diminished as that of America grew.* In the Middle East, its traditional sphere of influence, Britain henceforth would play second fiddle to America. British diplomats might not have liked it – 'the position of a junior partner being towed along in the wake of the Americans is . . . a very undignified one for Her Majesty's Government to accept', the ambassador in Jeddah grumbled in 1944 – but undignified or not, they had to put up with it. One by one British possessions were lost as American military and economic influence expanded. Hounded out of Palestine by Irgun terrorists, Britain washed her hands of the place in 1948 and Israel was born, following dextrous, well-funded Zionist lobbying in America. In 1952, the Free Officers' coup that removed Egypt's King Farouk saw the British knocked off their kingmakers' perch and reduced to spectators. Then, in 1956, came the ignominy of Suez, an Anglo-French humiliation and a political triumph for the charismatic Gamal Abdel Nasser, leader of a new, rabble-rousing pan-Arabism that rejected imperialism and electrified the masses across the region. In 1958, the British-supported monarchy in Iraq fell in a hail of bullets in Baghdad and the last strong client state had been lost. As the British prime minister Harold Macmillan ruefully remarked in 1952, from being 'a respected ally' of the US, Britain was now being treated with 'a mixture of patronising pity and contempt'.[29]

In 1968, Prime Minister Harold Wilson announced that British troops

---

* On 29 December 2006, the UK transferred £43 million to the US Treasury, the final payment on a $4.34 billion loan Washington extended to London in 1946.

would be withdrawn 'East of Aden', another bombshell that elicited withering scorn in Washington. 'For God's sake act like Britain,' US Secretary of State Dean Rusk said to his counterpart George Brown.[30] London's declaration also brought immediate apprehension to the Trucial States, which were ushered together, with British support, into the United Arab Emirates, founded in haste in 1971. Dubai was one of its six constituent emirates, along with Abu Dhabi (the richest and most powerful), Sharjah, Ajman, Umm al Quwain and Fujairah. They were joined by a seventh, Ras al Khaimah, in 1972. For an entirely new nation, hustled together from disparate sheikhdoms whose relations historically have been as much antagonistic as they have been brotherly, the UAE has proved astonishingly successful ever since, a beacon of political stability, religious moderation and economic growth in one of the world's most challenging regions.

Just as Baghdad surged up from Mesopotamian mud under the Abbasid caliph Al Mansur in the 760s, so Dubai mushroomed in size during the 1970s, as Sheikh Rashid launched project after common-sense-defying project. Again and again British advisers raised their eyebrows, sucked their teeth and poured cold water on the sheikh's latest plan. Far too risky, they tut-tutted, who would use it, what was the demand, where would the money come from? Again and again he proved them wrong, and Dubai grew and grew. In 1960, it was still a modest town of 60,000 crammed haphazardly into two square miles on and around the Creek. In 1970, it was a city of 100,000 spread across seven square miles. Five years later, it was home to 183,000 people living in eighteen square miles. By 1980 Dubai had exploded across thirty-two square miles with a population of 276,000.[31] It couldn't be done, everyone said. But it could, and was. From the time Rashid became ruler, Dubai's trading figures as a regional entrepôt accelerated at warp speed. In 1958, the year of his accession, imports stood at £3 million. A decade later, that had rocketed to £70 million.[32]

It was not all plain sailing, however. Dubai in the 1950s witnessed its own turbulence. With Gamal Abdel Nasser at Egypt's helm, revolution and anti-colonialism reverberated across the Arab world. Arab nationalism in Dubai found a growing voice through the Dubai National Front, founded a year after Egypt's military uprising. As Easa Saleh al Gurg, a Dubai banker and business tycoon, recalled in his memoir, there was a powerful 'sense of grievance' about the British and their effectively 'colonial presence' in the region; 'their readiness to intervene, in pursuit of their own ends, in the management of our society . . . was greatly resented'.[33] During riots in 1956, part of the British agent's house was burnt down by an angry mob. Ultimately, nationalism in Dubai was undermined and headed off by a combination of British power, Maktoum leadership, the removal of fired-up expatriate Arab teachers preaching Nasserism to their young charges, the reorganization of the police force and judicial system, and, perhaps most critical of all, the discovery of oil in 1966, which completely changed the equation.

The merchants had provided the steeliest challenge to the Maktoums in the 1930s. Henceforth the social contract between ruler and ruled relied to a great extent on enabling the merchants to make fortunes. Many of the richest men and women in Dubai today come from the old merchant families, like the Al Futtaims, Al Ghurairs and Al Habtoors, and the voice of business is invariably heard clearly at the ruler's *majlis*. Son of a successful merchant, Mohammed al Gergawi has been one of Sheikh Mohammed's ministers and closest advisers since 2006, one of the masterminds of the latest chapter in Dubai's development.

By the late 1960s, with Qatari and Saudi support, Dubai had got street lighting, its first proper bridge across the Creek and a tarmacked road to Ras al Khaimah. This was as nothing to what followed. Having ignored the cautious voices suggesting he was overdoing it, Rashid tore up the carefully planned blueprint to build a four-berth port and demanded it be revised to sixteen. Advisers swallowed hard. Port Rashid duly opened with sixteen berths in 1971. By 1976, such was the demand that it had to be expanded to thirty-five berths. At times Rashid's ambition seemed almost unhinged. Within a year of Port Rashid's inauguration, he had decided on another, vastly bigger deep-water port in Jebel Ali, a stretch of coral-studded sandy beach twenty miles from the Creek. It would have to be carved out in its entirety and, when finished, would offer more shipping space than San Francisco. There was a collective intake of breath from his advisers and the diplomatic community, but Rashid pressed on regardless, a man with a mission. There was no time to lose.

Amid this breakneck, helter-skelter construction, 1979 was a bumper year, with a royal visit from Queen Elizabeth II to inaugurate a series of landmark projects. Together with Sheikh Rashid, she opened the $1.6 billion, one-and-a-quarter-mile-long, sixty-six-berth Jebel Ali Port, one of the world's largest, and a vast dry dock that was greeted with immediate scepticism by the *Wall Street Journal*, whose inventively scoffing headline wondered 'Is Dry Dock in Dubai to be High and Dry and Pie in the Sky?'[34] The answer was no. Then there was Dubal, the $1.4 billion aluminium smelter, a key part of Dubai's plan to use its burgeoning oil revenues to diversify and industrialize, followed by Dugas natural gas plant in 1980 and Dubai Cabling Company in 1981. These were the early seeds of what grew into the behemoth of 'Dubai Inc.'.

As outlandish as Jebel Ali Port and Dubai Aluminium appeared at the time, by far the most startling of all, architecturally speaking, was the World Trade Centre, the city's first skyscraper, which frightened the superstitious and mystified the naysayers who considered it a white elephant and a waste of time. Located far away from the bustle of the Creek, apparently marooned in a mosquito-ridden patch of empty desert, the thirty-nine-storey tower (the British architect John Harris was going to build thirty-three but Rashid insisted he go higher) wasn't even within Dubai. It was a marker instead for where Dubai *would* go. It and the distant Jebel Ali were 'the testing ground for a new kind of urbanism: for the first time, large tracts of land were being disengaged from the city. Urbanisation was now linked to the non-urban.'[35] In the 1960s and 70s foreign business executives dipping their toes into Dubai often had to share hotel rooms with other guests. Now all of a sudden, they could book a suite and sit down to a dinner of Maine lobster on ice with a decent bottle of wine. The World Trade Centre stood at the gateway to what is now the most visually thrilling centrepiece of the twelve-lane Sheikh Zayed Road, a roaring highway that divides two battalions of battling skyscrapers, glistening beneath the desert sun. Rashid's tower was the concrete, apparently chimerical expression of the Maktoums' 'build it and they will come' philosophy and Sheikh Zayed Road, not to mention the rest of this endlessly expanding city-state, was its extraordinary realization. The Maktoums built it and the world came.

Apparently manic to the point of madcap and foolish, this rush and rash of development was in fact both wildly risk-taking and coolly rational. Long elusive, oil had been discovered in 1966 at the offshore Fateh (Conqueror) field and was in production from 1969, bringing in new revenues to Rashid's just created Dubai Petroleum Company, working in partnership with British, French, Spanish, German and American companies. The point was that the 4 billion barrels of reserves were of strictly finite value to Dubai, enabling Rashid, for a limited time only, to diversify his economy for the decades ahead. Relying on oil revenues for the foreseeable future, as oil-rich Abu Dhabi (with reserves of 92 billion barrels) and other Gulf monarchies were able to do, was never an option for Dubai. Most would now agree that this was a blessing. Peak production of 420,000 barrels per day was reached in 1991, from which time it has declined steadily. From representing around two-thirds of Dubai's economic output in its heyday, oil today accounts for less than 2 per cent of the economy.[36]

Oil has brought untold riches to the Gulf, raising living standards to undreamed-of heights in recent decades. 'Grandfathers who once lived in tents now live in villas in one of the top residential cities in the world,'

says Dahlia Kayed of the Sheikh Mohammed Centre for Cultural Understanding (motto: 'Open Doors Open Minds'), another symbol of Dubai's
tolerant atmosphere – with the notable exception of politics, which remains
strictly off limits.[37] One of the more negative consequences of this easy
money, in many cases, has been the parallel growth of a culture of indolence, entitlement, low productivity and a rentier-state reliance on foreign
labour.

All that lay ahead. There was nothing indolent about Sheikh Rashid,
a workaholic who famously put in eighteen-hour days. His schedule was
packed with personal inspections of his major infrastructure projects
before he returned home for his evening *majlis*, where he listened to problems and grievances in the traditional sheikhly manner deep into the night.
After a typically punishing day culminating in a banquet for India's Prime
Minister Indira Gandhi on 9 May 1981, he suffered a severe stroke from
which he never fully recovered.

In 1983, Rashid's wife Sheikha Latifa – whose wedding had played such
a critical role in facing down the merchants' challenges to Sheikh Said's
power back in 1939 – died suddenly while in London. After a marriage
that had lasted forty-four years, it was a desperate blow to the ailing ruler
on the eve of his seventy-first birthday. Those around him said he was
never the same again. Withdrawing from public life, he devolved more
and more power to his sons, as his father Said had to him decades earlier,
spending evenings gazing out over the city he had built from the terrace
of his modest Zaabeel Palace in the desert sands. At ten o'clock on the
night of 7 October 1990, he died, having ruled for thirty-two years.

'Sheikh Rashid was one of the most remarkable leaders I have ever met,'
his old friend Sheikh Zayed of Abu Dhabi told mourners at the funeral.
'Modern Dubai is a testimony to his vision.'[38] Tributes flew in from around
the world. The media hailed the 'merchant prince', who in a single generation had transformed a sleepy little Gulf town into a city that many now
compared with Hong Kong and Singapore as an icon of world trade. In
his youth Rashid had dreamed of putting Dubai on the map, of making
it a name and a place to be conjured with around the globe, somewhere
everyone knew about, admired and wanted to visit. Few gave him the
slightest chance of achieving this absurd ambition. Yet somehow this restless, dynamic sheikh had proved the legions of doubters wrong and made
Dubai famous the world over. 'Dubai was one man's vision,' says the
Emirati poet Khaled al Bodour. Rashid had taken his people on a journey
'more exciting than anything the Arabs had done in several hundred
years'.[39]

*

'What is there in Dubai to make it a tourist destination?' the Gulf minister sneered. 'You have nothing but humidity, red-hot sun, burning sand and barren desert.'[40] It was 1985 and at a meeting of Gulf leaders the thirty-six-year-old Sheikh Mohammed bin Rashid al Maktoum, who was taking on increasing responsibilities from his father, was weary of the predictably interminable discussions about Iran and the Palestinian situation. All hot air and no results. Why, he asked his colleagues, didn't the Gulf countries start thinking about making their region a centre for tourism? Dubai was planning to become one of the world's leading destinations. The only response was an awkward silence.

Undeterred by the complete lack of interest, Sheikh Mohammed threw his energies into creating a tourist sector from nothing. In the 1950s, visiting VIPs had no choice but to stay with the British Political Agent. Dubai's first hotel, the thirty-five-room Airlines Hotel in Al Rashidiya, opened its doors at the inauguration of the airport in 1960. Dubai's first bar, the Red Lion, a typical English pub, arrived in 1979, courtesy of the business magnate Khalaf al Habtoor, who, encouraged by Sheikh Rashid, built the Metropolitan Hotel on what then looked like an unpromising stretch of desert (today it is home to Al Habtoor City, a quartet of sky-scrapers on Sheikh Zayed Road containing three luxury hotels and a theatre offering 'a touch of Vegas').[41] By 1990, flush with oil revenues, booming with business, Dubai was attracting 600,000 visitors a year, who could choose from more than seventy hotels. By 2000, the number of international visitors had multiplied again to 3.4 million. In 2018 it was 15.9 million.

Dubai does not appeal to everyone. For some, its brashness, conspicuous consumption and paucity of historical monuments are simply uninviting. I visited for the first time on a journalistic assignment in 2002. *Time Out Dubai* set the scene with a picture of a glamorous Western couple, man in dinner jacket, woman in not very much apart from diamonds. 'Millionaires' Playground', said the headline. 'Fast cars, Cuban cigars, luxury yachts, bespoke building plots'. Red Ferraris and yellow Lamborghinis roared along Sheikh Zayed Road, which was already a forest of skyscrapers. In the lobby of the Fairmont, Dubai's then latest five-star hotel, a cosmopolitan cast of prostitutes was doing a brisk trade, while Emiratis in snow-white *dishdashas* and matching headdress gazed on, admiring the scenery. I wandered along the Creek, most faithful to the memories of old Dubai, still reeking of trade and sweaty sailors with laundry flapping on impromptu, on-board clothes lines, past dhows piled high with all the goods of the world, and into the shop-crammed *suqs*, a suddenly traditional world of spice merchants, fabric sellers, coffeehouses and old-school merchants. I hacked my way around the Montgomerie, a new course designed by the British golfer Colin Montgomerie, complete with the world's first 360-degree tee. Dubai loves a boast and a gimmick. The world's tallest building (Burj Khalifa, 828 metres), biggest shopping mall (Dubai Mall), largest indoor themed park (IMG Worlds of Adventure), heaviest doner kebab (468 kilograms), longest painting (10,850 metres), anything, no matter how weird and outlandish, to bring in the crowds and their money.[42]

It is easy to be down on Dubai. Critics assail it for a number of reasons. While journalists competed for superlatives and monikers to describe the city's boundary-busting boom of recent years – 'Manhattan-on-speed', 'a skyline on crack' and 'a capitalist dream on steroids' – there is also a dark side to the city's meteoric, no-questions-asked rise to riches.[43] The playground for Arabs and Western tourists has been built on the backs of South Asia's poorest workers. For each glittering new skyscraper that jousts its way into an ever-changing skyline, there is an army of poorly paid migrant workers living in substandard, sometimes appalling, conditions in guarded camps a world away from the luxury they have helped create. International media and human rights organizations have shone a disturbing light on the lives of exploited and abused workers operating in what has been described as a form of modern slavery in which millions of workers fly into Dubai and immediately have their passports confiscated before getting started. 'Right now I seriously wish the world would wake up and look beyond the glitter to the actual darkness which is there behind,' says Almass Pardiwala, a former recruitment agent.[44] For those outside the charmed circle of business and tourism – 71 per cent of Dubai's population of 2.5 million is Asian – the laissez-faire approach has had a high human cost. The famously light-touch regulation of a free port and regional trade hub has also attracted 'massive smuggling, gunrunning, human trafficking, and money-laundering operations', some of which have become intertwined with global terrorist networks.[45] In one of the more extreme instances of 'Dubai-bashing', a British journalist described the city as an 'Adult Disneyland' built on 'credit and ecocide, suppression and slavery'.

Dubai residents, long used to the barbs, roll their eyes and call out the 'smug, self-satisfying schadenfreude of the fly-in-fly-out reporter' who visits a couple of malls and a skyscraper and thinks he has the place covered. 'This is like me visiting Chicago for the first time ever and for ONE day and going to West Monroe and Garfield Park and then writing about what a violent, homicidal, dangerous city it is,' the influential Emirati commentator Sultan Sooud Al Qassemi tweeted recently of an

American magazine article on Dubai, 'The World's Vegas' and 'a non-place of a city'. 'Would the *New Yorker* allow me to publish that?'[46]

On my last trip to Dubai I stayed in Festival City, another thicket of glimmering towers on the south-eastern edge of the Creek towards Mirdif. In the years since my first visit an alphabet of sector-themed 'cities' had sprung up across town: Academic City, Golf City, Healthcare City, International Humanitarian City, Internet City, Logistics City, Maritime City, Media City, Motor City, Sports City, Studio City. Dubai had grown less like an inkstain spreading steadily across a map than water sloshed across it. Two giant, palm-shaped luxury developments protruded into the Arabian Gulf, and offshore the 300 islands of 'The World' awaited buyers in one of Dubai's latest hybrid demonstrations of vision and excess. A newspaper editor talked admiringly about Sheikh Mohammed's plans to make Maktoum International Airport the world's largest, with a capacity of more than 220 million passengers a year. A banker emphasized how Dubai had always been much more progressive than its neighbours, how it led on promoting women's role in society and women's rights, how there were many senior women in government and the foreign service.

Sheikh Nahyan Mubarak al Nahyan, the urbane Emirati minister of culture, had flown in by helicopter to open the annual literary festival which, like so many things in Dubai, has become the region's largest. His speech was a very Emirati call for inclusion and tolerance in a region being torn apart by sectarian conflict. 'Literature embraces every culture, ethnicity, gender, every language, country, religion, every philosophy, level of education, age, and every point of view,' he told a cosmopolitan audience of Arabs, Africans, Asians, Americans and Europeans. Where else in the Middle East other than Dubai would these words, this crowd and that multinational cast of writers, not to mention an extravagantly funded and meticulously organized event, have been possible? The festival was a microcosm of Dubai's growing soft power, underwritten by anything-goes economic and commercial success (in this case sponsored by Emirates airline) and a constantly changing multinational population.

To be a native of Dubai of a certain age is to have witnessed and survived extraordinary levels of urban change. Sheikh Mohammed, the 'CEO sheikh', has followed his father's lead by setting a pace his fellow citizens sometimes struggle to comprehend. 'I take decisions and I move fast, full throttle,' he says. The question of identity inevitably hangs over a city in which Emirati men and women make up only 10 per cent of the total population. 'You worry about culture and identity when you're not the majority,' says Dr Maryam Lootah, a political scientist at UAE University.

'The question of Emirati identity is still being moulded,' argues the retired banker Ammar Shams. 'The challenge is to grow at this rate and remain what we are and were.' The poet Khaled al Bodour says he has had to train himself to accept this bewildering, ongoing reinvention of the city of his birth, the loss of the old beach of Jumeirah, the replacement of empty sands with tourist crowds. 'Where it's going, I don't know, I sometimes don't care,' he says. 'I adapted. I had to. I live the moment and train myself not to live in the past and not worry about the future.' For Ruqaya al Bastaki, a senior ministry of health official whose family gave their name to the district of Bastakiya a century ago, it can sometimes feel as though you are a stranger in your own country. 'Dubai feels much more foreign now,' she says. 'It's changed totally and now you hear so many languages spoken.'[47] One of the many paradoxes of Dubai, an Arab city in the Arabian Gulf, is that it has become so global and English-speaking that the Arabic language itself is under threat.

If there is ambivalence about the lightning transformation of the urban landscape in such a short time, if there are thorny issues of identity to confront, there is equally understandable pride in having built such a remarkable city from empty desert. Crime may be higher, strange new neighbourhoods may have risen from the sands and childhood memories may have been razed by the bulldozers, but the indigenous love for this city remains visceral. 'Praise God we were born here,' says Ruqaya. 'What an amazing journey from what we were to what we have become. Dubai is now the best city in the world. I couldn't change it for any other. There's nothing like it.'

Others discreetly complain about 'a megalomaniac who is turning a pleasant city into a bloated megalopolis'.[48] The discretion is advisable, essential even, to avoid imprisonment. Sheikh Mohammed claims his inspiration for Dubai is tenth-century Cordoba, which may be less fanciful than such a comparison initially appears. The Andalusian capital was open, trade-friendly and cosmopolitan, a ferment of literary expression and laboratory of intellectual discovery. There is no reason to suppose, however, given the long-standing Arab tradition of autocratic rule, that Umayyad Cordoba was any more tolerant of political dissent or free speech than Maktoum Dubai. There is no free speech in Dubai, just as there is no free speech in almost any Arab country today, with the possible exception of Tunisia. Dubai is as open as any twenty-first-century Arab city gets, but criticism of the ruling family, or any other political activity, is absolutely prohibited.

The truth is that if you are not one of the many debt-ridden migrant South Asian workers toiling beneath the pitiless sun on the latest skyscraper or sheikh-inspired mega-project, if you are not a political activist, human rights campaigner or investigative journalist, Dubai is a city that works. Like all great cities it draws in the world, just as Baghdad did under the early Abbasid caliphs over 1,200 years ago. People from more than 200 countries have made it their home. It has its problems like any city, sustainability being one of the uppermost among them. Yet it has defied its critics for far too long now in terms of what it has already achieved to be written off glibly. It is one of the great success stories of the Arab world in recent decades, an urban phenomenon in its own right and a mind-bending Arab-global reimagining of the modern city.

Dr Rima Sabban, a professor of sociology at Zayed University in Dubai, smiles over her coffee. We are discussing some of the city's Arab detractors, who often dismiss Dubai as too new, too fake, too flashy, too lacking in history and culture, the cocky young kid on the block. Perhaps it all comes down to jealousy.

'Find me a Syrian, Iraqi, Lebanese, Tunisian, Algerian, Moroccan, Sudanese or an Egyptian who doesn't want to live in Dubai,' she says. 'They all do.'[49]

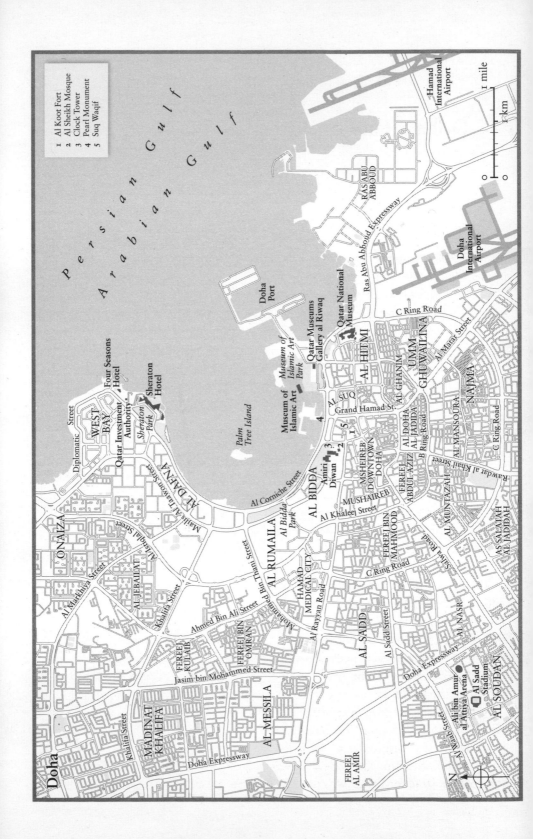

Doha

1 Al Koot Fort
2 Al Sheikh Mosque
3 Clock Tower
4 Pearl Monument
5 Suq Waqif

Persian Gulf

Arabian Gulf

Hamad International Airport

1 mile

1 km

RAS ABU ABBOUD

Ras Abu Abboud Expressway

C Ring Road

Doha International Airport

Al Matār Street

Doha Port

Museum of Islamic Art Park

Qatar Museums Gallery al Riwaq

Qatar National Museum

AL HITMI

UMM GHUWAILNA

Four Seasons Hotel

Qatar Investment Authority

Sheraton Park

Sheraton Hotel

WEST BAY

Diplomatic Street

Museum of Islamic Art

AL SUQ

Grand Hamad St.

AL GHANIM

AL DOHA AL JADIDA

NAJMA

C Ring Road

Palm Tree Island

Al Corniche Street

4

5

1

3
2

Amiri Diwan

MSHEIREB DOWNTOWN DOHA

FEREEJ ABDUL-AZIZ

B Ring Road

AL MANSOURA

Rawdat al Khail Street

AS SALATAH AL JADIDAH

AL DAFNA

AL BIDDA

Al Bidda Park

AL RUMAILA

MUSHAIREB

Al Khaleej Street

FEREEJ BIN MAHMOOD

AL MUNTAZAH

ONAIZA

Majlis Al Taawon Street

Al Istiqlal Street

AL JEBAILAT

Mohammed Bin Thani Street

HAMAD MEDICAL CITY

Al Rayyan Road

Salwa Road

C Ring Road

C Ring Road

Al Markhiya Street

Khalifa Street

Ahmed Bin Ali Street

FEREEJ BIN OMRAN

Jasim-bin Mohammed Street

AL SADD

Al Sadd Street

AL NASR

FEREEJ KULAIB

MADINAT KHALIFA

Khalifa Street

AL-MESSILA

Doha Expressway

Doha Expressway

FEREEJ AL AMIR

Al Waab Street

Al Ali bin Amur al Attiya Arena

Al Sadd Stadium

AL SOUDAN

N

15
Doha – City of Pearls (21st Century)

Change is happening so dramatically. It's a complete paradigm
shift. I lose my way around Doha all the time. New skyscrapers
are sprouting up everywhere, new roads, districts, shops,
restaurants and museums. It's all change. I absolutely love it.
Dr Mariam Ibrahim al Mulla, Qatar University

High in his office tower in West Bay, like an eagle in its eyrie, the billionaire Sheikh Faisal bin Qassim al Thani, founder, chairman and chief executive of Al Faisal Holding, remembers the early days of Doha. Outside this gleaming, air-conditioned skyscraper, headquarters of his sprawling business empire, palm trees wilt in the savage heat. Pigeons flap listlessly across the dazzling water. The Gulf sun is so strong here it casts a white stupor across the city. In this cauldron of radiating heat and shirt-staining humidity, for a moment indolence seems not only entirely forgivable but entirely appropriate.

Yet there is little in the remarkable career of this sixtysomething tycoon to suggest anything other than relentless industry and application. Back in the early 1960s, the teenage Sheikh Faisal, a distant relative of the ruling Emir of Qatar, Sheikh Tamim bin Hamad al Thani, started up a business selling car parts. Half a century later, standing at the helm of a diversified conglomerate encompassing property, construction, trading, transport, entertainment, education, information technology and hotels from the St Regis in Washington to the W in London and the Four Seasons in Cairo, the businessman is worth $2.1 billion.[1]

With little prompting Sheikh Faisal reminisces about the slow rise of what even in his lifetime was hardly more than a small pearl-fishing village. 'Doha was originally a place of refuge and safety, a sanctuary for tribesmen on the run. This was what made Doha and its history.' He says the greatest time for Qatar was not so much the extraordinary prosperity of the twenty-first century, but the period from 1800 to 1920, before the demise of the pearl trade in the 1930s and the ruinous advent of the Second World War, which devastated Doha, as it did Dubai and other coastal settlements across the Gulf. 'We went from a battle against weapons to a battle against hunger. The British and Germans were sinking ships all over the Gulf. Until 1944 people barely had clothes. The emir and everyone else went hungry. Many died of starvation.'

Though he is only in his late sixties, Sheikh Faisal already talks like an old man slightly discomfited by the modern age. 'The culture has changed a lot,' he says. 'In 1989 if you gave me 1 million riyals to have dinner outside my house with my family, it would be impossible and seen as shameful.' A pause. 'Now it's ok.' The Qatari capital has changed beyond recognition in the sheikh's lifetime. 'It was a much simpler time in those days,' he says of the Doha of his youth. 'I knew everyone in the country and I knew everyone's car.'[2]

That love of cars is impossible to miss at one of Doha's more eccentric visitor attractions. Thirteen miles along the Dukhan Highway north-west of the city (the distance shrinks as Doha, one of the world's fastest-growing cities, expands), a pastiche desert fort built in 1998 houses the Sheikh Faisal bin Qassim al Thani Museum, one man's idiosyncratic collection of 15,000 artefacts (and counting) amassed during his travels. They reflect his eclectic tastes: Jurassic fossils jostle for space with the world's smallest and largest Qurans. Qatari weaponry is juxtaposed with an astonishingly ornate Ottoman *kiswa* from 1910, emblazoned with gold and silver thread.* There are veteran pearl-fishing dhows, an entire eighteenth-century Syrian home transported to Qatar brick by brick, tile by tile. The sheikh's retired private plane, the 'Falcon of the Gulf', looms over a long hall rammed with Mercedes limousines and roadsters, American coupés and convertibles, antique carpets, the odd motorbike, a pair of diminutive cannon and a couple of mannequins dressed as traditional Arab tribesmen. In the next gallery lifesize models of horses and camels surrounded by gaudy paintings add a jaunty note to proceedings. This is a world of mementoes and memorabilia, rare and fabulously expensive treasures, kitsch and tourist tat. One of the strangest sections contains photographs of Muslim dervishes in the throes of religious passion, thrusting skewers and sticks through breasts and jaws. In terms of more orthodox Islamic boasting rights, the museum's greatest treasure is unquestionably the

---

* The *kiswa* is the vast, embroidered black cloth draped over the Kaaba annually during the *hajj* pilgrimage to Mecca.

slender golden key to the Kaaba door, whose acquisition was announced in January 2018.

The largest section here by far, though, is the sheikh's car collection of over 600 vehicles. Buicks, Pontiacs and Mustangs line up alongside Chevrolets, Cadillacs and Dodges. During my visit, rows and rows of unexceptional, mostly American cars, from 1950s muscle and two-seater sports cars to trucks and pickups in varying states of disrepair and neglect, quietly gathered dust, confounding the best efforts of the sheikh's curators to impose some kind of order onto this unruly collection. In an adjacent covered parking lot a procession of Bentleys, Rolls-Royces and Mercedes, together with motorbikes and early twentieth-century cars, awaited their turn with the restorers.

'The problem is, we're still expanding. He never stops buying!' said Abdulaziz, the weary curator of Islamic art. 'He got the collecting habit from his father. Whatever he sees of interest, he buys it. Boxes arrive all the time. He'll come in every night. Move that there, this here. Everything is constantly being rearranged. It's all about how things look. The narrative is not important. It's difficult for us with all the labelling and cataloguing when we're trying to run the museum professionally.'[3]

Ostensibly the Sheikh Faisal bin Qassim al Thani Museum is devoted to Islamic art, Qatari heritage, coins and currency, and American vintage cars. But it is much more than that. It is tempting to see in this eclectic museum a microcosm of Qatar itself: dizzying levels of wealth, acquisition and consumption, an assertion of power, status and Islamic heritage and, perhaps above all, an underlying quest for identity in a city whose inhabitants find themselves an increasingly small, sometimes bewildered, suddenly rich minority in their own country.*

Doha is still too much in its infancy to be considered the capital of a new Islamic Empire reimagined and rebranded for the twenty-first century, but there is no doubting there is a vigorous new Arab Muslim power on the international scene. Unafraid to assert itself, unprepared to genuflect any more to its neighbour Saudi Arabia, ready to intervene in multiple countries and conflicts and contract controversial alliances with myriad Islamists, underwritten by apparently endless funds, Doha has thrown off its traditional caution and conservatism and leapt onto the world stage.

---

* The Qatari royal family's ever-changing car collection, which in recent times has included such exotica as a one-off Pagani Zonda Uno, a special order Koenigsegg CCXR, a pair of £1.5 million Lamborghini Murciélago LP670–4 SuperVeloces, a Ferrari 599 GTB Fiorano and a purple, glow-in-the-dark Lamborghini Aventador is the conspicuous reminder – or warning? – that no one outdoes the ruling branch of the Al Thanis.

Assiduously, some would say impetuously, it has been positioning itself as a new Islamic force to be reckoned with.

Across town, on the seventh floor of another Doha tower block, Hussein Alfardan smiles benevolently among his treasures. They recall the original source of wealth in a city that is now booming from the income generated by the world's third largest natural gas reserves – upwards of 24 billion cubic metres, making Qatar the richest country in the world in terms of GDP per capita.[4] Alfardan, an owlish octogenarian, is the son of a famous pearl merchant. Haj Ibrahim Alfardan, the patriarch of the family, who died in 1981 aged well over a hundred, established the family in the pearl business and was known locally as 'The Surgeon' for his ability, over several weeks, to strip away the thin outer layers of an ugly *majhoolah* pearl to uncover a spectacular, lustrous gem beneath. As a boy Alfardan used to take pearling boats out to sea under the watchful eye of his father and witnessed the older man trade in pearls. In 1954, during the lean post-war period and fresh from a two-year stint as the first employee in Qatar's first bank (then Eastern Bank Limited, today Standard Chartered), Hussein Alfardan opened a small jewellery shop.

'We went through a very difficult period when the pearl trade came to an end,' he recalls. Many had to sell their homes amid sudden and terrible poverty across the region. It took 'many years for the oil wealth to trickle down to the ordinary people'.[5]

With one jewellery outlet to his name, the young man spent the next sixty years growing Alfardan Group into a multibillion-dollar family conglomerate invested in the jewellery, automotive, property, banking and hospitality sectors. In 2013 *Forbes* listed Alfardan as the forty-seventh richest Arab, with a net worth of $453 million.[6]

Part museum, part commercial space (once a pearl trader, always a pearl trader), Alfardan's Tawash Gallery is one of the world's largest collections of natural Gulf pearls. Illuminated cabinets showcase pearl jewellery of astounding rarity: cascading necklaces, including one worth $2 million, diamond- and pearl-encrusted feather headpieces, pearl-tasselled drop earrings, pearls and rubies, pearls and emeralds, pearls and sapphires, pearls and gold. The world's largest pearl, a 276-carat leviathan, artfully fashioned into a ring, would sit in pride of place among these piles of pearls, were it not for a trio of Fabergé eggs which compete for attention.

Perhaps another reason for Alfardan's lingering smile is his recent purchase of another. Unveiled in Doha only two months before our meeting, Fabergé's first Imperial Egg since 1917 (the most famous were made by

Peter Carl Fabergé for the Russian tsars Alexander III and Nicholas II in the late nineteenth and early twentieth centuries) caused a predictable international stir. Inspired by the formation of a pearl within an oyster and adorned with 3,305 diamonds, 139 natural pearls from Alfardan's private collection, carved rock crystal and mother of pearl set on white and yellow gold, the 'Pearl Egg' rotates on its base and opens in six sections to reveal a 12-carat grey Gulf pearl. It is the work of twenty highly skilled jewellers and took the best part of two years to complete. Accompanied by a Fabergé necklace of white pearls, diamonds and mother of pearl with a scallop motif and a 19-carat white pearl drop, the egg cost Alfardan an undisclosed seven-figure sum.[7]

The Fabergé treasure resonates historically in a place that once owed its living entirely to the pearl. 'We are all, from the highest to the lowest, slaves of one master – Pearl,' Mohammed bin Thani, the then ruler of Qatar, told William Gifford Palgrave, the English Arabic scholar and explorer, in 1863. It was a statement of fact. As Palgrave observed in the account of his Arabian travels, everything in Doha – 'all thought, all conversation, all employment' – turned on the pearl. Everything else was secondary.[8]

The pearl trade has long gone but, surrounded by a lifetime's prizes and awards, the elderly Alfardan still seems as motivated by business as he was sixty years ago. He mentions his company's massive property investment, an artificial island of almost 4 million square metres, a throng of tower blocks clustered in a circle around a smaller central island. Inevitably, it is called the Pearl. 'I took Berlusconi around the Pearl,' Alfardan says. 'He said, "Which crazy man came up with this idea?" I said it was me. It *was* crazy. With 0.5 billion riyals we built an 18 billion project now valued at over 80 billion (£15.5 billion).'

Alfardan ends our meeting with a dutiful encomium to the wisdom of the ruling Al Thani family, singling out for particular praise Sheikh Hamad bin Khalifa al Thani, the emir who ruled Qatar from 1995 until his surprising abdication in favour of his son Tamim in 2013. Today Qataris refer to him respectfully as the Father Emir.

'I've seen all the changes and I've been part of them,' Alfardan says. 'The changes were slow until the Father Emir came. Two years after he took over, the sun shone on Qatar. The market was open. When he came, the West Bay was nothing. We are lucky we have such great leaders. He gave everyone a chance to develop their country. He supported the banks, supported the companies, supported the people. He made Qatar.' It is the ritual, though no less heartfelt, Arab tribute to the all-powerful leader. Power is mediated here through deference, not democracy.

*

From its development in the early twenty-first century, West Bay in short order has become the quintessential image of Doha. It is little wonder that residents above a certain age can appear dazed by the swiftness of their city's transformation. As recently as the 1980s, minarets were the tallest structures in the city. The only building worthy of comment in West Bay was the Sheraton hotel, a fifteen-storey pyramid minus its triangular summit, built on reclaimed land and opened in 1982. Once alone on the water, today it is dwarfed by a petrified thicket of glass, 'starchitect'-designed skyscrapers. Foremost among them is Jean Nouvel's $125 million, 232-metre Burj Doha (Doha Tower), completed in 2012, sheathed in an aluminium mesh sunscreen, demonstrative of what the Frenchman calls a 'fully assumed virility', and popularly known as 'the Condom'.[9] Then there is the twisted, spiralling, shimmering Al Bidda Tower and the hyperbolic, lattice-clad Tornado Tower, supposedly reminiscent of a whirlwind in a desert storm and seen to best effect, like the rest of West Bay, by night. After the sun has sucked down the last of the dusk light and the sky is smudging into indigo, Doha's skyscrapers put on a lurid light show, with rainbow waves of colour tumbling down the towers and brilliant-white lights winking like stars. It is the Gulf's answer to Hong Kong, conceived and executed in little more than a decade.

West Bay, like Doha's wider development, is a source of pride for many Qataris and unmissable for the visitor to the city. But it also has its local detractors, some of whom are concerned that this pell-mell rush into the sky has not been properly thought through to create a liveable city for its residents. By day the towers throng with bankers, lawyers, accountants, oil men, property developers, public relations consultants, security advisers, growing numbers of Western expats lured by attractive, tax-free 'packages', and the far greater numbers of migrant workers, largely from the Indian Subcontinent, whose menial toil makes this city work. By night, marvels of the light show aside, West Bay is a ghost town.

'It's not properly designed,' says Mohammed Abdullah, a Qatari engineer. 'What's there at night? Nothing. There's nowhere to have coffee, no parking spaces, nowhere for walking. Foreign companies come in, they say you want a Central Business District, they build it and leave.'[10]

Foreign critics have been liberal with their gibes. The *Financial Times* wrote of a cityscape that smacked of 'developer greed' and 'architectural autism' with its 'dumb clusters of silly-shaped towers' springing up in isolation from their neighbours. 'There's no urban heritage here,' says Dena Qaddumi, a writer on Arab cities. 'There's strong culture, language and rituals but this city is mostly built by foreigners. There aren't many Qatari architects and only a couple of Qatari architectural practices.' The name

Dubai hovers on everyone's lips, Qatari and expatriate alike. 'There's real concern about losing identity and becoming another Dubai,' says a Western diplomat. While the Al Thanis profess a very different type of urban development, officially eschewing the anything-goes, flashy, mass tourism of their Emirati neighbour and supposedly adhering more closely to Islamic values, not all Qataris are convinced. 'The question is, why do people think we're not going down the Dubai route?' says Mohammed Abdullah. 'Everything is going that way. We have liquor in hotels, so do they. They say we're not Dubai. I say why not, what's the difference?' And this being an autocratic Arab monarchy, there is little or no opportunity to question the direction Qatar and its capital are taking. It is the Al Thani royal family, rather than the Qatari people, who set the pace and call all the shots. Like many Qataris, Mohammed finds the price of quickfire growth and success too high. 'I don't remember a month in my life when I haven't heard construction – hammers, digging, construction, house-building. People are starting to run away from all this noise to seek peace and quiet abroad. Those who can afford it buy houses in Paris and London. You can't live in a workshop and construction site.'[11]

Some would argue that this construction, however inconvenient (and working in Doha often feels like living on a giant building site), is the essential prelude to creating a modern, world-class city. Landmark buildings, such as Mangera Yvars's Qatar Faculty of Islamic Studies, an enthralling spaceship with twin pylon minarets, are genuinely great architectural totems. But for all these thrills of modernity and the built environment, the engineer Mohammed Abdullah arguably speaks for many Qataris when he complains of one of the most immediately obvious consequences of rapid development.

'Qataris are starting to feel they're a minority in their own capital city and it's not a good feeling. We're a tiny minority of 10 per cent and within a few years we might be less than that. Personally I feel that's dangerous. Those who take important decisions will not be Qatari – in municipalities, education, health, construction, you name it. We should be more cautious. We can't just say we're developing and we need more people and that's it.'

To the question, where is Qatar going, an uncertainty felt by many but expressed in public by very few, there is yet to be a satisfactory answer. Where the West likes to talk about openness and transparency, Al Thani Qatar deals in opacity. No one knows what will happen next. The only constant in twenty-first-century Doha is rapid change. The expectation on the part of the royal family that speedily rising living standards will constitute an answer carries all before it. But in the longer term, there are questions about governance, political rights and wider participation to address. Many Qataris, like Mohammed Abdullah, object to a model of development that consigns Qataris to tiny minority status in their own country. Doha may be a genuinely remarkable urban phenomenon, but for many observers what it says about the state of contemporary Arab governance is rather less spectacular.

Directly across the lagoon from West Bay, the perfect vantage point from which to survey the skyline, another new edifice offers a cultural counterpoint that has become a Doha icon. Immediately controversial to some Muslim critics, who deplored the absence of a dome, I. M. Pei's Museum of Islamic Art, designed when the architect was in his nineties, is a jewel in this city of pearls.

Set on its own island at the southern end of the corniche, which it now defines, the museum is approached via an esplanade fringed with palm trees. One of the region's most audacious buildings of recent times, it is a cool, Cubist composition of square and octagonal blocks piled on top of each other to form a fortress-like edifice of serene simplicity, strength and grace. Astounding outside, the museum also astonishes inside. In purchasing so much Islamic culture outright, the Al Thani royal family is following a long line of fantastically wealthy patrons of the arts, the rulers of past Islamic Empires. Here are treasures culled by Qatari petrodollars from the length and breadth of the Islamic world and the greatest dynasties that once ruled it: ninth-century ceramics and tenth-century brass astrolabes from Abbasid Iraq; the thirteenth-century Mamluk gilded and enamelled glass 'Cavour' Vase from Syria; a monumental carved emerald plaque, inscribed with a Muslim prayer, and a gem-set, enamelled gold falcon, from seventeenth-century Mughal India; a wondrous, sixteenth-century illuminated manuscript of the poet Ferdowsi's *Shahnameh*, Book of Kings, chronicling the history of the Persian Empire, from Safavid Iran; the glazed turquoise, cobalt and midnight blue ceramic cenotaph from fourteenth-century Uzbekistan, heart of Timur's world-spanning empire; a set of carved stone capitals from Umayyad Cordoba's palace-city of Medinat al Zahra; a nineteenth-century Turkish *zarf* coffee-cup holder of gold set with diamonds and rubies, opulent to the point of vulgarity. Gems aside, the museum has genuine literary jewels in its collection. One of the most beautiful is the delicately illustrated thirteenth-century manuscript by the famous Arab geographer and natural historian Zakariyya ibn Mohammed al Qazwini (1203–83), its title strangely appropriate for the museum, and for Doha itself: *Ajaaib al Makhluqat wa Gharaaib al Mawdujat, The Wonders of Creation and the Oddities of Existence.*

When it was unveiled to the world in 2008, many considered the Museum of Islamic Art a new wonder of the Islamic world. Yet, as Mariam

Ibrahim al Mulla, the former director of the Qatar National Museum and an outspoken history professor at Qatar University, recalls, there was vigorous local criticism of the landmark. 'People said, "It's completely destroying our identity." I said, "Why?" They said, "It's like a military building, there's no dome, it's all steel, it's not Islamic." This is a completely Qatari attitude. First they'll reject and criticize it, then they'll end up loving it. In the 1990s, they said Suq Waqif wasn't proper Qatari architecture. Now everyone loves it.'[12]

Like the jeweller-turned-tycoon Alfardan, Mulla pays tribute to the leadership of the former emir Sheikh Hamad bin Khalifa al Thani. She gives short shrift to critics who argue Qatar is losing its identity amid the great influx of foreigners. 'If you didn't open Qatar to expats, you wouldn't get it developing so rapidly,' she says briskly. 'The country didn't move forward before Sheikh Hamad.'

While the megaprojects hit the headlines, more domestic development continues at full tilt in pell-mell fashion. Historic neighbourhoods such as Al Asmakh and Al Najada, south-west of Suq Waqif, home to successive generations of lower-income migrant workers from the Indian Sub-continent, are threatened by the rising tide of new construction. A recent study revealed that around half of the buildings in Al Asmakh had been subject to demolition and eviction notices.[13]

Though today the ruling Al Thani Dynasty is synonymous with Qatar and its capital – black-and-white portraits of *Tamim al majd*, Tamim the Glorious, have adorned car bumpers, skyscrapers, shop windows, mobile phone cases, flags, posters and concrete walls ever since the diplomatic rupture in 2017 with Saudi Arabia, the UAE, Bahrain and Egypt – this is a comparatively recent phenomenon. The family's pre-eminence in Qatar dates only to the mid-nineteenth century and the rule of Sheikh Mohammed bin Thani (r. 1850–78), by which time Doha – then known as Bidaa – was well established in the sources.

The first description of Bidaa came in 1801, when Captain David Seton, the British representative in Muscat, sailed there with the Omani ruler. It was then a diminutive coastal settlement. 'On the Northern hillock is a fortified House with a Wall and Square tower, in the Valley a breast Work with two Guns, and on the southern hillock two large huts with some kind of defence, and half a Mile to the Southward near the ridge is another Square building with a flag staff . . .'[14]

Tellingly, this first British brush with the future Doha had a military purpose. Seton considered this settlement of Al Suwaidi tribesmen a pirate base that was a threat to British commercial interests. Frustrated by shallow waters in his efforts to get his warship close enough to bombard the little town, he abandoned the mission and returned to Muscat.

Twenty years later, in 1821, the British East India Company's brig *Vestal* managed what Seton had been unable to achieve, bombarding and destroying the town for its supposed violation of the maritime peace treaty. It mattered little to the British that the residents of Bidaa had neither signed up to the treaty nor knew the reason for the destruction of their town. The British action forced up to 400 tribesmen to seek temporary shelter on neighbouring islands. A year later, while Lieutenant Cogan and his colleagues were compiling their survey of neighbouring 'Debai', Lieutenant Houghton of the Bombay Marine was sketching 'El Biddah' from the deck of the *Discovery*. His skyscraper-free skyline of mud huts and fortress towers is the earliest visual representation of Qatar known in the India Office records.[15]

By the late 1830s, when the twin settlements of Bidaa and Doha were less than a mile apart (and therefore often conflated by visitors), in the absence of an all-powerful Qatari leader this stretch of the Gulf Coast was emerging as a sanctuary for pirates and outlaws. This resulted in another British bombardment in 1841 in retaliation for more attacks against shipping. Unable to pay the fine of $300 entirely in cash, Salemin bin Nasir al Suwaidi, the chief of the Sudan tribe at Bidaa, was reduced to offering the British an additional forty-two silver bracelets, a sword, a silver hair ornament, four pairs of gold earrings, two of silver, two daggers and nine bead necklaces.[16]

The rise and fall of desert tribes in the ever-shifting sands can seem opaque and puzzling. Dates may be uncertain, the written records limited, partial or non-existent. What is clear in Qatar is that sometime between 1848 and 1850, the Al Thani family moved from the northern Qatari settlement of Fuwairit to Doha, from where over the next half century they would boldly write their name into national pre-eminence. The Al Thanis belonged to the Maadhid tribe and claim descent from the Bani Tamim of central Arabia. Like many of their fellow tribesmen they roved among the desert from settlement to settlement, moving to southern Qatar in the eighteenth century, then onwards first to Zubara and then, in the nineteenth century, to Fuwairit, around fifty miles north of Doha. The opportunistic relocation by Sheikh Mohammed bin Thani to Doha, precipitated by the death of the powerful tribal leader Isa bin Tarif, head of the Al Bin Ali tribe, proved decisive.

Captain Charles Golding Constable and Lieutenant A. W. Stiffe of the Indian Navy provided a glimpse of Doha in 1860. Constable was a cartographer of good artistic pedigree, the second son of the landscape artist

John Constable. Their description of the town, together with the first detailed map of 'Al Bidda', was published in *The Persian Gulf Pilot* in 1879:

> Doheh [Doha] is a town partly walled round, with several towers, half a mile S.W. by W. from Ras Nesseh; it extends about 800 yards along the beach. The sheikh's house is at a large round tower with the flagstaff on the beach, about the centre of the town; to the west of this tower is a small bight, where boats are hauled up to repair.

Apart from a small cultivated area one-and-a-half miles south-east of Bidaa, 'the whole country is desert'.[17]

Around the same time, Palgrave left his own, highly unflattering account of the place. Like a number of other visitors, he confused the two main towns, wrongly believing he was staying in Bidaa when in fact he was in Doha. He found it 'the miserable capital of a miserable province', a country of barren, sun-scorched hills, muddy beaches of slimy quicksand rimmed with sludge and seaweed, pebble-choked, grass-starved pastures and villages of 'wretched, most wretched' earth cottages and palm-leaf huts which were 'narrow, ugly and low'. Making his way to the castle, which he thought offered accommodation more suitable for goods than men, he was introduced to the chief, Mohammed bin Thani:

> a shrewd, wary old man, slightly corpulent, and renowned for prudence and good-humoured easiness of demeanour, but close-fisted and a hard customer at a bargain; altogether, he had much more the air of a business-like avaricious pearl merchant (and such he really is) than of an Arab ruler.[18]

Mohammed bin Thani's shrewdness was never in doubt. Displaying the quintessential leadership expected of a desert sheikh, he played off his hostile neighbours, the Al Khalifa of Bahrain and the Saudi leader Faisal bin Turki, against each other in the 1850s in a bid to wrest off his Bahraini overlords. In 1867 a combined attack by Mohammed bin Khalifa al Khalifa and the Abu Dhabi ruler Sheikh Zayed bin Khalifa al Nahyan resulted in the sacking of Wakra, Bidaa and Doha in 'circumstances of peculiar barbarity'.[19] Devastating in the short term, the aggression proved auspicious for Al Thani leadership in the longer term, prompting the British to depose the ruler of Bahrain in 1868 on the one hand and recognize Al Thani leadership and independence from Bahrain on the other. Full independence, however, had to wait another century, and it was under Ottoman, rather than British, rule that Doha fell in 1871. At that time the town consisted of 1,000 houses and a population of 4,000. In 1893, the forces of Jassim bin Mohammed al Thani (r. 1878–1913), founder of modern Qatar, defeated the Ottomans at the Battle of Wajba, a modest military encounter but a defining moment in the formation of the nation, from which time the Sublime Porte was no longer a formidable force to be reckoned with on the Qatari Peninsula.

Ottoman rule, henceforth only slightly felt, lasted until 1915, when the arrival in the Gulf of British warships forced a Turkish evacuation. On 20 August, British troops 'landed without opposition', seized various weapons that had been abandoned, including a mountain gun, two field guns and fourteen rifles with 120 cases of ammunition, and 'on the advice of the Political Officer' handed the rifles and ammunition to 'the Sheikh of Qatar who has given us every assistance'.[20] The following year, after protracted negotiations between Sheikh Abdullah bin Jassim al Thani (r. 1913–49) and Major Percy Cox, the British half of the Sykes–Picot Agreement which secretly divided up the Middle East between the British and French in 1916, Doha became the capital of the new British Protectorate of Qatar, making it the ninth and last of the Trucial States.

Up until this time, it is fair to say that Qatar and its fledgling capital hardly intruded upon the world's consciousness. It was a distant corner of the British Empire, largely unknown to outsiders. In 1935, that started to change. Significant for Britain as the year of George V's silver jubilee, it was a milestone for Qatar. On 24 January, Britain's *Daily Express* published a sensationalist account of the first official visit ever made by a Qatari emir – to Britain to attend the jubilee celebrations. The headline – 'Pearl King with 84 Wives' – set the tone for the article about the 'Sheik of Arabia' that followed, incongruously sandwiched between an advertisement for dentures and the musings of a retired Victorian bantamweight boxer. Emir Abdullah, son of the founder of modern Qatar, Jassim bin Mohammed al Thani (r. 1878–1913), the newspaper told its readers, kept an exotic court of 'astrologers, jesters, dancing girls and dervishes alleged to be gifted with prophecy'. As the Qatari writer and businessman Mohammed al Thani acidly observed in his study of Emir Jassim, never 'let the facts get in the way of a good story'.[21]

The *Daily Express* article, followed by another, three days later in the *People*, complete with a similar Orientalist fantasy about Emir Abdullah lounging on silken cushions surrounded by his harem beauties and 4,000 slaves, was more than a lurid colour feature. Deliberately leaked to the press by an American oil company, it represented an unexpectedly public display of Anglo-American rivalry over oil in the Middle East.[22] Specifically, it was an American challenge to the secretive monopoly Britain had awarded itself over oil concessions in its Gulf possessions. The emir was allowed to sign agreements only with British approval. American challenges in the Gulf would become more forceful, and British ability to resist them steadily weaker, throughout the century. As the Conservative Party politician Enoch Powell warned his colleague and future prime minister Anthony Eden in the late 1940s, 'in the Middle East our great enemies are the Americans'.[23]

British negotiations with Emir Abdullah were protracted and testing. Reading British accounts of the fencing between the two sides recalls Palgrave's earlier comments about the 'business-like' Sheikh Mohammed bin Thani, 'a hard customer at a bargain'. Lt-Col Sir Trenchard Craven William Fowle, the magnificently named Political Resident, Curzon's 'uncrowned king of the Gulf', found the sheikh's regular stalling extremely frustrating, complaining in a letter to the India Office of Abdullah's 'almost childish suspicious nature'. There was nothing childish about the Qatari emir. His suspicion of British motives was entirely justified. Under pressure from his neighbour Ibn Saud not to sign any concession without Saudi approval, simultaneously pursued by the American company Socal, who were offering him apparently more favourable terms, he was determined to extract every last possible concession from the British, including political guarantees of protection against external attack and recognition of his son Hamad as his heir, the key to his dynasty's enduring preeminence over any future rivals. Heroically distrustful of the proposed British bank transfer, Abdullah insisted on physically seeing the money that was to be paid to him before finalizing the agreement – 400,000 rupees on signature, followed by 150,000 rupees for five years and then 300,000 rupees a year until the concession expired. In the event of oil being discovered, the ruler would be paid 3 rupees per ton. The wily emir finally signed the seventy-five-year agreement with the Anglo-Persian Oil Company, which was immediately transferred to Petroleum Development (Qatar) Limited, on 17 May 1935.[24]

Initial progress was encouraging. On 11 October 1939, the day Albert Einstein wrote to President Roosevelt arguing for the feasibility of the atomic bomb, the Bahrain Political Agent reported ground-breaking news in a telegram to the Political Resident. 'Petroleum Development Qatar have had slight show of oil in their test well near Zekrit. Drilling continues.' In a letter of 14 January 1940, the Political Agent wrote to Emir Abdullah 'to congratulate you most heartily on the discovery of oil in Qatar. I earnestly hope that the future drilling which the Company will undertake will prove that Qatar possesses a valuable oil field.'[25]

It did. Although they did not come immediately, delayed by the advent of world war, oil and later gas revenues would completely reorient the Qatari economy from its traditional reliance on the pearl. In time they

would utterly transform the sleepy town of Doha into a staggeringly prosperous, ever-expanding global city and put the tiny peninsula of Qatar
definitively onto the world map. From being one of the poorest places
on earth, Qatar was destined to become the most wildly prosperous in
the world.

That, though, lay decades ahead. The more immediate challenges to
endure and overcome were those of the Second World War and the total
collapse of the pearling industry. Photographs of Doha in 1947, clustered
around the historic centre of Suq Waqif, show swathes of the town completely devastated and in ruins. Around 1949, the year Qatar exported
its first shipment of crude oil, Sir John Arthur Wilton, the first British
Political Agent in Qatar, reported that Doha resembled 'the aftermath of
an air raid'.[26]

Seven decades later, Suq Waqif (Standing Market) is a place transformed.
Restored in a comprehensive, twenty-first-century redevelopment,
it sprawls across 164,000 square metres of land immediately south
of the old Dhow Harbour, south-west of the port and Museum of
Islamic Art.

Inside Suq Waqif Falcon Hospital, a hooded bird stands to attention
on a perch. Behind it a large screen displays X-ray images of what could
be mistaken for a scrawny supermarket chicken. Medical staff in pristine
blue scrubs bustle about the place impressively, consulting charts and
comparing notes on their feathered patients. With a multinational staff of
thirty vets and employees from right across the Muslim world, from Pakistan to Iraq, the hospital caters to the medical needs of falcons and their
deep-pocketed owners, passionate fans of falconry, the ancient sport of
kings. If your falcon is missing a feather after a nasty scrap with a houbara
bustard, the hospital has a well-stocked feather bank. A broken wing?
The bird is whisked off to orthopaedic surgery. Digestion issues? Time for
a fecal and blood check, perhaps some pharmaceutical and toxicology
analysis. This is seriously expensive, state-of-the-art equipment that would
embarrass many countries' national health services. 'We get people coming from Saudi Arabia, Kuwait and all over the Gulf bringing their falcons
in here,' says Alhakam, an Iraqi-British medical engineer.[27]

Suq Waqif dates back to around the mid-nineteenth century, long
before the Gulf's falcons were able to enjoy such extravagant healthcare,
and takes its name from the way locals and desert Bedouin once did business here, standing on the banks of the Wadi Msheireb River, trading in
fish, goats, sheep, camels and wool. By the late 1990s, by which time
Qataris had embraced Doha's air-conditioned shopping malls and

boutiques, the neglected market had fallen into disrepair, compounded by a devastating fire in 2003. Local voices called upon the authorities to preserve what little heritage remained in a city in thrall to the bulldozer and crane. Led by the Amiri Diwan, or royal court, of Sheikh Hamad and his wife Sheikha Moza bint Nasser (all decisions come from the top here), a huge restoration project guided by the Qatari artist Mohammed Ali Abdullah began in 2004. The entire site was purchased for 1 billion Qatari riyals (around £197 million) with an additional 300 million riyals (£59 million) spent on restoration. Modern buildings were demolished and metal sheet roofs replaced with the traditional roofs of *dangeel* wood and bamboo held together with a binding layer of clay and straw. Old buildings were rebuilt in the local vernacular of sun-baked brick pillars supporting exposed *dangeel* beams with walls rendered in mud.[28]

Today, though Suq Waqif might strike some visitors as ersatz, a *medina*-lite lacking in the ancient, monument-filled intensity, drama and squalor of the *suqs* of Damascus, Cairo, Fez or Istanbul, it has re-emerged as Doha's working heritage centre, used by local traders, residents and tourists alike. Qataris and foreigners wander through new-old alleys wreathed in the sweet smoke of *shisha*, bumping into *alhmalah* porters, immaculately turned out in maroon waistcoats as they manoeuvre their shopping-filled wheelbarrows. This is the place to hunt for *oud*, spices, grain, clothes, carpets, pashminas, antiques, chocolates and sweets, household goods, leather items, handbags, trinkets ('I ♥ QATAR' baseball caps, scarves emblazoned with pictures of Sheikh Tamim), taxidermy, embroidered *bukhnoq* head coverings for girls, all under the watchful eye of mounted police whose virgin-white uniforms date to the 1940s. In the pet section, canaries, budgerigars, lovebirds and chicks dyed pink, purple, green and orange maintain an upbeat chorus among cages – guaranteed to upset Western sensitivities – containing panting, heat-afflicted cats, rabbits and fluffy puppies.* When shoppers have had their fill, many flop into the restaurants lining the streets, or drop into the two-storey Bismillah Hotel, the oldest in Doha, to grab an ice-cream or coffee.

At Caffe Bormet on the edge of the *suq*, Khaled Abu Jassim, a fifty-something retired Qatar Airways pilot, keeps a lonely vigil, reminiscing about how everything has changed in a city he no longer knows. For people of his generation Suq Waqif represents a small, reassuring oasis of the familiar in a city hurtling into the unknown, clattering and reverberating to the ubiquitous sound of diggers, excavators, hydraulic piling

---

* In the summer of 2014, with temperatures advancing into the forties Celsius, thousands signed a petition calling for improved conditions for the animals after a number of deaths.

vibrators, roaring generators and humming cranes. 'Even if I miss just one day here I feel sad,' he says. 'This place is in my heart.'[29]

Back in the falcon hospital, I wonder what happens to those falcons the vets are unable to save, who have gone to chase bustards in the great hunting sky above? Are they buried? Alhakam shakes his head. 'We have an incinerator upstairs,' he says.

By the time Qatar declared its independence on 3 September 1971, following a diplomatic breakdown within the proposed union of nine emirates, Doha was a town that had grown from around 14,000 in the 1950s – a size that it more or less maintained for the first half of the century – to over 83,000. Qatari society at this time was still characterized by poverty and underdevelopment. The 1970 census found two-thirds of Qataris over the age of fifteen were illiterate.[30]

Independence changed the rules of the game. From 1972, an increasingly self-confident government held sway from its official seat in the Diwan al Emiri, prominently located at the southern end of the corniche across from Dhow Harbour at the western end of Old Doha. After what was seen as British exploitation in the dying days of empire, Qatar moved decisively to reassert total control of the energy sector. In 1973 it acquired a 25 per cent stake in Qatar Petroleum Company's onshore concessions and in the offshore concessions of Shell Company Qatar, active on the peninsula since the 1950s. A year later the government said it would acquire the remaining shares in both companies, and by 1977 nationalization was complete.

It was time to build a city. From 1974, led by the Emiri Diwan of Sheikh Khalifa bin Hamad al Thani (r. 1972–95), a massive dredging and land reclamation scheme of over 630 hectares was launched to create the 'New District of Doha', known locally as Dhafna (the buried). It reshaped Doha Bay into an elegant crescent whose tapered northern arm is today's West Bay business district, and provided large quantities of land for residential development, the diplomatic and government quarter, Qatar University's campus and the corniche park and promenade, one of the city's most visible public spaces. The corniche has remained the focal point of the city ever since, a semicircle from which a series of mirroring ring roads radiate inland towards the desert.

The 1970s saw a wave of compulsory acquisitions to control the direction of a city whose centre was 90 per cent privately owned. The bulldozers moved in and the growing population moved out to new suburban developments. Traditionally twisting narrow alleys gave way to roads wide enough for cars, mud-brick homes around small courtyards were replaced, first by two-storey modern villas, later by high-rise tower blocks. 'We had a lot of money and didn't know what to do with it,' says Harib Abdul Qadir, a senior government planner.[31]

More money, much more, would flow into the government's coffers once revenues from liquefied natural gas exports came onstream. Discovered offshore in the early 1970s, the world's largest gas field moved into production in 1991, generating fantastic sums, attracting new waves of migrants and funding continued expansion of the capital. Shared with Iran, the South Pars / North Dome gas field has reserves of 51 trillion cubic metres spread across an area of 3,700 square miles.

Natural gas, and the economic growth it unleashed, has effectively created a new country. At independence in 1971, GDP stood at $388 million. By 1974, it had shot to $2.4 billion, rising gently through the 1980s and 90s, before surging exponentially in the 2000s, from $17.8 billion in 2000 to a peak of $206 billion in 2014. This represents a virtually unfathomable fortune for a country whose population in 2017 was 2.6 million, of which Qataris numbered just 313,000, or 12 per cent of the total, behind Indians (650,000) and Nepalis (350,000).[32]

Blessed with this geological twist of fate, or the divine hand of Allah, Qatar has used the burgeoning revenues from its natural gas sector to fund ambitious development at home and an increasingly assertive foreign policy designed to win influence and prestige abroad.

Those in the outside world accustomed to dealing with a small, marginalized conservative Gulf state have found the hyperactive Qatari foreign policy since the mid-1990s something of a paradox and a difficult puzzle to crack. Notwithstanding the intense criticism levelled at Doha by allies and enemies alike, Qatar has not baulked at using its petrodollars to fund a much more interventionist stance in the Islamic world, consigning to history its traditional role as a quiet, behind-the-scenes mediator.

In 1996, a year after Sheikh Hamad became emir, Qatar became the first Gulf nation to establish relations with Israel. At the same time it strengthened ties on the one hand with neigbouring Iran – anathema to Washington and the Gulf's Sunni Arab states, especially Saudi Arabia – and on the other with the US, hosting two large military bases at Al Udeid and Sayliyah. In 2006, it supported both Hezbollah and Hamas in Gaza. During the Arab Spring protests that broke out against the region's oppressive regimes in 2011, Qatar actively backed democratic movements, while simultaneously financing and arming radical Islamist groups and, some argue, even terrorists – a charge Doha denies. When the Libyan revolution exploded onto the streets in the same year, Qatar took the unprecedented step of joining the NATO operation against the Gaddafi regime before secretly and unilaterally arming its favoured local brigades. It has also directly backed challenges to the Assad regime in Syria, while supporting the short-lived Islamist Muslim Brotherhood government in Egypt.[33]

Like neighbouring Dubai, Doha has also used its petrodollars to invest overseas in high-profile spending sprees and displays of financial muscle. Flagship international investments by the $335 billion Qatar Investment Authority and its subsidiaries have included Canary Wharf and the Shard skyscraper in London, the tallest structure in Europe, the retail emporium Harrods, Paris Saint-Germain football club, and stakes in some of the world's best-known companies such as Volkswagen, Deutsche Bank, Porsche, Rosneft, Glencore, Sainsbury's, Siemens and Credit Suisse. During a visit to Sheikh Hamad's fabulously restored, 4,000-square-metre, seventeen-bedroom London palace, Dudley House, at 100 Park Lane, the Queen was reportedly so impressed she said it made Buckingham Palace 'look rather dull' by comparison.[34]

The acceleration of Doha's urban sprawl in the second half of the century was no less remarkable than these economic figures and such lavish spending. The total urban area increased from a modest 130 hectares at mid-century to more than 7,100 hectares in 1995, the year the new emir Sheikh Hamad started to open Qatar up to the outside world with a series of liberalizing reforms.[35] Development of the energy sector, lukewarm during his more conservative father Sheikh Khalifa's time, accelerated apace.

In 1996, he established the satellite channel Al Jazeera, putting $150 million of his own money into the venture. In the stultified world of Arab media, which for decades had trotted out dreary regime propaganda from the shores of the Atlantic to the Gulf, Al Jazeera was a thunderbolt that struck at its heart with outspoken coverage of regional and international politics. By 1999 it was broadcasting twenty-four hours a day. The channel represented the media arm of Doha's bold new foreign policy and its influence was both immediate and controversial, infuriating policymakers and leaders the length and breadth of the Arab world, from Riyadh, Ramallah and Rabat, to Damascus, Baghdad, Cairo and Kuwait City, together with those in Washington, Jerusalem and many more cities besides.

On my first trip to Doha, in 2002, on assignment for the *Financial Times*, I checked into the city's newest hotel. Built on two man-made islands on what was then the bare northern fringes of the city (today it rubs shoulders with Hussein Alfardan's Pearl development, compared to which it already looks like the poor relation), the $545 million Ritz-Carlton was a byword for excess. Its Canadian interior designer had been told there was no budget to limit his imagination or spending. His mission was to make the hotel one of the most luxurious in the Middle East. With a seven-and-a-half-metre-high Swarovski teardrop chandelier of 2,000 crystals, acres of gold and silver leaf, Italian marble, eighteenth-century tapestries and umpteen suites of out-and-out opulence, he appeared to have succeeded. Yet the Qatari capital, if no longer a sleepy pearl-fishing village, was hardly exciting, either. In 2008, Lonely Planet rated it the most boring city on earth.[36]

I headed straight for Al Jazeera, which was then under fire from all sides, as it remains to this day. Ali Mohammed Kamal, the marketing director, was taking it all in his stride. 'The minister of information in Bahrain said Al Jazeera was owned by the Zionists,' he said with an ironic smile. 'Kuwait said we are an Iraqi voice. America said we're an Osama bin Laden medium, Israel that we're a Palestinian medium, the Palestinians that we're a Jewish medium. It's difficult to believe we have so many shareholders – Saddam, Sharon and Arafat all together.'[37]

If Al Jazeera has proved too strong meat for Qatar's Arab neighbours to stomach (as well as for the US, which bombed the network's offices in Kabul in 2001 and Baghdad in 2003), Doha's opportunist entry onto the world's political stage in the twenty-first century has been no less contentious. On 2 December 2010, to Doha's delight and the astonishment of the world, Sepp Blatter, the then president of world football's governing body FIFA, announced that Qatar had won the bid to host the 2022 World Cup. The shock decision was immediately overshadowed by accusations of bribery and corruption and the announcement of an FBI investigation, which eventually claimed the scalp of the hitherto impregnable Blatter. Qatar has always strenuously denied any accusations of wrongdoing.

Thrusting Qatar into the limelight has not been without its cost for the Al Thani ruling dynasty. Critics have repeatedly assailed the city-state for harbouring terrorists and extremists, such as the leadership of Hamas, together with members of the Taliban, Muslim Brotherhood and other controversial Islamists. Amid the purring limousines and dhows bobbing in the bay, 'Doha has become home to an exotic array of fighters, financiers and ideologues, a neutral city with echoes of Vienna in the Cold War, or a Persian Gulf version of the fictional pirate bar in the "Star Wars" movies.' The sudden projection of massive funding and power beyond its borders, together with an allegedly ambivalent attitude towards the fight against terrorists and extremists, led Saudi Arabia, the UAE, Bahrain and Egypt to sever diplomatic relations in 2017, resulting in an air and land blockade considered the most serious political crisis in the region in decades.[38] Saudi Arabia, long accustomed to primacy within the Gulf – it sees itself as the rightful leader of the Sunni Islamic world in opposition to Shia Iran – has not taken kindly to its upstart neighbour's efforts to conduct its own independent foreign policy. In 2018, the toxic diplomatic conflict between traditionally brotherly Riyadh and Doha worsened to the point where Saudi Arabia announced plans to turn Qatar into an island by digging a forty-mile channel along its border with its neighbour.[39]

Underlying the conspicuous munificence in Qatar and its audacious power plays is a straightforward desire to be noticed. To a considerable extent individual egos drive national policy within autocratic states like Qatar and Saudi Arabia, together with much of the region. 'There's tremendous one-upmanship here,' says a Western academic. 'The tradition is all about showing prestige and keeping one's followers. When Dubai builds towers, they feel they have to do the same. When Abu Dhabi gets the Louvre, it's the same thing.'[40]*

The spirit of ego-driven competition is evident in the built environment, too. Some argue that development in Doha has taken on 'a fetishistic quality' that pits Qatar against her Gulf neighbours, with Formula One racetracks, ever taller skyscrapers, sports stadiums, museums and university campuses emerging as 'the symbolic capital' by which the countries assert their position at the forefront of 'a cosmopolitan rendition of modernity'.[41]

Yet Qataris today are less inclined to worry about what foreign social scientists think of their city and are more focused on enjoying their newfound wealth and living the good life. Many young professionals are simply having the time of their lives. What may be discomfiting for older Qataris is an intoxicating blast of freedom and modernity for a younger generation as their fabulously rich country opens up to the world for the first time. The immense opportunities on offer to a generation of Qataris whose grandparents endured unimaginably tough and basic livelihoods elicit enormous pride and excitement. 'It's all change,' says Dr Mariam Ibrahim al Mulla over at Qatar University. 'I absolutely love it.'

Doha is, clearly, still a work in progress – but then so are all cities. They are dynamic, shifting centres, which ebb and flow, rise and decline, mirroring the fortunes of their residents and nations. As Herodotus – who I also quoted at the beginning of the book – remarked 2,500 years ago, 'those many cities which were once great, have mostly become small, and

---

* The Louvre Abu Dhabi was inaugurated on 8 November 2017 by French President Emmanuel Macron, UAE Vice President Mohammed bin Rashid al Maktoum and Crown Prince of Abu Dhabi Mohammed bin Zayed al Nahyan.

those that in my time were great, were in former times small'.[42] Doha, in the minds of its rulers and many of its residents, has both the ambition and resources to become great.

The greatness of the Dar al Islam, once written across the world in imperial might and splendour, with world-beating cities like Baghdad, Damascus, Cordoba, Fez, Cairo, Samarkand, Isfahan and Istanbul at its core, is far more difficult to discern in the early twenty-first century. The view across the Middle East from the tiny peninsula nation of Qatar is in fact profoundly disturbing.

Division and disorder rule. Conflict and bloodshed, instability, poverty, even humanitarian catastrophe in countries such as Yemen, Syria and Iraq, have become terrifyingly prevalent. From one end of the Middle East and North Africa to the other, vicious *fitna*, the age-old plague of division and strife, has erupted again.

My own experiences in Kabul, Tripoli and Baghdad have coincided with intensely controversial foreign interventions which have helped unleash and deepen such divisions and whose consequences will reverberate for years to come. Kabul's bitter recent experience, first under the Taliban from 1996 and later during the American-led war from 2001, thrust Afghanistan from the margins into the centre of international affairs. At one level the recent history of this turbulent country and its mountain-ringed capital is a case study of the troubled relationship between the West and the Muslim world. Tripoli today tells a disconsolate story that has evolved from the euphoria of revolution against a despised dictator to chaos, infighting and despair. And, hard on the heels of wars in Afghanistan and Iraq (branded a 'crusade' by President Bush), it sounds a warning on the perils of Western intervention in the Islamic world.

In its list of the causes of the Arab Spring protests, the world's most popular encyclopedia includes authoritarianism, dictatorship, political corruption, human rights violations, unemployment, inflation, kleptocracy, poverty and sectarianism. It is an accurate and excoriating charge sheet on the state of the Arab world and it ends with the self-immolation of Mohammed Bouazizi, a twenty-six-year-old Tunisian street vendor so relentlessly harassed by the authorities that he set himself on fire on 4 January 2011, igniting a series of revolutions across the region.[43] Eight years later, of all the countries which so recently reverberated to the roars of protesters – '*Al shaab yurid isqat al nizam!*', 'The people want to bring down the regime!' – only Tunisia has some semblance of freedom, though its people continue to battle poverty and unemployment on an immiserating scale.

Defying the hopes and dreams of its youthful revolutionaries, the Arab

Spring gave way to an Arab Winter characterized by renewed authoritarianism and, in places like Syria and Iraq, a resurgence of Islamist extremism
and terrorism. It is one of the many tragedies of recent decades that good
governance, once so integral to successive, world-spanning Islamic
Empires, seems to have become an oxymoron across much, though certainly not all, of the Islamic heartland. Egypt is once again a police state,
Iraq lurches in and out of bloody havoc, Libya is in turmoil, Yemen is the
world's worst humanitarian disaster, Afghanistan continues its endless
conflict and Syria has buried so many hundreds of thousands that precise
figures of the war dead are no longer possible to determine. Damascus,
one of the world's oldest cities, which until recently prided itself on lasting
peace, stability and harmony between its different communities, has
become synonymous with slaughter, sectarian strife and the grotesque
abuses of dictatorship. Almost a decade of conflict has left it hollowed out
and broken. The picture across the region has become so grim that it has
drawn comparisons with Europe's Thirty Years' War (1618–48), a devastating conflict founded on entrenched sectarian divisions and nation-state
rivalry that resulted in 8 million deaths.[44]

One of the most poignant differences between these cities at their apo-
gees and today can be discerned in the make-up of their populations. Over
time the heterogeneous has given way to the homogeneous. Most of these
cities were once vibrantly cosmopolitan, melting pots of two or three of
the Abrahamic faiths and a many-layered mosaic of different communities.
Within their collective walls Jews rubbed shoulders with Sunni and Shia
Muslims, Arabs with Afghans, Iranians, Kurds, Berbers, Franks, Greeks,
Genoese and Venetians, Turks, Tajiks and Turkmen, Hindus, Mongols,
Zoroastrians and Yazidis, and even the odd Englishman, Frenchman or
Italian, alongside Christians from a bewildering smorgasbord of sects –
Assyrian, Armenian Catholic, Coptic, Chaldean, Maronite, Melkite,
Nestorian, Jacobite, Syriac, Protestant and Orthodox.

Their strength as cities both derived from and engendered these diverse
populations. As recently as 1917, the Jews of Baghdad, one of the oldest
and most significant Jewish communities in the world, made up almost
40 per cent of the city's population and thrived as businessmen, financiers
and merchants. A century later, after constant hounding, a series of forced
expulsions, dispossessions and a pogrom in 1941, the Jewish community,
which had lived in Iraq for twenty-five centuries since Nebuchadnezzar
sacked Jerusalem and drove Jews into Babylonian captivity, had shrivelled
into single-figure oblivion. Outside Israel, the Jews of the Middle East are
a vanishing tribe and Christians, whose faith was born in these desert
sands, are becoming an endangered species from Egypt and Syria to Iraq.

Where there *is* order and stability in the Middle East and North Africa today, it invariably comes at a high cost, with freedom the most evident casualty. In contrast to much of the rest of the world, which in recent decades has made strides towards greater freedom and democracy, from Asia and Africa to South America, the Middle East, once testament to the Arab genius for civilization, has turned back the clock and shrivelled in on itself.

Islamic Empires were once quintessentially outward-looking, dynamic, intellectually curious and often exceptionally tolerant for their time. Now much of the region, assaulted from without and within, has become intro-verted, intolerant and stagnant, held hostage by strongmen – never women – who have failed to lead their people into a freer, safer modern world. The Dar al Islam reached its pinnacle when absolute monarchy was the norm in the West. While democracy steadily took root in Europe from the nineteenth century, the Islamic world of the Middle East never made a similar transition, despite stuttering efforts by ambitious modernizers in Cairo, Istanbul, Beirut and Tehran in the eighteenth and nineteenth centuries.[45] A crisis of governance remains at the heart of the region's agonies.

The two cities here which represent the twentieth and twenty-first centuries offer something more positive. Of the two, Dubai is the more interesting and most reminiscent of the great Arab cities of the past, with its deeply rooted policy of open doors, free trade and tolerance. Where it has had to rely on the ingenuity of its rulers to succeed in the absence of vast energy reserves, Doha has been able to sit back and watch the natural gas revenues pouring in. The two emirates have pursued markedly differ-ent approaches to development. While Dubai has concentrated on business and trade over politics, Qatar has espoused a much more political line in recent years. Its flirtation with Islamist movements has caused great upset within the region and won the emirate few friends internationally. Never-theless, in a replay of the economic boom enjoyed by Baghdad in the eighth and ninth centuries and Samarkand in the fourteenth, the world has beaten a path to both cities. Although each undoubtedly falls down on political freedom and inclusion, Dubai surely exemplifies the wisdom and benefits of tolerance, free trade and efficient governance. Arabs may sneer at Dubai as an arriviste on the world stage, light on history and long on hedonism, but that does not stop them flocking there in droves to make new lives and fortunes.

A city is an idea. It is the realization, however imperfect, of human-kind's aspiration for a better future. 'When a man rides a long time through wild regions he feels the desire for a city,' wrote the Italian novelist Italo Calvino. Every day migrants all over the world make this journey from wild regions to myriad cities in search of this elusive promise. For Ibn Khaldun in the fourteenth century, the city may have been 'a culturally refined but morally corruptive space', but that did not prevent countless millions of men and women from responding to the irresistible centripetal pull of Islamic cities over many centuries, right up to the present day.[46]

Today the great Islamic Empires are long gone, the lustre of their capital cities sadly dimmed. The best days of almost all the fifteen cities remembered in these pages are probably behind them, like those of other earlier empires headquartered in Athens, Rome and London. Yet in the Asian Century we now inhabit, we can perhaps still make out the echoes of their magnificence, tolerance and invention and their restless, cosmopolitan, risk-taking populations, in cities such as Dubai and Doha. Today, amid all the turmoil in the heart of the Islamic world, the great achievements of its history and the possibilities for its future should not be forgotten.

Notes

Preface

1. William Shakespeare, *Coriolanus*, Act 3 Scene 1.   2. 'Erdoğan: Turkey is the only country that can lead the Muslim world', Yeni Şafak, 15 October 2018 (https://www.yenisafak.com/en/world/erdogan-turkey-is-the-only-country-that-can-lead-the-muslim-world-3463638).

1. Mecca – Mother of All Cities

1. 'Saudis hit back over Mecca castle', BBC, 9 January 2002 (http://news.bbc.co.uk/1/hi/world/middle_east/1748711.stm).   2. For a highly critical commentary on the twenty first-century redevelopment of Mecca, see Ziauddin Sardar, *Mecca: The Sacred City*, pp. 345–7.   3. 'Mecca under threat: Outrage at plan to destroy the "birthplace" of the Prophet Mohamed and replace it with a new palace and luxury malls', *Independent*, 12 November 2014 (http://www.independent.co.uk/news/world/middle-east/mecca-under-threat-outrage-at-plan-to-destroy-the-birthplace-of-the-prophet-mohamed-and-replace-it-with-a-new-palace-and-luxury-malls 9857098.html).   4. 'Builders flock to Mecca to tap into pilgrimage boom', Reuters, 9 June 2011 (http://www.reuters.com/article/2011/06/09/us-saudi-mecca-development-idUSTRE7581G320110609).   5. For a summary of the redevelopment of Mecca and reactions to it, see 'Mecca's mega architecture casts shadow over hajj', *Guardian*, 23 October 2012 (http://www.theguardian.com/artanddesign/2012/oct/23/mecca-architecture-hajj1).   6. Bukhari, *Sahi Bukhari*, 1:2:48 (http://www.usc.edu/org/cmje/religious-texts/hadith/bukhari/002-sbt.php#001.002.048).   7. Author interview, 16 November 2014.   8. Quoted in Sardar, p. 106.   9. Henri Lammens, 'Mecca', *Encyclopedia of Islam*, vol. 5, p. 439; Henri Lammens, *Islam: Beliefs and Institutions*, p. 16.   10. Quoted in Francis E. Peters, *Mecca: A Literary History of the Muslim Holy Land*, p. 21.   11. Quran 14:37.   12. Lammens, 'Mecca', p. 439.   13. Ibn Ishaq, *The Life of Muhammad*, p. 46.   14. Mahmud Ibrahim, *Merchant Capital and Islam*, p. 35.   15. Peters, p. 3.   16. See Fred M. Donner, 'The Historical Context', in *The Cambridge Companion to the Quran*, p. 33; Patricia Crone, *Meccan Trade and the Rise of Islam*, p. 204; G. H. A. Juynboll, *Studies on the First Century of Islamic Society*, p. 2.   17. Fred Donner, *Muhammad and the Believers: At the Origins of Islam*, p. 51.   18. Crone, p. 134.   19. Tom Holland, *In the Shadow of the Sword: The Battle for Global Empire and the End of the Ancient World*, p. 303.   20. Azraqi, *Kitab Akhbar Makka*, 1:66, quoted in Zayde Antrim, *Routes and Realms: The Power of Place in the Early Islamic World*, p. 44.   21. See Quran 2:125–7.   22. Peters, p. 3.   23. Quran 6:92; 42:7.   24. Montgomery W. Watt and M. V. McDonald, *The History of al-Tabari*, vol. VI: *Muhammad at Mecca*, p. 52.   25. 'Scandal of the hajj pilgrims who are cheated by devious tour operators', *Guardian*, 8 October 2016 (https://www.theguardian.com/money/2016/oct/08/scandal-hajj-pilgrims-cheated-devious-tour-operators).   26. Karen Armstrong, *Muhammad: A Prophet for Our Time*, p. 28.   27. For a summary of this development, see Ibrahim, pp. 41–2.   28. M. J. Kister, 'Some Reports Concerning Mecca: From Jahiliyya to Islam', *Journal of the Economic & Social History of the Orient*, 15 (1972), p. 76.   29. A key figure among the

revisionists, Patricia Crone dropped a bombshell into the field with her sceptical and ground-breaking 1987 work, *Meccan Trade and the Rise of Islam*. For a summary of the debate and an overview of life in pre-Islamic Arabia, see Gene W. Heck, ' "Arabia without Spices": An Alternate Hypothesis: The Issue of "Makkan Trade and the Rise of Islam" ', *Journal of the American Oriental Society*. More recently Tom Holland has added further fuel to the controversy with his *In the Shadow of the Sword: The Battle for Global Empire and the End of the Ancient World*. For one of the latest academic contributions to this debate, see Glen Bowersock, *Crucible of Islam*, pp. 48–63.   30. This date is also problematic. It is more likely that Abraha's attack took place in around 547 since he is not thought to have ruled long after 553. The eighth-century historian Ibn al Kalbi writes that Mohammed was born twenty-three years after the Year of the Elephant. See Paul Gwynne, *Buddha, Jesus and Muhammad: A Comparative Study*, n. 45, p. 21.   31. For an extraordinary view from the top, see 'The Crescent atop the Makkah Clock Tower is Home to a Prayer Room' (http://www.urban-hub.com/landmarks/the-crescent-atop-the-makkah-clock-tower-is-home-to-a-prayer-room/).   32. Quran 96:1–5.   33. Ibn Ishaq, p. 106.   34. Ibid., p. 119.   35. Ibid., pp. 143–5.   36. Shibli Nomani, *Sirat al Nabi*, p. 242, quoted in Sardar, p. 47.   37. Ibid., p. 464.   38. Ibid.   39. For selected Muslim reactions to the massacre of the Qurayza, see Andrew G. Bostom (ed.), *The Legacy of Jihad: Islamic Holy War and the Fates of Non-Muslims*, pp. 17–19. For European reactions, see M. J. Kister, 'The Massacre of the Banu Qurayza: A Re-examination of a Tradition', *Jerusalem Studies in Arabic and Islam*, 8 (1986), p. 63.   40. Quoted in Francis E. Peters, *Muhammad and the Origins of Islam*, p. 225.   41. Ibn Ishaq, p. 547.   42. Ibid., p. 548.   43. Ibid., p. 552.   44. Peters, *Mecca*, p. 89.   45. Crone, p. 244.   46. Peters, *Mecca*, p. 91.   47. Azraqi, pp. 306–38.   48. For the full Tabari story, see G. R. Hawting, *The Idea of Idolatry and the Emergence of Islam: From Polemic to History*, pp. 130–32. For the version in Ibn Ishaq, see pp. 165–7.   49. Sardar, p. 360.

2. Damascus – The Perfumed Paradise

1. Acts 9:11. 'And the Lord said unto him, "Arise and go into the street which is called Straight, and inquire in the house of Judas for the one called Saul of Tarsus; for behold, he prayeth.'   2. A comprehensive damage assessment of Syria's largest cities conducted by the UN in 2018 found a total of 109,000 damaged structures, a quarter of which were in Damascus, second only to Aleppo. See 'Damage Caused by the Syrian Civil War: What the Data Say', 27 June 2018 (https://towardsdatascience.com/damage-caused-by-the-syrian-civil-war-what-the-data-say-ebad5796fca8).   3. Cited in Guy Le Strange, *Palestine under the Moslems: A Description of Syria and the Holy Land*, p. 237. Ibn Battuta, the peripatetic, fourteenth-century 'Traveller of Islam', deemed it 'the city which surpasses all other cities in beauty and takes precedence of them in loveliness'. See H. A. R. Gibb, *The Travels of Ibn Battutah*, vol. 1, p. 118.   4. Ibn Asakir, *Tarikh Madinat Dimashq*, 1:47–90, cited in Zayde Antrim, 'Ibn Asakir's Representations of Syria and Damascus in the Introduction to the *Tarikh Madinat Dimashq*', *International Journal of Middle East Studies*, 38 (2006), p. 113.   5. See Philip Hitti, *The Origins of the Islamic State. Being a Translation from the Arabic, Accompanied with Annotations, Geographic and Historic Notes of the Kitab Futuh al-Buldan of al-Imaam abu-l 'Abbas Aḥmad ibn Jabir al-Baladhuri*, p. 10. For Abu Bakr's rallying of Muslim warriors for the conquest of Syria, see p. 165.   6. Ibid., p. 187.   7. N. Elisséeff, 'Dimashq', *Encyclopedia of Islam 2*, vol. 2, p. 280.   8. Hugh Kennedy, *The Byzantine and Early Islamic Middle East*, p. 17.   9. R. Stephen Humphreys, 'Syria', in Chase F. Robinson (ed.), *The New Cambridge History of Islam*, vol. 1, p. 512.   10. Ross Burns, *Damascus: A History*, p. 103.   11. 'The zeal and virtue of Ali were never outstripped by any recent proselyte. He united the qualifications of a poet, a soldier, and a saint; his wisdom still breathes in a collection of moral and religious sayings; and every antagonist, in the combats of the tongue or of the sword, was subdued by his eloquence and valour. From the first hour of his mission to the last rites of his funeral, the apostle was never forsaken by a generous friend, whom he delighted to name his brother, his vicegerent, and the faithful

Aaron of a second Moses.' Edward Gibbon, *The Decline and Fall of the Roman Empire*, vol. 5, pp. 381–2. 12. Cited in Gérard Degeorge, *Damascus*, p. 31. 13. For a portrait of Umayyad Damascus, see Philip Hitti, *Capital Cities of Arab Islam*, pp. 61–84. 14. Cited in Burns, n. 25, p. 285. 15. Robert Hoyland, *In God's Path: The Arab Conquests*, pp. 228–9. 16. Peter Frankopan, *The Silk Roads: A New History of the World*, p. 90. 17. Yaqubi, *Tarikh ibn Wadih*, vol. 2, p. 283. Cited in Philip Hitti, *Capital Cities of Arab Islam*, p. 68. 18. J. B. Chabot (tr. and ed.), *Chronique de Michel le Syrien*, vol. 2, p. 475. Cited in Humphreys, p. 520. 19. Finbar Barry Flood, *The Great Mosque of Damascus: Studies on the Makings of an Umayyad Visual Culture*, p. 1. 20. Robert Hoyland (tr.), *Theophilus of Edessa's Chronicle*, pp. 199–200. 21. Ibn Asakir, *Tarikh Madinat Dimashq*, pp. 25–6, cited in K. A. C. Creswell, *Early Muslim Architecture, Part 1: Umayyads 622–750*, p. 102. 22. Le Strange, p. 233. 23. Tabari, *The History of al-Tabari, vol. 26: The Waning of the Umayyad Caliphate*, p. 194. 24. Oleg Grabar, *Formation of Islamic Art*, pp. 64–5. Cited in Humphreys, p. 521. 25. Flood, pp. 5–8. 26. R. J. C. Broadhurst (tr. and ed.), *The Travels of Ibn Jubayr*, pp. 306, 300. 27. 'Protesters stage rare demo in Syria', Al Jazeera, 15 March 2011 (https://www.aljazeera.com/news/middleeast/2011/03/20113151834383782. html). 28. N. Elisséeff, *La Description de Damas d'Ibn Asakir*, pp. 24–5. For a collection of Muslim writers' impressions of the Umayyad Mosque, see also Degeorge, pp. 35–8 and Nancy Khalek, *Damascus after the Muslim Conquest*, p. 137. 29. Mary's refuge is referred to in Quran 23:50; Abraham's Damascus connections are referenced in Genesis 14:15 and 15:2. 30. Cited in Creswell, p. 130. 31. Hoyland, *In God's Path*, pp. 171–2. 32. Ibid., p. 199. 33. Kenneth Baxter Wolf, *Conquerors and Chroniclers of Early Medieval Spain*, p. 145. 34. Edward Gibbon, *The History of the Decline and Fall of the Roman Empire*, vol. 6, p. 470. 35. Abul Faraj al Isfahani, *Kitab al Aghani*, vol. VI, p. 126. Cited in Robert Hamilton, *Walid and his Friends: An Umayyad Tragedy*, p. 20. 36. Betsy Williams, 'Walid II', Metropolitan Museum of Art, 12 June 2012 (https://www.metmuseum.org/exhibitions/listings/2012/byzantium-and-islam/blog/characters/posts/walid-ii). 37. Hoyland (tr.), p. 242. 38. Ibid., pp. 35–7. 39. Ibid., p. 246. 40. Ibid., p. 253. 41. Cyril Glassé, *The New Encyclopedia of Islam*, pp. 11–12. 42. Hugh Kennedy, *When Baghdad Ruled the Muslim World*, p. 8. 43. Roy Mottahedeh, 'The Abbasid Caliphate in Iran', in *The Cambridge History of Iran, vol. IV: The Period from the Arab Invasion to the Saljuqs*, p. 57. 44. See Chase F. Robinson, 'The Violence of the Abbasid Revolution', in Yasir Suleiman (ed.), *Living Islamic History: Studies in Honour of Professor Carole Hillenbrand*, p. 236. 45. Al Maqrizi, *Book of Contention and Strife Concerning the Relations between the Banu Umayya and the Banu Hashim*, p. 92. 46. Degeorge, p. 43. 47. Hitti, *Capital Cities of Arab Islam*, p. 70. 48. Hugh Kennedy, *The Early Abbasid Caliphate: A Political History*, p. 24. 49. Burns, p. 124. 50. Cited in Degeorge, pp. 42–3. 51. Humphreys, p. 525. 52. Ibid., pp. 533–5. 53. Hoyland, *In God's Path*, p. 230.

3. Baghdad – City of Peace, City of Blood

1. Al Muqaddasi, *The Best Divisions for Knowledge of the Regions*, p. 108. 2. 'Iraqi campus is under gang's sway', *New York Times*, 19 October 2009. 3. See Guy Le Strange, *Baghdad during the Abbasid Caliphate*, pp. 10–11. 4. Quoted in Gaston Wiet, *Baghdad: Metropolis of the Abbasid Caliphate*, pp. 10–11. 5. Cited in Jacob Lassner, *The Topography of Baghdad in the Early Middle Ages*, p. 56. 6. Ibid., p. 49. 7. Masudi, *The Meadows of Gold: The Abbasids*, p. 33. 8. Hugh Kennedy, *When Baghdad Ruled the Muslim World*, p. 132. 9. Ibid., p. 65; Edward Gibbon, *The History of the Decline and Fall of the Roman Empire*, vol. 1, p. 964. 10. Muqaddasi, p. 60. Cited in Peter Frankopan, *The Silk Roads: A New History of the World*, p. 94. 11. Philip Hitti, *Capital Cities of Arab Islam*, p. 94. 12. André Clot, *Harun al-Rashid and the World of the Thousand and One Nights*, p. 218. 13. Masudi, p. 123. 14. Ibn al Zubayr, *Kitab al Hadaya wa al Tuhaf (Book of Gifts and Rarities)*, pp. 121–2. 15. For a brief summary of the Darb Zubayda, see Marcus Milwright, *An Introduction to Islamic Archaeology*, pp. 162–4. 16. For accounts of Arib,

see Abu al Faraj al Isfahani, *Kitab al Aghani* (*The Book of Songs*), vol. XXII, pp. 348–59. See also Ibn Kathir, *Al Bidaya wal Nihaya* (*The Beginning and the End*), vol. XIV, p. 630.   17. Diarmaid MacCulloch, *A History of Christianity: The First Three Thousand Years*, p. 3.   18. Tabari, *The History of Al Tabari*, vol. I: *The Reign of Abu Jafar al Mansur 754–775*, p. 144.   19. MacCulloch, p. 264.   20. For Benjamin's description of Baghdad, see Marcus Nathan Adler, *The Itinerary of Benjamin of Tudela*, pp. 35–42.   21. See Tabari, vol. XXXI: *The War between Brothers: The Caliphate of Muhammad al Amin* AD 809–813/ AH 193–198, pp. 145–7.   22. Jim Al Khalili, *Pathfinders: The Golden Age of Arabic Science*, pp. 67–78.   23. Ibid., p. 78.   24. Quoted in Jonathan Lyons, *The House of Wisdom: How the Arabs Transformed Western Civilisation*, p. 73.   25. Al Khalili, p. 75.   26. Ibid., p. 149.   27. Ibid., p. 134.   28. Amira Bennison, *The Great Caliphs: The Golden Age of the Abbasid Empire*, p. 90.   29. For an entertaining discussion of Abu Nuwas's poetic life, see 'Dangling Locks and Babel Eyes: A Profile of Abu Nuwas', in Philip Kennedy, *Abu Nuwas: A Genius of Poetry*, pp. 1–19. See also Alex Rowell, *Vintage Humour: The Islamic Wine Poetry of Abu Nuwas*.   30. 'Mystery surrounds Iraqi statue's missing glass of wine', http:// www.al-monitor.com/pulse/originals/2015/08/iraq-baghdad-monuments-memorials-sabotage-destruction.html.   31. Ibn Khallikan, *Ibn Khallikan's Biographical Dictionary*, vol. I, p. 208.   32. Tabari, quoted in Kennedy, p. 120.   33. Gaston Wiet, *Baghdad: Metropolis of the Abbasid Caliphate*, pp. 76–7.   34. See Julia Ashtiany et al. (eds.), *Cambridge History of Arabic Literature*, vol. 2: *Abbasid Belles-Lettres*, p. 81.   35. See Charles Pellat, *The Life and Works of Jahiz*, pp. 265–7.   36. Wiet, p. 76; Kennedy, pp. 124–5.   37. Kennedy, p. 214.   38. Tabari, quoted in ibid., p. 285.   39. Masudi, p. 239.   40. For a full account of his visit to Baghdad, see Roland J. C. Broadhurst (tr. and ed.), *The Travels of Ibn Jubayr*, pp. 226–32.

4. Cordoba – Ornament of the World

1. Quoted in R. Hillenbrand, 'The Ornament of the World: Cordoba as a Cultural Centre', in Salma Jayyusi (ed.), *The Legacy of Muslim Spain*, p. 112.   2. Author interviews, 13–14 November 2016.   3. Enrique Sordo, *Moorish Spain*, p. 24.   4. Richard Fletcher, *Moorish Spain*, p. 53.   5. D. F. Ruggles, 'Madinat al Zahra and the Um Palace', in María Rosa Menocal, Raymond P. Scheindlin and Michael Sells (eds.), *The Literature of Al Andalus*, p. 27.   6. See Katharina Wilson, *Hrotsvit of Gandersheim: A Florilegium of Her Works*, p. 29.   7. Hugh Kennedy, *Muslim Spain and Portugal: A Political History of Al Andalus*, p. 83.   8. See Maribel Fierro, *Abd al Rahman III – The First Cordoban Caliph*, pp. 105–8.   9. Quoted in David. Wasserstein, *The Caliphate in the West: An Islamic Political Institution in the Iberian Peninsula*, p. 11.   10. Ibid., p. 14.   11. Fierro, p. 105.   12. On the challenges of Al Maqqari as a source and the wider historiography of Medinat al Zahra, see Ann Christys, 'Picnic at Madinat al-Zahra', in Simon Barton and Peter Linehan (eds.), *Cross, Crescent and Conversion: Studies on Medieval Spain and Christendom in Memory of Richard Fletcher*, pp. 87–108.   13. Sordo, pp. 29–30.   14. Ibid., pp. 30–31.   15. Quoted in Ann Christys, *Christians in Andalus 711–1000*, p. 64.   16. Nuha Khoury, 'The Meaning of the Great Mosque of Cordoba in the Tenth Century', in *Muqarnas*, vol. 13, p. 80.   17. Amira K. Bennison and Alison L. Gascoigne (eds.), *Cities in the Pre-Modern Islamic World: The Urban Impact of Religion, State and Society*, p. 76.   18. For a brief summary of Hakam II's additions to the Great Mosque, see María Rosa Menocal, *The Ornament of the World: How Muslims, Jews and Christians Created a Culture of Tolerance in Medieval Spain*, pp. 94–6.   19. Évariste Lévi-Provençal, *L'Espagne Musulmane*, vol. 3, p. 385.   20. Quoted in Menocal, p. 16.   21. 'Two arrested after fight in Cordoba's former mosque', *Guardian*, 1 April 2010 (http://www.theguardian.com/world/2010/apr/01/muslim-catholic-mosque-fight?INTCMP=ILCNETTXT3487); see also 'Cordoba rejects Catholic Church's claim to own mosque-cathedral', *Guardian*, 13 March 2016 (https://www.theguardian.com/world/2016/mar/13/cordoba-catholic-churchs-claim-mosque-cathedral).   22. Ruggles, p. 28.   23. Quoted in Menocal, p. 84.   24. See, for instance, Kennedy, p. 107; Fletcher, p. 65;

Fierro, p. 110. For a more sceptical view, see Christys, 'Picnic at Madinat al-Zahra'. *The New Cambridge Medieval History* prefers a population of 90,000 (vol. 3, *c. 900–c. 1024*, p. 68). On the reliability of Al Maqqari, see Christys, *Christians*, p. 15.   25. Sordo, p. 37; Fletcher, p. 65.   26. Ibn Hawqal, *Configuración del Mundo (Fragmentos Alusivos al Magreb y España)*, pp. 63–4. Quoted in Christys, *Christians*, p. 14.   27. Kennedy, pp. 98–9.   28. Quoted in Fletcher, p. 64.   29. Ibid., p. 63.   30. See Eliyahu Ashtor, *The Jews of Moslem Spain*, p. 284.   31. Menocal, p. 86.   32. Quoted in Menocal, Scheindlin and Sells (eds.), p. 83.   33. For a brief summary of Ziryab's remarkable career, see Dwight Reynolds, 'Music', in ibid., pp. 64–6. See also Robert W. Lebling Jr, 'Flight of the Blackbird', *Saudi Aramco World*, July–August 2003 (https://www.saudiaramcoworld.com/issue/200304/flight.of.the.blackbird.htm).   34. Menocal, Scheindlin and Sells (eds.), p. 308.   35. Ibid., p. 309.   36. Ibid., p. 313.   37. Ashtor, p. 255.   38. Sordo, p. 18.   39. For an opposing view to Menocal, *The Ornament of the World*, see, for example, Dario Fernandez Morera, *The Myth of the Andalusian Paradise: Muslims, Christians and Jews under Islamic Rule in Medieval Spain*.   40. Ibid., p. 55.   41. Fierro, p. 98.   42. Wilson, pp. 34–5.   43. Menocal, pp. 85–8.   44. See Ashtor, pp. 157–9.   45. Ibid., p. 182.   46. Georg Heinrich Pertz (ed.), *Vita Johannis Gorziensis, Monumentae Germanica Historiae* SS IV, pp. 335–77, quoted in Christys, p. 110.   47. Ibid., p. 111.   48. Quoted in Kenneth B. Wolf, 'Convivencia and the "Ornament of the World"', Address to the Southeast Medieval Association, Wofford College, Spartanburg, South Carolina, October 2007.   49. Quoted in Alexander E. Elinson, *Looking Back at Al-Andalus: The Poetics of Loss and Nostalgia in Medieval Arabic and Hebrew Literature*, pp. 6–7.   50. Christys, Picnic at Madinat al-Zahra', p. 6.   51. Menocal, p. 100.   52. Fletcher, p. 80.   53. Wasserstein, p. 27.

5. Jerusalem – The Contested City

1. Jerome Murphy-O'Connor, *The Holy Land: An Oxford Archaeological Guide from Earliest Times to 1700*, p. xix.   2. ' "This land is just dirt": A rooftop view of Jerusalem', *Guardian*, 23 October 2017 (https://www.theguardian.com/cities/2017/oct/23/jerusalem-rooftop-divided-israel-season-culture).   3. Paul M. Cobb, *Race for Paradise: Islamic History of the Crusades*, p. 20.   4. Ibid., pp. 20–21.   5. John Wolffe, *Religion in History: Conflict, Conversion and Coexistence*, p. 57.   6. Carole Hillenbrand, *Crusades: Islamic Perspectives*, p. 270.   7. Simon Sebag Montefiore, *Jerusalem: The Biography*, p. xx.   8. *The Itinerarium Burdigalense by The Anonymous Pilgrim of Bordeaux (333 AD)*, p. 28 (https://www.scribd.com/doc/37368846/The-Itinerarium-Burdigalense-by-The-Anonymous-Pilgrim-of-Bordeaux-333-a-d).   9. Cobb, p. 34.   10. Sebag Montefiore, p. 173.   11. Steven Runciman, *The First Crusade*, p. 1.   12. Sebag Montefiore, p. 175.   13. Author interview with Dr Hazem Nuseibeh, 4 June 2016.   14. Ibn Battuta, *Travels in Asia and Africa: 1325–1354*, p. 55.   15. Nancy Khalek, *Damascus after the Muslim Conquest*, p. 141.   16. Zayde Antrim, *Routes and Realms: The Power of Place in the Early Islamic World*, p. 50.   17. Runciman, p. 19.   18. Sebag Montefiore, p. 201.   19. Kamil Jamil Asali (ed.), *Jerusalem in History*, p. 118.   20. Hillenbrand, p. 49.   21. Moshe Gil, 'The Political History of Jerusalem During the Early Muslim Period', in Joshua Prawer and Haggai Ben-Shammai (eds.), *The History of Jerusalem: The Early Muslim Period, 638–1099*, n. 33, p. 30.   22. Robert Ousterhout, 'Rebuilding the Temple: Constantine Monomachus and the Holy Sepulchre', *Journal of the Society of Architectural Historians*, vol. 48, no. 1 (March 1989), pp. 66–78.   23. For his account of Jerusalem, see Nasir-i-Khusraw, *Diary of a Journey Through Syria and Palestine* (tr. Guy Le Strange).   24. Annalist of Nieder-Altaich, 'The Great German Pilgrimage of 1064–65' (tr. James Brundage) (https://legacy.fordham.edu/Halsall/source/1064pilgrim.asp).   25. A. C. S. Peacock, *The Great Seljuk Empire*, pp. 61–4.   26. There are five versions of Pope Urban's address. See August C. Krey, *The First Crusade: The Accounts of Eyewitnesses and Participants*, pp. 23–36; Dana C. Munro, 'Urban and the Crusaders', *Translations and Reprints from the Original Sources of European History*, vol. 1, pp. 5–8; Thomas F. Madden, *The Concise History of the Crusades*, p. 8; Dana C. Munro, 'The Speech of Pope

Urban II at Clermont, 1095', *The American Historical Review*, vol. XI, no. 2, pp. 231–42.   27. Jonathan Riley-Smith, *The First Crusade and the Idea of Crusading*, p. 1.   28. Hugh Goddard, *A History of Christian–Muslim Relations*, p. 90.   29. Andrew Sinclair, *Jerusalem: The Endless Crusade*, p. 50.   30. Amin Maalouf, *The Crusades Through Arab Eyes*, pp. 39–40.   31. Christopher Tyerman, *God's War: A New History of the Crusades*, p. 153.   32. James A. Brundage, 'Adhemar of Le Puy: The Bishop and his Critics', *Speculum*, vol. 34, no. 2 (April 1959), p. 201.   33. Riley-Smith, pp. 48–9.   34. Sebag Montefiore, p. 211.   35. Ibid., p. 212.   36. See Malcolm Lambert, *Crusade and Jihad: Origins, History and Aftermath*, p. 97.   37. Fulcher of Chartres in Edward Peters (ed.), *The First Crusade: The Chronicle of Fulcher of Chartres and Other Source Materials*, pp. 91–2.   38. Cobb, p. 101.   39. Maalouf, pp. 50–51.   40. Thomas Asbridge, *The First Crusade: A New History*, pp. 317–18.   41. Tyerman, p. 159.   42. Peters, p. 98.   43. Francesco Gabrieli, *Arab Historians of the Crusades*, p. 12.   44. Maalouf, p. xiii.   45. Ibn al Athir, *The Chronicle of Ibn al Athir for the Crusading Period from Al Kamil Fi'l-Tarikh*, Part I: *The Years 491–541/1097–1146 – The Coming of the Franks and the Muslim Response*, p. 22.   46. Maalouf, p. xvi.   47. Cobb, p. 103.   48. Author interview, 6 June 2016.   49. ' "This land is just dirt": A rooftop view of Jerusalem', *Guardian*, 23 October 2017 (https://www.theguardian.com/cities/2017/oct/23/jerusalem-rooftop-divided-israel-season-culture).

6. Cairo – The City Victorious

1. Stanley Lane-Poole, *The Story of Cairo*, p. 20.   2. André Raymond, *Cairo*, pp. 29–30.   3. Maria Golia, *Cairo: City of Sand*, pp. 52–3; Philip Hitti, *History of the Arabs*, p. 165; Nasser Rabbat, *The Citadel of Cairo: A New Interpretation of Royal Mameluk Architecture*, p. 3.   4. Max Rodenbeck, *Cairo: The City Victorious*, p. 68.   5. Heinz Halm, *Fatimids and Their Traditions of Learning*, pp. 73–4; Shafique N. Virani, *The Ismailis in the Middle Ages: A History of Survival, a Search for Salvation*, p. 92.   6. Raymond, p. 62.   7. Philip Hitti, *Capital Cities of Arab Islam*, p. 122.   8. Rodenbeck, p. 97.   9. A huge amount has been written about the Geniza documents. For an introduction and Cambridge University's digitized collection, see https://cudl.lib.cam.ac.uk/collections/genizah. The dowry list is available at https://cudl.lib.cam.ac.uk/view/MS-TS-NS-00264-00013/1. See also S. D. Goitein, *A Mediterranean Society: The Jewish Communities of the World as Portrayed in the Documents of the Cairo Geniza*.   10. See Judith Olszowy-Schlanger, 'Learning to Read and Write in Medieval Egypt: Children's Exercise Books from the Cairo Geniza', *Journal of Semitic Studies*, 48 (1) (Spring 2003), pp. 47–69.   11. Michael Brett, *The Rise of the Fatimids: The World of the Mediterranean and the Middle East in the Fourth Century of the Hijra, Tenth Century CE*, p. 338.   12. Maryanne Stroud Gabbani, 'The Mogamma Game in 2012' (http://miloflamingo.blogspot.com/2012/09/the-mogamma-game-in-2012.html).   13. Raymond, p. 45.   14. Rodenbeck, p. 101.   15. Raymond, p. 46.   16. See Doris Behrens-Abouseif, *Islamic Architecture in Cairo: An Introduction*, pp. 9–10; Raymond, pp. 59–60.   17. For the Mustansir Crisis, see Nelly Hanna (ed.), *Money, Land and Trade: An Economic History of the Muslim Mediterranean*, pp. 74–80; Halm, pp. 77–8; Rodenbeck, pp. 79–80.   18. For a detailed study of the Mosque of Al Hakim, see Jonathan M. Bloom, 'The Mosque of al-Hakim in Cairo', in Oleg Grabar (ed.), *Muqarnas I: An Annual on Islamic Art and Architecture*, pp. 15–36. For the Aqmar Mosque, see Doris Behrens-Abouseif, 'The Façade of the Aqmar Mosque in the Context of Fatimid Ceremonial', in Oleg Grabar (ed.), *Muqarnas IX*, pp. 29–38.   19. Lane-Poole, p. 71.   20. Raymond, p. 74.   21. Ibn al Athir, *Kamil al Tawarikh*, vol. XI, p. 242, cited in Hitti, *Capital Cities*, p. 124.   22. See Nasser Rabbat, *The Citadel of Cairo: A New Interpretation of Royal Mameluk Architecture*, pp. 3–8.   23. Ibn Jubayr, *The Travels of Ibn Jubayr*, p. 52.   24. Abdul Rahman Azzam, *Saladin: The Triumph of the Sunni Revival*, p. 145.   25. Golia, p. 57.   26. Jonathan Phillips, *The Crusades 1095–1204*, p. 162.   27. Azzam, p. 197.   28. Ibid., p. 135.   29. Rodenbeck, p. 81.   30. Herodotus, *Histories*, 1.5, p. 5.

7. Fez – The Athens of Africa

1. See Paul Bowles and Barry Brukoff, *Morocco*, pp. 32–9 (http://www.paulbowles.org/fez.html).   2. Mohammed Mezzine (ed.), *Fès Médiévale: Entre légende et histoire, un carrefour de l'Orient à l'apogée d'un rêve*, p. 40., quoted in Simon O'Meara, *Space and Muslim Urban Life: At the Limits of the Labyrinth of Fez*, p. 57.   3. For a summary of its growth over the centuries, see Al Qaraouiyine Rehabilitation Presentation Panels. Courtesy of Architect. Aga Khan Award for Architecture, 2010 (https://archnet.org/system/publications/contents/9386/original/DTP101869.pdf?1396260501). See also Fauzi M. Najjar, 'The Karaouine at Fez', *Muslim World*, vol. 48, issue 2 (April 1958), pp. 104–112; Edith Wharton, *In Morocco*, p. 96; Guinness World Records website (http://www.guinnessworldrecords.com/world-records/oldest-university) and 'Medina of Fez' on UNESCO's website (http://whc.unesco.org/en/list/170).   4. Leo Africanus, *The History and Description of Africa*, vol. II, p. 421. On the Pope Sylvester II story, see, for example, Mohammed Lebbar, 'La Ville de Fès et Sylvestre II' (http://wissensraum-mittelmeer.org/wp-content/uploads/2017/03/Lebbar_-_Sylvestre_II.pdf); Attilio Gaudio, *Fès: Joyau de la Civilisation Islamique*, p. 20. Author interviews, October 2017.   5. 'World's oldest library opens in Fez: "You can hurt us but you can't hurt the books"', *Guardian*, 19 September 2016 (https://www.theguardian.com/cities/2016/sep/19/books-world-oldest-library-fez-morocco); 'Profile: Khizanat al-Qarawiyyin, the oldest library in the world, set to re-open after multimillion-pound restoration', *The National*, 20 September 2016 (http://www.thenational.scot/world/14871162.Profile__Khizanat_al_Qarawiyyin__the_oldest_library_in_the_world__set_to_re_open_after_multimillion_pound_restoration/).   6. Abul Hassan al Jaznai, *Kitab Zahrat al As fi bina Madinat Fez*, p. 61 (tr. Alger, 1923, p. 132), quoted in Maya Shatzmiller, *The Berbers and the Islamic State: The Marinid Experience in Pre-Protectorate Morocco*, p. 110.   7. Ibn Abi Zar, *Roudh el Kartas*, p. 46 (tr., p. 40), quoted in O'Meara, p. 59.   8. Abul Hassan al Jaznai, p. 24 (tr., p. 50), quoted in O'Meara, p. 60.   9. For a summary of the foundation legends, see, for example, Roger Le Tourneau, 'Fas', *Encyclopedia Islamica*, pp. 818–21; 'Fès', in Aomar Boum and Thomas K. Park (eds.), *Historical Dictionary of Morocco*, pp. 188–9; Simon O'Meara, 'The foundation legend of Fez and other Islamic cities in light of the Prophet', in Amira K. Bennison and Alison L. Gascoigne (eds.), *Cities in the Pre-modern Islamic World*, pp. 27–42.   10. On the city's favourable location, see Roger Le Tourneau, *Fez in the Age of the Marinids*, pp. 3–5.   11. Ibn Khaldun, *The Muqaddimah: An Introduction to History*, pp. 63–4.   12. Rom Landau, *Morocco*, p. 87.   13. Susan Gilson Miller, Attilio Petruccioli and Mauro Bertagnin, 'Inscribing Minority Space in the Islamic City: The Jewish Quarter of Fez (1438–1912)', *Journal of the Society of Architectural Historians*, vol. 60, no. 3 (September 2001), p. 1; Titus Burckhardt, *Fez: City of Islam*, p. 1; Wharton, p. 79.   14. Leo Africanus, *The History and Description of Africa*, vol. II, p. 418; Abdelaziz Touri, 'L'oratoire de quartier', in Mezzine (ed.), p. 102; Ronald A. Messier, *The Almoravids and the Meanings of Jihad*, p. 218.   15. See Roger Le Tourneau and H. Terrasse, 'Fez', in C. Edmund Bosworth (ed.), *Historic Cities of the Islamic World*, p. 138.   16. Al Idrisi, *Description de l'Afrique et de l'Espagne par Edrisi*, pp. 87–8.   17. Ibn Abi Zar, quoted in Burckhardt, p. 42.   18. *Al Dhakhira al Saniya fi Tarikh al Dawla al Mariniyya*, p. 35, quoted in Shatzmiller, p. 50.   19. Ibn Abi Zar, p. 396. See also Burckhardt, p. 42.   20. For an excellent summary of the Marinid Dynasty, see Maya Shatzmiller, 'Marinids', in *Encyclopedia Islamica*, pp. 571–4; Burckhardt, p. 42.   21. Ibn Khaldun, *Histoire des Berbères*, vol. 4, pp. 39–41, quoted in Shatzmiller, *Berbers and the Islamic State*, p. 159.   22. See Hicham Rguig, 'Le Mellah de Fès: Genèse et évolution', in Said Ennahid and Driss Maghraoui (eds.), *Fez in World History: Selected Essays*, p. 84. See also Shatzmiller, *Berbers and the Islamic State*, p. 60.   23. Rguig, p. 86.   24. See Leo Africanus, vol. II, pp. 471–7.   25. Ibid., vol. III, p. 1018.   26. See Robert S. Lopez and Irving W. Raymond (trs.), *Medieval Trade in the Mediterranean World: Illustrative Documents*, pp. 74–5.   27. Al Jaznai, *Zahrat al As*, quoted in Halima Ferhat, 'Marinid Fez: Zenith and Signs of Decline', in Salma Jayyusi, Renata Holod, Attilio Petruccioli and André Raymond (eds.), *The City in the Islamic World*, pp. 248, 258.   28. For an essay on the gold trade and the economic foundations of the Marinid Dynasty, see Maya Shatzmiller,

'Marinid Fez: The Economic Background of the "Quest for Empire"', in Ennahid and Maghraoui (eds.), pp. 7–33. 29. Mohammed Hamdouni Alami, 'Contes et légendes', in Mezzine, p. 136; Landau, p. 98. 30. Quoted in O'Meara, p. 11. On Marinid *madrassas*, see also Sheila S. Blair and Jonathan M. Bloom, *The Art and Architecture of Islam, 1250–1800*, pp. 121–3. 31. Tim Mackintosh-Smith (ed.), *The Travels of Ibn Battutah*, pp. 275, 3. 32. Shatzmiller, *Berbers and the Islamic State*, p. 90. 33. Ibid., p. 61. 34. Ferhat, pp. 256–8. 35. Leo Africanus, vol. II, pp. 420–23. 36. Ibid., quoted in Ferhat, p. 248. 37. Author interview, 8 October 2017; Gwendolyn Wright, *The Politics of Design in French Colonial Urbanism*, p. 137; Bowles. 38. Burckhardt, p. 9.

8. Samarkand – Garden of the Soul

1. This chapter is based on Justin Marozzi, 'Samarkand, the "Pearl of the East": 1396–1398', in *Tamerlane: Sword of Islam, Conqueror of the World*, pp. 201–240; Christopher Marlowe, *Tamburlaine the Great*, Part 1, Act III, Scene iii, pp. 44–5. 2. Tacitus, *Agricola*, 1.30. 3. On loving Samarkand like a mistress, Marozzi, p. 207; Ruy González de Clavijo, *Embassy to Tamerlane 1403–1406*, p. 171. 4. Ibn Battuta, *Travels in Asia and Africa 1325–1354*, p. 174. 5. Ahmed ibn Arabshah, *Tamerlane or Timur the Great Amir*, p. 314; Clavijo, pp. 287, 142. 6. On Timur's 'soulless militarism', see J. J. Saunders, *The History of the Mongol Conquests*, p. 174. For Timur's removal of craftsmen to Samarkand, see Wilfrid Blunt, *The Golden Road to Samarkand*, p. 174; for a survey of Timurid architecture, see Lisa Golombek, 'From Tamerlane to the Taj Mahal', in Abbas Daneshvari (ed.), *Essays in Islamic Art and Architecture in Honour of Katharina Otto-Dorn*; Monika Gronke, 'The Persian Court between Palace and Tent: From Timur to Abbas I', in Lisa Golombek and Maria Subtelny (eds.), *Timurid Art and Culture: Iran and Central Asia in the Fifteenth Century*; Lisa Golombek and Donald Wilber, *The Timurid Architecture of Iran and Turan*. 7. Geoffrey Parker, *Power in Stone: Cities as Symbols of Empire*, p. 74. 8. Sharaf al Din Ali Yazdi, *The History of Timur-Bec, Known by the Name of Tamerlain the Great, Emperor of the Moguls and Tartars: Being an Historical Journal of his Conquests in Asia and Europe*, vol. 1, p. 529. 9. Battuta, p. 174. 10. For the Spanish ambassador's description of Samarkand, see Clavijo, pp. 218–300. See also Hilda Hookham, *Tamburlaine the Conqueror*, pp. 163–84; Harold Lamb, *Tamerlane the Earth Shaker*, pp. 105–112.

9. Constantinople – City of the World's Desire

1. C. Given-Wilson (tr. and ed.), *The Chronicle of Adam of Usk 1377–1421*, p. 121. For an account of Manuel II's remarkable visit, see Donald Nicol, *A Byzantine Emperor in England: Manuel II's Visit to London in 1400–01*; Cecily J. Hilsdale, *Byzantine Art and Diplomacy in an Age of Decline*, pp. 222–4. 2. Doğan Kuban, *Istanbul: An Urban History: Byzantion, Constantinopolis, Istanbul*, p. 33; Jelena Bogdanović, 'Tetrapylon', *Encyclopaedia of the Hellenic World, Constantinople* (http://www.ehw.gr/l.aspx?id=12429). 3. Quoted in Roger Crowley, *Constantinople: The Last Great Siege, 1453*, p. 18. 4. Edward Peters (ed.), *The First Crusade: The Chronicle of Fulcher of Chartres*, p. 62. 5. See Stephen Turnbull, *The Walls of Constantinople AD 324–1453*, pp. 11–16. 6. Crowley, p. 84. 7. Barnaby Rogerson, *The Last Crusaders: The Hundred-Year Battle for the Centre of the World*, p. 84. 8. Eugenia Kermeli, 'Osman I', in Gabor Agoston and Bruce Masters (eds.), *Encyclopedia of the Ottoman Empire*, pp. 444–5. 9. For Ibn Battuta's impressions of the city, see H. A. R. Gibb (tr. and ed.), *Ibn Battuta: Travels in Asia and Africa 1325–1354*, pp. 159–64. 10. Crowley, p. 35. 11. For his report on Constantinople, see Ruy González de Clavijo, *Embassy to Tamerlane 1403–1406*, pp. 71–90. 12. Donald M. Nicol, *The Last Centuries of Byzantium, 1261–1453*, p. 333; Turnbull, p. 44. 13. Stephen Reinert, 'Fragmentation (1204–1453)', in Cyril Mango (ed.), *The Oxford History of Byzantium*, p. 276. 14. Bertrandon de Brocquière, *The Travels of Bertrandon de Brocquière*, pp. 286–97. 15. Pero

Tafur, *Travels and Adventures 1435–1439*, pp. 144–5; Michael Angold, *The Fall of Constantinople to the Ottomans: Context and Consequences*, p. 181. 16. Roger Crowley, *1453: The Holy War for Constantinople and the Clash of Islam and the West*, p. 67. 17. Crowley, *Constantinople*, p. 46. 18. Donald M. Nicol, *Byzantium and Venice: A Study in Diplomatic and Cultural Relations*, p. 390. 19. Steven Runciman, *The Fall of Constantinople 1453*, p. xiii; Edward Gibbon, *The Decline and Fall of the Roman Empire*, vol. III (1185–1453), pp. 748–53, 761, 784. 20. Franz Babinger, *Mehmed the Conqueror and His Time*, pp. 112, 410. 21. Kritovoulos, *History of Mehmed the Conqueror*, p. 13. 22. Donald M. Nicol, *The Immortal Emperor: The Life and Legend of Constantine Palaiologos, Last Emperor of the Romans*, p. 52. 23. Gibbon, p. 760. 24. Kritovoulos, p. 28. 25. Quoted in Crowley, *Constantinople*, pp. 90–91. 26. Marios Philippides and Walter K. Hanak, *The Siege and the Fall of Constantinople in 1453: Historiography, Topography and Military Studies*, p. 451; Kritovoulos, p. 45. 27. For a brief study of Tursun Beg, see Halil İnalcik, 'Tursun Beg, Historian of Mehmed the Conqueror's Time', *Wiener Zeitschrift für die Kunde des Morgenlandes*, vol. 69 (1977), pp. 55–71. 28. Stefan Zweig, *Shooting Stars: Ten Historical Miniatures*, p. 51. 29. Quoted in Crowley, *Constantinople*, p. 170. 30. Kritovoulos, p. 35. 31. Nestor-Iskander, *The Tale of Constantinople: Of its Origin and Capture by the Turks in the Year 1453*, p. 81. 32. For Mehmed's call to arms, see Kritovoulos, pp. 60–66. 33. Ibid., pp. 68–9. 34. Ibid., p. 71. 35. Ibid., pp. 72, 75, 73. 36. See Halil İnalcik, 'Istanbul: An Islamic City', *Journal of Islamic Studies*, 1 (1990), pp. 1–23. 37. Kritovoulos, pp. 79–80. 38. Author interview, Istanbul, 30 January 2017. 39. Alev Çinar, 'National History as a Contested Site: The Conquest of Istanbul and Islamist Negotiations of the Nation', *Comparative Studies in Society and History*, vol. 43, no. 2 (April 2001), p. 379. 40. Author interview, Istanbul, 30 January 2017. 41. Gibbon, p. 779. 42. Halil İnalcik, *The Ottoman Empire: 1300–1600*, pp. 29–30. 43. Author interview, Istanbul, 30 January 2017. 44. Jan Morris, *Among the Cities*, p. 13; Savvas Tsilenis, 'The minority of Orthodox Christians in the official statistics of modern Turkey and the urban space' (http://www.demography-lab.prd.uth.gr/DDAoG/article/cont/ergasies/tsilenis.htm); 'The Greek Minority and its foundations in Istanbul, Gokceada (Imvros) and Bozcaada (Tenedos)', Hellenic Republic Ministry of Foreign Affairs website, 25 February 2018 (https://www.mfa.gr/en/issues-of-greek-turkish-relations/relevant-documents/the-greek-minority-and-its-foundations-in-istanbul-gokceada-imvros-and-bozcaada-tenedos.html). 45. Orhan Pamuk, *Istanbul: Memories and the City*, p. 85. On *hüzün*, see pp. 81–96. 46. Çiğdem Kafescioğlu, *Constantinopolis/Istanbul: Cultural Encounter, Imperial Vision and the Construction of the Ottoman Capital*, pp. 178–98. 47. Çiğdem Kafescioğlu, 'Heavenly and Unblessed, Splendid and Artless: Mehmed II's Mosque Complex in the Eyes of its Contemporaries', in Çiğdem Kafescioğlu and Lucienne Thys-Şenocak (eds.), *Aptullah Kuran için Yazılar/Essays in Honour of Aptullah Kuran*, p. 213. 48. Rabah Saoud, 'Muslim Architecture under Ottoman Patronage 1326–1924', *Foundation for Science, Technology and Civilisation*, July 2004, p. 3. 49. Kritovoulos, p. 140. For a survey of Mehmed's post-1453 construction in Istanbul, see Gülru Necipoğlu, *Architecture, Ceremonial and Power: The Topkapi Palace in the Fifteenth and Sixteenth Centuries*, pp. 3–13. See also Doğan Kuban, *Ottoman Architecture*, pp. 169–89 and Caroline Finkel, *Osman's Dream: The Story of the Ottoman Empire 1300–1923*, pp. 52–6. Seventeenth-century saying quoted in Philip Mansel, *Pillars of Monarchy*, p. 17. 50. İnalcik, *Ottoman Empire*, p. 29.

10. Kabul – A Garden in the Mountains

1. Ahmed Shah Massoud, 'A Message to the People of the United States of America' (1998) (http://www.afghan-web.com/documents/let-masood.html). 2. Nancy Hatch Dupree, *An Historical Guide to Afghanistan*, p. 88. 3. Ibn Battuta, *The Travels of Ibn Battuta: In the Near East, Asia and Africa, 1325–1354*, p. 98. 4. Babur, *The Baburnama*, p. 13. 5. Ibid., p. 92. 6. Quoted in Abraham Eraly, *Emperors of the Peacock Throne: The Saga of the Great Mughals*, p. 7. 7. Babur, pp. 198–9. 8. Stephen Frederic Dale, 'Steppe Humanism:

The Autobiographical Writings of Zahir Al-Din Muhammad Babur, 1483–1530', *International Journal of Middle East Studies*, vol. 22, no. 1 (1990) pp. 37–8; E. M. Forster, 'The Emperor Babur', in *Abinger Harvest*, pp. 301–303; John Leyden and William Erskine, *Memoirs of Zehir-Ed-Din Muhammad Babur, Emperor of Hindustan*, p. 432.   9. Babur, p. 627.   10. Ibid., p. 386.   11. For his description of Kabul, see ibid., pp. 199–227.   12. E. Denison Ross, 'Babur', in *Cambridge History of India*, vol. 4: *The Mughul Period*, pp. 1–20.   13. W. M. Thackston, 'Babur Mirza, *Baburnama*', in *A Century of Princes: Sources on Timurid History and Art*, p. 247.   14. Ibid., p. 273. For Babur's visit to Herat, see pp. 270–75.   15. Quoted in C. P. W. Gammell, *The Pearl of Khorasan: A History of Herat*, p. 119.   16. Babur, p. 340.   17. Ibid., p. 474.   18. See Stephen Dale, *The Gardens of Eight Paradises: Babur and the Culture of Empire in Central Asia, Afghanistan and India (1483–1530)*, pp. 17–18.   19. Ibid., p. 686.   20. Babur, p. 584.   21. Ibid., p. 518. For his portrait of Hindustan, see pp. 480–521.   22. Ibid., p. 525.   23. For the full letter see ibid., pp. 645–8.   24. John Richards, *The Mughal Empire*, p. 1.   25. Fergus Nicoll, *Shah Jahan*, p. 207.   26. Babur, p. 477.   27. Thackston, p. 258; Denison Ross, p. 20.   28. *The Akbarnama of Abul Fazl*, vol. 1, p. 413, quoted in Gammell, p. 136.   29. Gammell, p. 137.   30. Bayazid Bayat, *Tadkhira Humayun wa Akbar*, p. 205 (tr. Bruce Wannell).   31. *Akbarnama*, vol. 2, pp. 85, 56.   32. C. W. Woodburn, *The Bala Hissar of Kabul: Revealing a Fortress-Palace in Afghanistan*, p. 3.   33. Ruby Lal, *Domesticity and Power in the Early Mughal World*, p. 140.   34. *Akbarnama*, vol. 3, pp. 434, 532.   35. F. Lehman, 'Akbar I', *Encyclopaedia Iranica* (http://www.iranicaonline.org/articles/akbar-i-mughal-india).   36. Ibid.   37. For his assessment of Akbar, see Pierre du Jarric, *Akbar and the Jesuits: An Account of the Jesuit Missions to the Court of Akbar*, pp. 203–208.   38. Author interviews, 15 March 2017 and 13 November 2018; Babur, p. 217. See also Robin Lane Fox, 'The Garden King of Kabul: Babur's legacy lives on in Afghanistan', *Financial Times*, 5 February 2016 (https://www.ft.com/content/5631b7ae-c4ed-11e5-808f-8231cd71622e); Lalage Snow, 'Kabul's hidden gardens offer Afghans haven from war', *Financial Times*, 13 September 2013 (https://www.ft.com/content/f1b9f768-1635-11e3-a57d-00144feabdco).

11. Isfahan – Half the World

1. See Rudi Matthee, 'Was Safavid Iran an Empire?', *Journal of the Economic and Social History of the Orient*, vol. 53, nos. 1/2 (2010), pp. 233–65.   2. Sussan Babaie, *Isfahan and its Palaces: Statecraft, Shiism and the Architecture of Conviviality in Early Modern Iran*, pp. 73–4.   3. Ibn Battuta, *Travels in Asia and Africa 1325–1354*, p. 91.   4. Ahmed ibn Arabshah, *Tamerlane or Timur the Great Amir*, p. 45.   5. See Roger Savory and Ahmet Karamustafa, 'Esmail I Safawi', *Encyclopaedia Iranica* (http://www.iranicaonline.org/articles/esmail-i-safawi).   6. H. R. Roemer, 'The Safavid Period', in Peter Jackson and Laurence Lockhart (eds.), *The Cambridge History of Iran*, vol. 6, pp. 189–350; Roger Savory, 'Abbas I', *Encyclopaedia Iranica* (http://www.iranicaonline.org/articles/abbas-i).   7. Sebouh Aslanian, *From the Indian Ocean to the Mediterranean: The Global Trade Networks of Armenian Merchants from New Julfa*, p. 1; David Blow, *Shah Abbas: The Ruthless King Who Became an Iranian Legend*, p. 174.   8. Michael Axworthy, *Iran: Empire of the Mind: A History from Zoroaster to the Present Day*, p. 136.   9. For a comprehensive survey of Isfahan's Safavid architecture, see Sussan Babaie with Robert Haug, 'Isfahan X: Monuments (1): A Historical Survey', *Encyclopaedia Iranica* and following essays (http://www.iranicaonline.org/articles/isfahan-x1-a-historical-survey).   10. Eskandar Beg Monshi, *History of Shah Abbas the Great* (tr. Roger Savory), vol. 2, p. 977.   11. Robert Byron, *The Road to Oxiana*, p. 153.   12. Sussan Babaie, Kathryn Babayan, Ina Baghdiantz-McCabe and Massumeh Farhad, *Slaves of the Shah: New Elites of Safavid Iran*, p. 1.   13. Byron, p. 199.   14. Ibid., p. 196.   15. Monshi, vol. 2, pp. 1038–9.   16. Jean de Thévenot, *The Travels of Monsieur de Thévenot into the Levant*, vol. 2, p. 81.   17. Wilfrid Blunt, *Isfahan: Pearl of Asia*, pp. 91, 73.   18. Quoted in Blow, p. 199. For a potted biography of Mirza Beg Junabadi, see Stephen Blake, *Time in Early Modern Islam: Calendar, Ceremony and Chronology in the*

Safavid, Mughal and Ottoman Empires, p. 116.   19. See Rudi Matthee, 'Safavid Iran through the Eyes of European Travellers', *Harvard Library Bulletin*, vol. 23, nos. 1–2 (Spring–Summer 2012), pp. 10–24.   20. Blow, p. 204.   21. Sir John Chardin, *Travels in Persia 1673–1677*, p. 146.   22. Jean-Baptiste Tavernier, *The Six Voyages of John Baptista Tavernier*, p. 153.   23. Blow, pp. 203–204.   24. De Thévenot, vol. 2, p. 79; John Fryer, *A New Account of East India and Persia Being Nine Years' Travels 1672–1681*, p. 260; Tavernier, pp. 149–50.   25. Rudi Matthee, 'Between Aloofness and Fascination: Safavid Views of the West', *Iranian Studies*, vol. 31, no. 2, *Historiography and Representation in Safavid and Afsharid Iran* (Spring 1998), pp. 227–8. For more on Father Paul Simon, see H. Chick (ed.), *A Chronicle of the Carmelites in Persia: The Safavids and the Papal Mission of the 17th and 18th Centuries*, pp. 155–163.   26. Quoted in Matthee, 'Between Aloofness and Fascination', p. 241.   27. Ibid., pp. 223–34.   28. Ibid., p. 226. For the story of this fraternal triumvirate, see also Sir Anthony Sherley, *The Three Brothers, or The Travels and Adventures of Sir Anthony, Sir Robert and Sir Thomas Sherley in Persia, Russia, Turkey, Spain etc.*   29. Matthee, 'Safavid Iran', p. 21.   30. Blow, p. 206; Clare Williamson, 'Safavid Persia through the Eyes of French Travellers', *La Trobe Journal*, no. 91 (June 2013), p. 19.   31. For the full obituary notice, see Monshi, pp. 1301–307.   32. Rudi Matthee, *The Pursuit of Pleasure: Drugs and Stimulants in Iranian History, 1500–1900*, p. 54.   33. Ibid., p. 56.   34. See Sussan Babaie, 'Shah Abbas II, the Conquest of Qandahar, the Chihil Sutun, and its Wall Paintings', *Muqarnas*, 11 (1994), pp. 125–42. See also Wolfram Kleiss, 'Safavid Palaces', *Ars Orientalis*, vol. 23 (1993); Gülru Necipoğlu, 'Framing the Gaze in Ottoman, Safavid, and Mughal Palaces', *Ars Orientalis*, vol. 23 (1993).   35. Babaie et al., *Slaves of the Shah*, p. 44.   36. Babaie with Haug.   37. Rudi Matthee, 'Soltan Hosayn', *Encyclopaedia Iranica* (http://www.iranicaonline.org/articles/soltan-hosayn).   38. Roy Mottahedeh, *The Mantle of the Prophet: Religion and Politics in Iran*, p. 204.   39. Matthee, 'Soltan Hosayn'.   40. Roemer, pp. 325–6; Michael Axworthy, *The Sword of Persia: Nader Shah, from Tribal Warrior to Conquering Tyrant*, p. 88.

12. Tripoli – Pirates' Lair

1. George Francis Lyon, *A Narrative of Travels in Northern Africa in the Years 1818–20*, p. 53.   2. Massimiliano Munzi, 'Italian Archaeology in Libya: From Colonial Romanità to Decolonization of the Past', in Michael L. Galaty and Charles Watkinson (eds.), *Archaeology Under Dictatorship*, p. 85.   3. On migrant-smuggling in Sabratha, see 'Libya's hub for migrant smuggling empties after controlling militia is ousted', *The Star*, 1 January 2018 (https://www.thestar.com/news/insight/2018/01/01/libyas-hub-for-migrant-smuggling-empties-after-controlling-militia-is-ousted.html). For a brief summary of Daesh's role in post-revolution Libya, see 'When the Islamic State came to Libya', *The Atlantic*, 10 February 2018 (https://www.theatlantic.com/international/archive/2018/02/isis-libya-hiftar-al-qaeda-syria/552419/).   4. On Louis XIV and Leptis, see Nancy Thomson de Grummond (ed.), *Encyclopedia of the History of Classical Archaeology*, p. 675. For the Crown Estate's use of the ruins, see 'The Leptis Magna Ruins', https://www.thecrownestate.co.uk/media/5311/leptis-magna-ruins.pdf.   5. Mary Berenson, *A Vicarious Trip to the Barbary Coast*, p. 23.   6. Aristotle, 'History of Animals', in *Complete Works of Aristotle*, vol. 1, p. 946.   7. John Wright, *A History of Libya*, p. 65.   8. Ibid., p. 68; Miss Tully, *Narrative of a Ten Years' Residence at Tripoli in Africa*, p. 2; Ali Bey, *Travels of Ali Bey in Morocco, Tripoli, Cyprus, Egypt, Arabia, Syria and Turkey between the Years 1803 and 1807*, p. 233; Hisham Matar, *The Return: Fathers, Sons and the Land in Between*, pp. 123–4.   9. Ludovico Micara, 'Ottoman Tripoli: A Mediterranean Medina', in Salma Jayyusi, Renata Holod, Attilio Petruccioli and André Raymond (eds.), *The City in the Islamic World*, vol. 2, p. 386; Simonetta Ciranna, 'Roman Persistence and Re-use of Ancient Remains', in *The Mediterranean Medina: International Seminar*, p. 297; Werner Diem and Marco Schöller, *The Living and the Dead in Islam: Studies in Arabic Epitaphs*, vol. 3, pp. 292–3.   10. Jayyusi et al. (eds.), p. 387.   11. For a modern survey of Barbary Coast piracy, see Robert C. Davis, *Christian Slaves, Muslim Masters: White Slavery in the Mediterranean, the Barbary Coast, and Italy, 1500–1800*;

Fernand Braudel, *The Mediterranean and the Mediterranean World in the Age of Philip II*, vol. 2, p. 885; Barnaby Rogerson, *A Traveller's History of North Africa*, p. 229; Glen O'Hara, *Britain and the Sea Since 1600*, p. 48.   12. Hugh Bicheno, *Crescent and Cross: The Battle of Lepanto 1571*, p. 278.   13. Herodotus, *The Histories*, 6.112; H. G. Wells, *The Outline of History*, p. 332.   14. Henry Teonge, *The Diary of Henry Teonge: Chaplain on H.M.'s Ships Assistance, Bristol and Royal Oak 1675–1679*, p. 125.   15. For Baker and Ibn Ghalbun's comments, see C. R. Pennell, *Piracy and Diplomacy in Seventeenth-Century North Africa: The Journal of Thomas Baker, English Consul in Tripoli, 1677–1685*, p. 61; Wright, p. 78.   16. Seton Dearden, *A Nest of Corsairs: The Fighting Karamanlis of the Barbary Coast*, p. 35.   17. Ibid., p. 50.   18. Ibid., pp. 62–3, 58.   19. Ronald Bruce St John, *Libya: From Colony to Independence*, p. 34.   20. 'People for sale', CNN, 14 November 2017 (https://edition.cnn.com/2017/11/14/africa/libya-migrant-auctions/index.html).   21. For an early nineteenth-century perspective on the Saharan trade, see Lyon, pp. 152–60.   22. Ettore Rossi, 'Tripoli', in *Encyclopedia of Islam*, p. 816.   23. René Basset, 'Karamanli', in *Encyclopedia of Islam*, pp. 746–7; Ali Bey, p. 235; Wright, p. 80.   24. For her eyewitness account of the plague in Tripoli, see Miss Tully, pp. 79–106.   25. Ibid., pp. 5–6.   26. Ibid., p. 6.   27. *The Speeches of Mr. Wilberforce, Lord Penrhyn, Mr. Burke, Sir W. Young, Alderman Newnham ... &c. &c. on a motion for the abolition of the slave trade, in the House of Commons, May the 12th, 1789. To which are added, Mr. Wilberforce's twelve propositions*, p. 8.   28. Justin Marozzi, *South from Barbary: Along the Slave Routes of the Libyan Sahara*, p. 23.   29. Miss Tully, p. 273.   30. Dearden, p. 129.   31. St John, p. 36.   32. Ibid., p. 40.   33. James Parton, *Life of Thomas Jefferson: Third President of the United States*, p. 299.   34. Joseph Wheelan, *Jefferson's War: America's First War on Terror 1801–1805*, p. 70.   35. For the American accounts of their captivity in Tripoli, see John Wright, *Travellers in Turkish Libya 1551–1911*, pp. 68–71.   36. Joshua London, *Victory in Tripoli: How America's War with the Barbary Pirates Established the U.S. Navy and Shaped a Nation*, p. 165.   37. Spencer C. Tucker (ed.), *The Encyclopedia of the Wars of the Early American Republic, 1783–1812: A Political, Social and Military History*, p. 433; Alexander Slidell Mackenzie, *Life of Stephen Decatur, a Commodore in the Navy of the United States*, p. 122.   38. John Wright, *Libya, Chad and the Central Sahara*, p. 62.   39. M. H. Cherif, 'Algeria, Tunisia and Libya: The Ottomans and their Heirs', in B. A. Ogot (ed.), *General History of Africa*, vol. 5: *Africa from the Sixteenth to the Eighteenth Century*, p. 260.   40. For the demise of the Karamanli dynasty see Wright, *A History of Libya*, p. 81.   41. Kola Folayan, *Tripoli during the Reign of Yusuf Pasha Qaramanli*, pp. 145–6.

13. Beirut – Playground of the Levant

1. Herodotus, *The Histories*, 7.44.   2. Nina Jidejian, *Beirut through the Ages*, p. 54.   3. Philip Mansel, *Levant: Splendour and Catastrophe on the Mediterranean*, p. 92.   4. See William Persen, 'The Russian Occupations of Beirut, 1772–4', *Journal of The Royal Central Asian Society*, vol. 42, issue 3–4 (1955), pp. 275–86.   5. Quoted in Samir Kassir, *Beirut*, p. 109.   6. Stephen Olin, *Travels in Egypt, Arabia Petræa, and the Holy Land*, vol. 2, p. 457; Kassir, pp. 6, 11.   7. T. J. Gorton (ed.), *A Beirut Anthology: Travel Writing through the Centuries*, pp. 33–5; Kassir, p. 98.   8. Mansel, p. 93.   9. Samir Khalaf, *Heart of Beirut: Reclaiming the Bourj*, p. 53; Mansel, p. 93; Kassir, p. 106; Leila Tarazi Fawaz, *Merchants and Migrants in Nineteenth-Century Beirut*, p. 61.   10. For a survey of the Tanzimat reforms, see the 2011 paper by Ishtiaq Hussain, *The Tanzimat: Secular Reforms in the Ottoman Empire*, pp. 5–11 (http://faith-matters.org/images/stories/fm-publications/the-tanzimat-final-web.pdf).   11. Jens Hanssen, *Fin de Siècle Beirut: The Making of an Ottoman Provincial Capital*, p. 32.   12. Frederick Arthur Neale, *Eight Years in Syria, Palestine and Asia Minor: From 1842 to 1850*, pp. 208–9; Mansel, p. 98.   13. Mansel, p. 97; Hanssen, p. 122; Kassir, p. 180.   14. Eugene Rogan, *The Arabs: A History*, p. 92.   15. Leila Tarazi Fawaz, *An Occasion for War: Civil Conflict in Lebanon and Damascus in 1860*, p. 226.   16. Ibid., p. 60.   17. For a breakdown of the nineteenth-century population, see ibid.,

pp. 131–2.   18. Ibid., pp. 108, 115.   19. Edward Atiyah, *An Arab Tells His Story: A Study in Loyalties*, pp. 10, 132.   20. Ibid., p. 11.   21. 'The place to see and be seen: Beirut's legendary museum rises from the ashes', *Guardian*, 7 October 2015 (https://www.theguard ian.com/artanddesign/2015/oct/07/beirut-sursock-museum-reopening).   22. Fawaz, *Merchants and Migrants*, p. 91.   23. Ibid., pp. 93–4; Lorenzo Trombetta, 'The Private Archives of the Sursuqs, a Beirut Family of Christian Notables: An Early Investigation', *Rivista degli Studi Orientali*, Nuova Serie, vol. 82, fasc. 1/4 (2009), pp. 197–228.   24. Fawaz, *Merchants and Migrants*, p. 84.   25. Mansel, p. 93.   26. Kassir, pp. 154, 219; Mansel, p. 150.   27. Quoted in Hanssen, pp. 231, 107.   28. Kamal Salibi, *A House of Many Mansions: The History of Lebanon Reconsidered*, p. 179.   29. Fawwaz Traboulsi, *A History of Modern Lebanon*, p. 67. On Ibrahim al Yaziji and the poem, see Alex Rowell, 'Translation of Ibrahim al-Yaziji's "Awaken and arise, O Arabs"' (http://thedisgraceofgod.blogspot.co.uk/2015/04/ translation-of-ibrahim-al-yazijis.html). On Midhat Pasha's downfall, see Leila Hudson, *Transforming Damascus: Space and Modernity in an Islamic City*, pp. 28–9.   30. Kassir, p. 168.   31. For a brief portrait of Yaziji *père et fils*, see ibid., pp. 165–6.   32. Ibid., pp. 172–3; Mansel, p. 149; Gorton, p. 58.   33. For a recent review of *Leg over Leg*, see Robyn Creswell, 'The First Great Arabic Novel', *New Yorker*, 8 October 2015 (http://www. nybooks.com/articles/2015/10/08/first-great-arabic-novel/#fn-1). On Mohammed Arslan and the Syrian Scientific Society, see George Antonius, *The Arab Awakening: The Story of the Arab National Movement*, p. 53; Kassir, p. 167.   34. Hanssen, pp. 195–6; Mansel, p. 153.   35. Khalaf, p. 188. On Beirut's Red Light district and Marica Espiredone, see Khalaf, pp. 211–22; Emad Bazzi, 'Inside Beirut's Most Notorious Brothels during the "Mad Years"' (http://raseef22.com/en/life/2017/03/22/inside-beiruts-notorious-brothels-mad-years/).   36. Hanssen, pp. 55, 219.   37. Ibid., p. 243; Khalaf, p. 64.   38. For the full letter, see Hanssen, pp. 243–4.   39. For an illustrated history of the Kaiser's visit, see Sawsan Agha Kassab and Khaled Omar Tadmori, *Beyrouth et le Sultan: 200 photographies des albums de Abdul Hamid II (1876–1909)*; for the official account of the visit, see *Das Deutsche Kaiserpaar im Heiligen Lande im Herbst 1898 (The German Imperial Couple in the Holy Land in Autumn 1898)*, p. 378.   40. Gorton, p. 1.   41. Nadia Tuéni, *Lebanon: Poems of Love and War*, p. xxviii.   42. For his views on Solidere, see Khalaf, pp. 137–48. See also Saree Makdisi, 'Beirut, a City without History?', in Ussama Makdisi and Paul Silverstein (eds.), *Memory and Violence in the Middle East and North Africa*, p. 212; Assem Salam, 'The Role of Government in Shaping the Built Environment', in Peter G. Rowe and Hashim Sarkis (eds.), *Projecting Beirut: Episodes in the Construction and Reconstruction of a Modern City*, p. 132; Craig Larkin, 'Remaking Beirut: Contesting Memory, Space, and the Urban Imaginary of Lebanese Youth', *City & Community*, vol. 9, issue 4 (December 2010) (https://www. researchgate.net/publication/229919784_Remaking_Beirut_Contesting_Memory_Space_ and_the_Urban_Imaginary_of_Lebanese_Youth); Ghenwa Hayek, *Beirut, Imagining the City: Space and Place in Lebanese Literature*, p. 131; Tarek Saad Ragab, 'Who Won the Battle of Beirut Downtown? Revisiting the Crisis of Cultural Identity in Rehabilitating Post-War Beirut', in Roderick Lawrence, Hulya Turgut and Peter Kellett (eds.), *Requalifying the Built Environment: Challenges and Responses*, p. 129; Hadi Makarem, 'Downtown Beirut: Between Amnesia and Nostalgia' (http://blogs.lse.ac.uk/mec/2012/10/17/downtown-beirut- between-amnesia-and-nostalgia/); Saree Makdisi, 'Laying Claim to Beirut: Urban Narrative and Spatial Identity in the Age of Solidere', *Critical Inquiry*, vol. 23, no. 3, *Front Lines/ Border Posts* (Spring 1997), p. 674; 'Is Beirut's glitzy downtown redevelopment all that it seems?', *Guardian*, 22 January 2015 (https://www.theguardian.com/cities/2015/jan/22/ beirut-lebanon-glitzy-downtown-redevelopment-gucci-prada).   43. Tarek Osman, *Islamism: What it Means for the Middle East and the World*, p. 134.

14. Dubai – Build It and They Will Come

1. Robert A. Carter, *Sea of Pearls: Seven Thousand Years of the Industry that Shaped the Gulf*, p. 4.   2. Andrew George (tr.), *The Epic of Gilgamesh*, p. 98.   3. Gasparo Balbi,

Viaggio dell'Indie Orientali, p. 49.   4. Quoted in Carter, p. 79.   5. 'Trigonometrical Plan of the Back-water of Debai by Lieut. R. Cogan under the direction of Lt. J. M. Guy, H. C. Marine. 1822. Drawn by M. Houghton' (1/2), British Library Map Collections, IOR/X/3690 (https://www.qdl.qa/en/archive/81055/vdc_100024141117.0x000002).   6. For a summary of this argument, see James Onley, 'Britain and the Gulf Shaikhdoms, 1820–1971: The Politics of Protection', Occasional Paper No. 4, Center for International and Regional Studies, Georgetown University of Foreign Service in Qatar (2009), pp. 1–10 (https://repository.library. georgetown.edu/bitstream/handle/10822/558294/CIRSOccasionalPaper4JamesOnley2009. pdf).   7. Michael Quentin Morton, *Keepers of the Golden Shore: A History of the United Arab Emirates*, p. 70.   8. Ibid.; Jim Krane, *Dubai: The Story of the World's Fastest City*, pp. 33–4.   9. Christopher Davidson, *Dubai: The Vulnerability of Success*, p. 68.   10. Frauke Heard-Bey, *From Trucial States to United Arab Emirates: A Society in Transition*, p. 242.   11. Author interview, Dubai, 12 December 2014.   12. John Gordon Lorimer, *Gazetteer of the Persian Gulf, Oman and Central Arabia*, vol. 2: *Geographical and Statistical*, pp. 455–6.   13. 'Dubai Inc.', *Forbes*, 3 March 2006 (https://www.forbes.com/2006/03/02/ dubai-DPWorld-Emmar_cx_daa_0302dubai.html).   14. Bilal Khamis's story is told in his own words in Julia Wheeler and Paul Thuybaert, *Telling Tales: An Oral History of Dubai*, pp. 22–5. For Jumaa al Batishi's recollections, see 'The perils of the pearl divers', *The National*, 21 June 2009 (https://www.thenational.ae/uae/the-perils-of-the-pearl-divers-1.559014). On pearling vocabulary, see Eileen Khoury, 'Servants of the Pearl', *Aramco World*, vol. 41, no. 5 (September/October 1990) (http://archive.aramcoworld.com/issue/199005/ servants.of.the.pearl.htm).   15. Graeme Wilson, *Rashid's Legacy: The Genesis of the Maktoum Family and the History of Dubai*, p. 56. On the Seddiqi family business, see the group's website (http://www.seddiqi.com/en/article/the-origins/the-story.html).   16. Anthony Mayo, Nitin Nohria, Umaimah Mendhro and Johnathan Cromwell, 'Sheikh Mohammed and the Making of "Dubai Inc."', Harvard Business School Case 410-063 (February 2010, revised August 2010), p. 2.   17. Morton, pp. 90–92.   18. Krane, pp. 28–9.   19. See Rosemarie Said Zahlan, *The Origins of the United Arab Emirates: A Political and Social History of the Trucial States*, p. 161; Morton, p. 115.   20. Wheeler and Thuybaert, p. 100; Krane, p. 42.   21. Wilfred Thesiger, *Arabian Sands*, p. 220.   22. Wheeler and Thuybaert, p. 66.   23. Wilson, p. 130; author interview, Dubai, 11 November 2014.   24. Sheikh Mohammed bin Rashid al Maktoum, *My Vision: Challenges in the Race for Excellence*, p. 86.   25. Graeme Wilson, *Rashid: Father of Dubai*, p. 126.   26. Wilson, *Rashid's Legacy*, p. 178.   27. Davidson, pp. 109–10.   28. Jacques Benoist-Mechin, *Turkey 1908–1938: The End of the Ottoman Empire*, p. 222.   29. James Barr, *Lords of the Desert: Britain's Struggle with America to Dominate the Middle East*, pp. 58, 150.   30. Ibid., p. 338.   31. Krane, pp. 76–7.   32. Donald Hawley, *The Trucial States*, p. 200.   33. Quoted in Davidson, pp. 39–40.   34. Krane, p. 78.   35. 'Story of cities #43: How Dubai's World Trade Centre sold the city to the world', *Guardian*, 16 May 2016 (https://www.theguardian.com/cities/2016/ may/16/story-of-cities-43-dubai-world-trade-centre-turned-sand-gold-uae).   36. 'Dubai is stronger for steering clear of oil-based economy', *The National*, 10 May 2015 (https://www. thenational.ae/business/dubai-is-stronger-for-steering-clear-of-oil-based-economy-1.126843); 'Go inside the Middle East's ultramodern city of extravagance', *National Geographic*, 20 November 2018 (https://www.nationalgeographic.com/travel/destinations/asia/united-arab-emirates/dubai/pictures-globalization-tourism-middle-east/).   37. Author interview, Dubai, 8 March 2016.   38. Wilson, *Rashid's Legacy*, p. 502.   39. Author interview, Dubai, 11 March 2016; Krane, p. viii.   40. Pranay Gupte, *Dubai: The Making of a Megapolis*, p. 188.   41. 'Al Habtoor City: The Dawn of a New City' (http://alhabtoorcity.com).   42. '8 "world's biggest" records held by Dubai', *ShortList*, 19 September 2016 (http://www.short listdubai.com/around-town/article/10048-8-worlds-biggest-records-held-by-dubai).   43. Syed Ali, *Dubai: Gilded Cage*, p. 1.   44. See 'The Slaves of Dubai', a film by the BBC reporter Ben Anderson, 8 August 2012 (https://www.youtube.com/watch?v=gMh-vlQwrmU).   45. Davidson, p. 277.   46. Justin Thomas, *Psychological Wellbeing in the Gulf States: The New Arabia Felix*, p. 4; 'Why Dubai bashing is not clever', *Arabian Business*, 13 May 2010 (https://www.arabianbusiness.com/photos/why-dubai-bashing-is-not-clever-269236.

html?page=0&img=0). See also 'Sultan Al Qassemi's response to the latest Dubai-bashing article is perfect', *What's On*, 27 April 2017 (http://whatson.ae/dubai/2017/04/sultan-al-qassemis-response-latest-dubai-bashing-article-perfect/).   47. Mayo, Nohria, Mendhro and Cromwell, p. 16; author interview, Dubai, 10 March 2016; author interview, Dubai, 11 November 2014; author interview, Dubai, 11 March 2016; author interview, Dubai, 9 March 2016.   48. Author interview, Dubai, 9 March 2016; Krane, p. 191.   49. Author interview, Dubai, 14 November 2014.

15. Doha – City of Pearls

1. 'Faisal Bin Qassim Al Thani', *Forbes*, 30 January 2018 (https://www.forbes.com/profile/faisal-bin-qassim-al-thani/).   2. Author interview, Doha, 28 April 2015.   3. Author interview, Doha, 25 April 2015. Names have been changed where indicated.   4. 'Qatar Facts and Figures', OPEC website (http://www.opec.org/opec_web/en/about_us/168.htm), consulted 12 February 2018; according to the World Bank, GDP per capita in Qatar was $127,728 in 2016. The figures for the US and UK were $57,638 and $43,081 respectively (http://databank.worldbank.org/data/reports.aspx?source=2&series=NY.GDP.PCAP.PP.CD&country=).   5. Author interview, Doha, 29 April 2015; Eileen Khoury, 'Servants of the Pearl', *Aramco World*, vol. 41, no. 5 (September/October 1990), (http://archive.aramcoworld.com/issue/199005/servants.of.the.pearl.htm); 'From pearls to skyscrapers – Qatar's Alfardan sticks to family model', Reuters, 8 November 2015 (https://uk.reuters.com/article/us-qatar-alfardan-family/from-pearls-to-skyscrapers-qatars-alfardan-sticks-to-family-model-idUKKCN0SX0RO20151108).   6. 'The World Richest Arab 2013', *Forbes* (https://www.forbesmiddleeast.com/en/list/the-world-richest-arab-2013/item/47/).   7. 'Fabergé revives the tradition', Fabergé website, 25 February 2015 (https://www.faberge.com/news/an-objet-d-art-masterpiece-the-faberge-pearl-egg-191); 'Fabergé Unveils New "Imperial Egg" at Baselworld 2015 and Names its Buyer', *Forbes*, 23 March 2015 (https://www.forbes.com/sites/anthonydemarco/2015/03/23/faberge-unveils-new-imperial-egg-at-baselworld-2015-and-names-its-buyer/#fod83b367b77).   8. William Gifford Palgrave, *Narrative of a Year's Journey Through Central and Eastern Arabia 1862–63*, vol. 2, p. 387.   9. 'Vanity Mirror: Jean Nouvel's Message in a Bottle', *Vanity Fair*, April 2008 (https://www.vanityfair.com/news/2008/04/beauty-ysl-nouv).   10. Author interview, Doha, 8 January 2015. His name has been changed.   11. 'Bridge in the Gulf', *Financial Times*, 11 February 2011 (https://www.ft.com/content/dd454d60-3563-11e0-aa6c-00144feabdco); author interviews, Doha, 7–8 January 2015.   12. Author interview, Doha, 27 April 2015.   13. On the threats to historic Doha neighbourhoods, see Ashraf M. Salama, Simona Azzali and Florian Wiedmann, 'The everyday urban environment of migrant labourers in Gulf Cities: The case of the old centre of Doha, Qatar', in *City, Territory and Architecture*, vol. 4, 5 (February 2017) (https://cityterritoryarchitecture.springeropen.com/articles/10.1186/s40410-017-0061-5).   14. Sultan Mohammed al Qasimi (ed.), *The Journals of David Seton in the Gulf 1800–1809*. For a useful timeline of Doha, see 'A History of Doha and Bidda: Historical References to Doha and Bidda before 1850', Origins of Doha and Qatar Project, led by Dr Robert Carter of UCL Qatar (https://originsofdoha.files.wordpress.com/2015/03/a-history-of-doha-and-bidda1.pdf).   15. Habibur Rahman, *The Emergence of Qatar: The Turbulent Years 1627–1916*, p. 31. The 1823 'Trigonometrical plan of the harbour of El Biddah on the Arabian side of the Persian Gulf' is available at Qatar Digital Library (https://www.qdl.qa/en/archive/81055/vdc_100000010848.0x000001).   16. Rosemarie Said Zahlan, *The Creation of Qatar*, p. 34.   17. *The Persian Gulf Pilot*, archive editions.   18. Palgrave, pp. 386–7.   19. For more on this attack, see Rahman, pp. 75–6.   20. Ibid., p. 260.   21. Zahlan, p. 11; Mohammed al Thani, *Jassim the Leader*, p. xi.   22. Khaled Adam, 'Rediscovering the Island: Doha's Urbanity from Pearls to Spectacle', in Yasser Elsheshtawy (ed.), *The Evolving Arab City: Tradition, Modernity and Urban Development*, pp. 219–20; Zahlan, p. 11.   23. James Barr, *Lords of the Desert: Britain's Struggle with America to Dominate the Middle East*, p. xi.   24. In 1963 Petroleum Development (Qatar) Ltd became

Qatar Petroleum Company, today's Qatar Petroleum. The 1935 Qatar Oil Concession can be seen at https://www.qdl.qa/en/archive/81055/vdc_100023599463.0x000002. 25. For the telegram of 11 October 1939, see Dr Mark Hobbs, 'Qatari History: Pivotal Moments Revealed in India Office Records', Qatar Digital Library (https://www.qdl.qa/en/qatari-history-pivotal-moments-revealed-india-office-records). The letter of 14 January 1940 can be seen at Qatar Digital Library (https://www.qdl.qa/en/archive/81055/vdc_100024164774.0x000065). 26. *A History of Doha and Bidda*, p. 19. 27. Justin Marozzi, 'Welcome to the falcon hospital of Doha', BBC, 26 May 2015 (http://www.bbc.co.uk/news/magazine-32842338). 28. For the story of Suq Waqif's restoration, see Hassan Radoine, *Souk Wakif On-site Review Report*, edited by Aga Khan Award for Architecture, 2010 (https://archnet.org/system/publications/contents/8722/original/DTP101221.pdf?1396271815). See also Djamel Boussaa, 'Rehabilitation as a Catalyst of Sustaining a Living Heritage: The Case of Souk Waqif in Doha, Qatar', *Art and Design Review*, vol. 2, no. 3 (2014) (http://file.scirp.org/Html/4-1250021_49452.htm). 29. Author interview, Doha, 29 April 2015. 30. For the growing size of the city, see Florian Wiedmann, Ashraf M. Salama and Alain Thierstein, 'Urban evolution of the city of Doha: An investigation into the impact of economic transformations on urban structures', *METU Journal of the Faculty of Architecture*, vol. 29, no. 2 (December 2012), p. 41 (https://pureportal.strath.ac.uk/files-asset/38618741/Urban_evolution_of_the_city_of_Doha_Wiedmann_Salama_Thierstein_35_61_8_.pdf). On the 1970 census, see Kristian Coates Ulrichsen, *Qatar and the Arab Spring*, p. 24. 31. Sharon Nagy, 'Dressing up Downtown: Urban development and government public image in Qatar', *City & Society*, vol. 12, issue 1 (June 2000), p. 134. 32. See World Bank data for Qatar at https://data.worldbank.org/country/Qatar; on Qatar's demographics, see 'Population of Qatar by Nationality – 2017 report', Priya DSouza Communications, 7 February 2017 (http://priyadsouza.com/population-of-qatar-by-nationality-in-2017/). 33. For a discussion of Qatar's foreign policy, see Faisal Mukhyat Abu Sulaib, 'Understanding Qatar's Foreign Policy, 1995–2017', *Middle East Policy*, vol. XXIV, no. 4 (Winter 2017); Marc Pierini, 'Qatar's Foreign Policy Under the New Emir', Carnegie Europe, 28 June 2013 (https://carnegieeurope.eu/strategiceurope/52236). 34. On the Qatar Investment Authority, see, for example, 'Qatar's investment arm streamlines its strategy', Oxford Business Group report 2016 (https://oxfordbusinessgroup.com/analysis/new-approach-country%E2%80%99s-investment-arm-streamlining-its-strategy). On Sheikh Hamad's restoration of Dudley House, see 'Sheikh Shack', *Vanity Fair*, February 2015 (https://www.vanityfair.com/style/2015/01/dudley-house-london). 35. Wiedmann, Salama and Thierstein, p. 44. 36. See Ali A. Alraouf, ' "Dohaization": An Emerging Interface between Knowledge, Creativity, and Gulf Urbanity', in George Katodrytis and Sharmeen Syed (eds.), *Gulf Cities as Interfaces*, pp. 47–68. 37. Justin Marozzi, 'Get the Message from the Gulf: The US and Baghdad both Criticise Al Jazeera, the Arabic Language Satellite Station. Perhaps It Is Doing Something Right', *Financial Times*, 14 September 2002. 38. See, for instance, Kristian Coates Ulrichsen, 'Qatar and the Arab Spring: Policy Drivers and Regional Implications', Carnegie Endowment for International Peace, 24 September 2014 (http://carnegieendowment.org/2014/09/24/qatar-and-arab-spring-policy-drivers-and-regional-implications-pub-56723); Tom Keatinge, 'Why Qatar is the focus of terrorism claims', Centre for Financial Crime and Security Studies, BBC, 13 June 2017 (http://www.bbc.co.uk/news/world-middle-east-40246734); 'How Qatar is funding the rise of Islamist extremists', *Daily Telegraph*, 20 September 2014 (http://www.telegraph.co.uk/news/worldnews/middleeast/qatar/11110931/How-Qatar-is-funding-the-rise-of-Islamist-extremists.html); 'Qatar Opens Its Doors to All, to the Dismay of Some', *New York Times*, 16 July 2014 (https://www.nytimes.com/2017/07/16/world/middleeast/doha-qatar-blockade.html). 39. 'Saudi Arabia may dig canal to turn Qatar into an island', *Guardian*, 1 September 2018 (https://www.theguardian.com/world/2018/sep/01/saudi-arabia-may-dig-canal-to-turn-qatar-into-an-island). 40. Author interview, Doha, 28 April 2015. 41. On sustainability in Doha, see Andrew M. Gardner, 'How the City Grows: Urban Growth and Challenges to Sustainable Development in Doha, Qatar', in Paul Sillitoe (ed.), *Sustainable Development: An Appraisal from the Gulf Region*, pp. 343–66. 42. Herodotus, *Histories*, 1.4. 43. 'Arab Spring',

Wikipedia (https://en.wikipedia.org/wiki/Arab_Spring).   44. See, for example, Brendan Simms, Michael Axworthy and Patrick Milton, 'Ending the New Thirty Years' War', *New Statesman*, 26 January 2016 (https://www.newstatesman.com/politics/uk/2016/01/ending-new-thirty-years-war). For a counter view, see Lorenzo Kamel, 'There is no Thirty Years' War in the Middle East', *The National Interest*, 29 August 2016 (https://nationalinterest. org/feature/there-no-thirty-years-war-the-middle-east-17513). See also Peter H. Wilson, *The Thirty Years War: Europe's Tragedy*, p. 4.   45. See, for example, Christopher de Bellaigue, *The Islamic Enlightenment: The Modern Struggle Between Faith and Reason*.   46. Italo Calvino, *Invisible Cities*, p. 7; Gardner, 'How the City Grows', in Sillitoe (ed.), *Sustainable Development*.

Bibliography

General Reading

Ajami, Fouad, *The Dream Palace of the Arabs: A Generation's Odyssey* (New York, 1998)

Allawi, Ali A., *The Crisis of Islamic Civilization* (New Haven, Connecticut; London, 2009)

Atiyah, Edward, *The Arabs* (London, 1955)

Bennison, Amira K., and Gascoigne, Alison L. (eds.), *Cities in the Pre-modern Islamic World: The Urban Impact of Religion, State and Society* (London, 2007)

Blair, Sheila S., and Bloom, Jonathan M., *The Art and Architecture of Islam, 1250–1800* (New Haven, Connecticut; London, 1994)

Bosworth, C. Edmund (ed.), *Historic Cities of the Islamic World* (Leiden, 2007)

Dawood, N. J. (tr.), *The Koran* (London, 2000)

Gibb, H. A. R., *The Travels of Ibn Battutah* (Cambridge, 1958)

Hitti, P. K., *Capital Cities of Arab Islam* (Minneapolis, Minnesota, 1973)

—, *History of the Arabs* (New York, 1937)

Hourani, Albert, *A History of the Arab Peoples* (London, 2013; reprint of 1991 original)

—, and Stern, S. M. (eds.), *The Islamic City* (Oxford, 1970)

Hoyland, Robert G., *Arabia and the Arabs: From the Bronze Age to the Coming of Islam* (London, 2001)

Irwin, Robert, *Night, Horses and the Desert: The Penguin Anthology of Classical Arabic Literature* (London, 2000)

Jayyusi, Salma, Holod Renata, Petruccioli, Attilio, and Raymond, André (eds.), *The City in the Islamic World* (Leiden, 2008)

Kassir, Samir, *Being Arab* (London, 2006, reprint and translation of *Considérations sur le Malheur Arabe*, 2004)

Kennedy, Hugh, *The Great Arab Conquests: How the Spread of Islam Changed the World We Live In* (Cambridge, Massachusetts, 2007)

Khaldun, Ibn, *The Muqaddimah: An Introduction to History* (London, 1978)

Lewis, Bernard, *The Arabs in History* (Oxford, 2002; reprint of 1950 original)

—, *The Muslim Discovery of Europe* (London, 2000)

Mackintosh-Smith, Tim, *Arabs: A 3,000-Year History of Peoples, Tribes and Empires* (New Haven, Connecticut, 2019)

Mitchell, George (ed.), *Architecture of the Islamic World* (London, 1978)

Robinson, Chase F. (ed.), *The New Cambridge History of Islam* (Cambridge, 2010)

—, *Islamic Historiography, Themes in Islamic History* (Cambridge, 2003)

Rogan, Eugene, *The Arabs: A History* (London, 2012; reprint of 2009 original)

1. Mecca – Mother of All Cities

Antrim, Zayde, *Routes and Realms: The Power of Place in the Early Islamic World* (Oxford, 2012)

Armstrong, Karen, *Muhammad: A Prophet for Our Time* (New York, 2006)

Bostom, Andrew G. (ed.), *The Legacy of Jihad: Islamic Holy War and the Fates of Non-Muslims* (Amherst, New York, 2008)

Bowersock, Glen, *Crucible of Islam* (Cambridge, Massachusetts; London, 2017)

Bukhari, *Sahi Bukhari* (https://www.sahih-bukhari.com)

Crone, Patricia, *Meccan Trade and the Rise of Islam* (Princeton, New Jersey, 1987)

Donner, Fred M., *Muhammad and the Believers: At the Origins of Islam* (Cambridge, Massachusetts, 2010)

—, 'The Historical Context', *The Cambridge Companion to the Quran* (Cambridge, 2006)

Grabar, Oleg, 'Upon Reading Al-Azraqi', *Muqarnas Online*, vol. 3, issue 1 (1985) (https://brill.com/view/journals/muqj/3/1/article-p1_2.xml)

Gwynne, Paul, *Buddha, Jesus and Muhammad: A Comparative Study* (Chichester, 2014)

Hawting, G. R., *The Idea of Idolatry and the Emergence of Islam: From Polemic to History* (Cambridge, 1999)

Heck, Gene W., ' "Arabia without Spices": An Alternate Hypothesis: The Issue of "Makkan Trade and the Rise of Islam" ', *Journal of the American Oriental Society* (Ann Arbor, Michigan, 2003)

Holland, Tom, *In the Shadow of the Sword: The Battle for Global Empire and the End of the Ancient World* (London, 2012)

Ibrahim, Mahmud, *Merchant Capital and Islam* (Austin, Texas, 1990)

Ishaq, Ibn, *The Life of Muhammad*, translated by A. Guillaume (London, 1955)

Juynboll, G. H. A., *Studies on the First Century of Islamic Society* (Carbondale, Illinois, 1982)

Kister, M. J., 'The Massacre of the Banu Qurayza: A Re-examination of a Tradition', *Jerusalem Studies in Arabic and Islam*, 8 (Jerusalem, 1986)

—, 'Some Reports Concerning Mecca: From Jahiliyya to Islam', *Journal of the Economic & Social History of the Orient*, 15 (1972)

Lammens, Henri, *Islam: Beliefs and Institutions* (Oxford, 2013; reprint of 1929 original)

Mubarak, Safiur Rahman (ed.), *History of Makkah* (Riyadh, London; Darussalam, 2002)

Peters, Francis E., *Mecca: A Literary History of the Muslim Holy Land* (Princeton, 2017; reprint of 1994 original)

—, *Muhammad and the Origins of Islam* (Albany, New York, 1994)

Sardar, Ziauddin, *Mecca: The Sacred City* (London, 2014)

Smith, Martyn, *Religion, Culture, and Sacred Space* (New York, 2008)

Watt, Montgomery W., 'Mecca – The pre-Islamic and early Islamic periods', in *Encyclopedia of Islam*, vol. 5 (Leiden, 2008)

—, and McDonald, M. V., *The History of al-Tabari*, vol. VI: *Muhammad at Mecca* (Albany, New York, 1988)

Wolfe, Michael, *One Thousand Roads to Mecca: Ten Centuries of Travelers Writing about the Muslim Pilgrimage* (New York, 1997)

2. Damascus – The Perfumed Paradise

Al Isfahani, Abul Faraj, *Kitab al Aghani* (Cairo, 1905)

Al Maqrizi, *Book of Contention and Strife Concerning the Relations between the Banu Umayya and the Banu Hashim* (Manchester, 1980)

Antrim, Zayde, 'Ibn Asakir's Representations of Syria and Damascus in the Introduction to the *Tarikh Madinat Dimashq*', *International Journal of Middle East Studies*, 38 (Cambridge, 2006)

Asakir, Ibn, *Tarikh Madinat Dimashq* (Beirut, 1997)

Broadhurst, R. J. C. (tr. and ed.), *The Travels of Ibn Jubayr* (London, 1952)

Burns, Ross, *Damascus: A History* (London, 2005)

Creswell, K. A. C., *Early Muslim Architecture*, Part 1: *Umayyads 622–750* (Oxford, 1969)

Degeorge, Gérard, *Damascus* (Paris, 2004)

Elisséeff, N., 'Dimashq', *Encyclopaedia of Islam 2*, vol. 2 (Leiden, 1965)

—, *La Description de Damas d'Ibn Asakir* (Damascus, 1959)

Flood, Finbar Barry, *The Great Mosque of Damascus: Studies on the Makings of an Umayyad Visual Culture* (Leiden, 2001)

Frankopan, Peter, *The Silk Roads: A New History of the World* (London, 2015)

Gibbon, Edward, *The History of the Decline and Fall of the Roman Empire* (London, 1911)

Glassé, Cyril, *The New Encyclopaedia of Islam* (London, 2013)

Grabar, Oleg, *Formation of Islamic Art* (New Haven, Connecticut, 1973)

Hamilton, Robert, *Walid and his Friends: An Umayyad Tragedy* (Oxford, 1988)

Hawting, G. R., *The First Dynasty of Islam: The Umayyad Caliphate AD 661–750* (London, 1986)

Hitti, Philip, *The Origins of the Islamic State. Being a Translation from the Arabic, Accompanied with Annotations, Geographic and Historic Notes of the Kitab Futuh al-Buldan of al-Imaam abu-l 'Abbas Ahmad ibn Jabir al-Baladhuri* (New York, 1916)

Hoyland, Robert, *In God's Path: The Arab Conquests* (Oxford, 2013)

— (tr.), *Theophilus of Edessa's Chronicle* (Liverpool, 2011)

Humphreys, R. Stephen, 'Syria', in Chase F. Robinson (ed.), *The New Cambridge History of Islam*, vol. 1 (Cambridge, 2010)

Kennedy, Hugh, *The Byzantine and Early Islamic Middle East* (Aldershot, 2006)

—, *When Baghdad Ruled the Muslim World: The Rise and Fall of Islam's Greatest Dynasty* (Cambridge, Massachusetts, 2005; US edition of *The Court of the Caliphs*, London, 2005)

—, *The Early Abbasid Caliphate: A Political History* (London, 1981)

Khalek, Nancy, *Damascus after the Muslim Conquest: Text and Image in Early Islam* (New York, Oxford, 2011)

Le Strange, Guy, *Palestine under the Moslems: A Description of Syria and the Holy Land* (London, 1890)

Mottahedeh, Roy, 'The Abbasid Caliphate in Iran', in *The Cambridge History of Iran*, vol. IV: *The Period from the Arab Invasion to the Saljuqs* (Cambridge, 2008)

Robinson, Chase F., 'The Violence of the Abbasid Revolution', in Yasir Suleiman (ed.), *Living Islamic History: Studies in Honour of Professor Carole Hillenbrand* (Edinburgh, 2012)

Rowson, Everett K., and Robinson, Chase, *The Works of Ibn Wadih al-Yaqubi: An English Translation* (Leiden, 2017)

Tabari, *The History of al-Tabari*, vol. 26: *The Waning of the Umayyad Caliphate* (Albany, New York, 1989)

Wolf, Kenneth Baxter, *Conquerors and Chroniclers of Early Medieval Spain* (Liverpool, 1990)

3. Baghdad – City of Peace, City of Blood

Abbott, Nabia, *Two Queens of Baghdad: Mother and Wife of Harun al Rashid* (London, 1986; reprint of 1946 original)

Abdullah, Thabit, *A Short History of Iraq: From 636 to the Present* (London, 2003)

Adler, Marcus Nathan, *The Itinerary of Benjamin of Tudela* (Oxford, 1907)

Ahsan, Muhammad Manazir, *Social Life Under the Abbasids* (London, 1979)

Al Isfahani, Abul Faraj, *Kitab al Aghani* (*Book of Songs*) (Cairo, 1905)

Al Khalili, Jim, *Pathfinders: The Golden Age of Arabic Science* (London, 2010)

Al Muqaddasi, *The Best Divisions for Knowledge of the Regions*, a translation of Ahsan al Taqasim fi Ma'rifat al Aqalim by Basil Anthony Collins (Reading, 1994)

Al Tikriti, Abd al Rahman, *Al Amthal al Baghdadiyya al Muqarana, Comparative Proverbs of Baghdad*, 4 vols. (Baghdad, 1969)

Al Zubayr, Ibn, *Kitab al Hadaya wa al Tuhaf* (*Book of Gifts and Rarities*), translated and annotated by Ghada al Hijjawi al Qaddumi (Cambridge, Massachusetts, 1996)

Ali, Sayed Amir, *The Spirit of Islam: A History of the Evolution and Ideals of Islam with a Life of the Prophet* (London, 1922)

Arberry, A. J., *Arabic Poetry* (Cambridge, 1965)

Armstrong, Karen, *A History of God: From Abraham to the Present: The 4,000-year Quest for God* (London, 1999; reprint of 1993 original)

Ashtiany, Julia, et al. (eds.), *Abbasid Belles-Lettres, Cambridge History of Arabic Literature*, vol. 2 (Cambridge, 1990)

Baig, Sulaiman Faiq, *The History of Baghdad*, translated by Mousa Kadhim Nawras (Baghdad, 1962)

Bell, Gertrude, *Diaries* and *Letters*, available in Newcastle University's Gertrude Bell Archive, http://www.gerty.ncl.ac.uk

Bennison, Amira, *The Great Caliphs: The Golden Age of the Abbasid Empire* (London, 2009)

Broadhurst, Roland J. C. (tr. and ed.), *The Travels of Ibn Jubayr, Being the Chronicle of a Mediaeval Spanish Moor Concerning his Journey to the Egypt of Saladin, the Holy Cities of Arabia, Baghdad the City of the Caliphs, the Latin Kingdom of Jerusalem, and the Norman Kingdom of Sicily* (London, 1952)

Clot, André, *Harun al-Rashid and the World of the Thousand and One Nights*, translated from the French by John Howe (London, 2005)

Coke, Richard, *Baghdad: The City of Peace* (London, 1927)

De Slane, Baron Mac Guckin (tr.), *Ibn Khallikan's Biographical Dictionary*, 4 vols. (Paris, 1842–71)

Duri, A. A., 'Baghdad', *Encylopaedia of Islam 2*, vol. 1 (Leiden, 1965)

Gibbon, Edward, *The History of the Decline and Fall of the Roman Empire* (London, 1835)

Gruendler, Beatrice, *Medieval Arabic Praise Poetry* (London, 2002)

Irwin, Robert, *The Arabian Nights: A Companion* (London, 2004)

Kathir, Ibn, *Al Bidaya wal Nihaya (The Beginning and the End)* (Al Mostafa e-library; www.al-mostafa.com)

Kennedy, Hugh, *When Baghdad Ruled the Muslim World: The Rise and Fall of Islam's Greatest Dynasty* (Cambridge, Massachusetts, 2005; US edition of *The Court of the Caliphs*, London, 2005)

Kennedy, Philip, *Abu Nuwas: A Genius of Poetry* (Oxford, 2005)

Lassner, Jacob, *The Topography of Baghdad in the Early Middle Ages* (Detroit, 1970)

Le Strange, Guy, *Lands of the Eastern Caliphate: Mesopotamia and Central Asia from the Moslem Conquest to the Time of Timur* (Cambridge, 1905)

—, *Baghdad during the Abbasid Caliphate* (Oxford, 1900)

Lyons, Jonathan, *The House of Wisdom: How the Arabs Transformed Western Civilisation* (London, 2008)

Lyons, Malcolm (tr.), *The Arabian Nights: Tales of 1001 Nights*, 3 vols. (London, 2008)

MacCulloch, Diarmaid, *A History of Christianity: The First Three Thousand Years* (London, 2009)

Marozzi, Justin, *Baghdad: City of Peace, City of Blood* (London, 2014)

Masudi, *The Meadows of Gold: The Abbasids*, translated and edited by Paul Lunde and Caroline Stone (London, 1989)

Mathers, Powys, *The Thousand Nights and One Night*, 4 vols. (London, 2005, 1996; reprint of 1949 original)

Milwright, Marcus, *An Introduction to Islamic Archaeology* (Cambridge, 2010)

Nicholson, Reynold Alleyne, *A Literary History of the Arabs* (London, 1914; reprint of 1907 original)

O'Leary, De Lacy, *How Greek Science Passed to the Arabs* (London, 1948)

—, *Arabic Thought and its Place in History* (London, 1922)

Pellat, Charles, *The Life and Works of Jahiz* (London, 1969)

Rowell, Alex, *Vintage Humour: The Islamic Wine Poetry of Abu Nuwas* (London, 2018)

Shaban, M. A., *The Abbasid Revolution* (Cambridge, 1979)

Shamash, Violette, *Memories of Eden: A Journey Through Jewish Baghdad* (London, 2008)

Spuler, Bertold, *The Muslim World*, vol. 1: *The Age of the Caliphs* (Leiden, 1960)

Tabari, *The History of Al Tabari*, vol. XXXI: *The War between Brothers: The Caliphate of Muhammad al Amin AD 809–813/AH 193–198* (1992)

—, *The History of Al Tabari*, vol. I: *The Reign of Abu Jafar al Mansur 754–775* (Albany, New York, 1989)

—, *The History of Al Tabari*, vol. XXX: *The Abbasid Caliphate in Equilibrium: The Caliphates of Musa al Hadi and Harun al Rashid* AD 785–809/AH 169–193 (1989)

—, *The History of Al Tabari*, vol. XXXV: *The Crisis of the Abbasid Caliphate: The Caliphates of al Musta'in and al Mu'tazz* AD 862–869/AH 248–255 (1985)

Wiet, Gaston, *Baghdad: Metropolis of the Abbasid Caliphate* (Norman, Oklahoma, 1971)

4. Cordoba – Ornament of the World

Ashtor, Eliyahu, *The Jews of Moslem Spain* (Philadelphia, Pennsylvania, 1992)

Catlos, Brian A., *Kingdoms of Faith: A New History of Islamic Spain* (London, 2018)

Christys, Ann, 'Picnic at Madinat al-Zahra', in Barton, Simon, and Linehan, Peter (eds.), *Cross, Crescent and Conversion: Studies on Medieval Spain and Christendom in Memory of Richard Fletcher* (Leiden, 2008)

—, *Christians in Andalus 711–1000* (Richmond, 2001)

Elinson, Alexander E., *Looking Back at Al-Andalus: The Poetics of Loss and Nostalgia in Medieval Arabic and Hebrew Literature* (Leiden, 2009)

Fierro, Maribel, *Abd al Rahman III – The First Cordoban Caliph* (Oxford, 2005)

Fletcher, Richard, *Moorish Spain* (Berkeley, California, 2006; reprint of 1992 original)

Hillenbrand, R., 'The Ornament of the World: Cordoba as a Cultural Centre', in Jayyusi (ed.)

Jayyusi, Salma (ed.), *The Legacy of Muslim Spain* (Leiden, 1992)

Kennedy, Hugh, *Muslim Spain and Portugal: A Political History of Al Andalus* (London, 1996)

Khoury, Nuha, 'The Meaning of the Great Mosque of Cordoba in the Tenth Century', in *Muqarnas*, vol. 13 (1996)

Lévi-Provençal, Évariste, *L'Espagne Musulmane*, vol. 3 (Paris, Leiden, 1950)

Menocal, Maria Rosa, *The Ornament of the World: How Muslims, Jews and Christians Created a Culture of Tolerance in Medieval Spain* (London, 2003)

—, Scheindlin, Raymond P., and Sells, Michael (eds.), *The Literature of Al Andalus* (Cambridge, 2000)

Morera, Dario Fernandez, *The Myth of the Andalusian Paradise: Muslims, Christians and Jews under Islamic Rule in Medieval Spain* (Wilmington, Delaware, 2016)

Smith, Colin (tr. and ed.), *Christians and Moors in Spain*, vol. 1 (Liverpool, 1988)

Sordo, Enrique, *Moorish Spain* (London, 1963)

Wasserstein, David, *The Caliphate in the West: An Islamic Political Institution in the Iberian Peninsula* (Oxford, 1993)

Wilson, Katharina, *Hrotsvit of Gandersheim: A Florilegium of Her Works* (Cambridge, 1998)

Wolf, Kenneth B., 'Convivencia and the "Ornament of the World"', Southeast Medieval Association, Wofford College, Spartanburg, South Carolina, October 2007 (https://scholarship.claremont.edu/cgi/viewcontent.cgi?referer=https://www.googl.com/&https redir=1&article=1042&context=pomona_fac_pub)

5. Jerusalem – The Contested City

Annalist of Nieder-Altaich, 'The Great German Pilgrimage of 1064–65', translated by James Brundage (https://legacy.fordham.edu/Halsall/source/1064pilgrim.asp)

Asali, Kamil Jamil (ed.), *Jerusalem in History: 3,000 BC to the Present Day* (London, 1997)

Asbridge, Thomas, *The First Crusade: A New History* (New York, London, 2004)

al Athir, Ibn, *The Chronicle of Ibn al Athir for the Crusading Period from Al Kamil Fi'l-Tarikh*, Part I: *The Years 491–541/1097–1146 – The Coming of the Franks and the Muslim Response* (London, 2017)

Battuta, Ibn, *Travels in Asia and Africa: 1325–1354*, translated by Reverend Samuel Lee (Mineola, New York, 2013)

Brundage, James A., 'Adhemar of Le Puy: The Bishop and his Critics', *Speculum*, vol. 34, no. 2 (April 1959)

Cobb, Paul M., *Race for Paradise: Islamic History of the Crusades* (Oxford, 2014)

Gabrieli, Francesco, *Arab Historians of the Crusades* (London, 2009)

Gil, Moshe, 'The Political History of Jerusalem During the Early Muslim Period', in Joshua Prawer and Haggai Ben-Shammai (eds.), *The History of Jerusalem: The Early Muslim Period, 638–1099* (Jerusalem, 1996)

Goddard, Hugh, *A History of Christian–Muslim Relations* (Edinburgh, 2000)

Hillenbrand, Carole, *Crusades: Islamic Perspectives* (New York, 2000; reprint of 1999 original)

The Itinerarium Burdigalense by The Anonymous Pilgrim of Bordeaux (333 AD) (https://www.scribd.com/doc/37368846/The-Itinerarium-Burdigalense-by-The-Anonymous-Pilgrim-of-Bordeaux-333-a-d)

Khalek, Nancy, *Damascus after the Muslim Conquest* (New York, Oxford, 2011)

Khusraw, Nasir-i-, *Diary of a Journey Through Syria and Palestine*, translated by Guy Le Strange (London, 1893)

Krey, August C., *The First Crusade: The Accounts of Eyewitnesses and Participants* (London, 2016; reprint of 1921 original)

Lambert, Malcolm, *Crusade and Jihad: Origins, History and Aftermath* (London, 2016)

Maalouf, Amin, *The Crusades Through Arab Eyes* (London, 1984)

Madden, Thomas F., *The Concise History of the Crusades* (Lanham, Maryland, 1983)

Montefiore, Simon Sebag, *Jerusalem: The Biography* (London, 2011)

Munro, Dana C., 'The Speech of Pope Urban II at Clermont, 1095', *The American Historical Review*, vol. XI, no. 2 (1906)

—, 'Urban and the Crusaders', *Translations and Reprints from the Original Sources of European History*, vol. 1 (Philadelphia, 1894)

Murphy-O'Connor, Jerome, *The Holy Land: An Oxford Archaeological Guide from Earliest Times to 1700* (Oxford, 1998; reprint of 1992 original)

Ousterhout, Robert, 'Rebuilding the Temple: Constantine Monomachus and the Holy Sepulchre', *Journal of the Society of Architectural Historians*, vol. 48, no. 1 (March 1989)

Peacock, A. C. S., *The Great Seljuk Empire* (Edinburgh, 2015)

Peters, Edward (ed.), *The First Crusade: The Chronicle of Fulcher of Chartres and Other Source Materials* (Philadelphia, 1998; reprint of 1971 original)

Riley-Smith, Jonathan, *The First Crusade and the Idea of Crusading* (London, 2009; reprint of 1986 original)

Runciman, Steven, *The First Crusade* (Cambridge, 1980)

Sinclair, Andrew, *Jerusalem: The Endless Crusade* (London, 1996)

Tyerman, Christopher, *God's War: A New History of the Crusades* (London, 2007)

Wolffe, John, *Religion in History: Conflict, Conversion and Coexistence* (Manchester, New York, 2004)

Wright, Thomas (ed.), *Early Travels in Palestine* (London, 1968; reprint of 1847 original)

6. Cairo – The City Victorious

Al Athir, Ali ibn, *Kamil al Tawarikh*, 14 vols. (Leiden, 1851–76)

Azzam, Abdul Rahman, *Saladin: The Triumph of the Sunni Revival* (Cambridge, 2014)

Behrens-Abouseif, Doris, 'The Façade of the Aqmar Mosque in the Context of Fatimid Ceremonial', in *Muqarnas IX: An Annual on Islamic Art and Architecture* (1992), edited by Oleg Grabar

—, *Islamic Architecture in Cairo: An Introduction* (Cairo, 1989)

Bloom, Jonathan M., 'The Mosque of al-Hakim in Cairo', in *Muqarnas I: An Annual on Islamic Art and Architecture* (1983), edited by Oleg Grabar

Brett, Michael, *The Rise of the Fatimids: The World of the Mediterranean and the Middle East in the Fourth Century of the Hijra, Tenth Century* CE (Leiden, 2001)

Goitein, S. D., *A Mediterranean Society: The Jewish Communities of the World as Portrayed in the Documents of the Cairo Geniza* (Los Angeles, 2000; reprint of 1967–85 original)

Golia, Maria, *Cairo: City of Sand* (London, 2004)

Halm, Heinz, *Fatimids and Their Traditions of Learning* (London, New York, 2001)

Hanna, Nelly (ed.), *Money, Land and Trade: An Economic History of the Muslim Mediterranean* (London, 2002)

Lane-Poole, Stanley, *The Story of Cairo* (Nendeln, Liechtenstein, 1971; reprint of 1902 original)

Olszowy-Schlanger, Judith, 'Learning to Read and Write in Medieval Egypt: Children's Exercise Books from the Cairo Geniza', *Journal of Semitic Studies*, 48 (1) (Spring 2003)

Phillips, Jonathan, *The Crusades 1095–1204* (London, New York, 2014)

Rabbat, Nasser, *The Citadel of Cairo: A New Interpretation of Royal Mameluk Architecture* (Leiden, 1995)

Raymond, André, *Cairo* (Cambridge, Massachusetts; London, 2000)

Rodenbeck, Max, *Cairo: The City Victorious* (Cairo, 2005; reprint of 1999 original)

Virani, Shafique N., *The Ismailis in the Middle Ages: A History of Survival, a Search for Salvation* (New York, Oxford, 2007)

7. Fez – The Athens of Africa

Abi Zar, Ibn, *Roudh el Kartas: Histoire des Souverains du Maghreb et Annales de la Ville de Fès* (Paris, 1860)

Africanus, Leo, *The History and Description of Africa*, vol. II (London, 1896)

Al Idrisi, *Description de l'Afrique et de l'Espagne par Edrisi* (Leiden, 1866)

Al Jaznai, Abul Hassan, *Kitab Zahrat al As* (Algiers, 1923)

Boum, Aomar, and Park, Thomas K. (eds.), *Historical Dictionary of Morocco* (Lanham, Maryland, 2016)

Bowles, Paul, and Brukoff, Barry, *Morocco* (New York, 1993)

Burckhardt, Titus, *Fez: City of Islam* (Cambridge, 1992)

Ennahid, Said, and Maghraoui, Driss (eds.), *Fez in World History: Selected Essays* (Ifrane, Morocco, 2011)

Ferhat, Halima, 'Marinid Fez: Zenith and Signs of Decline', in Jayyusi, Salma (ed.), *The City in the Islamic World* (Leiden, 2008)

Gaudio, Attilio, *Fès: Joyau de la Civilisation Islamique* (Paris, 1982)

Khaldun, Ibn, *The Muqaddimah: An Introduction to History*, translated by Franz Rosenthal (London, 1958)

—, *Histoire des Berbères*, vol. 4 (Paris, 1925–56)

Landau, Rom, *Morocco* (London, 1967)

Lebbar, Mohammed, 'La Ville de Fès et Sylvestre II' (http://wissensraum-mittelmeer.org/wp-content/uploads/2017/03/Lebbar_-_Sylvestre_II.pdf)

Le Tourneau, Roger, 'Fas', *Encyclopedia Islamica* (Leiden, 2008)

—, *Fez in the Age of the Marinids* (Norman, Oklahoma, 1974; reprint of 1961 original)

—, and Terrasse, H., 'Fez', in Bosworth, C. Edmund (ed.), *Historic Cities of the Islamic World* (2007)

Lopez, Robert S., and Raymond, Irving W. (trs.), *Medieval Trade in the Mediterranean World: Illustrative Documents* (New York, 2001; reprint of 1955 original)

Mackintosh-Smith, Tim (ed.), *The Travels of Ibn Battutah* (London, 2002)

Messier, Ronald A., *The Almoravids and the Meanings of Jihad* (Santa Barbara, California, 2010)

Mezzine, Mohammed (ed.), *Fès Médiévale: Entre légende et histoire, un carrefour de l'Orient à l'apogée d'un rêve* (Paris, 1992)

Miller, Susan Gilson, Petruccioli, Attilio, and Bertagnin, Mauro, 'Inscribing Minority Space in the Islamic City: The Jewish Quarter of Fez (1438–1912)', *Journal of the Society of Architectural Historians*, vol. 60, no. 3 (September 2001)

Najjar, Fauzi M., 'The Karaouine at Fez', *Muslim World*, vol. 48, issue 2 (April 1958)

O'Meara, Simon, *Space and Muslim Urban Life: At the Limits of the Labyrinth of Fez* (London, 2007)

—, 'The foundation legend of Fez and other Islamic cities in light of the Prophet', in Bennison, Amira K., and Gascoigne, Alison L. (eds.), *Cities in the Pre-modern Islamic World*, (London, 2007)

Shatzmiller, Maya, in *Encyclopedia Islamica* (2008)

—'Marinids', *The Berbers and the Islamic State: The Marinid Experience in Pre-Protectorate Morocco* (Princeton, New Jersey, 2000)

Wharton, Edith, *In Morocco* (London, 1920)

Wright, Gwendolyn, *The Politics of Design in French Colonial Urbanism* (Chicago, London, 1991)

8. Samarkand – Garden of the Soul

Adshead, S. A. M., *Central Asia in World History* (London, 1993)

Andrews, Peter, 'The Tents of Timur', in *Arts of the Eurasian Steppelands*, edited by Philip Denwood (London, 1978)

Arabshah, Ahmed Ibn, *Tamerlane or Timur the Great Amir*, translated by J. H. Sanders from *The Arabic Life* by Ahmed ibn Arabshah (London, 1936)

Barthold, V. V., 'The Burial of Timur', in *Iran, Journal of the British Institute of Persian Studies*, XII (London, 1974)

Blunt, Wilfrid, *The Golden Road to Samarkand* (London, 1973)

Boyle, J. A., *The Successors of Genghis Khan*, translated from the Persian of Rashid al-Din (New York, 1971)

Browne, Edward G., *A Literary History of Persia*, 4 vols. (Cambridge, 1928)

The Cambridge History of Central Asia (Cambridge, 1990)

Clavijo, Ruy González de, *Embassy to Tamerlane 1403–1406*, translated from the Spanish by Guy Le Strange (London, 1928)

Flecker, James Elroy, *Hassan: The Story of Hassan of Bagdad and How He Came to Make the Golden Journey to Samarkand* (London, 1922)

Forbes Manz, Beatrice, *The Rise and Rule of Tamerlane* (Cambridge, 1999)

—, 'Temür and the Problem of a Conqueror's Legacy', *Journal of the Royal Asiatic Society*, third series, vol. 8, no. 1 (April 1998)

—, 'Tamerlane and the Symbolism of Sovereignty', *Iranian Studies*, vol. XXI, nos. 1–2 (1988)

Golombek, Lisa, 'From Tamerlane to the Taj Mahal', in Daneshvari, Abbas (ed.), *Essays in Islamic Art and Architecture in Honour of Katharina Otto-Dorn* (Malibu, 1981)

—, and Subtelny, Maria (eds.), *Timurid Art and Culture: Iran and Central Asia in the Fifteenth Century* (Leiden, 1992)

—, and Wilber, Donald, *The Timurid Architecture of Iran and Turan* (Princeton, New Jersey, 1988)

Grabar, Oleg, Review of A. A. Semenov's 'Inscriptions on the tombs of Temur and descendants in the Gur e Amir', *Ars Orientalis*, 2 (1957)

Gronke, Monika, 'The Persian Court Between Palace and Tent: From Timur to Abbas I', in Golombek and Subtelny (eds.)

Hookham, Hilda, *Tamburlaine the Conqueror* (London, 1962)

Howorth, Henry H., *History of the Mongols: From the 9th to the 19th Century*, 4 vols. (London, 1876, 1928)

Jamaluddin, Syed, *The State under Temur: A Study in Empire Building* (New Delhi, 1995)

Juvayni, Ata-Malik, *The History of the World Conqueror (1252–1260)*, translated by John Andrew Boyle, 2 vols. (Manchester, 1958)

Khwandamir, *A Literal Translation of Habeeb-us-Siyar, Life of Tamerlane*, parts V & VI and parts VII & VIII (Bombay, 1900)

Lamb, Harold, *Tamerlane the Earth Shaker* (London, 1929)

Marlowe, Christopher, *Tamburlaine the Great* (London, 2014; reprint of epic 1590 original)

Marozzi, Justin, *Tamerlane: Sword of Islam, Conqueror of the World* (London, 2004)

Morgan, David O., *Medieval Persia: 1040–1797* (London, 1992)

Nicolle, David, *The Age of Tamerlane: Warfare in the Middle East c.1350–1500* (London, 2001)

—, *The Mongol Warlords: Genghis Khan, Kublai Khan, Hülegü, Tamerlane* (Poole, 1990)

Oman, C. W. C., *The Art of War in the Middle Ages* A.D. 378–1515 (Ithaca, New York, 1953; reprint of 1885 original)

Parker, E. H., *A Thousand Years of the Tartars* (London, 2002)

Parker, Geoffrey, *Power in Stone: Cities as Symbols of Empire* (London, 2014)

Polyakova, E. A., 'Timur as Described by the 15th Century Court Historiographers', *Iranian Studies*, vol. XXI, nos. 1–2 (1988)

Saunders, John Joseph, *The History of the Mongol Conquests* (London, 1971)

Shami, Nizam ad-Din, *Histoire des Conquêtes de Tamerlan Intitulée Zafarnama, par Nizam-uddin Sami*, ed. F. Tauer, vols. I and II (Prague, 1937, 1956)

Wellard, James, *Samarkand and Beyond: A History of Desert Caravans* (London, 1977)

Woods, John E., 'Timur's Genealogy', in *Intellectual Studies on Islam* (Salt Lake City, Utah, 1990)

Yazdi, Sharaf al Din Ali, *The History of Timur-Bec, Known by the Name of Tamerlain the Great, Emperor of the Moguls and Tartars: Being an Historical Journal of his Conquests in Asia and Europe*, 2 vols. (London, 1723)

9. Constantinople – City of the World's Desire

Angold, Michael, *The Fall of Constantinople to the Ottomans: Context and Consequences* (New York, 2014; reprint of 2012 original)

Babinger, Franz, *Mehmed the Conqueror and His Time* (Princeton, New Jersey, 1978)

Çelebi, Evliya, *Narrative of Travels in Europe, Asia, and Africa, in the Seventeenth Century*, translated by Joseph Freiherr von Hammer-Purgstall (London, 1834, 1850)

Çinar, Alev, 'National History as a Contested Site: The Conquest of Istanbul and Islamist Negotiations of the Nation', *Comparative Studies in Society and History*, vol. 43, no. 2 (April 2001)

Crowley, Roger, *1453: The Holy War for Constantinople and the Clash of Islam and the West* (London, 2006)

—, *Constantinople: The Last Great Siege, 1453* (London, 2005)

De Brocquière, Bertrandon, *The Travels of Bertrandon de Brocquière* (Hafod Press, 1807)

Finkel, Caroline, *Osman's Dream: The Story of the Ottoman Empire 1300–1923* (London, 2005)

Gibbon, Edward, *The Decline and Fall of the Roman Empire*, vol. III (1185–1453) (various editions)

Given-Wilson, C. (tr. and ed.), *The Chronicle of Adam of Usk 1377–1421* (Oxford, 1997)

Hilsdale, Cecily J., *Byzantine Art and Diplomacy in an Age of Decline* (New York, 2014)

Hughes, Bettany, *Istanbul: A Tale of Three Cities* (London, 2017)

İnalcik, Halil, *The Ottoman Empire: 1300–1600* (London, 2000; reprint of 1973 original)

—, 'Istanbul: An Islamic City', *Journal of Islamic Studies*, 1 (1990)

—, 'Tursun Beg, Historian of Mehmed the Conqueror's Time', *Wiener Zeitschrift für die Kunde des Morgenlandes*, vol. 69 (1977)

Kaçar, Hilmi, *An Islamic City: Konstantiniyye/Istanbul: Constructing an Empire on a City* (Ghent, 2013) (http://www.academia.edu/2197840/An_Islamic_City_Kostantiniyye_Istanbul_constructing_an_empire_on_a_city)

Kafescioğlu, Çiğdem, *Constantinopolis/Istanbul: Cultural Encounter, Imperial Vision and the Construction of the Ottoman Capital* (University Park, Pennsylvania, 2009)

—, 'Heavenly and Unblessed, Splendid and Artless: Mehmed II's Mosque Complex in the Eyes of its Contemporaries', in Çiğden Kafescioğlu and Lucienne Thys-Şenocak (eds.), *Aptullah Kuran için Yazılar/Essays in Honour of Aptullah Kuran* (Istanbul, 1999)

Kermeli, Eugenia, 'Osman I', in Agoston, Gabor, and Masters, Bruce (eds.), *Encyclopedia of the Ottoman Empire* (New York, 2009)

Kritovoulos, *History of Mehmed the Conqueror* (Westport, Connecticut, 1970)

Kuban, Doğan, *Istanbul: An Urban History: Byzantion, Constantinopolis, Istanbul* (Istanbul, 1996)

Mango, Cyril (ed.), *The Oxford History of Byzantium* (Oxford, New York, 2002)

Mansel, Philip, *Pillars of Monarchy* (London, 1984)

Morris, Jan, *Among the Cities* (London, 1985)

Muslu, Cihan Yüksel, *The Ottomans and the Mamluks: Imperial Diplomacy and Warfare in the Islamic World* (London, 2014)

Necipoğlu, Gülru, *Architecture, Ceremonial and Power: The Topkapi Palace in the Fifteenth and Sixteenth Centuries* (Cambridge, Massachusetts; London, 1991)

Nestor-Iskander, *The Tale of Constantinople: Of its Origin and Capture by the Turks in the Year 1453* (New Rochelle, New York, 1998)

Nicol, Donald, *The Immortal Emperor: The Life and Legend of Constantine Palaiologos, Last Emperor of the Romans* (Cambridge, 1992)

—, *Byzantium and Venice: A Study in Diplomatic and Cultural Relations* (Cambridge, 1988)

—, *The Last Centuries of Byzantium, 1261–1453* (Cambridge, 1993; reprint of 1972 original)

—, *A Byzantine Emperor in England: Manuel II's Visit to London in 1400–01* (Birmingham, 1971)

Pamuk, Orhan, *Istanbul: Memories and the City* (London, 2006; reprint of 2005 original)

Philippides, Marios, and Hanak, Walter K., *The Siege and the Fall of Constantinople in 1453: Historiography, Topography and Military Studies* (London, 2017)

Reinert, Stephen, 'Fragmentation (1204–1453)', in Mango, Cyril (ed.), *The Oxford History of Byzantium* (Oxford, New York, 2002)

Rogerson, Barnaby, *The Last Crusaders: The Hundred-Year Battle for the Centre of the World* (London, 2009)

Runciman, Steven, *The Fall of Constantinople 1453* (Cambridge, 1965)

Saoud, Rabah, 'Muslim Architecture under Ottoman Patronage 1326–1924', *Foundation for Science, Technology and Civilisation* (July 2004)

Tafur, Pero, *Travels and Adventures 1435–1439* (London, 1926)

Tsilenis, Savvas, 'The minority of Orthodox Christians in the official statistics of modern Turkey and the urban space' (http://www.demography-lab.prd.uth.gr/DDAoG/article/cont/ergasies/tsilenis.htm)

Turnbull, Stephen, *The Walls of Constantinople AD 324–1453* (London, 2014)

Zweig, Stefan, *Shooting Stars: Ten Historical Miniatures* (London, 2013)

10. Kabul – A Garden in the Mountains

Alam, Muzaffar, and Subrahmanyam, Sanjay (eds.), *The Mughal State 1526–1750* (Delhi, 1998)

Babur, *The Baburnama (Memoirs of Babur)*, translated by Annette Susannah Beveridge (London, 1922)

Bayat, Bayazid, *Tadkhira Humayun wa Akbar*, translated by Bruce Wannell for the Aga Khan Trust for Culture (Kabul, 2008)

Dale, Stephen Frederic, *The Gardens of Eight Paradises: Babur and the Culture of Empire in Central Asia, Afghanistan and India (1483–1530)* (Leiden, 2004)

—, 'Steppe Humanism: The Autobiographical Writings of Zahir Al-Din Muhammad Babur, 1483–1530', *International Journal of Middle East Studies*, vol. 22, no. 1 (1990)

Denison Ross, E., 'Babur', in *Cambridge History of India*, vol. 4: *The Mughul Period* (Cambridge, 1937)

Du Jarric, Pierre, *Akbar and the Jesuits: An Account of the Jesuit Missions to the Court of Akbar* (London, 2004)

Dupree, Nancy Hatch, *An Historical Guide to Afghanistan* (Kabul, 1971)

Eraly, Abraham, *Emperors of the Peacock Throne: The Saga of the Great Mughals* (London, 2000)

Faruqui, Munis D., *Princes of the Mughal Empire, 1504–1719* (Cambridge, 2012)

Fazl, Abul, *The Akbarnama of Abul Fazl*, translated by H. Beveridge, 3 vols. (Calcutta, 1897–1921).

Forster, E. M., 'The Emperor Babur', in *Abinger Harvest* (London, 1953)

Gammell, C. P. W., *The Pearl of Khorasan: A History of Herat* (London, 2016)

Lal, Ruby, *Domesticity and Power in the Early Mughal World* (Cambridge, 2005)

Lamb, Harold, *Babur the Tiger: First of the Great Moguls* (London, 1962)

Lane Fox, Robin, 'The Garden King of Kabul: Babur's legacy lives on in Afghanistan', *Financial Times*, 5 February 2016 (https://www.ft.com/content/5631b7ae-c4ed-11e5-808f-8231cd71622e)

Lehman, F., 'Akbar I', *Encyclopaedia Iranica* (http://www.iranicaonline.org/articles/akbar-i-mughal-india)

Leyden, John, and Erskine, William, *Memoirs of Zehir-Ed-Din Muhammad Babur, Emperor of Hindustan* (London, 1921)

Nicoll, Fergus, *Shah Jahan* (London, 2009)

Richards, John, *The Mughal Empire* (Cambridge, New York, 1993)

Rushbrook Williams, L. F., *An Empire Builder of the Sixteenth Century: A Summary Account of the Political Career of Zahir-ud-din Muhammad, surnamed Babur* (London, 1918)

Schinasi, May, *Kabul: A History 1773–1948* (Leiden, 2016)

Thackston, W. M., 'Babur Mirza, *Baburnama*', in *A Century of Princes: Sources on Timurid History and Art* (Cambridge, Massachusetts, 1989)

Woodburn, C. W., *The Bala Hissar of Kabul: Revealing a Fortress-Palace in Afghanistan* (Chatham, 2009)

11. Isfahan – Half the World

Arabshah, Ahmed Ibn, *Tamerlane or Timur the Great Amir*, translated by J. H. Sanders from *The Arabic Life* by Ahmed ibn Arabshah (London, 1936)

Aslanian, Sebouh, *From the Indian Ocean to the Mediterranean: The Global Trade Networks of Armenian Merchants from New Julfa* (Berkeley, California; London, 2011)

Axworthy, Michael, *The Sword of Persia: Nader Shah, from Tribal Warrior to Conquering Tyrant* (London, 2009)

—, *Iran: Empire of the Mind: A History from Zoroaster to the Present Day* (London, 2008)

Babaie, Sussan, *Isfahan and its Palaces: Statecraft, Shiism and the Architecture of Conviviality in Early Modern Iran* (Edinburgh, 2008)

—, with Babayan, Kathryn, Baghdiantz-McCabe, Ina, and Farhad, Massumeh, *Slaves of the Shah: New Elites of Safavid Iran* (London, 2004)

—, with Haug, Robert, 'Isfahan X: Monuments (1): A Historical Survey', *Encyclopaedia Iranica* and following essays (http://www.iranicaonline.org/articles/isfahan-xi-a-historical-survey)

—, 'Shah Abbas II, the Conquest of Qandahar, the Chihil Sutun, and its Wall Paintings', *Muqarnas*, 11 (1994)

Blow, David, *Shah Abbas: The Ruthless King Who Became an Iranian Legend* (London, 2014)

Blunt, Wilfrid, *Isfahan: Pearl of Persia* (London, Toronto, 1966)

Byron, Robert, *The Road to Oxiana* (London, 2000; reprint of 1937 original)

Chardin, Sir John, *Travels in Persia 1673–1677* (New York, London, 1988)

Chick, H. (ed.), *A Chronicle of the Carmelites in Persia: The Safavids and the Papal Mission of the 17th and 18th Centuries* (London, 2012)

De Thévenot, Jean, *The Travels of Monsieur de Thévenot into the Levant*, vol. 2 (London, 1687; reprint of 1674 original)

Fryer, John, *A New Account of East India and Persia Being Nine Years' Travels 1672–1681* (London, 1698)

Kleiss, Wolfram, 'Safavid Palaces', *Ars Orientalis*, vol. 23 (1993)

Matthee, Rudi, 'Safavid Iran through the Eyes of European Travellers', *Harvard Library Bulletin*, vol. 23, nos. 1–2 (Spring–Summer 2012)

—, 'Was Safavid Iran an Empire?', *Journal of the Economic and Social History of the Orient*, vol. 53, nos. 1/2 (2010)

—, *The Pursuit of Pleasure: Drugs and Stimulants in Iranian History, 1500–1900* (Princeton, 2005)

—, 'Between Aloofness and Fascination: Safavid Views of the West', *Iranian Studies*, vol. 31, no. 2, *Historiography and Representation in Safavid and Afsharid Iran* (Spring 1998)

—, 'Soltan Hosayn', *Encyclopaedia Iranica* (http://www.iranicaonline.org/articles/soltan-hosayn)

Monshi, Eskandar Beg, *History of Shah Abbas the Great*, translated by Roger Savory, vol. 2 (Boulder, Colorado, 1978)

Mottahedeh, Roy, *The Mantle of the Prophet: Religion and Politics in Iran* (Oxford, 2000; reprint of 1988 original)

Necipoğlu, Gülru, 'Framing the Gaze in Ottoman, Safavid, and Mughal Palaces', *Ars Orientalis*, vol. 23 (1993)

Roemer, H. R., 'The Safavid Period', in Jackson, Peter, and Lockhart, Laurence, (eds.), *The Cambridge History of Iran*, vol. 6 (Cambridge, 1997; reprint of 1986 original)

Savory, Roger, 'Abbas I', *Encyclopaedia Iranica* (http://www.iranicaonline.org/articles/abbas-i)

—, and Karamustafa, Ahmet, 'Esmail I Safawi', *Encyclopaedia Iranica* (http://www.iranicaonline.org/articles/esmail-i-safawi)

Sherley, Sir Anthony, *The Three Brothers, or The Travels and Adventures of Sir Anthony, Sir Robert and Sir Thomas Sherley in Persia, Russia, Turkey, Spain etc.* (London, 1825)

Tavernier, Jean-Baptiste, *The Six Voyages of John Baptista Tavernier* (London, 1678)

Williamson, Clare, 'Safavid Persia Through the Eyes of French Travellers', *La Trobe Journal*, no. 91 (June 2013)

12. Tripoli – Pirates' Lair

Austen, Ralph A., 'The Trans-Saharan Slave Trade: A Tentative Census', in Gemery, Henry A, and Hogendorn, Jan S. (eds.), *The Uncommon Market: Essays in the Economic History of the Atlantic Slave Trade* (New York, London, 1979)

Badoglio, Pietro, *Italy in the Second World War*, translated by Muriel Currey (Oxford, 1948)

Basset, René, 'Karamanli', in *Encyclopedia of Islam* (Leiden, 1913–36)

Berenson, Mary, *A Vicarious Trip to the Barbary Coast* (London, 1938)

Bey, Ali, *Travels of Ali Bey in Morocco, Tripoli, Cyprus, Egypt, Arabia, Syria and Turkey between the Years 1803 and 1807* (London, 1816)

Bicheno, Hugh, *Crescent and Cross: The Battle of Lepanto 1571* (London, 2003)

Bovill, E. W., *Caravans of the Old Sahara* (Oxford, 1933)

Braudel, Fernand, *The Mediterranean and the Mediterranean World in the Age of Philip II*, vol. 2 (Berkeley, California, 1995)

Cherif, M. H., 'Algeria, Tunisia and Libya: The Ottomans and their Heirs', in Ogot, B. A. (ed.), *General History of Africa*, vol. 5: *Africa from the Sixteenth to the Eighteenth Century* (Paris, London, 1978–93)

Ciranna, Simonetta, 'Roman Persistence and Re-use of Ancient Remains', in *The Mediterranean Medina: International Seminar*, pp. 297–300 (Rome, 2011)

Cooley, John K., *Libyan Sandstorm* (London, 1983)

Davis, Robert C., *Christian Slaves, Muslim Masters: White Slavery in the Mediterranean, the Barbary Coast, and Italy, 1500–1800* (Basingstoke, 2003)

Dearden, Seton, *A Nest of Corsairs: The Fighting Karamanlis of the Barbary Coast* (London, 1976)

De Grummond, Nancy Thomson (ed.), *Encyclopedia of the History of Classical Archaeology* (London, 2015)

Diem, Werner, and Schöller, Marco, *The Living and the Dead in Islam: Studies in Arabic Epitaphs* (Wiesbaden, 2004)

Fisher, Sir Godfrey, *Barbary Legend: War, Trade and Piracy in North Africa 1415–1830* (Oxford, 1957)

Folayan, Kola, *Tripoli during the Reign of Yusuf Pasha Qaramanli* (Ife, Nigeria, 1979)

London, Joshua, *Victory in Tripoli: How America's War with the Barbary Pirates Established the U.S. Navy and Shaped a Nation* (Hoboken, New Jersey, 2005)

Lyon, George Francis, *A Narrative of Travels in Northern Africa in the Years 1818–20* (London, 1985; reprint of 1821 original)

Mackenzie, Alexander Slidell, *Life of Stephen Decatur, a Commodore in the Navy of the United States* (Boston, 1848)

Mantran, R., 'Karamanli', in *Encyclopedia of Islam*, vol. 5 (Leiden, 1975)

Marozzi, Justin, *South from Barbary: Along the Slave Routes of the Libyan Sahara* (London, 2001)

Matar, Hisham, *The Return: Fathers, Sons and the Land in Between* (London, 2016)

McLachlan, K. S., 'Tripoli and Tripolitania: Conflict and Cohesion during the Period of the Barbary Corsairs (1551–1850)', *Transactions of the Institute of British Geographers*, vol. 3, no. 3, *Settlement and Conflict in the Mediterranean World* (1978)

Micara, Ludovico, 'Ottoman Tripoli: A Mediterranean Medina', in Jayyusi, Salma, Holod, Renata, Petruccioli, Attilio and Raymond, André (eds.), *The City in the Islamic World*, vol. 2 (Leiden, 2008)

Munzi, Massimiliano, 'Italian Archaeology in Libya: From Colonial Romanità to Decolonization of the Past', in Galaty, Michael L., and Watkinson, Charles (eds.), *Archaeology Under Dictatorship* (New York, London, 2004)

O'Hara, Glen, *Britain and the Sea Since 1600* (New York, Basingstoke, 2010)

Parton, James, *Life of Thomas Jefferson: Third President of the United States* (Boston, 1874)

Pennell, C. R., *Piracy and Diplomacy in Seventeenth-Century North Africa: The Journal of Thomas Baker, English Consul in Tripoli, 1677–1685* (London, 1989)

Richardson, James, *Travels in the Great Desert of Sahara in the Years of 1845 and 1846* (London, 1970; reprint of 1848 original)

Rogerson, Barnaby, *A Traveller's History of North Africa* (London, 2008; reprint of 1998 original)

Rossi, Ettore, 'Tripoli', in *Encyclopedia of Islam* (Leiden, 1913–36)

St John, Ronald Bruce, *Libya: From Colony to Independence* (Oxford, 2008)

Teonge, Henry, *The Diary of Henry Teonge: Chaplain on H.M.'s Ships Assistance, Bristol and Royal Oak 1675–1679* (London, 2014)

Tucker, Spencer C. (ed.), *The Encyclopedia of the Wars of the Early American Republic, 1783–1812: A Political, Social and Military History* (Santa Barbara, California, 2014)

Tully, Miss, *Narrative of a Ten Years' Residence at Tripoli in Africa* (London, 1983; reprint of 1817 original)

Vandewalle, Dirk, *Libya Since Independence: Oil and State-Building* (London, 1998)

Wheelan, Joseph, *Jefferson's War: America's First War on Terror 1801–1805* (New York, 2004)

Wright, John, *Tripoli: A History* (Oxford, 2015)

—, *A History of Libya* (London, 2012)

—, *Travellers in Turkish Libya 1551–1911* (London, 2011; reprint of 2005 original)

—, *Libya, Chad and the Central Sahara* (London, 1989)

13. Beirut – Playground of the Levant

Antonius, George, *The Arab Awakening: The Story of the Arab National Movement* (London, 1938)

Atiyah, Edward, *An Arab Tells His Story: A Study in Loyalties* (London, 1946)

Fawaz, Leila Tarazi, *An Occasion for War: Civil Conflict in Lebanon and Damascus in 1860* (London, 1994)

— (ed.), *State and Society in Lebanon* (Oxford, 1991)

—, *Merchants and Migrants in Nineteenth-Century Beirut* (Cambridge, Massachusetts, 1983)

Gorton, T. J. (ed.), *A Beirut Anthology: Travel Writing through the Centuries* (Cairo, 2015)

Hanssen, Jens, *Fin de Siècle Beirut: The Making of an Ottoman Provincial Capital* (Oxford, 2005)

Hayek, Ghenwa, *Beirut, Imagining the City: Space and Place in Lebanese Literature* (London, New York, 2015)

Herodotus, *The Histories* (London, 2003)

Hudson, Leila, *Transforming Damascus: Space and Modernity in an Islamic City* (London, 2008)

Hussain, Ishtiaq, *The Tanzimat: Secular Reforms in the Ottoman Empire* (http://faith-matters.org/images/stories/fm-publications/the-tanzimat-final-web.pdf)

Jidejian, Nina, *Beirut through the Ages* (Beirut, 1973)

Kassab, Sawsan Agha, and Tadmori, Khaled Omar, *Beyrouth et le Sultan: 200 photographies des albums de Abdul Hamid II (1876–1909)* (Beirut, 2002)

Kassir, Samir, *Beirut* (Berkeley, California; London, 2010)

Khalaf, Samir, *Heart of Beirut: Reclaiming the Bourj* (London, 2006)

Larkin, Craig, 'Remaking Beirut: Contesting Memory, Space, and the Urban Imaginary of Lebanese Youth', *City & Community*, vol. 9, issue 4 (December 2010)

Makarem, Hadi, 'Downtown Beirut: Between Amnesia and Nostalgia', 17 October 2012 (http://blogs.lse.ac.uk/mec/2012/10/17/downtown-beirut-between-amnesia-and-nostalgia/)

Makdisi, Saree, 'Beirut, a City without History?', in Makdisi, Ussama, and Silverstein, Paul (eds.), *Memory and Violence in the Middle East and North Africa* (Bloomington, Indiana, 2006)

—, 'Laying Claim to Beirut: Urban Narrative and Spatial Identity in the Age of Solidere', *Critical Inquiry*, vol. 23, no. 3, *Front Lines/Border Posts* (Spring 1997)

Mansel, Philip, *Levant: Splendour and Catastrophe on the Mediterranean* (London, 2010)

Neale, Frederick Arthur, *Eight Years in Syria, Palestine and Asia Minor: From 1842 to 1850* (London, 1851)

Olin, Stephen, *Travels in Egypt, Arabia Petræa, and the Holy Land*, vol. 2 (New York, 1843)

Osman, Tarek, *Islamism: What it Means for the Middle East and the World* (New Haven, Connecticut, 2016)

Persen, William, 'The Russian Occupations of Beirut, 1772–4', *Journal of The Royal Central Asian Society*, vol. 42, issue 3–4 (1955)

Ragab, Tarek Saad, 'Who Won the Battle of Beirut Downtown? Revisiting the Crisis of Cultural Identity in Rehabilitating Post-War Beirut', in Lawrence, Roderick, Turgut, Hulya, and Kellett, Peter (eds.), *Requalifying the Built Environment: Challenges and Responses* (Oxford, 2012)

Salam, Assem, 'The Role of Government in Shaping the Built Environment', in Rowe, Peter G., and Sarkis, Hashim (eds.), *Projecting Beirut: Episodes in the Construction and Reconstruction of a Modern City* (Munich, London, 1998)

Salibi, Kamal, *A House of Many Mansions: The History of Lebanon Reconsidered* (London, 1998)

Traboulsi, Fawwaz, *A History of Modern Lebanon* (London, 2012; reprint of 2007 original)

Trombetta, Lorenzo, 'The Private Archives of the Sursuqs, a Beirut Family of Christian Notables: An Early Investigation', *Rivista degli Studi Orientali*, Nuova Serie, vol. 82, fasc. 1/4 (2009)

Tuéni, Nadia, *Lebanon: Poems of Love and War* (Beirut, 2006)

14. Dubai – Build It and They Will Come

Ali, Syed, *Dubai: Gilded Cage* (New Haven, Connecticut; London, 2010)

Al Maktoum, Sheikh Mohammed bin Rashid, *My Vision: Challenges in the Race for Excellence* (Dubai, 2006)

Balbi, Gasparo, *Viaggio dell'Indie Orientali* (Venice, 1590)

Barr, James, *Lords of the Desert: Britain's Struggle with America to Dominate the Middle East* (London, 2018)

Benoist-Mechin, Jacques, *Turkey 1908–1938: The End of the Ottoman Empire* (Zug, Switzerland, 1989; reprint of 1980 original)

Carter, Robert A., *Sea of Pearls: Seven Thousand Years of the Industry that Shaped the Gulf* (London, 2012)

Cogan, Lieut R., 'Trigonometrical Plan of the Back-water of Debai by Lieut. R. Cogan under the direction of Lt. J. M. Guy, H. C. Marine. 1822. Drawn by M. Houghton' (1/2), British Library Map Collections, IOR/X/3690 (https://www.qdl.qa/en/archive/81055/vdc_100024141117.0x000002)

Davidson, Christopher, *Dubai: The Vulnerability of Success* (Oxford, 2008)

George, Andrew (tr.), *The Epic of Gilgamesh* (London, 2000; reprint of 1999 original)

Gupte, Pranay, *Dubai: The Making of a Megapolis* (New Delhi, 2011)

Hawley, Donald, *The Trucial States* (London, 1970)

Heard-Bey, Frauke, *From Trucial States to United Arab Emirates: A Society in Transition* (London, 1996; reprint of 1982 original)

Khoury, Eileen, 'Servants of the Pearl', *Aramco World*, vol. 41, no. 5 (September/October 1990) (http://archive.aramcoworld.com/issue/199005/servants.of.the.pearl.htm)

Krane, Jim, *Dubai: The Story of the World's Fastest City* (London, 2013; reprint of 2009 original)

Lorimer, John Gordon, *Gazetteer of the Persian Gulf, Oman and Central Arabia*, vol. 2: *Geographical and Statistical* (Calcutta, 1908)

Mayo, Anthony, Nitin, Nohria, Umaimah, Mendhro, and Cromwell, Johnathan, 'Sheikh Mohammed and the Making of "Dubai Inc."', Harvard Business School Case 410-063 (February 2010, revised August 2010)

Morton, Michael Quentin, *Keepers of the Golden Shore: A History of the United Arab Emirates* (London, 2016)

Onley, James, 'Britain and the Gulf Shaikhdoms, 1820–1971: The Politics of Protection', Occasional Paper No. 4, Center for International and Regional Studies, Georgetown University of Foreign Service in Qatar (2009) (https://repository.library.georgetown.edu/bitstream/handle/10822/558294/CIRSOccasionalPaper4JamesOnley2009.pdf)

Thesiger, Wilfred, *Arabian Sands* (London, 1960)

Thomas, Justin, *Psychological Wellbeing in the Gulf States: The New Arabia Felix* (Basingstoke, 2013)

Wheeler, Julia, and Thuybaert, Paul, *Telling Tales: An Oral History of Dubai* (Dubai, 2006)

Wilson, Graeme, *Rashid's Legacy: The Genesis of the Maktoum Family and the History of Dubai* (London, 2006)

—, *Rashid: Father of Dubai* (Kuala Lumpur, Malaysia, 1999)

Zahlan, Rosemarie Said, *The Origins of the United Arab Emirates: A Political and Social History of the Trucial States* (London, 2016; reprint of 1978 original)

15. Doha – City of Pearls

Adam, Khaled, 'Rediscovering the Island: Doha's Urbanity from Pearls to Spectacle', in Elsheshtawy, Yasser (ed.), *The Evolving Arab City: Tradition, Modernity and Urban Development* (London, 2008)

Al Qasimi, Sultan Mohammed (ed.), *The Journals of David Seton in the Gulf 1800–1809* (Exeter, 1995)

Alraouf, Ali A., ' "Dohaization": An Emerging Interface between Knowledge, Creativity, and Gulf Urbanity', in Katodrytis, George, and Syed, Sharmeen, *Gulf Cities as Interfaces* (Cambridge, 2012)

—, 'A Tale of Two Souqs: The Paradox of Gulf Urban Diversity', *Open House International*, vol. 37, no. 2 (June 2012)

Al Thani, Mohammed, *Jassim the Leader* (London, 2012)

Boussaa, Djamel, 'Rehabilitation as a Catalyst of Sustaining a Living Heritage: The Case of Souk Waqif in Doha, Qatar', *Art and Design Review*, vol. 2, no. 3 (2014) (http://file.scirp.org/Html/4-1250021_49452.htm)

Calvino, Italo, *Invisible Cities* (London, 1997)

Carter, Robert, 'A History of Doha and Bidda: Historical References to Doha and Bidda before 1850', Origins of Doha and Qatar Project, led by Dr Robert Carter of UCL Qatar (https://originsofdoha.files.wordpress.com/2015/03/a-history-of-doha-and-bidda1.pdf)

—, 'Bringing Doha's Past to Life: Discoveries from the UCL Qatar project that is shedding new light on the history of Doha', *The Foundation*, monthly magazine of Qatar Foundation, issue 68 (August 2014)

—, with contributions by Sakal, Ferhan, Eddisford, Daniel, and Roberts, Kirk, 'Highlights of the Latest Archaeological Discoveries in Doha', Qatar Museums Workshop, 21 October 2014

Gardner, Andrew M., 'How the City Grows: Urban Growth and Challenges to Sustainable Development in Doha, Qatar', in Sillitoe, Paul (ed.), *Sustainable Development: An Appraisal from the Gulf Region* (New York, 2014)

—, 'The Transforming Landscape of Doha: An Essay on Urbanism and Urbanization in Qatar', *Jadaliyya*, 9 November 2013 (http://www.jadaliyya.com/Details/29778)

—, 'Gulf Migration and the Family', *Journal of Arabian Studies*, 1.1 (June 2011)

Hobbs, Mark, 'Qatari History: Pivotal Moments Revealed in India Office Records', Qatar Digital Library (https://www.qdl.qa/en/qatari-history-pivotal-moments-revealed-india-office-records)

Kamrava, Mehran, *Qatar: Small State, Big Politics* (Ithaca, New York, 2013)

Keatinge, Tom, 'Why Qatar is the focus of terrorism claims', Centre for Financial Crime and Security Studies, BBC, 13 June 2017 (http://www.bbc.co.uk./news/world-middle-east-40246734)

Moe, Tammi, Al Obaidly, Fahad Ahmed, and Forehand, Leslie, 'The Transitional Generations of Doha: A Case Study of Culture and the Built Environment', Virginia Commonwealth University Qatar (undated) (www.academia.edu/11413106/The_transitional_generations_of_Doha_A_case_study_of_culture_and_the_built_environment)

Nagy, Sharon, 'Making Room for Migrants, Making Sense of Difference: Spatial and Ideological Expressions of Social Diversity in Urban Qatar', *Urban Studies*, vol. 43, no. 1 (January 2006)

—, 'Dressing up Downtown: Urban development and government public image in Qatar', *City & Society*, vol. 12, issue 1 (June 2000)

—, 'Social diversity and changes in the form and appearance of the Qatari house', *Visual Anthropology*; published in cooperation with the Commission on Visual Anthropology, 10:2–4 (1998)

Palgrave, William Gifford, *Narrative of a Year's Journey Through Central and Eastern Arabia 1862–63*, vol. 2 (London, 1868)

Pierini, Marc, 'Qatar's Foreign Policy Under the New Emir', Carnegie Europe, 28 June 2013 (https://carnegieeurope.eu/strategiceurope/52236)

Radoine, Hassan, *Souk Wakif On-site Review Report*, edited by Aga Khan Award for Architecture (2010) (https://archnet.org/system/publications/contents/8722/original/DTP101221.pdf?1396271815)

Rahman, Habibur, *The Emergence of Qatar: The Turbulent Years 1627–1916* (London, 2005)

Salama, Ashraf M., Azzali, Simona, and Wiedmann, Florian, 'The everyday urban environment of migrant labourers in Gulf Cities: The case of the old centre of Doha, Qatar', in *City, Territory and Architecture*, vol. 4, 5 (February 2017)

Sulaib, Faisal Mukhyat Abu, 'Understanding Qatar's Foreign Policy, 1995–2017', *Middle East Policy*, vol. XXIV, no. 4 (Winter 2017)

Ulrichsen, Kristian Coates, *Qatar and the Arab Spring* (London, 2014)

—, 'Qatar and the Arab Spring: Policy Drivers and Regional Implications', Carnegie Endowment for International Peace, 24 September 2014 (http://carnegieendowment.org/2014/09/24/qatar-and-arab-spring-policy-drivers-and-regional-implications-pub-56723)

Wiedmann, Florian, Salama, Ashraf M., and Thierstein, Alain, 'Urban evolution of the city of Doha: An investigation into the impact of economic transformations on urban structures', *METU Journal of the Faculty of Architecture*, vol. 29, no. 2 (December 2012)

Zahlan, Rosemarie Said, *The Creation of Qatar* (London, 2016)

Acknowledgements

I first started travelling to the Middle East and North Africa as a teenager and over the following thirty years have never stopped. In the course of my travels I have incurred numerous debts – and enjoyed the humbling hospitality of hosts from one end of the region to the other.

To acknowledge these in the order in which they appear in the book, in **Damascus** I am grateful to Hussein Hinnawi, a font of knowledge about the city he has seen destroyed by the civil war, eight years old and counting as I write, and to Professor Stephen Humphreys of the University of California, Santa Barbara.

I gave thanks to the many people who helped me in **Baghdad** in my last book, *Baghdad: City of Peace, City of Blood*. I thank them all here again, with special mention to Lieutenant Colonel Tim Spicer OBE, Brigadier James Ellery CBE, Dr Thair Ali and Manaf al Damluji.

I am immensely grateful to Monica Vinader and Nick Zoll for putting together a research- and Rioja-filled itinerary in **Cordoba**, brilliantly curated by Pablo Mansilla and Santiago Muñoz-Machado. It is not every day you get a famous bullfighter (José Luis Moreno Ruiz) and musician (Manuel Ruiz 'Queco') to take you around the city they know and love so well. Thank you to Sebastián de la Obra of Casa de Sefarad, a historical treasure trove of Andalusian Jewry; María Jesus Viguera Molins and María Sierra Yébenes Roldán of the Biblioteca Viva de Andalus; David Luque Peso, deputy mayor of Cordoba; Kamal Mekhelf, president of the Muslim Association of Cordoba; Manuel Gonzalez Muñana, canon of Cordoba Cathedral; and my old tutor Professor David Abulafia, Professor of Mediterranean History at Cambridge University.

Thank you to Professor Bashar Nuseibeh, Dr Hazem Nuseibeh and Professor Sari Nuseibeh for sharing their bittersweet memories of **Jerusalem**.

I first visited **Cairo** to learn Arabic aged eighteen and have been returning ever since. There are too many people to thank here, but I am particularly grateful to Mandi Mourad, who always helped find all the right people: from experts in interfaith relations, such as Ali Gomaa, the

Grand Mufti of Egypt; Mouneer Anis, the Anglican Bishop of Egypt; and Dr Ali al Semman of the Supreme Council for Islamic Affairs, to trailblazing feminists like film director Inas al Deghedy and Hind al Hinnawy, the country's most famous and infamous single mother, who both glory in breaking taboos. Thanks also to Gamila Ismail, Amir Salem, Laila Soueif, Hani Shukrallah, Professor Assem Deif, Heba Saleh, Alaa Al Aswany, Bahaa Taher, Max Rodenbeck, Galal Moawad, Issandr al Amrani, Bothaina Kamel, Khaled Abul Naga, Professor Salima Ikram, Ehab Gaddis, Dr Nasry Iskander, Director General of Conservation and Preservation in the Egyptian Antiquities Organization, widely considered the Daddy of Mummies at the Egyptian Museum, Abd al Monem Abu al Futuh of the Muslim Brotherhood, Saad Eddin Ibrahim, chairman of the Ibn Khaldun Centre for Democracy Studies and Rabab Abdelaziz Othman, who is (as far as I know) the only one of my interlocutors who can dance with a blazing candelabrum on her head.

Fez is another city I first experienced as a teenager. I travelled here twice with my old friend Anthony Pask, first in the late 1980s, then twenty-five years later to sell a crumbling *riad* townhouse we owned in the Rif Mountains. As to my most recent visit to study the city's Marinid heyday in the thirteenth century, my thanks to Ahmed Sentissi and Hassan Janah of the Conseil Régional du Tourisme de Fès-Boulemane, the architect Aziza Chaouni, the historian Said Ennahid, the perfumer Rachid Ouedrhiri and my wife Julia, who visited for the first time in 2017.

In Samarkand my thanks to Alisher Faizullaev, Uzbek Ambassador to the Court of St James's, and his colleague Mardon Yakubov, the journalist Eric Walberg and my translator Farkhad, a patient guide as we pursued Timur, or Tamerlane, across desert, steppe and mountain. I am grateful to the Timurid historians Professor Omonullo Boriyev and Turgun Faiziev at the Institute of Oriental Studies; Dr Anvar Shakirov at Samarkand State University; Dr Asom Urinboyev; Nozim Khabibullaev, Director of the Amir Timur Museum; Murad Gulamov, the Librarian at the Tellya Sheikh Mosque; the archivist Gulsara Ostonova; Misrob Turdiev, Dean of International Relations and Diplomacy at Tashkent State University; the poet and historian Akbar Piruzi; the historian Fazlidin Fakhridinov; and Ahmed Rustamov, the imam of the Khoja Abdi Darun Mosque.

While focusing on Sultan Mehmed II and his world-changing conquest of Constantinople in 1453, I was fortunate to speak to many distinguished experts. They include the Boğaziçi University professors of history Çiğdem Kafescioğlu and Edhem Eldem, recently elected International Chair of Turkish and Ottoman History at the Collège de France, and the Anglophile sociologist and historian Professor Faruk Birtek, who generously reviewed Chapter 9. Thank you to the historians Professor Norman Stone, Philip Mansel, Caroline Finkel, Nilay Özlü, Roger Crowley, Hilmi Kaçar, John Scott, Özalp Birol, head of the Suna and İnan Kiraç Foundation's Pera Museum and the Istanbul Research Institute, Yasmine Seale, Alev Scott, Ismini Palla and Agah Karliaga of Bahçeşehir University. I treasure the memory of a grand, high-spirited Divan Dinner on the Bosphorus organized by Jeremy Taylor and Tom Sutherland of the Travellers Club and hosted by Ömer M. Koç, which brought together an Anglo-Turkish crowd including Jason Goodwin, Anthony Sattin, Barnaby Rogerson and Jeremy Seal. And thank you to my wife Julia and friend Ned Cranborne for accompanying me along the massive Theodosian walls in 2018.

The late Nancy Hatch Dupree, director of the Afghanistan Center at Kabul University, nicknamed 'the grandmother of Afghanistan', was a warm and generous guide to the history of **Kabul** when I started my research on Babur. She paved the way to Mohammed Fahim Rahimi, Director of the National Museum of Afghanistan, and Jawan Shir Rasikh, who were both astonishingly helpful from afar. Great thanks to Bruce Wannell and Charlie Gammell for a host of introductions, including to Tommy Wide of Turquoise Mountain, the organization which has done so much to restore and preserve Kabul's heritage, and Jolyon Leslie, the architect who played a leading role in the Aga Khan Trust for Culture's rehabilitation of Babur's Gardens. I salute Engineer Abdul Latif Kohistani, the heroic, motorbike-riding, plant-collecting chief horticulturalist for his memories of that work. More recently thanks to Bryony Taylor, Emily Poyser and Sophie Wheale of the Cabinet Office for getting me back to Afghanistan after a number of years.

When it comes to **Isfahan**, I owe especial thanks to Hillary Sheridan, director of British Council Iran, and Professor Ali Ansari, head of the British Institute of Persian Studies, for their assistance with the city during its Safavid zenith in the seventeenth century, and Dr Niloofar Kakhi for her generous support, which included reviewing Chapter 11.

I owe my first experience of **Tripoli** to my late father, Silvio Marozzi, who unwittingly planted the seeds of an expedition by camel across the Libyan Sahara years later. Although I suspect he would have preferred me to continue the family business, I maintained an interest in Libya but as a writer, journalist and historian. Sir Wilfred Thesiger, the last great desert explorer, was a mine of useful advice on that desert journey with Ned Cranborne, as were Shane Winser of the Royal Geographical Society and Dr Noel Guckian, British Consul in Tripoli. During the Libyan Revolution of 2011, the bloody convulsions from which still shake the country, I reported alongside journalist friends including the late Marie Colvin,

Anthony Loyd, Jon Lee Anderson, Suliman Ali Zway, Osama al Fitory, Ruth Sherlock and Portia Walker, and I thank Simon Haselock for making these visits possible. More recently I have been travelling to Tripoli as an adviser to the Libyan government, a role in which I owe thanks to many people, among them successive British ambassadors Peter Millett and Frank Baker and their excellent teams, especially Iona Thomas, Angus McKee, Helena Owen, Alero Adetugbo, Mohammed Saffar, Nameer al Hadithi, Nicholas Jaques, David True, Ellie Gunningham, Youcef Marzooq, Asma Siyala, Louise Hopper, Charlotte North and Emmeline Carr. On the Libyan side, thank you to Prime Minister Faiez Serraj and his team: Jalal Othman has been a resolute friend and colleague, together with Fadeel Lameen, Serraj Alhammel, Moayed Othman, Hassan al Huni, Tarek Erwimed, Mazin Ramadan, Moutaz Ali, Huda Abuzeid, Omar Matoq, Rafaat Belkhair, Ali Sherif and Nayla Muntasser. Thank you to Gavin Graham and the Gardaworld team for keeping me safe during monthly visits from 2016. Huge thanks to Adel and Rula Dajani for their endless hospitality in Tunis. Historians love tracing connections between the past and the present. What could give greater pleasure, then, than interviewing Ahmed Fadl Karamanli and Ibrahim Karamanli, descendants of the remarkable Karamanli Dynasty that gloried in its defiance of the Ottoman Empire and the Great Powers of Europe – and the US – from Tripoli for much of the eighteenth and nineteenth centuries, the focus of Chapter 12.

Beirut, where my father was born in 1938, is a beautiful, fragile city, home to so many of the divisions that tear the region and its peoples apart. I am grateful to Professor Eugene Rogan, Professor of Modern Middle Eastern History at Oxford University, for steering me in the right direction, to my friend David Gardner, the *Financial Times'* long-time Beirut correspondent and sage guide to the Middle East, to Fayed Abushammala, former correspondent for the BBC Arabic Service, and to Ghassan Salamé, Lebanese academic, politician and current head of the UN's mission to Libya. I am also indebted to the late Samir Kassir's history *Beirut*.

Sneered at by so many for its materialist excesses and lack of history, Dubai has managed to avoid the turmoil that has engulfed so many of its neighbours. It must be doing something right. Thank you to His Excellency Sulaiman Almazroui, the United Arab Emirates' Ambassador to the UK, and in Dubai a huge thank you to Isobel Abulhoul OBE, founder of the Emirates Airline Festival of Literature. I am grateful to her excellent team, especially Sam al Hashimi, who assisted with interviews with Khaled Budour, Dahlia Kayed, Heyam al Bastaki, Noura Noman and Dr Rafia Ghubash. Thank you to Clare Dight and Nicholas Leech of *The*

National newspaper for both generous commissions and helpful ideas, to Jamal bin Huwaireb and Wes Harry of the Sheikh Mohammed bin Rashid al Maktoum Foundation, Ammar Shams, Omar Hadi, the incorrigible Justin Doherty, Professors Chris Brown and Justin Thomas of Zayed University, the *FT*'s Dubai correspondent Simeon Kerr, Pamela Grist, publisher of a wonderful oral history of Dubai (which I have freely raided), Michael Quentin Morton, author of a fine new history of the UAE, Professor Jane Bristol-Rhys and the excellent Dr Rima Sabban, whose acute remarks form the final words of Chapter 14. I must also thank His Highness Sultan bin Mohammed al Qasimi, also known by the surely unique moniker Sheikh Sultan III, Ruler of Sharjah, for his hospitality both in London and in the UAE with the Sharjah International Book Festival, splendidly supported by Tony Mulliken, Steven Williams and their team at Midas PR.

Writers are not always blessed with limitless funds, so I pay tribute to the generosity of the British Council who flew me to **Doha** and arranged a series of excellent interviews there. Thank you to the then British Ambassador Nicholas Hopton, the then head of British Council Qatar Martin Hope and his colleague Sophie Partarrieu. Fahad al Obeidly, oral historian and couturier, was a courteous guide to his city, as were Abdulaziz Al Mahmoud, Abdul Rahman Azzam, historian and adviser to the royal family, Dena Qaddumi, Abdullah Naimi, Sahar Hassan Saad, Hamad al Naimi, Ali Willis, old friends and Doha expatriates Paul Jessup and Sholto Byrnes, and the redoubtable Dr Mariam Ibrahim al Mulla of Qatar University, former director of the Qatar National Museum whose enthusiastic comments open Chapter 15. The story of Doha begins with pearls, and I am indebted to Hussein Alfardan, pearl-trader-turned-tycoon, for his reminiscences about the city in which he made his fortune. The story of Doha was also written by the Al Thani family and I am grateful to Sheikh Faisal bin Qassim al Thani, founder, chairman and chief executive of Al Faisal Holding, a royal tycoon who was happy to share memories of the Doha of his youth. Thanks also to Matthew Teller, Burhan Wazir and Louis Allday. Finally I would like to thank Dr Robert Carter, University College London's Doha-based Professor of Arabian and Middle Eastern Archaeology, mastermind of the 'Origins of Doha and Qatar' project combining archaeology, historical research and oral histories, who somehow and very kindly found time to review my chapter on Doha.

Sincere thanks to the historian Robert Irwin, who reviewed the entire manuscript, provided a number of insights and corrected a number of errors. Any which remain are, of course, entirely my own. Thank you to my superb agent Georgina Capel for launching us into what sometimes felt like an epic undertaking.

At Allen Lane, many thanks indeed to Stuart Proffitt for commissioning this book, to Helen Conford for editing it, and to the indefatigable Bela Cunha, who did amazing close work on the text and who maintained morale with bacon and avocado sandwiches. Thank you also to Richard Duguid, Holly Hunter, Ben Sinyor and Pen Vogler. I am indebted to Cecilia Mackay for tracking down the wonderful pictures which illustrate this volume. Thank you to Ed Merritt for his handsome maps.

Finally, my heartfelt thanks to my long-suffering wife Julia, who has always been here while I have been there, and our daughter Clemmie for their love and patience over the past several years. I can only hope it was worth it.

Index